Introduction to Children's Literature

SECOND EDITION

JOAN I. GLAZER

Rhode Island College

Merrill,
an imprint of Prentice Hall
Upper Saddle River, New Jersey   Columbus, Ohio

Library of Congress Cataloging-in-Publication Data

Glazer, Joan I.
     Introduction to children's literature / Joan I. Glazer. — 2nd ed.
       p. cm.
     Includes bibliographical references and index.
     ISBN 0-02-344111-9
     1. Children—Books and reading. 2. Children—United States—Books and reading. 3. Children's literature—Study and teaching. 4. Children's literature—Study and teaching—United States.   I. Title.
    Z1037.A1G57   1997   96-34809
    028.5'—dc20   CIP

Cover art: M. T. O'Keefe / H. Armstrong Roberts
Editor: Bradley J. Potthoff
Developmental Editor: Linda James Scharp McElhiney
Production Editor: Christine M. Harrington
Photo Coordinator: Anthony Magnacca
Design Coordinator: Julia Zonneveld Van Hook
Text Designer: STELLARViSIONs
Cover Designer: Brian Deep
Production Manager: Laura Messerly
Electronic Text Management: Marilyn Wilson Phelps, Matthew Williams, Karen L. Bretz, Tracey Ward
Illustrations: Jane Lopez
Director of Marketing: Kevin Flanagan
Advertising/Marketing Coordinator: Julie Shough

This book was set in Galliard by Prentice Hall and was printed and bound by Quebecor Printing/Book Press. The cover was printed by Phoenix Color Corp.

Photo credits: Gordon E. Rowley, pp. 1, 6, 11, 17, 22, 37, 41, 50, 59, 63, 69, 90, 101, 105, 109, 117, 123, 130–133, 151, 157, 188, 189, 193, 197, 205, 236, 259, 264, 271, 297, 309, 325, 357, 391, 419, 427, 432, 451, 479.

Printed in the United States of America

10 9 8 7 6 5 4 3 2 1

ISBN: 0-02-344111-9

Prentice-Hall International (UK) Limited, *London*
Prentice-Hall of Australia Pty. Limited, *Sydney*
Prentice-Hall of Canada, Inc., *Toronto*
Prentice-Hall Hispanoamericana, S. A., *Mexico*
Prentice-Hall of India Private Limited, *New Delhi*
Prentice-Hall of Japan, Inc., *Tokyo*
Simon & Schuster Asia Pte. Ltd., *Singapore*
Editora Prentice-Hall do Brasil, Ltda., *Rio de Janeiro*

 # Preface

Although this is officially the second edition of *Introduction to Children's Literature,* it is in fact an almost completely revised book. The focus is now on the early years of children's interactions with books, from preschool through grade four. The organization reflects the central focus literature for children has taken in many elementary schools and puts information about how teachers can help children develop into avid and knowledgeable readers before the chapters on types of literature. Chapter 1 defines literature for children and then sets the stage for the remaining chapters by reviewing child growth and development and identifying the philosophy that underlies the suggestions within the text.

Chapter 2 classifies books by both format and genre and explores children's responses to literature. Chapter 3 then shows how teachers and librarians can create a community of readers among their students by creating an atmosphere that encourages a variety of shared responses. Chapters 4 and 5 show how literature can be explored for its own value and how it can be the focal point for curricular studies. With this as background, Chapters 6 through 11 explore the various genres in depth, with examples of how teachers have presented each genre.

The book concludes with a chapter that shows how society's view of the child has affected what literature is considered appropriate for children. This chapter also provides contemporary viewpoints about literature for children.

The following special features can be found in this text:

- Annotated bibliographies of Touchstone Books are included. These are books that many critics consider outstanding and that can provide a beginning point for reading and a point of comparison for other books.

- Multicultural books are integrated throughout the text, modeling the use of books with characters, authors, and illustrators representing a diversity of backgrounds.

- Many examples are taken from actual classrooms showing how children responded to a book or to an activity.

- Content and methodology are integrated, with examples in the genre chapters showing how teachers have involved children.

&☙ Figures titled "On Second Thought" show how teachers have reflected on how they have engaged children with literature and how they might improve their interactions the next time they present that piece of literature.

&☙ Sections at the end of each chapter suggest ways for students to explore their personal responses to literature; to apply literary criteria to books for children, preparing to share literature with children; to engage children with literature; and to analyze children's responses to literature.

What has remained constant in both editions of this book is the belief that an introduction to exploring children's literature and involving young readers with it should be as fresh and intriguing as children's books themselves. Such a book should reflect the vitality of the literature and the joy that is generated when children first meet books they will never forget. It should encourage students to search for the books described, or ones like them, and make them eager to share their responses. I've tried to write such a book.

ACKNOWLEDGMENTS

Many people helped to make this book possible. A thank you and a hug go to my husband, Wes Miller, for his love and support and for his gentle reminders to stop letting the "urgent but unimportant" take precedence over my writing.

Then there are the Lindas who made this book a reality: Linda Peterson, who began as editor, changed roles but not interest and influence; Linda Montgomery, who with Christine Harrington, guided the book through production with efficiency and good humor; and especially Linda James Scharp McElhiney, who served as insightful editor, wise counselor, strong advocate, and friend.

A thank you goes to Gordon E. Rowley, photographer extraordinaire, for capturing the children and teachers at the Henry Barnard School as they engaged in literature-related activities. Thanks also to the administration and faculty of the school for their cooperation, and for being so good at what they do: Celeste Bowler, Marybeth Cannon, Carolyn Carrara, Mary Fitzgerald, Phyllis Humphrey, Miriam Aroesty O'Connell, Jeanmarie Saulnier, Haven Starr, and Ronald Tibbetts.

David Nelson, Dean of the School of Education and Human Development at Rhode Island College, gave the kind of support a professor needs: time to write in the initial stages of the book and moral support throughout the project.

Many, many teachers and librarians have shared their ideas and their enthusiasm, and I cannot begin to name all of them. Those whose work appears in figures or whose ideas are quoted, even if their names have been changed in the book, are Martha Aurelio, Christine Beard, Cherylann Bertoncini, Sr. Debra Bow, Julie Butler, Janet Caretti, Bethany Carter, Erica Cross, Barbara Cunniff, Jennifer Darling, Diana Daunis, Marie England,

Brenda Franco, Leslie Gibbons, Stephanie Good, Diane Hunter, Cheryl Hvisdoz, Colleen Johnston, Connie Lamansky, Debbie LaTour, Mary Beth Letendre, Deb Marciano, Trish Morgan, Jill Patrie, Margaret Rock, Julie Rossi, Mary Ryder, Kerri Shaw, Karen Smith, Priscilla Sousa, Bethany Tonderys, Linda Whittaker, Joan Wilkinson, Elizabeth Wilcox, Patricia Wolf, Julie Woolman-Bonilla, and Sookyung Yoo. Thank you all.

Thanks also to the reviewers of this text for their most helpful suggestions: Susan A. Burgess, Framingham State College; John J. Carney, University of New Hampshire; Susan A. Cooper, University of Kentucky; Alice Denham, Texas Tech University; Carol J. Fisher, University of Georgia; Barbara N. Kupetz, Indiana University of Pennsylvania; Pose Lamb, Purdue University; JoAnn Mullen, University of Northern Colorado; Marilyn Ohlhausen, University of Nevada, Las Vegas; Pat Tipton Sharp, Baylor University; Marilou R. Sorenson, University of Utah; Dixie M. Turner, Olivet Nazarene University; William J. Valmont, University of Arizona; and Judith Washburn, California State University, Los Angeles.

And finally, thank you to Charlotte Huck, an inspiration to me throughout my teaching career and a friend who has never given me bad advice (and I've asked her advice often!).

 # Brief Contents

 # Contents

§ THREE §

The Classroom or Center: Creating a Community of Readers   69

§ FOUR §

Planning a Curriculum: Literature at the Center   117

§   F I V E   §

Books for the Early Years: Helping Children Become Literate   157

§   S I X   §

Picture Books: A Balance Between Text and Illustrations   205

§ SEVEN §

Poetry: Bringing Poems for Children to Life   259

§ EIGHT §

Traditional Literature: Familiar Tales, Different Voices   309

§   N I N E   §

Modern Fantasy: A Small Step From Reality   *357*

§   T E N   §

Realism: Fiction Out of Fact   *391*

§ ELEVEN §

Biography and Informational Books: Factual Portraits and Explorations   427

§ TWELVE §

Changes Over Time: Society's View of the Child   461

§ A P P E N D I X A §

§ A P P E N D I X B §

 **Chapter One**

Literature and Children:
Making Choices

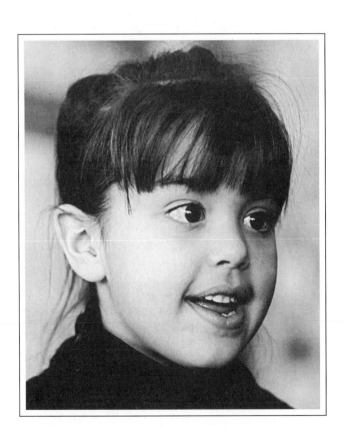

*I*f you are going to work with literature, whether with children or adults, you must be able to use your imagination. So let's begin right now.

USE YOUR IMAGINATION

Imagine you are an incredibly talented writer. You can develop characters with keen understanding; you can create plots that hold your readers breathless; you can write movingly in either prose or poetry; you can compose with authority on any subject. Your literary talent is matched only by your skill in art—you are a preeminent illustrator. Your editor calls, begging you to write a book for children. You agree. But now it is time for you to make some decisions.

What will be the subject of your book?

For what age range is it intended?

Will it be prose or poetry? Fiction or nonfiction?

Will it be illustrated? If so, how?

What will be special about your book?

Answer the previous questions about the book *you* would write. For each answer, describe *why* you made each decision.

Figure 1-1 shows how three children described what type of stories they would write. Figure 1-2 shows how three teachers answered the same questions you were asked. And in Figure 1-3 three children's authors describe their work. Compare your descriptions with theirs and look for similarities among the responses. For example, Larry, a second grader, Jeannine, a teacher, and Jean Little, an author, all talk about what they read as children. And both Ken, a teacher, and Eloise Greenfield, an author, have knowledge and feelings that they want to convey to their readers. All of us have ideas about children, what they read and should read, what makes a good book,

These children were asked to tell about the kind of book they'd write for other children if they had a publisher who was "just waiting to get their manuscript so the book could be put into print."

Eliani (kindergarten): I want to be a teacher when I grow up and I want to teach in a kindergarten, just like Mrs. Hicken [her teacher]. I'd write a book just like the ones she reads to us.

Larry (grade 2): I'd write about my friend Michael, and I'd put some mystery things in it 'cause I like to read mysteries. I do that when I write at school. And I'd draw the pictures for my story.

Jenna (grade 4): I'd do a story about animals because I love animals—you know, dogs and cats and puppies. I live on a farm but I can't have many pets because my sister's allergic to them. But I do have six chickens, and I've named them all after celebrities. The feathers are sort of the color of the star's hair. Bonnie Raitt has reddish feathers. That might make a story kids would like.

Figure 1-1   Three children describe books they'd like to write.

These teachers were asked what kind of book for children they'd write if they had all the necessary skill and talent.

Jeannine: If I had the ability to write a book, I would write a sports book. It would be fiction for third, fourth, fifth graders involving a female main character. I have always been interested and involved in sports. As a young reader, I would often select books about sports because that's what I was interested in, but I was aware that I was a little girl reading a "boy's" book. I feel that we've come a long way regarding men and women portrayed in very traditional roles. However, there is still room for improvement.

Ken: I would like to write so that children can read and know what's "normal" about growing up. I recently had jury duty. Some of the kids had been molested and thought it was normal; they thought every child went through this. It horrified me that they felt this way. I'd like to write something so they could get help and know that what was happening to them was wrong.

Marita: I would write a book about animals. Living in a wooded area, we see many wild animals. I would be able to share my experiences and thoughts with small children. I would try to write some poems to put in the book. Pictures of animals would also be in it. Some of the animals we see are deer, foxes, opposums, wild rabbits, coyotes, and skunks. The man who lives down the street has three llamas and a baby llama.

Figure 1-2   Three teachers describe books they'd like to write.

These authors have written about their own published writing for children.

David Wiesner: When I graduated and began working as an illustrator, my goal was eventually to publish a wordless picture book of my own. . . . *Free Fall* was the culmination of many ideas about an impressionistic kind of storytelling that I had been forming since art school.

There were many other possibilities I wanted to explore. I longed to do a book that was wildly humorous, almost slapstick. . . .

A wordless book offers a different kind of an experience than one with text, for both the author and the reader. There is no author's voice telling the story. Each viewer reads the book in his or her own way. The reader is an integral part of the storytelling process. . . . As the author of a wordless book, I don't have to concern myself about whether the reader's interpretation of each and every detail is the same as mine. My own view has no more (and no less) validity than that of any other viewer. Since my intent was for the book [*Tuesday*] as a whole to make people laugh, all that matters is that the pictures are funny.

Quote by David Wiesner from his Caldecott Acceptance
Speech, reprinted by permission of the author.

Eloise Greenfield: One of my primary goals in writing for children is to hold up a mirror that accurately reflects African American life. All cultures have strengths and flaws, but the media, for the most part, do not give us the full picture.

I try, in my work, to provide a balanced portrayal of the African American family, the one we see in real life. Some of this work is done on a conscious level, because I see the need for it, but much of it surfaces simply because of the images that form inside me . . . images inspired by the reality of the many people who treat their children with love and responsibility, and who make sacrifices to give their children good lives.

Quote by Eloise Greenfield, copyright 1996 by Eloise Greenfield.
Used by permission of Scott Treimel, New York.

Figure 1-3   Three children's authors discuss their work.

and what we think is important. Thus the field of children's literature comprises a wide range of ideas, opinions, types of books, and styles of writing and illustrating.

In this chapter, children's literature is defined, what is known about children's reading interests is discussed, how children's growth and development influence their reading is reviewed quickly. You might want to think about how your book meets the needs and interests of children and what impact it might have on its readers. This chapter delineates the approach to literature taken in this text, particularly the importance of selecting books that authentically reflect the diversity of our country and the world.

Jean Little: As a child . . . I knew that my own house, which I loved, would never be in a book. Mary Lennox of *The Secret Garden* was just like me—selfish, bad-tempered, lazy, and entirely alive—but Misselthwaite Manor was unlike any place I had ever seen. Only one book I read as a child had a setting I recognized. In *Jane of Lantern Hill* (Bantam), Jane started out living at 60 Gay Street in Toronto. She soon departed for Lantern Hill on Prince Edward Island, but for a third of the book she actually lived in a city where I, too, had lived. . . .

Why not write books about people like me and Jane. I wanted my heroes to be Canadians who weren't from "the island." I wanted my readers to discover that ordinary boys and girls like themselves made perfectly fine literary protagonists. I wanted them to grow up feeling confident that stories worthy of being written down could happen as easily in Toronto as in Paddington—or Avonlea, for that matter. There were lots of books "to take them worlds away." I wanted to bring them home.

"Homecoming," by Jean Little, *The Horn Book Magazine* May/June 1991, p. 289, reprinted by permission of The Horn Book, Inc. 11 Beacon St., Suite 1000, Boston, MA 02108.

Figure 1-3 *continued*

DEFINING LITERATURE FOR CHILDREN

The term *literature* generally refers to imaginative writing that results in an aesthetic experience for the reader. That experience is guided by the writer, who shapes a story through a series of decisions. What events shall be told? What will happen first? Will the events be told in direct chronological order or through flashbacks? Should there be dialogue? Shall time be telescoped to make the story more interesting? What exact words or phrases can be used to describe the wanted image? How can ideas be woven into the text so that their interrelationships will be implicit? What can be done to create a coherent whole?

Literature provides a structured look at a real or imagined experience rather than a transcript of the sometimes mundane, disjointed, and undecipherable happenings of daily life. In both its meaning and in the words and images that convey that meaning, literature encourages a thoughtful, aesthetic response.

For a quick look at how an author has incorporated the technique of flashback, that is, inserted an episode of past action into the present action of the story, read any of the following picture books: *Miss Rumphius* by Barbara Cooney, *How My Parents Learned to Eat* by Ina R. Friedman, or *What's Under My Bed?* by James Stevenson.

A Sense of Audience

Literature for children differs from adult literature in degree rather than kind. The same themes or topics may be addressed and the same elements manipulated, but the experiences and understanding of children determine whether a book is "for" them. Any piece of literature can be looked at in terms of its **implied audience,** the readers for whom the book seems intended. To identify the implied audience, consider what sort of person is

The implied audience for many alphabet books is the preschool child who enjoys identifying and talking about the objects pictured.

likely to appreciate a book most, what background knowledge would be helpful, and what ways of looking at the world would enhance understanding. For example, the implied audience of many alphabet books is preschool children who can point to the pictures, identify them, talk about them, and begin to recognize and associate letter names with the print on the page.

The implied audience for Beverly Cleary's story *Muggie Maggie* is second-, third-, or fourth-grade children who have, like Maggie, had to switch from printing to cursive writing and have endured the teasing of classmates.

Perry Nodelman points out that thinking about the implied audience of a text is a useful strategy for one's own understanding and enjoyment of the writing, but he cautions about the danger of overgeneralizing or making inaccurate generalizations. As an example Nodelman notes that some of his adult students felt that "The Owl and the Pussycat" by Edward Lear was not a good poem for children because it included difficult words. Yet the adults had enjoyed it—and they were unable to define the "difficult" words themselves. (Some of the words were made up by Lear). They were so intent on generalizing about the implied audience that they ignored their own responses (16–17).

Many authors write with a child audience in mind. Beatrix Potter wrote *Peter Rabbit* first in letter format to the son of her former governess, a very specific child audience. Other authors write for children in general, telling a

Beatrix Potter first wrote Peter Rabbit *in letter format to the son of her former governess. (Source:* Illustration from THE TALE OF PETER RABBIT by Beatrix Potter. Copyright © Frederick Warne & Co., 1902, 1987. Reproduced by permission of Frederick Warne & Co.)

story that seems to fit a young audience and developing it based on their knowledge of or assumptions about this audience. Isaac Singer, for instance, when asked about his writing for children, responded:

> I try to give a happy ending to a story for a child because I know how sensitive a child is. If you tell a child that a murderer or a thief was never punished and never caught, the child feels that there is no justice in the world altogether. And I don't like children to come to this conclusion, at least not too soon. (54)

Some authors say they write with no particular audience in mind, and some adult literature has been taken over by children. Folktales, for example, were originally told for the entertainment of adults, but have become in their retellings almost exclusively for children.

Singer has retold Jewish folktales as well as writing original stories. Look for *Zlateh the Goat, When Shlemiel Went to Warsaw,* and *Mazel and Shlimazel.*

Complexity and Emphasis

A few obvious differences set contemporary children's books apart from those for adults. One difference is that they tend to be shorter than adult novels, and plots are simpler. The main characters themselves are often children, and often more emphasis is placed on the actions than on the thoughts of the characters. But authors of children's books are free to write on almost any subject, to use bold and imaginative language, to please the reader. They may write for a specific child, for the children they picture in their own minds, or for no particular readership. The book becomes a children's book when children read, enjoy, and understand it.

Folktales, originally told for adults, have become in their retellings almost exclusively for children. (Source: Illustration by Lulu Delacre from THE BOSSY GALLITO by Lucia M. Gonzales, Illustration Copyright © 1994 by Lulu Delacre. Reprinted by permission of Scholastic Inc.)

CHILDREN'S READING INTERESTS

The question of whether there are patterns in the kinds of books children like has been well researched and the results remain fairly consistent (Haynes). Before age 9, there are few differences in reading interests between boys and girls, but their interests begin to diverge between the ages of 10 and 13 (Isaacs 139).

It also appears that children of varying abilities like the same types of books, with gifted children preferring books that are liked by a slightly older age group, reading more books, and having a wider range of interest than readers of average ability (Russell 394–395).

Many states and organizations give annual awards to authors and illustrators of children's books. You might want to see what awards are given in your area of the country.

Each year the International Reading Association and the Children's Book Council conduct a project in which children read and vote on newly published books. Publishers send books to review teams in five different regions of the United States, where the books are read in classrooms. Children vote in March, and the list of favorites, known as "Children's Choices," is published each October in *The Reading Teacher,* a journal of the International Reading Association. This annotated list can give you a picture of children's current interests.

However, no one can say with certainty what a specific child will like. That depends on a child's interests and experiences as well as developmental aspects.

Children should often be left alone in a library to choose their own books and, as a fundamental principle, should not be forced to read books that are meaningless to them, no matter how good the books are. But at times, children will look naturally to adults and to other children to help them find good books.

Parents, teachers, and librarians sometimes become brokers between literature and children, so adults need to arm themselves with a strong sense of what is good literature. They also need to recognize individual differences in how children grow and what they like. It does little good, warns critic Northrop Frye, to tell a young boy that the book he has just plucked off the shelf is no good.

> He has to feel values for himself, and should follow his individual rhythm in doing so. In the meantime, he can read almost anything in any order, just as he can eat mixtures of food that would have his elders reaching for the baking soda. A sensible teacher or librarian can soon learn how to give guidance to a youth's reading that allows for underdeveloped taste and still doesn't turn him into a gourmet or dyspeptic before his time. (116).

There are two key steps to providing literary guidance: identifying good literature and then meeting the child's particular interests. Before you know the child well, you can begin with what you know generally about children of different ages. Figure 1-4 describes key features in children's development and reading preferences to suggest beginning points for selecting books for children of particular ages.

HOW CHILDREN GROW AND LEARN

Much of our knowledge about children comes from research that often is tied to specific theories of child development. Some researchers study a cross-section of children. That is, they look at a large group of children who are the same age and look for the characteristics the children share. Then they describe what children are like at this particular age or stage. This process is similar to the discovery a teacher makes as she looks out at a class of second graders and sees that many of them have front teeth missing. She notes that a characteristic of the physical development of 7-year-old children is that they are losing their baby teeth and gaining their permanent teeth.

Other researchers study children longitudinally. That is, they follow the growth and development of a child or group of children over a period of time. This process is similar to a parent's observation of his son's physical changes. For instance, his son gets his first tooth at 7 months and acquires more until, at age 3, he has a full set of 20 baby teeth. At age 6 and a half he begins to lose his baby teeth and by age 12 has all his permanent teeth. Because the father sees these changes in incremental steps, he can describe the pattern of change.

We learn from both types of studies. The cross-sectional results describe the general characteristics of children at a particular age. The longitudinal results describe the pattern of development—what has come before and is likely to come after a snapshot in time. In general, children are similar in their

AGE	LOOK FOR BOOKS THAT . . .	AN EXAMPLE IS
0 to 2 years	• Have clear, brightly colored illustrations. • Are about everyday objects or routines. • Have strong rhythm and rhyme. • Are interactive (allow the child to participate by pulling or touching.) • Are of laminated cardboard for easy handling.	• *At Home* by Eric Hill. (New York: Random, 1983) • *Sleeping* by Jan Ormerod. (New York: Lothrop, 1985) • *Barnyard Banter* by Denise Fleming. (New York: Holt, 1994) • *Pat the Puppy* by Edith Kunhardt. (Racine, WI: Golden, 1993) • *Say Goodnight* by Helen Oxenbury. (New York: Macmillan, 1987)
2 to 4 years	• Are short enough to be completed in one sitting. • Develop concepts. • Have rhythm, rhyme, or both. • Have structured plots (such as folktales). • Have a happy ending, with poetic justice.	• *Oh, What a Noisy Farm!* by Harriet Ziefert. (New York: Tambourine, 1995) • *How Many?* by Debbie MacKinnon. (New York: Dial, 1993) • *Going to Sleep on the Farm* by Wendy Lewison. (New York: Dial, 1992) • *Hattie and the Fox* by Mem Fox. (New York: Bradbury, 1986) • *The Three Billy Goats Gruff* by Marcia Brown. (New York: Harcourt, 1957)
4 to 7 years	• Are in picture book format and have a strong plot. • Include humor or fantasy. • Are retellings of folktales. • Have rhyme or pattern that makes the story predictable. • Have no words so the child can look at the illustrations and tell the story.	• *The Fortune Tellers* by Lloyd Alexander. (New York: Dutton, 1992) • *Duckat* by Gaelyn Gordon. (New York: Scholastic, 1992) • *Nine-in-One Grr! Grr!* by Blia Xiong. (San Francisco: Children's Press, 1989) • *Brown Bear, Brown Bear, What Do You See?* by Bill Martin. (New York: Holt, 1983) • *Frog Goes to Dinner* by Mercer Mayer. (New York: Dial, 1974)
7 to 9 years	• Has chapters requiring sustained reading. • Presents humor or adventure. • Is about life in the past or the future, or life in other lands. • Is a biography. • Is a mystery or includes puzzles or problem solving.	• *Amber Brown Is Not a Crayon* by Paula Danziger. (New York: Putnam, 1994) • *Rats!* by Pat Hutchins. (New York: Greenwillow, 1989) • *The Most Beautiful Place in the World* by Ann Cameron. (New York: Knopf, 1988) • *Ahyoka and the Talking Leaves* by Peter and Connie Roop. (New York: Lothrop, 1992) • *Boys at Work* by Gary Soto. (New York: Delacorte, 1995)

Figure 1-4 Appropriate books for different ages.

Children may go through recognizable patterns of development, but each child is unique.

development at particular ages, and in general, they go through recognizable patterns of development.

But each child is unique. One seven-year-old may always select nonfiction reading selections; another requests that the same fairy tale be read aloud each bedtime, day after day. One child may progress steadily, whereas another grows in a series of spurts and changes. Knowing how children develop helps you to understand them and decide which books may be most appropriate for them. Knowing children as individuals allows you to plan in meaningful ways and not be surprised when children of the same age select very different books.

Cognitive Development

Cognitive, or intellectual, development refers to how children think and how their thinking and reasoning change over time. The Swiss psychologist Jean Piaget found that the ability to organize experience grows as the child grows, in regular stages, but that the pace varies from child to child (Piaget *Psychology*). He suggested that there are four stages in the growth of natural ability and that they always follow the same order. The stages applying to preschool and primary grade children are summarized in Figure 1-5, with the implications for book selection indicated for each stage.

Piaget found that children have ideas about the physical world that they have not learned in the classic sense. For example, many young children believe that anything that moves is alive—including such things as windblown curtains, and waves.

STAGE	KEY CHARACTERISTICS OF CHILDREN	IMPLICATIONS FOR LITERATURE SELECTION
Sensorimotor Birth to 2	• Explore the world through senses and motor ability	• Books that the children handle themselves should be plastic or laminated cardboard, since children of this age are likely to touch, smell, and taste them. • Select books that invite participation through such devices as flaps to move or fabric to touch.
Preoperational 2 to 6 or 7	• Focus on the present • Begin to use symbols to represent objects • Often see things only from their own point of view	• Select concept books to encourage exploration and refinement of generalizations. • Select fiction that is in picture book format and has patterns or repetition and a clear plot structure. • Plan to reread many of the books you select.
Concrete Operational 7 to 11 or 12	• Use logic as well as sensory data to explain phenomona they observe • Can see from other points of view • Can understand past and future	• Select chapter books that have more complex stories than most picture books. • Present biographies so that children can under- stand lives in the past.

Figure 1-5 Piagetian stages and implications for book selection.

Humans organize experience into categories, or *schemata*. If new experiences make sense and fit well within that organization, they are *assimilated* into, or added to, the schemata. If new experiences are at odds with the categories and do not fit, then the schemata must be modified, a process Piaget called *accommodation*. This process is continual in both adults and children, and it defines us all as active processors of information, not as passive recipients, an important point to remember as we work with children. As children hear stories, they develop a schema for what a story is, and this guides their expectations. They know, for example, that "Once upon a time" signals a fairy tale, and that if two similar events have occurred, a third is likely. Figure 1-6 shows how two children, one five and one nine, process the information in *Piggybook* by Anthony Browne. Notice how the younger child focuses on a literal interpretation whereas the older one sees beyond the surface to underlying meanings, a function of age and intellectual development.

Moral Development

No one can know a child's learning ability or maturity simply from knowing how old the child is. Similarly, no one can predict how a child will judge right and wrong just by knowing the child's age. But there are general patterns of change. Piaget identified two basic stages in children's development of thinking about moral choices, which correspond with intellectual development (Piaget *Moral Judgment*). Very young children have difficulty seeing the point of view of another person and label acts as totally right or totally wrong. They also tend to judge an act by the consequences, not by intentions. For them, if a person meant to bring a bouquet of flowers and in doing so ruined part of a garden, that person was wrong and should be punished severely. Around eight or nine years of age, children develop better skill at understanding the viewpoints of others and become less absolute in their judgments. They also consider intentions more carefully; the person who cut the flowers meant well, and that is important.

It appears that males and females may approach moral decisions from different points of view. Lawrence Kohlberg, a researcher at Harvard University, based his work on that of Piaget and, working only with males, contended that everyone passes through the same sequence of moral stages. At each of six stages, males have a different view of law, civil liberties, authority, and other areas where questions of right and wrong are debated. Kohlberg verified the stages through an 18-year study in which researchers interviewed 50 American males every three years from ages 10 to 28, each time presenting a moral dilemma in story form. Kohlberg looked at the reasoning the participants used rather than at the specific course of action they recommended. Figure 1-7 summarizes the stages described by Kohlberg.

Males grow in their ability to reason about moral questions by hearing arguments representing the next highest stage. To facilitate this growth, teachers often encourage children to give their reasons for decisions about moral issues raised in the books they are reading.

Linda was interested in how her own children responded to ideas within books and to know exactly what they seemed to understand. She decided to share *Piggybook* by Anthony Browne (New York: Knopf, 1986) with her son Nathan, who was almost five, and her daughter Jillian, who was nine. She read and discussed the book with each child individually, asking the same questions and tape-recording the responses.

The cover of *Piggybook* shows a woman carrying a man piggyback, and on his back are two boys, riding in the same way. She is looking straight ahead seriously, but the man and the boys are smiling. The book introduces the Piggott family, with Mr. Piggott and the boys giving orders to the mother, who not only does all the housework but also works outside the home. In first a subtle fashion, and then very overtly, a pig motif appears. The flowers on the wallpaper become pig snouts, the shadow of Mr. Piggott's head is a pig. Then Mrs. Piggott walks out, leaving a note for her family that says, "You are pigs." Mr. Piggott and the boys are not successful in taking care of themselves. As the house becomes more and more like a pigsty, they take on the physical characteristics of pigs. When Mrs. Piggott returns, they beg her to stay. She does, but now they assume responsibility for household tasks. The last page shows Mrs. Piggott fixing the car, which has the license plate "SGIP 321."

Linda's Questions	Nathan's Reponse (5-years-old)	Jillian's Response (9-years-old)
(Prior to reading) When you look at the picture on the cover of this book, what do you think this book might be about?	"Us." (**Linda:** "Us? You mean our family?") "Yea."	"I think its going to be about a family and how they're silly or something. The dad and boys are trying to be silly and the mom is trying to be serious."
(After reading) What kind of book is this?	"A nice book. I liked it."	"It's about how you shouldn't be lazy. You're not supposed to just sit there and let somebody else do work that you can do, that you're able to do."
What sort of people are Mr. Piggott and his sons?	"Pigs."	"At the beginning, they were lazybones, frankly."
How do you know?	"Because they had faces like pigs."	"Because they wouldn't do anything by themselves. In the book they explained that they had to come home from this very important job and she would always have to do the cooking, the washing. They would just sit around saying, 'When's supper ready?' and 'When's breakfast ready?'"

Figure 1-6   Two children respond to *Piggybook*.

Linda's Questions	Nathan's Reponse (5-years-old)	Jillian's Response (9-years-old)
Why did Mrs. Piggott leave?	"Because they were pigs."	" 'Cause she was tired of being pushed around."
Where do you think she went?"	"I think she went here." (**Linda:** Where's here?) "Here at our house."	"I think she went . . . well, maybe she went to her mom's house."
Why did Mrs. Piggott come back?	"Because they changed back to people."	"Because she wanted to see how they acted now. And she probably thought, 'Well, things are going to be different now that they know how it feels.'"
Did you learn something from this book?	(No response, just shrugged his shoulders.)	"Yes. I shouldn't be lazy, and I should get things that I can get by myself."

Linda related the responses of her son and daughter to their ages.

The five-year-old focused on the transformation of the characters from human to pig form without regard for cause-and-effect relationships. In a leap of faith, he accepted the change of Mr. Piggott and his sons with no need to ask why the change occurred. Nathan did not identify Mrs. Piggott's problem beyond the fact that she was suddenly dealing with pigs rather than people. I think he interpreted her departure from the house as logical under the circumstances. He didn't seem to grasp the sequence of events very clearly. The moral lesson embodied in the story was lost on this five-year-old.

In addition, Nathan relied heavily on visual cues. Mr. Piggott and his sons were pigs because their faces had become pig-like, not because of their behavior prior to the transformation. Nathan enjoyed looking for pigs and pig-like objects in the artwork throughout the book.

The nine-year-old, however, used her developing problem-solving skills to zero in on the relationship between Mrs. Piggott and her family. Even while answering the opening question, Jillian observed in the cover artwork the serious expression of the mother in contrast to the smiling faces of the husband and sons. Jillian was able to grasp the subtle aspects of the story and expand on them to apply the moral to her own life experience.

I was surprised by the responses of both children to the question that asked why Mrs. Piggott returned to her home. I had anticipated that the children would identify the motive for her return to be love of the family despite their boorish ways. Instead both children attributed the return to something else; in one case to curiosity and in the other case to a simple return to human form. Somehow, that concept of the mother's love seemed to be overlooked.

I must say, my whole family read and enjoyed the book. We spent the weekend pointing out "Piggott" behavior. I think I even remember a few grunts from my husband!

Figure 1-6 *continued*

Preconventional Morality

Level 1 • Obedience and Punishment (It is right if the person in power says it is. It is wrong if it will bring punishment.)

Level 2 • Rewards and Reciprocity (It is right if it is rewarded and satisfies own needs. It is right if it represents an equal exchange.)

Conventional Morality

Level 3 • Orientation Toward Pleasing Others

• Conformity Toward Role Behaviors (It is right if it is what "good" boys or girls would do.)

Level 4 • Respect for Authority

• Desire to Maintain Social Order (It is right if that is what the law says. Laws represent what most people want and are necessary for an orderly society.)

Beyond Conventional Morality

Level 5 • Social Contract (It is right if it brings the greatest good for the greatest number.)

Level 6 • Universal Ethical Principles (It is right if it follows self-chosen ethical principles.)

Figure 1-7 Kohlberg's stages of moral development.

Children could discuss actions in *The Sweetest Fig* by Chris Van Allsburg. This book provides opportunities for children to explore both personal principles and relationships.

Carol Gilligan found in her study that women based their reasoning about moral dilemmas on being considerate of others and on maintaining relationships more than the men did and attended to how their decisions would affect others. Gilligan noted that women are socialized to consider the consequences of their actions on others rather than to focus on personal principles. As boys and girls explore their reactions to the actions of characters in books, they may be making judgments using different frames of reference that are gender based.

Age designations mean little by themselves. You cannot identify children's moral reasoning approach by asking how old they are. Children often switch back and forth between stages, sometimes thinking at one stage and acting in another. But books present many opportunities for children to explore and explain moral reasoning as they discuss motivations and actions of characters.

Social and Emotional Development

Social development in children is related to their intellectual development, particularly in their ability to take the viewpoint of another (Shaffer). As with other aspects of development, experience contributes to the child's growing understanding. The older a child is, the more likely it is that he or she will see multiple aspects of a situation (Mussen et al.). A nine-year-old, for example, is more likely to take into account the actions leading up to an event in judging that event than is a preschooler.

Observation of how others behave is a powerful tool in social development. Social learning theorists note that the behavior modeled and the situation together influence children (Bandura). This influence may be apparent in the classroom when children, for example, read to one another and hold the book just as the teacher does. One teacher described her young students reading aloud to the wall, stopping to show the illustrations in slow, sweeping movements. The influence may be even more subtle. For example, a child who sees adults avoid sitting next to or talking with members of particular groups may begin to avoid those groups without being able to state any clear reason for doing so. The behaviors observed, the situations in which they occur, and the child's perceptions of reinforcement given all influence the child's learning.

Most children experience close friendships. These relationships are important because they let children practice social skills, help children develop a sense of their own identity, and provide the sense of security that comes from group membership. Children interacting with each other are equals; they must learn to resolve conflicts, communicate their wants clearly, and interact effectively. In fact, children's friendships have the same characteristics as adult friendships (Rubin).

Social interaction also influences children's **personality development.** Children learn about themselves and develop their **self-concept**—their idea of their own capabilities—as parents, guardians, teachers, and friends respond to them in positive or negative ways. Their **self-esteem**—the value

The powerful effect of observing others is one reason that it is important for children to see parents and other care givers reading.

Close friendships help children develop a sense of their own identity.

they place on themselves—is similarly influenced. We know, for example, that people often respond to physically attractive children in positive ways; as a result, such children come to think positively about themselves.

How children deal with their emotions changes as they get older (Schickedanz). At ages 2 and 3, they can talk about their feelings. From 4 to 7, they can match appropriate emotional responses to a situation. At this period, they do not report having conflicting emotions in a single situation, and they may have difficulty understanding that concept. Not until they are 11 or 12 do they report conflicting emotions, such as being "happy" to move to a new home but also being "scared" to leave their old friends. Earlier combinations of emotions are all of the same valence, such as "happy and excited" or "scared and nervous." Social and emotional growth and personality development develop simultaneously, each influencing the other.

Language Development

Children seem to race from random crying and babbling, to talking in mono-syllables, to intuitively grasping rules of language—all before the first day of kindergarten. Throughout the early school years, children gradually learn standard grammar and the exceptions to the rules; their sentence structure becomes increasingly complex. Although the greatest growth in language occurs in the preschool years, development continues throughout the elementary years.

Children are also exploring the world of print. Harste, Woodward, and Burke found that children at age three had a mark that they used to symbolize their name, and they could distinguish between art and writing. When observers pay attention to process rather than product, they discover that even very young children know quite a lot about the written word. Although it may appear as a scribble to the adult, the child can tell what his or her just-completed writing says.

Children's understanding of print is often evident in their manipulation of books. When a child listener no longer covers the print with her hand or turns the pages rapidly when there is text but no picture, she is showing that she understands that the print carries the message. Gradually the child begins to match the words on the page with the words being read. Hearing the same story repeated while watching the page and hearing a story so often that it is known by heart and can be "read" independently contribute to the child's growing concept of print and of the reading process. Home environments in which adults or older siblings read regularly set the stage for children to become readers themselves.

Experiencing good literature contributes to children's growth in vocabulary and syntax (Cohen; Nagy, Hermann, and Anderson; Chomsky). They encounter a variety of words and sentence constructions that they might not hear in everyday conversation, and they see how language can be used creatively. Figure 1-8 gives excerpts from several children's books. Note the effective use of language in vocabulary choice, description, syntax, dialect, and aesthetic and creative appeal.

One reason for having books with many different cultures and groups represented is that it helps children who belong to these groups see themselves in a positive light.

These excerpts from children's books show several ways in which language is being used effectively. Children learn the possibilities of language when they experience such literature. Each selection has more than one strong point, and each fits within a carefully developed story, even though only one aspect is highlighted.

Vocabulary

Lilly's parents were amused when Julius blew a bubble.
"Can you believe it?" they exclaimed.
But if Lilly did the exact same thing, they said,
"Lilly, let's mind our manners, please."

Lilly's parents were dazzled when Julius babbled and gurgled.
"Such a vocabulary!" they exclaimed.
But if Lilly did the exact same thing, they said,
"Lilly, let's act our age, please."

Lilly's parents were amazed when Julius screamed.
"What lung capacity!" they exclaimed.
But if Lilly did the exact same thing, they said,
"Lilly, let's restrain ourselves, please."

> Text excerpt from *Julius, The Baby of the World* by Kevin Henkes. Copyright 1990 by Kevin Henkes. Reprinted by permission of Greenwillow Books, a division of William Morrow and Company, Inc.

Descriptive Language

My father's hands are big and strong, scooping up earth and lifting sacks of seeds. Thin cracks run down my father's fingers. Dirt fills every line and edges each nail black. Planting, watering, weeding, my father's hands shape a patch of earth into our garden.

> Quoted from *My Father's Hands* by Joanne Ryder. Text Copyright 1994 by Joanne Ryder. Reprinted by permission of Morrow Junior Books, a division of William Morrow and Company, Inc.

Variety in Sentence Structure

With the half-moon half helping, Zeke threaded his way through a confusion of trees and tangled vines. The world around him was still. Even the trees were asleep.

But then, out of that silence, came a frightful yowling . . .

Two nanoseconds later a death-dealing coyote had him pinned to the ground. Zeke was so scared he couldn't breathe. But when the coyote's claws pierced his flesh, he somehow squeezed out the opening bars of the only song that came to mind: "Show Me the Way to Go Home."

> From *Zeke Pippin* by William Steig. Copyright 1995 by William Steig. Reprinted by permission of HarperCollins Publishers.

Figure 1-8   Examples of effective language in books for children.

Dialect

Mama sat down at the table and started playin' with the salt shaker. "What you mean, Nobie?"

"I mean, if you could have yourself one wish, what would it be for?"

Mama put the salt back on a straight line with the pepper and got the look on her face like when she tellin' me the wise old stuff.

"Good friends, Nobie. That's what we need in this world. Good friends." Then she went back to playin' with the table.

Well, I didn't think she was gonna say that! Usually when I hear grown people talkin' 'bout different things they want, they be talkin' 'bout money or a good car or somethin' like that. Mama always do come up with a surprise.

Excerpt from *Three Wishes* by Lucille Clifton. Copyright 1974 by Lucille Clifton. Used by permission of Bantam Books, a division of Bantam Doubleday Dell Publishing Group, Inc.

Aesthetic and Creative Appeal

Behind the mill rose huge piles of black shiny coal and rich red iron ore, and a hill of rusting scrap metal. A crane that to us looked like a dinosaur with huge jaws was constantly at work picking up twisted, jagged pieces of metal and dropping them into railroad cars to be taken into the mill. Sometimes we would imagine that the mill itself was a huge beast, glowing hot, breathing heavily, always hungry, always needing to be fed. And we would run home, not stopping once to look back over our shoulders.

From *No Star Nights* by Anna Smucker. Copyright 1989 by Anna Smucker. Reprinted by permission of Alfred A. Knopf, Inc.

Figure 1-8 *continued*

Aesthetic Development

As children grow, they develop in both their appreciation of beauty in art and their ability to create. In the visual arts, children begin by first scribbling; at this stage, art is basically a physical activity. Gradually they identify what the scribbling signifies—it is a dog, or a flower, or a friend (Lowenfeld). During the preschool years they develop the ability to create identifiable shapes but use color more for preference than accuracy (Cox). Around age four-and-a-half or five they begin to formulate the idea for their drawing before they begin.

The artwork of elementary children becomes increasingly complex as they begin to be aware of relative size and to use techniques such as the overlapping of shapes. Placing all figures on a baseline and representing the sky as a band of blue across the top of the picture are common for young children. By fourth or fifth grade, most children place figures in more varied arrangements and are concerned with perspective.

Young children often draw all the figures on a baseline and represent the sky by a band of blue across the top of the picture.

Sharing picture books introduces children to media and style in art and demonstrates to them the many possibilities for representing ideas and feelings. In addition, teachers use terminology that helps children focus on techniques and composition as they talk about pictures that the children have created and those in books. The chapter on picture books presents information about artistic elements and suggests ways to guide children's appreciation and understanding of the visual arts.

Words to use in helping children describe art work include *line* (thick, thin, wavy, bold); *space* (white, negative, balanced); *shape* (solid, overlapping, repeated); *color* (warm, cool, bright, quiet); and *texture* (soft, smooth, rough).

CHILDREN'S CONCEPT OF STORY

Children's concept of what a story is develops as a result of the interaction between their reading experiences and their developing intellectual maturity. They refine their ideas about the role of truth within stories and develop expectations for how stories are told.

Arthur Applebee analyzed the patterns children used in telling stories and the responses they gave when asked about fiction and fictional characters to determine what their concept of story was. Many young children view stories more as histories than as fictional constructs. Here is an interview with Joseph, age six years and three months.

Is Cinderella a real person?   No.

Was she ever a real person?   Nope, she died.

Did she used to be alive?   Yes.

When did she live?   A long time ago, when I was one years old.

Are stories always about things that really happened?   Yes.

When did the things in Little Red Riding Hood *happen?*   A long time ago when I was a baby, they happened. There was witches and that, a long time ago. So when they started witch . . . they saw two good people and they made some more good people, so did the more horrible people. And they made more good people and the bad people got drowned.

Are there still people like that?   Nope, they were all killed. The police got them. (44)

Joseph is combining his experience with folktales with his television viewing and his knowledge of the biblical story of Noah.

At age six nearly three-fourths of the children interviewed were not certain about whether stories were real. By age nine, however, all of the children said that stories were make-believe.

Adults help children develop a sense of story by sharing literature with them regularly.

To find out what children expected as a framework for a story, Applebee asked youngsters aged two to five to tell a story. Even at age two, children recognized some conventions of story. Seventy percent of the two-year-olds began their story with "Once upon a time," concluded it with "and they lived happily ever after," or used the past tense to tell it.

As children matured, they became better at chaining events within a story, and they were more definitive about recognizing roles that particular characters played, such as a fox being clever or a witch being evil. Adults guide this development by sharing stories regularly, by selecting stories of various genre, by telling children the authors and illustrators of each book, and by encouraging children to compare one story with another.

AN APPROACH TO SELECTING LITERATURE FOR CHILDREN

Four specific beliefs underlie the suggestions in this text for selecting and sharing literature with children:

1. Literary quality is a key criterion in selecting books for children.
2. The range of books shared with children must include characters, authors, and illustrators from culturally diverse populations.
3. Choice in book selection is vital for both children and teachers.
4. Grouping books around a theme or topic and integrating literature and the content areas enhance literary understanding.

We will examine each suggestion in depth in the following sections.

High Quality Literature

When children have read and heard many examples of books high in literary and aesthetic quality, they become more discerning readers themselves. They develop an appreciation for clever or beautiful language or a carefully crafted story. Because literature is a means for exploring the human condition, it is important for children's literature to provide a depth of understanding and challenge readers to consider new ideas and share new emotions.

Thus throughout this book, you will find suggestions for assessing the literary quality of books for children, with Chapter 2 focusing on general criteria. To share high quality literature with children, you must be able to recognize it yourself. The lists of books labeled "Touchstone" are examples of books of particular genre that critics have evaluated as superior in literary quality. They are included so you can read them and use them as standards for comparing other books. Just as basalt was once a touchstone, used to test the quality of gold or silver by comparing the streak left on it by one of these metals with that of a standard alloy, other books can be compared with these touchstones to see what "mark" they make.

Cultural Diversity

Culture has been defined as "a way of perceiving, believing, evaluating and behaving" (Gollnick and Chinn 6). It involves all aspects of our lives—how we communicate with one another, how we decide what is ethical, how we relate to our families, and how we live within a group. We learn our culture from other people.

Culture reflects national or ethnic origin, age, gender, socioeconomic level, primary language, religion, geographical region, and handicapping or exceptional conditions (Gollnick and Chinn 15). Selecting books with an eye toward **cultural diversity** means making certain that the books within the chosen collection have characters that are of various cultural groups, and that their authors and illustrators also represent different cultural groups.

Cultural diversity in books for children is important because books provide a means of socialization through which children begin to understand themselves and others. We live in a diverse world, and all of us need to learn respect for ourselves and for others. Children who see people like themselves presented positively in books gain a measure of self-esteem and pride in their own heritage and background. Violet Harris writes:

> Multiethnic literature . . . enables children of color to know and understand how their people and culture have contributed and continue to contribute to human life. They can begin to perceive themselves, their communities, and their cultures as valued elements of schooling. In a sense, their worth as human beings is affirmed, and they can become empowered through increased knowledge. (176)

Children who read books about people from cultures different from their own have the opportunity to understand how others think and live.

Cultural diversity is a social rather than a literary criterion in selecting books for children. As Rudine Sims Bishop writes, "Multicultural literature is one of the most powerful components of a multicultural education curriculum, the underlying purpose of which is to help to make the society a more equitable one" (40).

Multicultural Education

Because terminology changes over time, and because different people within a group may prefer different words to describe them, it is often useful to ask members of a group what designation they would like you to use for them.

The movement toward **multicultural education** has been described by Banks as "designed to restructure educational institutions so that all students, including white middle-class males, will acquire the knowledge, skills, and attitudes needed to function effectively in a culturally diverse nation and world" (23). One result of this movement has been changes in the lists of books to be read, the literary cannon, to include the works of authors from parallel cultures. Another result has been the inclusion in textbooks of content that reflects the lives and influence of African Americans, Native Americans, Asian Americans, and Hispanic/Latino Americans as well as European Americans.

It is predicted that by the year 2020, about 45.5% of the school-age population in the United States will be people of color (Banks 24). Research also indicates that "by age 4 African American, white, and Mexican American children are aware of racial differences and show racial preferences favor-

Seeing books from a variety of cultures helps children learn respect for themselves and for others. (Source: Illustration from FAMILY PICTURES/CUADROS DE FAMILIA by Carmen Lomas Garza. Reprinted with permission from Children's Book Press, San Francisco, CA.)

ing whites. Students can be helped to develop more positive racial attitudes if realistic images of ethnic and racial groups are included in teaching materials in a consistent, natural, and integrated fashion" (Banks 26). Adults can present these realistic images through the books they select for children and in their method of presentation.

In addition to literary criteria, then, adults must look at the cultural portrayal of characters in individual books. Bishop (44–46) divides such portrayals into three categories.

1. The **culturally specific** book describes the experiences of a character in a particular nonwhite cultural group. Details about specifics such as family relationships, religion, values, and attitudes add depth and texture and give readers insight into the daily lives of the characters.
2. The **generic** book features characters of color but has few details that identify them as members of a particular culture. They are more universal, more generically American (or British or Canadian).
3. A third category is the **culturally neutral** book. These books have characters who are people of color but are basically about something else. The illustrations in these books often show cultural diversity.

Fox Song *is a culturally specific book about a child and her Abenaki Indian grandmother.* (*Source:* Text and illustration reprinted by permission of Philomel Books from FOX SONG, text Copyright © 1993 by Joseph Bruchac, illustrations Copyright © 1993 by Paul Morin.)

Fox Song by Joseph Bruchac is a culturally specific book. Young Jamie remembers her Grama Bowman, an Abenaki, cutting bark from a birch tree, explaining that the Indian name for the tree was *Maskwa,* meaning blanket tree, and noting that one only took what was needed and took it carefully so the tree would not die. She remembers the basket they made that day from the bark and spruce roots. And Jamie remembers the bits of wisdom her Grama shared with her, and that when she sang the song used to greet the day or to welcome someone, she would never be alone. An endnote explains that the author had been given a song by a Native elder and had sung it to a fox, just as Jamie did in the story. The song quoted in the story is not that special song but is instead an Abenaki greeting song sung by one group of Abenaki people after being welcomed by another.

Yo! Yes? by Chris Raschka is an example of a generic book. Two characters, one black and one white, make friends, but the focus is not on race but on personality. One child is an extrovert who opens with an enthusiastic "Yo!" The other, timid and shy, responds with a quiet and tentative "Yes?" Through a series of one- or two-word exchanges, accompanied by clear body language, the shy one takes a chance on friendship, and both go "YOW!" as they slap high fives.

What Shape? by Debbie MacKinnon is culturally neutral. This book for toddlers about basic shapes features one child with each of eight shapes, and the children are from different racial backgrounds. There is no real cultural content, but there is the very clear message that diversity is valued.

Guidelines for Selecting Culturally Diverse Books

Providing for cultural diversity means evaluating individual books and planning a balanced collection of books. When looking at an individual book that is culturally specific, evaluate the literary quality of the book and look for authenticity in the cultural portrayal.

Yo! Yes! has one black character and one white character, but the interplay is on personality, not race. (*Source:* From YO! YES! by Chris Raschka. Illustrations Copyright © 1993 by Chris Raschka. Reprinted by permission of the Publisher, Orchard Books, New York.)

While this book does not include cultural content, it does give a clear message that diversity is valued. (*Source:* Photo and text excerpt from WHAT SHAPE? by Debbie MacKinnon, Photos by Anthea Sieveking. Copyright © 1992 by Debbie MacKinnon, text. Used by permission of Dial Books for Young Readers, a division of Penguin USA Inc.

A. Accuracy

- The information in both text and illustrations should accurately portray the culture.
- The information should be up-to-date in stories with contemporary settings.

B. Portrayal of Characters

- The characters should be unique individuals, not stereotyped representatives of a culture.
- The language spoken by the characters should be accurate and appropriate to their background and the social situation in which the action takes place.
- The characters should have names that are authentic within their culture.
- The characters' lives should be enriched and guided by their cultural background.
- The characters should be proactive, that is, demonstrate the abilty to be leaders, to solve problems, to take the initiative.

C. Language

- The text should avoid terms that are demeaning or offensive.

Figure 1-9   Guidelines for evaluating cultural content in books for children.

Figure 1-9 gives guidelines for evaluating the cultural content of literature for children. It is based on the work of Bishop (49–50), Aoki (122–123), Harris (111–116), MacCann (161), and Slapin and Seale.

As you apply these criteria, you will need to read for both implied and stated information and attitudes, and you will need to think about how you will present the book to children. Some stereotypes may be blatant and require little analysis to recognize—for example, the Native Americans whose vocabulary consists of "Ugh!" and "How," or the Asian Americans who all bow politely at every opportunity. At other times, however, inaccuracies may be more subtle. What message is being conveyed when a culture's religious beliefs are described as "superstitions" or a people's everyday clothing as "costumes?" What happens when a culture's view of the role of women is presented as contemporary when in fact that view has changed over time and is now very different from the description given? What message is delivered when characters from one cultural group always look to members of another group for leader-

D. Perspective

- The text should view cultural diversity in our country as an asset and should portray culturally diverse traditions and language as valuable.
- The text should show that it is not necessary to give up non-mainstream cultural values to be successful.
- The text should present characters from diverse cultures as being part of American society, not as outsiders.
- The text should not be paternalistic in tone.

E. Illustrations

- The illustrations should be culturally accurate.
- The illustrations should enhance natural appearances, showing unique physical qualities, such as body build or hair styles, and avoiding stereotypical caricatures.
- The illustrations should show variety in the physical features among members of any group.
- The illustrations should present specific rather than generic aspects of a culture.

F. Overall Effect

- The book should have a positive, or neutral, effect on the self-esteem of a reader who is a member of the culture portrayed.
- The book should have a positive, or neutral, effect on the attitudes of readers from other cultural groups toward members of the group portrayed.

Figure 1-9   *continued*

ship and problem solving? It may help to try to imagine yourself as a member of the group being portrayed. How would it make you feel?

At times, particularly in nonfiction or historical fiction, a character expresses an attitude toward a cultural group or uses terminology that is clearly offensive. How you present the book, if you choose to use it, is central to children's understanding. If you used the nonfiction book *Off the Map* by Peter and Connie Roop, which contains selected excerpts from the journals of Lewis and Clark, you would find that the term *squaw* is used regularly. Children should be told that this was the term used by whites at that time, and that Lewis used it in a descriptive rather than a derogatory manner. Children might also try to identify Lewis's attitudes toward various tribes and Native Americans in general by reading these journal entries, inferring from the content the attitudes he held.

When you are unfamiliar with a particular culture, it can be difficult to know whether elements within the story are authentic or not. It is useful to read books by authors who are members of that group to gain insight into how they describe characters and events within the culture.

Remember also that there is variety within any culture and that groups develop and change. When you present books to children, you will want many examples of a culture during the course of the year. This will let them see not only the diversity of cultures, but the diversity within a single culture.

A balanced collection includes many examples within a culture, many different cultures, varied perspectives on events, and books that fill in omissions or correct distortions of any single book in the collection. Such a collection will have biographies of individuals revered in that culture as well as those honored by the mainstream culture. It will help children learn to appreciate the diverse world in which they live.

Different viewpoints of the arrival of Christopher Columbus in America can be seen by comparing *Encounter* by Jane Yolen (New York: Harcourt, 1992), the view of a Taino boy, with *Pedro's Journal: A Voyage with Christopher Columbus August 3, 1492–February 14, 1493* (Honesdale, PA: Boyds Mills, 1991), told in journal-entry form by a young Spanish boy on the *Santa Maria*.

Guidelines for Presenting Culturally Diverse Books
As you continue to build your knowledge about books representing diverse groups, you will also want to think about how you present these books. Here are some basic guidelines:

1. Present culturally diverse books throughout the year, not just at "special" times, such as holidays or Black History Month.
2. Group books so that children see commonalities among peoples. A book about a child with a handicapping condition achieving a goal could be paired with the story of another child reaching a goal. The feeling is the same, even though the goal may be different.
3. If the book contains words from a language you don't speak, have a speaker of that language help you learn the pronunciation. If the dialogue is in a dialect you are uncomfortable with or unskilled at reading, read the words without attempting the tones and stresses.
4. Encourage children in your class to share their own cultural experiences and to amplify elements within the book.
5. Be as specific as possible when introducing a story or an author or illustrator. For example, Gary Soto is a Mexican American author, not just "Hispanic" or "Latino." *Tree of Cranes* is about a Japanese child, not just an "Asian" child.
6. Keep a record of what you have shared with children so you can work toward a balance both among groups and within groups. For example, check to see that you have read about elderly characters as well as about new siblings and that those characters have varied interests and capabilities, lifestyles, and ethnic backgrounds.

International Literature and Global Awareness
Just as literature can introduce children to different cultures within their own country, it can also introduce them to cultures worldwide. Generally, the term **international literature** in the United States refers to books published originally in another country and then published in the United States.

When presenting culturally diverse books, one should be as specific as possible, noting that the boy in Tree of Cranes *is Japanese, not just "Asian." (Source: Illustration from TREE OF CRANES, Copyright © 1991 by Allen Say. Reprinted by permission of Houghton Mifflin Company.)*

They may have been written in English, or in another language and translated into English.

Such literature gives readers a feel for the country and for the lives of at least some of its people. However, translation can be a problem sometimes, particularly if the translator, in trying to make the story easily understood by its new audience, makes changes that alter the meaning or tone of the story. In addition to applying the criteria for all books presenting cultural diversity, look also for a smooth-reading text, names and places that have not been changed, and phrases and content that have not been Americanized.

To show children that good stories are written by people in many countries, let them know that many of the classics in literature for children first appeared in countries other than the United States. Among them are *The Tale of Peter Rabbit* (England), *Bambi* (Germany), *Pippi Longstocking* (Sweden), *The Adventures of Pinocchio* (Italy), and *The Story of Babar* (France).

In addition to books first published in other countries, other books are published in the United States but set in other countries. Sometimes the author has moved to the United States and is writing about his or her homeland. Omar Castañeda, for example, was born in Guatemala City, Guatemala, and moved to the United States when he was a child. His book *Abuela's Weave,* is set in Guatemala and tells about Esperanza and her grandmother, who go to the market hoping to sell the *huipiles,* tablecloths, skirts, and a special tapestry they have woven.

In other books the author has visited the country or learned about it in some other way. Ann Cameron was born in the United States but currently lives in Panajachel, Guatemala, a town she has named "San Pablo" in her book *The Most Beautiful Place in the World.* Illustrator Trina Schart Hyman used Cameroon as the setting for *The Fortune-Tellers,* written by Lloyd Alexander, as a way to introduce her grandson to his father's homeland and to thank the people there for their hospitality during her visit.

Books such as these help children to identify with people who may live very different lives from the readers and to see beyond appearance and action into thoughts and feelings.

Choice

Both children and adults need to have choice in the books they select. Children may be asked to read particular selections at times and for specific purposes, but both in school and out, they should be allowed to choose reading material themselves. This text assumes that children will be reading books they have chosen themselves and presents ways of encouraging children to share their reading and their responses.

Teachers also should have choice in the books they bring to their classes and should select literature based on the needs and interests of the students in their class. Teachers who are knowledgeable about literature for children are in a far better position to do this well than are those with limited literary experience.

Integration

Integrating materials in a coherent whole makes material more meaningful and more memorable. This text focuses on having children integrate ideas from literature with experiences in their own lives, with other books, and with other content areas. In addition, many important aspects of literary study and life in classrooms are integrated into each chapter. The text also includes books with characters from diverse cultures within each genre and for each theme studied rather than in a separate chapter. Suggested teaching methods are integrated into the genre chapters, both in the text and in the figures. Assessment is a part of the ongoing experiences with literature and is addressed throughout the text, as well as in a short, focused section. This text both advocates and models integration.

SUMMARY

The term *literature* refers to imaginative writing that results in an aesthetic experience for the reader. Literature for children fits this definition, and differs from adult literature in degree rather than kind. The experience and the understanding of children determine whether a book is for them.

To help select books that are appropriate for children of particular ages and experiences, adults rely on their knowledge of children's growth and reading preferences. As children mature, they become better able to understand the point of view of others, thus giving them more insight into complex plots and the motivations of characters. Their reasoning about moral issues changes from one focusing on results to one including intentions as well, and they begin looking more at justice and the consequences to others rather than just whether they will be rewarded or punished. They become skilled themselves at reading and writing, and their vocabulary and the complexity of their sentence structures develops. All these changes mean that children are able to comprehend more complex plots, more involved sentence structures, more sophisticated literary techniques, and more points of view as they mature. They also begin seeing story as fiction and recognize a variety of literary conventions. The adult looks at books with all these factors, plus a knowledge of children's reading preferences, in mind when deciding whether a particular book is likely to be understood and enjoyed by a group of children.

This textbook reflects a specific position on the sharing of literature with children. First, if children are to become discerning readers themselves, then the literature adults bring to them must be of high literary and aesthetic quality. Second, that literature should reflect the cultural diversity of our country and our world, helping children to value their own heritage and understand people with other backgrounds. Diversity should be reflected in both the fictional characters of the books, and in the authors and illustrators who create them. Third, choice in reading material is essential to both children and the educators who teach them. And fourth, individual works of literature can be combined with one another, and with activities in the content area, to present a more unified, integrated approach to learning. This textbook is organized around these ideas, and the belief that imagination permeates not just good literature, but good lives as well.

⌒ EXPLORE ON YOUR OWN

1. **Explore Your Personal Response.** Ask five teachers to tell you the title of one book they've read aloud to their class and why they chose to read it. List their reasons and identify underlying assumptions about children and about literature. Decide which reasons you believe are valid.

   or

   Read a book for children whose characters share your cultural background. Tell how authentic the book seems to you. Analyze your emotional reactions to the book.

2. **Apply Literary Criteria.** Select two books for children, one picture book and one chapter book. Tell what each might contribute to a child's language growth by looking carefully at the author's use of language. Support your conclusions with quotations from the books.

3. **Prepare to Share Literature With Children.** Select one book for a child in each of the three age designations shown in Figure 1-5. Tell why you think each book would be appropriate.

   or

   Browse through the picture section of a library. Find four books whose illustrations give cultural information about parallel cultures within the United States.

∞ EXPLORE WITH CHILDREN

1. **Explore Children's Responses.** Try reading the same picture book to children of different ages. Plan three or four questions you will ask. Analyze the children's responses just as the teacher who read *Piggybook* did.

2. **Engage Children With Literature.** Read a story to a group of children. When you've finished, ask them to close their eyes and "picture" the story. Then have them draw what

they pictured. How much variety is there? How would you explain this?

or

Ask a child to select a children's book for you to read. After you've completed it, let the child lead a discussion about the book with you, asking you questions or telling you how he or she responded to the book.

∞ SUGGESTED PROFESSIONAL REFERENCES

Applebee, Arthur N. *The Child's Concept of Story: Ages Two to Seventeen.* Chicago: The University of Chicago Press, 1978. § The author describes patterns in the stories children tell and in their responses to stories they hear and shows how the patterns relate to Piaget's stages of development.

Au, Kathryn H. *Literacy Instruction in Multicultural Settings.* New York: Holt, 1993. § This text addresses both theory and practice in how teachers may approach the teaching of reading and writing to children of diverse cultural and linguistic backgrounds.

Coles, Robert. *The Call of Stories: Teaching and the Moral Imagination.* Boston: Houghton Mifflin, 1989. § Coles shows how literature has influenced him and his students.

Elkind, David. *The Hurried Child: Growing Up Too Fast Too Soon.* Reading, MA: Addison-Wesley, 1981. § Elkind posits that children are under too much pressure, and he discusses in one chapter the role of books and media in hurrying them.

Fisher, Margery. *The Bright Face of Danger.* Boston: The Horn Book, Inc., 1986. § Fisher examines the special characteristics of the adventure story and compares stories written in that genre for adults with those written for children.

Gollnick, Donna M., and Chinn, Philip C. *Multicultural Education in a Pluralistic Society.* 3rd ed. Upper Saddle River, NJ: Merrill/Prentice Hall, 1990. Originally published in Columbus, OH: Charles E. Merrill. § The authors explore a full range of multicultural education issues in separate chapters on class, race, gender, exceptionality, religion, language, and age.

Harris, Violet, ed. *Teaching Multicultural Literature in Grades K–8.* Norwood, MA: Christopher-Gordon, 1992. § Writers from various national and ethnic backgrounds discuss literature from specific cultures, giving guidelines for selection and suggested titles.

Hazard, Paul. *Books Children & Men.* 1944. Trans. Marguerite Mitchell. Boston: The Horn Book, Inc., 1967. § This classic text celebrates both children and their books and discusses national traits found in children's books.

Lamme, Linda, Suzanne Krogh, and Kathy Yachmetz. *Literature-Based Moral Education.* Phoenix, AZ: Oryx, 1992. § After describing stages of children's moral development, the authors suggest ways of encouraging children to respond to specific books and moral issues.

Langer, Judith. *Envisioning Literature: Literary Understanding and Literature Instruction.* Newark, DE: International Reading Association, 1995. § Langer presents a theory of literature instruction that focuses on the development of "literature communities" in the classroom.

Nodelman, Perry. *The Pleasures of Children's Literature.* 2nd ed. New York: Longman, 1996. § Nodelman presents contexts and strategies for both adults and children to help them understand and enjoy literature for children.

Purves, Alan C., and Dianne L. Monson. *Experiencing Children's Literature.* Glenview, IL: Scott Foresman, 1984. § Theories of child development and of response to literature are presented as they relate to the presentation of literature to children.

✑ CHILDREN'S BOOKS CITED

Alexander, Lloyd. *The Fortune-Tellers*. Ill. by Trina Schart Hyman. New York: Dutton, 1992.

Browne, Anthony. *Piggybook*. New York: Knopf, 1986.

Bruchac, Joseph. *Fox Song*. Ill. by Paul Morin. New York: Philomel, 1993.

Cameron, Ann. *The Most Beautiful Place in the World*. Ill. by Thomas B. Allen. New York: Knopf, 1988.

Castaneda, Omar S. *Abuela's Weave*. Ill. by Enrique O. Sanchez. New York: Lee & Low, 1993.

Cleary, Beverly. *Muggie Maggie*. Ill. by Kay Life. New York: Morrow, 1990.

Collodi, Carlo. *The Adventures of Pinocchio*. 1891. New York: Knopf, 1988.

De Brunhoff, Jean. *The Story of Babar*. New York: Random, 1967.

Lindgren, Astrid. *Pippi Longstocking*. New York: Viking, 1950.

MacKinnon, Debbie. *What Shape?* Ill. by Anthea Sieveking. New York: Dial, 1992.

Potter, Beatrix. *The Tale of Peter Rabbit*. New York: Warne, 1902.

Raschka, Chris. *Yo! Yes?* New York: Orchard, 1993.

Roop, Peter, and Connie Roop. *Off the Map: The Journals of Lewis and Clark*. Ill. by Tim Tanner. New York: Walker, 1993.

Salten, Felix. *Bambi*. 1929. Cutchogue, New York: Buccaneer Books, 1983.

✑ CHAPTER REFERENCES

Aoki, Elaine. "Turning the Page: Asian Pacific American Children's Literature." Ed. Violet Harris. *Teaching Multicultural Literature in Grades K–8*. Norwood, MA: Christopher-Gordon, 1992, 109–135.

Applebee, Arthur N. *The Child's Concept of Story*. Chicago: The University of Chicago Press, 1978.

Bandura, Albert. *Social Learning Theory*. Englewood Cliffs, NJ: Prentice Hall, 1977.

Banks, James A. "Multicultural Education: Development, Dimensions, and Challenges." *Phi Delta Kappan*, 75.1 (Sept. 1993): 22–28.

Bishop, Rudine Sims. "Multicultural Literature for Children: Making Informed Choices." Ed. Violet Harris. *Teaching Multicultural Literature in Grades K–8*. Norwood, MA: Christopher-Gordon, 1992, 37–53.

Chomsky, Carol. "Stages in Language Development and Reading Exposure." *Harvard Educational Review* 42 (Fall 1972): 1–33.

Cohen, Dorothy. "The Effect of Literature on Vocabulary and Reading Achievement." *Elementary English* 45 (Feb. 1968): 209–213.

Cox, Maureen V. *Children's Drawings*. New York: Penguin, 1992.

Frye, Northrop. *The Educated Imagination*. Bloomington: Indiana University Press, 1964.

Gilligan, Carol. *In a Different Voice: Psychological Theory and Women's Development*. Cambridge, MA: Harvard University Press, 1984.

Gollnick, Donna M., and Philip C. Chinn. *Multicultural Education in a Pluralistic Society*. 3rd ed. Upper Saddle River, NJ: Merrill/Prentice Hall, 1990. Originally published in Columbus, OH: Charles E. Merrill.

Harris, Violet. "Continuing Dilemmas, Debates and Delights in Multicultural Literature." *The New Advocate* 9.2 (Spring 1996): 107–122.

Harris, Violet. "Multiethnic Children's Literature." Eds. Karen D. Wood and Anita Moss. *Exploring Literature in the Classroom*. Norwood, MA: Christopher-Gordon, 1992, 169–201.

Harste, Jerome, Virginia Woodward, and Carolyn Burke. *Language Stories and Literacy Lessons*. Portsmouth, NH: Heinemann, 1984.

Haynes, C. "Explanatory Power of Content for Identifying Children's Literature Preferences." *DAI* 49 (1988): 3617.

Isaacs, Kathleen T. *"Go Ask Alice:* What Middle Schoolers Choose to Read." *The New Advocate* 5.2 (Spring 1992): 129–141.

Kohlberg, Lawrence. *The Philosophy of Moral Development*. Vol. 1. San Francisco: Harper, 1981.

Lowenfeld, Viktor, and W. Lambert Brittain. *Creative and Mental Growth*. 8th ed. Upper Saddle River, NJ: Merrill/Prentice Hall, 1987. Originally published in Columbus, OH: Charles E. Merrill.

MacCann, Donnarae. "Native Americans in Books for the Young." Ed. Harris, Violet. *Teaching Multicultural*

Literature in Grades K–8. Norwood, MA: Christopher-Gordon, 1992, 137–169.

Mussen, Paul Henry, et. al. *Child Development and Personality.* 7th ed. New York: Harper, 1990.

Nagy, William, Patricia Hermann, and Richard Anderson. "Learning Words from Context." *Reading Research Quarterly* 20 (1985): 233–253.

Nodelman, Perry. *The Pleasures of Children's Literature.* 2nd ed. New York: Longman, 1996.

Piaget, Jean. *The Grasp of Consciousness: Action and Concept in the Young Child.* Trans. Susan Wedgewood. Cambridge, MA: Harvard University Press, 1976.

Piaget, Jean. *The Moral Judgment of the Child.* New York: Macmillan, 1932, 1955.

Piaget, Jean, and Barbel Inhelder. *The Psychology of the Child.* New York: Basic Books, Inc., 1969.

Rubin, Zick. *Children's Friendships.* Cambridge, MA: Harvard University Press, 1984.

Russell, David. *Children Learn to Read.* Boston: Ginn, 1961.

Schickedanz, Judith A. *Understanding Children.* Mountain View, CA: Mayfield, 1990.

Shaffer, David R. *Developmental Psychology.* 2nd ed. Pacific Grove, CA: Brooks/Cole Publishing, 1989.

Singer, Isaac Bashevis. "On Writing for Children." Ed. Francelia Butler and Richard Rotert. *Reflections on Literature for Children.* Hamden, CT: Library Professional Publications, 1984, pp. 51-57.

Slapin, Beverly, and Doris Seale. *Through Indian Eyes: The Native Experience in Books for Children.* 3rd ed. Philadelphia, PA: New Society Publishers, 1992.

Weisner, David. "1992 Caldecott Acceptance Speech." *Journal of Youth Services to Children* 5.4 (Summer 1992): 359–360).

 **Chapter Two**

Literature for Children: Learning About Literature

A small book, only 58 pages long, won the Newbery Award in 1986. The American Library Association gave this annual award to *Sarah, Plain and Tall* as the most distinguished contribution to children's literature published in the United States during the preceding year.

The story tells of Anna and Caleb and their father Jacob, of their life on the prairie, of Sarah, who comes from Maine in answer to the advertisement for a wife that Jacob had placed. The author of the book, Patricia MacLachlan, described in her acceptance speech how she came to write it. Her mother had told her about the real Sarah, who had come from Maine to North Dakota to marry a great uncle and to be a mother to his children. Patricia had known the story for years. When two of her children were preparing to leave home for college, Patricia's parents had taken the whole family to North Dakota to see the farm where her father had been born and to stand on the vast prairie themselves.

Now her mother was suffering from Alzheimer's disease, and little by little the memories were disappearing. Patricia MacLachlan explains:

> When I began *Sarah,* I wished for several things and was granted something unexpected. Most of all I wished to write my mother's story with spaces, like the prairie, with silences that could say what words could not. I began the story as a picture book, and it is clear to me that I wanted to wrap the land and the people as tightly as I could and hand this small piece of my mother's past to her in a package as perfect as Anna's sea stone, as Sarah's sea. But books, like children, grow and change, borrowing bits and pieces of the lives of others to help make them who and what they are. And in the end we are all there, my mother, my father, my husband, my children, and me. We gave my mother better than a piece of her past. We gave her the same that Anna and Caleb and Sarah and Jacob received—a family. (412)*

---

* Quote by Patricia MacLachlan from Newbery Medal Acceptance reprinted by permission of the author.

Where does this book fit in the whole range of literature for children? And what is it that made this "gift" an award-winning children's book?

CLASSIFICATION BY FORMAT

The many terms used to classify books for children focus on different aspects and thus do not fit into a single system. The two most frequently used systems are **format** and **genre,** within which are terms that do not fit into a neat outline.

Format refers to the physical makeup of a book: its size, shape, quality of paper and binding, typography, illustrations, and design. The format should be appropriate to the book's content and should make the book more effective.

Author/illustrator Eric Carle experiments regularly with format in his picture books. In *The Very Hungry Caterpillar,* for example, a caterpillar eats his way through a variety of fruit; with holes in the pages showing his nibbling path. In *The Grouchy Ladybug,* a rather ill-tempered ladybug argues with each animal she meets, suggesting that they fight. The pages are not full width, and as the ladybug meets larger and larger animals, the pages increase in size. The yellow jacket takes up a two-inch page, while the whale takes six full pages and an extra half page for his tail. The passage of time can be seen as the sun rises in the sky, peaks, and then begins to set.

Other creative formats employed by Carle include a spider web that is raised in *The Very Busy Spider,* so that its construction can be felt as well as seen, and a sound chip that is activated as readers turn the last page of *The Very Quiet Cricket,* so the no-longer silent cricket can be heard.

When books are described as toy books, board books, wordless books, picture books, illustrated books, chapter books, or junior novels, they are being classified by format. Figure 2-1 shows the classification of books by format with examples of books in each category.

Toy Books

Toy books are those that have some feature that makes them part toy, part book. Such books may have tabs to pull or materials to feel, or they may be shaped like a truck, complete with wheels so that the book can be rolled along the floor. Scratch-and-sniff books have areas which, when scratched, give off a fragrance. Also available are plastic books that float in the bathtub and books with pop-up figures that startle the reader on the second reading as well as the first. Usually toy books are for very young children.

Two interesting toy books designed for older children are *Leonardo DaVinci* by Alice and Martin Provensen and *Robot* by Jan Pienkowski.

Board Books

Board books, too, are usually for toddlers. These books are printed on heavy cardboard and are often laminated. The pages can be easily turned by young hands and can withstand a reasonable amount of licking and chewing. Amy MacDonald's *Let's Make a Noise,* for example, contains seven pages, with the

Figure 2-1 Classification of books by format.

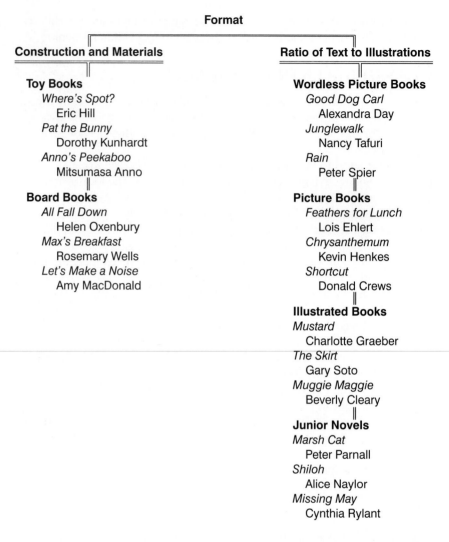

Format

Construction and Materials	Ratio of Text to Illustrations
Toy Books	**Wordless Picture Books**
Where's Spot?	*Good Dog Carl*
Eric Hill	Alexandra Day
Pat the Bunny	*Junglewalk*
Dorothy Kunhardt	Nancy Tafuri
Anno's Peekaboo	*Rain*
Mitsumasa Anno	Peter Spier
Board Books	**Picture Books**
All Fall Down	*Feathers for Lunch*
Helen Oxenbury	Lois Ehlert
Max's Breakfast	*Chrysanthemum*
Rosemary Wells	Kevin Henkes
Let's Make a Noise	*Shortcut*
Amy MacDonald	Donald Crews
	Illustrated Books
	Mustard
	Charlotte Graeber
	The Skirt
	Gary Soto
	Muggie Maggie
	Beverly Cleary
	Junior Novels
	Marsh Cat
	Peter Parnall
	Shiloh
	Alice Naylor
	Missing May
	Cynthia Rylant

story beginning on the inside front cover and ending on the inside back cover. The left page has text in the pattern of "Let's make a noise like a _____," and then the noise. The right pages shows the animal or object. All are familiar—a cat, a dog, a train. Two-year-olds grasp the pattern quickly, like to participate by making the noise, and can turn the pages by themselves.

Wordless Picture Books

Toy books, board books, and wordless picture books are all picture books—books in which the illustrations are as important as the text in telling the story. Toy and board books are set apart because of the construction or materials used.

Wordless books, sometimes called textless books, are just what their name implies—books that have no words. *Tabby,* for example, opens with a

A child who has early experiences with board books, printed on heavy cardboard, learns to handle books with ease.

little girl and her father headed toward an animal shelter, the father carrying an empty cage. Once inside they select a kitten, then walk home, where they are met by the little girl's mother and two neighbor children. The focus is on the kitten's activities, but other action occurs as well. The mother is pregnant as she greets the new kitten, and later in the book the girl is shown cuddling a baby. The change of seasons shows the passage of time, and the book concludes with the celebration of Tabby's first birthday. The main story line is clearly shown through the illustrations alone.

Look in Chapter 6 for ideas for using wordless books.

Picture Books

By contrast, in the **picture book** *Feathers for Lunch,* Lois Ehlert uses text and pictures equally to recount the story. The title page shows a bird on a bush being watched by a cat staring out the window, paws on the pane. The illustrations show the cat's tail.

The illustrations in this wordless book convey the plot and the feelings of the characters clearly. (Source: From TABBY by Aliki Brandenburg. Reprinted by permission of HarperCollins Publishers.)

Uh-oh
Door's left open
just a crack.

The next page shows the cat behind the geraniums.

My cat is out
and he won't
come back!*

As the cat prowls, various birds are shown and identified, but the bell he wears warns the birds, and the cat gets only "feathers for lunch." The text lets us know that the cat prefers something wild to the food he'd get from a can. The illustrations show us what birds he sees, which ones he goes after, and how he is caught in the end by two human hands. Together text and illustrations tell the complete story.

Illustrated Books

In **Illustrated books** the text gains importance. In these books the illustrations add to the story, but there are fewer of them and the text itself could stand alone. In *Mustard*, eight-year-old Alex realizes that the family cat is

---

* Excerpt from FEATHERS FOR LUNCH, Copyright © 1990 by Lois Ehlert, reprinted by permission of Harcourt Brace & Company.

old and that his heart is not strong. But Alex is not ready to accept the reality that Mustard may soon die. However, when the cat has a heart attack, cannot see or walk steadily, and begins to cry in pain during the night, Alex realizes that Mustard is not going to get better. Mustard is taken to the veterinarian, who gives him something "to help him die in peace." The family buries Mustard in the backyard.

Each chapter begins with an illustration of Mustard engaged in one of the activities described in that chapter. In addition, one full-page illustration in each chapter usually portrays the emotion of the humans as they are involved with Mustard. The illustrations all relate to the story and depict clearly what is happening, but they do not give new information or expand on what is already known. The text is more important than the illustrations.

Other examples of illustrated books are *Muggie Maggie* by Beverly Cleary, *I'll Meet You at the Cucumbers* by Lilian Moore, and *Rats!* by Pat Hutchins.

Junior Novels

The final step in the continuum of number and importance of illustrations is the **junior novel.** These books may contain no illustrations at all, an illustration or design introducing each chapter, or just a few illustrations. The focus is clearly on the text. Peter Parnall's *Marsh Cat*, a 128-page book, has only

Although the illustrations for this junior novel capture the setting and mood of the story, they are necessary for an understanding of the book. (Source: Illustration from MARSH CAT by Peter Parnall reprinted with the permission of Atheneum Books for Young Readers, an imprint of Simon & Schuster, Copyright © 1991 Peter Parnall.)

seven illustrations. While these beautiful pen-and-ink sketches certainly capture the setting and the appearance of Cat, they are not an integral part of the book. The text alone conveys to the reader the life of this huge, black, wild cat, how it came to live in the marsh, how it followed the small cat Puffer to the barn and wintered there, how it learned to accept the little girl, and how it eventually returned to its wild habitat.

Both *Mustard* and *Marsh Cat* are technically **chapter books** because both are divided into chapters. However, the term *chapter book* is most often used to denote short and easily read books with chapters. These books mark a young reader's transition from picture books to longer and more text-dependent books.

CLASSIFICATION BY GENRE

The second system commonly used to classify children's books is **genre,** defined by Lukens as "a kind or type of literature in which the members share a common set of characteristics" (11). Terms such as *fantasy, folktale, poetry,* and *contemporary realism* refer to genre. So, too, do more specific terms such as *mystery, sports story,* and *adventure novel.* Lukens warns that these classifications are not as clear-cut as they sound because in literature both variations and similarities occur within each genre classification. There are many kinds of poetry, for example, and not all poetry looks alike. Also, a single book may fit into more than one genre—it may be both contemporary realism, for example, and a sports story.

Prose and Poetry

Writing can be categorized as either prose or poetry, a prime example of a distinction that is not always clear-cut. **Prose** is sometimes described as "ordinary writing," though much prose contains poetic qualities. **Poetry** possesses economy of language, relies on the sounds and images of language to help convey its message, has an imaginative quality, and often expresses emotion. Because not all poems contain all of these general characteristics, readers must judge whether what they are reading is poetry. Of course, the form of the text often indicates what the author intended.

Fiction and Nonfiction

The difference between poetry and prose is determined by the ways words are used and the overall sound and form of the writing. The difference between **fiction** and **nonfiction** is determined by the content of the writing. **Fiction** is created from an author's imagination, whether pure fancy or based on actual happenings. *Sarah, Plain and Tall* is fiction, for MacLachlan wove her own story around a thread of fact, creating new characters, deciding how they would look and what they would say, and putting the events into a chronological narrative. Nonfiction is factual. MacLachlan's book could have been **nonfiction** had she told only what was known to have happened. Had she focused on the life of her great uncle or his bride, she would have written a **biography**; had she focused on the westward movement or described this couple's life on the prairie, she would have written an **informational** book. Figure 2-2 shows how a librarian worked with a group of elementary school children to explore how books could be categorized, with both fiction and nonfiction in the stack of 11 books being grouped in various ways.

Fiction is further categorized into **realism, fantasy,** and **traditional literature.** Four of the books discussed in the description of format are about cats. All are **contemporary realism,** for all tell stories that could happen

---

Leslie, an elementary school librarian, wanted the small group of students to understand that books can be classified in a variety of ways and to begin to find clues to genre classifications. When the students came in, she gave them time to look through the following books displayed on a large table:

The Sun, Our Nearest Star by Franklin Branley. Ill. by Don Madden.

The Sun, Our Nearest Star by Franklin Branley. Ill. by Helen Borton.

Eclipse: Darkness in Daytime by Franklin Branley.

The Sun, Our Neighborhood Star by David Darling.

Why the Sun and the Moon Live in the Sky. Retold by Elphinstone Dayrell.

"Early Morning," "Firefly Light," and "Shadow Play." Poems in *Poetry* by Leland Jacobs.

Under the Sun by Ellen Kandoian.

The True Book of Sun, Moon, and Stars by John Lewellen.

The Sun by Seymour Simon.

"The Moon" by Robert Louis Stevenson

Clouds by Robert Tallon.

Then she gave each student a turn to select some of the books that would form a group and explain why. Each student had to come up with a different reason for categorizing books. As each student gave a grouping, the rest of the children were encouraged to see if there were any other books that belonged in that group. Leslie recorded their categories on chart paper:

Figure 2-2   Children look at ways of grouping books.

Here are the groups the children devised:

    Books with the same title
    Books about the sun
    Books only about the sun
    Books about the moon
    Books with lots of information
    Books that are true or real
    Books that are make-believe or made up
    Books that tell a story
    Poems
    Nighttime books
    Books with the sun on the cover

Then Leslie ask them to group all of the books into only two groups. They decided on:

    Books with a story
    Books with lots of information

The next day, Leslie read *The Magic Schoolbus, Lost in the Solar System* by Johanna Cole to them. This book combines factual information with fantasy. Before she began reading, she told the children that they would have to decide in which group or groups the book might belong. After the reading, each child wrote the name of the group or groups, or could describe a new group. Leslie read their groupings and the children discussed each one. Then she asked them to come up with a new group that included all their choices. Their new, inclusive group for *The Magic Schoolbus, Lost in the Solar System* was

    A made-up story about the solar system with lots of information

In these two days, the children had addressed various genre, explored the two major categories of fiction and nonfiction, and grappled with the problem of a book that seems to fit into more than one genre.

Figure 2-2   *continued*

and all have a contemporary setting. A little girl could get a kitten from an animal shelter as in *Tabby;* cats do roam outdoors in search of birds as in *Feathers for Lunch;* cats, no matter how loved, do get older and die as in *Mustard;* and feral cats do live in the wild as in *Marsh Cat.* Realism set in the past is called historical realism, or **historical fiction,** and *Sarah, Plain and Tall* is an example.

Fantasy includes at least one action that could not happen in the world as we know it. In another cat story, *Catwings* by Ursula Le Guin, Mrs. Tabby and her four winged kittens talk with one another, and the kittens can fly. Thus the story is fantasy because the actions are impossible according to our present knowledge. **Science fiction** is a form of fantasy in which the story usually stresses scientific or technological inventions and is frequently

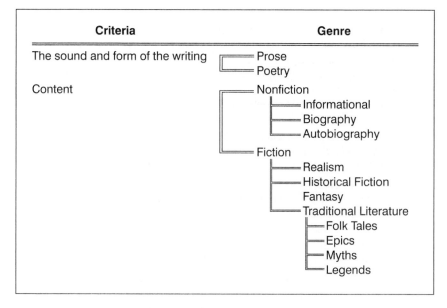

Criteria	Genre
The sound and form of the writing	Prose Poetry
Content	Nonfiction 　Informational 　Biography 　Autobiography Fiction 　Realism 　Historical Fiction 　Fantasy 　Traditional Literature 　　Folk Tales 　　Epics 　　Myths 　　Legends

Figure 2-3　Classification of books by genre.

set in the future. A cat aboard a space ship to another galaxy would be part of a science fiction story.

Ashley Bryan wrote about a cat and a rat in *The Cat's Purr*. His story is a retelling of a West Indian folktale and, as such, is a part of **traditional literature. Folktales, epics, myths, legends**—all the stories that began with storytellers and were part of the oral tradition—are traditional literature. Authors who retell and adapt these tales usually give their source and often will indicate on the title page that the story is a "retelling." Bryan includes the source and the complete tale of "Why Cat Eats Rat," the basis for his version.

Figure 2-3 summarizes classification by genre.

EVALUATING THE ELEMENTS OF LITERATURE

Even though the many ways of looking at literature and the varied backgrounds of readers may bring a variety of responses to the same piece of writing, it is important to understand how an author uses the elements of literature. At the very least, this understanding helps people talk about literature using a common language. At best, it permits people to engage in a critical aesthetic response, going beyond an initial precritical reaction to a more thoughtful, more analytic response. The elements of *plot, setting, characterization, theme, style,* and *point of view* are basic to all literature. Figure 2-4 lists guidelines for evaluating these elements in books for children.

Here is how these elements are developed and interact in *Sarah, Plain and Tall.*

Plot should
- be interesting.
- be original.
- be constructed logically, with reasonable cause and effect tying actions together.
- create tension and build to a climax.

Setting should
- set the stage for the action without intruding.
- give details that make the plot more believable.
- be accurate if a specific place or time is indicated.

Characterization should
- reveal the characters in many ways—through their actions, their thoughts, their speech, the thoughts of others about them, and the actions of others toward them.
- be clear and consistent.
- show both strengths and weaknesses of the characters.
- let characters change in believable ways.
- avoid stereotyping.

Theme should
- grow naturally out of the story, whether explicit or implicit.
- be presented in a subtle rather than an overpowering fashion.
- be worth imparting.

Style should
- be appropriate for the content of the story.
- create mood and set the pace within the story.
- include only *accurate* dialect if the author has chosen to use dialect.

Figure 2-4   Guidelines for evaluating the elements of literature.

Plot

"It's about a family that lives on the prairie," begins a young reader's description of *Sarah, Plain and Tall.*

Children often identify a book by its plot, by what happens. When they love a book, they pass on the plot to friends in a breathless synopsis: "And when Sarah said her first word was *dune,* Caleb was sad, but Papa said that they had dunes and took them out to a haystack."

Here is a full synopsis of MacLachlan's book:

> Anna and Caleb learn that their father Jacob has placed an advertisement in the newspaper for a mail-order bride. Their mother died the day after Caleb's birth, and the three of them have managed, although Anna notes that their father no longer sings. They hear from a woman in Maine, Sarah, who agrees to come for one month to see if the arrangement will work out. She describes herself as "plain and tall" and explains that she has lived with her brother but that he is soon to marry.

During the month with Sarah, both Anna and Caleb want desperately for her to stay. They listen as she describes the sea and they worry about her missing it. They cling to every positive comment in the hope that each means she will stay. If she dries spring flowers so that they can have flowers in the winter, that means she may be there in the winter! They worry when she learns to drive the wagon herself and goes to town alone. She returns, though, bringing with her colored pencils so she can add the colors of the sea to the drawing she had done of the storm-whipped prairie. In the end, Sarah does stay, telling the children that she will always miss her old home, but if she left, she would miss them even more.

The plot of *Sarah, Plain and Tall* is sometimes called **progressive** because it progresses toward a climax, or peak event: Sarah returns from town and tells the worried children that she will stay. Other books are built on **parallel** plots, with two sets of action occurring simultaneously. Usually the parallel lines of plot come together at the end of the book. Some novels have a major plot and one or more **subplots,** less important story lines that support the main action. Another large group of books for children have **episodic** plots. Each chapter tells a different tale, each with its own climax, complete in itself, but linked together by common characters or a common theme.

Novelist E. M. Forster once developed a simple test for plots. If a book says, "The king died and then the queen died," that is merely a report of two unconnected events. If a book says, "The king died and then the queen died of grief," that is a plot (130).

Sarah, Plain and Tall is built on a good plot. Events interlock. Anna and Caleb long for a mother before they learn that their father has advertised for a wife. Sarah leaves the seacoast she loves because once her brother marries, she will no longer occupy the same place in the household. Tension is created by the question of whether she will stay and is kept alive in the pattern of her actions, which alternate between those that show her homesickness and those that show her adaptability to a new situation.

In a good plot, the events happen logically, not by coincidence, and the events are often foreshadowed. It is no surprise that Sarah would leave the barn to rescue her chickens from a storm when earlier she has allowed them to follow her into the house.

For examples of books that have strong and interesting plots, look at the fantasy stories of William Steig and the realistic stories of Carol Carrick.

Setting

In some books, setting is specific. *Sarah, Plain and Tall* is set on the American prairie in the late 1800s. In other books, authors emphasize the universality of their stories by deliberately leaving place and time vague.

When the setting is specific, it must be true to the author's perception of time and place. Novels set in the past therefore require painstaking research. The work of historians often provides the foundation for such stories, a panorama from which authors pick important detail.

After such research, authors may be tempted to drop in more of the setting than the reader wants to know. But successful settings never intrude. Place and time enter gently, often with references to what is seen, heard, tasted, touched, or smelled by characters in the story.

*Reading fiction about a partic-
ular time, place, or person may
stimulate a child to seek more
information about the topic.*

The setting for *Sarah, Plain and Tall* is conveyed to the reader through Anna's senses. She describes Sarah's arriving in the spring: "She came through green grass fields that bloomed with Indian paintbrush, red and orange, and blue-eyed grass" (16). She looks at the land as spring blends into summer: "The dandelions in the fields had gone by, their heads soft as feathers. The summer roses were opening" (38). The following quote describes the storm and the barn where they go to be safe:

> The grasses flattened. There was a hiss of wind, a sudden pungent smell. Our faces looked yellow in the strange light. Caleb and I jumped over the fence and found the animals huddled by the barn. I counted the sheep to make sure they were all there, and herded them into a large stall. A few raindrops came, gentle at first, then stronger and louder, so that Caleb and I covered our ears and stared at each other without speaking. (46)*

Time and place here are more than a backdrop. The details of prairie life make the plot more believable. Fields are prepared by horse-drawn plows;

* *Source:* From SARAH, PLAIN AND TALL by Patricia MacLachlan. Copyright © 1985 by Patricia MacLachlan. Reprinted by permission of HarperCollins Publishers.

bread dough is kneaded on a marble slab; the children bathe in a wooden tub. It is a time when advertising for a wife is not unusual, and when the danger of Sarah's becoming too lonely to stay is emphasized by a visit from neighbors who know what it is to miss their friends and to be several hours away from their nearest neighbors.

For examples of books in which the setting influences the plot, look at *Mirandy and Brother Wind* or *Nettie Jo's Friends* by Patricia McKissick; or *Island Boy* or *Hattie and the Wild Waves* by Barbara Cooney.

Characterization

Learning about characters in literature is like learning about people we've just met. We see what they do, hear what they say, listen at times to what they think, and hear what others say about them. When we put these things together, we feel that we know them. Readers learn about characters such as Sarah through techniques of **character delineation**—portrayal—used in all literature.

Sarah is revealed through her actions. Her love of animals is shown in the way she treats her cat Seal, in her letting the sheep lick her fingers and naming them after her two aunts in Maine, in her immediate clucking back to the chickens that were "for eating" according to Maggie, and in her scattering of Caleb's hair so that the birds could use it in their nests. We don't have to be told how she feels because her actions show us.

In many stories, readers learn what a character is thinking. In *Sarah, Plain and Tall,* Anna tells the story, so we learn her thoughts, but not what Sarah is thinking. Sarah does reveal something of herself through her letters, however. In her first letter to Jacob, she writes that she has never been married, although it is not because she has not been asked. And she gives her own view of her personality. "I am strong and I work hard and I am willing to travel. But I am not mild mannered" (9).

Her sense of humor shows in her letter to Caleb, where she answers his question by saying that she doesn't know if she snores because her cat has never told her.

Sarah's speech also provides an introduction, one that reinforces her independence. MacLachlan never says, "Sarah is a strong-willed woman, capable of making her own decisions." Instead we hear Sarah respond to Papa's comment that the cat would be good in the barn with an immediate, "She will be good in the house, too" (19). Sarah announces that she is not afraid to climb up the haystack "dune," and she insists, rightly, that she knows how to fix a roof.

Sarah is shown further in the way others see her. Anna notes that she really is plain and tall, just as she had said, and notices that her hands are "large and rough" (19). And it is Anna who sees Sarah's eyes fill with tears when Maggie asks her if she is lonely, and who notices the sadness in Sarah's eyes when she holds a sea shell to her ear and listens to the sea. Anna describes Sarah's emotional responses, but others see her independence. Maggie meets her and assumes that she will be able to drive a wagon. Papa says, "Sarah is Sarah. She does things her own way, you know" (55). And

MacLachlan develops the character of Sarah fully through her actions, thoughts, speech, and the ways others view her.
(Source: From SARAH, PLAIN AND TALL by Patricia MacLachlan. Copyright © 1985 by Patricia MacLachlan. Reprinted by permission of HarperCollins Publishers.)

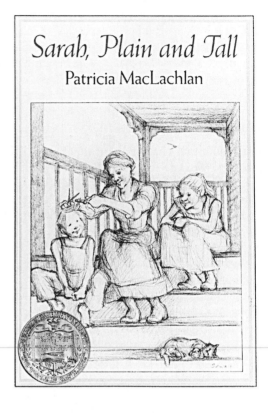

Papa doesn't ask her if she can really fix a roof, but rather "Are you fast?" (46) because the storm is approaching quickly.

The portrait of Sarah that emerges is clear and consistent but not static. She changes during her time on the prairie, in small, believable ways. She still misses the sea and her life in Maine, but she has come to love Anna and Caleb and Jacob so that she would miss them even more were she to return east. MacLachlan makes this change, this **character development,** believable by having it happen slowly and naturally.

Good writers tell about their characters in a variety of ways, just as MacLachlan does. Their characters emerge naturally from what they do, think, and say. Their characters show weaknesses as well as strengths, and if they change during the course of the book, the pace of the change is believable. At the end of the book, the reader knows enough about the characters to imagine what might happen if the book continued.

For strongly delineated characters, look at the picture books of Rosemary Wells, the chapter books of Beverly Cleary, and both picture and chapter books by Kevin Henkes.

Theme

"It's about a woman who comes to be a wife and mother."

"It's a book about living on the prairie a long time ago."

"It's about how Anna and Caleb try to make Sarah stay."

Different readers may focus on character, setting, or plot to describe *Sarah, Plain and Tall.* But underlying all three elements is a **theme,** a fundamental truth.

A theme may be explicit, with a character voicing it at some point in the story, or implicit, interwoven in all that happens. Often a book has more than one theme. Thus different readers may focus on differing underlying ideas. One reader may say that the theme of *Sarah, Plain and Tall* is the importance of family. Another may suggest that the basic theme is that people need to be flexible and able to change in order to find happiness. A third might say that the theme is that love and acceptance grow slowly. All are identifying what is for them the significant point of the story.

The theme in a well-written book never overwhelms the plot or attempts to teach a lesson. Over centuries, books for children have often turned into tracts; themes have popped out like messages in a fortune cookie, surrounded by hollow characterization and a dry plot. Good books, however, are based on complex and important themes, presented with subtlety through plot, setting, and characterization.

To practice identifying theme, look at the picture books of Leo Lionni, Eve Bunting, Lynne Cherry, Faith Ringgold, Allen Say, or Chris Van Allsburg.

Style

The presentation itself, the choice of words and the way they are put together, can either draw readers into the book or drive them away. MacLachlan captures readers through natural and compelling dialogue. Caleb's persistent questions and Anna's answers both move the story forward and show how these characters are feeling.

Authors face questions about style as they begin a book. They can use dialect in the characters' speech if that will help establish identity. They may use figurative language. MacLachlan uses figurative language when she has Anna describe hail as "ice marbles" (49) and Sarah describe her aunts by saying, "There are three old aunts who all squawk together like crows at dawn" (40).

Writers can also choose the pace of their story, the speed of Sarah's trip to town, for instance. They can make events in the plot whisk by like markers on a highway, or they can slow the pace to take a close look at one scene or to listen to one character's anxiety about what is happening.

Style permeates every sentence. It sets mood. MacLachlan often uses short sentences, the kind a young child like Anna might use in her everyday conversation. She uses verbs and adverbs to give clear yet succinct pictures of the action. Jack, the horse, "nipped" at Sarah's overalls, and Sarah answers a question "crisply." The right word eliminates the need for a sentence of explanation.

MacLachlan's style meets several criteria of vivid language use. The language itself flows smoothly. She chooses active verbs. She thrusts readers into scenes by letting them experience the sounds, smells, tastes, and textures as well as the sights. She varies sentence length and frees characters to speak conversationally with room to take a breath. Best of all, her style is never more noticeable than the story. It presents a clear picture of Anna's world.

To see how style contributes to and matches content, compare *On a Starry Night* with *The Bear That Heard Crying,* both by Natalie Kinsey-Warnock.

Point of View

Who is telling the story and how much the narrator knows constitutes **point of view.** An author may choose to tell the story in the first person, taking the role of one of the characters, usually the main character. *Sarah, Plain and Tall* is told through the eyes of Anna. First person narratives create a sense of comradeship with the teller. It limits what is told, though, to what that character knows and observes. We witness only what Anna witnesses and know only Anna's thoughts and interpretations.

MacLachlan wrote the screenplay for a television movie of *Sarah* and in it switched the perspective. The story was no longer seen through Anna's eyes, but through the eyes of the camera. Action previously not seen was shown. MacLachlan explains:

> I had always agreed with my collaborators (her term to describe the relationship between herself and actress Glenn Close and producer William Self) that the point of view should be an adult one. While the book was in Anna's voice, and the story was seen from the children's point of view, I welcomed the chance to deepen the vision; to go beyond the original. The book *Sarah* was filled with the understatements of children; of spaces filled by unspoken and unobserved moments that I knew or imagined were there, happening as the children waited to see if Sarah would stay. The reader only saw Sarah and Jacob when the children were present, and for me there was always an intense undercurrent; writing the screenplay allowed me to look into the lives beyond the words. (221)

Two children have drawn and captioned snapshots, one as though taken by Anna and the other by Sarah.

MacLachlan used the screenplay to develop the relationship between Sarah and Jacob, exploring the difficulties created by Jacob's unwillingness to face his grief over the death of his wife, and Sarah's reasons for coming.

The point of view of the camera is that of **third person,** an objective observer who tells but does not interpret. More often in books, the third person will be either **omniscient** or **limited omniscient** rather than **objective.** The **omniscient** view is all-knowing. The narrator can tell what each character is thinking, add details of past or future, and add interpretations to the action. **Limited omniscient** means that the narrator is limited to the main, or only a few, characters. The reader still knows more than a first person account would allow, but not as much as an omniscient point of view. Third person books allow authors to present several perspectives on the action.

Once an author has selected a point of view, the narration must be consistent with it. Young Anna, for example, doesn't question what her father might have put in his advertisement that would have caused Sarah to leave her beloved Maine and move inland. As MacLachlan wrote the screenplay, with its adult focus, she had to address this. Her answer was that Sarah was a realist and that she wanted her life to matter. She decided that Jacob's advertisement would have read:

> Needed: A kind woman to share a life with a widower and his two young children. To make a difference. (222)

Making a difference. This is what would have caused Sarah to come.

All the elements of literature work together in a well-written book. One element may stand out, as the characterization in *Sarah, Plain and Tall* does, but they blend to form a unified whole. The reader gets caught up in the experience of the story and only later adopts a critical stance to see how the writing contributed to the experience.

APPROACHES TO LITERARY CRITICISM

When individuals say a book is "good," or "bad," or "well-written," or "inappropriate," they are applying a set of standards, perhaps consciously, perhaps unconsciously. For the literary critic, the standards may be those of a particular approach to criticism. For the student, the standards may be those that a teacher or professor has said should apply. For the parent selecting a book for a child, the standards may be related to the anticipated reaction of the child or to the values in the story.

Often several systems come into play simultaneously, especially when individuals are assessing literature for children. It is important to identify the standards being used and the assumptions being made in both one's own and others' responses to literature.

Theories of literary criticism grow and change over time, and more than one theory will be in use in any one period. Critical theories can be described by what they emphasize without detailed descriptions of particular approaches or critics. In general, critical theory focuses on the **text** itself, or on the **context** in which the text is created or read, or on the **interaction between the text and its reader.** This last approach, **reader-response,** is currently being emphasized at all levels, and has been an enduring though frequently unrecognized approach to literature for children.

Text-Focused Approach

Focusing on the text means examining the work and seeing how its elements interact or looking at the work in relation to a larger body of literature. The discussion of *Sarah, Plain and Tall* earlier focused on the text. A comparison of it with other books of historical fiction or with other works by MacLachlan would also fit into a text-focussed approach to criticism.

The more experience readers have with literature, the more likely they are to see how one work fits in with a body of similar works. Experience also gives readers a set of expectations about literature that makes comprehension easier and a set of standards against which new texts can be measured. This development of literary standards is the rationale for reading books that are considered to be of very high quality or are labeled "classics." The lists of recommended children's books, the "Touchstone" lists, in this book indicate some of the books that critics consider excellent literature. The classics in literature for children are books that have maintained a readership from one generation to another.

While most authorities agree that *Charlotte's Web* and *Where the Wild Things Are* are classics, there is much discussion and seldom total agreement about which books **must** be included on a list of children's classics.

Charlotte's Web *is considered a classic in children's literature. (Source:* Illustration of "Wilbur" from CHARLOTTE'S WEB by E. B. White. Illustrations Copyright Renewed © 1980 by Garth Williams. Selection reprinted by permission of HarperCollins Publishers.)

Context-Focused Approach

Critical theory that **focuses on context** looks at the setting from which the text emerged. The political and social conditions of the time of the book's writing are assumed to have influenced the writing. Understanding them will thus enhance the understanding of the book.

Biographical studies of authors, as well as notations of their age, class, gender, and nationality are undertaken in context-focussed approaches to literary criticism. For example, knowing that Patricia MacLachlan was trying to preserve a part of her family history would be used in a context-focused interpretation of *Sarah, Plain and Tall*.

Sometimes a specific contemporary context is assumed, and literature is measured against that standard. Feminist criticism, for example, asserts that most literature has been written—and interpreted—from a male viewpoint. Feminist critics see a need for recognition and acceptance of a different reader stance.

A good source for learning about authors and illustrators is the series of books *Something About the Author* edited by Anne Commire (Gale Research), usually found in the reference section in the children's room of the library.

Response-Centered Approach

The **response-centered** approach to literary criticism focuses on the **interaction between reader and text** by looking at how meaning is constructed as a reader encounters a text. Louise Rosenblatt calls this a **transaction** (*The Reader . . .* 16). Meaning is neither solely in the literature nor solely in the background of the reader. It is, rather, what is constructed as the reader interacts with a text.

RESPONSE TO LITERATURE

The three boys huddled around their grandfather as he read several of the short stories from American folklore collected by Alvin Schwartz. *More Scary Stories to Tell in the Dark* had scary stories, the kind that can make hikers shiver as they listen to them around the campfire. The boys sat close, their shoulders touching, as they heard about John Sullivan, who wondered why everyone was startled to see him—until he learned he had been killed in an automobile accident the previous day, and about the undertaker who solved the problem of the woman who wanted her husband buried in a brown rather than a blue suit by simply switching his head with that of another corpse already dressed in a brown suit.

Several times the boys responded to a tale with an immediate, "Read it again!" They were experiencing the literature fully, enjoying the scary thoughts, gaining security from being together, shuddering at the wavery ghostlike voice their grandfather used. Louise Rosenblatt would describe this experience with literature as an **aesthetic** stance, an interaction with literature in which the experience is the important factor. This is at one end of a continuum, the other being **efferent** reading, where the purpose is to gain information. In both approaches to literature, meaning is created as the reader's or listener's background and understanding combine with the words of the author, and perhaps the pictures of the illustrator, in what Rosenblatt describes as a **transaction.** In addition, the context in which the transaction takes place can influence response. In this case, the words conjured up frightening images; the boys' knowledge of ghost stories helped them put the events being described into the realm of fantasy and to understand the stories literally; and their closeness with each other and with their grandfather provided a cushion of safety.

The Wide Range of Response

Still, the boys' responses were not identical; each had a different favorite story. There were parts of several stories that one of the two younger brothers did not understand and had to ask about. And only the oldest said he would like to read the stories on his own.

In fact, their responses to reading and to literature in general varied. The previous Christmas all three had received books as gifts. The oldest, age 11, had been the first to open a package that contained books. He had sat down where he was and begun to read a few pages of each book, oblivious to his unopened gifts still under the tree. The youngest, age 7, had come to his set of books soon after that. He was standing up and, seeing what he had, said calmly, "Oh . . . books," and simply dropped the package on the floor and reached for another gift. The middle brother had checked the titles of the books he was given, smiled with pleasure, added them to his collection of gifts, and continued opening his presents.

These three brothers attended the same school and had many of the same teachers, yet they responded quite differently to the books they received. They also had different reading interests. The 11-year-old liked adventure stories, considered Gary Paulson his favorite author, and read whenever he had the chance. The middle brother liked fantasy, having heard *The Hobbit* (Tolkien) read to him by his mother when he was 7 and again when he was 8. He was also enthralled with dinosaurs and liked both fiction and nonfiction on the subject. The youngest liked to be read to but didn't like reading on his own. He liked stories that could be finished in one sitting.

Age, gender, interests, and personal experiences with literature all may influence an individual's choice of what to read and, indeed, whether to read at all. A teacher working with a classroom of children will have not three individuals to consider, but 20 to 30.

How a teacher shares literature and teaches reading can strongly influence how children respond to literature. Here are some factors controlled by the teacher that have been shown to be related to how children react to literature.

1. A classroom in which children are expected to read and to write and in which they regularly share their reading and writing will stimulate children to value and enjoy literature and literacy and will help them become more discerning in their assessment of literature. (Hickman; Hickman and Hepler; Kiefer; McClure; Short; Turner)

2. The teacher's approach to the purpose of literature will influence what children expect. That is, if a teacher sees literature only as a source of information and asks literal questions about what has been read, children will read for detail. If a teacher reads only light, humorous stories, children may not understand or be open to other types of literature (Galda). If, however, a teacher expects children to talk about their personal responses to literature and encourages diversity, children will gain confidence in their own reactions (Hickman).

3. Choice in reading material will stimulate children to take personal responsibility for reading behavior and growth and will enhance enthusiasm (Cox and Many; Hickman).

4. Children may respond differently and with more depth when a book is read more than once (Jacques; Mackey; Martinez and Roser).

Educators have observed how children respond, sometimes in the context of a research study and other times as individual teachers planning and evaluating a literature program. Both literary theorists and educators have categorized responses in an attempt to understand and explain what they observe.

Critic and writer Northrop Frye suggests that there are two kinds of responses to literary experience. One occurs while reading a book or watching a play. "If our experience is limited, we can be roused to enthusiasm or carried away by something," he writes. The second kind of response occurs later: "the conscious, critical response we make after we've finished reading or left the theatre." Frye argues that practicing this second response makes the first response "more sensitive and accurate, or improves our taste" (104). Discussion or other activities after reading can provide this perspective for readers of all ages.

Children may respond differently and in more depth when they read a book a second time.

Yet classroom activities need not involve criticism to sharpen taste. Students who savor a scene from a book or interpret it in spontaneous play or lively discussion are obliged to look back on what they have read. Was the book as exciting as they first thought? What elements made it work or fail? How are others in the class reacting to it? Answering questions like these requires taking a second look at the literature, a look that can reveal flaws and strengths.

Kristo observed children and categorized responses as nonword —children might grin; literal—they might say the refrain along with the teacher; evaluative—they might say how good they thought a story was; and extension—they might dramatize a story or draw a picture about it. It is possible to categorize responses by what happens before a story, during the sharing of a story, and after a story. It is also possible to divide responses into those that are unsolicited, that happen spontaneously, and those that are solicited, as when a child is asked his or her opinion or directed to write a response. Whatever system is used, it is necessary to listen and watch carefully as children let others know what they think or feel about a story.

The Value of Response Activities

We devote time in schools to the activities we value. Sharing literature regularly and building time for children to share and respond are valued for several reasons. The primary reason is that reading literature from an aesthetic stance, that is, taking part in the experience and allowing one's feelings to surface, is key to the development of lifelong enjoyment of literature (Galda).

In addition, when children share with each other their thoughts and questions about what they have read, they are exposed to the thinking of others, and this contributes to their own construction of meaning. Figure 2-5 shows how Sara, a first grader, compared her interpretation of *Shortcut* by Donald Crews with that of a classmate. The child who hears another describe when the action took place or how she thinks a character must have felt and why now has another point of view to consider.

Experience with many forms of literature helps children develop a sense of story. As they recognize, often intuitively, how a story is structured, they have expectations for new stories they encounter. They have a schema into which new stories fit and which helps them make sense of what they are reading.

As children share responses in journals, through the arts, or in discussion, they build relationships with each other and with the teacher. Often a book provides the impetus for a discussion that might not otherwise occur. Lehr, for example, found that fourth graders reading books about the flight of refugees expanded their views about personal freedom and social injustice (194). Children also tell about their own lives as they relate them to those of characters in books, and they make connections to other books they have read. Further, they gain in social and language growth by making clear to others their own reactions.

The teacher, as either observer or participant, learns how children are interpreting what they are reading and hearing. This may be useful informa-

During read-aloud time, the teacher shared *Shortcut* by Donald Crews with the class. In the brief picture book, Crews relates a memory from his childhood. He tells about deciding with his cousins, when they were all visiting his grandparents, to take a shortcut home. The shortcut was on the railroad tracks, and when a train came, they were all forced to jump off the tracks into the briers that covered the slopes beside the tracks. They make it home safely—but they don't tell what happened, and they don't take the shortcut again.

Tanya, a first grader, began talking about the book with her friend Sara. She said that it had happened in the morning because the sky was grayish in the illustrations. Sara argued that it happened in the evening, and that the children were hurrying so they'd get home before dark. When Tanya wasn't convinced, Sara showed her that the sky was black when the children reached home. Listening to someone else talk about the story and present evidence for a different interpretation, Tanya changed her opinion.

The two girls looked again at the illustrations. Although Sara liked the pages where the train goes by, and there are no words, Tanya stayed with her initial preference for the part "where the train is really close and the WHOO is really loud."

Figure 2-5   A child's response.
Source: Illustration from SHORTCUT by Donald Crews. Text Copyright © 1992 by Donald Crews. Reprinted by permission of Greenwillow Books, A Division of William Morrow & Company, Inc.

tion for planning future experiences and for assessment. When Chris discussed her reading of *Jumanji* (Van Allsburg) with her third-grade class, she found that several of her English as a Second Language students had missed the sarcastic tone, and thus the meaning, of several of the statements. For example, they had not understood that Peter's tone of voice as he said "how exciting" gave the phrase the exact opposite meaning. The discussion helped the students make more sense of the story and of the character's reaction. It let Chris understand why her students were confused and helped her identify areas in which she might plan language lessons in the future.

Figure 2-5   *continued*

Together they decided to draw a picture about the story. They drew the children jumping from the tracks and landing in the briers. This was an exciting part, they both said, and they wondered why the author didn't make a picture of it.

The opportunity to talk about the book allowed both girls to share their reactions and preferences and to explore and clarify meanings. Time to draw, and an atmosphere that encouraged response to literature, let them work comfortably to create on paper what had been created in their minds by the words of an author.

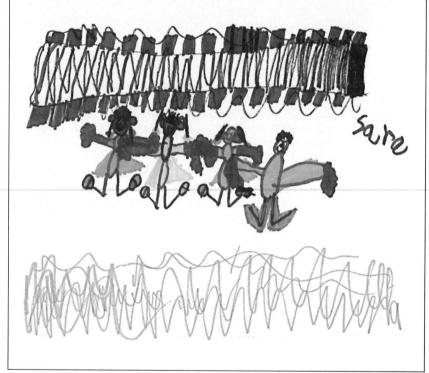

The Teacher's Role in Response

The basic role of the teacher is to facilitate the flow of ideas among students and to ensure that students are challenged and growing in their understanding of literature.

This role can be broken down into several discrete functions:

1. The teacher devises a classroom structure that facilitates participation. Examples of such structure are given in the section on discussion.
2. The teacher gives students the opportunity to choose what they read and determine what form their response may take.

One role of a teacher is to facili-tate the flow of ideas among students.

3. The teacher listens to what children say and shows respect for their opinions, thus encouraging them to listen to one another.
4. The teacher understands the cultural communication patterns of the children in the class and structures discussion to accommodate these patterns. An example given by Hepler is that of a group of Polynesian children whose discussions were better when they overlapped comments than when they took structured turns (74).
5. The teacher models and provides examples of ways to express responses to literature and shows students how to support their opinions by refer-ring back to the story.
6. The teacher helps students go beyond what they may initially notice, often by responding to their comments or using prompts for writing or art. Teachers with a strong background in literature are better able than those with a limited background to guide students toward literary understandings in free-flowing discussions (Eeds and Wells).
7. The teacher builds on the teachable moment. Figure 2-6 shows how one teacher noticed the comments her first graders made and with them wrote a story about "The Three Dinosaurs Gruff."
8. The teacher analyzes children's responses for clues to their understand-ing and as a measure of the effectiveness of the literature program and specific experiences.

In October Debra told the story of *The Three Billy Goats Gruff* to her class of 18 kindergartners. They had not been particularly interested. In February she read the story from a big book, and they noticed that the print got larger as the goats got larger and spoke louder. They also read along. They asked to dramatize the story, and for the two weeks that followed, small groups did dramatizations on their own. They also compared this story with *The Three Bears* and *The Three Little Pigs* by charting the characters, what their problems were, and what happened to them.

In March, Debra and the class were looking at pictures and talking about spatial relationships. One picture showed a dinosaur going over a bridge and a person under the bridge. One child said, "Hey. That's like *The Three Billy Goats Gruff."* Another said, "The Three Dinosaurs Gruff." The opportunity was too good to let pass. Debra had the children bring the portable chalkboard to the group. She wrote "The Three Dinosaurs Gruff" at the top and asked them how a story about Dinosaurs Gruff might begin. Throughout the story, the class gave and discussed suggestions, and when consensus was reached, the sentences were added to the story. Several times they stopped and read all that they had written, making changes in wording or sentence structure that they thought were necessary.

Here is their story:

Once upon a time there were three dinosaurs, a pterodactyl, a triceratops, and a tyrannosaurus. The dinosaurs went to cross the bridge to eat some grass and get chubby. There was a girl under the bridge. The pterodactyl went across the bridge . . . click, clack, click, clack. The girl said, "Who's crossing my bridge?"

"It's only me, the pterodactyl. I'm the smallest one. Wait until my brother comes. He's bigger. Don't eat me."

The girl said, "Just go on."

The triceratops went over the bridge . . . clip, clap, clip, clap. The girl said, "Who's that going over my bridge?"

"It's me, the triceratops. Don't eat me. I'm middle-size. Wait until my biggest brother comes." The girl said, "Just go on."

The tyrannosaurus crossed the bridge . . . boom, boom, boom, boom. The girl said, "Who's going over my bridge?"

"It's me, the tyrannosaurus. I'm going to push you off the bridge!"

And that's what he did. The dinosaurs ate lots of grass and got chubby and lived happily ever after.

The end

The next day Debra put the children in pairs, teaming up children she thought would work well together. She gave each pair a sentence and asked them to draw a picture as a team to illustrate that sentence. When they were finished, she added the words and put the book together. And, in her words, "We've been enjoying it ever since."

Debra recognized the opportunity for her students to create a story. They had made the connection between the events in the picture they were seeing and the story they had heard earlier, and were eager to participate. It was a natural time for them to review the structure of the story and the way the refrains helped build the action. Their debates over word choice and sentence structure showed their commitment to creating an effective tale, and they expressed their pride in the finished product as they read and reread *The Three Dinosaurs Gruff.* Building on her students' enthusiasm and insight let Debra guide them at the height of their enthusiasm and let them know that the connections they made were valued.

Figure 2-6   A teachable moment—*The Three Dinosaurs Gruff.*

SUMMARY

Individuals preparing to work with children need to understand literature and how it can be evaluated so that they can select quality literature and plan for balance in a literature program. In addition, they need to recognize that children respond in a variety of ways to literature read and heard.

The term *literature* generally refers to imaginative writing that results in an aesthetic experience for the reader. Writers of children's literature sometimes write for a specific child, or for their own concept of the child audience, or for no specific audience. These books become books for children when children read, enjoy, and understand them.

Children's books are classified in two common ways—by format and by genre. Format refers to the physical makeup of the book and often indicates the ratio of words to pictures in a book. Format determines whether a book is termed a toy book, a board book, a wordless book, a picture book, an illustrated book, or a chapter book. Genre is a classification of literature in which members share common characteristics. Some typical classifications of genre are fiction or nonfiction, prose or poetry, realism, or fantasy.

While the many ways of looking at literature and the varied backgrounds of readers bring a variety of responses to the same piece of writing, it is important to be able to examine how an author uses the elements of literature. The plot should be interesting and logical, with events interlocking rather than happening by coincidence. The setting should be accurate if it is a specific time and place and should support but not intrude on the story. Characters should be presented through several techniques and should emerge clearly and consistently. The theme should be significant, growing naturally out of the plot, setting, and characterization. Style should be appropriate to the story. Once the author selects a point of view, the narration should be consistent with it. All the elements work together in a well-written book.

Approaches to literary criticism often focus on either the text itself, the context in which the writing occurred, or the interaction between the reader and the text. This last approach, in which a reader constructs meaning as he or she reads, is most viable in work with children and literature.

Children respond to literature in a variety of ways that are influenced by age, gender, interests, and personal experiences. Teachers can help children acquire an aesthetic stance toward literature by developing a classroom in which children see themselves as readers and writers, have choice in what they read, have opportunities to share their thoughts about their reading, and are challenged to extend their thinking while still having their opinions respected.

∽ EXPLORE ON YOUR OWN

1. **Explore Your Personal Response.** Read three books that are often thought of as "classics" in literature for children. Do you think children should be required to read all or any of these? On what do you base your decision?
2. **Apply Literary Criteria.** Look at two reviews of the same book. Compare the content and

conclusions of the reviews. Identify the criteria each reviewer seems to be using.
3. **Prepare to Share Literature With Children.** Select and read a book for children. Write three questions you might ask a child that would elicit a personal response and three that would guide the child to evaluate the literary merit of the selection.

∽ EXPLORE WITH CHILDREN

1. **Explore Children's Responses.** Read the first two pages of three different books to several children. Have each one tell you which of the three books they would choose to read and why. Which of their statements relate to the books? Which relate to their own backgrounds?
                              or
Select a folktale in a trade book edition and a Disney edition. Read both to at least three children.

Have them tell you which they prefer and why. What seems to be influencing their responses?
2. **Engage Children With Literature.** Read a story to a group of children. Have them select one of the characters; then as a group list what they know about that character. Have them tell you how they know it. Discuss with them the different ways the author has let them know about that character.

∽ SUGGESTED PROFESSIONAL REFERENCES

Eagleton, Terry. *Literary Theory: An Introduction*. Minneapolis: University of Minnesota Press, 1983. § Eagleton describes modern literary theories in this book, which is designed for readers with little background knowledge of the field.

Cameron, Eleanor. *The Seed and the Vision: On the Writing and Appreciation of Children's Books*. New York: Dutton, 1993. § In 12 essays Cameron discusses both specific literary works and current critical theories.

Hazard, Paul. *Books Children & Men*. 1944. Trans. Marguerite Mitchell. Boston: The Horn Book, Inc., 1967. § A classic text that celebrates both children and their books and discusses national traits in relation to children's books.

Hunt, Peter. *Criticism, Theory, & Children's Literature*. Cambridge, MA: Basil Blackwell, 1991. § Hunt explores how critical theory can help in understanding what happens when we read and when we make selective judgments about books.

Lukens, Rebecca J. *A Critical Handbook of Children's Literature*. 5th ed. New York: HarperCollins, 1995. § Major genres and common elements of literature are explained, then illustrated with examples from books for children.

May, Jill P. *Children's Literature and Critical Theory*. New York: Oxford University Press, 1995. § May describes different schools of literary criticism and shows how literary criticism can be a part of elementary classroom practice.

Meek, Margaret, Aidan Warlow, and Griselda Barton. *The Cool Web: The Pattern of Children's Reading*. New York: Atheneum, 1978. § This collection of 50 essays focuses on how readers relate books to their own lives, how authors see their role, how certain critics apply their skills to literature for children, and how specialists in various fields approach children's books.

Nodelman, Perry. *The Pleasures of Children's Literature*. 2nd ed. New York: Longman, 1996. § Nodelman presents contexts and strategies for both adults and children to help them understand and enjoy literature for children.

Nodelman, Perry, ed. *Touchstones: Reflections on the Best in Children's Literature*. West Lafayette, IN: Children's Literature Association. Volume I, 1985; Volume II, 1987; Volume III, 1989. § This collection of critical essays is organized by genre and focuses on specific books for children.

Rees, David. *The Marble in the Water.* Boston: The Horn Book, Inc., 1980. § Rees, a contemporary British critic, analyzes the work of 10 American and 8 British authors of fiction for children.

Rees, David. *Painted Desert, Green Shade.* Boston: The Horn Book, Inc., 1984. § Rees presents critical essays on 12 authors of works for children and young adults.

Rosenblatt, Louise. *Literature as Exploration.* 1938. New York: Noble and Noble, 1968. § Rosenblatt examines the literary experience as being concerned with the book, the reader, and the interaction of the two.

Rosenblatt, Louise. *The Reader the Text the Poem: The Transactional Theory of the Literary Work.* Carbondale, IL: Southern Illinois University Press, 1978. § In this full development of the theory that reading is a "transaction" between reader and text, Rosenblatt shows how reader and text both contribute to the construction of meaning.

Short, Kathy G., ed. *Research and Professional Resources in Children's Literature: Piecing a Patchwork Quilt.* Newark, DE: International Reading Association, 1995. § Short and her coauthors categorize and review research, professional journals, and professional books on literature for children.

Sloan, Glenna Davis. *The Child as Critic.* 3rd ed. New York: Teachers College Press, 1991. § Sloan addresses the importance of a strong literature program based on literary theory within the context of "literature-based" classrooms.

Smith, Lillian H. *The Unreluctant Years: A Critical Approach to Children's Literature.* Chicago: American Library Association, 1991. § In this book, originally published in 1953, Smith presents criteria for assessing the literary quality of children's books.

Whale, Kathleen B., and Trevor J. Gambell, eds. *From Seed to Harvest: Looking at Literature.* Canada: The Canadian Council of Teachers of English, 1985. § These essays present issues and reflections on literature and response to literature.

White, Mary Lou. *Children's Literature: Criticism and Response.* Upper Saddle River, NJ: Merrill/Prentice Hall, 1976. Originally published in Columbus, OH: Charles E. Merrill. § Essays on literary criticism of literature for children are grouped within the framework of four theories: psychological, sociological, archetypal, and structural.

∽ CHILDREN'S BOOKS CITED

Aliki. *Tabby.* New York: HarperCollins, 1995.

Bryan, Ashley. *The Cat's Purr.* New York: Atheneum, 1985.

Carle, Eric. *The Grouchy Ladybug.* New York: Crowell, 1977.

Carle, Eric. *The Very Busy Spider.* New York: Philomel, 1984.

Carle, Eric. *The Very Hungry Caterpillar.* Cleveland: World, 1969.

Carle, Eric. *The Very Quiet Cricket.* New York: Philomel, 1990.

Ehlert, Lois. *Feathers for Lunch.* San Diego: Harcourt, 1990.

Graeber, Charlotte. *Mustard.* Ill. by Diane Diamond. New York: Macmillan, 1982.

Le Guin, Ursula K. *Catwings.* Ill. by S. D. Schindler. New York: Orchard, 1988.

MacDonald, Amy. *Let's Make a Noise.* Ill. by Maureen Roffey. Cambridge, MA: Candlewick Press, 1991.

MacLachlan, Patricia. *Sarah, Plain and Tall.* New York: Harper & Row, 1985.

Parnall, Peter. *Marsh Cat.* New York: Macmillan, 1991.

Schwartz, Alvin. Collector. *More Scary Stories to Tell in the Dark.* Ill. by Stephen Gammell. New York: Lippincott, 1984.

Tolkien, J. R. R. *The Hobbit.* Boston: Houghton, 1938.

Van Allsburg, Chris. *Jumanji.* Boston: Houghton, 1981.

∽ CHAPTER REFERENCES

Cox, Carole, and Joyce E. Many. "Toward an Understanding of the Aesthetic Response to Literature," *Language Arts* 69.1 (Jan. 1992): 28–33.

Eeds, Maryann, and Deborah Wells. "Grand Conversations: An Exploration of Meaning Construction in Literature Study Groups." *Research in the Teaching of English* 23.1 (Feb. 1989): 4–29.

Forster, E. M. *Aspects of the Novel.* New York: Harcourt, 1954.

Frye, Northrop. *The Educated Imagination.* Bloomington: Indiana University Press, 1964.

Galda, Lee. "How Preferences and Expectations Influence Evaluative Responses to Literature" Eds. Kathleen Holland, Rachael Hungerford, and Shirley Ernst.

Journeying: Children Responding to Literature. Portsmouth: Heinemann, 1993, 303–316.

Hepler, Susan. "Picking Our Way to Literacy in the Classroom Community." Eds. Charles Temple and Patrick Collins. *Stories and Readers: New Perspectives on Literature in the Elementary Classroom.* Norwood, MA: Christopher-Gordon, 1992, 67–83.

Hickman, Janet. "A New Perspective to Response to Literature: Research in an Elementary School Setting." *Research in the Teaching of English* 15.4 (Dec. 1981): 343–354.

Hickman, Janet, and Susan Hepler. "The Book Was OK, I Love You." *Theory Into Practice* 21.4 (Autumn 1982): 278–283.

Jacques, Deborah G. "The Judge Comes to Dinner." Ed. Kathleen Holland, Rachael Hungerford, and Shirley Ernst. *Journeying: Children Responding to Literature.* Portsmouth: Heinemann, 1993, 43–51.

Kiefer, Barbara. "Picture Books as Contexts for Literary, Aesthetic, and Real World Understandings." *Language Arts* 65.3 (Mar. 1988): 260–271.

Kristo, Janice V. "Reading Aloud in a Primary Classroom: Reaching and Teaching Young Readers." Eds. Kathleen Holland, Rachael Hungerford, and Shirley Ernst. *Journeying: Children Responding to Literature.* Portsmouth: Heinemann, 1993, 54–71.

Lehr, Susan. "Struggling for Freedom: Children's Responses to Stories About the Flight of Refugees." *The New Advocate* 7.3 (Summer 1994): 193–203.

Lukens, Rebecca. *A Critical Handbook of Children's Literature.* 5th ed. New York: HarperCollins, 1995.

McClure, Amy. "Children's Responses to Poetry in a Supportive Literary Context." Eds. Kathleen Holland, Rachael Hungerford, and Shirley Ernst. *Journeying: Children Responding to Literature.* Portsmouth: Heinemann, 1993, 151–172.

Mackey, Margaret. "Many Spaces: Some Limitations of Single Readings." *Children's Literature in Education* 24.3 (Sept. 1993): 147–163.

MacLachlan, Patricia. "Newbery Medal Acceptance." *The Horn Book Magazine* 62 (July/Aug. 1986): 407–413.

MacLachlan, Patricia. "Painting the Air." *The New Advocate* 3.4 (Fall 1990): 219–225.

Martinez, Miriam, and Nancy Roser. "Read It Again: The Value of Repeated Readings During Storytime." *The Reading Teacher* 38.8 (Apr. 1985): 782–786.

Rosenblatt, Louise. "The Literary Transaction: Evocation and Response." *Theory into Practice* 21.4 (Autumn 1982): 268–277.

Rosenblatt, Louise M. *The Reader the Text the Poem.* Carbondale: Southern Illinois University Press, 1978.

Short, Kathy G. "Making Connections Across Literature and Life." Ed. Kathleen Holland, Rachael Hungerford, and Shirley Ernst. *Journeying: Children Responding to Literature.* Portsmouth: Heinemann, 1993, 284–301.

Turner, Julianne C. "The Influence of Classroom Contexts on Young Children's Motivation for Literacy." *Reading Research Quarterly.* 30.3 (July/Aug./Sept. 1995): 410–441.

 **_Chapter Three_**

The Classroom or Center:
Creating a Community of Readers

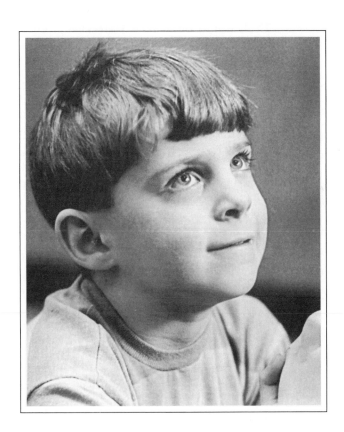

Stephanie wanted to get to know her second graders as the new year began. During the first few weeks, she talked with the children individually, finding out about their interests, their attitudes toward reading and writing, and what they hoped to learn in the coming year. They were candid as they responded to the question, "How do you pick out books that you think you'll enjoy?"

"Well, I like cats, and if I see a cat on the cover I know I'll like it. And if it's, like, a dance book, I'll get it."

"I know the kind of books that I like. Like, fact books. Fact books about things like animals. And I like mystery stories."

"Well, first I look at the pages. And then I read some of the pages to see if it's interesting."

"Well, usually I look at a book and I read the title. And if it sounds interesting I look at the back and I see the paragraph they wrote on it. And if it sounds interesting, I read it."

"In the library the books are faced the title way; they're faced with the pages at the back of the wall. So I look at the titles and I pick the titles I can read 'cause I know I've already read them."

"If there aren't hard words I pick them out. And if I like the pictures. If they don't have good pictures, I don't pick them out."

"Well, I usually, um, I look to see how hard the words are. And the pictures. Well, it doesn't have to have really good pictures if it has a lot of words."

"I just look through them and read a couple of sentences."

"I chose this book in the school library—it's called *Cam Jansen and the Stolen Diamonds*—because I read some of the Cam Jansen books at school and we did these activities, and I liked them. So I just, like, wanted to read some more of them. So I went to the library and they had some."

"Well, I usually look at the author. Like, I like—um, my dad read me a Stephen King book once. I couldn't even see the words, they were so small! And I like Tomie dePaola. I like Eric Carle."

These children expressed a wide variety of reasons and strategies for selecting books, many of which we as adults also use. We like the subject or the genre, the book looks interesting, the blurb on the cover makes it sound good, the book is long or short, easy or difficult, or we know and like the series or the author. These are valid ways of choosing books for individual reading.

STRUCTURING THE CLASSROOM ENVIRONMENT

How a teacher sets up the classroom directly influences how children interact with the teacher and with each other, what content and skills are learned, and whether children are motivated to read (Palmer and Codling). Both the physical arrangement and the procedures to be followed determine the level of formality, the expectations for student behavior, and the learnings that are valued. When Stephanie interviewed each of her students about how they selected books and what they liked to read, she was demonstrating to them that reading was important, that she would encourage individual choice of books, and that she would pay attention to each individual—that *each* child mattered.

A classroom can be arranged so that children know their experiences with literature are important and that their responses are valued. Frank Smith describes developing classrooms where children become a community of readers, where it is expected that they will enjoy reading and participate in discussing what they and others have read. Teachers are central in developing such a community.

The Physical Arrangement

There is, obviously, no one "right" or "perfect" way to arrange the furniture and allocate the space within a classroom. Teachers usually work with what the school provides, at least primarily, and there will be great variance in this. Some classrooms have tables, other desks, for example. The way the tables or desks are aligned gives a message. Straight rows with space between desks indicates that work is to be done independently. Small groupings of desks or chairs around a table are conducive to conversation and sharing. Desks all facing the front of the room focus atten-

Look at the arrangement of furniture in several of your college classes. What does this tell you about expectations for students' behavior?

tion on the teacher. Desks in a circle or horseshoe provide for students to attend more easily to the comments of their classmates. To develop a community of readers in the classroom, desks and spaces should be arranged to encourage easy conversation about books. Many teachers also bring in a rocker or other comfortable chair to use as they read aloud to their classes. This helps to create a place for sharing literature that is warm and homey.

To encourage the reading and discussion of good literature, a teacher should make certain that good books are plentiful and displayed attractively. This usually means a library area where books are on shelves with the covers, and not just the spines, showing. The books can be easily reached and removed for perusal. Children have a comfortable place to sit while they look at the books, on a rug, squares of carpet samples, or bean bag chairs. Figure 3-1 describes how one kindergarten teacher uses baskets for storing books and how the children have learned to care for the library area themselves.

Sketching a plan for the classroom arrangement and then visualizing children and activity within the class can be very helpful. You may notice,

---

Cheryl thought about how she could organize a library area so that her first-grade children would have easy access to the books, so that they could help keep it in order and learn about books in the process, and so that it would be an inviting and attractive area. She decided to use plastic baskets.

The baskets were upright on the floor and a low shelf. Children could move a basket and look at all the books in it. Cheryl made certain that baskets did not become crammed.

The books in each basket fit a particular category. Some baskets were arranged by topics the children were studying such as farm life or seasons. Some were categorized by author or illustrator. Other baskets contained easy reading. Each basket was labeled so children could locate particular books quickly. When children returned books to the baskets, they could look at the titles and the pictures to find the right place for the book. With illustrators, they often recognized the style of art. They could also match the author and illustrator names with the names of books already in a basket. Knowing the people and topics being discussed in their class helped the children narrow the possible categories. On Fridays, it was the job of children in the class who could read to check the baskets to see that the books had been filed correctly.

Cheryl also found that this system had an added benefit. When she wanted to talk with the children about a topic or do activities related to it, she could quickly grab the right basket and bring it to the discussion group, having resources at her fingertips.

Figure 3-1   Baskets for organizing the classroom library.

for example, that the reading area is between the sink and the art supplies, creating a traffic pattern that may disrupt children's concentration in the reading area. You may see that the science corner is next to the reading area and realize that this will be very effective as you teach children to find information using nonfiction books.

Change any problems in the physical arrangement of the classroom and observe the effects. Often children can be included in the problem solving. "Our library corner seems to be a good book-choosing place in the mornings, but in the afternoons, while we are waiting for different bus dismissal times, it seems to be noisy and crowded. Does it seem this way to you? What might we do to make it better?"

Procedures and Atmosphere

Just as the physical arrangement of a classroom affects the work within the classroom, so too do the procedures and general atmosphere. The following procedures encourage the development of reading skill and enhance children's enjoyment of reading:

1. There is a regular time for independent reading, often labeled Sustained Silent Reading (SSR) or Drop Everything and Read (DEAR). Everyone, including the teacher, takes time to read. Teachers often begin with only short periods of time—perhaps as little as three or four minutes for first graders—then gradually lengthen the time.
2. Children are given time to talk about their reading and to share their reactions informally. Often teachers take a few minutes following Sustained Silent Reading for children to tell about their books. Some classrooms have graffiti boards in the library area where children write comments about the books they're reading. After they have finished a book, children can make comments on strips of paper clipped to the first page of each book. Others in the class then can see what their classmates thought. This procedure can be very motivating for children as they select books. Of course, there is also the chance that the first child who reads a book dislikes it and dissuades others from reading it.
3. Children engage in response activities and have a regular opportunity to share their journals, art, and writing.
4. Children can take books from the library as they finish a book, not just at the scheduled weekly library time.
5. Special events focus attention on books and reading. Such events include book fairs, book clubs, participation in the Reading is Fundamental program, guest readers, or author visits. Figure 3-2 shows how two kindergarten teachers send books home for parents and children to read together.

Figure 3-2 Book bags
for home reading.

Kim and Sookyung, friends who taught kindergarten in the same school, went to an afterschool workshop together. There the presenter talked about "book bags," a system of putting a book, a suggestion for the parent about reading the book with the child, an activity that could be done to accompany the book, and sometimes a toy or artifact in a cloth bag that the child could borrow. The purpose was to involve the parent in reading with the child, reinforce the idea that reading was fun, give the child added practice in reading, and set up a system of communication with the parent.

They decided to develop "book bags" themselves. They were able to secure funds from the PTO for 20 books and 20 canvas bags. Together they made a list of the books, with Kim taking 10 and Sookyung taking 10. They would share the bags.

The bag for *Owen* by Kevin Henkes (New York: Greenwillow, 1993) suggested that the parents read to their child the story about Owen and his love and need for the fuzzy yellow blanket he had had since he'd been a baby. Then they could go back and let the child point to and tell what he or she noticed in the pictures. After that, they could work with their child to make something a child could carry from the 18-inch square of yellow cloth that was included. In the story, Owen's mother cuts his blanket in small handkerchiefs that he can carry with him.

Kim and Sookyung wrote to the parents explaining the purpose and procedure of the book bags and began letting children borrow them once they had five completed. The children began showing what they had made or telling what they had done, and the popularity of the book bags grew. The "Owen" creations began filling a shelf, and children were eager to borrow that bag.

The teachers became aware as they developed bags that they needed to include more variety in the activities. Responses from parents let them know when directions were not clear. They plan to continue developing new bags and to revise their original ones.

SELECTING BOOKS

When teachers select books to use in their classrooms, they, like Stephanie's second graders, pay attention to genre, author and illustrator, subject, level of reading ability required, and how interesting the book appears. But they have other criteria as well, often depending on the intended use of the book.

Books for Reading Aloud

Books to be read aloud to children should be of high literary quality. Given the limited number of books that can be shared in this way, it makes sense not to waste the time of either teacher or the child on poor or mediocre books.

As you select books, plan to include a variety of genre such as prose and poetry, realism and fantasy, contemporary and historical; a variety of new books and classic stories; and variety of art and illustration styles. This is your opportunity to demonstrate to children the breadth of literature available and to introduce them to enjoyable books they might not select themselves. Some books, such as those with heavy dialect in the speech of the characters, may be difficult for children to read themselves. When you share such books orally, you bring new literature to children and you help them hear variety in spoken English.

Make certain also that many cultures are represented in both the characters in the books and in the authors and illustrators who created them. Children need to see themselves represented in the literature they hear and to hear about other groups as well. They need to know that peoples from all groups tell stories.

Keep your audience in mind. Think about the interests of the children you are teaching, their backgrounds, and their understanding level. Look for similarities between their lives and the story. Often this will be people or emotions children will recognize. Wendy Hartmann's book *All the Magic in the World* is set in her home of South Africa, yet American children can identify with familiar feelings about what it is like to feel clumsy and to believe in special magic items. It is the emotion more than the setting that provides contact.

Books with varieties of spoken English include books *Obadiah the Bold* by Brinton Turkle, *Flossie and the Fox* by Patricia McKissack, and *Clancey's Coat* by Eve Bunting.

Children can identify with the emotions of characters even if the setting is new to them. (Source: From ALL THE MAGIC IN THE WORLD by Wendy Hartman, illustrated by Niki Daly. Copyright © 1993 by Wendy Hartman for Text. Copyright © 1993 by Niki Daly for Illustrations. Used by permission of Dutton Children's Books, a division of Penguin Books USA, Inc.)

Many teachers find it helpful to keep a record of what they have read to their classes. Some note it in a plan book; others keep a log. The record helps them maintain a balanced selection over time without feeling constrained to have "one of each" for variety in each group of read-aloud books.

Books for Classroom Libraries

Selecting books for a classroom library is similar to the selection of books for oral reading, but there are several additional criteria. First, reading level as well as interest and understanding level must be considered. You need to know the range of reading levels within your class and select books that allow children of varying reading abilities to find appropriate books. Many word processing programs can assess the reading level of a selection when samples of 100 words are typed in. Various readability formulas are used, most relying on the length of the sentences and the difficulty of the words. You may want to use such a procedure to help you learn to estimate reading levels or to assess books you are unsure about. Another approach is to take copies of the books to class and ask several children to read a few pages. You will see how the books match your students' reading levels and interests and will build your own skill in quickly assessing approximate reading level.

If children are selecting books to read and discuss in groups, you may want to have several books on a similar theme that vary in reading level. Generally teachers select books that are available in paperback editions so ordering multiple copies will be cost effective. For example, Trent, a third-grade teacher, presented four books about friendship, all with school settings. *Randall's Wall* (Fenner) is on a fourth-grade reading level; *Amber Brown is Not a Crayon* (Danziger) third-grade level; and *December Secrets* (Giff) and *Arthur's Great Big Valentine* (Hoban) on a second-grade level. He briefly introduced each book, left all four out for the day so the children could browse through them, and then had each child select a book to read. Children can learn to select books at an appropriate level, and when he first began this system, Trent allowed children to change groups after two days if the reading was too difficult or too easy. By having books on the same theme, Trent could have children first discuss a common reading within one group and then have them form new groups comprised of children who had read different books. The first group deepened their understanding through discussion, and the second summarized their book, listened to others, and looked for commonalities.

SHARING LITERATURE

The key to a good presentation of literature is preparation. Mastering the material before you introduce it ensures that you will present it well and frees you to ride out distractions, to be aware of children's reactions, to change the program on the spot when necessary, and to make the literature fresh and new.

Reading Aloud

As a teacher, you will be reading aloud to your students no matter what the grade level. If you are teaching fourth grade, you will probably be reading a few chapters a day from a novel or sharing short stories. If you are teaching second or third grade, you will likely be sharing a combination of picture books and chapter books. If you are working with preschoolers, kindergartners, or first graders, you will be reading picture books, often reading more than once a day to your class.

Whatever the grade level, it is essential that you read the book yourself before sharing it with children. This allows you to assess its literary quality and appropriateness for your class. This preview also lets you identify any unfamiliar words, dialect, or special expressions that you want to practice saying aloud. In addition, it will eliminate surprises in the content and, if you read it orally, will help you estimate the time a particular reading will take.

As you prepare a story, picture yourself sharing it with children:

- You begin by making certain that all of the children can see the book, and you give them a moment to get settled. You introduce the story by telling the title, author, and illustrator and perhaps giving other information, such as other books by the author or why you decided to read this particular book. You briefly introduce the story and do not give away the main points. (Imagine yourself being given a mystery with an introduction like this: "You'll love reading this story and learning how the maid managed to poison the whole family without getting caught.") Telling too much can ruin a story for children as well as for adults.

- You hold the book so that your face is not obscured, and you look up and make eye contact with your students. This increases the sense of shared enjoyment and keeps you aware of the children's reactions.

- If you are reading a picture book, you share the pictures by either looking down over the top of the book as you read or by holding the book to the side. If there is a lot of text, you might read first and then show the illustrations.

- Your book is an appropriate size for the number of children listening and for the distance between the children and the book. Denise Fleming's *Barnyard Banter,* for example, is 9 by 12 inches and is big enough for reading to a group of 20 children. They can see the brightly colored illustrations of the barnyard animals and answer the repeated question, "But where's goose?" with not just "where," but by describing the goose's actions as well, as it attempts to catch an insect.

- You set general expectations for student behavior during reading, and you tell students if there will be a change. Many teachers ask students to refrain from making comments until the reading is completed. This maintains the flow of the story and keeps the mood intact. Other teachers encourage children to comment as illustrations are shown to heighten involvement and stimulate interaction.

Much of the plot of Tough Boris *is conveyed through the illustrations. (Source:* Illustration from TOUGH BORIS by Mem Fox, illustrations Copyright © 1994 by Kathryn Brown, reproduced by permission of Harcourt Brace & Company.)

The book itself may provide the key for specific reading, regardless of the general pattern. If you were reading *Tough Boris* by Mem Fox to a group of kindergartners, for example, you might tell them that for the first reading, you are going to read the page and then ask them to tell you what they see in the illustrations. You would do this because the illustrations have a story that parallels the story in the text. Thus you would read that Boris is a tough pirate, and scruffy, and greedy, but that when his parrot dies, he cries. As the children look at the pictures, they would add the following comments: that the pirates had found a treasure chest, that it held a violin in addition to gold, that the cabin boy took the violin from Boris, and that when the parrot died, pirate and cabin boy put the body into the violin case and both cried. They could then recognize that the boy is the narrator of the story. On a second reading, you might have children repeat the phrases they recognize, aided by the clear patterning in the text. Find a style that fits your purposes and is comfortable for the children, but be willing to change and adapt when a different style is indicated.

Reading well requires practice, but because it is often hard for people to hear their own voices, you may want to ask for help from friends or family in identifying your strengths and weaknesses. One way to get a clear idea of how you sound to others is to read one or two books, perhaps a picture book and an excerpt from a chapter book, aloud to several adults. Ask them to rate your reading frankly on copies of a chart such as the one shown in Figure 3-3.

Your evaluators need not sign their names. Look for patterns when you read the charts and then try to correct weak points. Practice. Recording yourself when you read to children and later listening to the tape may also give surprising insight on how you could be a better reader. Even experienced teachers find that tapes can turn up irritating quirks of expression, as well as examples of good phrasing and expression. When the tapes are well

ORAL READING RATING SHEET			
	Excellent	**Satisfactory**	**Needs Improvement** (Specify the problem)
Rate			
Volume			
Enunciation			
Expression			
Eye Contact			
Showing of Illustrations (if appropriate)			
Comments:			

Figure 3-3   Rating sheet for reading aloud.

done, you can add them to the listening library in your classroom, allowing children to hear a favorite story again.

Storytelling

Preparation for storytelling should not involve line-by-line memorization. Instead, storytellers either plot out the main elements of action and any refrains or language they want to use, and practice retelling; they read and reread the story until a retelling comes naturally. Some books translate to spoken stories better than others. Written stories that adapt well for telling have concise, action-filled plots, begin boldly, and build toward a climax. They offer drama and emotional appeal and usually have only a few characters. They also are not dependent on either the illustrations or the exact wording of the text.

Chapter 8 has more detailed suggestions for telling folktales.

The Three Wishes as retold and illustrated by Margot Zemach would be a good story for telling. In this traditional tale a hard-working man and wife help an imp who is trapped under a tree in the forest. In gratitude for their kindness, he grants them three wishes—and *only* three. They are delighted and begin discussing how they will use their wishes. When the wife says that they might wish to never go hungry again, the husband says that at the moment he'd just wish for a pan of sausages for their dinner. The wish is granted. When the wife sees what a foolish thing her husband has done, she responds in anger that she wishes the sausages were hanging from his nose. Whoops. Wish granted. Now they must use their third wish to remove the sausages from his nose. They are not totally disillusioned, however, because they do have the sausages.

The plot is clear and dramatic, the conclusion satisfying, the characters easy to portray. And while the story is well written and beautifully illustrated, it can be told quite effectively in other language and without pictures.

Tough Boris, on the other hand, would be an excellent choice for reading, but a poor choice for telling. Much of the action, as well as characterization, is conveyed through the illustrations. The text is spare, with every word essential, and is in rhyme. This story would be lost in a retelling.

Storytellers sometimes memorize the opening and concluding sentences of a story. Occasionally they will memorize phrases from the body of the story, particularly when the words are repeated. Like the beginning and closing bars of a jazz composition, these sentences and phrases provide a frame around improvisation in the middle of the piece. But like jazz-note variations, the words in the body of the tale will vary with each telling. The composition will remain the same, but the story will sound fresh each time it is told.

Telling the story to different groups of children can help you understand how to shape material for your listeners. Practicing also improves technique. A change in the pitch of the voice, for instance, might help establish one character compared with another. In dialogues, a slight turn of the head from one side to the other can indicate that the speaker has changed. Gestures should be used sparingly, however, or they will siphon interest away from the material.

Similarly, aids to presenting literature, such as audiovisual media based on books, are most valuable when they focus attention on the literature itself.

Using Media and Technology

Videotapes, recordings, films and filmstrips, CDs, and computer programs have poured into school media centers, classrooms, and libraries in recent years. Many children are accustomed to using individual cassette recorders, videotape players, and computers in addition to more traditional audiovisual material such as records and slides.

Available for use are videos based on children's books, sometimes using **live action** and other times either adding motion through **animation,** or using a moving camera method called **iconographic technique.** Stories can

1. **The material should be based on good literature.**
   Filming or recording a story or poem that lacked literary merit in the original is unlikely to result in anything better.

2. **The medium should be appropriate to the story.**

3. **The material should have aesthetic integrity, whether or not it deviates from the original.**

4. **The technical quality should be high.**
   For example, the voices of characters should be clear and easy to understand, and music or sound effects should not cover voices.

5. **The presentation should be authentic.**
   If there is dialect, for instance, it should be spoken accurately. The setting of a film or video should be authentic to the time and place represented.

6. **The material should be appropriate for the intended audience.**

Figure 3-4   Guidelines for selecting audiovisual materials.

be experienced on CD ROM, and children can learn about books through programs accessible on the Internet. Computer programs that test children on books they've read are also available.

As a teacher, you will have the opportunity to select from the media your school system provides and to recommend new purchases. A good question to ask yourself is whether you would use the book, the test, or the list in its paper form. If not, then there is no need to use it in electronic form. For stories, ask yourself what makes the electronic presentation better than or equal to reading the book. Perhaps the illustrations can be seen more easily by the entire class, or the voices used add drama and variety, or it introduces a new author to your class.

It is essential that you preview any material before sharing it with your students. Figure 3-4 lists guidelines for selecting media based on literature.

Once you have selected the material, be certain you understand how to run the equipment needed. While not every blip can be anticipated, you should be at ease with basic loading and running of tapes and programs. You might also want to find out who is considered the building "expert," so that if you need help, you can go immediately to the most promising source.

ENCOURAGING RESPONSE

Presenting literature regularly and allowing time for reading are basic to a literature program and to the development of reading interest and skill. Figure 3-5 shows 10 strategies that have been proven effective in encouraging children to read and to share thoughtful responses to their reading.

1. Read aloud daily to your class, including poetry.
2. Reread the children's favorite books or passages.
3. Develop an inviting classroom library area with books that vary in genre, reading level, and topic.
4. Provide time for children to read books they have selected themselves.
5. Encourage children to read with a friend or classmate.
6. Have children discuss books among themselves in small groups.
7. Guide children in comparing books using a graphic recording of data, such as a Venn diagram.
8. Have children depict aspects of a story artistically, either in two-dimensional art, sculpture, music, or movement.
9. Let children dramatize stories or scenes from stories.
10. Encourage children to keep and share response journals.

Figure 3-5   Effective strategies for eliciting response to literature.

BOOK DISCUSSIONS

Book discussions are one of the primary ways children and adults express what they think about what they have read. Yet effective discussions do not just happen in a classroom. Taking part in a discussion is a learned behavior that involves listening to others; developing, corroborating or challenging their ideas; and introducing new ideas within the flow of ongoing comments. That means that teachers must help children understand the process of discussion as well as the content being discussed. Figure 3-6 shows how a teacher can structure experiences in discussion so that students are successful and gain in skill.

Approaches to Discussion

Discussions may be run by students on their own, by students and teacher together as equals, or by the teacher, often through preplanned questions. Student-led discussions often produce complex and rich exchanges of ideas (Almasi). Short described a study in which she and her colleagues observed as third graders and sixth graders met to discuss sets of books on a similar topic or theme. They were interested in seeing the connections children made between books, between books and life experiences, and between various elements of literature. They found that groups operated in a variety of ways. In some groups each member became an expert on one book. In other groups nearly everyone read all the books. Some brainstormed ideas, some made webs. Short writes, however:

Teachers can help children learn to participate effectively in student-centered discussions by at first controlling three crucial variables: *group size, length of discussion,* and *complexity of the task.*

For example, students might learn to carry on their own discussions by working in pairs, a few minutes at a time, on simple questions. They could explore the theme of friendship before reading books on that topic by drawing up a list of things they like to do with friends, one list per pair. A time limit, say four minutes, should be set.

Children with more experience might work in groups of three on a slightly more complicated task. For example, they might answer the question What is friendship? The threesomes could be given six or seven minutes to interpret what characters in a book thought about friendship. Then the students would write a definition satisfying every member of the group. They would also have to choose someone to report how the group felt.

Students with even more experience in group work might be assigned to groups of five to weigh the question Should friends always tell each other the truth? They might begin by interpreting the actions of a character in a story and then call on their own experiences with juggling tact and truthfulness. Twenty minutes would be an appropriate time limit for this activity.

In each of these discussions, students begin with a specific task. Vague directions such as "Discuss courage" generate superficial reports. Specific instructions such as "Decide who was the more courageous character, Sarah or Jacob, and produce evidence to support your decision" stimulate students to probe deeper into books and to test and sharpen their reactions to them.

Figure 3-6   Structuring experiences in discussion.

While there was a great deal of choice and student involvement in this strategy, there was also a supportive structure within which students made choices. As teachers, we were responsible for establishing broad structures that would support the students' decision making. We established processes for choosing topics for the sets and signing up for the groups, got the groups started with reading and discussing, suggested strategies they might use in their groups, set aside a reflection time when groups could share their strategies with each other, and provided materials and time for presentations. Often we joined groups during brainstorming and suggested additional ideas and connections that the group might consider in their discussions. Some groups invited us to join them because they were having difficulty, either with the group dynamics or with a particular issue. (298)

As you think about establishing book discussions in your classroom, plan for time, space, and your role. One approach for book discussions is to divide the entire class into small groups that discuss books simultaneously. This means deciding how group membership will be established (perhaps

A useful source for learning about cooperative learning strategies is *Cooperative Learning: Resources for Teachers* by Kagan (Riverside, CA: University of California, 1985).

based on the books they've chosen to read); allowing adequate space between groups so that they do not distract each other; deciding how long the discussions will last, either ahead of time or by watching the progress groups are making; and deciding if you will stay with one group or move around the room. In this pattern, most teachers move from group to group or cruise the room unobtrusively. Cooperative learning strategies work well in this pattern.

Another approach is to have some students read quietly and others work on writing or art or projects related to their reading as a third group discusses. Usually the teacher sits with the discussion group, and the other children are expected to work independently. In such an approach, children participate in each activity for a short time. That is, a child might read, then come to discussion group, and then work on an activity. Another child might first discuss, then work on the activity, and then read. This approach assumes continuity from day to day so that children have always read before they come to discuss, even if they read one day and engage in the discussion the next.

Still another approach is a reading workshop in which students select their own books and read at their own rate. In addition to reading, they may also write about what they have read. Figure 3-7 shows a sheet that a first-grade teacher, Patricia McClure, working with Thomas Newkirk, had her students keep in their reading folders.

Note that the children were to read the book themselves, then read it to a friend, and write about it. Once they had completed the work, they would sign up as being ready to discuss their book. When four or five children had signed up, the teacher would call them together. Each would tell about his or her book and listen to and ask questions of the others. As one group was discussing, the

---

Name: _____

READING RECORD

Book Read:

                                                                    Date

Choose the book and practice reading.   [_____]

Read to a partner and talk about it.   [_____]

Write about the book.   [_____]

Share the book in a group.   [_____]

Figure 3-7   A child's record of reading involvement.

other children were reading. This, too, is an ongoing approach that is used from day to day. In this approach the teacher participates in the discussion group and keeps a record of what book is discussed, when each child has discussed a book, and any special comments. The teacher also needs to see that all students participate regularly and that children not in the group work independently.

You may decide to focus on one approach because it works well for both you and your class, or you may change or interchange patterns. You might also devise your own pattern for structuring book discussions. The point is, a clear structure will help children function effectively in groups.

Student-Centered Discussions

Any of the approaches just discussed can work when students assume responsibility for the discussion. Some teachers help children gain this independence by participating themselves in early discussions and then gradually withdrawing, first by not asking prepared questions and then by making fewer comments.

Other teachers use a direct approach, explaining to children that they will be running discussions and modeling appropriate behavior. Figure 3-8 shows how one fourth-grade teacher began discussion groups with her class. As you can see, it includes both prompts for literary responses and a structure for how the groups are to operate. It also engages the children in deciding what is appropriate group behavior and then rating themselves. In this early stage of group work with children who had little prior experience of this sort, the teacher was cognizant of the importance of process and of having children accept responsibility from the beginning.

Teacher-Led Discussions

Approaches for group discussion, except when several groups are discussing simultaneously, can function with the teacher as the group leader. There also may be times when the teacher will lead the whole class in a discussion. A teacher may decide to lead the discussion to model a particular strategy for working with ideas. For example, the teacher may have students compare two books using a Venn diagram. Two circles are drawn so that portions overlap. Elements that are common to both books are listed in the space where the circles overlap. Elements that are in only one of the books appear in only one of the circles. Figure 3-9 shows a Venn diagram and two other charts for recording information when comparing books. Creating visual representations of information can be a useful strategy for children to use in their own discussions. Other strategies that may be helpful to model are webbing, in which ideas are recorded around a central theme, often categorized as they are written; and story mapping, in which the setting and action of the story are represented as a map or in chart form. It makes sense to use **graphic organizers** such as these when they will aid children's comprehension of a story. Not all graphic organizers do this. It is possible, for example, to use a "story frame" in which children list the characters, setting, problem, and solution, as a memory exercise with no interpretations given, no new

Figure 7-1 shows a web; Figure 6-10 a story map; and Figure 2-3 a lesson that involves categorization.

Connie's fourth graders had very little experience working in groups. She wanted them to be able to conduct their own literature discussions, but realized she would have to spend time on the process. She decided on a four-step procedure:

1. She would explain what they would be doing and why.

2. She would work with them in developing questions based on reading so that they could develop their own questions as a basis for their early discussions.

3. She would guide them in developing and using a set of rules for effective discussion.

4. She would give them time in class for the reading and writing necessary for the group work.

On Monday, Connie told the class that there were many ways of choosing and sharing books. They were going to all read the same book and then discuss it in small groups. To get ready for the discussions, they would write some of their questions. One person in each group would serve as leader, reading the questions they had written and encouraging everyone to participate.

Then she read the poem "Not in a Hundred Years" by Claudia Lewis. Lewis recalls her own fourth grade and the day that Milton, a boy who had never read, stumbled through his first words, the teacher encouraging him. The poem ends with the narrator saying she had seen something she never thought she'd see in a hundred years, "great tears in my teacher's eyes." Connie modeled the kinds of questions the children might want to ask. For example,

1. **Something that puzzles you.**
   Why would a teacher cry when a child read? Shouldn't she be happy?

2. **Something that interests you and you'd like to talk about.**
   Why is it so surprising to see a teacher cry?

3. **Something about the way the author wrote.**
   How would the effect of this poem change if it were written in rhyme?

She commented that these were real questions for her, not questions to see if they had understood the poem. Then she read the poem again, asking the children to visualize the situation as she read. Each child then wrote one question. (Several asked, "How did Milton get to fourth grade if he couldn't read?) Connie collected them and read them aloud. The class took time to respond to some of the questions. Connie pointed out that questions that require more than a yes/no answer are usually more interesting. She noted to herself that about half the questions were factual, and that she would work again on asking questions that were real for the asker.

She then introduced the book *Stay Away from Simon* by Carol Carrick (Clarion, 1985). It is also set in the past and begins in a school setting. Connie knew that it was within the reading level of all her students.

Figure 3-8   Introducing student-centered discussion.

She gave them time to begin reading. They were to read for about 20 minutes and then write two questions, each on a separate index card. As they read, she was available if students needed her.

In the afternoon, students were again given reading and writing time. The six children who had not completed the book took it home with them to finish.

On Tuesday, Connie began by having the whole class dictate rules for effective work in groups. They came up with about 20, too many to use efficiently. Connie then suggested that they select the five or six most important ones. They selected these:

1. Each person gets a turn.

2. More than one person should be allowed to ask questions.

3. Only talk when you're asking or answering a question.

4. Alternate turns.

5. Don't talk too loudly.

6. You might go clockwise.

Connie changed her original plan of having one student serve as leader when the class wanted to take turns asking the questions. She also agreed to their idea of going clockwise for whose turn it was to be leader since they felt it was important.

She then divided the class into groups of five, collecting and shuffling the question cards from each group. They were to read and respond to all the questions, and the earlier-finishing groups were to find and share parts of the story they particularly liked. As they talked, Connie moved from group to group. She was pleased that they stayed on task and seemed genuinely involved with book. She knew that the discussions lacked a logical flow, since questions were asked at random, but she accepted this as part of a first step toward independence in groups.

When they had all finished, Connie asked each group to rate itself from 1 (perfect) to 5 (we really need to work on this) on each of the six rules for discussion. Most rated themselves just as Connie would have. They felt they did a good job taking turns, but they had sometimes talked when not asking or answering a question, and they had sometimes talked too loudly. They were excited about their discussions and eager to continue working in groups.

In the weeks that followed, the students began selecting which books they wanted to read and formed groups based on book choice. They no longer required "clockwise" turns nor did they need a designated leader, although Connie sometimes asked a particular student to lead. Connie varied her prompts for responses to be shared in the groups and moved to response journals rather than questions, although students frequently brought up questions in the context of their writing. Throughout the year Connie had the students discuss and evaluate their participation in discussion groups.

Figure 3-8   *continued*

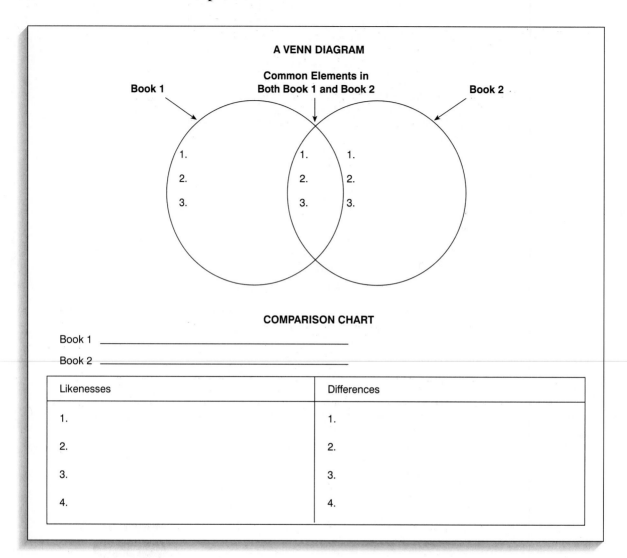

Figure 3-9   Graphic organizers for book comparisons.

understandings developed, and all the excitement of the old-fashioned book report.

   Another reason a teacher may want to lead the discussion is to involve children who tend not to participate often. Listening to children respond to questions may provide the teacher with insight into the child's understanding and allow informal assessment.

   A teacher may also chose to lead a discussion to guide children to consider specific elements within a story. Perhaps the children have been responding only to the plots of the stories. A teacher-led discussion is one

COMPARISON CHART

	Book 1	Book 2	Book 3
Category of Comparison (for example, main character)			
Category of Comparison (for example, the problem the character had)			
Category of Comparison			
Category of Comparison			

Figure 3-9   *continued*

way to expand their view. Questions may also stretch children's thinking and stimulate them to consider aspects of a books that they might otherwise have overlooked.

Questioning Techniques

Judith Langer, in her research on response-based literature instruction, found that a literary orientation toward reading material causes a person to explore possibilities and thus continually clarify and modify understandings.

This teacher is using a Venn diagram to help children compare what they've read about whales with what they've read about fish.

There is never total closure because "continually raising questions about the implications and undersides of what one understands precludes closure and invites ambiguity" (205).

A teacher may decide to use very open questions and then develop the discussion by building on the responses children give. Patricia Kelly (466) used just such an approach, based on the work of David Bleich, with three basic questions:

1. What did you notice in the story?
2. How did the story make you feel?
3. What does this story remind you of in your own life?

Her third graders responded to these questions orally at the beginning of the year, and later wrote their responses in their journals. She followed their lead by phrasing questions that helped them expand and clarify their responses.

The questions a teacher prepares for a literature discussion should be what have been termed **higher-order questions.** This means that the children should be involved in thinking that requires them to compare, interpret, infer, or evaluate, not just recall what they have read. Figure 3-10 gives examples of higher-order questions that might apply to any book.

Often, however, a teacher-led discussion has questions that relate specifically to a particular book or aspect of the book. The teacher selects a

The following questions address story content in terms of form and structure. Thus they can apply to any book. They are taken from *The Child as Critic: Teaching Literature in Elementary and Middle Schools* by Glenna Davis Sloan (New York: Teachers College Press, 1991), 119–124.

Type of Story

What signs and signals indicate that this story will be fanciful or realistic?

If the world created by the author is far different from the one we know, how does the author make the story seem possible and believable?

Setting and Plot

Where and when does the story take place? How do you know? If the story took place somewhere else or in a different time, how would it be changed?

What incident, problem, conflict, or situation gets the story started?

What is the basic shape of the story? (for example, home-adventure-home)

What does the author do to create suspense, to make you want to read on to find out what happens? Is what happens made credible and plausible? How? Did the author prepare you for what happens? How?

How is the story ordered for telling?

Trace the main events of the story. Is it possible to change the order? Leave any of them out? Why or why not?

Suppose you thought of a new ending for the story. How would the rest of the story have to be changed to fit the new ending?

Did the story end as you expected it to? What clues did the author offer to prepare you to expect this ending? Did you recognize these clues as important to the story as you first read or listened to it? Why are these clues important to your overall reaction to the story?

Figure 3-10   General questions for book discussions.

focus for the discussion and plans questions that guide children to discuss that focus in depth. Suppose the class had heard *An Extraordinary Egg* by Leo Lionni. In this picture book, one of three frogs, Jessica, returns from a day of exploration with what she thinks is a beautiful stone. Her friend Marilyn tells her that it is a chicken egg, while the third frog, August, listens. Jessica has never heard of chickens, but Marilyn explains that there are some things you just know. It is an egg, but what hatches is an alligator, not a chicken. The three frogs refer to it as a chicken, however, and even when it finds its mother, and she calls it her sweet little alligator, Jessica persists in calling it a chicken. When she tells Marilyn and August what

Characters

Who is the main character in the story? What kind of person is this character? How do you know? Do you sympathize with the character? Are you interested in the character's fate? Why? Can you figure out from the story why the characters behave as they do? Do you recognize here any character types that you know from other stories?

Do any characters change in the course of the story? If so, how are they different at the end? What changed them? Does the change seem believable?

Some characters play small but important roles in a story. Pick out a bit player from a story. Why is this character necessary to the story?

Point of View

Who tells the story? How does point of view affect tone, characterization, and credibility?

Mood or Tone

Does the story as a whole create a definite mood or feeling? How is it created? Does the mood or tone change during the course of the story? How does the author signal this change?

Did you have any strong feelings throughout the story?

What did the author do to make you feel strongly?

Style

Does the style of writing fit the subject? Do the characters speak naturally and in keeping with their setting? Is the language rich in imagery and in memorable ways of expressing ideas? Does it flow rhythmically when it is read aloud?

Theme

What is the idea *behind* the story that gives point to the whole?

Making Connections

Is this story, though different in content, like any other story you have read or watched in its form and structure?

Think of all the characters in the story. Are any of them the same or similar to characters in other stories, cartoons, comics, movies?

Figure 3-10   *continued*

This illustration from An Extraordinary Egg *shows Jessica and the chicken, whose mother calls her a sweet little alligator. (Source:* From AN EXTRAORDINARY EGG by Leo Lionni. Copyright © 1994 by Leo Lionni. Reprinted by permission of Alfred A. Knopf, Inc.)

happened and what was said, all three frogs have good laugh at the silly thing uttered by the chicken's mother.

The teacher might decide to focus the discussion on a theme within the book, for example, that if one assumes one is right, one may miss clues to more accurate information.

In planning this discussion, the teacher should keep in mind five basic criteria:

1. There should be a focus to the discussion.
2. The focus should match the strengths of the book.
3. The discussion should revolve around the book and lead back to it.
4. The questions should progress in a logical sequence.
5. The questions should structure a discussion but not limit it.

Figure 3-11 shows questions a teacher might ask following the reading of *An Extraordinary Egg* and the rationale for each question.

The planned questions are a roadmap, and a teacher may decide to take a detour to follow up on something a child has said. Suppose, for example, that after several responses to question 5 in Figure 3-11 about why the frogs laughed at the comments by the "chicken's" mother, a child says, "I thought that was the funniest part of the book. This was a funny book." This is a perfect time for the teacher to ask what makes the book so funny. If you use prepared questions as a guide only, you will be better able to judge when to follow such detours without limiting your discussions unnecessarily.

FOCUS: Theme—Learning New Things/Keeping an Open Mind

QUESTION	REASON FOR THE QUESTION
1. Why did Jessica believe Marilyn when Marilyn said it was a chicken egg?	Calls for children to analyze the experience the frogs had with chickens and Marilyn's self-confident assertion that she knew.
2. Why didn't the frogs know it was a baby alligator when it hatched?	Again relates to experience as a source for knowledge and begins look at holding to an idea in the face of conflicting evidence.
3. How do we know what things are?	Asks children to relate idea within the book to their own lives.
4. Do you think what something is called matters? Why do you think this?	Encourages divergent responses and has children's assess differing opinions.
5. Why did the frogs think that the mother's calling her child "my sweet little alligator" was a silly thing to do?	Helps establish the frogs' inability to address new evidence.
6. What would you do to convince Marilyn, August, and Jessica that their friend was an alligator, not a chicken.	Asks students to engage in problem solving within the context of the story.
7. What advice on how to learn about new things would you give the frogs?	This advice should address the problem of paying attention to new information and lead to discussion of the theme.

Figure 3-11   Sample discussion questions for *An Extraordinary Egg.*

DRAMATIC AND ORAL EXPRESSION: THE CLASSROOM AS PRIVATE THEATRE

Rikki's first graders bounce in their seats, nod their heads, and clap softly as she reads an alphabet rhyme with pulsing rhythm. It is about letters climbing up a coconut tree.

They have caught the pattern and are reciting the refrain they've come to recognize. Soon they will act out the whole story of *Chicka Chicka Boom Boom* (Martin and Archambault), each child having a letter as they respond with actions as Rikki reads the text. For these children, oral response and dramatic activity are common and enjoyable responses.

Bill Martin, Jr. has many books that have strong rhythm and catchy refrains.

Oral Expression

Reading along with the teacher or coming in on recognized refrains is only one way children can respond orally to literature. Certainly discussion is an oral response, and chiming in as the teacher reads is another. Figure 3-12 suggests ways of extending books through oral language and drama.

Wordless Books

Wordless books give children the opportunity to add a text of their own with the story line provided. A book can be passed around a group with each child taking a turn at continuing the narrative. They can tell the story through dialogue, by taking the various roles and saying what they think that character might say when the teacher or leader points to it. Different groups or different children might tape-record their telling of the story and then play the tapes and compare versions. Children could be asked what

Figure 6-3 shows many ways of involving children with wordless books.

Here are some oral language and dramatic activities for children, and examples of books that lend themselves to such activities.

ACTIVITY	APPROPRIATE BOOK
Children look at an illustration and describe what they see. A variation is to focus on detail, action, or use of descriptive langauge.	*Only the Cat Saw* by Ashley Wolff. (New York: Dodd, 1985) *Tuesday* by David Weisner. (New York: Clarion, 1991)
Children pantomime the action as the teacher reads. Can be done with each child doing each action or with parts assigned.	*Possum Come a-Knockin'* by Nancy Van Laan. (New York: Knopf, 1990) *Pretend You're a Cat* by Jean Marzollo. (New York: Dial, 1990)
Children engage in choral reading of the story, taking parts or entering on a refrain.	*Yo! Yes!* by Chris Raschka. (New York: Orchard, 1993) *THUMP, THUMP, Rat-a-Tat-Tat* by Gene Baer. (New York: Harper, 1989)
Children read dual books, with one group reading the English, the other the Spanish (or other language).	*Radio Man* by Arthur Dorros. (New York: Harper Collins, 1993) *The Bossy Gallito: A Traditional Cuban Folktale* by Lulu Delacre. (New York: Scholastic, 1994)
Children learn the verse or poem, add motions, and then teach the verse and the motions to their classmates.	*Whiskers & Rhymes* by Arnold Lobel. (New York: Greenwillow, 1985)
Children add sound effects as the teacher reads the story.	*Nothing at All* by Denys Cazet. (New York: Orchard, 1994) *Barnyard Banter* by Denise Fleming. (New York: Holt, 1994)

Figure 3-12   Extending books through oral language and drama.

stands out about each of the tellings? Wordless books provide the plot, but the teller adds style and explains emotions and motivation.

Many wordless books are available in filmstrip or video format that allows children to see the illustrations clearly. A video can be put on "pause" while students speak. Teachers sometimes prepare their own slides of books, although copyright laws require that the copyright holder, usually the publisher, grant permission in advance even when copies are made for use in one classroom.

Voices in Chorus

Chanting what they can of nursery rhymes or predictable books prepares children for later choral reading (or speaking, if they have memorized the words), most often of poetry.

All methods of choral reading rely on careful selection of good poems children like. A class could begin with a simple poem, such as "I Want You to Meet . . . " by David McCord:

I Want You to Meet . . .
Meet Ladybug.
her little sister Sadiebug,
her mother, Mrs. Gradybug,
her aunt, that nice oldmaidybug,
And Baby—she's a fraidybug.*

They might first read it in **unison,** with everyone reciting at the same time. You might have individuals read one line each, sometimes called **line-a-child.** Children could be divided into five groups, with each group reading one line. In their groups they would decide how they should read it—how their voices should sound—and practice before coming back to the whole class for the full reading. Children better understand and appreciate poetry when they interpret it themselves.

Certain poems lend themselves to particular kinds of reading. Some are set up in a question-and-answer format and are easily read by two groups. Poetry reading in which two groups recite parts of the poem back and forth to one another is called **antiphonal.** If you are making a copy of such a poem on a chart, you might use two colors to differentiate the parts. Other poems have several lines and then a refrain, easily divided into single voices for a line or two and then the entire class for the refrain or last line. It might be effective to have a just a few voices read the first line, then with each line add more readers.

Another interesting technique is the use of **obbligato,** a spoken accompaniment to choral reading in which a background of words or sounds is made by one group while a second group reads the poem. For example, half

---

* From ONE AT A TIME by David McCord. Copyright © 1961 by David McCord. By permission of Little, Brown and Company.

the class might repeat the refrain of "Hip Hip Hooray for Bears!" or a rhythmic "Rat-a-tat-tat, Rat-a-tat-tat," while the other half reads the words to "Bear Parade" by Jane Yolen.

Bear Parade
I can hear the sound of their marching feet
And a great drumroll and a rat-a-tat beat
As the bears come marching down my street,
Singing *Hip Hip Hooray for Bears!*

There's a bear in red with a great big stick,
And a teddy bear with a honey lick,
And a hundred more who are stepping quick,
Singing *Hip Hip Hooray for Bears!*

There's a bear with a bunch of bright balloons,
And a pair of bears playing big bassoons,
And they're shouting out their favorite tunes,
Singing *Hip Hip Hooray for Bears!*

Now you may prefer being out on the sea,
Or in front of a roaring fire with your tea,
But the bears' parade is the place for me,
Singing *Hip Hip Hooray for Bears!**

They might explore other phrases or sounds that would fit with the rhythm, or perhaps have their own parade as they recite the words.

Readers Theatre
Readers theatre emphasizes oral expression, in which a child reads dialogue, but does so as though taking part in a radio play, where an actor reads the script but generally stays in place. A quick approach to readers theatre is to select plays for students to read. Another approach is to select books or parts of books that include much dialogue. The teacher or the teacher and students together mark each reader's part and usually have a narrator read the parts that are descriptive. Look at *Rats on the Roof* and *Rats on the Range* by James Marshall as examples of books that lend themselves to readers theatre. These two collections of short stories are heavy with dialogue, short, and humorous. They give children the opportunity to be expressive, and they have a limited number of characters so that following the text does not become confusing.

Dramatic Expression

In Meg's kindergarten class, students take turns being Jack and jumping over a candlestick as she reads "Jack Be Nimble." In Art's class, a fourth

---

* "Bear Parade" from THE THREE BEARS RHYME BOOK by Jane Yolen, Copyright © 1987. Reprinted by permission of Harcourt Brace & Company.

The stories in Rats on the Roof *can be adapted easily for readers' theatre. (Source:* From RATS ON THE ROOF by James Marshall. Copyright © 1991 by James Marshall. Used by permission of Dial Books for Young Readers, a division of Penguin Books USA Inc.)

grader takes the role of Harriet in *Harriet's Hare* (King-Smith) and explains to the alien visitor what he, disguised as a hare, must know about farm life in order to survive.

In both of these instances, children used drama to extend their experience with books. They became actors and actresses without an audience or formal scripts, using body movements, dramatic voices, or both to express literature and to learn as they performed.

In this section four types of projects for dramatizing good books are presented: **interpreting** a story dramatically, **improvising, role playing,** and **puppetry.** Like the oral activities discussed in the previous sections, these explorations in drama permit children to respond to literature on many levels, from jumping over the candlestick just like Jack to making up scenes based only loosely on the text provided by the book.

Interpreting

Interpreting a story or poem means following the story line literally while presenting it dramatically. Interpretation, however, never depends on speaking the author's words. An adult can read the book while children pantomime the story or add only occasional fragments of dialogue, or children can add their own words to carry the plot forward.

Stories with repeating patterns lend themselves well to interpretation by children just learning dramatic expression. In Pat Hutchins' *What Game Shall We Play?* Duck and Frog go out to play but have trouble deciding what game. They search for Fox, hoping he will have an idea. He doesn't, so all three go in search of Mouse—and the pattern continues. Finally, Duck, Frog, Mouse, Rabbit, and Squirrel find Owl and ask him what game they should play. Owl, who has been watching all the searches from the air, suggests Hide and Seek. They agree, Owl closes his eyes, and the animals scurry to hide, each in its original spot. The irony is not lost, even on young children.

Groups of six children can dramatize the story as the teacher reads, or they add their own dialogue. The pattern helps them remember the sequence of action.

Sometimes the whole class can interpret a single story. To do this, look for stories where the number of characters is indeterminate. In *Dance Away* (Shannon), for example, a "group" of rabbits has a friend who loves to dance and engages them in dancing with him whenever he meets them. When a fox captures some of the rabbits, the dancing rabbit gets all his rabbit friends to grab the fox in a mad dance. They dance until they can leap across the river, where they let go of the fox and he drops into the water. The rabbits continue home safely. The only "major" parts are those of the dancing rabbit and the fox, which means that the rest of the class can be rabbits, dancing to the refrain and responding to what fox and rabbit do.

To prepare children for dramatizing a story, first have the children describe the characters in the story, who they are, what they did, and how

Any number of children can dramatize this story about a rabbit who loves to dance. (Source: From DANCE AWAY by George Shannon, illustrations copyright © 1982 by Jose Aruego and Ariane Dewey. By permission of Greenwillow Books, a division of William Morrow and Company, Inc.)

they may have felt. Children might pantomime an action or respond in a voice they think the character might have used. Then have children orally reconstruct the plot sequence of the story.

Depending on your purpose and your knowledge of the children, you determine how roles will be decided. If you have one very strong child and others who are uncertain, you might assign that child to the key part. After others have seen how dramatization can be done, switch the roles. You might let children draw names to see who will play particular characters. Another strategy is to say to the first child, "Which character would you like to be?" Then go around the group, letting children choose. The next time the story is enacted, the order is reversed so that different children get first choice of roles. The class then decides on the set, which means blocking out areas of the classroom. For *Dance Away,* a kindergarten class moved several tables to the perimeter of the classroom to make more space. They decided where the rabbits' home would be, where the fox would hide, where he would take the rabbits he captured, and where the river would be. The teacher put what she called her "all-purpose water," a piece of blue fabric, on the floor for the river and quickly taped down the edges. In this instance, children also did several pantomimes of "capturing" a rabbit and "running" from the fox. If some of the action in a story has the potential to get out of hand, have children work with that segment before enacting the whole story so that acceptable ways of dramatizing can be modeled.

After the story has been dramatized, encourage the children to talk about it. What was especially good about their dramatization? How might they solve the problem of several characters talking at once? Should any changes be made in the set? After this discussion, the roles are changed, and a new dramatization takes place. Each version will be slightly different.

Improvising

Children who are interpreting a story use the book's story line as a basis for their acting. Another dramatic activity, **improvisation,** involves some departure from the story. Much of the material comes from the children themselves, inspired by the story as a kind of premise.

The teacher may pose a question to stimulate an improvisation. For example, What will the rabbits do the next time they see the fox? Or What will the fox say to his family when he returns home without any rabbit dinner? Often a change in point of view provides a fresh way of looking at a story and viable alternatives for improvisation.

Intermediate grade children might identify the structure or theme of a story and use that to build their own story. Folktales often are good sources. In the story of *The Little Red Hen,* the main character is a hard-working hen who gets no help from her friends. The other animals answer, "Not I," every time she requests aid on jobs like planting wheat. But after she has planted the wheat, tended it, harvested it, taken it to be ground into flour, and used that flour to bake a cake, all the other animals are willing to join in and have some cake.

Whether interpreting or improvising, children produce their own dialogue rather than working from scripts.

Children first identify the underlying premise, that one character does all the work but others want to share the rewards. To improvise on that premise, children pick a new setting and new characters and perhaps even create a few twists of plot. In a fourth-grade class, four groups brainstormed ideas, selected one, and developed their own improvisation. One group enacted a school project to be done by a group, where one conscientious student did all the work but kept quiet about it only when those who did not participate offered to share their lunch treats. Two groups set their stories at home, where siblings argued over chores. The last group had a cadre of space travelers, where all had to help if any were to survive. In the original, the industrious hen kept the rewards for herself. In improvisation, the main character may decide to share rewards or win no reward at all. One of the other characters might decide to help after all, leaving the other slackers to quibble about whether they should join too. The directions depend on the participants, but in following their own ideas, children get a better sense of how they compare and contrast with the hen in the original tale. In the discussion that followed the improvisations of the fourth-grade class, the students decided that the Little Red Hen was like a mother—she did a lot of work with very little help.

Role Playing

Some improvisation focuses on exploring solutions to a problem expressed in the literature. In **role playing** students first decide what the problem is and then take the roles of characters to explore what is wrong and what might be done. Third graders could read *The Skirt* (Soto) and examine the Miata's problem and possible solutions. It is Friday afternoon, and she has left her folklórico skirt on the school bus. She had planned to wear it for a dance she was to perform on Sunday. Children could take the roles of Miata and her friend Ana as they try to find a solution, and perhaps the roles of Miata's mother or father as they become part of the attempted solution.

After each role-playing session, students should have the chance to say how they felt living in that role. The activity can put them in close touch with a character at the same time they delve into a theme.

Puppetry

Another dramatic activity, **puppetry,** can be used to interpret literature or to improvise on it. Some children find it easier to manipulate a puppet than to face a class themselves. Puppets provide a kind of cloak or disguise, which frees students to concentrate on dramatizing what they have read or to improvise from it in shows made up on the spot.

Hand or stick puppets work better than marionettes that require dexterous string pulling. Puppets are easily made from paper bags, cylinders of all kinds, socks, or construction materials. Children should make the puppets themselves, adding hair and features. For stick puppets, children first draw

Children can role-play Miata and Ana as they try to find a solution to Miata's problem. (Source: "Art Work" by Eric Velasquez, Copyright © 1992 by Eric Velasquez. From THE SKIRT by Gary Soto, Illustrated by Eric Velasquez. Used by permission of Bantam Doubleday Dell Books for Young Readers.)

characters and then cut out their drawings and paste them on heavy paper or cardboard. They then paste the cardboard to a stick—a ruler, a straw, a popsickle stick. As in all dramatic activities, whether they interpret or improvise on literature, children produce their own dialogue, without working from scripts or memorizing lines. Generally they perform only for themselves, with the simplest of props and setting. There is no need for an elaborate stage, curtain, costumes, or spotlight. The activity spotlights the literature itself and the children's responses to it.

WRITTEN EXPRESSION: BEYOND THE BOOK REPORT

"Read a book and write a report of at least two paragraphs. Be sure to include the title and the author." For decades, this dreaded and vague assignment led children to write dull prose, rehashing the plot until the required length had been reached. It was used primarily to see if the child had read the book.

Response Journals

Today's teachers want children's writing to be more thoughtful, useful, and interesting. Many have children keep **response journals** in which they record their personal reactions to what they read. Usually a teacher initiates such journal writing by modeling his or her own response. The entry might focus on what the reading made the teacher think of or on people, places, or events. It might be what the teacher liked or disliked about the story. The entry could describe what stood out to the reader or list questions that came to mind. The child writes his or her own free response in a notebook set aside for this purpose. The teacher also makes clear that the emphasis is on content, not on spelling and mechanics of writing.

The teacher or the teacher and the children plan how the journals will be shared. They may be used as the basis for discussion in a group; they may be given to the teacher, who responds in writing; or they may be shared with a classmate, who writes back. They are shared with someone in some way.

When Julie Woolman-Bonilla began using journals with her fourth graders, she was clear in telling them not to simply retell the story. She also had them brainstorm a list of ways to respond, after modeling several ways herself. Then during the year, she noted the types of responses they gave and how she could reply to support their efforts and enhance their understanding. Here she describes the replies she wrote to students:

> My replies focused upon the content of their letters and tended to
> a. affirm ideas and feelings ("I'm glad you liked the book. It made me look at animals differently too.")
> b. provide information ("*Wrung* comes from *wring*. You can wring out a towel by twisting and squeezing it . . . ")

c. request information related to students' responses ("Do you like Simon Turtle?")

d. model elaboration ("It *is* realistic! The author describes bacon and eggs so well you can almost see, smell, and taste them.")

e. guide children to examine their ideas and discover new insights ("What do you think gives Ellen the courage to ask him?") (118)

The responses you provide for children should both support their thinking and teach using the observations you make or the questions you ask. Figure 3-13 shows a child's response to *The War With Grandpa* by Robert

Figure 3-13 Responding to student writing.

Here is what Alan wrote in his journal after he had completed the book *The War With Grandpa* by Robert Kimmel Smith.

> I liked the book alot, But it did'nt have much of Jenny Don't you think some of Peter's tricks were kind of nasty. Like stealing his dencers! That was funny. I have to amit! Even Grand pa did some nasty tricks like stealing his underwear. I wish the war kept going on I don't know the next book I'll read.
>
> Alan

Here are three examples of what a teacher might write in response to Alan's comments.

Alan,
   I laughed as I read the book, too. It's interesting how a trick can seem both nasty and funny. Why do you suppose this is so?

Alan,
   Would you like to have read more about Jenny? She is what is called a minor character in a story, one who plays only a small part, but who lets us know more about the main characters or the action. Without her, we wouldn't have seen Grandpa and Pete work together to cover up their war (Chapter 30).

Alan,
   You might want to look at other books by Robert Kimmel Smith, such as *Bobby Baseball, Chocolate Fever,* or *Jelly Belly.* Many of his books are humorous.

Kimmel Smith, and three possible comments a teacher might write back. In the book, fifth grader Peter Stokes is angry and hurt that he has to give up his bedroom when his grandfather moves in, even though he loves him. He wages a silent war of tricks against his grandfather, who proves to be able to retaliate with tricks of his own.

When the journal writing is to be used for discussion, the teacher may give a prompt. For example, one day the students who were reading *The War with Grandpa* were asked to write about what bothered them in their own lives. One child wrote:

1. My sister in the morning.
2. Things that are unfair.
3. Getting yelled at.

Another wrote,

> I hate it when Kevin gets out of the shower and is Mr. Cool Dude. He spikes his hair and looks realy dum. And when where at the park he wants to go alone with Willie on the roller coaster.

Then in their discussion group, they shared their writing and told how thinking about what bothered them helped them understand Peter's feelings in the book.

Sharing written responses to a book can provide the stimulus for a group discussion

Another fourth-grade teacher had students write several quotes and the page number on one side of the page, and their response on the other. One child wrote, from *The Sign of the Beaver* (Speare 11), "On the day of their great adventure, Attean had come without his dog. So there was no warning." Across from the quotation, he wrote, "It gives me the feeling something exciting is going to happen." Generally it is a good idea to have students write the page number of the quote or content they are responding to, so that it can be found quickly and shared. Frequently used prompts include making predictions early in the reading (doing so later either frustrates children who want to read ahead or is ineffective because they have read ahead), noting something that happened and how the student felt about it, and writing and responding to quotations (quotes the student liked, metaphoric language, language that was difficult to understand, something that was funny—whatever fits the book and the purpose of the entry). As children share their writing, you will see how effective a particular prompt was. Look at the lesson and the reflections about it shown in Figure 3-14. In this case, the prompts used did not elicit the kind of thinking the teacher envisioned.

It may be useful to let children in kindergarten or first grade talk about the book before they begin to record their responses in a journal. Woolman-Bonilla, in a later study with first graders, found that encouraging comments before writing helped the children write or draw better responses and did not interfere with their writing individual ideas and feelings (Woolman-Bonilla 567).

Literature as a Stimulus for Writing

In addition to journal writing, books provide a stimulus for writing from both their content and their form. The clearest provision of content is writing the narration to tell a story in a wordless book. Yet students can do more than retell. They might write what will happen to the character in the year after the story ends, write a different ending to the book, or write a letter from one character to another.

They might choose to create all new content, but use the existing form. Reading mysteries, for example, can help children see how clues are scattered throughout a story but gain meaning at the end; mysteries also prepare children to write their own who-done-it. They might use postcards, letters, or diaries as formats for what they have to say.

Figure 3-15 shows several ways to extend books through writing, with the ideas grouped under *content* and *form*. These are by no means the only ways, but they will give you a starting point to get you and your students thinking about writing related to books. Some writing projects become even more interesting to students when combined with artistic expressions such as drawing, painting, photography, and three-dimensional constructions.

THE LESSON, AS PLANNED AND TAUGHT	REFLECTIONS . . .

Rationale

George decided to read *Fly Away Home* by Eve Bunting (Clarion, 1991) to his second-grade class because the book is about homeless people, and he knew that two of his students had been homeless at one time; several were currently in foster care. He felt that the book would help the children understand that under given conditions, anyone could become homeless. He also wanted to give students the opportunity to express their feelings about having been homeless or being in foster care.

George was clear in his purpose and selected a well-written book appropriate to the age and experience of his students. Reading it orally allowed all the students to share the knowledge and the base for his planned writing activity.

The Lesson

After reading the book aloud to the class, George had students write a story on what they thought it would be like to be homeless. He wrote the following guide questions on the board but told the students they could write their stories any way they wished.

1. What would it be like to be homeless?
2. How would you feel if you were homeless?
3. Where would you live?
4. Do you know anyone who is homeless?
5. Are the homeless bad people or just in need of help?
6. How do people become homeless?
7. Why did the boy tell the bird "Don't stop trying" when the bird tried to get out of the airport?

George was disappointed because the students did not seem to express personal feelings about the topic, even when sharing their stories. Some did not address the topic at all. Others wrote about homeless animals rather than homeless people. Still others wrote sentences that answered each question but did not form a coherent paragraph. It did appear, however, that the children understood that circumstances might cause "good" people to become homeless.

A discussion rather than a writing assignment might have elicited more responses because students would be stimulated by each other's comments and reactions. They could work together to construct meaning.

If the questions had been grouped and sequenced, they might have been more helpful. That is, a story that dealt with questions 1, 2, and 3 would focus on the child's perception of what it would be like to be homeless. Questions 4 and 6 would focus on homeless people the child may have known.

Question 5 is a leading question and should be rephrased—perhaps, "Based on *Fly Away Home*, what do you think homeless people may be like?"

Question 7 stands alone, the only one that takes the students back to the book. It addresses the theme of the book and would be better used for discussion.

If George were to use his questions in a discussion, he might reorder them as follows: 7, 5 (rephrased), 4, 6, 2, 3, omit 1, and add, for closure, "Why is a home important to most people?" This would provide a more logical flow to the thought and discussion and provide a sense of completeness to the discussion.

Figure 3-14   On second thought: Using prompts/questions effectively.

Books may stimulate writing through their content

- Write the text, or the dialogue, for a wordless book.
- Write a diary entry for one character in a book.
- Retell a story or part of a story from another point of view.
- Write a new ending for the story.
- Write further adventures of one of the characters.
- Write a letter from one of the characters to another.
- Create a newspaper with cartoons, editorials, news stories, obituaries, and sports pages, using events from books.
- Write the dialogue between characters from different stories who meet.
- Prepare interview questions for a character.
- Write an advertisement for the book.
- Write a book jacket statement for the book.

Books may stimulate writing through their form

Letters

Dear Mr. Henshaw by Beverly Cleary. (New York: Morrow, 1983)

The Jolly Postman by Janet and Allan Ahlberg. (Boston: Little, 1986)

Kate Heads West by Pat Brisson. (New York: Bradbury, 1990)

Postcards

Stringbean's Trip to the Shining Sea by Vera Williams. (New York: Greenwillow, 1988)

Diaries

A Gathering of Days by Joan Blos. (New York: Scribner's, 1979)

Cartoons

The Flying Acorns by James Stevenson. (New York: Greenwillow, 1993)

Storyboards

The Bionic Bunny Show by Marc Brown. (Boston: Little, 1984)

Memoirs

The Land I Lost by Huynh Quang Nhuong. (New York: HarperCollins, 1982)

Autobiographies

Bill Peet: An Autobiography by Bill Peet. (Boston: Houghton, 1989)

Figure 3-15   Extending books through writing.

ARTISTIC EXPRESSION: PERSPECTIVE BEYOND WORDS

Artistic expressions inspired by literature are more than decorations for classroom or library walls and shelves. Like other activities suggested in this chapter, student artwork can help readers recall, interpret, and share what they have read, turning a line of plot directly into lines of an action-filled drawing or an author's character sketch into a painted portrait. Rosenblatt writes that activities such as "drawing, painting, playacting, and dance" can "offer an aesthetic means of giving form to a sense of what has been lived through in the literary transaction. This can give evidence of what has caught the young reader's attention, what has stirred pleasant or unpleasant reactions. This can lead back to the text" (276). Thus art provides a channel through which children can express their reactions to books. Just as they share their writing, or participate together in planning a dramatization, they need time to explain their art, what they did and how it represents their feelings.

Work in different media can help students appreciate how artists create picture books. Chapter 6 contains descriptions of major media. Watercolors, collage, crayon, and opaque paint are easy to use in the classroom. Students can also make pictures of characters or book settings in scratchboard by coloring paper with heavy wax crayon, painting over the crayon

Children can explore the use of various media in their own art, gaining an appreciation of how artists create the illustrations in picture books.

with thick tempera, letting the paint dry, and scratching the surface to reveal the crayon beneath.

Books can also influence the way students draw a classroom scene, color a painting of a schoolyard, or shade a sketch of a friend. As with other activities, student artists can use a book as a springboard into fresh experiments with self-expression.

Literature as Artistic Subject

In some artistic activities, literature is the subject. Students cast an artist's eye on literary elements such as plot, characterization, or setting and then reproduce what they see.

They might, for example, retell a story in a series of drawings within frames on a roll of paper. Like scenes in a slide show, episodes come into view as the roll is unwound. Students can construct a box to hide the roll, with a hole cut in the side to see the drawings. Making a roll requires deciding on the key elements of plot. Writing a script to accompany the show or captions on each picture builds communication skills.

Often an art project can be a stimulus for discussion. This mural provided a focus for a discussion of personified animals.

Second graders in Delia's class made a mural based on books they had read, all books that included mice. The painting brought to one canvas such characters as Owen, Julius and his sister Lily, and Chrysanthemum in books by Kevin Henkes; Frederick and Geraldine from books by Leo Lionni; and Amos from *Amos and Boris* by William Steig. Their mural showed what they knew of each of these characters, and they later created a dialogue balloon for each one.

Literature as Vantage Point

In other activities, books give students fresh perspective for viewing the world around them artistically. After one group of second graders had listened to their teacher read *Two Bad Ants* by Chris Van Allsburg and seen how he had shown the entire story from the perspective of the ants, they took a new look at their classroom—crouching on the floor and looking up. They tried putting their faces at desk level, as though they were ants walking across a table. Some even imagined themselves crawling up the wall. Then each selected his or her own subject and sketched how it would look to an ant.

Having materials readily available will encourage children to respond artistically. Paints, crayons, chalk, different kinds of paper, construction materials such as milk cartons, pipe cleaners, egg cartons, and decorative items such as ribbon, sequins, and yarn can be kept in a place where children are free to select what they need.

Figure 3-16 suggests some ways to think about artistic responses to literature that are appropriate for elementary and middle school children. You, and the children you teach, will think of many others.

Here are some ways that children might use art, music, or movement to extend or respond to a book.

Think about forms of art, music, and movement.

Collage	Dancing
Mural	Singing
Mosaic	Playing an instrument
Drawing	Puppets
Painting	Diorama
Printing	Shadow box
Montage	Mask
Mobile	Roller movie
Sculpture	Filmstrip
Photography	Video
Rubbing	Flannelboard characters
Wax resist	Scratchboard
Carving	Papier mâché

Think about media and equipment.

Crayon	Records
Paint	Compact discs
Chalk	Videotapes
Clay	Audiotapes
Construction paper	Orf instruments
Tissue paper	Rhythm instruments
"Found" objects	Child-constructed instruments
Colored pencils	
Fabric	

Think about where art, music, and movement appear.

Book jackets	Posters
Travel brochures	Time lines
Photo albums	Flags
Maps	Greeting cards
Quilts	Commercials
Cartoons	Parades
Endpapers	Dances
Borders	Games
Friezes	Storytelling
Chapter headings	Television shows
Advertisements	Radio shows
Wall hangings	

Figure 3-16 Extending books through artistic expression.

EVALUATING COMMERCIAL MATERIALS

Many companies produce materials to be used with literature for children, usually guides that suggest questions and activities. Most begin with a summary of the story, a little information about the author and illustrator, prereading ideas, questions and activities, and finally a list of several other related books.

You should evaluate these materials using the same criteria suggested for book-related ideas you develop yourself. That is, discussion questions should elicit higher-order thinking, diverse responses, and connections with the book. Extension activities should provide for the sharing of responses to the book and expand understanding and enjoyment. In addition, both questions and activities should be appropriate for your students and should match your purposes. They should allow for student choice and not be overwhelming. One company produces booklets of activities that have more pages than the books they accompany.

Here are three activities from a guide to the picture book *Alexander and the Terrible, Horrible, No Good, Very Bad Day* by Judith Viorst. The first is to make a list of things Alexander saw in his dad's office. This requires only that the child recall the information. Rosenblatt would call this "efferent reading," not an aesthetic stance appropriate to literature.

A second activity is for the child to draw the four scenes from the book that are described on the activity sheet. At best, this is another recall activity; at worst, it could be done without the book ever having been read.

A third activity notes that Alexander and his family had cereal for breakfast and directs the child to design a new cereal box for Alexander's family. This activity at least allows for some creativity, but it has nothing to do with key ideas in the story.

In contrast, here are three activities from a guide to *Anastasia Krupnik* by Lois Lowry. The first is that after the teacher reads Chapter 1 aloud, he or she asks the students how they would describe Anastasia and why they think she keeps a list. Both questions require interpretation and inference and set the stage for the rest of the story.

A second activity is for children to draw an important or funny scene from the book and write about what they've shown. Here the students must select the scene themselves and be able to explain it.

A third activity is to design a birth announcement for Anastasia's new baby brother and fill it in as a Krupnik might. This relates to the story directly, as Anastasia's reaction to her mother's pregnancy is central to the story, and it requires the child to follow the character development of Anastasia, her mother, and her father. Each is clearly delineated, and each would fill out the announcement differently.

If you decide to purchase commercial materials, read them carefully beforehand to assess their quality. Once you've obtained them, be selective about which parts you use. Think of them as a resource for ideas rather than a lesson plan to be followed.

SUMMARY

Teachers can design the physical arrangement and procedures of their classroom so that children will read and respond thoughtfully to books. When teachers read aloud regularly, allow children time to read independently and with classmates, set up attractive library areas, and encourage choice of and discussion about books, they demonstrate to children that literature is important.

Small-group book discussions give students an opportunity to exchange ideas, clarify their thoughts, and consider the ideas of others. These discussions may be student centered or teacher led. Teachers help children succeed in book discussions by structuring the event, by modeling the expected behavior, and by encouraging children to take responsibility for the effectiveness of the group work. When teachers lead the discussion, they may prepare higher-order questions to focus the discussion on a particular topic or ask questions that fit any book and use the student comments to guide the discussion.

Throughout the year, children should have the opportunity to express their responses to literature through dramatic and oral expression, through writing, and through the arts. They may engage in choral reading or speaking, in dramatizing a story or event within a story, in puppetry, in singing, in drawing, in making roll stories, in making diary entries for a character. And they may respond to stories by writing in their journals, using these to communicate with the teacher and with their classmates and as a basis for group discussions about a book. Whether teachers use all their own ideas or use commercial materials, the activities they suggest for children should emphasize the literary experience as an aesthetic one.

⌒ EXPLORE ON YOUR OWN

1. **Explore Your Personal Response.** Keep a response journal as you read a novel or a novel for children. Record your thoughts at least three different times. Try to predict what may happen in the story for one of your entries. Read back through your responses. How does this compare to other writing about books you've been required to do?
2. **Apply Literary Criteria.** Select any three questions from Figure 3-10 and answer them about a children's book you've read. For each, identify the literary understandings inherent in the questions or responses.
3. **Prepare to Share Literature with Children.** Select and read one book for children. Then, using the ideas in Figures 3-12, 3-15, and 3-16, brainstorm a list of specific activities for extending the book.

⌒ EXPLORE WITH CHILDREN

1. **Explore Children's Responses.** Look at entries in a response journal of several children. Select two or three entries and write what you as a teacher might write back to the child, using the criteria described by Woolman-Bonilla in this chapter.
2. **Engage Children with Literature.** Read two picture books, two short stories, or two folktales to a group of children. Have them compare the books as you record the information. Look back at Figure 3-9 for examples of three graphic organizers that would be appropriate for this activity.

☙ SUGGESTED PROFESSIONAL REFERENCES

Barton, Bob, and David Booth. *Stories in the Classroom. Storytelling, Reading Aloud and Roleplaying with Children*. Portsmouth, NH: Heinemann, 1990. § The authors describe, with many examples, how to build a "story culture" in the classroom, with emphasis on child participation and interaction.

Beaty, Janice J. *Picture Book Storytelling: Literature Activities for Young Children*. San Diego: Harcourt, 1994. § After an introduction on storytelling and story reading, the author presents 10 topics, each with appropriate picture books and many extension activities.

Bromley, Karen D'Angelo. *Webbing With Literature: Creating Story Maps With Children's Books*. 2nd ed. Needham Heights, MA: Allyn & Bacon, 1996. § This handbook shows types of webs and strategies for using them, with the webs drawn, purposes and grade levels suggested.

Brown, Hazel, and Brian Cambourne. *Read and Retell*. Portsmouth, NH: Heinemann, 1990. § The authors present in detail a strategy in which children retell stories they have heard or read, both for their own growth and as a way of allowing a teacher to assess their comprehension of text and control over language.

Chambers, Aidan. *The Reading Environment*. Great Britain: The Thimble Press, 1991. § Chambers describes the social context of reading and how teachers, librarians, and parents can create an environment that enables children to become avid readers.

Cooper, Patsy. *When Stories Come to School: Telling, Writing, & Performing Stories in the Early Childhood Classroom*. New York: Teachers & Writers Collaborative, 1993. § Cooper shows the importance of story in young children's development and in their acquisition of literacy.

Dyson, Anne Haas, and Celia Genishi, eds. *The Need for Story: Cultural Diversity in Classroom and Community*. Urbana, IL: National Council of Teachers of English, 1994. § The contributors to this book show the function and power of story in the classroom and its connections to the diverse sociocultural groups in our society.

Fox, Mem. *Teaching Drama to Young Children*. Portsmouth, NH: Heinemann, 1987. § Fox presents 36 specific creative dramatic activities, with poems and books suggested, and how a teacher might approach the topics with primary grade children.

Graves, Donald. *Build a Literate Classroom*. Portsmouth, NH: Heinemann, 1991. § This guide suggests actions teachers can take as they rethink and perhaps change their approach to the teaching of reading, literature, and writing.

Heinig, Ruth Beall. *Improvisation With Favorite Tales*. Portsmouth, NH: Heinemann, 1992. § The author uses 19 traditional tales as springboards for improvisations and a wide range of dramatic activity.

Hickman, Janet, and Bernice Cullinan, eds. *Children's Literature in the Classroom: Weaving Charlotte's Web*. Needham Heights, MA: Christopher-Gordon, 1989. § In this collection of essays, several educators explore how various genre can be used in a classroom and how teachers have structured their classrooms to be literature based.

Holland, Kathleen E., Rachael A. Hungerford, and Shirley B. Ernst, eds. *Journeying: Children Responding to Literature*. Portsmouth, NH: Heinemann, 1993. § Key researchers in children's response to literature report their findings with many classroom examples.

McCaslin, Nellie. *Creative Drama in the Classroom and Beyond*. 6th ed. New York: Longman, 1996. § This classic text thoroughly describes dramatic techniques, with chapters addressing the needs of special students and the role of the arts in a multicultural society.

McClure, Amy A., and Janice V. Kristo, eds. *Inviting Children's Responses to Literature*. Urbana, IL: National Council of Teachers of English, 1994. § Activities and related books accompany a brief plot summary for each of the 57 Notable Trade Books in the Language Arts selected for inclusion.

Moss, Joy F. *Focus on Literature: A Context for Literacy Learning*. Katonah, NY: Richard C. Owen, 1990. § Moss presents a literary curriculum made up of units that serve as a resource for developing children's literary, language, and thinking skills.

Phelan, Patricia, eds. *Literature & Life: Making Connections in the Classroom*. Urbana, IL: National Council of Teachers of English, 1990. § All 28 articles show how teachers helped children respond to and interact with literature in this book in the Classroom Practices series.

Newkirk, Thomas, and Patricia McLure. *Listening In: Children Talk About Books (and Other Things)*. Portsmouth, NH: Heinemann, 1992. § The transcripts of children in a first- and second-grade classroom talking about books shows how they interpret and respond to what they are reading. The authors' comments analyze the importance of the children's responses in the learning process.

Purves, Alan C., Theresa Rogers, and Anna O. Soter. *How Porcupines Make Love II: Teaching a Response-Centered Literature Curriculum.* New York: Longman, 1990. § The authors show the implications of reader response theory for literature instruction with many examples, most from middle to high school level.

Short, Kathy, and Kathryn Pierce, eds. *Talking About Books: Creating Literate Communities.* Portsmouth, NH: Heinemann, 1990. § Fourteen teachers and teacher educators write about how and why they use literature in their classrooms and share many transcripts of student discussion and examples of student response.

Stewig, John. *Dramatizing Literature in Whole Language Classrooms.* 2nd ed. New York: Teachers College Press, 1994. § The role of drama in children's language growth is central to the methods and activities described in practical and concrete terms.

Temple, Charles, and Patrick Collins, eds. *Stories and Readers: New Perspectives on Literature in the Elementary Classroom.* Norwood, MA: Christopher-Gordon, 1990. § Approaches and issues in the exploration of literature in elementary classrooms are placed in the larger context of schooling in the United States by many of the writers contributing to this book.

Trelease, Jim. *The New Read-Aloud Handbook.* New York: Penguin, 1989. § After addressing the importance and techniques of reading aloud, Trelease presents an annotated list of recommended read-aloud books.

Woolman-Bonilla, Julie. *Response Journals: Inviting Students to Think and Write About Literature.* New York: Scholastic, 1991. § Woolman-Bonilla presents several ways teachers can reply to student writing about literature so that learning is extended. Each technique is illustrated with examples of both student writing and teacher responses.

CHILDREN'S BOOKS CITED

Danziger, Paula. *Amber Brown is Not a Crayon.* Ill. by Tony Ross. New York: Putnam's, 1994.

Fenner, Carol. *Randall's Wall.* New York: McElderry, 1991.

Fleming, Denise. *Barnyard Banter.* New York: Holt, 1994.

Fox, Mem. *Tough Boris.* Ill. by Kathryn Brown. San Diego: Harcourt, 1994.

Giff, Patricia Reilly. *December Secrets.* 1984. Ill. by Blanche Sims. New York: Delacorte, 1986.

Hartmann, Wendy. *All the Magic in the World.* Ill. by Niki Daly. New York: Dutton, 1993.

Henkes, Kevin. *Chrysanthemum.* New York: Greenwillow, 1991.

Henkes, Kevin. *Julius the Baby of the World.* New York: Greenwillow, 1990.

Henkes, Kevin. *Owen.* New York: Greenwillow, 1993.

Hoban, Lillian. *Arthur's Great Big Valentine.* New York: Harper, 1989.

Hutchins, Pat. *What Game Shall We Play?* New York: Greenwillow, 1990.

King-Smith, Dick. *Harriet's Hare.* Ill. by Roger Roth. New York: Crown, 1995.

Lionni, Leo. *An Extraordinary Egg.* New York: Knopf, 1994.

Lionni, Leo. *Frederick.* New York: Pantheon, 1967.

Lionni, Leo. *Geraldine, the Music Mouse.* New York: Pantheon, 1979.

Lowry, Lois. *Anastasia Krupnik.* Boston: Houghton, 1979.

McCord, David. *Every Time I Climb a Tree.* Ill. by Marc Simont. Boston: Little, Brown, 1967.

Marshall, James. *Rats on the Range.* New York: Dial, 1993.

Marshall, James. *Rats on the Roof.* New York: Dial, 1991.

Martin, Bill Jr., and John Archambault. *Chicka Chicka Boom Boom.* Ill. by Lois Ehlert. New York: Simon, 1989.

Shannon, George. *Dance Away.* Ill. by Jose Aruego and Ariane Dewey. New York: Greenwillow, 1982.

Smith, Robert Kimmell. *The War With Grandpa.* New York: Delacorte, 1984.

Soto, Gary. *The Skirt.* Ill. by Eric Velasquez. New York: Delacorte, 1992.

Speare, Elizabeth. *The Sign of the Beaver.* Boston: Houghton, 1983.

Steig, William. *Amos & Boris.* New York: Farrar, 1971.

Van Allsburg, Chris. *Two Bad Ants.* Boston: Houghton, 1988.

Viorst, Judith. *Alexander and the Terrible, Horrible, No Good, Very Bad Day.* New York: Atheneum, 1972.

Yolen, Jane. *The Three Bears Rhyme Book.* Ill. by Jane Dyer. San Diego: Harcourt, 1987.

Zemach, Margot. *The Three Wishes, An Old Tale.* New York: Farrar, 1986.

∽ CHAPTER REFERENCES

Almasi, Janice. "The Nature of Fourth Graders' Sociocognitive Conflicts in Peer-Led and Teacher-Led Discussions of Literature." *Reading Research Quarterly* 30.3 (July/Aug./Sept. 1995): 314–351.

Bromley, Karen D'Angelo. "Buddy Journals Make the Reading-Writing Connection." *The Reading Teacher* 43.2 (Nov. 1989): 122–129.

Eeds, Maryann, and Deborah Wells. "Grand Conversations: An Exploration of Meaning Construction in Literature Study Groups." *Research in the Teaching of English* 23.1 (Feb. 1989): 4–29.

Kelly, Patricia R. "Guiding Young Students' Response to Literature." *The Reading Teacher* 43.7 (Mar. 1990): 464–470.

Langer, Judith A. "Focus on Research: A Response-Based Approach to Reading Literature." *Language Arts* 71 (Mar. 1994): 203–211.

Palmer, Barbara, and Rose Marie Codling. "In Their Own Words: What Elementary Students Have to Say About Motivation to Read." *The Reading Teacher* 48.2 (Oct. 1994): 176–178.

Rosenblatt, Louise. "The Literary Transaction: Evocation and Response." *Theory into Practice* 21.4 (Autumn 1982): 268–277.

Short, Kathy G. "Making Connections Across Literature and Life." Eds. Kathleen Holland, Rachael Hungerford, and Shirley Ernst. *Journeying: Children Responding to Literature*. Portsmouth, NH: Heinemann, 1993. 284–301.

Short, Kathy, and Kathryn Pierce. *Talking About Books: Creating Literature Communities*. Portsmouth, NH: Heinemann, 1990.

Smith, Frank. *Joining the Literacy Club*. Portsmouth, NH: Heinemann, 1988.

Woolman-Bonilla, Julie. "Reading Journals: Invitations to Participate in Literature." *The Reading Teacher* 43.2 (Nov. 1989): 112–121.

Woolman-Bonilla, Julie, and Barbra Werchadlo. "Literature Response Journals in a First Grade Classroom," *Language Arts* 72.8 (Dec. 1995): 562–570.

 **Chapter Four**

Planning a Curriculum:
Literature at the Center

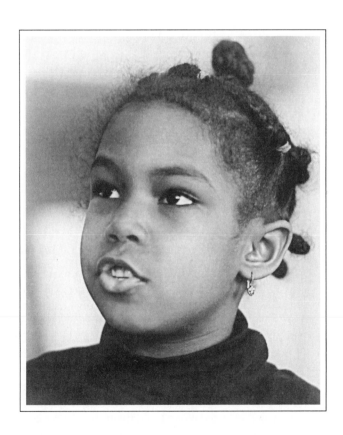

Violet sat with her class discussing foods the children liked. After they had decided that pizza was the favorite, followed closely by ice cream, she asked them to tell about a food that grown-ups like but children often do not.

Their list:

shrimp—"It tastes bad."

broccoli

lentil soup—"I hate those brown hard things."

cottage cheese—"My mom eats it at lunch. Oh . . . it's gross. Yuck!"

Then she asked, "What food do you dislike now that you think you might like when you're a grown-up?"

Their list:

carrots—"I like them regular now, but not when you cook them. Probably when I'm grown-up I'll like them cooked."

shrimp—"My parents really think it's great."

broccoli

cheese—"I always eat the pepperoni off the pizza but not the cheeses."

This discussion fit into an exploration of change. During the previous week, the children had brought in pictures of themselves as babies that they used to create a "Who Am I?" bulletin board; interviewed their parents or guardians about what they were like when they were toddlers; and responded to *Birthday Presents* by Cynthia Rylant. Rylant's book is told from the point of view of the parents, who describe the child on each birthday from age one to age six. On her second birthday, the parents give the child a clown cake and invite the child's friends over, but the child was interested only in the presents. Before her sixth birthday, however, she has picked flowers and made cards for her parents' birthdays and told them that she loves them, just as they have been telling her that they love her. Violet knew that after the children had looked at changes in themselves, both physical and emotional, she would be introducing several books in a literature unit that would show characters over a much longer period of time. She thought of it as the "Living a Lifetime" unit.

LITERATURE UNITS

A **unit** is a small set of four or five books related by theme, style, story situation, or other common element. Teachers group books into units for many reasons. A well-designed unit offers a variety of reading experiences for a diverse class. At the same time, the thread tying the books in the unit together will also unify the group of children, particularly as they explore a common subject through discussion and activities. Further, comparing and contrasting books on the same subject will sharpen students' understanding of the individual titles.

A unit arrangement often enhances enjoyment. If students like one book, they will be more receptive to a second book when the teacher introduces it as "another story about a mouse" or "another book by Leo Lionni."

Finally, creating a unit makes sense because the field of literature itself is composed of related books. While individual books may mark out separate plots, even very young children can begin to see that these plots are related. Critic Northrop Frye offers a similar rationale for grouping books together rather than presenting and responding to them merely as a stack of separate titles. Frye suggests that all themes, characters, and stories in literature belong to "one big interlocking family." He continues:

> You can see how true this is if you think of such words as *tragedy* or *comedy* or *satire* or *romance:* certain typical ways in which stories get told. You keep associating your literary experiences together: you're always being reminded of some other story you read or movie you saw or character that impressed you. For most of us, most of the time, this goes on unconsciously, but the fact that it does go on suggests that perhaps in literature you don't just read one novel or poem after another, but that there's a real subject to be studied, as there is in a science, and that the more you read, the more you learn about literature as a whole. This concept of "literature as a whole" suggests something else. Is it possible to get in, in however crude and sketchy a way, some bird's eye view of what literature as a whole is all about: considered, that is, as a coherent subject of study and not just a pile of books? (Frye 48–49)

Frye's answer is yes. He suggests that all modern stories relate to primitive tales, and ultimately to one tale about a hero "whose adventures, death, disappearance and marriage or resurrection are the focal points of what later became romance and tragedy and satire and comedy in fiction . . . " (55).

Violet need not lead her students in a search for ancient literary roots to give them a sense of the family of literature and a framework for understanding other books they read. She can begin by simply introducing some closely related members of the family. Then her students can discover their relationships.

What are the relationships? There are as many as there are in human families. Some books grow out of ancient themes involving human emotions such as fear or jealousy, although their plots may be quite contempo-

The term *unit* has varied meanings in educational discussions, so it is sensible to check how a writer or speaker is using it.

PRESCHOOL AND KINDERGARTEN

Situation/Topic: Bedtime

Bierhorst, John. *On the Road of Stars: Native American Poems and Sleep Chants.* New York: Macmillan, 1994.

Brown, Margaret Wise. *Goodnight Moon.* Ill. by Clement Hurd. New York: Harper, 1947.

Ginsburg, Mirra. *Asleep, Asleep.* Ill. by Nancy Tafuri. New York: Greenwillow, 1992.

Leviston, Wendy Cheyette. *Going to Sleep on the Farm.* Ill. by Jean Wijngaard. New York: Dial, 1992.

Winthrop, Elizabeth. *Asleep on a Heap.* New York: Holiday, 1993.

Theme: Jealousy

Brown, Marc. *Arthur's Chicken Pox.* Boston: Little, 1994.

Clifton, Lucille. *Everett Anderson's 1-2-3.* Ill. by Ann Grifalconi. New York: Holt, 1977.

Henkes, Kevin. *Julius the Baby of the World.* New York: Greenwillow, 1990.

Hoban, Russell. *A Baby Sister for Frances.* Ill. by Lillian Hoban. New York: Harper, 1964.

McCully, Emily. *My Real Family.* New York: Harcourt, 1994.

Genre: Nursery Rhymes

Agard, John, and Grace Nichols. *No Hickory, No Dickory, No Dock: Caribbean Nursery Rhymes.* Ill. by Cynthia Jabar. Cambridge, MA: Candlewick, 1995.

Ahlberg, Janet, and Allan Ahlberg. *Each Peach Pear Plum.* New York: Scholastic, 1978.

Demi. *Dragons and Dragonflies: A Collection of Chinese Nursery Rhymes.* New York: Harcourt, 1986.

Lamont, Patricia. *Ring-a-Round-a-Rosy. Nursery Rhymes, Actions Rhymes and Lullabies.* Boston: Little, 1990.

Watson, Wendy. *Wendy Watson's Mother Goose.* New York: Lothrop, 1989.

Author or Illustrator: Pat Hutchins

Hutchins, Pat. *The Doorbell Rang.* New York: Greenwillow, 1986.

Hutchins, Pat. *Little Pink Pig.* New York: Greenwillow, 1994.

Hutchins, Pat. *Rosie's Walk.* New York: Macmillan, 1968.

Hutchins, Pat. *Tidy Titch.* New York: Greenwillow, 1991.

Hutchins, Pat. *What Game Shall We Play?* New York: Greenwillow, 1990.

Other Common Element: Personified Animals

Browne, Anthony. *Willie and Hugh.* New York: Knopf, 1991

Fox, Mem. *Koala Lew.* Ill. by Pamela Lofts. New York: Harcourt, 1989.

Henkes, Kevin. *Owen.* New York: Greenwillow, 1993.

Lobel, Arnold. *Frog and Toad Are Friends.* New York: Harper, 1970.

Marshall, James. *George and Martha.* Boston: Houghton, 1972.

Wells, Rosemary. *Shy Charles,* New York: Dial, 1988.

Figure 4-1   Sample units.

rary. Some groups of books spring like siblings from the same author or illustrator. You may find yourself seeing how books relate to one another, discovering their **intertextuality,** as you read chapters later in this book. It is evident, at least, that books fall naturally into different groups depending on their genre. Violet built her "Living a Lifetime" unit based on books with the same situation and strong characterization. Figure 4-1 presents some examples of units. As you read widely, you will find that there are titles you could fill in for each of these units.

PRIMARY

Situation/Topic: Dragons

de Paola, Tomie. *The Knight and the Dragon.* New York: Putnam, 1980.

Leaf, Margaret. *Eyes of the Dragon.* Ill. by Ed Young. New York: Lothrop, 1987.

Prelutsky, Jack. *The Dragons Are Singing Tonight.* Ill. by Peter Sis. New York: Greenwillow, 1993.

Shannon, Margaret. *Elvira.* New York: Ticknor, 1993.

Williams, Jay. *Everyone Knows What a Dragon Looks Like.* Ill. by Mercer Mayer. New York: Four Winds, 1976.

Theme: Trickery

Goble, Paul. *Iktomi and the Buzzard: A Plains Indian Story.* New York: Orchard, 1994.

Greene, Jacqueline Dembar. *What His Father Did.* Ill. by John O'Brien. Boston: Houghton, 1992.

Knutson, Barbara. *Sungura and Leopard: A Swahili Trickster Tale.* Boston: Little, 1993.

McKissack, Patricia. *Flossie and the Fox.* Ill. by Rachel Isadora. New York: Dial, 1986.

Spagnoli, Cathy, and Blia Xiong. *Nine-in-One Grr! Grr! A Folktale from the Hmong People of Laos.* San Francisco: Children's Book Press, 1989.

Genre: Cumulative Tales

Gonzalez, Lucia M. *The Bossy Gallito/El gallo de bodas: A Traditional Cuban Folktale.* Ill. by Lulu Delacre. New York: Scholastic, 1994.

Kimmel, Eric A. *The Old Woman and Her Pig.* New York: Holiday, 1992.

Neitzel, Shirley. *The Bag I'm Taking to Grandma's.* Ill. by Nancy Winslow Parker. New York: Greenwillow, 1995.

Williams, Linda. *The Little Old Lady Who Was Not Afraid of Anything.* Ill. by Megan Lloyd. New York: Harper, 1986.

Wood, Audrey. *The Napping House.* Ill. by Don Wood. New York: Harcourt, 1984.

Author or Illustrator: Tomie de Paola

de Paola, Tomie. *The Art Lesson.* New York: Putnam, 1989.

de Paola, Tomie. *The Legend of the Bluebonnet: A Tale of Old Texas.* New York: Putnam, 1983.

de Paola, Tomie. *The Legend of the Poinsettia.* New York: Putnam, 1994.

de Paola, Tomie. *Strega Nona.* New York: Simon & Schuster, 1975.

de Paola, Tomie. *Tom.* New York: Putnam, 1993.

Other Common Element: Life Story

Cooney, Barbara. *Island Boy.* New York: Viking, 1988.

Houston, Gloria. *My Great-Aunt Arizona.* Ill. by Susan Condie Lamb. New York: HarperCollins, 1992.

Mitchell, Margaree Kind. *Uncle Jed's Barbershop.* Ill. by James Ransome. New York: Simon & Schuster, 1993.

Say, Allen. *Grandfather's Journey.* Boston: Houghton, 1993.

Schertle, Alice. *Maisie.* Ill. by Lydia Dabcovich. New York: Lothrop, 1995.

Figure 4-1 *continued*

Teachers begin to build a unit by weighing particular interests and abilities in the classroom and by defining their teaching goals. They may begin with one or two books that they know well and then ask other teachers or librarians for help in finding other books to fill out a unit. They will also use journals about children's books, and reference books that include brief annotations. Figure 4-2 describes several of these sources. These and other similar guides enable teachers to list related books in just a few minutes of cross-checking between index and book descriptions. The next step in building a unit is paring down the list to a usable number.

Figure 4-2 Finding the right book—selection guides.

The following books and journals can help you select individual books and group them into units.

Books

Adventuring With Books, edited by Julie Jensen and Nancy Roser and published by the National Council of Teachers of English, 10th edition, 1993, annotates recommended books, listing them first by genre and then by more specific subheadings. The index lists books by title, author, and subject.

Kaleidoscope, a Multicultural Booklist, edited by Rudine Sims and published by the National Council of Teachers of English, 1994, annotates books about people of color; usually identifies the country, nationality, or ethnic group of the characters; and groups titles by genre or theme rather than cultural group.

Our Family, Our Friends, Our World: An Annotated Guide to Significant Multicultural Books for Children and Teenagers, published by R. R. Bowker, 1992, gives critical annotations of over 1,000 titles, with chapters focusing on specific groups or countries and chapters divided by the age level of the intended audience.

Journals

Book Links, published bimonthly by Booklist Publications, an imprint of the American Library Association, contains articles in which many books on a single topic are listed and annotated, suggestions for response activities for single books, discussions with authors and artists about their work, and reviews of new books.

The Horn Book Guide, published twice each year by The Horn Book, Inc., contains brief reviews of all children's books published in the United States during the preceeding six months, grouped by genre. The index lists books by title, author, and subject.

The Horn Book Magazine, published six times per year by The Horn Book, Inc., contains reviews of new children's books and articles about literature for children.

School Library Journal, published 11 times per year by Bowker Publishers, contains reviews of children's books that often include suggestions of other books on the same topic or by the same author as well as articles about literature for children.

In part, of course, selection depends on what is available in a school or local library or on what can be obtained. Final choice is also swayed by how much time the teacher wants to spend on the unit. Once these issues are considered, however, the teacher then matches the books to a particular class by answering these questions:

Will the readers understand each of the books?

Will they be interested?

Will the selection extend their experience with literature?

Beyond these criteria for selecting individual titles, teachers should also be concerned with matching each book to other books in the unit. Answering the following questions will help you make wise choices:

Does the collection provide variety within itself, even though all entries relate to a common theme?

Can books be compared and contrasted to sharpen perspective on each title?

Do the books naturally generate different activities to enhance the students' response to literature?

Violet decided to create a unit of books in which all or most of the main character's life is portrayed. This literature unit would fit within her broader curriculum theme of change, specifically "Change is a part of life." The children had looked at how they had changed since they were babies. Now she wanted to extend their thoughts so that they might see how people change over a lifetime, yet often maintain their interests and their values. She also wanted to deepen their understanding of how one person can affect another.

Since one of Violet's basic teaching goals was to foster enjoyment of good literature, she planned to read the unit aloud. That would give her

Children's understanding of individual books is sharpened when they compare books on the same subject.

freedom to choose highly interesting books that would have been too difficult for some in her class if they had tried to read them on their own.

Violet found 10 books that fit the topic. Two she immediately eliminated because they were poorly written. She selected *Island Boy* by Barbara
Cooney, *My Great-Aunt Arizona* by Gloria Houston, *Uncle Jed's Barbershop*
by Margaree Mitchell, *Grandfather's Journey* by Allen Say, and *Maisie* by
Alice Schertle. Four of the five began when the main character was a child
and the fifth when the character was a young man. All of the characters lived
long and interesting lives. Represented in this group of books were both
men and women; an African American family, a Japanese American family,
and three European American families; characters who married and characters who stayed single; and characters living in different parts of the country.
All characters were well delineated. Violet eliminated *Miss Rumphius*
(Cooney) because the children knew the book well already. She decided not
to use *Now Let Me Fly* (Johnson), which traces the life of an African American slave from her kidnapping in Africa to her raising of four children on a
plantation, because its central theme—the inhumanity of slavery—would fit
better in another unit she was planning. She decided not to use *Yonder*
(Johnson) in the unit because, while it shows a full lifetime, the characters
are not unique individuals. She kept it, though, to put it on the table for the
children to read on their own and to enjoy the poetic language and impressionistic illustrations.

Unit planning takes time and careful thought. Figure 4-3 shows how
one teacher selected good literature for a unit, yet could have made the unit
stronger by attending more to the ethnic, racial, and socioeconomic diversity of the characters in the books.

After selecting the books, Violet planned the order in which she would
present them and the activities that would help children explore the topic
and see the relationships among the books. She thought it would take at
least seven days to complete the unit, but she knew she could extend that
time if necessary. Here are the time frame and the activities in the unit.

Day 1

Violet opened the unit by reading *My Great-Aunt Arizona* to the children. She
opened with this book because it was the most straightforward of the books
and she thought it would provide a good base of understanding. The children
had listened to how Arizona loved to read, sing, and dance as a child in the
Blue Ridge Mountains; how she had left school to care for her father and
younger brother after her mother died; how she had finally become a teacher,
married, had a daughter, and continued teaching in a one-room school for 57
years. They then discussed what she had taught her young pupils and how she
was remembered by them all their lives. The children wrote what they would
teach children if they were teachers. They also began a chart that would be
used throughout the unit. Violet listed the name "Arizona" on the left side of
the chart. Then the children contributed items in two columns. Under the first
column heading, "Stayed the Same," they listed aspects of Arizona's life and

Many teachers keep data banks or card files on books they've read even if they do not plan to use them immediately. Such files can save duplication of effort.

There is no *one* right order, but some make more sense than others and lead to more successful units.

THE LESSON, AS PLANNED AND TAUGHT	REFLECTIONS . . .

Rationale

Sherri was planning a theme cycle on families, and decided that one of her literature units would focus on grandparents. She began collecting books on the topic and then narrowed the unit to five books.

The Lesson

Sherri presented the following books:

*   *Grandma Gets Grumpy* by Anna Grossnickle Hines. (New York: Clarion, 1988)

*   *Grandmas at Bat* by Emily Arnold McCully. (New York: Harper-Collins, 1995)

*   *Grandaddy and Janetta* by Helen Griffith. Ill. by James Stevenson. (New York: Greenwillow, 1993)

*   *Song and Dance Man* by Karen Ackerman. Ill. by Stephen Gammell. (New York: Knopf, 1988)

*   *Tom* by Tomie de Paola. (New York: Putnam, 1993)

In the course of the unit, the children made a class book, with each child writing a description of one or more grandparent; compared the grandfathers in *Tom* and *Song and Dance Man* using a Venn diagram; role-played the grandmother and the children in *Grandma Gets Grumpy;* and made a chart of words selected from the books that were good for describing grandparents.

Sherri was pleased with the children's participation and understanding of the concepts within the unit.

Sherri's topic was appropriate for the class she was teaching, both for their age level and for their interactions with grandparents. Although there was great variety in how often these children saw or talked with a grandparent, all of them knew at least one of their grandparents.

Sherri's exploration of the unit theme was thorough and stimulating. The books she chose were all outstanding literature, and the grandparents described displayed an array of different personality traits.

However, all of the characters were white and from a middle class socioeconomic background. Sherri could have strengthened this unit by including a more diverse ethnic or economic group of grandparents. For example, she might have included one or more of the following books:

*   *Fox Song* by Joesph Bruchac. Ill. by Paul Morin. (New York: Philomel, 1993). Native American.

*   *Grandfather and I* by Helen Buckley. Ill. by Jan Ormerod. (New York: Lothrop, 1994). New issue with African American characters.

*   *Papa's Luck Shadow* by Niki Daly. (New York: Macmillan, 1992). Black characters, South African.

*   *Pablo's Tree* by Pat Mora. Ill. by Cecily Lang. (New York: Macmillan, 1994). Latino characters.

*   *Tanya's Reunion* by Valerie Flournoy. Ill. by Jerry Pinkney. (New York: Dial, 1995). African American characters.

Figure 4-3   On second thought: Planning for diversity.

personality that remained consistent. Under the second column heading, "Changed," they listed things that did not remain the same.

Day 2

Violet held up the book *Island Boy* and asked the children to look at the cover to get clues about where the story might take place and what they could tell about the little boy. The children noted the ocean, the island, and the baby gull the boy was holding. In this story, young Matthias loves his home on Tibbetts Island, sliding down the snow-covered hill in winter, watching the birds, and helping his father and brothers with the planting and wood chopping. All the children leave the island when they grow up, with Matthias going to sea on a schooner; only Matthias returns. He marries and raises his family there, and when he dies, he is buried on the island.

The children add Matthias to their chart and then begin a photo album of their own lives. They draw pictures of themselves doing things they enjoy, mount them in an "album," and write captions for each picture. Violet encourages them to look again at the baby and toddler pictures they had brought in earlier and to make some pictures of themselves when they were younger for their album.

Day 3

Violet again asks the children to make predictions based on the cover of the book she is about to read. This time they look at *Grandfather's Journey,* noting that the young boy is on a ship, the waves are high, and he is very dressed up. They recognize that he is on a trip. The book tells about the author's

The illustrations in Island Boy *give readers detailed information about the setting.* *(Source:* Illustration from ISLAND BOY by Barbara Cooney. Copyright © 1988 by Barbara Cooney Porter. Used by permission of Viking Penguin, a division of Penguin Books USA Inc.)

grandfather coming to the United States from Japan, settling in California, and eventually returning with his family to Japan, homesick for the mountains and rivers of his childhood. He is glad to be home, but he misses California. However, his plans to visit the United States again are changed by the World War II. The author, raised in Japan and now living in California, concludes the book by saying that he, too, is homesick for whichever country he has left, and that he understands his grandfather better now. Violet guides the children in looking carefully at the illustrations, noting the sepia-toned initial illustration of the grandfather and the matching "photo" of him that concludes the book. The children add this character to their chart. Then they talk about "getting to know" someone better. Each child selects an adult to interview, and they decide to ask the people what has remained the same about them and their lives and what has changed. They discuss how to interview and take notes and then practice by interviewing each other.

Day 4

The children bring to class the notes from their interviews. Violet has set up the outline for another Same/Change chart. This time each child gives the name of the person interviewed and tells what information was gathered. They read over the chart and make several generalizations about change in these people's lives.

Maisie maintains her compassion for animals all her life. (Source: Illustration from MAISIE by Alice Schertle, illustrations by Lydia Dabcovich. Copyright © 1995 by Alice Schertle.)

Day 5

Violet reads *Maisie* to the children. The book opens with Maisie's birth, tells about her childhood, even how she traded a pencil for a frog just so she could let the animal go. Maisie marries, moves to a house in a suburban area, raises her own children, and then lives to see her grandchildren come to visit with children of their own. On her 90th birthday, her whole family, including 31 great-grandchildren, helps her celebrate. The story concludes as Maisie and her youngest great-granddaughter, Elizabeth, let the frog that Elizabeth has caught go free.

The children look at the changes in clothing styles represented in the book and talk about their own family celebrations. They then add Maisie to the chart. Violet leads a discussion about Maisie, asking the children whether they think she is more like Arizona or more like Matthias, and why they think that.

Day 6

When you select books, think about what children may want to discuss and how you can guide them to further understanding.

Violet reads *Uncle Jed's Barbershop* to the class. This story opens when Jed is already grown and is the only black barber in the county. He goes from house to house with his clippers, but his dream is to have his own barbershop. He saves money, but one time he spends it to pay for an operation for his niece. He saves again but loses the money when the banks fail in the Depression. Finally, at age 79, he opens his own shop. The author says he died soon after, but that he died a happy man and that he taught her to dream. The children tell what they think the last line about dreaming means and then describe some of their own dreams. Many are surprised by the descriptions of segregation in the book, and they talk about basic civil rights. Violet suggests that they add pictures to their photo album showing what they hope they will be like or be doing in the future. They add Jed to their chart.

Day 7

The children look at the completed chart and make generalizations about how these characters both changed and stayed the same over a lifetime. They look at the illustrations in each book to see how the artists have portrayed the changes. They discuss how each of the characters influences other people. Then Violet suggests that if these five characters were to meet, they would probably have much to talk about. She has the children role-play in groups of five, with each child in a group playing being a different character. Before they begin, she has all of the Jed's and all the Maisie's—each character—meet in a group and reread the book. Then they make a name tag for themselves. When the children are in groups, she has them introduce themselves to each other and ask each other questions about their lives. She gives two more prompts—they tell something special about themselves and they tell each other about their grandchildren.

Violet puts the books on a table under the chart so children can look at them for the week that follows, even as new books are being shared. In the course of the year, Violet engages the children with many literature units. After several units, children develop a stronger understanding that books, members of the family of literature, are related by such things as theme, subject, and genre. Moving from unit to unit and encountering single titles between units, they gain a surer sense that stories in different books sometimes tend to follow the same patterns and that traditional styles survive in fresh forms.

A LITERATURE CURRICULUM

A **literature curriculum** is a course of study including a set of books, often divided into units and single titles, and a set of activities related to these books. In written form, a complete curriculum contains a book list, brief descriptions of how titles will be used, a suggestion for sequencing materials, a statement of goals, and suggestions for evaluating whether the goals have been met. The focus is on the literature itself. Jon Stott has developed a literature curriculum he calls the "Spiralled Sequence Story Curriculum (151–154)." It is based on a structuralist approach to the study of literature and emphasizes the patterns in stories. The stories are sequenced so that children see the same themes, characters types, and other literary conventions in increasingly complex literature. Stott sees this curriculum as helping children become better readers of literature by giving them ways to approach literature.

Teachers often develop their own literature curricula, individually or in grade level groups or perhaps in school or district-wide committees. They select books they know are of high literary quality, will be interesting to students, and match their goals. By planning the curriculum, teachers can achieve the balance they strive for in planning a unit. A full year's program will comprise realism and fantasy, classic as well as contemporary titles, poetry to balance prose, humorous and serious stories, and nonfiction as well as fiction.

Figure 4-4 shows how Deb Marciano, a second-grade teacher, planned for a visit from author/illustrator Michael Emberley as part of her literature curriculum. Although her class read the works of several "awesome authors" during the year, the visit from Emberley was special and depended on much advance preparation.

A **literature-based curriculum** is a course of study for all subjects that uses literature as the focal point, with both fiction and nonfiction books supplying the information and suggesting process. In some schools systems, topics and specific content for each grade level have been determined, and teachers select the materials they will use to guide children in studying that content. In other systems, teachers, or teachers and children, select the topics or themes and identify what is to be learned.

Two of the most common patterns in literature-based instruction are thematic organization and literature integrated with other subject areas.

SEPTEMBER

Second-grade teacher Deb Marciano finds an announcement in her school mailbox about Chapter II mini-grants. The proposals are due in two weeks. She talks with her principal and gets the application form. Each year she has spotlighted different authors and illustrators of children's books as part of her on-going literature program. Students listen to, read, and do various projects based on the work of that month's "Awesome Author." She would like to have an author visit this year's class. Because the deadline for the application is so close, she writes for what she calls "a generic author." That is, the author is to be selected when and if the funds are granted.

NOVEMBER

The mini-grant is awarded. There is a limit on total funds and a state-imposed cap on the honorarium. The $100.00 for the purchase of the author's books for the school library is funded in full.

Deb writes to several publishers asking for lists of local authors. Given the funds available, she knows she cannot offer overnight accommodations or much in travel expenses.

She looks at the lists that arrive. She eliminates two excellent authors because, "Even though they are in state, they don't serve the purposes I want." Both write for intermediate grades rather than primary children. She eliminates several others because she cannot afford their fees.

Deb goes to the library and rereads works she knows by the "finalists" and also looks for any of their works that may be new to her. She makes her selection—Michael Emberley. His work is varied and witty, appropriate for primary children, and he lives in Boston—just over an hour's drive to her school in Rhode Island.

DECEMBER

Deb contacts Little, Brown & Co., Michael Emberley's publisher. She learns from them that he would like her to call him directly. She leaves her message on his answering machine.

Figure 4-4   A classroom visit by an "Awesome Author."

JANUARY

Michael Emberley accepts the invitation. He and Deb decide on March 9 as the day he will visit. He will do presentations in the morning and autograph books in the afternoon.

Deb talks with the three other second-grade teachers in her school and invites them to participate. They are delighted to do so.

Deb reads *Ruby* and *The Present* to her class without informing them that the author/illustrator will be coming.

She arranges with Little, Brown to have a sale of Emberley's books. Orders will be taken, money collected, and the books delivered before his visit so that on March 9, the children will have books to be autographed.

FEBRUARY

In mid-February Deb tells her class about the plans for Emberley's visit. All of the second-grade classes read and discuss his books. Deb has waited until three and a half weeks before his visit so that the children's interest will be at a peak.

Deb sends notes to parents describing the visit, the books Michael Emberley has written, the prices, and the deadline, a week and a half away, for placing an order. In several places, in large letters, parents are assured that the purchase of books is optional. Deb collects the money, phones in the order to Little, Brown, and the books are delivered to the school. The publisher has offered the books at a discount. Deb uses 10% of the discount to pay the cost of shipping and handling, passing the rest on to the book purchasers.

Figure 4-4   *continued*

FEBRUARY/MARCH

The last part of February and the first part of March are spent in projects that focus on Emberley's work and are integrated with the on-going curriculum.

Deb reads *Ruby* and *The Present* again, this time encouraging the children to tell what they notice about the illustrations and the language of the stories.

In social studies, the children are studying urban, suburban, and rural areas. They work with the art teacher to create an urban mural depicting the setting of *Ruby.* After Deb rereads *Ruby* to them, they make the characters and add them to their mural.

Children try their hands at following Emberley's drawing instructions, using copies of *How to Draw Dinosaurs* and *More Dinosaurs and Other Prehistoric Animals.*

Interest is high. Children try to determine exactly what Michael Emberley looks like by squinting at the author's picture on book jackets.

The other second-grade classes are engaged in similar book sharing and projects.

Ruby
Small mouse
walking, reading, visiting,
She didn't like Reptile
Granny

Figure 4-4 *continued*

MARCH 9

Michael Emberley speaks to the four second-grade classes, illustrating as he talks. Children learn how he has used the scenes around his Boston studio in *Ruby.* They learn about his work habits and hobbies. They learn how he plans his stories and illustrations. They watch him demonstrate how to show movement and speed in an illustration. He also reads *Ruby* and then *Drummer Hoff,* written and illustrated by his parents, to the classes.

After lunch he autographs books, and for children who do not have books, he autographs cards or bookplates. Deb takes a photo of each child standing beside Emberley as he signs the books and gives each child the print.

MARCH/APRIL

Deb places nine auto-graphed copies of Emberley's books and several original sketches in the school library.

The children continue to use Emberley's ideas and books in their draw-ing. They remove all the characters from their mural, arrange them to spell HAPPY BIRTHDAY and send this as a birthday card to Emberley.

Deb and the class begin to study a different author.

APRIL

The class makes and sends get-well cards to Emberley when they learn he has broken his wrist. He sends back a sketch from his latest book, a sketch drawn with his left hand.

JUNE

One child tells Deb that he is going to Boston for a Red Sox game. "Maybe I'll stop and see Michael Emberley on the way home," he says.

The class gives Deb a gift certificate from a local bookstore with instructions that it is to be used to buy the next book by Michael Emberley.

Figure 4-4   *continued*

LITERATURE IN THEMATIC UNITS

A **thematic unit** is an interdisciplinary unit that integrates literature, language arts, science, social studies, mathematics, and the arts. The term is used for units that have either a theme or a topic as the focal point. A theme is usually stated in sentence form, such as "Change is a part of life." A topic just names the subject, such as "pets" or "ocean life." Some educators prefer themes over topics, believing that themes are more dynamic (Shanahan, Robinson, and Schneider, 718), but other educators group both under the title of thematic unit or topical unit.

Topic as a Focal Point

Topics and themes are used to organize concepts to be explored and activities to be experienced. The literature within the unit provides a narrative structure that often helps children connect the topic with their own lives (Smith and Johnson, 198) and approach a topic in a natural and interesting way. Figure 4-5 shows a web built on the idea that change is a part of life, demonstrating one approach to the planning of a unit.

Here the teacher has begun by listing the key ideas that will be a part of the unit. She has looked at many areas of change and decided on those that will help children understand the basic theme and that will be meaningful to them. Thus she has decided on looking at how seasons, plants, animals, people, and places change over time. She has then found high quality literature that addresses the topic. Both fiction and nonfiction are represented. Next she adds activities keyed to the topic that relate to the books. The literature unit that Violet developed fits within this larger thematic unit. Her class looked carefully at fiction books exploring the concept that people change over a lifetime. Each topic in this web could be expanded just as that portion was. Also, activities may be added even though they do not build directly on one of the books.

The unit draws on several content areas: science for the study of plants and animals and seasons; social studies for both psychological and physical changes in people and for the effects of progress on specific places; reading and writing throughout the unit; mathematics as children observe, describe, and tally changes; and the arts as they portray the changes they observe and see how others have portrayed them. A teacher who starts unit planning by listing the key ideas will go back to see if other subjects need to be added.

The web in Figure 4-5 shows the books that the teacher will share with the class. There will be many more books in the classroom on the unit topic. Children will want to read more about a particular topic within the unit so there will need to be books that explore these concepts in more depth. Children will be reading at different levels, so the books should represent a range of reading difficulty. And there should be many books just for browsing to stimulate and expand children's interest in the topic.

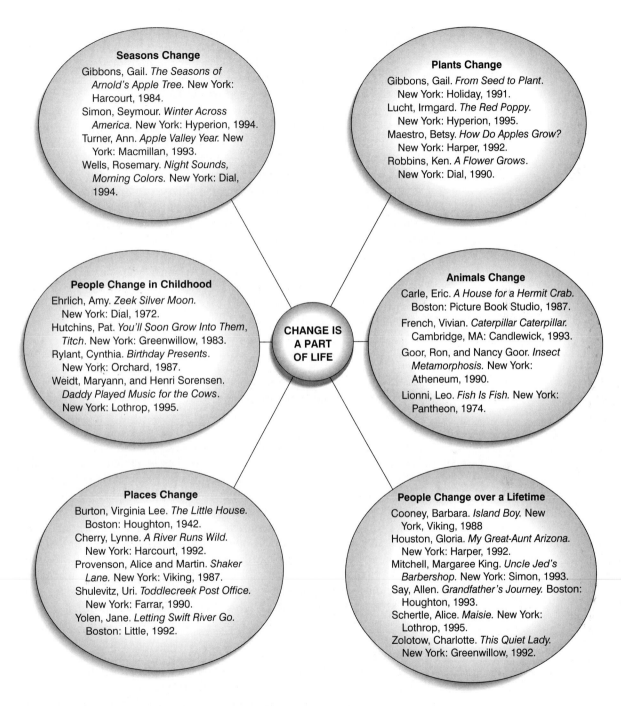

Figure 4-5 A web on change: Topic as focal point.

The web contains a central node "CHANGE IS A PART OF LIFE" connected to six surrounding nodes:

Seasons Change
Gibbons, Gail. *The Seasons of Arnold's Apple Tree*. New York: Harcourt, 1984.
Simon, Seymour. *Winter Across America*. New York: Hyperion, 1994.
Turner, Ann. *Apple Valley Year*. New York: Macmillan, 1993.
Wells, Rosemary. *Night Sounds, Morning Colors*. New York: Dial, 1994.

Plants Change
Gibbons, Gail. *From Seed to Plant*. New York: Holiday, 1991.
Lucht, Irmgard. *The Red Poppy*. New York: Hyperion, 1995.
Maestro, Betsy. *How Do Apples Grow?* New York: Harper, 1992.
Robbins, Ken. *A Flower Grows*. New York: Dial, 1990.

People Change in Childhood
Ehrlich, Amy. *Zeek Silver Moon*. New York: Dial, 1972.
Hutchins, Pat. *You'll Soon Grow Into Them, Titch*. New York: Greenwillow, 1983.
Rylant, Cynthia. *Birthday Presents*. New York: Orchard, 1987.
Weidt, Maryann, and Henri Sorensen. *Daddy Played Music for the Cows*. New York: Lothrop, 1995.

Animals Change
Carle, Eric. *A House for a Hermit Crab*. Boston: Picture Book Studio, 1987.
French, Vivian. *Caterpillar Caterpillar*. Cambridge, MA: Candlewick, 1993.
Goor, Ron, and Nancy Goor. *Insect Metamorphosis*. New York: Atheneum, 1990.
Lionni, Leo. *Fish Is Fish*. New York: Pantheon, 1974.

Places Change
Burton, Virginia Lee. *The Little House*. Boston: Houghton, 1942.
Cherry, Lynne. *A River Runs Wild*. New York: Harcourt, 1992.
Provenson, Alice and Martin. *Shaker Lane*. New York: Viking, 1987.
Shulevitz, Uri. *Toddlecreek Post Office*. New York: Farrar, 1990.
Yolen, Jane. *Letting Swift River Go*. Boston: Little, 1992.

People Change over a Lifetime
Cooney, Barbara. *Island Boy*. New York, Viking, 1988
Houston, Gloria. *My Great-Aunt Arizona*. New York: Harper, 1992.
Mitchell, Margaree King. *Uncle Jed's Barbershop*. New York: Simon, 1993.
Say, Allen. *Grandfather's Journey*. Boston: Houghton, 1993.
Schertle, Alice. *Maisie*. New York: Lothrop, 1995.
Zolotow, Charlotte. *This Quiet Lady*. New York: Greenwillow, 1992.

Units may be connected to one another in a theme cycle that continues for a full year, with one unit blending into the next. For example, one rural school system has developed a theme cycle for the third grade that begins in the fall with a study of apples and apple production, which are economically important in the area. This unit leads to a study of the town itself, its history and development. A part of this development is the fact that the original village was flooded to create a reservoir to supply water for the surrounding towns. The history leads to a study of the need for water, the water cycle, and ways of maintaining clean water. Each portion of the cycle has closure, but each leads naturally to the next part of the cycle.

Another approach to planning thematic units is to draw directly on each content area. In this approach, a teacher begins with the topic in the center of the web but lists books and ideas under subject area headings such as science or social studies or writing.

In general, beginning with the key ideas gives a more natural and cohesive form to the unit than does trying to make every subject fit into it. And, of course, units change as they are taught, for children bring in ideas and books and make suggestions. The web is a plan and can be modified as necessary.

A Book as a Focal Point

A single book can serve as the core of a unit. Such a book has to have the potential for extended exploration and ties to many ideas that are of interest and of value. Figure 4-6 shows a web built on *The Relatives Came* by Cynthia Rylant.

The web here is constructed like the one in which the topic is developed through the stating of key ideas. The teacher has identified areas that build directly on the book and are extensions of it rather than looking for subject-area coordination. Thus there are activities grouped around books by Rylant, books illustrated by Stephen Gammell, books about families, books with Appalachian settings, and activities that build directly on *The Relatives Came*. There is strong potential for developing a sensitivity to language and dialect, for seeing how writers use language to describe settings, and for observing the art in picture books in detail. The section on family life and on activities can help children make connections between the book and their own lives. Units built on a single book are particularly effective in showing children how a book fits into the context of their lives and the world of literature.

Webbing as a Planning Strategy
There are many advantages to using webbing as a planning strategy. First, it allows you to see all of the pieces of a unit at once, determining how they relate to one another and what may be missing. Second, webbing encourages flexibility because ideas can be added to any section at any time. And third, it can be done with children or shared with children as they experience the unit, giving them an overview of the topic and the opportunity for input.

Other Books Illustrated by Stephen Gammell

Ackerman, Karen. *Song and Dance Man*. New York: Knopf, 1988.
Blos, Joan. *Old Henry*. New York: Morrow, 1987.
Gammell, Stephen. *Git Along, Old Scudder*. New York: Lothrop, 1983.
Haseley, Dennis. *The Old Banjo*. New York: Macmillan, 1983.
Lyon, George-Ella. *Come a Tide*. New York: Watts, 1990.
Rosenberg, Liz. *Monster Mama*. New York: Philomel. 1993.

Other Books Written by Cynthia Rylant

All I See. New York: Orchard, 1988.
Best Wishes. Katonah, New York: Richard C. Owen, 1992.
Henry and Mudge and the Best Day of All. New York: Macmillan, 1995.
Miss Maggie. New York: Dutton, 1983.
Mr. Putter and Tabby Bake the Cake. New York: Harcourt, 1994.
When I Was Young in the Mountains. New York: Dutton, 1982

The Relatives Came

Books with an Appalachian Setting

Gibbons, Faye. *Mountain Wedding*. New York: Morrow, 1996.
Johnston, Tony. *Amber on the Mountain*. New York: Dial, 1994.
Ransom, Candice. *When the Whipoorwill Calls*. New York: Tambourine, 1995.
Rylant, Cynthia. *Appalachia: The Voices of Sleeping Birds*. Harcourt, 1991. (Also *Miss Maggie* and *When I Was Young in the Mountains*.)

Books about Extended Families

Adoff, Arnold. *Black Is Brown Is Tan*. New York: Harper, 1973.
Caseley, Judith. *The Cousins*. New York: Greenwillow, 1990.
de Paola, Tomie. *Bonjour Mister Satie*. New York: Putnam, 1991.
Hoffman, Mary. *Boundless Grace*. New York: Dial, 1995.
Soto, Gary. *Too Many Tamales*. New York: Putnam, 1993.

Activities Related to *The Relatives Came*

• Make a book about a time you visited relatives or they visited you.
• Plan a menu for dinner for the family and a visiting friend.
• Compare the illustrations in three different Rylant books set in Appalachia.
• Read Rylant's autobiography, *Best Wishes*, and write the questions you'd like to ask her.

Figure 4-6 A web of *The Relatives Came:* A single book as focal point.

A single book such as The Relatives Came *can provide the focal point for a unit. (Source:* Illustration and text reprinted with the permission of Simon & Schuster Books for Young Readers from THE RELATIVES CAME by Cynthia Rylant, illustrated by Stephen Gammell. Illustrations Copyright © 1985 Stephen Gammell.)

INTEGRATING LITERATURE AND OTHER CURRICULAR AREAS

Literature is integrated with other curricular areas to provide a wider base of knowledge, to address the interests and capabilities of diverse groups of students, and to provide an up-to-date source of data. Students learn to see that literature overlaps many areas of knowledge; it is not isolated or irrelevant to the other work they do. They come to recognize that literature, while often imaginative, can be constructed from fact. And the perspective of a writer of literature is different from that of a writer of textbooks and may sharpen a student's understanding of other subjects. The library's listing of books by subject is useful in finding books on a particular topic. Books on science and social studies topics, the solar system, or the colonial period in American history, for example, can usually be found more easily than those that develop the language arts. Several professional organizations produce yearly lists of recommended books for children in particular fields, using as criteria both the literary merit of the selection and its accuracy of content. Figure 4-7 describes three such sources, for science, social studies, and language arts.

Combining curricula makes sense, but teachers planning to match literature with other subjects have to be careful to avoid two mistakes. The first is misus-

---

Outstanding Science Trade Books for Children
The books in this bibliography are selected by a book review panel appointed by the National Science Teachers Association in cooperation with the Children's Book Council. Selection is based on three criteria: the information in the book is consistent with current scientific knowledge; the book is readable; and the format and illustrations are pleasing. The list appears each year in the March issue of *Science and Children.*

Notable Children's Trade Books in the Field of Social Studies
The books in this bibliography are selected by a Book Review Panel of the National Council for the Social Studies and the Children's Book Council Joint Committee. The books selected emphasize human relations, represent diversity, present an original theme or fresh look at a traditional topic, and are of high literary quality. The list appears each year in the April/May issue of *Social Education.*

Notable Children's Trade Books in the Language Arts
The books in this bibliography are selected by a committee of The Children's Literature Assembly of the National Council of Teachers of English. These books are considered to be diverse and finely crafted and have the potential to stimulate and extend children's language use. Suggestions for involving children with each book are given. The list appears in the *Journal of Children's Literature.*

Figure 4-7   Notable trade books for children.

ing the literature. For example, turning literature into a source of vocabulary words to be memorized or testing students on the dates that appear incidentally in historical fiction is a misuse of literature. The second mistake to be avoided is mismatching literature. Some children's books can undermine teaching goals in other subjects. For example, a process-oriented science program would include student-run experiments to give practice in the processes, the general techniques, of scientific inquiry. The results of the experiments are less important in such a program than the approaches students take to get results. Consequently, a book about science experiments that explains what will happen and why can lessen the incentive for the child to discover the process behind the experiment.

A respect for the literature and an understanding of goals in other subject areas are prerequisites to bringing children's books into the broad school curriculum.

Science and Social Studies

Goals in many subject areas cluster around three general categories: knowledge, skills, and attitudes. For example, in the thematic unit on change as a part of life (Figure 4-5) a knowledge goal might be an understanding of the policy of eminent domain. In the book *Shaker Lane* by Alice and Martin

Books often fit into discussions of several different topics and can be reread for new insights or connections.

Provensen, the County Land Agent comes to talk with the residents of Shaker Lane and explains to them that a reservoir is to be built on their land, that they must move, and that the county will pay them for their land. An illustration shows the notice that one respondent received.

A process- or skill-oriented goal might be for students to read the many quotations from the residents, then interview people about a topic and write the responses in paragraph form, attempting to keep the exact words used and correctly enclosing those words in quotation marks.

Attitudes and values could be explored by reading *Toddlecreek Post Office* by Uri Shulevitz. The book raises the question of when change is for the better in its depiction of the closing of the Toddlecreek Post Office when the postal inspector finds that the office is used as a gathering place for the local residents. She declares that a post office is for post office business only and that Toddlecreek is such a small village that it doesn't have enough postal business to merit keeping the office open. Within the one portion of this thematic unit, the goals of knowledge, skills, and attitudes are all addressed.

Science and social studies topics can provide the stimulus for writing, often taking a literary approach. Figure 4-8 describes how two fourth-grade

Figure 4-8 Integrating science and poetry.

Jennifer and Diana, both fourth-grade teachers in the same school, began discussing their plans for a science unit on space as they ate lunch. Jennifer was reading a book recommended to her by the curriculum director—*Whole Learning: Whole Language and Content in the Upper Elementary Grades* by Pat Cordeiro (Katonah, NY: Richard C. Owen, 1992). In one section, the author described "moonwatching," and noted the importance of having children begin their learning by observing and collecting their own data. Jennifer and Diana decided that they would begin their unit by having the children make lunar observations and that they would incorporate language arts into the study.

After two weeks of carefully recording what they had seen, the children began to describe the pattern of when and where the moon was visible. They shared their drawings of the moon's shape. Jennifer and Diana then read several poems about the moon, and the children compared the kind of language and observation used in poetry with that used in science. The children then combined their "scientific" observations with their "poetic" observations and created a group poem:

> Cold as ice and snow
> Dry as desert sand
> Bumpy like pot holes in the road
> When it's setting, we're rising
> Ring of light surrounds it
>   Sprinkled with powder
>   Scribbled with a Crayola pencil
>
> THE MOON

teachers worked on a science unit on the moon, using much literature, and then guided their students to use both scientific and poetic observations of the moon in creating a class poem about the moon.

Reading and Writing

All literature units can involve extensive reading and writing. Children gain in sophistication in their skills and their attitudes about literacy as they have more experience. Figure 4-9 reports on an interview with children from preschool through grade four. Each is asked about what they've read lately and enjoyed and about stories they have written. As you look at their responses, notice the patterns between what they say about reading and what they write themselves.

Again, the goals of knowledge, skills, and attitude can be addressed. Children can look at the effect of various writing styles on themselves as readers. Look at the three lead sentences quoted in Figure 4-10. Decide which of the three books you would read based on these opening sentences, and then try to analyze what it was about the style or content of the author's words that made one book seem more appealing to you than the others. Such activities focus children's attention on writing and give them knowledge of how style functions.

Many books for children use figurative language effectively, presenting another aspect of writing. Weller, in *Matthew Wheelock's Wall,* describes that wall.

> "Old Matthew Wheelock built this wall. A hundred years ago and more, he laid the stony necklace round his fields, from road to river." (n.p.)

Just hearing such language regularly helps children understand the power that language can have.

Children practice reading and writing skills as they read regularly, use a variety of materials and types of literature, and respond in writing to what they've read. Just as children may focus on writing style, they may also focus on organization. Both Graves (316–324) and Freeman note that nonfiction can provide a model for reports that students write themselves. They can see how an author presented information, whether chronologically, using cause and effect, and by related topics. They can begin to discuss what organization makes sense for the information they wish to present in their reports.

Attitudes about reading and writing are shown in fiction, sometimes as the central theme and sometimes incidentally. In *Shark in School,* Patricia Reilly Giff takes her protagonist, Matthew Jackson, from an unskilled reader who hates to read to a reader who wants to talk about what he is learning and reading, all the result of being in Miss Bass' classroom. She has numerous books around, loves to read herself, and expects everyone in her class to read. Matthew begins by pretending to read and ends up actually reading—and liking it!

Walter Dean Myers tells an original fable in *The Story of Three Kingdoms,* one in which the People can rule the earth because they have overcome the

Chapter 3 has suggestions for helping children respond to books in writing.

Name and Grade of Child	Tell me about a good story you've read lately. Why did you enjoy it?	Tell me about a story you have written.	What do authors include in stories to make them good?
Larry (preschool)	Clifford the dog is a dog who has a birthday.	I tell the teacher about my dog at my house.	No answer.
Katie (kindergarten)	*Grumpy Bears.* It's really funny. The bears get confused about cheese.	It's a story about a tiny teddy bear looking for a place to stay.	An author draws pictures and writes words. He puts in funny things.
Amy (grade 1)	I liked the *Berenstein Bears Trouble with Money.* I like stories about bears. They're funny.	It's a story about my friend Tara and playing with her. We played and then I went home.	They put pictures, words, and the name on the front.
Chris (grade 2)	*The Lion, the Witch, and the Wardrobe.* It was interesting and had a lot of mystery. I like to read mystery stories.	I wrote a story about a boy who liked to swim. He only knew the dog paddle.	He makes mysteries in his stories.
Tara (grade 3)	*Sweet Valley Twins Out of Place.* I like this series because it's so interesting and I don't know what will happen in each episode.	I write stories about people in my family. Also about places I go on vacation.	He includes the setting of the story, the ending, and things that happen. He includes color pictures.
Erin (grade 4)	*Kristy's Great Idea,* which is one of the Babysitters Club books series. I like to find out about the characters' personalities in each book of the series.	It was called "The Hero Who Went to School." A girl went to school and found a man holding up the principal and kids. She ran to the police for help and won a trophy.	They include imagination, exciting things, good adjectives, and happy endings. I just learned about adjectives in school.

Figure 4-9   Children talk about reading and writing.

Read these sentences from the opening, or lead, from a picture book about a river. Decide which book you would read and think about what influenced your decision. Then picture yourself using examples such as these from books to show children how an author's choice of words can influence a reader's reaction.

Book 1

"Once there were two boys named Josh and Aaron who lived with their family in a big yellow house. Nearby was a river that flowed gently into the sea."

Book 2

"Long ago a river ran wild through a land of towering forests. Bears, moose and herds of deer, hawks and owls all made their homes in the peaceful river valley."

Book 3

"When I was six years old the world seemed a very safe place. The wind whispered comfortable through the long branches of the willow by my bedroom window."

Book 1 is *Where the River Began* by Thomas Locker (NY: Dial, 1984). It tells how Josh and Aaron and their grandfather follow the river from the house to its source, camping along the way.

Book 2 is *A River Ran Wild* by Lynne Cherry (NY: Harcourt, 1992). It is about the history of the Nashua River in New Hampshire, beginning before the arrival of the white settler when the river was pristine, showing the changes as land use changed and manufacturing polluted the river, and finally tracing the efforts of one woman to have the river cleaned up.

Book 3 is *Letting Swift River Go* by Jane Yolen (Ill. by Barbara Cooney. Boston: Little, 1992). A young girl describes how her hometown was abandoned and then submerged as the Quabbin Reservoir in Massachusetts was created. She returns as an adult, looking down through the water at places she used to play.

A good lead sets the tone for a book and lets readers know the mood of a story. It should draw readers in. Having children compare and evaluate the language used by professional authors can help them think about how they are using language in their own writing.

Figure 4-10 Which book would you read?—Learning about leads

Source: Excerpts from A RIVER RAN WILD, Copyright © 1992 by Lynne Cherry, reprinted by permission of Harcourt Brace & Company. Text excerpt from LETTING SWIFT RIVER GO by Jane Yolen. Text Copyright © 1992 by Jane Yolen, Illustrations Copyright © 1992 by Barbara Cooney. By permission of Little, Brown and Company.

Elephant, the Shark, and the Hawk. They have told stories about what has happened to them and learned from their stories. But then they decide that they do not need to be the masters of the earth, because with the gift of story came wisdom, and they can share the earth because it is wise to do so. The theme that there is wisdom in stories is clear. Children could discuss the value of stories, expressing their own attitudes and comparing them with that of the people in the story.

Much literature, of course, addresses more than one goal. Vera Williams, in *Stringbean's Trip to the Shining Sea*, tells the whole story of Stringbean's trip with his brother from Kansas to the Pacific Ocean through the postcards he writes home to his family. The fronts of the cards show the variety one sees on the rack, from photographs of places to maps to charts. The backs show how the card is addressed, but also

The People in The Story of Three Kingdoms *recognize that the gift of story brings wisdom. (Source:* Illustration from THE STORY OF THREE KINGDOMS by Walter Dean Myers. Copyright © 1995 by Ashley Bryan. Reprinted by permission of HarperCollins Publishers.)

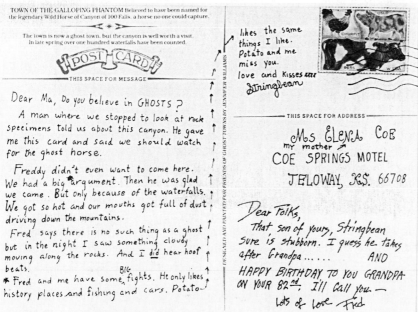

TOWN OF THE GALLOPING PHANTOM Believed to have been named for
the legendary Wild Horse of Canyon of 100 Falls. a horse no one could capture.

⊰⊱

The town is now a ghost town, but the canyon is well worth a visit.
In late spring over one hundred waterfalls have been counted.

POST CARD

THIS SPACE FOR MESSAGE

Dear Ma, Do you believe in GHOSTS?

A man where we stopped to look at rock
specimens told us about this canyon. He gave
me this card and said we should watch
for the ghost horse.

Freddy didn't even want to come here.
We had a big argument. Then he was glad
we came. But only because of the waterfalls.
We got so hot and our mouths got full of dust
driving down the mountains.

Fred says there is no such thing as a ghost
but in the night I saw something cloudy
moving along the rocks. And I did hear hoof
beats.
* Fred and me have some BIG fights. He only likes
history places and fishing and cars. Potato—

likes the same
things I like.
Potato and me
miss you.
love and kisses xxx
Stringbean

THIS SPACE FOR ADDRESS

Ms ELENA COE
my mother →
COE SPRINGS MOTEL
JELOWAY, KS. 66708

Dear Folks,
That son of yours, Stringbean
sure is stubborn. I guess he takes
after Grandpa...... AND
HAPPY BIRTHDAY TO YOU GRANDPA
ON YOUR 82nd. I'll Call you—
Lots of love Fred

The postcards Stringbean sends provide models for writing to family and friends, writing brief descriptions of places, designing postcards and stamps, and addressing letters. (Source: Illustrations from STRINGBEAN'S TRIP TO THE SHINING SEA *by Vera B. Williams and Jennifer Williams. Copyright © 1988 by Vera B. Williams and Jennifer Williams. Reprinted by permission of Greenwillow Books, a division of William Morrow and Company, Inc.)*

captured the style of writing for postcards: how to convey much information in a small space. Knowledge about how to address and write postcards, skills in doing so if the students write using these as a model, and attitudes toward conveying information and feelings are all a part of this book.

Tony Johnson, in *The Iguana Brothers,* intersperses Spanish words into this story of Dom and Tom, two iguanas. The text is written so that readers can glean the meaning of the Spanish words from the context. Here is an example.

> Dom said, "You will get thin, Tom. You will get *flaco, flaco, flaco.*"
> "I would rather be *flaco* than eat bugs."
> "You will get pale, Tom," said Dom. You will get *palido, palido, palido.*"
> "Bugs make me pale already."
> "And you tail will drop right off," said Dom. (n.p.)

Children hearing this story are caught up in the humor and the repetition, but they are also learning words in Spanish and seeing another language as valued and effective for communication. In fact, sharing bilingual books, in which the text is in two languages, is a way for young children to learn about other languages and perhaps see their own represented in a book shared with the whole class. Figure 4-11 lists suggestions for presenting bilingual books and specific recommended examples.

Mathematics

Real problems that require mathematical solutions may be presented in books for children. In Pat Hutchins' *The Doorbell Rang,* Victoria and Sam have just sat down to share a plate of 12 cookies when the doorbell rings. Tom and Hannah from next door come in, and now the cookies must be shared by four children rather than two. Thus begins a series of new arrivals, and the necessity of refiguring how many cookies each child gets. Children hearing the story can apply their own problem-solving skills and will probably also empathize with the characters who see their share of the snack getting smaller and smaller. Fortunately, just when there seem to be too many people, grandma arrives with more cookies.

Perhaps one of the best-known authors for children who writes about mathematical topics is Mitsumasa Anno. His books range from simple counting books to ones that explore complex mathematical topics and logic. In *The Magic Seeds* he shows multiplication. Each time Jack plants a seed, the plant that grows produces two seeds. The plot thickens, however, when he eats some, saves some, and otherwise changes the formula. Each illustration shows the seeds, so that students can figure out how many and count to check their answers.

A caution for integrating literature and mathematics is not to stretch the connection to absurd limits just to make a connection.

Check the list of professional references at the end of this chapter to find sources of lists of books that have potential for correlation with math activities and learning.

A. With the following books, children can learn or repeat phrases. They enjoy hearing the sound of other languages and have fun playing with words.

Bozylinsky, Hannah Heritage. *Lala Salama.* New York: Philomel, 1993.

Dabcovich, Lydia. *The Keys to My Kingdom: A Poem in Three Languages.* New York: Lothrop, 1992.

Feder, Jane. *Table, Chair, Bear: A Book in Many Languages.* New York: Ticknor, 1995.

Griego, Margot, et al. *Tortillitas Para Mama.* Ill. by Barbara Cooney. New York: Holt, 1981.

Hall, Nancy Abraham, and Jill Syverson-Stork. *Los Pollitos Dicen/ The Baby Chicks Sing: Traditional Games, Nursery Rhymes, and Songs from Spanish-Speaking Countries.* Ill. by Kay Chorao. Boston: Little, Brown, 1994.

Mora, Pat. *Listen to the Desert/Oye al desierto.* Ill. by Francisco Mora. New York: Clarion, 1994.

Pomerantz, Charlotte. *The Tamarindo Puppy.* Ill. by Byron Barton. New York: Greenwillow, 1980.

Yolen, Jane, ed. *Sleep Rhymes Around the World.* Honesdale, PA: Boyds Mills, 1994.

B. Children can use the pictures in the following books to tell the story. The pictures can help them build their language competence, lead to writing, and encourage children whose native language is not English to share words in their language.

Asch, Frank, and Vladmir Vagin. *Here Comes the Cat!* New York: Scholastic: 1989.

Burstein, Fred. *The Dancer/La bailarina/*Ill. by Joan Auclair. New York: Bradbury, 1993.

de Mariscal, Glanca Lopez. *The Harvest Birds/Los pajaros de la cosecha.* San Francisco: Children's, 1995.

Ehlert, Lois. *Moon Rope/Un lazo a la luna.* San Diego: Harcourt, 1992.

C. Let children hear the following stories in two languages and then discuss them in English. If you do not read the second language, use tapes or work with an ESL teacher to present the literature.

Dorros, Arthur. *Radio Man.* New York: HarperCollins, 1993.

Dorros, Arthur. *This Is My House.* New York: Scholastic, 1992.

Hammond, Anna, and Joe Matunis. *This Home We Have Made/ This House We Have Made.* New York: Crown, 1993.

Figure 4-11   Bilingual books.

D. In reading the following books, children can summarize the key points of a paragraph using either the English or the Spanish text and then point out in the illustrations what the text describes.

Ancona, George. *The Pinata Maker/El Pinatero.* San Diego: Harcourt, 1994.

Garza, Carmen Lomas. *Family Pictures/Cuadros de familia.* Emeryville, CA: Children's Book Press, 1990.

Roe, Eileen. *Con Mi Hermano/With My Brother.* New York: Bradbury, 1991.

Rohmer, Harriet. *Uncle Nacho's Hat/El Sombrero del Tio Nacho.* Ill. by Veg Reisberg. Emeryville, CA: Children's Book Press, 1989.

Winter, Jeanette. *Diego.* New York: Knopf, 1991.

E. Children can play language games using the following books.

Guess the animal:

De Zutter, Hank. *Who Says a Dog Goes Bow-wow?* Ill. by Suse MacDonald. New York: Doubleday, 1993.

Find synonyms:

Gonzalez, Lucia M. *The Bossy Gallito/El gallo de bodas: A Traditional Cuban Folktale.* Ill. by Lulu Delacre. New York: Scholastic, 1994.

Poulin, Stephane. *Ah! Belle Cite!/ A Beautiful City ABC.* Montreal: Tundra, 1985.

Torres, Leyla. *Subway Sparrow.* New York: Farrar, 1993.

Compare structure:

What do you notice?

Ekoomiak, Normee. *Arctic Memories.* New York: Holt, 1988.

Han, Suzanne Crowder. *The Rabbit's Judgment.* Ill. by Yumi Heo. New York: Holt, 1994.

Nomura, Takaaki. *Grandpa's Town.* New York: Kane Miller, 1991.

Figure 4-11   *continued*

The Arts

Talking to the Sun by Koch (New York: Holt, 1985) and *Go In and Out the Window* by Fox (New York: Holt, 1987) combine artwork from the Metropolitan Museum of Art with poetry and songs and provide brief explanations.

Picture books are works of art in themselves, so sharing these with children is the beginning of art education. Books for children give full expression to music, drama, dance, and the visual arts. Nonfiction can give knowledge, but so can such books as *When Clay Sings* by Byrd Baylor, which describes and depicts the art on prehistoric Indian pottery.

Many books provide the stimulus to explore various media, and certainly attitudes toward the arts are expressed. Some are very direct. In *Daddy Played Music for the Cows* by Maryann Weidt and Heri Sorensen, a child remembers how music was a part of her life from the time she was a toddler and how important it was, and is, to her.

and rang.

Each time a new child arrives, the children must decide how to divide the cookies evenly.
(Source: Illustration from THE DOORBELL RANG by Pat Hutchins, Copyright © 1985 by Pat Hutchins. Reprinted by permission of Greenwillow Books, a division of William Morrow and Company, Inc.)

Children can use the illustrations to help them answer the questions about how many seeds Jack has. (Source: Illustration from ANNO'S MAGIC SEEDS. Copyright © 1995 by Mitsumasa Anno.)

The next year—that is, the *fifth* year—in the spring all the sprouts came up, and in the fall the new seeds were made. That winter, Jack ate 1 seed and he buried the rest of them in the ground.

How many seeds did he bury?

George does not appreciate Martha's critical comments about his painting. (Source: Illustration from GEORGE AND MARTHA ROUND AND ROUND. Illustration copyright © 1988 by James Marshall. Reprinted by permission of Houghton Mifflin Co. All rights reserved.)

In the short story "The Artist" in *George and Martha Round and Round,* James Marshall contrasts Martha's sensitivity to George's comments about her painting with George's confidence about his own paintings and ability to shrug off Martha's comments. The idea that artists differ is presented, but so too is the attitude that one makes a painting to suit oneself, not others.

ASSESSING THE LITERATURE PROGRAM

Assessment begins with the goals and objectives of a program. You must have an idea of what you hope to accomplish if you are to devise a plan for measuring your success. Here are commonly agreed on goals for a literature program:

1. Children will read widely in a variety of genre.
2. Children will choose to read.
3. Children will recognize different types of reading material and will read for different purposes.
4. Children will make connections between literature and their own lives.
5. Children will make connections among different books.
6. Children will have confidence in their own responses to literature.
7. Children will respect the responses of others to literature.
8. Children will become lifelong readers.

When evaluating their literature program, teachers look at their own behaviors, how they structure the classroom, and the behavior of their students. Here is a checklist the teacher who has the goals stated earlier might use to guide the evaluation process:

Do I

1. read aloud to the children every day?
2. read a variety of genre, including poetry, to the children?
3. provide time for children to read books they've chosen themselves?
4. provide many books of various genre in the classroom?
5. provide books that represent ethnic and racial diversity?
6. guide children to read for different purposes?
7. encourage children to share their responses to books in a variety of ways?
8. respect differences of opinions about specific books?
9. encourage children to make connections among works of literature and between literature and life?
10. work with parents and librarians to stimulate children's interest in reading?

This same teacher would also want to know how children are responding to the literature program. Often teachers sense when something is going well, but a strong evaluation is structured and systematic. For example, a teacher might review the sign-up sheets for literature discussion groups to see what patterns exist for individual children and for the group about books chosen, number of books read, types of books read, and frequency of participation in discussion groups.

A strong literature program stimulates children to read and enjoy literature.

Or the teacher might use notes made during small-group discussions. Some teachers put these notes on gummed labels so they can transfer them quickly to a folder for the child involved. These quick anecdotal records may show the depth of response and, when several are reviewed, can show patterns of growth.

Observation can be a powerful assessment tool if carefully done. Once again, a structured and systematic approach will yield more valid results than a teacher's simply thinking back about the program. For example, if you are interested in how children use their Sustained Silent Reading time, then observe regularly and take notes. Write down how many children are engaged in reading, what behaviors besides reading are occurring, and who is reading and who isn't. You may want to observe specific children on regularly scheduled days if there is too much activity to make notes on all of it.

Children's work and their comments about it give insight into how the program is functioning and into what individual children are thinking. Response journals kept by students can be read. Many teachers also have students keep **portfolios.** Children may keep a log of what they've read and periodically select a sample of their work to put in the portfolio. For literature, it might be one entry each month from their response journal, with a comment on why they selected this particular piece. They might also put in another response activity, again giving the rationale for their selection.

Usually a combination of data will help give a clear picture of the effect of your literature program—observational notes on children's behaviors, reviews of children's portfolios and response journals, and analyses of group participation, for example.

Assessing your program allows you to plan effectively, keeping those aspects that enhance the achievement of your goals and modifying those that don't. Curricular planning is a continuous process that involves initial planning, implementation, evaluation and reflection, and then another round of planning that takes into consideration the results of the evaluation and reflection.

SUMMARY

A **unit** is a set of books related by theme, style, story situation, or other common element. Well-planned units offer a variety of reading experiences for a diverse class while illustrating relationships among books. Creating units makes sense because the field of literature itself is composed of related books, and placing them together encourages children to see and discuss the similarities.

A **literature curriculum** is a course of study including the books, often divided into units and single titles, and a set of activities related to them. This differs from a **literature-based curriculum,** which is a course of study for all subjects that uses literature as the focal point, with both fiction and nonfiction books supplying information and suggesting process.

Literature is often used in thematic or topical units in which many subject areas of the curriculum are integrated. For example, a class may study a theme such as "Most things and most people change over time," or a topic such as "pets" or "ocean life." While exploring the theme or topic, children learn science, social studies, reading and writing, and the arts. A single book may serve as the focal point for an integrated unit.

Literature may also be integrated with specific subject areas. A careful integration of subjects maintains the integrity of both. For example, a nonfiction book about science experiments will not tell how each experiment will conclude as the experiment is introduced. Nor will it be chosen and used exclusively to "teach" science, with no thought about its literary quality or children's responses to it.

Assessment begins with the goals and objectives of a program and moves to see if they have been met. Teachers look at both their own behaviors and structuring of the classroom and the behavior of their students for evaluating their literature program. A checklist may help guide evaluation of elements controlled by the teacher, and observations of children and the reading of their response journals and portfolios may provide insight into the children's knowledge and growth. Assessing your program allows you to plan effectively.

⌒ EXPLORE ON YOUR OWN

1. **Explore Your Personal Response.** Read three books from the Touchstone lists in the chapters on traditional literature, fantasy, realism, or nonfiction and biography. Select the three books from three different lists. If you were going to reread one of the books, which would it be and why?

2. **Apply Literary Criteria.** Find at least seven nonfiction books that would fit within a curriculum unit topic you have chosen. Select the book you think is the best of the group and the book you think is the weakest. Describe the differences in these two books.

3. **Prepare to Share Literature With Children.** Using a listing of books on the same topic, from an issue of *Book Links* or other reference, select three fiction books that would fit well as a literature unit and decide in what order you would present them to children. Be prepared to give the rationale for your plan.

⌒ EXPLORE WITH CHILDREN

1. **Explore Children's Responses.** Interview five children from the same classroom individually. Ask them to tell you how books are used in their classroom. You may want to prompt them by asking such questions as, "What different kinds of books do you have in your classroom?" or "How often do you usually read in school?" From their responses, decide how central they perceive literature to be to their classroom work.

2. **Engage Children With Literature.** Find a fiction book on a topic children are studying. Read the book to them and ask them to identify ways the book relates to the topic. Record their responses in web form.

∽ SUGGESTED PROFESSIONAL REFERENCES

Bosma, Betty, and Nancy DeVries Guth, eds. *Children's Literature in an Integrated Curriculum.* New York: Teachers College Press, 1995. § Teachers share their methods of relating curriculum to literature for children, with the editors providing the theory underlying the recommended practices.

Cecil, Nancy Lee, and Phyllis Lauritzen. *Literacy and the Arts for the Integrated Classroom.* New York: Longman, 1994. § Practical approaches are blended with theory in chapters that present ways to integrate art, poetry, drama, singing, photography, and dance into classroom activities.

Danielson, Kathy Everts, and Jan La Bonty. *Integrating Reading and Writing Through Children's Literature.* Needham Heights, MA: Allyn & Bacon, 1994. § The authors present examples of methods and strategies for using children's books to teach children reading and writing skills and to foster comprehension.

Cox, Carole, and James Zarrillo. *Teaching Reading With Children's Literature.* Upper Saddle River, NJ: Merrill/Prentice Hall, 1993. Originally published in Columbus, OH: Charles E. Merrill. § A thorough description of literature-based models of reading instruction is supplemented by sections on using literature across the curriculum.

Griffiths, Rachel, and Margaret Clyne. *Books You Can Count On: Linking Mathematics and Literature.* Portsmouth, NH: Heinemann, 1988. § The authors give plans for integrating math and literature for specific books, including extension activities and suggestions for further reading, with entries indexed and charted.

Hancock, Joelie, and Susan Hill, eds. *Literature-Based Reading Programs at Work.* Portsmouth, NH: Heinemann, 1987. § Experienced teachers share how they began and maintained literature-based reading in their classrooms.

Irwin, Judith W., and Mary Anne Doyle, eds. *Reading/Writing Connections: Learning From Research.* Newark, DE: International Reading Association, 1992. § The contributing authors analyze research and theory on reading and writing, emphasizing the implications for classroom instruction.

Laughlin, Mildred Knight, and Claudia Lisman Swisher. *Literature-Based Reading: Children's Books and Activities to Enrich the K–5 Curriculum.* Phoenix, AZ: Oryx, 1990. § Suggested activities are organized by grade level and topic or skill.

Laughlin, Mildred Knight, and Patricia Payne Kardaleff. *Literature-Based Social Studies: Children's Books and Activities to Enrich the K–5 Curriculum.* Phoenix, AZ: Oryx, 1991. § Suggested activities are organized by grade level and then by social studies topic.

National Education Association. *Student Portfolios.* Washington, DC: NEA Professional Library Publication, 1993. § Six teachers describe how they, their colleagues, or school system used portfolios to assess student progress, including time lines, charts, and record-keeping sheets.

Sheffield, Stephanie. *Math and Literature (K–3), Book Two.* White Plains, NY: Math Solutions Publications, 1995. § The author shows how 21 specific books can be integrated with mathematics, usually showing how the same book could be used at more than one grade level.

Sorensen, Marilou, and Barbara Lehman. *Teaching With Children's Books: Paths to Literature-Based Instruction.* Urbana, IL: National Council of Teachers of English, 1995. § Classroom teachers and college educators share the history of literature-based reading and examples from contemporary classrooms.

Stewig, John Warren. *Read to Write: Using Children's Literature as a Springboard to Writing.* 3rd ed. Katonah, NY: Richard C. Owens, 1990. § Stewig ties writing suggestions to elements of literature such as characterization, plot, and point of view.

Thiessen, Diane, and Margaret Matthias, eds. *The Wonderful World of Mathematics.* Reston, VA: The National Council of Teachers of Mathematics, 1992. § This annotated book list is organized in four sections: early number concepts, number (extensions and connections), measurement, and geometry and spatial sense.

Tompkins, Gail E., and Lea M. McGee. *Teaching Reading With Literature: Case Studies to Action Plans.* Upper Saddle River, NJ: Merrill/Prentice Hall, 1993. Originally published in Columbus, OH: Charles E. Merrill. § A full reading program, from planning to assessment, demonstrates how such a program can be structured and implemented.

Wepner, Shelley B., and Joan T. Feeley. *Moving Forward with Literature.* Upper Saddle River, NJ: Merrill/Prentice Hall, 1993. Originally published in Columbus, OH: Charles E. Merrill. § The authors show how teachers have used literature in both basal reading programs and trade book programs.

Yopp, Hallie Kay, and Ruth Helen Yopp. *Literature-Based Reading Activities.* 2nd ed. Needham Heights, MA: Allyn & Bacon, 1996. § These reading activities are categorized into those for prereading, during reading, and postreading.

Zarnowski, Myra, and Arlene F. Gallagher. *Children's and Social Studies.* Dubuque, IA: Kendall/Hunt, 1993. § Members of the Book Review Subcommittee of the National Council of the Social Studies Children's Book Council describe how they selected and used notable books in social studies education.

⚭ CHILDREN'S BOOKS CITED

Anno, Mitsumasa. *Anno's Magic Seeds.* New York: Philomel, 1995.

Baylor, Byrd. *When Clay Sings.* Ill. by Tom Bahti. New York: Scribner's, 1972.

Cooney, Barbara. *Island Boy.* New York: Viking, 1988.

Cooney, Barbara. *Miss Rumphius.* New York: Viking, 1982.

Giff, Patricia Reilly. *Shark in School.* Ill. by Blanche Sims. New York: Delacorte, 1995.

Houston, Gloria. *My Great-Aunt Arizona.* Ill. by Susan Condie Lamb. New York: HarperCollins, 1992.

Hutchins, Pat. *The Doorbell Rang.* New York: Greenwillow, 1986.

Johnson, Dolores. *Now Let Me Fly.* New York: Macmillan, 1993.

Johnson, Tony. *The Iguana Brothers.* Ill. by Mark Teague. New York: Scholastic, 1995.

Johnson, Tony. *Yonder.* Ill. by Lloyd Bloom. New York: Dial, 1988.

Marshall, James. *George and Martha Round and Round.* Boston: Houghton, 1988.

Mitchell, Margaree King. *Uncle Jed's Barbershop.* Ill. by James Ransome. New York: Simon & Schuster, 1993.

Myers, Walter Dean. *The Story of Three Kingdoms.* Ill. by Ashley Bryan. New York: HarperCollins, 1995.

Provensen, Alice, and Martin Provensen. *Shaker Lane.* New York: Viking, 1987.

Rylant, Cynthia. *Birthday Presents.* Ill. by Sucie Stevenson. New York: Orchard, 1987.

Rylant, Cynthia. *The Relatives Came.* Ill. by Stephen Gammell. New York: Bradbury, 1985.

Say, Allen. *Grandfather's Journey.* Boston: Houghton Mifflin, 1993.

Schertle, Alice. *Maisie.* Ill. by Lydia Dabcovich. New York: Lothrop, 1995.

Sharmat, Marjorie. *Gila Monsters Meet You at the Airport.* Ill. by Byron Barton. New York: Puffin, 1980.

Shulevitz, Uri. *Toddlecreek Post Office.* New York: Farrar, 1990.

Weller, Frances Ward. *Matthew Wheelock's Wall.* Ill. by Ted Lewin. New York: Macmillan, 1992.

Williams, Vera, and Jennifer Williams. *Stringbean's Trip to the Shining Sea.* New York: Greenwillow, 1988.

⚭ CHAPTER REFERENCES

Freeman, Evelyn B. "Informational Books: Models for Student Report Writing." *Language Arts* 68.6 (Oct. 1991): 470—473.

Frye, Northrop. *The Educated Imagination.* Bloomington, IN: Indiana University Press, 1974.

Graves, Donald. *A Fresh Look at Writing.* Portsmouth, NH: Heinemann, 1994.

Shanahan, Timothy, Bonita Robinson, and Mary Schneider, eds. "Integrating Curriculum." *The Reading Teacher* 48.8 (May 1995): 718—719.

Smith, J. Lea, and Holly Johnson. "Models for Implementing literature in Content Studies." *The Reading Teacher* Vol 48 No 3 (November 1994), pp. 198-209.

Stott, Jon. "The Spiralled Sequence Story Curriculum: A Structuralist Approach to Teaching Fiction in the Elementary Grades." *Children's Literature in Education* 18.66 (Fall 1987): 148—162.

 **Chapter Five**

Books for the Early Years: Helping Children Become Literate

Eric Hill was working at home as a freelance artist when he created his first book, *Where's Spot?* He had been designing advertising that used flaps. He took some of his work into his two-year-old son's room, and watched as young Christopher giggled as he lifted the flaps and discovered pictures underneath. This reaction caused Hill to think about the books he had shared already with Christopher. He concluded that, "Although they were marvelous books, they were too intricate, the illustrations too detailed, the text too small for a two year old" (Frith 578).

He created *Where's Spot?* just for Christopher. In it, Sally, the mother, is looking for her puppy, Spot. On each page Hill asks "Is he in here?" with the answer under a flap. The type is very large, the illustrations bold and clear on a white background, and the flaps sturdy. About six months after its publication, *Where's Spot?* was a best seller in London. Since then Hill has created a series of books about Spot in which the yellow puppy with the brown spot has various adventures. Spot makes trips to the beach, the park, the farm, and the circus. He celebrates his birthday, Easter, and Christmas. Each book features flaps that, when lifted, reveal more of the story. In *Spot Goes to the Park*, for example, Spot kicks a rubber ball and doesn't know where it has gone. "Oops! Where did the ball go?" asks the text. Lines denoting motion lead to a newspaper reader sitting on a park bench. When the flap is bent down, the newspaper is lowered, disclosing an irritated elephant with the ball wedged between its trunk and its chest. "It's right here," grumbles the elephant, his response shown in a dialogue balloon.

Eric Hill is one of many authors creating books for very young children. Most of his works fit into the category of toy book or board book. Other authors' and illustrators' work present Mother Goose rhymes, explore concepts, or use language in a way that enhances children's knowledge of and beginning skill at reading. These materials help introduce children to the joys of literature and the skills of literacy.

Eric Hill has several series of books for young children. Some are also about Spot, such as *Spot Looks at Shapes* and other concept books and Spot books in many sizes and materials. Others are about Baby Bear. *At Home* and *My Pets* are examples of wordless board books, and *Good Morning, Baby Bear* is an example of a book with paper pages for very young children.

The books about Spot have flaps that when lifted answer questions or reveal more of the story. (Source: From SPOT GOES TO THE PARK, copyright Eric Hill © 1991. Reprinted by permission of Ventura Publishing Limited.)

TOY AND BOARD BOOKS

Toy books are those that have a toy-like element that encourages children to play with the book. These elements include flaps to be lifted, levers to be pulled, fabric to be touched, movable parts to be manipulated, pop-ups to be startled by, and various other attributes that go beyond print on flat sheets of paper. Sometimes these books are referred to as **participation books,** although this term may also refer to any book in which children participate in the reading, such as by repeating a refrain. One bookstore shelves these books under the classification "Novelty Titles," another under "Interactive Books."

    Board books have a standard book format, but they are printed on heavy cardboard and are often laminated. Both toy and board books have been a staple of mass market publication and can often be found at the grocery or drug store checkout counter. However, the ample supply of books with *pudgy* or *chubby* as part of the title have been joined by toy and board books by recognized authors and illustrators of quality literature for children.

Uses and Value

Because toy and board books are most often shared by parent and child, they help develop closeness and mutual enjoyment. The parent reads the simple text and waits for the child to answer the question and pull the flap for Spot or to touch the fabric in *Pat the Bunny* (Kunhardt) and *The Touch Me Book* (Witte). Mitsumasa Anno's *Peekaboo* has an inset between each pair of facing pages of two hands held up side by side as though to cover one's eyes. What they cover, however, is about two thirds of the face of a person or animal. The child sees ears or hair, clues to what might be there. Then the

Try having children create their own "touch" books. They can begin searching for thin objects with texture that can be mounted on paper or cardboard. Children then write or dictate a sentence about each object, often describing how it feels.

hand page can be turned and the full picture revealed. Adults can engage children in playing peekaboo with this book and in guessing what might be hidden behind the hand pages.

Board books and toy books both encourage participation. For board books, the activity is the child's turning the pages. The heavy cardboard is easier to grip, and the books usually have only a few pages. Parents can give the child control of a sharing session by having him or her turn the pages when ready. The child might also look at the book alone. Dorothy Butler in *Babies Need Books* believes that the only justification for board books is that they do allow babies to handle books by themselves. She admits, however, that for her, a book is a book only if it is printed on paper. Others, though, believe that learning how to handle a book is a valid reason for giving board books to very young children.

Helen Oxenbury's board book *I See* has a picture of a round-faced toddler lying on his back in the grass, pointing toward the sky. Opposite pages show a close-up of what he sees and then the object and boy together, giving scale. A book with clearly illustrated objects or places and little or no plot is often called a **naming book.** Children look at the pictures, point, and name what they see. In Oxenbury's book, objects included are an airplane, a butterfly, a frog, a friend, and a flower. Adults can encourage discussion, perhaps telling the child that the flower is a daffodil or asking the child if he or she thinks the boy will catch the butterfly.

Some board books present information; others tell stories. Big Friend, Little Friend *explores the theme of friendship. (Source:* Illustration and excerpt from BIG FRIEND, LITTLE FRIEND copyright © 1991 by Eloise Greenfield and Jan Spivey Gilchrist. Used by permission of Scott Treimel New York.)

Board books may function in their content just as other books for children do. Some may present information, others tell stories. Eloise Greenfield's *Big Friend, Little Friend* contrasts what a small boy does with his big friend, an older girl, and his little friend, a smaller boy. In most of the examples, the bigger friend helps him, and he helps the smaller friend. It concludes with statements that he likes both his friends and they like him. This very simple book explores the ideas that people can have many friends, that friends are valuable for different reasons, and that people need not be exactly alike to be friends.

Guidelines for Evaluation

Big Friend, Little Friend and *I See* are what Marilyn Apseloff calls "pre-literature," that is, they "encourage children to explore the possibilities of narrative, fancy, and art" (65). Apseloff says that toy or board books get their fundamental validity from the closeness they foster between parent and child, but that they may also introduce a child to narrative structure, various styles of art, the world of the imagination, and ways of verbalizing experiences. Thus these early books are pre-literature.

Evaluating toy and board books means considering aspects of both the toy and the book. As with other toys, they should be safe, they should withstand normal use, and the child should enjoy playing with them. Be sure they are made from nontoxic materials—babies tend to lick and chew as well as look. Be certain that there are no buttons or other parts that a child might choke on. Try the tabs or pop-ups to see if they are strong enough to be pulled and pushed by young hands. Then watch the child's reaction.

Linda Lamme videotaped and analyzed mothers reading to their infants and verified the results through further observations and interviews. A key conclusion was that the success of sharing books with infants was "the degree to which the mothers adjusted their bookreading behavior to the developmental level of their infants" (504). This meant being willing to let the child who was fascinated with turning pages but didn't respond to the content of the book just turn pages. It also meant being very aware of the child's visual behavior. If an infant looked away without any distraction, such as a noise, and the parent stopped reading, the session ended well. If the parent kept on reading, the child frequently became fussy. Successful book sharing required an observant and responsive parent.

Evaluating toy and board books as literature means looking at the text and illustrations as well as safety and durability. The language should be natural, not stilted or simplified. The content should be familiar to young children and accurate. Illustrations should be clear, uncluttered, and follow the story line.

Nancy Tafuri in *Where We Sleep* uses three-word sentences and accurate vocabulary to tell where various animals sleep—"Bunnies have burrows," for example. The illustrations clearly show the animal and what its habitat looks like. The pattern in the language is consistent. By contrast, *The Little Engine*

Finger rhymes are popular with preschoolers. Marc Brown gives rhymes and illustrates the motions that go with them in *Hand Rhymes* and *Finger Rhymes*, published by Dutton.

```
┌─────────────────────────────────────────────────────────────────┐
│  Toy Books                                                        │
│  Eric Carle              Jan Pienkowski                           │
│  Eric Hill                                                        │
│  Board Books                                                      │
│  Dick Bruna              Leo Lionni           Ronald Peppe        │
│  John Burningham         Jan Ormerod          Nancy Tafuri        │
│  Eric Hill               Helen Oxenbury       Rosemary Wells      │
└─────────────────────────────────────────────────────────────────┘
```

Figure 5-1   Creators of quality toy or board books.

That Could Pudgy Word Book (Ong) opens with an illustration of the little engine pulling two cars along a track, with the words placed confusingly on the page. Beneath the red car and tracks is the word *wheels,* beneath the yellow car and tracks are the words *yellow car,* and beneath the engine and tracks is the word *track.* To use the book successfully, the adult would need to ignore the labeling (the child would not be reading it anyway) in this book rather than build on it.

Figure 5-1 lists selected authors and illustrators who have created high quality toy or board books. Looking at their work will help you see the possibilities in these formats.

MOTHER GOOSE

The British call them nursery rhymes. In the United States they are called Mother Goose rhymes, but these old verses for children are the same by either name. Along with alphabet, counting, and concept books, which are discussed later in this chapter, Mother Goose is an introduction to more advanced kinds of literature to children. Unlike alphabet books, though, most of Mother Goose was not originally meant for children.

Origins

Most Mother Goose rhymes collected and illustrated for children today were made up in their original wording by adults for adults. British writers Iona and Peter Opie point out in their introduction to *The Oxford Dictionary of Nursery Rhymes* (3–4) that some of the verses, such as "One Misty Moisty Morning," are taken from ballads or folk songs. Other rhymes are converted drinking songs ("Nose, Nose, Jolly Red Nose"), songs of battle ("At the Siege of Belle Isle"), or political commentary ("William and Mary, George and Anne").

A few come from popular songs of this century, but most verses are much older. The Opies found that close to 10% of the rhymes they studied were in existence a century before the American Revolution (7). Tradition holds that some counting rhymes (such as "eeny, meeny, mony, my," used to select a child to be "it" in games), are older than that—as old as rites used by

Druids, ancient priests in Gaul and Britain. There is no proof, but legend holds that these priests used such rhymes to choose human sacrifices (12).

The Opies conclude "almost without hesitation" (4) that the only rhymes written especially for children before 1800 were rhyming alphabets, lullabies, and verses accompanying children's games. All of the other rhymes now in the family of Mother Goose were written for mature audiences.

One reason these rhymes infiltrated the nursery was the attitude parents had toward their offspring two centuries ago when the poems were first published for children. The Opies point out that in the seventeenth and eighteenth centuries, children were treated as "grown-ups in miniature."

> In paintings we see them wearing clothes which were replicas of those worn by their elders . . .
>   Many parents saw nothing unusual in their children hearing strong language or savouring strong drink. (5)

Another reason was that parents, faced with a damp or squalling child to amuse, relied with little thought on songs they liked themselves.

Was There a Real Mother Goose?

There is confusion about who this stouthearted lady was. There also is no clear explanation of why she became associated with early collections of children's verse, although it is reasonably certain that her association in English dates from the eighteenth century. One persistent legend is that she was an American, Elizabeth Goose of Boston. The story is that one of her sons-in-law, a printer named Thomas Fleet, heard Mrs. Goose telling old tales to one after another of his children. He collected his mother-in-law's stories in a book he called *Songs for the Nursery, or Mother Goose's Melodies for Children.* Supposedly, the book was printed in 1719. The title page displayed a goose-like animal with a long neck, apparently honking.

No scholar takes the story seriously today. There is no trace of Fleet's book, and the strongest advocate of its existence is suspect: a man named John Eliot Fleet, great grandson of Thomas Fleet, who did not claim to have seen the book himself.

A more reliable trail leads to France, where the phrase *Conte de la Mere Oye* (Mother Goose Story) has been tracked to writings from the middle of the seventeenth century. A French author named Charles Perrault printed a book with the frontispiece "Contes de ma Mere L'Oye" in 1696–1697. It included such classic stories as "Sleeping Beauty" and "Little Red Riding Hood" and was translated into English in 1729, the first-known appearance of the famous lady in our language (39). Later in the eighteenth century, Mother Goose became associated exclusively with children's rhymes.

Appeal to Children

As interesting as all this may be, the origin of Mother Goose is of no import to children. It does not even matter that some of the words are strange. Ask a four-year-old what "curds and whey" are and you are likely to hear either "I don't know" or "Something to eat."

Mother Goose has survived not because it teaches moral or historical lessons, but because of the strength of the rhymes. Generations of editing by parents and children have winnowed down the words until they are most appealing, most magical, to children. Mother Goose succeeds as literature in several ways. As you look at Figure 5-2, think of Mother Goose rhymes you know that fit each category.

Figure 5-2   The appeal of Mother Goose.

APPEAL	EXAMPLE

Rhythm of the language	This is the way the gentlemen ride,
	    Gallop-a-trot,
	    Gallop-a-trot,
	This is the way the gentlemen ride,
	    Gallop-a-gallop-a-trot!

Rhyme	Here am I, Little Jumping Joan: When nobody's with me I'm always alone.

Content—narrative humor	Little Boy Blue,
	    Come blow your horn,
	The sheep's in the meadow,
	    The cow's in the corn.
	Where is the boy
	    Who looks after the sheep?
	He's under a haystack,
	    Fast asleep.
	Will you wake him?
	    No, not I,
	For if I do,
	    He's sure to cry.

Participation	Ring-a-ring o'roses, A pocket full of posies, Tisha! Tisha! We all fall down.
Associations with home where rhymes may have been heard first	This little pig went to market; This little pig stayed at home; This little pig had roast beef; This little pig had none; This little pig said, "Wee, wee wee, wee, wee! I can't find my way home."

Nursery Rhymes From Many Cultures

English-speaking societies are not the only ones that have a strong collection of nursery rhymes for children, and Mother Goose's repertoire is expanding to include verses from many different languages and cultures. Some of these rhymes are available in book form. Others can be learned from the children themselves or from their parents and grandparents.

Tortillitas Para Mama (Griego et al.) is a collection of Latin American nursery rhymes, with text in both Spanish and English. Try this one:

> Uno, dos, tres, cho-
> Uno, dos, tres, -co-
> Uno, dos, tres, -la-
> Uno, dos, tres, -te.
> Bate, bate, chocolate.

This rhyme is fun to say, even without the hand motions of counting and rubbing hands together as though stirring the chocolate with a beater. Listening to these sounds, children begin to realize the power of words. For some children such rhymes offer a chance to learn a verse in a "new" language; others enjoy the excitement of seeing and hearing their native tongue in the school setting.

Demi, in *Dragon Kites and Dragonflies*, adapted and illustrated Chinese nursery rhymes. The adaptation has resulted in verses that rhyme in English, unlike those in *Tortillitas Para Mama*, where the English translation is more literal and rhyme is not often achieved. Here is one from *Dragon Kites and Dragonflies*:

As a teacher, you might ask children to have their parents teach them a nursery rhyme or write it out for them. Make a class book of "family" rhymes to be read and enjoyed.

The text for these nursery rhymes is in both English and Spanish. (Source: From TORTILLITAS PARA MAMA, selected and translated by Margot C. Griego, Betsy L. Bucks, Sharon S. Gilbert, Lauren H. Kimball, illustrated by Barbara Cooney. Text copyright © 1981 by Margot C. Griego, Betsy L. Bucks, Lauren H. Kimball, and Sharon S. Gilbert. Illustrations copyright © 1981 by Barbara Cooney. Reprinted by permission of Henry Holt and Co.)

> Little silk worms, if you please,
> Eat up all the mulberry leaves.
> Make cocoons as white as milk,
> And we'll make clothes of purest silk.

Again, children will delight in the sound of the words and might well act out the action.

Children who experience nursery rhymes from other cultures and in other languages learn about the culture—whether about a favorite drink (chocolate) and how it is made or about silkworms—and begin to appreciate differences and recognize commonalities.

Uses and Value

The appeal of Mother Goose rhymes makes them useful for preschool and primary grade teachers. Adult readers of the rhymes will find an interested audience: Many children will have heard the words before, in a pleasant setting, and the repetition helps combat the unfamiliarity of the classroom. Others will find the poems new, but soon be captivated by the language.

Lines such as "Peter Piper picked a peck of pickled peppers" help children develop a feeling for **alliteration,** the repetition of the same consonant sound. Simple rhyming patterns, "Jerry Hall, He is so small; A rat could eat him, Hat and all." make the verse easy to remember and stimulate the creation of mental images.

Teachers often build on the dramatic possibilities of Mother Goose verses by having children act out the story line. All children may participate in reciting clear narratives and simple plots such as when Bo Peep looks for her sheep or Jack and Jill start their climb. Children recite the rhyme, or the parts they know, as they show the action. They are learning about story sequence and structure in the context of an activity they enjoy. Figure 5-3 shows some ways to involve children with Mother Goose rhymes.

Charts with familiar Mother Goose rhymes encourage children to attempt to read the verses themselves. Because children already know the verse, they concentrate on matching what they know the words say with the print on the chart. This is an important step in understanding how print works and in discovering that one word may have several syllables. A five-year-old who announces that she is "reading" the chart will no doubt be told by an older sibling that she is not reading, that she has just memorized the words. The teacher, however, knows that this is an important prereading step that builds the child's self-confidence and heightens her desire to read.

---

* *Source:* Excerpts from DRAGON KITES AND DRAGONFLIES by Demi Hitz, copyright © 1986 by Demi, reprinted by permission of Harcourt Brace Company.

Dramatizing—One Character

These rhymes have only one character doing the action, they so can be dramatized by many children at once, each doing his or her own interpretation.

"Here I Am, Little Jumping Joan"
"I Had a Little Hen"
"It's Raining, It's Pouring"
"Jack Be Nimble"
"Little Miss Muffet"
"Old Mother Hubbard"
"Oh Where, Oh Where, Has My Little Dog Gone?"

Dramatizing—Two or More Characters

These rhymes have interaction among characters. They can be dramatized by children after deciding which part each will play. Change parts often.

"Jack and Jill Went Up the Hill"
"Jack Spratt Could Eat No Fat"
"Little Poll Parrot"
"Pat-a Cake, Pat-a-Cake, Baker's Man"
"The Queen of Hearts"
"Simple Simon Met a Pieman"
"Three Little Kittens"

Reading from Charts

These rhymes have repetition. Children seeing them on charts can begin to pick out lines and words.

"Baa, Baa, Black Sheep"
"Humpty Dumpty Sat on a Wall"
"Polly Put the Kettle On"
"Rain on the Green Grass"
"Rain, Rain Go Away"
"Sally Go Round the Sun"
"There Was a Crooked Man"

Choral Speaking or Reading

These rhymes have a question-and-answer format. They lend themselves to choral speaking or reading with two parts.

"Baker, Baker, Shave a Pig"
"I Went Up One Pair of Stairs"
"Little Girl, Little Girl, Where Have You Been?"
"Mother, May I Go Out to Swim?"
"Old Woman, Old Woman, Shall We Go a-Shearing?"
"One, Two, Three, Four, Five,
   Once I Caught a Fish Alive"
"Pussy Cat, Pussy Cat, Where Have You Been?"

Figure 5-3   Involving children with Mother Goose rhymes.

Evaluating Mother Goose Books

The rhymes themselves do not change much with age. Some were rewritten in the late 1700s to sanitize the bawdiness of the original adult songs. A few writers in this century have tried to contribute new or rewritten verses. But most of the words remain the same. There are, however, major differences in the way they are presented in the dozens of Mother Goose editions available today. The quality of the artwork is a major criterion in judging collections of Mother Goose rhymes and individually illustrated rhymes in picture book format.

Illustrations

Illustrations should capture the spirit of the rhyme. There is more than one way to do this. James Marshall has his Old Mother Hubbard a rather stout but nonetheless energetic lady whose chubby cheeks bear a strong resemblance to the jowls of her equally chubby bulldog. When she goes to the cupboard, she slides down the bannister to get there. Her cupboard is bare—no bone—but it does have two mice sitting at a small table with a checkerboard tablecloth, having coffee or tea, and their mouse waiter elegantly holding his tail until he is needed again. The stunned and hungry bulldog is saying in a cartoon balloon that he can scarcely believe it. The full rhyme bounces along as Mother Hubbard goes from shop to shop to get items for the dog. Careful viewers will notice many details, such as the bulldog in the last scene wearing the beanie that Mother Hubbard had pointed to as she talked with the hatter. Marshall embellishes the story, adding wordless subplots and humor that complement the poetry. A model for this

James Marshall's illustrations for Old Mother Hubbard *embellish the story with humor and wordless subplots. (Source:* Illustration from OLD MOTHER HUBBARD AND HER WONDERFUL DOG by James Marshall. Illustrations copyright © 1991 by James Marshall. Reprinted by permission of Farrar, Straus & Giroux, Inc.)

approach is Randolph Caldecott, a nineteenth-century illustrator who set standards that today's artists are still trying to meet.

Caldecott extends the action of the poem "Three Jovial Huntsmen," for example, in his *Picture Book No. 1,* published around 1880 and still available today. The poem is about three red-coated, horn-tooting horsemen galloping breakneck through rolling English hills, looking for foxes. They find only a scarecrow, a grinding stone, farm animals, children, and lovers in the course of a "rattlin' day."

But there is action in Caldecott's detailed drawings that never appears in the words. At one point, one rider falls off his horse, who prances away up a hill without him. The man's two boisterous friends, holding their hats, are so caught up in the hunt that they never notice the empty saddle behind them. The lone rider picks up his hunting horn and blows a blast. The other mounts are now over the first hill and climbing a second, far away. In desperation, the lost rider climbs a tree and blows again, and now one of his friends waves reassurance while the other reins in the riderless horse.

All of this is told in just three pictures on two pages (24 and 25). The words of the poem never refer to the adventure.

A second approach to illustration is more literal: The artist faithfully captures the scene described in the poem without augmenting its meaning or extending its story. Kate Greenaway's delicate drawings for *Mother Goose or the Old Nursery Rhymes,* also published in the 1880s and still available, are static compared to those of Caldecott. She illustrates the setting with warm details: Jack Horner's corner is in an old-fashioned

Randolph Caldecott extended the action of the poems he illustrated and set standards still in effect today. (Source: From Randolph Caldecott's PICTURE BOOK NO. 1. Frederick Warne & Co.)

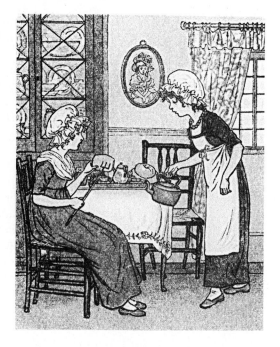

Kate Greenaway gave a literal interpretation to the rhymes she illustrated. (Source: From Kate Greenaway's MOTHER GOOSE by Frederick Warne & Co.)

kitchen with a brick oven and a few cooking utensils. The figure of Jack looking at a plum is pensive and still. It is as though the moment were captured in a snapshot.

Lorinda Cauley uses this approach in her illustrations for *Three Blind Mice.* The rural setting is established in the first picture as the mice walk down a dirt road through green fields. One carries a comb, their only luggage, just as the rhyme says. The pictures are warm and realistic in style, full of charming details. The pictures show these lively and adventurous mice making merry as they eat the cheese the farmer has given them and feeling distraught as they fall into brambles and are blinded.

Both the interpretative and the more literal approaches have value. Being aware of these differences allows a teacher to offer several different editions, in several illustrative styles, to match individual tastes.

Format

The Greenaway drawings are only four and a half inches long and two and a half inches wide; most of the figures are about as big as Tom Thumb. That may be a cozy size for individual readers, but groups of children sitting some distance from a teacher holding the book may come to think that all Mother Goose characters look alike. Both the Cauley and the Marshall books, with their large pictures, are more appropriate for sharing with a group.

In *The Real Mother Goose,* a famous collection that has gone through more than 75 printings since it first appeared in 1916, many of the drawings

Lorinda Cauley's illustrations for Three Blind Mice *establish a rural setting. (Source:* Illustration and text from THREE BLIND MICE by Lorinda Bryan Cauley, © 1991 by Lorinda Bryan Cauley. Reprinted by permission of G. P. Putnam's Sons.)

are large enough for group use. But in this classic collection, another problem arises: So many poems are printed per page that a child may have difficulty telling which of Blanche Fisher Wright's cheerful illustrations go with which poem. Some illustrations are beside the poem they match; others are underneath or above it. The layout may not be a problem for children hearing the poems read to them, but a young student trying to read the poems independently and counting on pictures to help with difficult words may find the format confusing.

A better choice for these emergent readers might be *The Baby's Lap Book* (Chorao), carefully organized so that there is one poem and one picture on a page, or so that two poems of similar content are illustrated together. In one full-page illustration, the Little Girl with a Curl—the one who when she was bad was horrid—sits on a garden wall maliciously emptying water from a sprinkling can on an understandably irritated Contrary Mary, working in her garden with its silver bells and cockle shells. Both poems appear opposite the character they describe on the clear white facing page.

Compare the 1990 with the 1977 edition of *The Baby's Lap Book* by Kay Chorao. The illustrations in the newer edition are in color. What is the effect of this change?

Coverage and Appropriateness

The Real Mother Goose is useful in a classroom library because it includes more than 160 rhymes. It can fill almost any request. Smaller collections should be judged in part by what rhymes are presented. A few unusual rhymes can add zest. Also note how much of the rhyme is included. Most collections include only the verse about Old Mother Hubbard finding the cupboard bare, though some may tell all of her adventures. The basic verse may be all that you want for a particular young audience. However, books such as the small eight-page cloth booklets from *The Real Mother Goose* (Rand McNally, publisher) are inadequate because they give only

Aylesworth, John. *My Son John.* Ill. by David Frampton. New York: Holt, 1994. Building on the rhyme about "My Son John," Aylesworth creates 14 new poems about other children, maintaining the rhyme and rhythm of the original Mother Goose.

Chorao, Kay. *The Baby's Lap Book.* New York: Dutton, 1991. The new edition of this collection maintains the effective placement of the rhymes and the original illustrations, but with color.

de Paola, Tomie. *Tomie de Paola's Mother Goose.* New York: Putnam's, 1985. Over 200 poems are included, each clearly and cleverly illustrated with vintage de Paola characters.

Edens, Cooper, selector. *The Glorious Mother Goose.* Ill. by "the best artists from the past." New York: Atheneum, 1988. Eden has selected Mother Goose illustrations from many artists of the late 1800s and early 1900s, giving readers the opportunity to see the work of Leslie Brooke, Arthur Rackham, Randolph Caldecott, Kate Greenaway, and many others.

Griego, Margot C. *Tortillitas Para Mama.* Ill. by Barbara Cooney. New York: Holt, 1981. These Latin American nursery rhymes are presented in both Spanish and English, with warm-toned illustrations.

Hague, Michael. *Mother Goose, A Collection of Classic Nursery Rhymes.* New York: Holt, 1984. Hague's illustrations have a classic appeal, and the format of one poem per page makes them easy for young children to follow.

Jeffers, Susan. *Three Jovial Huntsmen, A Mother Goose Rhyme.* New York: Bradbury, 1973. The illustrations in this Caldecott Honor book have many hidden animals as the huntsmen search unsuccessfully for their quarry.

Lamont, Priscilla. *Ring-a-Round-a-Rosy.* Boston: Little, Brown, 1990. This collection of nursery rhymes, action rhymes, and lullabies has illustrations of both the literal meaning of the rhymes and the actions that go with them.

Figure 5-4   Touchstone editions of Mother Goose.

the first line of each rhyme. Both story and language appreciation are lost when all that is said is that "There was an old woman who lived in a shoe."

Some witty collections, of course, are inappropriate for children. Eve Merriam, in *The Inner-City Mother Goose,* rewrote verses to focus on urban problems. One verse:

There was a crooked man
And he did very well. (11)

The message is clear, clever, and vital—but not for three-year-olds. See Figure 5-4 for other editions of Mother Goose rhymes.

Lobel, Arnold. *The Random House Book of Mother Goose.* New York: Random House, 1986. This lively collection is a good resource of both familiar and less common rhymes, with humor in many of the illustrations.

Marks, Alan. *Ring-a-Ring O'Roses & a Ding, Dong, Bell. A Book of Nursery Rhymes.* Saxonville, MA: Picture Book Studio, 1991. Poems are carefully paired, with illustrations that embellish the story.

Opie, Iona, and Peter Opie. *Tail Feathers From Mother Goose.* Boston: Little, Brown, 1988. Rhymes collected by the Opies from a wide range of sources are illustrated by well-known children's illustrators.

Patz, Nancy. *Moses Supposes His Toeses are Roses and 7 Other Silly Old Rhymes.* San Diego: Harcourt, 1983. The silly characters about whom the rhymes are written romp through their own poems and those about others.

Spier, Peter. *And So My Garden Grows.* 1969. New York: Dell, 1992. One of several Spier Mother Goose books, this one is illustrated with sketches Spier did while in Italy, giving it a flavor different from many English editions.

Stow, Jenny. *The House That Jack Built.* New York: Dial, 1992. The Caribbean setting gives a fresh look to this old rhyme, with lush vegetation and clear, bright colors.

Sutherland, Zena. *The Orchard Book of Nursery Rhymes.* Ill. by Faith Jaques. New York: Orchard, 1990. Beautifully placed illustrations and large type make this a good edition for children to read themselves.

Tripp, Wallace. *Granfa' Grig Had a Pig and Other Rhymes Without Reason.* Boston: Little, Brown, 1976. Tripp's illustrations have a zany humor, with characters speaking as in cartoon strips, that will appeal to older children and adults.

Figure 5-4 *continued*

CONCEPT BOOKS

A nimble rabbit leaps over a snail. A carrier pigeon floats above some telephone wires. A four-engined jet flies over a wagon drawn by eight oxen. An old oak stands next to a straggly pea vine with unruly tendrils. To a child first looking at two adjoining pages of a book called *Fast-Slow High-Low* (Spier), the pictures at first may appear haphazard and puzzling.

Then the child takes several intellectual steps. Step one: Many of the objects—the plane, rabbit, and telephone lines—are familiar. Why are they grouped together on these two pages? Even preschool children who cannot read the only two words on the pages, "fast-slow," can begin to climb to the next step. The rabbit is more fleet than the snail. The plane beats the oxcart.

Though it may take some explaining, preschool children soon understand that the telephone does the job faster than the carrier pigeon, and the pea grows more rapidly than the oak. Part of the initial puzzle has been solved. These are drawings of fast versus slow animals and objects.

Other pages in the book, by artist and writer Peter Spier, illustrate full versus empty, light versus dark, and other contrasting characteristics. Now the child can climb the next step: This is a book about opposites.

Spier's *Fast-Slow* is an example of a **concept book,** a book in which a jumble of data falls into patterns under a general concept or idea. The concept helps the reader create order out of the clutter: It makes the pieces fit. Unlike Mother Goose, which is colored with mystery and dreamlike images, concept books bring the everyday world into sharp focus for young children. In much the same way that children must look at everyday happenings and bring them into their own schema—their mental organization of data—these books organize specific objects or events into larger categories.

Some concept books, such as this one by Spier, explore abstract concepts. Others present many facets of a single idea. In *Let's Eat,* True Kelley has pages for favorite foods, breakfast, lunch, and dinner, eating equipment, and even "food tricks." (Can you toss a grape into the air and catch it in your mouth? Balance a carrot on your nose? Make your bacon and eggs look like a face on your plate?) Each page has many illustrations and many opportunities for conversation.

Michelle Koch, in *Hoot Howl Hiss,* explores the concepts that animals make sounds and that different animals have different habitats. Woods, pond, jungle, and farm each have three animals and the sounds they make—lions roar, pigs grunt. Very young children may just identify the animals, others may make the sounds, and others may begin to see the connections and groupings.

One child's strategy in reading a concept book may be **inductive:** jumping from picture to picture, perhaps pointing, until the specific examples suggest the concept—"Oh. You use all these things to eat with." Another child's strategy may be **deductive:** recognizing the concept first, then finding examples and labeling each picture—"That's a plate, that's a fork, that's a knife, that's a straw."

Some concept books appear to favor one strategy over another. Most alphabet books first present an abstract symbol and then show how it is used in particular instances. But many concept books, including alphabet and counting books, are flexible enough to match the child's style. You can start with the examples and move to the symbol, jump back and forth between general and specific, or skip pages. Many of these books can be adapted on the spot to meet individual curiosities. Figure 5-5 provides guidelines for evaluating concept books.

Uses and Value

Concept books both introduce and clarify concepts. Bruce McMillan's *Growing Colors* will not be the first experience children have had with color names. However, in photographing fruits and vegetables to illustrate the colors,

Think of a concept you feel is appropriate for kindergarten or first-grade children to explore. List at least six facets or examples of that concept. How would you organize your ideas if you were creating a concept book?

1. **Is the information accurate?**
   This applies to facts, descriptions, and relationships. For example, in a concept book about taste, it is not accurate to use *crisp* as a taste along with *sour* and *spicy. Crisp* describes texture. Nor should information be omitted if the result is a misrepresentation of the concept.

2. **Is the information presented clearly?**
   Both text and illustrations contribute to clarity. For example, if a counting book shows the number 5, it should show five objects rather than a starfish with five arms. Examples given should be within children's range of experience and understanding.

3. **Does the book have artistic merit?**
   Look at the design of each page, at the skill of the illustrator, at the special creative touches and imaginative approaches.

4. **Does the book extend the child's thinking?**
   An alphabet book that gives many examples for each letter may help a child generalize about the sound that letter makes. A counting book may help a child categorize as well as count. A concept book may lead a child to understand that terms such as *heavy* and *light,* or *large* and *small* are relative.

Figure 5-5   Guidelines for evaluating concept books.

McMillan made a conscious choice to include certain lesser-known varieties. The concept of a brown pepper or a purple bean may be new to many children.

Often teachers have several books addressing the same concept. A teacher might well have *Growing Colors* as well as *Red Bear* (Rikys) and *Samuel Todd's Book of Great Color* (Konigsburg). In *Red Bear,* the left page is the color named on it, beginning with red, and opposite it is a red bear. As each color is introduced, the bear puts on a piece of clothing of that color. Children can match the colors and name the clothing. Samuel Todd tells about colors he likes and leads from one color to another. Bananas are yellow except for the spots, which are brown like freckles, and of course, chocolate. The books reinforce the concept of color names, yet introduce other ideas as well. Samuel Todd comments that they say pink is for girls, but that boy flamingos are just as pink as girl flamingos.

The discussion that attends the sharing of a concept book leads to growth in vocabulary and language skills. Children may describe the pictures they see. They learn new words as they listen to others use those words in context. Some concept books will present new vocabulary. Anne and Harlow Rockwell's *The Toolbox* gives one sentence for each tool pictured. Children see pliers, a drill, and wire cutters in father's toolbox and they learn the names of these common tools. Venice Shone's *Tools* goes further, picturing and labeling tools used in various occupations and differentiating more

Ahlberg, Janet, and Allan Ahlberg. *The Baby's Catalogue.* 1982. London: Puffin, 1984. Each page shows the variety in a single class of objects or people in the lives of babies.

Anholt, Catherine, and Laurence Anholt. *All About You.* New York: Viking, 1992. Everyday life is explored through illustration and questions to the readers about their own lives.

Barton, Byron. *Trucks.* New York: Crowell, 1986. Trucks are shown in use, with a sentence giving names and uses.

Carle, Eric. *The Grouchy Ladybug.* New York: Crowell, 1977. The sun rises higher in the sky, a clock shows the time, and a grouchy ladybug attempts to pick a fight with increasingly larger animals.

Crews, Donald. *Freight Train.* New York: Morrow, 1978. As the train travels along the tracks, through tunnels and over tressles, the colors of its cars (each named) blend.

Falwell, Cathryn. *Clowning Around.* New York: Orchard, 1991. This clown's act includes moving letters around to form new words that match his actions.

Fisher, Leonard Everett. *Look Around! A Book About Shapes.* New York: Viking, 1987. Shapes are named, illustrated singly and in a group of objects, and described with their defining characteristics.

Hoban, Tana. *Colors Everywhere.* New York: Greenwillow, 1995. The photographs in this wordless book show many tones and shades; each page has a color graph that represents the proportions of the colors in the pictures.

Hoban, Tana. *Look Up, Look Down.* New York: Greenwillow, 1992. Color photographs show what can be seen by looking either up or down, capturing perspective and patterns.

MacDonald, Suse. *Sea Shapes.* New York: Gulliver, 1994. Clear shapes on a white page are transformed to sea creatures in their underwater world. A triangle, for example, can be seen as the teeth of a shark.

Figure 5-6   Touchstone concept books.

finely. There is an electric drill and a hand drill, pliers and pincers, a hacksaw, a handsaw, and a jigsaw. The tools are grouped by use, so that a wallpaper brush, wallpaper paste, a utility knife, and scissors appear on the same page. Children learn terminology, but they are also encouraged to talk about what they know about these tools. How are these implements used in putting up wallpaper? What is the process? What has to be done before the wallpaper can be hung? Concept books raise as well as answer questions. Figure 5-6 lists some excellent concept books.

Two specific kinds of concept books help children to understand relationships between common abstract symbols and their use in everyday expressions. Many **alphabet** and **counting books** follow the same formula:

MacKinnon, Debbie. *Things to Eat.* Ill. by Geoff Dann. New York: Bantam (Rooster), 1994. This board book, like the others in the series, shows photographs of familiar objects against a white background.

McMillan, Bruce. *Step by Step.* New York: Lothrop, 1987. The relationship of age to motor skills is explored through a series of photographs showing a baby from age 4 months to 14 months.

McMillan, Bruce. *Super Super Superwords.* New York: Lothrop, 1989. Comparative forms of adjectives are illustrated with photographs of a kindergartner's day.

Miller, Margaret. *Whose Shoe?* New York: Greenwillow, 1991. A double-page spread with a photograph of a shoe and the question "Whose shoe?" is followed by another double-page spread with the answer, such as "hockey player," and illustrations of the owner and of a child using the footgear.

Rockwell, Anne. *Bear Child's Book of Hours.* New York: Crowell, 1987. Very clear and simple illustrations show a clock and what bear child is doing, while a sentence tells the time.

Schwartz, David. *How Much Is a Million?* Ill. by Steven Kellogg. New York: Lothrop, 1985. Marvelossissimo the Mathematical Magician demonstrates the meaning of a million through comparisons and with seven pages of stars that add up to only 100,000.

Skofield, James. *'Round and Around.* Ill. by James Hale. New York: HarperCollins, 1993. Dan and his father take a walk and find circles in nature; they then continue to see the shape after returning home.

Ward, Cindy. *Cookie's Week.* Ill. by Tomie de Paola. New York: Putnam's, 1988. Each day of the week, the mischievous cat Cookie gets into some kind of trouble.

Figure 5-6 *continued*

a lefthand page introduces the symbol, and pictures and text on the right-hand page put the symbol to work or show what it represents. But like other concept books, there is variety in style, complexity, and purpose.

Alphabet Books

Today *A* doesn't always stand for apple, and not every alphabet book is for very young children. *A* may be for aardvark, as it is in *Aardvarks, Disembark!* (Jonas), where it stands for this and for other endangered or extinct species such as the aoudad and the anoa. The alphabet is incidental, significant only because when Noah calls the names of the animals to leave the ark, and when he walks past all those whose names he did not know, the animals are in alphabetical order. What is important in this book is the number and variety of endangered animals and the strongly implied theme when Noah bids them good-bye and tells them to take care of themselves. Five of the animals shown are extinct and 70 are endangered. The content, vocabulary and theme are more appropriate for second and third graders than for preschoolers.

Other alphabet books include lessons in science, short stories, or word and picture tours through the city or countryside. Some books appeal to adult as well as children's interests. *Anno's Alphabet,* by Japanese artist Mitsumasa Anno, is designed around paintings of wooden letters, realistic down to their splinters. Several of the letters are optical illusions, and many show elaborate engineering. Anno's *P,* for instance, converts to *R* by unlatching part of the *P,* sliding it out of the groove, and allowing it to drop down. The appeal of this wizardry spans generations.

Anno's book is appropriate for all ages, but many alphabet books are not. The choice, from a wide and expanding shelf, depends on the role the book is expected to play and the developmental level of the child.

Figure 5-7 shows various types of alphabet books. An adult selecting such books should first clarify the purpose for their use and then choose accordingly.

Figure 5-8 presents a list of recommended alphabet books. When you read these or other alphabet books, think about the ways they might be used with children.

Figure 5-9 describes some ways alphabet books can be used in the classroom.

Counting Books

Counting books, too, can provide pictures for young children to discuss, introduce numerals (the written symbols for numbers), tell stories, develop themes, or challenge the imagination. The concepts conveyed by these books are not always as simple as 1, 2, 3.

The endpapers of Lois Ehlert's *Fish Eyes* are covered with fish with neon pink eyes, except for one whose eye is the same rich blue as the background on which the fish are swimming. This little fish says that if it could swim down rivers and seas, it would see first one green fish and then two fish that are jumping, and so on. The eyes of these brightly colored and patterned fish are holes, so that the colors from the pages behind them show through. The child looking at the illustrations can identify the number of shapes easily, for they are clearly defined—a basic criterion for beginning counting books. If the book is to help the child gain the concept of number, then the number must be represented unambiguously. In addition, the numeral must be shown. Ehlert does this and also includes the written word for each number. In the corner of each page, the small fish tells how

TYPE	EXAMPLE	USE	CRITERIA MET
A Book of Pictures	*26 Letters and 99 Cents*, Hoban. One object for each letter is photographed and presented against a clear white background.	To identify objects For vocabulary development To encourage discussion	The illustrations are clear and uncluttered. The objects are familiar to young children.
A Book of Letters	*Action Alphabet*, Neumeier and Glaser. The letter and word for the objects are on the left page; the letter as part of a drawing appears on the right page.	To reinforce letter recognition	Both upper- and lowercase letters are shown. The objects are clear and familiar.
A Book of Sounds	*Grandpa's Great City Tour*, Stevenson. Each double-page spread of city life is filled with objects beginning with the chosen letter.	To reinforce sounds individual letters make	The objects are likely to be called by only one name (*robot*—not rabbit or bunny). Initial letters are sounded (not *knife* for *K*)
A Book That Tells a Story	*The Folks in the Valley*, Aylesworth. The life of a Pennsylvania Dutch family is described in rhyme.	To share a story or information To see the letter in the context of word, sentence, and story	The entries fit the alphabetic structure naturally. There is continuity in the story line. The story is interesting.
A Book That Develops a Theme	*Jambo Means Hello*, Feelings. One Swahili word for each letter in that alphabet is used to introduce this African culture.	To explore many facets of a single topic or idea	The objects presented are important to the general topic and a reasonable part of it.
A Book That Stimulates the Imagination	*Alphabatics*, MacDonald. Each letter goes through a transformation from letter to object. A *T* sprouts branches and becomes a tree, for example.	To stimulate creative thinking	The letters are presented in a creative way. Problem solving is encouraged.

Figure 5-7 Types of alphabet books.

Bowen, Betsy. *Antler, Bear, Canoe—A Northwoods Alphabet Year.* Boston: Little, Brown, 1991. With two or three letters for each month, Bowen explores life in northern Minnesota throughout the year.

Burningham, John. *John Burningham's ABC.* 1964. New York: Crown, 1993. Clear and lively illustrations abound with energy and invite comment.

Ehlert, Lois. *Eating the Alphabet: Fruits and Vegetables from A to Z.* San Diego: Harcourt, 1989. Several fruits and vegetables are shown for each letter, all carefully labeled.

Fisher, Leonard Everett. *The ABC Exhibit.* New York: Macmillan, 1991. One object, illustrated in a scene, represents each letter, with the word printed clearly above it.

Geisert, Arthur. *Pigs From A to Z.* Boston: Houghton, Mifflin, 1986. A group of piglets work to construct a tree house, with each letter represented by several of them forming the letter with their bodies. Forms of each letter are hidden in each illustration.

Hoban, Tana. *A, B, See!* New York: Greenwillow, 1982. Photographs of a group of objects for each letter provide many examples. The entire alphabet is printed at the bottom of each page, with the letter being illustrated large and in bold print.

Kellogg, Steven. *Aster Aardvark's Alphabet.* New York: Morrow, 1987. Wild, tongue-twisting sentences explain the problems and foibles of a variety of animals.

Kitamura, Satoshi. *From Acorn to Zoo.* New York: Farrar, 1992. Each page has a question to be answered by careful perusal of the illustration, with its many labeled objects and characters.

Lear, Edward. *A Was Once an Apple Pie.* Ill. by Julie Lacome. Cambridge, MA: Candlewick, 1992. Lear's verses play with the sounds of language as they tell what each letter "once was."

Lobel, Anita. *Alison's Zinnia.* New York: Greenwillow, 1990. Each girl, beginning with Alison, obtains a flower beginning with the same letter for another girl whose name begins with the following letter.

Figure 5-8   Touchstone alphabet books.

many would be there if it too were counted. Children can use this book to count the fish, to find words and numerals, to talk about words that describe the fish, and perhaps to tell if these imaginary fish remind them of any real fish.

Other counting books may be for the child who wants to test his or her skill in counting. Quite often these books involve skills of observation and of categorization. In *How Many Snails?* author Paul Giganti, Jr. poses a series of questions on each page, questions that can be answered by looking carefully at the illustrations by Donald Crews. On the page with

Aylesworth, Jim. *One Crow: A Counting Rhyme.* Ill. by Ruth Young. New York: Harper, 1988. Animals in farm scenes represent the numbers, with a descriptive rhyme for each.

Bang, Molly. *Ten, Nine, Eight.* New York: Greenwillow, 1983. A father and young child count backward from 10 to 1 until the child gets sleepy and is ready for bed.

Dunrea, Olivier. *Deep Down Under.* New York: Macmillan, 1989. In this cumulative rhyme a moudiewort (Scottish for mole) digs underground, causing others to wiggle, scurry, scamper, and otherwise react to the sound.

French, Vivian. *One Ballerina Two.* Ill. by Jan Ormerod. New York: Lothrop, 1991. Two ballerinas, one an older girl and the other quite young, practice their steps from 10 plies to 2 final curtsies and 1 happy hug.

Gretz, Susanna. *Teddy Bears 1 to 10.* New York: Four Winds, 1986. A series of teddy bears go through the process of getting first dirty, then clean, before 10 of them have tea together.

Hughes, Shirley. *When We Went to the Park.* New York: Lothrop, 1985. A little girl and her grandpa go to the park where the things they see are named and counted—except for the leaves because there were too many to count.

Jonas, Ann. *Splash!* New York: Greenwillow, 1995. A child and several animals climb, and fall, in and out of a backyard pond, with the questions of how many are in the pond stimulating counting activities.

Kitchen, Bert. *Animal Numbers.* New York: Dial, 1987. Hanging on to each numeral is a female and the number of babies the numeral represents, up to 10; then 15 pigs, 25 garter snakes, 50 seahorses, 75 leatherneck turtles, and 100 common frogs.

MacDonald, Suse, and Bill Oates. *Puzzlers.* New York: Dial, 1989. The puzzle is to find the numeral, part of an abstract representation of an animal, as it is described on the preceeding page—upside down, wide, or paired.

Figure 5-10   Touchstone counting books.

Merriam, Eve. *Twelve Ways to Get to Eleven.* Ill. by Bernie Karlin. New York: Simon, 1993. The challenge is to find 11 in each of the double-page spreads as combinations of items can be added to achieve this goal.

Morozumi, Atsuko. *One Gorilla.* New York: Farrar, 1990. One gorilla wanders through forest, field, and garden where other creatures blend with the landscape.

Moss, Lloyd. *Zin! Zin! Zin! A Violin.* Ill. by Marjorie Priceman. New York: Simon, 1995. Ten orchestral instruments are introduced, along with a counting game and terms for numerical groupings such as *solo.*

Peek, Merle. *The Balancing Act: A Counting Song.* New York: Clarion, 1987. At Elephantland, one elephant begins to balance on the high wire and is joined by others, one by one, until the 10th one causes the wire to break (but there is a net!).

Peek, Merle. *Roll Over!* Boston: Houghton Mifflin, 1981. The song tells of 10 in the bed, with the little one saying to roll over until only she is left.

Sheppard, Jeff. *The Right Number of Elephants.* Ill. by Felicia Bond. New York: Harper, 1990. Going from 10 to 1, this book prescribes how many elephants would be needed for each of the comic situations presented.

Sis, Peter. *Going Up! A Color Counting Book.* New York: Greenwillow, 1989. Ordinal numbers are illustrated as Mary gets into the elevator on the first floor and watches as it stops at every floor, where a character wearing a different color gets in. At the 12th floor they all get off for a surprise party for Mary's mother.

Sis, Peter. *Waving: A Counting Book.* New York: Greenwillow, 1988. Mary's mother waves for a taxi and two bicyclists wave back, thus beginning a series of waves—until Mary and her mother walk home.

Tafuri, Nancy. *Who's Counting?* New York: Greenwillow, 1986. A puppy looks at animals on each page until the last when he is joined by nine other puppies.

Figure 5-10   *continued*

BOOKS FOR EMERGENT READERS AND WRITERS

The authors of *Becoming a Nation of Readers,* the report of the Commission on Reading, concluded that "The single most important activity for building the knowledge required for eventual success in reading is reading aloud to children" (Anderson et al. 23). Thus any book shared with preschool children is in one sense a book for an emergent reader.

Young children develop their understanding of reading and writing gradually and naturally, particularly when they are in an environment where they witness important adults in their lives engaged in these processes and when they have the opportunity to experiment with reading and writing themselves (Holdaway). Brian Cambourne (33 and 187) lists several conditions that lead to children's learning to read and write as naturally as they learned to speak:

- Immersion
- Demonstration
- Expectations
- Responsibility
- Employment
- Approximations
- Response

First is **immersion**—that is, children need to see print all around them. For example, children see print on signs and the like and also as they sit in their parents' laps, looking at a book as it is read to them. The second condition is **demonstration,** seeing how adults use written language, and that adults read and write for information and for enjoyment. The **expectation** that children will become literate is subtle but essential. **Responsibility** and **employment** mean having books and writing supplies readily available so children can experiment frequently with reading and writing whenever they or their parents choose. They will be active learners, determining what they want to learn. **Approximation** means allowing children to try reading, even though their words will likely not match the written text exactly. And last, **response,** or feedback, is giving children a chance to talk about their reading and writing with others and to see its effect on others. Response puts reading and writing in a social context.

These conditions prevail in many, but obviously not all, households. They do prevail for three-year-old Tony. His house is filled with reading material—newspapers that his parents read daily, magazines, and books that his two older brother own. He already has a collection of paperbacks purchased by his parents and hard cover books given as gifts by his grandparents and aunt. There are pencils, crayons, and paper in his bedroom, in the den, and in the kitchen. He watches his mother and brother use a word processor, sees his parents write and read letters, and sees everyone else in his family reading for pleasure. He has watched his father study material to earn a promotion on his job. His parents read to him at least once a day. Sometimes he echoes what the reader has just read; sometimes he tells a story himself while looking at the pictures in a book and recalling some of the actual language; sometimes he chimes in with the reader for stories he asks to have read often and knows well.

He goes to bookstores with his mother and brothers and knows that he can look at the books, that he is not to tear the pages or damage them

Visualize your room and your home when you were a child. What in your own childhood environment contributed to your literary development?

Alphabet and counting books help children develop and extend their understanding of words and numbers.

in any way, and that often he may select one paperback book that he would like. His family assumes that he too will be a reader. At bedtime, his mother reads library books and also whatever book he wants read from their own collection. Sometimes he listens to stories being read to his brothers even though he doesn't understand all he hears. When he asks questions, he is given information to help him make sense of what he's hearing.

Tony is an emergent reader. He has a fund of knowledge about reading and writing, and he continues to make connections and to refine his understanding. While all books contribute to this emerging literacy, some have qualities that make them particularly effective.

Predictable Books

Predictable books have patterns that allow the reader to figure out, or predict, what is going to happen next. Events may be repeated, as is often the case in folktales. For example, the three Billy Goats Gruff attempt to cross the bridge, each one being stopped by the voice of the ugly troll. Once the first two have been stopped, the probability is high that the third one will also be stopped.

In *My Old Teddy* (Mansell), the leg comes off her teddy bear and the child says "Poor old Teddy." She takes Teddy to the Teddy doctor, which the illustrations show is her mother. The "doctor" stitches the leg back on. Then Teddy loses an arm (somewhat violently, actually, as a younger brother rips it off). "Poor old Teddy." And it's off to the doctor again. The pattern is set, and when Teddy loses an ear, we know what the child will say and where Teddy is going. When Teddy loses his head, though,

An environment that includes good books attractively displayed encourages children to want to learn to read.

the doctor fixes it but suggests that Teddy needs to rest. The doctor gives the child a new Teddy, whom she likes, but of course, poor old Teddy is still loved best.

This book contains a second quality that gives predictability, and that is the repetition of language. The events are described each time with the same phrases and followed by the lament, "Poor old Teddy."*

When rhythm and rhyme are used, phrases become even more memorable. Wendy Lewison has a pajama-clad boy sitting on the floor playing with toy animals in *Going to Sleep on the Farm*. Endpapers showing sunset and moonrise on the farm establish the setting. Next to the boy is his father, stretched out on the floor, head on pillow, book in hand. The child asks:

> "How does a cow go to sleep—tell me how?
> How does a cow go to sleep?"

---

* Extracts from MY OLD TEDDY by Dom Mansell reproduced with permission of Walker Books Ltd. Copyright © 1992 Dom Mansell. Published in the US by Candlewick Press, Cambridge, MA.

Chapter Five

The next double-page spread shows the cow in the barn.

> "A cow lies down in the soft, sweet hay, in a cozy barn, at the end of
> day."

And continues:

> "And that how a cow goes to sleep—Moo-moo.
> That's how a cow goes to sleep."

As the child plays with the duck, he asks:

> "How does a duck go to sleep—tell me how?
> How does a duck go to sleep?" (n.p.)

The pattern is established—the question is asked and repeated. The
answer is given in rhyme, and the concluding statement ends with the sound

The rhyme and patterned language in Going to Sleep on the Farm *help a child predict
what will happen. (Source: From* GOING TO SLEEP ON THE FARM *by Wendy
Cheyette Lewison, pictures by Juan Wijngaard. Copyright © 1992 by Wendy
Cheyette Lewison. Copyright © 1992 by Juan Wijngaard, pictures. Used by permission of Dial Books for Young Readers, a Division of Penguin Books USA Inc.)*

the animal makes. The illustrations show the child getting sleepier and sleepier until the father carries him to bed. A child having this story read aloud can predict what will happen midway through the book. After subsequent readings, the child may be able to tell the entire story using the pictures as cues. Often these retellings, or reenactments as they are sometimes called, incorporate much of the original language.

Repetition of both story events and language occurs in **cumulative tales.** These are stories in which each event builds on the previous one, and all are repeated each time a new event occurs. *The Little Old Lady Who Was Not Afraid of Anything* (Williams) is a cumulative tale in which the brave heroine heads out into the woods to collect herbs and seeds. As she starts home in the moonlight, she comes upon two shoes blocking her path. The shoes are going "CLOMP CLOMP." She tells them she is not afraid and walks on. Behind her she can hear the shoes going "CLOMP CLOMP." Then she encounters a pair of pants. The pants go "WIGGLE WIGGLE." She is not afraid of them either, but now behind her she hears the shoes going "CLOMP CLOMP" and the pants going "WIGGLE WIGGLE." By the time she reaches her cottage, she is being followed by shoes, pants, shirt, gloves, hat, and a scary pumpkin head, each making its own sound or motion. The repetition reinforces the plot and is great fun to say along and to act out. Figure 5-11 lists the titles of some predictable books.

Other books are predictable because they follow a known sequence such as days of the week or increasingly larger numbers. *Busy Monday Morning* (Domanska), a translation of a Polish folk song, repeats its refrain and each verse with a new day and then names the activity for that day. On Monday Father mows the hay, on Tuesday rakes it, on Wednesday dries it. The work conveniently takes six days so that Father and his helper who tells the story can rest on Sunday. The use of days of the week sets the sequence. The predictability of this text is greatly strengthened by the repetition of the refrain.

Uses and Value

Many predictable books have more than one element of repetition or sequence. As children use these elements, they gain control over the story. They can say it along with the person reading, and they often announce that they are "reading" the book as they look at the illustrations and recite the text. Such reading-like behaviors help children learn to read naturally in much the same they learned to talk. The more they hear the stories the more closely their renditions will approximate the text (Sulzby; Teale and Sulzby). Reading remains exciting and an activity that children assume they will do successfully.

Aardema, Verna. *Bringing the Rain to Kapiti Plain.* Ill. by Beatriz Vidal. New York: Dial, 1981. This cumulative tale from Kenya is much like "This is the House That Jack Built" in its structure and rhythm.

Burningham, John. *Mr. Gumpy's Outing.* New York: Holt, 1971. Mr. Gumpy lets the animals come aboard his boat, one by one, with a similar warning to each to behave, but of course, they forget.

Carle, Eric. *The Very Busy Spider.* New York: Philomel, 1984. Animal after animal asks the spider to join it, but she is too busy spinning her web.

Fox, Mem. *Hattie and the Fox.* Ill. by Patricia Mullins. New York: Macmillan, 1987. Hattie the hen sees something in the bushes revealed bit by bit until she recognizes the fox in this book with repetitive refrains and a cumulative plot.

Fox, Mem. *Shoes from Grandpa.* Ill. by Patricia Mullins. New York: Orchard, 1990. In a cumulative plot, a young girl's relatives each buy her something to go with the shoes Grandpa has given her.

Galdone, Paul. *Cat Goes Fiddle-i-fee.* New York: Clarion, 1985. This cumulative English folk song has rhythm, rhyme, patterning, and a host of animal sounds.

Ginsburg, Mirra. *Asleep, Asleep.* Ill. by Nancy Tafuri. New York: Greenwillow, 1992. Simple, quiet text that answers that each animal is asleep, until the wind sings the child to sleep also.

Ginsburg, Mirra. *The Chick and the Duckling.* Ill. by Jose Aruego and Ariane Dewey. New York: Macmillan, 1972. For everything the duckling does, the chick says "Me too" and follows along, even to going for a swim.

Lindbergh, Reeve. *The Day the Goose Got Loose.* Ill. by Steven Kellogg. New York: Dial, 1990. Each verse begins and ends with "The day the goose got loose" in this hilarious rhyming description of the events.

Figure 5-11   Touchstone predictable books.

BIG BOOKS

Big books are just what the name implies—large-format books that are in the range of 20 by 30 inches or so, depending on the shape of the book. A group of children can see the text and the illustrations clearly and gain some of the same experience that individual children acquire when adults sit next to them and read to them. Big books are published by companies that specialize in materials for whole language instruction, by trade book publishers that produce in this larger format books that were originally a standard size, and by certain companies that specialize in paperback books.

Uses and Value

Big books are used for enjoyment and reading instruction. Where a parent reading a predictable book does so for the child's enjoyment and takes cues from the child's behavior, the teacher adds to these an element of planned instruction. Figure 5-12 shows the pattern one teacher uses as she presents a

Martin, Bill, Jr. *Brown Bear, Brown Bear, What Do You See?* Ill. by Eric Carle. New York: Holt, 1983. The answer to the question in the title is, "I see a redbird looking at me," and this leads to the next question of what the redbird sees in this patterned book that also presents colors.

Martin, Bill, Jr. *Polar Bear, Polar Bear, What Do You Hear?* Ill. by Eric Carle. New York: Holt, 1990. This companion book to *Brown Bear* uses the same pattern of questions and answers.

Neitzel, Shirley. *The Jacket I Wear in the Snow.* Ill. by Nancy Winslow Parker. New York: Greenwillow, 1989. This cumulative tale builds as a child adds all the clothing needed for going outside in the snow.

Sendak, Maurice. *Chicken Soup With Rice.* New York: Harper, 1962. Month-by-month this snappy verse extols the virtues of chicken soup with rice.

Shannon, George. *April Showers.* Ill. by Jose Aruego and Ariane Dewey. New York: Greenwillow, 1995. The recurring refrain and the strong rhythm and rhyme make it easy for children to join in as these frogs celebrate spring.

Sheppard, Jeff. *Splash, Splash.* Ill. by Dennis Panek. New York: Macmillan, 1994. The repetition of animal sounds as one animal after another falls into the lake reveals a pattern that is easy and fun to follow.

Van Laan, Nancy. *Possum Gone a-Knockin'.* Ill. by George Booth. New York: Knopf, 1990. The language as well as the repetition—Granny was "a-knittin'" and Pappy was "a-whittlin"—make this fun to read.

Wood, Audrey. *The Napping House.* Ill. by Don Wood. San Diego: Harcourt, 1984. On a rainy afternoon, the pile of characters napping on the bed grows larger and larger until a flea starts a chain reaction that wakes everyone.

Figure 5-11 *continued*

This teacher is guiding children as they read a big book together.

Day 1:   Robin, the kindergarten teacher, puts a big book copy of Mirra Ginsburg's book *The Chick and the Duckling* (Ill. by Jose Aruego and Ariane Dewey. New York: Macmillan, 1972) on an easel and calls the class to come sit on the carpet in front of the easel. She reads the title and author, and then asks the children to look at the picture on the cover. "What do you notice?" she asks. Hands are in the air immediately.
"I see butterflies"
"The chicken and the duck are both yellow."
"There are flowers all over."
    "What do you think might happen in this story?" Robin asks.
"They might become friends."
"They go on a picnic together."
"They get lost."
    "Well, let's see what the author says. As I read the book, if you know what the words say, say them along with me." With that, Robin reads the story of the chick who hears each thing the duckling says it is doing, annnounces "Me too," and follows suit. Catching a butterfly and taking a walk are fine, but when the chick follows the duckling for a swim, it sinks to the bottom of the pond. The duckling must rescue it. The next time the duckling announces that it is going for a swim, the chick responds "Not me."
    By the third page the children are chiming in on the "Not me's." They laugh at the ending and want to hear the story again. Robin reads it again, and this time the children are saying the refrain from the beginning. "They kind of went on a picnic," says one child. "That wasn't a picnic," says another. "They just live outside." "They were friends," volunteers another, as they think about the predictions they made from the title and cover.

Figure 5-12   Teaching with big books.

big book to a group of kindergartners. Notice the actions she takes to help children respond to the story and learn about how print functions.

The use of big books and the shared reading experience simulate reading at home, where children see the print as they hear the words being read. These books allow children to participate at a level that is comfortable for them and to gain fluency through multiple readings. Reading is placed in a social context, as the children join together to discuss and participate in the story.

BEGINNING BOOKS

As children begin to build a sight vocabulary and gain decoding skills, they are eager to read books on their own. They may reread the predictable books they know, either in standard or big book format. They may also begin to read books that are written specifically for beginning readers. Com-

Day 2: Robin read *The Chick and the Duckling* to the group again. This time she moves her hand under the print as she reads. Sometimes she doesn't read the refrain herself but just moves her hand as the children say it. After completing the book, she turns back to an earlier page and asks, "Who can find the words that say, 'Me too?'" A child comes up and frames the words with her hands. Robin turns the pages and asks children to identify other phrases. Sometimes she lets children show any sentences, phrases, or words that they know.

Day 3: Robin involves the children with print in a variety of ways. She has one child use a pointer to guide the children as they now read the book in unison. She reads one line, and the children read the next. With other books she has had children repeat after she reads or read part of a sentence and wait as the children complete it.

Day 4: Robin encourages the children to read the book on their own by leaving it where they can handle it easily. She has five small copies of the book, and she lets the children borrow these to take home and read to their parents. She has the children retell the story; then she lets pairs of children act out the two parts. She introduces another big book.

Day 5: Robin puts *The Chick and the Duckling* in the box of books they've heard and may choose to hear again. She knows that she will return to it later. She will use it to have children isolate the letters that make the "ch" sound and the "d" sound when she begins to help children focus on individual letters. In the meantime, she watches as children act out the story on their own and gain fluency as they read the story repeatedly themselves. She is pleased to see how much the children enjoy literature and how confident they are about their own developing literacy.

Figure 5-12   *continued*

panies use various names—Easy to Read, I Can Read, Ready to Read—but all attempt to control the difficulty level of the reading by controlling, to some degree, the length of the sentences and the difficulty of the vocabulary.

The quality of these books varies widely. Some authors tell a good story with short sentences and common vocabulary. Others produce stilted, boring books.

Here is a selection from *Frog and Toad Are Friends* in which author Arnold Lobel has stayed within the confines of a beginning reading book but written with skill and humor.

One day in summer
Frog was not feeling well.
Toad said, "Frog,
you are looking quite green."
"But I always look green,"
said Frog. "I am a frog."

"Today you look very green
even for a frog," said Toad.
"Get into my bed and rest."* (16)

The books about Frog and Toad have captivated many young readers.

There are books of fantasy, like the Frog and Toad stories, and realistic fiction, both contemporary and historical. Teachers may also use beginning-to-read poetry and folk literature. Teachers can select so that children have a variety of genre as they begin to read on their own. Figure 5-13 suggests several authors who have written beginning-to-read books that reflect effective use of language and interesting plots.

Uses and Value

The basic value of beginning-to-read books is that they allow children to attack new material on their own with a strong chance of success. These books give children the opportunity to figure out the meaning of a story using what they know of the world, what they know about print, and what they know about story structure.

Beginning-to-read books can be used for "buddy reading," in which a pair of children read together, helping one another and discussing what they have read. Children learn to use a table of contents and to see the relationship of chapters within a single story or stories within a book. Most importantly, these books can reinforce for children the idea that they are readers who choose their own materials based on their interests. The instructional context for literacy, that is, the kinds of reading and writing tasks that chil-

---

Nathaniel Benchley—historical fiction
Lilian Hoban—books about Arthur; fantasy
Lee Bennett Hopkins (selector)—poetry
Leonard Kessler—sports stories
Arnold Lobel—books about Frog and Toad and other fantasy stories
Edward Marshall—books about Lolly, Spider, and Sam; realism
James Marshall—books about Fox; fantasy
Else Minarik—books about Little Bear; fantasy
F. N. Monjo—biography
Cynthia Rylant—books about Henry and Mudge; realism
Joan Sandin—historical fiction
Jean Van Leeuwen—books about Amanda Pig; fantasy

Figure 5-13   Authors of beginning-to-read books.

---

* *Source:* From FROG AND TOAD ARE FRIENDS by Arnold Lobel. Copyright © 1970 by Arnold Lobel. Reprinted by permission of HarperCollins Publishers.

These boys are engaged in buddy reading, taking turns reading a page aloud and discussing the story.

dren do in school, strongly affects their motivation to read and write. When children can control the materials they use and can engage in collaborative activities, they are likely to spend more time on the task and to engage in a wider variety of reading strategies (Turner).

EVALUATING PREDICTABLE BOOKS, BIG BOOKS, AND BEGINNING-TO-READ BOOKS

What sets these three books apart is their contribution to children's initial reading competence, but they fit within the broader category of literature for children. Thus they can be assessed by two sets of standards. The first is their quality as literature, and for this, the same standards apply as would to any book for children. Poor literature is not an effective vehicle for demonstrating the value and enjoyment of reading. The second standard is what contribution they make to children's learning to read. If they qualify as good literature, then the second standard really is a question of how they are used rather than the quality of the materials themselves. Predictable books read only once are enjoyed, but the learning that comes only with several readings is lost. Big books that are read, but without discussion, involvement of the children, or any focus on how print functions, serve no special purpose. Beginning-to-read books presented too soon or required for book reports will not stimulate good feelings about reading or self-confidence in reading. Knowing how to assess literature helps teachers involve children in ways that address both literature and literacy (Allen, Freeman, Lehman, and Scharer).

Adults play many roles as they help children construct meaning in their interactions with books. They may initiate response to the literature by sharing their own reactions and asking the children to share theirs. They may provide information that will help the child understand. Often they direct the activity, selecting the book and the time for sharing (Roser and Martinez). Figure 5-14 shows how one kindergarten teacher prepared to introduce a book and reflected on the success of the activity.

Parents and adults working with preschool children help children gain meaning from a text through their conversation.

Here a mother and her 23-month-old child are sharing *Spot's First Walk* (Hill). The print on the page says, "What have you found?"

> Child: What's the dog doing?
> Mother: He's digging in the dirt looking for his bone. Look what he found in there.
> Child: Oh.
> Mother: What have you found, Spot?
> Child: A doggy bone.
> Mother: Yes, he's found a doggy bone. He's having fun outside.
> Child: Yeah.
> Mother: What is he doing with his feet?
> Child: What's he doing with his feet, Mom?
> Mother: He's digging.
> Child: He's digging.

Next the printed text says, "Now for a drink."

> Mother: Look what he's doing next. He's getting a drink. Now for a drink of water.

And then, as the text says, "Don't fall in."

> Child: There's a fish.
> Mother: There's a fish saying, "Don't fall in, don't fall in."
>   (Altwerger 479)

The mother is surrounding the actual pictures and text with her own conversation, helping the child focus on the action in the illustrations, indicating who is talking, and encouraging the child to talk. She is paying attention to the meaning of the story and adding to or altering the text to make the meaning clearer. Gradually, as the child internalizes the story-reading

THE LESSON AS PLANNED AND TAUGHT	REFLECTIONS . . .
Rationale Marti wanted to set the stage for introducing the big book edition of Pat Hutchins *The Surprise Party* to her class of 25 kindergartners. In the book, Rabbit whispers to Owl that he's having a party but that it's a surprise. Each animal passes the message along, and each one gets it a little more garbled. Marti decided to have the class play telephone, where a message is whispered from person to person around a circle; then beginning and ending messages are compared.	Engaging children in an activity related to a book before reading can heighten interest and aid in understanding.
The Lesson The children were seated in a circle and Marti began. "We're going to be reading a book about some animals who pass a message from one to the other. Before we begin our book, we're going to try passing a message. Some of you may have played a game like this called "Telephone." I'm going to whisper something in Darian's ear, and he will tell June, who will tell Ricki, until it goes all the way around our circle. Bryan, the last person, will tell us what the message is. But—here's a rule that makes it more challenging. You can only say the message once—no repeating. So each of you will need to speak clearly and listen well." She then whispered, "It's a bright, blue, sunshiny day today" in Darian's ear.	Giving a reason for the activity helped children understand. The directions were clear and Marti did not give away the possible outcome of a changed message, so she did not predispose the children to make changes.
When the message reached Rob, who had forgotten the directions, he whispered in Xia'a ear, "You're a dummy." "You're not supposed to say that," she complained. Several children giggled. While Marti explained the directions again to Rob, many of the children grew restless waiting for a turn and began talking. Marti had to settle them for the game to continue, and they seemed to be losing interest.	Marti might have had several students model the passing of a message, first aloud so the process was known, and then by whispering. As the activity was structured, it required sustained silence and inactivity for too long a period. Marti might have had small groups of five or six children form circles and pass the message. This would have ensured that no child would have had to wait long before participating. One member from each group could then report the final message, perhaps recorded by Marti. The whole group could then look at ways the message may have changed.
Evaluation Marti felt the lesson was good, but that it wasn't as effective as she had expected. The message was changed considerably, but the children couldn't remember what they had heard or passed on. She wanted a way to focus their attention on how and why the message changed.	

Figure 5-14   On second thought: Keeping children actively involved.

process, she will do less of this. Some parents and caregivers, like Eric Hill, start children on the road to literacy by creating a book just for their child; many, many others read to their toddlers, just as the mother in the transcript did. Teachers continue to guide children's literacy development by presenting quality literature and helping children explore how print works and how authors and readers work together to create meaning.

SUMMARY

There are books appropriate for children from infancy onward. Toy and board books are often children's introduction to the world of literature. Board books offer children the opportunity to handle a book successfully, and both toy and board books can be shared so that children participate. Youngsters turn the pages, pull tabs and flaps, and name what they see. Children also recognize repetition in language or events, and this knowledge of a pattern lets them "read" along with the adult. Teachers often select just such predictable books so that children can begin to put print and oral language together, a first step in understanding the reading process.

Concept books help children explore and understand both concrete and abstract ideas. Most can be approached in a variety of ways, particularly alphabet and counting books. The purpose for use is a key criterion is evaluating alphabet and counting books.

Mother Goose verses trigger laughter and participation, with language that has strong rhythm and rhyme, stories that are fun, and often associations with pleasant surroundings. Nursery rhymes in languages other than English are becoming part of many classrooms and homes as they reflect different cultures and demonstrate that the sound of language can be appealing even if the words are unknown.

How parents and teachers present books influences the children's responses. Parents who are aware of infants' attention and who add context to stories as they read to toddlers set the stage for meaningful interactions between child and book. Preschool and kindergarten teachers build on home experiences by replicating them but adding the dimension of instruction. Thus, emergent readers and writers look at the print in a big book as they chime in on phrases they know; they "read" Mother Goose rhymes from a book or chart; they write their own stories. Soon they are reading books whose language they know and deciphering words for themselves in easy-to-read books. Adults can share these first books with children in ways that are enjoyable and that encourage further exploration with literature.

✆ EXPLORE ON YOUR OWN

1. **Explore Your Personal Response.** Find a toy book that you like. What about it appeals most to you? Evaluate it first as a toy and then as literature, using the guidelines described in the text. Were you attracted more by the playful aspects or the literary quality of this book?

2. **Apply Literary Criteria.** Go to a discount or grocery store and to a bookstore. Look at the collection of board books they carry. How would you characterize the books at each place? What seem to be the major differences and how might these differences be explained?

3. **Prepare to Share Literature With Children.** Look through the beginning-to-read section for children in a library or bookstore. Select three books. Tell what you might say about each book to interest young children in choosing to read it with a "buddy."

∽ EXPLORE WITH CHILDREN

1. **Explore Children's Responses.** Read a book to an infant. When the child looks away, stop reading. When he or she looks back, start to read again. Then try reading continuously, whether the child appears to be attending or not. What do you notice about the infant's behavior in each instance?

or

Ask several first or second graders to tell you about a book they liked when they were "really young." What did they like about it? Ask them what *they* think they learned from that book.

2. **Engage Children With Literature.** Select a book that has elements of predictability. Read it to two children or two groups of children, telling them to say the words with you whenever they know them. Note how quickly each child or group recognizes the pattern.

∽ SUGGESTED PROFESSIONAL REFERENCES

Burke, Eileen. *Literature for the Young Child.* Boston: Allyn & Bacon, 1990. § Statements about the value of literature for young children and approaches for sharing literature are amply illustrated with specific titles.

Butler, Dorothy. *Babies Need Books.* 2nd ed. New York: Penguin, 1988. § Writing from her experience as a mother, grandmother, and an expert on children's books, Butler suggests specific books and ways of sharing them with children ages one through five.

Butler, Dorothy. *Cushla and Her Books.* Boston: The Horn Book, 1980. § This moving account of books in the life of a child with a severe disability is a tribute both to literature and to her parents' faith and perseverance.

Clay, Marie M. *Becoming Literate: The Construction of Inner Control.* Portsmouth, NH: Heinemann, 1991. § Clay describes how successful readers become independent readers and writers even though they may be learning in differing systems.

Cochran-Smith, Marilyn. *The Making of a Reader.* Norwood, NJ: Ablex, 1984. § The author describes what children in a preschool she observed know about books and how they came to know it.

Glazer, Joan I. *Literature for Young Children.* 3rd ed. Upper Saddle River, NJ: Merrill/Prentice Hall, 1991. Originally published in Columbus, OH: Charles E. Merrill. § The author describes ways in which literature supports young children's language, intellectual, social, moral, aesthetic, and personality development, and lists recommended books and activities.

Greene, Ellin. *Books, Babies, and Libraries: Serving Infants, Toddlers, Their Parents and Caregivers.* Chicago, IL: 1991. § Greene reviews current research on emergent literacy, recommends specific books, and shows how a library can be receptive to the needs of its youngest patrons.

Holdaway, Don. *The Foundations of Literacy.* Sydney: Ashton Scholastic, 1979. § This New Zealand educator presents the method and rationale for teaching beginning reading through shared book experiences.

Lynch, Priscilla. *Using Big Books and Predictable Books.* New York: Scholastic, 1986. § This brief booklet gives explicit directions on how big books can be used to guide children's literacy development.

McCord, Sue. *The Storybook Journey: Pathways to Literacy Through Story and Play.* Upper Saddle River, NJ: Merrill/Prentice Hall, 1995. Originally published in Columbus, OH: Charles E. Merrill. § Based on a model of child development, this text shows how caring adults can guide children toward literacy in a variety of ways, with emphasis on the importance of story.

Morrow, Lesley Mandel. *Literacy Development in the Early Years.* Upper Saddle River, NJ: Merrill/Prentice Hall, 1989. Originally published in Columbus, OH: Charles E. Merrill. § Morrow describes the development of literacy in children from birth to age seven, with emphasis on literature and writing in both the home and the school setting.

Morrow, Lesley Mandel, Diane Tracey, and Caterina Marcone Maxwell, eds. *A Survey of Family Literacy in the United States.* Newark, DE: International Reading Association, 1995. § This research report describes success rates of programs involving young children's development of literacy, most often within the context of the family.

Opie, Iona, and Peter Opie. *The Oxford Dictionary of Nursery Rhymes.* Oxford: Clarendon Press, 1973. § This general introduction to nursery rhymes is a useful reference that includes over 500 rhymes and their history.

Slaughter, Judith Pollard. *Beyond Storybooks: Young Children and the Shared Book Experience.* Newark, DE: International Reading Association, 1993. § This useful handbook for teachers contains techniques for engaging preschool and primary age children in shared reading with predictable books and an annotated bibliography.

Strickland, Dorothy, and Leslie Mandel Morrow, eds. *Emerging Literacy: Young Children Learn to Read and Write.* Newark, DE: International Reading Association, 1989. § Well-known researchers explore both reading and writing at home and at school, focusing on a natural and gradual development.

Taylor, Denny, and Catherine Dorsey-Gaines. *Growing Up Literate.* Portsmouth, NH: Heinemann, 1988. § Taylor and Dorsey-Gaines describe Black urban poor families as their children become literate and as they struggle with unsupportive schools.

Taylor, Denny, and Dorothy Strickland. *Family Storybook Reading.* Portsmouth, NH: Heinemann, 1986. § The authors describe how various families have shared books, giving many suggestions for effective ways of presenting books within the family.

Wells, Gordon. *The Meaning Makers.* Portsmouth, NH: Heinemann, 1986. § With 15 years of research, Wells documents the importance of reading aloud to preschoolers for later success in school.

∽ CHILDREN'S BOOKS CITED

Anno, Mitsumasa. *Anno's Alphabet.* New York: Crowell, 1975.

Anno, Mitsumasa. *Anno's Counting Book.* New York: Crowell, 1977.

Anno, Mitsumasa. *Anno's Peekaboo.* New York: Philomel, 1987.

Aylesworth, Jim. *The Folks in the Valley.* Ill. by Stefano Vitale. New York: HarperCollins, 1992.

Butler, Dorothy. *Babies Need Books.* 2nd ed. New York: Penguin, 1988.

Caldecott, Randolph. *Picture Book No. 1.* London: Warne.

Cauley, Lorinda Bryan. *Three Blind Mice.* New York: Putnam's, 1991.

Chorao, Kay. *The Baby's Lap Book.* 1977. New York: Dutton, 1990.

Demi. *Dragon Kites and Dragonflies. A Collection of Chinese Nursery Rhymes.* San Diego: Harcourt, 1986.

Domanska, Janina. *Busy Monday Morning.* New York: Greenwillow, 1985.

Ehlert, Lois. *Fish Eyes, A Book You Can Count On.* San Diego: Harcourt, Brace, 1990.

Feelings, Muriel. *Jambo Means Hello: Swahili Alphabet Book.* Ill. by Tom Feelings. New York: Dial, 1974.

Feelings, Muriel. *Moja Means One: Swahili Counting Book.* Ill. by Tom Feelings. New York: Dial, 1972.

Giganti, Paul Jr. *How Many Snails?* Ill. by Donald Crews. New York: Greenwillow, 1988.

Greenaway, Kate. *Mother Goose or the Old Nursery Rhymes.* London: Warne.

Greenfield, Eloise. *Big Friend, Little Friend.* Ill. by Jan Spivey Gilchrist. New York: Black Butterfly Children's Books, 1991.

Griego, Margot C., Betsy Bucks, Sharon Gilbert, and Laurel Kimball, sel. and trans. *Tortillitas Para Mama.* Ill. by Barbara Cooney. New York: Holt, 1981.

Hill, Eric. *Spot Goes to the Park.* New York: Putnam's, 1991.

Hill, Eric. *Spot's First Walk.* New York: Putnam's, 1981.

Hill, Eric. *Where's Spot?* New York: Putnam's, 1980.

Hoban, Tana. *26 Letters and 99 Cents.* New York: Greenwillow, 1987.

Hutchins, Pat. *1 Hunter.* New York: Greenwillow, 1982.

Jonas, Ann. *Aardvarks, Disembark!* New York: Greenwillow, 1990.

Kelley, True. *Let's Eat!* New York: Dutton, 1989.

Koch, Michelle. *Hoot Howl Hiss.* New York: Greenwillow, 1991.

Konigsburg, E. L. *Samuel Todd's Book of Great Colors.* New York: Atheneum, 1990.

Kunhardt, Dorothy. *Pat the Bunny.* 1940. Racine, WI: Golden, 1968. Lewison, Wendy. *Going to Sleep on the Farm.* Ill. by Juan Wijngaard. New York: Dial, 1992.

Lobel, Arnold. *Frog and Toad Are Friends.* New York: Harper, 1970.

MacDonald, Suse. *Alphabatics.* New York: Bradbury, 1986.

McMillan, Bruce. *Growing Colors.* New York: Lothrop, 1988.

Mansell, Dom. *My Old Teddy.* Cambridge, MA: Candlewick, 1992.

Marshall, James. *Old Mother Hubbard and Her Wonderful Dog.* New York: Farrar, 1991.

Merriam, Eve. *The Inner City Mother Goose.* Ill. by Laurence Rutzkin. New York: Simon & Schuster, 1969.

Neumeier, Marty, and Bryon Glaser. *Action Alphabet.* New York: Greenwillow, 1985.

Ong, Christina. *The Little Engine That Could Pudgy Word Book.* New York: Grosset & Dunlap, 1988.

Oxenbury, Helen. *I See.* London: Walker Books, 1985.

The Real Mother Goose. (cloth book). Rand McNally: Taiwan, 1986.

Rikys, Bodel. *Red Bear.* New York: Dial, 1991.

Rockwell, Anne, and Harlow Rockwell. *The Toolbox.* New York: Macmillan, 1971.

Shone, Venice. *Tools.* New York: Scholastic, 1991.

Spier, Peter. *Fast-Slow High-Low.* 1972. Garden City, NY: Doubleday, 1988. Stevenson, James. *Grandpa's Great City Tour.* New York: Greenwillow, 1983.

Tafuri, Nancy. *Where We Sleep.* New York: Greenwillow, 1987.

Williams, Linda. *The Little Old Lady Who Was Not Afraid of Anything.* Ill. by Megan Lloyd. New York: Crowell, 1986.

Witte, Pat, and Eve Witte. *The Touch Me Book.* Ill. by Harlow Rockwell. Racine, WI: Western, n.d.

Wright, Blanche Fisher. *The Real Mother Goose.* Chicago: Rand McNally, 1991. Copyright 1916.

∽ CHAPTER REFERENCES

Allen, Virginia, Evelyn Freeman, Barbara Lehman, and Patricia Scharer. "*Amos and Boris:* A Window on Teachers' Thinking about the Use of Literature in Their Classrooms." *The Reading Teacher* 48.5 (Feb. 1995): 384–390.

Altwerger, Bess, Judith Diehl-Faxon, and Karen Dockstader-Anderson. "Read-Aloud Events as Meaning Construction." *Language Arts* 62.5 (Sept. 1985): 476–484.

Anderson, Richard C. et al. *Becoming a Nation of Readers: The Report of the Commission on Reading.* Champaign, IL: Center for the Study of Reading, 1985.

Apseloff, Marilyn. "Books for Babies: Learning Toys or Pre-Literature?" *Children's Literature Association Quarterly,* Vol. 12, No. 2 (Summer, 1987), pp. 63 -66.

Cambourne, Brian. "Toward an Educationally Relevant Theory of Literacy Learning: Twenty Years of Inquiry." *The Reading Teacher* 49.3 (Nov. 1995): 182–190.

Cambourne, Brian. *The Whole Story—Natural Learning and Acquisition of Literacy in the Classroom.* Auckland, New Zealand: Ashton-Scholastic, 1988.

Frith, Margaret. "Interview with Eric Hill." *The Horn Book* (Sept./Oct. 1987): 577–587.

Holdaway, Don. *The Foundations of Literacy.* Sydney: Scholastic Ashton, 1979.

Lamme, Linda. "Bookreading Behaviors of Infants." *The Reading Teacher* 39.6 (Feb. 1986): 504–509.

Opie, Iona, and Peter Opie. *The Oxford Dictionary of Nursery Rhymes.* Oxford: Clarendon Press, 1973.

Roser, Nancy, and Miriam Martinez. "Roles Adults Play in Preschoolers' Response to Literature." *Language Arts* 62.5 (Sept. 1985): 485–490.

Sulzby, Elizabeth. "Children's Emergent Reading of Favorite Storybooks: A Developmental Study." *Reading Research Quarterly* 20.4 (Summer 1985): 458–481.

Teale, William, and Elizabeth Sulzby, eds. *Emergent Literacy: Writing and Reading.* Norwood, NJ: Ablex, 1986.

Turner, Julianne V. "The Influence of Classroom Contexts on Young Children's Motivation for Literacy." *Reading Research Quarterly* 30.3 (July/Aug/Sept. 1995): 410–441.

NOTE: In Canadian Edition: Illustration from ACORN TO ZOO by Satoshi Kitamura. Copyright © 1992 Satoshi Kitamura. Published by Andersen Press, London and Farrar, Straus & Giroux, NY.

Chapter Six

Picture Books: A Balance Between Text and Illustrations

Tarvone was five when he made his first trip from California to New York. He and his parents flew to visit his aunt, uncle, and cousins. The trip was long, the plane ride frightening, and the noise and activity overwhelming. But when he walked into the room he was to share with his cousins, he found a friend—a copy of *Where the Wild Things Are* by Maurice Sendak. It was a book he had heard many times at kindergarten and at home. He could repeat phrases from it and tell the entire story when he looked at the pictures.

Together the family sat down and read about Max, who made so much mischief that his mother called him a wild thing. When Max responded that he would eat her up, he was sent to bed without his supper. Then a forest grew in Max's room, a small boat appeared on the ocean at the forest's edge, and Max sailed off to the land of the wild things. There the monsters "roared their terrible roars and gnashed their terrible teeth and rolled their terrible eyes and showed their terrible claws" (n. pag.).[1] But Max stared into their eyes until they were subdued and declared that he was king. As king, Max announced that the wild rumpus could begin. Three full double-page spreads show Max and the wild things as they cavort in the jungle. And even though the wild things beg him to stay, Max leaves them and sails home to his room, where he finds his supper awaiting him, still hot. *Where the Wild Things Are* has been called a classic among picture books, both for its lasting popularity and for the quality of the text and illustrations. For Tarvone it provided a connection to the secure world he had left. Here were pictures he knew and words he could recite. Here was a story that spoke to him of forgiveness and security. Here was a friend to be with him on this first night away from home. Look at Figure 6-1 and see if there are "friends" you recognize.

---

[1] *Source:* Excerpt from WHERE THE WILD THINGS ARE by Maurice Sendak. Copyright © 1963 by Maurice Sendak. Reprinted by permission of HarperCollins Publishers.

TRY THIS: See if you can match the names in the left column with the descriptions in the right column. These are from picture books often considered "classics." You may have read them when you were a child.

a.   Amelia Bedelia   1. ____ a little girl who lives in Paris

b.   Curious George   2. ____ the smallest child in the family

c.   Frog   3. ____ a mother who raises her little ones in the
                                   Boston Public Gardens

d.   George   4. ____ a boy who sails from his bedroom to a
                                   special place

e.   Horton   5. ____ a character whose best friend is Toad

f.   Madeline   6. ____ a housekeeper who takes all directions
                                   literally

g.   Mrs. Mallard   7. ____ a silly goose who becomes very proud

h.   Max   8. ____ a character whose best friend is Martha

i.   Petunia   9. ____ an elephant who is faithful 100 percent

j.   Titch   10. ____ a monkey who often gets into trouble

(See footnote below for the answers.)

Figure 6-1   From your own childhood.

VARIETY IN MODERN PICTURE BOOKS

Where the Wild Things Are is a **picture story book,** with the words and illustrations being equally important in presenting the narrative. The text tells us that Max was making mischief; the illustrations show us Max in his wolf suit chasing the dog. The text tells us that Max wants the "wild rumpus" to begin; the illustrations show us the creatures dancing in the moonlight, swinging rhythmically from the trees, honoring Max as their king. The text builds to a climax as Max becomes king of the wild things; the illustrations show this as they get larger and larger until there is no text at all—only pictures. The illustrations then become smaller as the action subsides. Text and illustrations combine to tell a story, each contributing to the whole.

Picture Books

The term **picture book** applies to any book in which the illustrations are as important as the text. This includes the books presented in Chapter 5, such as concept books and board books, and all of the books discussed in this chapter.

Not all picture books have a story as such, with a problem to be solved or characters in conflict. Many are descriptive. Cynthia Rylant wrote about the place where she grew up in *Appalachia, The Voices of Sleeping Birds.* She tells about the people:

In the summer many of the women like to can. It seems their season. They sit on kitchen chairs on back porches and they talk of their lives while they snap beans or cut up cucumbers for pickling. It is a good way for them to catch up on things and to have time together, alone, for neither the children nor the men come around much when there is canning going on. (17)[2]

She tells about the place:

Morning in these houses in Appalachia is quiet and full of light and the mountains out the window look new, like God made them just that day. Night in these houses is thick, the mountains wear heavy shawls of fog, and giant moths flap at the porch lights while cars cut through the dark hollows like burrowing moles. (13)

She gives the book coherence through the flow of the language, the logic of the topics, and her references to the dogs in Appalachia. The book opens with a mention of the dogs being country dogs, full of muscles. At various points she talks about the dogs, noting, for example, that they are not allowed on the beds and that they are used for hunting. The book closes with how the people look forward to each season; that in winter they feel "safe till the next year begins, Prince or King running the mountains like all good dogs in Appalachia" (22).

Barry Moser's watercolor illustrations in Rylant's book match what is described in the text—the opening illustration is of a dog facing the reader and stretching, and the closing illustration is of the same dog, again stretching, but this time facing the opposite page. But the illustrations do more than that; they give added information. When the text tells about children walking with their dogs on dirt roads, the illustration shows not only this, but also that the children are barefoot and that one carries an umbrella as protection against the sun. When the text presents possible reasons many of the men are coal miners, the illustration shows a miner in work clothes. When the text says that many of the people put photographs of their families on the walls, the illustration shows these photographs. The miner pictured is white; the family in the photographs black. While not mentioned in the text, the fact that there are both white and black residents of Appalachia is made clear in the illustrations. Both Rylant and Moser are from Appalachia, and together they have created a picture book that shares the ethos of a place and its people.

Just as Rylant often writes about Appalachia, other authors and illustrators are associated with particular regions. Barbara Cooney often sets her stories in New England; Patricia McKissack in the south; Byrd Baylor in the southwest.

Picture Story Book

A **picture story book** is a narrative, with a recognizable plot structure, that is in picture book format. It may be very simple. In *Who Is the Boss?* by Josse Goffin, two toy-like men and a duck are aboard a toy boat. The men get

---

[2] *Source:* Excerpts from APPALACHIA, THE VOICES OF SLEEPING BIRDS, Copyright © 1991 by Cynthia Rylant, reprinted by permission of Harcourt Brace & Company.

Rylant's text and Moser's illustrations vividly portray this book's Appalachian setting. Source: Illustration from APPALACHIA, THE VOICES OF SLEEPING BIRDS by Cynthia Rylant, illustration by Barry Moser, Copyright © 1991 by Pennyroyal Press, Inc., reproduced by permission of Harcourt Brace & Company.)

into an argument about who is the boss, each, of course, seeing himself as the boss. While they are busy trading statements about their capabilities, the boat crashes into a rock. The book ends with their having to ride on the back of the duck as the boat sinks, with the closing line, "Now! Who is the boss?" (n.p.). The story has a clear plot, as well as a theme about arguments and about focusing on what is important.

A more complex narrative is told in *Miss Rumphius* by Barbara Cooney. It opens with the narrator describing her Great-aunt Alice, Miss Rumphius, in present tense. Then the story flashes back to Miss Rumphius' childhood, when as a young girl she hoped to travel and eventually to live by the sea. Her artist grandfather adds a third goal: that she do something to make the world more beautiful. Miss Rumphius achieves her first two goals, but the third eludes her until she sees the lupines from her garden spread to a neighboring hillside. She buys five bushels of lupine seed and tosses it all along the stone walls and into the fields. She

Answers to Figure 6-1: 1. f. Bemelmans, Ludwig. *Madeline.* New York: Viking, 1939. **2.** j. Hutchins, Pat. *Titch.* New York: Macmillan, 1971. **3.** g. McCloskey, Robert. *Make Way for Ducklings.* New York: Viking, 1941. **4.** h. Sendak, Maurice. *Where the Wild Things Are.* New York: Harper, 1963. **5.** c. Lobel, Arnold. *Frog and Toad Are Friends.* New York: Harper, 1970. **6.** a. Parish, Peggy. *Amelia Bedelia.* New York: Harper, 1963. 7. i. Duvoisin, Roger. *Petunia.* New York: Knopf, 1950. **8.** Marshall, James. *George and Martha.* Boston: Houghton Mifflin, 1972. **9.** e. Geisel, Theodor (Dr. Seuss). *Horton Hatches the Egg.* New York: Random House, 1940. **10.** b. Rey, H. A. *Curious George.* Boston: Houghton Mifflin, 1941.

makes the world more beautiful as each spring the flowers brighten the area with blue and purple and pink.

The story then goes back to the narrator, young Alice, great-niece of Miss Rumphius. She and her friends are invited into the house, where Miss Rumphius tells Alice that she too must do something to make the world more beautiful. When the book ends, Alice doesn't yet know what she will do. Figure 6-2 shows how two different groups of children responded to *Miss Rumphius.*

This plot concerns the life of Miss Rumphius and how she solved the problem of how to fulfill her grandfather's instructions. It begins and ends with young Alice, now faced with the same dilemma. And like *Who Is the Boss?* it has a theme children can identify and discuss.

Black and White by David Macaulay is a sophisticated picture book with four stories being told simultaneously. Each double-page spread is divided into quadrants, with each quadrant having its own text and illustrations. The four stories are interrelated, with events in one story having import for the other stories. For example, the "boulders" that the boy sees from the train are the cows from another story. The strange behavior of the parents as they arrive home wearing newspapers can be explained by following the story in which a crowd of passengers wait for a delayed train, eventually

As a substitute teacher, Colleen often took good books with her to share with her students for the day. She discovered that different groups sometimes had very different responses to the same book. Here is how two classes of second graders responded to and interpreted *Miss Rumphius* by Barbara Cooney. The comments quoted are representative of the discussion in each group.

1. Before reading the book, Colleen showed the cover, read the title and author, and then turned to the title page. She asked if anyone knew what the flowers there were called. No one did, so she gave the name, lupines.

   Group 1
   The class was quiet and attentive. They said they thought the flowers were pretty.

   Group 2
   The class was quiet and attentive. Several children referred to the flowers as trees, even when reminded that they were flowers.

2. After reading the part in which Miss Rumphius is trying to decide what she could do to make the world more beautiful, Colleen asked the children to predict possible actions Miss Rumphius might take.

   Group 1
   "She might paint pictures."
   "She might pick up trash."

   Group 2
   "Miss Grumpy (child's pronunciation) might get rid of all those rocks."
   "She might change the color of the trees."

3. When the book was finished, children in both groups talked about Miss Rumphius, the kind of person she was, and what they thought of the book.

   Group 1
   "She was kind—she cared about her grandfather and what he asked her to do."
   "I liked the book because it teaches you something."
   "Did this story really happen?"

   Group 2
   "She was young and then she got old."
   "She planted trees all over."
   "She got rid of those rocks."

Figure 6-2   Responses differ: Two classes, same presentation.

making hats and clothing out of the newspapers they have long since finished reading. As children look at the book, the initial challenge is how to begin, how to make sense of what is going on. Then it becomes a game of putting events and characters together. This is a picture story book with multiple **parallel plots.**

What makes all of these books fit the same category of picture story book is that all are narratives, and all use text and illustrations equally to convey the message. In accepting the 1995 Caldecott Award for his illustrations for *Smoky Night* (Bunting), David Diaz expressed this idea when he said, "I wanted *Smoky Night* to achieve a balance between the text, the design, the painted illustrations, and the collaged backgrounds. I wanted each element to add to the book and to create a cohesive unit" (345–346).

During the discussion with both groups, Colleen encouraged the children to support and to expand on their initial responses. Interpretations were clarified and sometimes revised. As Colleen compared the groups, she noted that the comments of children in the second group were at a literal level and that several of the children repeated comments of their classmates rather than describing what had actually been shown in the book.

Colleen thought of several possible explanations:

- She read *Miss Rumphius* to Group 2 in the fall of the year and to Group 1 in the spring. A year's maturation might have made the difference in the children's ability to think about the ideas in the book.

- Also, the children in Group 1 had just completed a unit on ecology when she shared the book, whereas those in Group 2 did not have this context for the story.

- She wondered about the number of stories each group of children had heard and discussed. The children in Group 1 followed up on one child's question of whether the story was true, deciding that it probably wasn't, but that it could be. They seemed accustomed to responding to books and to the ideas of one another. The children in Group 2 made decisions based more on the illustrations than the text, and once an idea had been expressed, they repeated it even after the text and illustrations showed it to be false.

- Finally, Colleen tried to reconstruct exactly how she had introduced the book to each group. She knew that helping children bring their background of understanding to a new book or idea can help them make sense of it.

Colleen used her experiences and her analysis of the responses to *Miss Rumphius* as she planned how she would select and present other books in various primary classrooms.

Figure 6-2   *continued*

Macaulay tells four interrelated stories simultaneously in Black and White. *(Source:* Illustration from BLACK AND WHITE. Copyright © 1990 by David Macaulay. Reprinted by permission of Houghton Mifflin Company. All rights reserved.)

Wordless Books

Wordless books are exactly what the name implies; they have illustrations only, with no text, although some books with only a few words are sometimes put into the "wordless" category. Raymond Briggs opens his wordless book *The Snowman* with a little boy awakening to a heavy snowfall, getting out of bed and making a snowman, complete with muffler and hat. The snowman comes to life, exploring with the boy the wonders of modern living—light switches, ice cubes, skateboards. Though the snowman seems innocent and bumbling indoors, he is competent outside, even able to fly. Snowman and boy fly through the night to distant countries, returning just before daybreak. The boy returns to bed, this time awakening to a sunlit sky—and a melting snowman.

Briggs uses a variety of picture sizes in the book, from pages that have the format of comic books, with many panels showing the action, to double-page spreads of one illustration. The smaller panels often show a sequence of action in detail, such as the snowman looking at, then grabbing, and then squeezing a plastic bottle of dishwashing soap. The large illustrations emphasize the dramatic moments, with two consecutive double-page spreads providing the climax, as boy and snowman rise into the snowy night sky and fly over the buildings below. Readers need to know the convention of left-to-right and top-to-bottom reading as they look at this book.

Geisert limits his picture configuration in *Oink* to either one or two pictures per page and does use one word—*oink*. The dialogue is well-chosen since the book is about eight piglets and their mother. Adults sharing this book with children can have fun with it as they and the children read the different "oinks" with expression: the piglet's contented oinks as they nurse; their obedient oinks as they follow their mother on a walk; their loud and lingering oinks as they leap from the edge of the hillock onto a tree branch; and the sow's "Follow me" oink and her "Get out of that tree this minute!" oink.

Geisert helps place the action by switching from close-ups of the pigs to distant pictures of the farm and surrounding countryside. He indicates the passage of time by showing the sun first on the horizon and then higher in the sky. Geisert and other illustrators rely on readers' understanding that time is passing between panels. Action is captured at key moments, but the reader must convert the single pictures into continuous narrative.

Wordless books lend themselves to language activities in which children add the text themselves, giving their interpretations of the action. Figure 6-3 suggests several approaches for using wordless books and lists outstanding books that have potential for each category.

Children who are learning English as their second language may be particularly intrigued by wordless books because they can understand the story on their own. They also can use their native language patterns and prior knowledge to make sense of the story (Flatley and Rutland 277). Teachers may use this opportunity to supply the English words for objects or actions that appear in the story. Lindauer (138) suggests also that it may be easier for teachers to use the children's native language as they tell the story of a wordless book than to translate a book with English text.

The Snowman by Raymond Briggs was published in Britain as a wordless book. It is now available in a miniature edition (London: Hamish, 1989), in an edition with words (London: Hamish, 1990), and in a film and video version (Weston Woods).

Many of John Goodall's books, such as *The Story of a Main Street* (New York: Macmillan, 1987), are excellent for research because they show the same scene as it changes over time. Students may observe and describe specific changes, such as those in transportation, or make more general observations about "progress."

ACTIVITY	PURPOSE	GOOD WORDLESS BOOKS TO USE
Children create the narrative orally, passing the book around a small group, each child continuing the story for his or her pages.	Builds idea of narrative structure, of use of language to express actions and ideas. Encourages the use of descriptive language.	Felix, Monique. *The Wish.* New York: Stewart, 1991. Hutchins, Pat. *Changes, Changes.* New York: Macmillan, 1971. McCully, Emily Arnold. *Picnic.* New York: Harper, 1984. Rohmann, Eric. *Time Flies.* New York: Crown, 1994.
Children take the parts of the characters, creating the dialogue for each scene. Big book editions or slides of the illustrations are useful because they allow all to see, and you can orchestrate if you wish by pointing to each character to indicate turns for speaking. Giving children cards with the name or picture of the character can help both child and teacher remember who is taking which role.	Encourages natural sounding speech in a literary context. Encourages attention to facial expressions, body language, and emotional reactions.	Mayer, Mercer. *Ah-choo.* New York: Dial, 1976. Mayer, Mercer. *Frog Goes to Dinner.* New York: Dial, 1974. Mayer, Mercer. *Hiccup.* New York: Dial, 1976. Mayer, Mercer. *Oops.* New York: Dial, 1977.
Different children tape-record their telling of the narrative as they look at the illustrations; then they listen to several, or parts of several, tellings (beginnings, for example) and compare.	Allows children to explore how a story may be interpreted, and to hear various ways of expressing an idea.	Bang, Molly. *The Grey Lady and the Strawberry Snatcher.* New York: four winds, 1980. Ormerod, Jan. *Moonlight.* New York: Kestrel, 1982. Sara. *Across Town.* New York: Orchard, 1991. Turkle, Brinton. *Deep in the Forest.* New York: Dutton, 1976.
Children "read" the book in pairs, alternating telling the story as they turn the pages.	Allows prereaders or beginning readers to "read" successfully. Gives children experience in working *together.*	Bonners, Susan. *Just in Passing.* New York: Lothrop. 1989. Collingwood, Peter. The Midnight Circus. New York: Knopf, 1993. Krahn, Fernando. *Who's Seen the Scissors?* New York: Dutton, 1975 Tafuri, Nancy. *Junglewalk.* New York: Greenwillow, 1988.

Figure 6-3 Involving children with wordless books.

ACTIVITY	PURPOSE	GOOD BOOKS TO USE
Children write the text to accompany the illustrations. They may attach the paper with their writing to the book using removable tape. This can be done as a group or an individual project.	Encourages children to read and enhances success because all the words written are in the children's vocabularies.	de Paola, Tomie. Sing, *Pancakes for Breakfast*. New York: Harcourt, 1978. McCully, Emily Arnold. *School*. New York: Harper, 1987. Tafuri, Nancy. *Do Not Disturb*. New York: Greenwillow, 1987.
Children write descriptions of what they see on a single page. Other children read the description and try to locate the page.	Encourages close attention to detail and the use of descriptive language.	Anno, Mitsumasa. *Anno's USA*. New York: Philomel, 1983. Goodall, John. *The Story of a Main Street*. New York: Macmillan, 1987. Monro, Roxie. *The Inside-Outside Book of New York City*. New York: Dodd, 1985.
Children, as a group, see how many things they notice in each illustration. You might have them identify elements in the pictures that are essential to the story.	Presents the idea that artists plan illustrations carefully. Encourages close attention to visual elements.	Goodall, John. *Little Red Riding Hood*. New York: Macmillan, 1988 Spier, Peter. *Rain*. Garden City, NY: Doubleday, 1982. Weisner, David. *Free Fall*. New York: Lothrop, 1988.
Children use the wordless format to create stories of their own and then share their books with one another.	Encourages clear sequence of events in the plot. Helps children tell a story in a form other than words.	Day, Alexandra. *Carl Goes to Daycare*. New York: Farrar, 1993. Rikys, Bodel. *Red Bear*. New York: Dial, 1992. Young, Ed. *The Other Bone*. New York: Harper, 1984.

Figure 6-3 *continued*

215

Understanding wordless books usually requires going beyond a simple literal interpretation. Readers must make judgments about the characters' feeling and motivations, about what might be happening that is not shown directly in the illustrations, and about how the events shown in pictures are related to one another. A child looking at *One Frog Too Many* by Mayer and Mayer sees an early illustration where the boy opens his present with a big smile on his face. His dog looks eagerly into the box, but the frog glares at its contents. This sets the stage for later action by the frog— biting the leg of what was in the box. . . . another frog. Facial expressions and body language of both human and animals give information about their feelings. The reason for the frog's unhappiness, his jealousy of the new frog, must be inferred from what the characters are doing and the way they look.

Sometimes you can assess children's understanding of a wordless book by just watching them as they look at it. Children looking at David Wiesner's *Tuesday* laugh and point as they see the frogs flying out of the swamp on their lily pads. Their laughter grows as they see the frogs enter the town, knocking down laundry, entering a room where a woman has fallen asleep in front of her television, and chasing dogs before they return to their pond to sit pensively on fresh lily pads. They see the puzzled detective and police officers looking at the evidence left from the night's activities. The following Tuesday there is a pig-shaped shadow on the side of the barn, and the rump and tail of a pig, almost at roof level, show next to a building. Some children make the connection immediately, and their laughter grows. Others need to turn the page, where pigs are flying above the weather vane, tumbling though the air just as the frogs had done.

The body language and facial expressions of characters give information about their feelings. (Source: Illustration from ONE FROG TOO MANY by Mercer and Marianna Mayer. Copyright © 1975 by Mercer and Marianna Mayer. Used by permission of Dial Books for Young Readers, a division of Penguin Books USA Inc.)

Encouraging children to talk about what they see and what they think it means lets them hear the thought processes of others and work together to construct meaning from the illustrations.

Because most wordless books do present a story, readers usually expect this and may have to rethink their assumptions when they encounter a wordless book such as Josse Goffin's *OH!* The central figure on each page is transformed when the fold-out flap is extended, and an object from the flap is the central figure of the next page. When the alligator from the first illustration appears in the last, the changes have come full circle. Still, many readers flip back and forth, trying to find the key to the narrative that they seem to have missed. Figure 6-4 shows some visual games using illustrations that teachers can use with children.

VISUAL GAMES

Who hid the toothbrush?

In kindergarten, a group of children sat with their teacher pointing out the objects hidden in the pictures— and giggling at their success.

Second graders looked for the hidden creatures early in a unit on oceans. Later they worked together to create a mural of "hidden" sea creatures, adding their own fish and animals.

Figure 6-4   Visual games.

Sources: Illustration from WHO HID IT? by Taro Gomi, Copyright © 1991 by Taro Gomi, and reprinted by permission of The Millbrook Press, Inc. § Illustration by Demi reprinted by permission of Grosset & Dunlap from DEMI'S FIND THE SEA CREATURES, copyright © 1991 by Demi. § Illustration reprinted from THE ELEVENTH HOUR: A CURIOUS MYSTERY by Graeme Base. Copyright © 1988 by Doublebase Pty Ltd. Publishing in 1989 by Harry N. Abrams, Inc. New York. All rights reserved. § Illustration from WHERE'S WALDO? by Martin Handford. Copyright © 1987 by Martin Handford. By permission of Walker Books Ltd. London.

In fourth grade, five teams of children kept track of the clues they found in the pictures as well as their ideas, as each team worked to solve the mystery.

In second grade, children played "I Spy" in pairs as they looked at various pages.

In fourth grade, children often looked at the book for ideas when they were looking for a writing topic.

Figure 6-4   *continued*

Wordless books are thus not simpler than other picture books. The reader adds the narrative or interpretation, so language is not a factor, but the skills of careful observation and interpretation are necessary for understanding.

Picture Books of Poetry and Song

Poems and songs lend themselves to picture book format because of their relatively brief texts, appropriate for a book that is usually around 32 pages long. Many are also narrative, telling a story that can be expanded through illustrations. Folk songs in particular have stories to tell that can be entertaining whether read or sung.

Teachers often find illustrated songs and poems particularly useful with emergent readers because of the repetition in lyrics and verses. They read or sing with the children, who learn the words by heart. Then when the children see the words in the book, they can match the words they know with the words they see printed. A child who has sung, "Go tell Aunt Rhody, Go tell Aunt Rhody, Go tell Aunt Rhody, That the old gray goose is dead," can pick up the illustrated version by Aliki and "read" it immediately. Poems and songs with a steady rhythm and often with refrains function as predictable literature.

There are also collections of songs, with each song illustrated. Examples are Gonna Sing My Head Off: American Folk Songs for Children, collected by Kathleen Krull and illustrated by Allen Garns (New York: Knopf, 1992) and Go In and Out the Window from the Metropolitan Museum of Art (New York: Holt, 1987), in which songs are matched with paintings, sculpture, and prints.

Poetry and Verse

Poem picture books are discussed in Chapter 7, the chapter on poetry. However, many picture books are written in rhyme. The classic *Madeline* by Ludwig Bemelmans begins,

> In an old house in Paris
> that was covered with vines
> lived twelve little girls in two straight lines.
> In two straight lines they broke their bread
> and brushed their teeth
> and went to bed. (n.p.)[3]

The narrative in entirely in verse. The book has remained a favorite with children because Madeline is lively and appealing and because both text and illustrations are filled with humor. In addition, one has the sense that the story determined the verse, not the verse the story. There is nothing stilted in either plot or language. Generally picture books written in verse are not identified as such in card catalogues or book lists. You may want to begin your own list of high-quality books in verse.

---

[3] *Source:* Excerpt from MADELINE by Ludwig Bemelmans. Copyright 1939 by Ludwig Bemelmans, renewed © 1967 by Madeleine Bemelmans and Barbara Bemelmans Marciano. Used by permission of Viking Penguin, a division of Penguin Books USA Inc.

Song

Jolongo and Bromley write that, "Song picture books hold special appeal for children of all ages because of their potential for involvement" (840). The most obvious involvement is singing either the entire song or the refrain. Children hearing *The Hippopotamus Song: A Muddy Love Song* by Michael Flanders are eager to join in with:

> Mud! Mud! Glorious Mud!
> Nothing quite like it for cooling the blood.
> So follow me, follow, down to the hollow,
> And there let us wallow in glorious mud. (n.p.)[4]

The rhythm and rhyme of the words and the rollicking tune beg for children to join in. Children might add accompaniment with rhythm instruments.

Many songs for children, such as "London Bridge Is Falling Down," fit the category of nursery rhyme and also have actions that go with the words. Figure 6-5 suggests ways of involving children with song books. Of course, many of these books lend themselves to more than one method of involvement.

As with books written in verse, song books in picture book format can be a challenge to locate in some libraries. Baird (142) found them listed under 49 different headings, ranging from "Folk Songs—American" to "Games with Music" to simply "Picture Books."

Picture Books for Older Children

Some picture books are appropriate only for intermediate grade or older children, and some can be understood and enjoyed by children in grade 2 or grade 4 and beyond. In books for older children, either the content or the style is beyond the understanding of most six- to eight-year-olds.

An example of such a book is *Rose Blanche* by Roberto Innocenti. The book opens with the story being told in first person by Rose Blanche, a young German girl who remembers the day a truck came and many men dressed as soldiers left. The illustrations show the soldiers boarding an open truck as German officials watch from a porch and civilians look on from the street and from open windows. Bright red flags with black swastikas on a circle of white stand out against the muted red of the brick building and the dull olive of the truck, uniforms, and pavement. Rose continues to describe events in the town from the perspective of a young child. She sees tanks come through the town; she watches as the mayor of the town, wearing a red swastika armband, stops a young boy who has jumped from the back of a truck and allows soldiers to recapture him; and she follows the tracks of the truck into a forest where she discovers hungry children imprisoned behind an electric barbed wire fence.

---

[4] *Source: HIPPOPOTAMUS SONG,* by Michael Flanders and Donald Swann, © Chappell Music Ltd. (PRS). All Rights administered by Chappell & Co. & ASCAP. All Rights Reserved. Used by Permission of WARNER BROS. PUBLICATIONS U.S. INC., Miami, FL. 33014.

ACTIVITY	SUGGESTED BOOKS
Sing either the refrain or the entire song.	Delacre, Lulu, ed. *Arroz Con Leche: Songs and Rhymes from Latin America.* New York: Scholastic, 1989. Hellen, Nancy. *Old MacDonald Had a Farm.* New York: Orchard, 1990. Jonas, Carol. *This Old Man.* Boston: Houghton, 1990. Paparone, Pam. *Who Built the Ark?* New York: Simon, 1994.
Read and then sing during the rereading.	Hurd, Thatcher. *Mama Don't Allow.* New York: Harper, 1984. Young, Ruth. *Golden Bear.* Ill. by Rachael Isadora. New York: Viking, 1992.
Sing or chant with motions.	Hawkins, Colin, and Jacqui Hawkins. *I Know an Old Lady Who Swallowed a Fly.* New York: Putnam, 1987. Westcott, Nadine. *Peanut Butter and Jelly.* New York: Dutton, 1987.
Sing and dramatize.	Gerstein, Mordicai. *Roll Over!* New York: Crown, 1984. Raffi. *Five Little Ducks.* Ill. by Jose Aruego and Ariane Dewey. New York: Crown, 1989.
Make up verses of their own.	Carle, Eric. *Today Is Monday.* New York: Philomel, 1993. Halpern, Shari. *What Shall We Do When We All Go Out?* New York: North-South, 1995. Peek, Merle. *Mary Wore Her Red Dress.* New York: Clarion, 1985. Zelinsky, Paul O. *The Wheels on the Bus.* New York: Dutton, 1990.
Compare different illustrations for the same song	Galdone, Paul. *Cat Goes Fiddle-i-fee.* New York: Clarion, 1985. Sweet, Melissa. *Fiddle-i-Fee: A Farmyard Song for the Very Young.* Boston: Joy Street, 1992. Ivemey, John. *Three Blind Mice.* Ill. by Victoria Chess. Boston: Little, Brown, 1990. Ivemey, John. *Three Blind Mice.* Ill. by Paul Galdone. New York: Clarion, 1987. Conover, Chris. *Froggie Went A-Courting.* New York: Farrar, 1986. Langstaff, John. *Frog Went A-Courtin'.* Ill. by Feodor Rojankovsky. New York: Harcourt, 1955. Aliki. *Hush Little Baby: A Folk Lullaby.* Englewood Cliffs, NJ: Prentice Hall, 1968. Zemach, Margot. *Hush Little Baby.* New York: Dutton, 1976. Spier, Peter. *The Fox Went Out on a Chilly Night.* 1961. New York: Dell, 1993. Watson, Wendy. *Fox Went Out on a Chilly Night.* New York: Lothrop, 1994.

Figure 6-5   Involving children with song books.

Rose begins taking food from home to give to the children with the bright yellow stars pinned on their shirts. Then the soldiers start coming back to town at night, weary and beaten. One day they and the townspeople flee. Rose walks back through the forest and finds the compound empty, but there are soldiers in the fog and a shot is fired. Rose's mother waits but her child does not come home. Spring comes, and the clearing is now filled with wildflowers, spots of bright red and pink and purple among the grasses. The final illustration shows a strand of barbed wire with a wilted periwinkle draped over it—the flower Rose had been holding against the wire in the last illustration in which she appeared.

Because the topic of World War II and the imprisonment of Jews in concentration camps requires background information that young children are not likely to have, primary grade readers may not be able to make sense of the story. For example, the text does not tell what the swastika symbolizes; it does not tell why the boy was taken or why people were behind barbed wire; it does not tell why the town was evacuated. The reader who knows about the topic can understand the action. The reader who does not is left wondering what is going on.

The style of both text and illustration has a sophistication that is beyond primary age children. The title, *Rose Blanche,* was chosen because it was the name of a group of young German citizens who protested the war, symbolism likely to be lost on young listeners. The point of view changes from first person to third person in the middle of the book, right after Rose discovers the concentration camp. This allows the personal involvement and childlike perspective at the beginning and the death of Rose at the end. Small spots of bright red in the illustrations catch the eye and focus attention on key elements—the Nazi flags and armbands, the ribbon in Rose's hair, the gate that blocks the road to the camp, the flowers that grow around the destroyed and deserted prison.

Teachers of grade 4 and up often use *Rose Blanche* in conjunction with *Number the Stars* by Lois Lowry, a novel about the courage shown by one Danish family and the Jewish people they help escape to Sweden. They also use the book as part of a unit on the Holocaust or World War II. For these children, what is unspoken in the text and symbolized in the illustrations

Some picture books, such as Rose Blanche, *are more appropriate for intermediate than primary grade children.* (*Source:* Illustration from ROSE BLANCHE by Christophe Gallaz and Roberto Innocenti Copyright © 1985, reprinted with the permission of Creative Education, Mankato, MN.)

adds power to the story and deliver an emotional impact. Figure 6-12 at the end of this chapter lists picture books for older children.

Other picture books may be understood and enjoyed by both primary and intermediate grade children. Fourth-grade teachers use picture books with their students for a variety of reasons. Enjoyment, of course, is a key reason. Fourth graders laugh at *Tuesday* as readily as their younger brothers and sisters. Teachers also share picture books for the aesthetic appeal of both text and illustrations, as a quick way to study literary elements, for information that can be gathered from the illustrations, and as an addition to a topic being discussed. *Shaker Lane* by Alice and Martin Provensen, can be understood and enjoyed by both young children and intermediate grade children. It is the story of the changes on Shaker Lane, from the days when the Herkimer sisters began to sell portions of their farm, to the growth of a small community, to the flooding of that community for the creation of a reservoir, to the new community—on what was left of Shaker Lane, now named "Reservoir Road." The story itself captures the human reaction of many of the residents to these changes, including Old Man Van Sloop, who stays by moving to a houseboat. Focal points in sharing this book with children could include the following approaches:

1. Seeing techniques used by the illustrators, such as double-page spreads, a cutaway view of a house, close-ups, and long shots.
2. Identifying the possible themes, such as change is inevitable, not all change is progress, perseverance pays.
3. Discussing the information given in the illustrations, such as how the families lived, how the land changed, what is meant by eminent domain.
4. Comparing it with other books, such as *Letting Swift River Go* by Jane Yolen, or with actions and changes within their own community.

Picture books have much to offer the intermediate grade student, and teachers are seeing the possibilities in books designed for an older audience and in those that span the range of elementary years.

ILLUSTRATIONS IN PICTURE BOOKS

Just as authors make choices about content and style, so too do illustrators. Their choices determine how the pictures function with the text. In some picture books, the illustrations simply *reflect* what the text says. Both tell the same story, one visually and one with words. In other picture books, the illustrations may *clarify* or *interpret* the text, showing what the words mean and giving added detail. In still other picture books, the illustrations *extend* the text, adding story elements, sometimes even telling a story of their own. All of these approaches may apply to the literary elements of plot, characterization, setting, theme, and mood. That is, an illustrator may draw pictures that clearly show the plot, paint pictures that go beyond the words in giving information about the setting, or use colored chalk to establish the mood of a tale. The questions in Figure 6-6 ask children to compare the illustrations in an old and new edition of *Evan's Corner.*

Sometimes different artists have illustrated books about the same character. Look at *Some of the Days of Everett Anderson* or *Everett Anderson's Christmas Coming* by Lucille Clifton. They are illustrated by Evaline Ness. Then look at any of the other books about Everett Anderson. They are illustrated by Ann Grifalconi. See if you think the illustrations develop the character.

Figure 6-6 How illustrations give information.

Sources: From EVAN'S CORNER by Elizabeth Starr Hill, illustrated by Nancy Grossman. Illustrations copyright © 1967 by Nancy Grossman. Reprinted by permission of Henry Holt and Co., Inc. $ Illustration and text from EVAN'S CORNER by Elizabeth Starr Hill, illustrated by Sandra Speidel. Text Copyright © 1991 by Elizabeth Starr Hill, illustrations Copyright © 1991 by Sandra Speidel. Used by permission of Viking Penguin, a division of Penguin Books USA Inc.

Evan's Corner was first published in 1967. Twenty-three years later, in 1991, a new edition was published with new illustrations. Each illustrator interpreted the story in her own way. Look at the illustrations below. They are from the first page of the story, when Evan, on his way home from school, stops to look in the window of a pet shop. Then for each one, decide:

1. How old is Evan?
   What makes you think this?

2. How is Evan feeling? What might he be thinking?
   How can you tell?

3. What is Evan's neighborhood like?
   How can you tell?

DESIGN—LOOKING AT BORDERS

What other books might Westcott have selected for this song about a clambake? (Source: From A REAL NICE CLAMBAKE by Nadine Bernard Westcott. Text Copyright © 1945 by Williamson Music, Inc. © Renewed courtesy of Rodgers & Hammerstein Organization. Illustrations Copyright © 1992 by Nadine Bernard Westcott. By permission of Little, Brown and Company.)

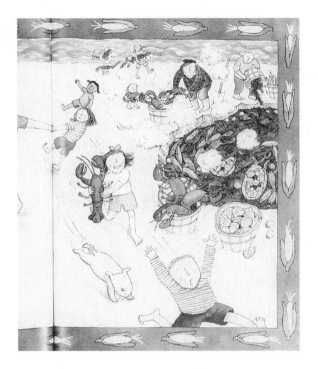

How does this border fit a short story from Iran? (Source: "Nabookin," from DIANE GOODE'S BOOK OF SILLY STORIES AND SONGS by Diane Goode, illustrations. Copyright © 1992 by Dutton Children's Books, collection. Illustrations copyright © 1992 by Diane Goode. Used by permission of Dutton Children's Books, a division of Penguin Books USA Inc.)

DESIGN—LOOKING AT BORDERS

What information is provided in this border? (Source: Excerpts from A RIVER RAN WILD, Copyright © 1992 by Lynne Cherry, reprinted by permission of Harcourt Brace & Company.*)*

What does this border add to the illustration? (Source: Illustration and text excerpt from "MORE, MORE, MORE, SAID THE BABY" by Vera B. Williams, Copyright © 1990 by Vera B. Williams. Reprinted by permission of Greenwillow Books, a division of William Morrow and Company, Inc.*)*

DESIGN—LOOKING AT BORDERS

How does this border augment the story? (Source: Illustrations and text from BERLIOZ THE BEAR by Jan Brett, copyright © 1991 by Jan Brett. Reprinted by permission of G. P. Putnam's Sons.)

But watercolors can be used quite differently, layered to achieve deep colors or outlined with ink to give sharp edges. In *Half a Moon and One Whole Star,* artist Jerry Pinkney has used watercolor pastels and colored pencil to create the bright red of the parrot, the variable tones of the leaves, and the delineation of the feathers. **Pastel** is a dried paste made of ground chalk and other materials. It is the medium used by Ed Young for *I Wish I Were a Butterfly.*

John Steptoe's final illustration for *Mufaro's Beautiful Daughters* shows the use of **crosshatching,** crisscross patterns of lines, to add shading to the painting. It appears on the wings and necks of the birds and is used to create clouds in the sky. He has used an **opaque paint,** paint heavy enough to prevent light from passing through it.

There are several kinds of opaque paint. **Acrylics,** which are quick-drying paints made from plastics, appear vivid and shining on the page. **Tempera,** made by mixing coloring powder into a sticky substance such as egg yolk and thinning with water, gives a comparatively flat look. **Oils,** made with coloring powder and linseed oil, can give a bright, rich effect that calls out to be touched. The illustrations for *Family Farm* and for *Yonder,* also in the previous photo section, are done in oils.

The birds in the illustrations for *Who Says a Dog Goes Bow-Wow?* are **collages,** made by cutting or tearing pieces of paper and gluing them on a background. Suse MacDonald used hand-colored tissue paper. When you look at the book, you can see how the colors on the paper were blended, how sharp the cut paper is, and the way that figures are overlapped.

David Wisniewski went even further in constructing the illustrations for *Rain Player.* He drew and then cut out each piece, assembled the pieces into each scene, lit the assembled pieces to create shadows, and photographed it. When you look at the overlapping, you will see the depth created by this technique. Notice how slits in the paper create veins on the leaves and define the mountain, for instance.

Artists continually explore new media and mix media as they illustrate picture books, as well as apply techniques that have been used effectively for years. Pen and ink, **scratchboard** (covering a board with black ink, then scratching away at the blackness to reveal some of the white beneath), photography, crayon, pencil, and all types of paints are represented in picture books.

Style

Pat Cummings has compiled a book of interviews with illustrators of children's books titled *Talking with Artists* (New York: Macmillan, 1992). It is an excellent source for finding out about techniques and seeing examples of various media as well as discovering interesting facts about the illustrators.

Different artists may use the same medium in different ways and portray the same content in different ways. Differences in the use of blank space, line, solids, and color define **style.** Artistic style, the particular way an artist uses media, can be as individual as a signature or a smile. Tomie dePaola's round-faced, curly-headed characters, for example, are easily recognizable.

Style has a second meaning. Look at the illustrations of trees in the photo section. Each picture fits a general category of style depending on how realistic it is. Thomas Locker's paintings for *Family Farm* show the scenes and the people almost as they would look through a camera's viewfinder. Locker paints in a **realistic** or **representational** style. The trees in *Yonder,* on the other hand, are painted in an **impressionistic** style, and the hundreds of small brush strokes impart a sense of the way light reflects and sparkles. Real trees do not look like points or strokes of light. Impressionism, developed in the 1870s in France, calls on the viewer to supply the reality suggested in the painting.

The trees in the illustration from *The Tunnel* may look realistic at first, but take a second look. Hidden in the bark are the figures of a wolf and a bear, making this scene even more frightening. Anthony Browne embedded the images of animals into the trees and placed a single tombstone in the middle of the forest. The style of art in which objects are combined in unnatural ways or images are juxtaposed is called **surrealism.**

Expressionistic art varies color and proportion rather than content. Figures may be in colors that reflect how the artist feels about the subject, not the natural colors. The illustrations for *Who Says a Dog Says Bow-Wow?* are expressionistic. In other expressionistic art, the size of objects may reflect their importance, or the perspective may be distorted to emphasize meaning.

Farther still from the camera's eye is the **cartoon** style of *Goldilocks and the Three Bears.* Two trees grow together, forming an archway that spells out "SHORT CUT." Goldilocks herself has eyes, nose, and mouth depicted by simple lines with just the right twist to reveal her smirk as she heads down the path.

Finally, some styles bear only distant similarities to reality. The **gouache** paintings of Gerald McDermott for *Zomo the Rabbit* are reminiscent of African **folk art.** He draws the rabbit and the palm tree with more concern for evoking a traditional style than for recreating an animal or a tree.

Some artists work well in several of these stylistic categories, whereas others are best known in one style. McDermott, for instance, illustrates folktales and models his art after the folk art of the tale's origin. Whether the pictures are realistic or abstract, good picture books have a style that, like the medium, is wedded to the story.

Visual Literacy

While children need not be able to identify the style of art or the exact medium used, they can learn to talk about the art in the books they are reading. John Stewig writes:

> If children are seldom encouraged to study illustrations, they are even less often asked to translate what they have learned in this visual mode into the oral mode. Putting thoughts about what was learned visually into spoken words is an important challenge all children should experience. (56)

Visual literacy means being able to construct meaning from visual images, or "decode" pictures. Stewig posits three steps in the process.

To build your knowledge of illustrators, their styles, and techniques, read the "Visual Links" features in *Book Links,* a journal published by the American Library Association.

1. First, have children bring their own background to bear on what they are seeing—what they notice and how it compares with what they have experienced.
2. Second, have children pay attention to individual units within the larger context—looking at an artist's use of line, space, or color within a page or an entire book.
3. Third, have children make aesthetic judgments about the relative merit of one picture or book over another (12–16).

Children can explore how artists have used particular elements. Look at the illustrations from *Owl Lake* and *Who Says a Dog Says Bow-Wow?* See how the white space is used, heightening the black "V" of action as the owl plummets to the water and snatches the fish or giving a clean and clear background for the birds. Notice the picture within a picture in *Half a Moon and One Whole Star.*

Books can be grouped so that specific characteristics can be compared. In the special photo section are five books in which the artists have put a border around the illustrations. Look at them and decide for yourself. What is the effect of each? Why did the artist choose that particular border? What information can be gained from looking at the border?

"More, More, More," Said the Baby is a short book with three stories in which the parent or grandparent of each baby catches and cuddles the child. *A Real Nice Clambake* illustrates the Rodgers and Hammerstein's song of the same name. "Nabookin" is a short story from Iran in a collection of short stories and poems from various countries. *Berlioz the Bear* is a story about a group of musicians who come to the village to give a concert. And *A River Ran Wild* tells the history of the Nashua River, its pollution and eventual cleanup.

Teachers help children learn terms such as "endpapers" and "title page" by using them as they share books aloud.

Barbara Keifer describes a classroom she visited in which the children seemed especially insightful about the books they were reading.

> While Mrs. Harbert was not an expert in art history or art appreciation, she was knowledgeable about criteria for choosing picture books, about illustrators, and about book production; and she shared this knowledge with children, using terms like "endpages," "title page," "wood block prints," or "acrylics" as she talked about books. She also loved picture books and was enthusiastic as she shared good picture books with children. "I have a special new storybook to share with you. Come up close, very, very close. It's one of *those* books," she'd say—a signal to children to look carefully and think deeply about what was to come as she read aloud. During read-aloud sessions she encouraged children to look for "secrets" in picture books, to find the unexpected or deeper meaning conveyed by so many illustrators. Her questions invited children to be meaning makers. "What does this remind you of?" "Where have you heard that name before?" "What do you think the story will be about just from looking at the pictures?" she might ask as she introduced a new book. She allowed comments and questions to flow among the children as she read each page and paused for many moments to invite discussion. Her own comments and questions: "What are you thinking as you're looking at this page?" "How does this book make you feel?" "Why would you say that?" encouraged the children to develop what she called a "careful eye, a careful attention to detail, to noticing and appreciating. (268)

This teacher's approach allows learning by both teacher and students as they look carefully at books being shared and encourages higher-order thinking skills, judgments, and expression of the characters. Look at some of the books on the Touchstone list in Figure 6-13 at the end of this chapter to see picture books that many critics consider to be outstanding. As Elleman has stated, "picture books are ideal to stimulate classroom discussion; often filled with lyrical prose, they make good writing models; multilayered in story and content, they work in numerous connections across the classroom; and containing a wealth of art styles and mediums, they offer rich aesthetic opportunities" (5).

The size of a book becomes important when you plan to read it to a group of children. The book must be large enough for the children to see the illustrations.

THE LEGACY OF CRUIKSHANK, CRANE, GREENAWAY, AND CALDECOTT

The sophistication evident in today's children's literature came slowly to picture books. For centuries after the invention of the printing press in the mid-1400s, most book illustrators had to cut their designs into wood. They would gouge the surface of a flat board, leaving raised areas where they wanted lines or blocks of print. The projection of the wood surface above the hollows is called a **relief.** Then artists would apply ink to the wood and press the wet, carved block against paper. Pictures showed white space above the indentations in the block and black lines where the inky relief met the paper. There are sharp contrasts in these early woodcuts, as if scenes were lit by a harsh spotlight that burned away color.

Printing from flat metal plates offered an alternative to woodcuts as early as the late fifteenth century. Artists etched pictures into copper, brass, or zinc; covered the plate with ink; and wiped the surface clean. Enough ink remained in the hollows cut into the metal to flow onto the paper placed under pressure against the plate. The method, the opposite of relief printing, is called **intaglio** printing. Intaglio comes from Latin words meaning "to cut in."

Until the beginning of the last century, children's books printed by either method were black-and-white, unless someone hired by the publisher, or readers themselves, added hues by hand to the printed page. The content of pictures was somewhat gray as well, offering static, idealized people frozen in statuelike poses. Printers had experimented for several hundred years with techniques of adding colors—using two woodcuts inked separately and then fitted together, for instance. Results were often blotchy.

In the 1800s new techniques of printing took hold. One major advance was **lithography,** a method that was neither relief nor intaglio. Artists drew designs with greasy ink on the surface of a smooth, flat stone. Then they brushed the whole surface of the stone with ordinary ink and washed it with water. The rinsing carried away the ink except where it was held in the water-repellent grease. They pressed paper against the stone, and inky areas transferred the drawing. Other advances permitted more use of color.

Content became more colorful, too, as several artists in the 1800s began creating imaginative books, some of which are still in circulation today.

George Cruikshank (1792–1878) was one of these pioneering artists. Son of a political cartoonist, George himself began roasting politicians—Tories, Whigs, and Radicals alike—when he was still a teenager. He illustrated his first book in 1820 with spirited and funny drawings in a version of fairy tales collected by Jakob and Wilhelm Grimm. Cruikshank favored wild costumes for his characters and sometimes drew enlarged heads, a style developed by seventeenth-century artists and still used by cartoonists.

Walter Crane (1845–1915), son of a portrait painter, learned his trade as apprentice to a wood engraver and studied Italian master painters and Japanese color prints. In the mid-1860s, he turned to children's books. Working with a famous printer named Edmund Evans, he published a series of nursery rhyme books including *Baby's Opera.* It presented words and music to popular children's verse and featured dignified but upbeat drawings. His illustration for "Old King Cole" shows the fiddlers three in formal pose and uniform. Yet each member of the trio—one with long curly hair, one with short straight hair, and one bald—is curiously individual, scratching out the music in his own way as a parrot perched on the king's throne conducts.

Two other illustrators, both born in 1846, set standards followed by children's book artists ever since.

Kate Greenaway (1846–1901) was shy of public recognition, but her pink-cheeked children with placid faces were so well dressed they influenced styles in children's clothes wherever her books appeared.

As a child, Randolph Caldecott (1846–1886) liked to cut wood into the shapes of animals. But his father, an accountant, apparently thought art was not

Look back to pages 169 and 170 to see illustrations done by Caldecott and Greenaway.

a proper field for his son, and young Caldecott became a banker. One of his banks was located in the farmlands of Shropshire. Here in the country, he lived with a farmer who helped introduce Caldecott to prancing pigs and horses and cows and dogs that later romped through his book illustrations. He switched from banking to books in the 1870s, moving to London but continuing his studies of animals, sometimes dissecting them to study their structure. In his art, his subjects were usually mobile and lively, though Caldecott himself in later years suffered rheumatic fever and had trouble climbing two flights of stairs.

One of his illustrations for *The Diverting History of John Gilpin: Showing How He Went Farther Than He Intended, and Came Home Safe Again,* by William Cowper, shows Gilpin clinging to a runaway horse as it gallops through a village, disrupting geese and astounding staid country folk. In 1938, the American Library Association began giving an annual award for the most distinguished illustrations in an American picture book. The design of the medal struck for the award is adapted from the picture of grim Mr. Gilpin on his wild horse ride.

Like many twentieth-century artists, Caldecott did not begin his career as a children's book illustrator. His first major job, in 1875, was illustrating a book for adults, Washington Irving's *Sketch-Book* (Carus 148).) Like all other trend-setting artists in the nineteenth century, and the best of those who followed them, Caldecott was a mature craftsman, careful of detail even when he was most whimsical.

EVALUATING PICTURE BOOKS

Being able to help children enjoy and appreciate good picture books means being able to make judgments yourself about the quality of specific books. Then you are able to match the books with the child or class. Figure 6-7 lists nine criteria that can be applied. As you read them, review for yourself what

---

1. Text and illustrations should both build the story.
2. The style and medium of the illustrations should be appropriate for the text.
3. The language should be clear and evocative.
4. Characters should be well delineated and possibly developed.
5. The text and illustrations should be free of stereotypes.
6. The setting, if specific, should be presented accurately in both text and illustrations.
7. The book's tone should not be condescending.
8. The book's size, type, jacket, title page design, and spacing of text and illustrations should be appropriate for the content of the book.
9. The paper and binding should be durable and of high quality.

Figure 6-7   Guidelines for evaluating picture books.

you have just read about text and illustrations working together. Reread the language quoted from *Appalachia, the Voices of the Singing Birds.* Think about how the books described meet these criteria.

SELECTING PICTURE BOOKS

Whether selecting books far in advance while planning a unit of study or finding just the right book to fit the mood of the class during a lunch break, teachers keep in mind the need to choose books of high literary quality. But they frequently use other criteria as well. Key among these are content, literary or artistic elements, author and illustrator, and multicultural representation.

Content

Watching her first graders struggle with their coats and boots, look for lost mittens, and fumble with zippers and buttons, Diane felt sympathy for the hassle they were experiencing. "Do we have to wear our boots?" they asked. "It's not cold—I don't need to look for my mittens." She knew just the book for them—*Thomas' Snowsuit* by Robert Munsch. Thomas' mother gives him a new brown snowsuit, which Thomas immediately declares is ugly and in the same breath says he will not wear. His mother responds that they'll see about that, and the contest begins. She gets him into it and sends him to school, where he again says "no" to the snowsuit. When the teacher tries to get him into it, they have "an enormous fight," with her ending up in the snowsuit and Thomas in her dress. When the principal intervenes, the clothes get switched again. The slapstick comedy of both text and illustration delights the children, who want to hear the book reread immediately and who eagerly follow the teacher's suggestion that they join with Thomas each time he says, "No."

Diane chose the book because of its content. It fit what was going on in the classroom, and she read it to the whole class. Earlier in the year she had brought in a book just for Carla, who was going to the zoo *with* her aunt, and *without* any of her six siblings. It was to be a very special day. Diane gave her *Just Us Women* by Jeanette Caines, knowing she would empathize with the little girl who travels by car to North Carolina with her Aunt Martha. They eat what they want, stop along the way, and enjoy the trip for just the two of them, a trip for "just us women."

The content in both books related to the lives of the children. For both groups and individuals, there will be many times when books seem to fit naturally. A book may fit the lighter moments, such as debating over a snowsuit; the important times, such as a special trip with a special person; or even the very difficult times, such as adjusting to the divorce of parents or the death of a grandparent.

Diane also chose books for their content as she and the children explored the topic of oceans. Both fiction and nonfiction filled the classroom. Diane knew that a wide selection of picture books would allow the

Picture books may show street signs, advertisements, other environmental print, and a variety of forms of print. Young children can point out the print and see if they can identify any of the words.

A young girl and her aunt plan a trip to North Carolina together. (Source: Illustration from JUST US WOMEN by Jeannette Caines, Illustration by Pat Cummings. Copyright © 1982 HarperCollins Publishers. Reprinted with permission.)

children to see many facets of the topic, to select books whose text and illustrations they understood, to read together, to learn how information can be found in books, and to expand their knowledge of oceans and ocean life.

Literary or Artistic Element

Teachers help children learn about literature when they select books with literary or artistic elements in mind and build on the strength of these elements in discussions and other book-related activities with children. The children's work in Figure 6-8 shows exploration of both plot and setting. In drawing the **story maps,** the children had to keep in mind the structure of the story (What happened when Pearl left school?). And they had to add the setting, putting in the forest, the boulder, and Pearl's home. They also saw the relationship between these two elements. Yet this was not a formal lesson about plot, but rather an activity that allowed the children to show their understanding of the story and to retell it in their own words.

Mary wanted her small class of ESL students to learn about the work of several authors and illustrators, to hear English used effectively, and to begin visualizing the action of a story as they listened. Over the course of a week, she read several books by William Steig, and the children compared his characters, how they talked and how they looked, how their personalities were similar and different. By the end of the week, the children could identify a Steig book and were taking them out of the library on their own.

When Mary read *The Amazing Bone* (Steig, William. New York: Farrar, 1976), she showed the illustrations and encouraged the children to think about where the action was taking place. After the reading, the children listed the characters and the settings.

Characters	*Places* (Setting)
Pearl Pig	school
three robbers	city
fox	forest
Pearl's parents	big boulder
	fox's house
	Pearl's home

In the story, Pearl Pig dawdles around town before heading home from school, takes her time walking in the forest between her home and the school, finds a bone that can talk, is accosted by three robbers who had hidden behind a boulder, is captured by a fox who takes Pearl and the bone to his home, and finally gets away when the bone says magic words that shrink the fox. She and the bone go to her home where her parents had been "frazzled with worry." Pearl, her parents, and the talking bone settle down to a happy life.

Mary discussed maps with the children, and together they drew a map showing the route from their classroom to the school library. Then the children listened to a second reading of *The Amazing Bone*, knowing that they were each going to create a map of the places in the story and place the characters somewhere on the map.

Once the maps were completed, the children shared them with one another and retold the story, moving their fingers to show the route of the characters. In making the maps, the children had to visualize the places and their relationship to one another, which in turn related to the action of the story. Retelling focused on the sequence of the action and involved cause and effect. Mary was able to hear the language the children used and assess their understanding as they participated in the retellings.

Figure 6-8   Creating and using story maps.

Young children can learn to recognize plot structures through such activities. They will see that many folktales have a cumulative plot; that some stories have a similar structure of a character leaving home, completing a task, and returning home a changed person even though the characters are very different from one another; and that books such as *If You Give a Mouse a Cookie* (Numeroff) and *Look Out Bird!* (Janovitz) have circular plots. And recognizing that a pattern of organization underlies most stories helps children know what to expect and how to interpret stories. Figure 6-9 shows how one teacher rethought an activity that was designed to help children recognize pattern within a story.

Looking at setting encourages children to be aware of the descriptive language used in the text and to be observant of detail in the illustrations. Picture

Here are maps drawn by three of the children.

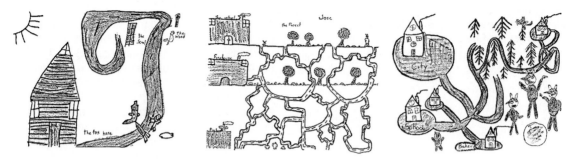

The schoolhouse is shown in all three, even though it is not shown but only mentioned in the story.

1. The first picture shows a direct story line, with the path from the school through the woods to the fox's house a single road. The child continued the story to end at Pearl's house even though her map ends at the fox's. She saw the action as Pearl leaving the safety of her school, facing danger in the woods, and finally arriving at the safety of her home.

2. In the second picture, Jose has made a maze of paths, all feasible given the story line. He showed more of the characters, and his retelling was filled with details.

3. In the third picture, the places shown were all mentioned, but their relationship to one another is confused. The bakery, the school, and the city are represented as three distinct places, rather than the bakery and the school being in the city. Pearl Pig's home is shown as near the school and the fox's house as far off in the woods. There is no reason, using this map, for Pearl to be walking in the woods to return home. When Hector retold the story using this map, he had difficulty moving the characters from place to place. His strength in the retelling was his recounting of Pearl's escape from the robbers.

Mary found that these story maps helped the children follow the action of the story, encouraged their use of oral language in the retellings, and gave her valuable information about how each child's understanding of the story, its plot, its setting, and its characters.

Figure 6-8   *continued*

books can be travelogues for young viewers. Peter Parnall's illustrations for *Hawk, I'm Your Brother* (Baylor) capture the spaciousness of the southwest. Trina Schart Hyman's illustrations for *The Fortune Tellers* (Alexander) set this tale in Cameroon and depict the beauty of the landscape, the activities in a small village, and the intricacy of the designs on fabric and pottery. Children should be given time to look closely at the illustrations, to talk about what they see, and to compare the settings in the books with places they know.

As you select books, it may be helpful to read what people from the country represented have to say about them. In one study of Chinese as portrayed in picture books, the researcher noted that the main flaw was the lack of cultural authenticity, but recommended the work of Ed Young, Lily Toy Hong, Demi, Allen Say, and Thomas Handforth, among others (Cai 187).

THE LESSON AS PLANNED AND TAUGHT	REFLECTIONS . . .
Rationale Elena wanted her third graders to understand story structure. She also wanted them to be aware of sequencing when retelling a story.	The reason for accurate sequencing in retelling a story is to maintain the logic of the plot and to show the development of relationships. In *Jumanji* the beginning in which the two children find the game and the ending where they see two others picking it up must be held constant. The internal events, where the game becomes real and landing on a square on the board causes a series of animals to invade the house, could come in any order, with no disruption to the story. Thus this activity was more a memory test than an explication of logic or structure in a story.
The Lesson Elena began by showing the cover of *Jumanji* by Chris Van Allsburg (Boston: Houghton, 1981) and asking what *jumanji* might mean. Following this discussion she told the children that they were to listen carefully because each student in this group of seven would help retell the story in order. After the reading, they talked about the story, then retold it, with different students continuing plot. Elena then asked each student to select one event and illustrate it. She made a list so that events would not be duplicated. When the illustrations were completed, they were pasted in sequence onto a large sheet of posterboard. Each student retold the part of the story represented by his or her picture.	Elena decided that next time she would select a story where events had to be correctly sequenced for it to make sense. Then children could see how events were related. She might also use this as a means, rather than an end in itself. If the students made pictures, perhaps they could retell the story for the rest of the class. They might want to recall exact sequencing to dramatize the story.

Figure 6-9   On second thought: Activities involving sequencing.

Selecting books based on their themes provides an opening for discussing abstract ideas and a concrete experience on which that discussion can be built. Seeing Osa in *Osa's Pride* (Grifalconi) become so proud that she thinks that her believing can make something true or not is an opening for children to discuss the possibility of being too proud. Figure 6-10 shows the writing three first-grade children did after listening to *Jim Meets the Thing* (Cohen) and talk-

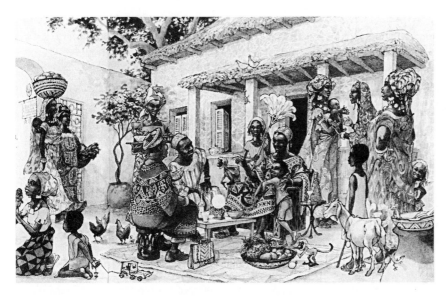

The illustrations in The Fortune Tellers, *set in Camaroon, show the intricacy of the designs on fabric and pottery. (Source:* Illustration from THE FORTUNE-TELLERS by Lloyd Alexander, illustrated by Trina Schart Hyman. Copyright © 1992 by Trina Schart Hyman, illustrations. Used by permission of Dutton Children's books, a division of Penguin Books USA Inc.)

ing about their own fears. These children were able to identify the theme when the teacher phrased her question, "In this story, what did Jim learn?"

Certain characters in picture books could almost be called celebrities because they are so well known. Madeline remains her assertive self through a series of books about her by Ludwig Bemelmans, and saying "big red dog" to kindergartners will usually bring the immediate response of "Clifford!" (Bridwell). Teachers help children explore characterization by sharing books that have the same character in a variety of situations, such as the series of books about Everett Anderson (Clifton) or those that have Christopher (Carrick) as the protagonist. They may ask children to describe characters, what they think they are like and how they've reached those conclusions. Hearing *Flossie and the Fox* (McKissack), children note that Flossie is clever because she is able to trick the fox, and that the fox is not so clever, because he spends his time trying to convince Flossie that he *is* a fox and thus does not steal the eggs she is carrying. They contrast the way each speaks, Flossie with a Black dialect of the rural south and the fox with the vocabulary and syntax of an upper-class "gentleman." When children dramatize the story, they think even more about what they know and feel about the characters.

McKissack's use of the two dialects is one aspect of style. The effects of an author's writing style are evident when primary grade children use vocabulary or phrases in their own writing from stories they've heard. Selecting books with a variety of styles demonstrates to children the possi-

Plan: Jill loved sharing the books of Miriam Cohen with her first-grade students. Set in classrooms very much like their own, Cohen's books show life as it is for many children—with their concerns about friendship, learning to read, taking tests, learning from those who are different from oneself, coping with life when you are five- or six- or seven-years-old. On this day she reads *Jim Meets the Thing* (Cohen, Miriam. Ill. by Lillian Hoban. New York: Greenwillow, 1981) to the whole class.

In the book, Jim and many of his classmates had watched "The Thing" on television. Jim had nightmares and was still frightened when he arrived at school, but his friends thought it was great. When they suspect his fear, he denies it. Later in the day, however, Jim is the only one not afraid of a praying mantis that has landed on Danny's shoulder. His brave removal of the insect and his carrying it to a safe spot earn him the name of "Mantis Man" and lead to the conclusion that everybody gets scared sometimes.

After the story, the children began telling about things that frightened them and expressed much empathy for Jim. They were surprised to hear their teacher say that she, too, was afraid at times. The children were asked to think about one thing they were afraid of and why. They then wrote about their fears and illustrated their stories if they wished.

Response: Here are three of the children's stories. They have used invented spelling, that is, used the words they want and spelled them as they think the words might be spelled. The teacher was pleased that the children felt comfortable enough with her and with their classmates to describe their fears. When they shared their words and pictures, they decided that just like Jim's class, different people sometimes were afraid of different things. They concluded their discussion by talking about what they could do when they were afraid.

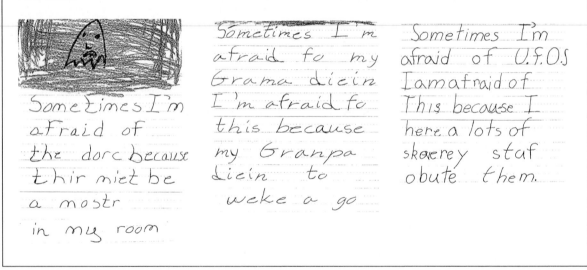

Figure 6-10   A discussion about fear: *Jim Meets the Thing.*

bilities that exist for telling a story. It may be nearly all narrative; it may rely heavily on dialogue to advance events; or it may be in a specialized form. *Farm Boy's Year* by David McPhail is in the form of a diary, with the 12-year-old boy describing his life on a New England farm in the 1800s, with one entry for each month.

As children experience the excitement of good stories, they also see a variety of styles of art and a range of media. When teachers group books so that children can see several that have expressionistic illustrations or watercolors, children can begin to make generalizations for themselves. Sometimes teachers encourage children to experiment with the media they have seen in picture books, making collage illustrations themselves or seeing how they can rub chalk to give soft edges to the objects they have drawn.

Author/Illustrator

One of the most successful ways of helping children become aware of style in either text or illustration is the study of an author or illustrator. The work of author/illustrators such as Tomie dePaola, Pat Hutchins, William Steig, and many others is so distinctive that children develop a feel for their work and can identify it, even before being able to describe it. The class that made story maps of *The Amazing Bone* (Figure 6-8) did so as part of a unit on the books of Steig. They came to view him as a real person and to see books as being the work of individuals who created stories just as they did.

Multicultural Representation

As the cultural diversity of the students has increased, educators have become more aware of the need to present literature that represents a variety of cultural backgrounds and experiences. In thinking about selecting such materials, Junko Yokoto writes:

> Students from nonmainstream cultures can profit from having opportunities for understanding and developing pride in their heritage and for building a positive self-concept. In addition, for *all* students, multicultural literature provides vicarious experiences from cultures other than their own; and these experiences help them understand different backgrounds, thereby influencing their decisions about how they will live in this culturally pluralistic world. (156)

Thus teachers make a conscious effort to include books that represent various cultural groups, both within their own country and globally. They share them in ways that encourage children to empathize with the characters. Aoki suggests that one way to do this is to have students pretend they are the character and answer questions about how they feel and why they have behaved in particular ways (127).

Teachers also make a conscious effort to find literature that accurately reflects the lives and beliefs of various groups. This means locating the books, assessing their accuracy, and presenting them to children with the most specific information you have. That is, the characters are Mexican, or Puerto Rican—not just Hispanic. It is an Ashanti folktale, not just an African folktale. A teacher sharing *Crow Boy* by Taro Yashima would tell children that the story is set in a village in Japan where the author grew up. The book was published in 1955, and if the author was around 30 years old, then the story would have taken place around 1930. This is important information for the children to have. It will help them recognize that cultures are diverse and continually changing and evolving.

Literature allows the reader to see similarities among groups as well as to appreciate differences. Figure 6-11 gives pairs or triads of picture books that have similar topics or themes, yet represent different cultural groups.

The following books are grouped by topic or theme with characters that represent differing ethnic, racial, or national groups.

Ekoomiak, Normee. *Arctic Memories.* New York: Holt, 1988. The author/artist describes his childhood in arctic Canada with a series of pictures accompanied by text in both English and Inuikitut. (Quebec—Inuit)

Garza, Carmen Lomas. *Family Pictures.* San Francisco: Children's Book Press, 1990. The author/artist describes her childhood in a Hispanic community in Texas in a series of pictures accompanied by text in both English and Spanish. (US—Hispanic {Mexican})

Hoffman, Mary. *Amazing Grace.* Ill. by Caroline Binch. New York: Dial, 1991. Grace's classmates tell her she can't play the part of Peter Pan because she is female and black, but she knows she can be anything she wants and gets the part. (US—African American)

Say, Allen. *El Chino.* Boston: Houghton Mifflin, 1990. Bong Way Wong, called Billy after he emigrates from China to Arizona, believes his father when he says that BIlly can be whatever he wants; Billy becomes the first Chinese matador—even though he is not Spanish. (US—Chinese American)

Marzollo, Jean. *Close Your Eyes.* Ill. by Susan Jeffers. New York: Dial, 1978. The illustrations for this lullaby show the father getting his son ready for bed and the words to the lullaby as well. (US—Caucasian)

Osofsky, Audrey. *Dreamcatcher.* Ill. by Ed Young. New York: Orchard, 1992. As the baby drifts off to sleep, big sister weaves a net to catch the bad dreams. (US—Native American {Ojibway})

Lee, Jeanne M. *Silent Lotus.* New York: Farrar, 1991. Lotus, a young Cambodian girl who cannot speak or hear, is taken to the city where she sees the temple dancers, learns to dance, performs for the royal court, and eventually becomes a famous dancer herself. (Cambodia)

Schroeder, Alan. *Ragtime Tumpie.* Ill. by Bernie Fuchs. Boston: Little, Brown, 1989. Based on an incident in the life of Josephine Baker, this book tells about Tumpie's desire to dance to ragtime music and her winning of a silver dollar in a dance contest as a child. (US—African American)

Bunting, Eve. *The Wednesday Surprise.* Ill. by Donald Carrick. New York: Clarion, 1989. Anna's surprise for the family is that she has taught her grandmother to read. (US—Caucasian)

Heide, Florence Parry, and Judith Heide Gilliland. *The Day of Ahmed's Secret.* Ill. by Ted Lewin. New York: Lothrop, 1990. Ahmed's surprise for his family, when he returns from his work of delivering fuel, is that he has learned to write his name. (Cairo)

Figure 6-11   Multicultural representations in books with similar topics or themes.

Miles, Miska. *Annie and the Old One.* Ill. by Peter Parnall. Boston: Little, Brown, 1971. Annie's grandmother helps Annie understand that there is a time for all things to return to the earth, and that time cannot be held back. (US—Native American {Navajo})

Nodar, Carmen Santiago. *Abuelita's Paradise.* Ill. by Diane Paterson. Morton Grove, IL: Whitman, 1992. Marita sits in her grandmother's rocking chair and remembers the stories her grandmother told her about growing up in Puerto Rico, and her mother consoles her over her abuelita's death. (US and Puerto Rico—Hispanic)

Dorros, Arthur. *Abuela.* Ill. by Elisa Kleven. New York: Dutton, 1991. Rosalba imagines flying over Manhattan with her grandmother, looking down at the buildings and activity below. A glossary translates Spanish words and phrases interspersed in the English text. (US—Hispanic)

Ringgold, Faith. *Tar Beach.* New York: Crown, 1991. Cassie Louise Lightfoot imagines herself leaving the tar beach, the rooftop of the Harlem apartment building where she lives, and flying over the city, free to go wherever she wants. (US—African American)

Caines, Jeannette. *Daddy.* Ill. by Ronald Himler. New York: Harper, 1977. The child of divorced parents described waiting for her father to pick her up and the things she does on her visit with him. (US—African American)

Christiansen, C. B. *My Mother's House, My Father's House.* Ill. by Irene Trivas. New York: Atheneum, 1989. A little girl describes living half the week at her mother's and half the week at her father's, and says that when she grows up she will have one house for all the time. (US—Caucasian)

Bunting, Eve. *Fly Away Home.* Ill. by Ronald Himler. New York: Clarion, 1991. Andrew and his father are making the airport their home until his father earns enough money for them to rent an apartment. (US—Caucasian)

Heide, Florence Parry, and Judith Heide Gilliland. *Sami and the Time of the Troubles.* Ill. by Ted Lewin. New York: Clarion, 1992. Sami and his family live in the basement of his uncle's house, emerging only when there is a break in the fighting and gunfire. (Beirut)

Crews, Donald. *Bigmama's.* New York: Greenwillow, 1991. The author describes his childhood trips to visit his grandmother in Cottondale, Florida. (US—African American)

Hines, Anna Grossmickle. *Grandma Gets Grumpy.* New York: Clarion, 1988. Five children learn that there is a limit to what their grandmother will allow when she babysits with them for an evening. (US—Caucasian)

Nomurs, Takaaki. *Grandpa's Town.* Translated by Amanda Stinchecum. New York: Kane/Miller, 1991. When Yuuta visits his grandfather and goes with the old man on his daily schedule, he learns that his grandfather has many friends and is not lonely living alone. Text in English and Japanese. (Japan)

Figure 6-11 *continued*

Dorros, Arthur. *Radio Man.* New York: HarperCollins, 1993. Diego relies on his radio for company as he and his family drive through several western states picking fruits and vegetables. In English and Spanish. (US—Hispanic {Mexican})

Williams, Sherley Anne. *Working Cotton.* Ill. by Carole Byard. San Diego: Harcourt, 1992. Shelan describes working in the cotton fields near Fresno, from the early morning bus ride through the long day in the fields. (US—African American)

Friedman, Ina R. *How My Parents Learned to Eat.* Ill. by Allen Say. Boston: Houghton Mifflin, 1984. The American sailor and the Japanese schoolgirl each learned to use the utensils of the other. After they were married, the family eats with chopsticks some days and knives and forks on others. (Japan, US—Japanese, Caucasian)

Medearis, Angela Shelf. *Dancing with the Indians.* Ill. by Samuel Byrd. New York: Holiday, 1991. In the 1930s a young girl goes with her family to an Indian powwow, joining in the dances and remembering that the Seminoles had rescued their grandfather from slavery. (US—African American, Native American) {Seminole})

Polacco, Patricia. *Mrs. Katz and Tush.* New York: Bantam, 1992. As Larnel helps Mrs. Katz care for an abandoned kitten, he learns about her coming to the United States from Poland and about her Jewish heritage. (US—Jewish, African American)

Figure 6-11   *continued*

Sharing these books with children can let them explore the common feelings or experiences among characters while also learning about the culture of the characters.

In addition, some picture books that, through their content or theme, directly address cultural differences and the understanding of those differences. Peter Spier's *People* describes and pictures people all over the world and shows how different groups engage in particular activities. What do they eat, what are their religions, what do they wear, what makes them laugh? This quick overview shows that people are not all alike, but that they have comparable needs. Lankford looked at just one small item—the game of hopscotch—in her book *Hopscotch Around the World.* Almost like the story of Cinderella, this game has made its way around the world with variations on a recognizable underlying structure. Playing the games is a way to begin to build acceptance and positive attitudes toward others.

The issue of stereotypical thinking can be addressed with a discussion following the reading of *Somewhere in Africa* (Mennen and Daly) or *Gila Monsters Meet You at the Airport* (Sharmat). In the first book, Ashraf, who lives in Africa, is reading a book about Africa that is filled with pictures of lions and zebras; it is Ashraf's favorite book. He likes reading about these animals because he has never seen them—he lives in an African city.

In the second book, a boy from New York city is moving "Out West," and his friend Seymour tells him what to expect. There will be cactus everywhere, he'll have to ride a horse to school, everybody will be named Slim or Tex, and, of course, gila monsters will meet him at the airport. At the airport "Out West" he meets a boy who is moving East and who knows that in the East, gangsters with flowers in their lapels fill the streets, and people sit on top of each other as they ride the subway cars to work. Both books can stimulate children to examine their own thinking about particular places and peoples.

Tarvone, the five-year-old from California who flew to New York with his family, learned firsthand about a new place. But there are many places he will never see and many peoples he will never encounter in person. Picture books let him learn about a larger world and help him develop an attitude of openness to and interest in the human condition.

SUMMARY

There is great variety in children's picture books, those books in which illustrations are as important as the text in presenting information or telling a story. Children can respond to these books in many ways. Foremost, of course, is listening to an adult read the book and simply enjoying the story. Often, however, teachers and other adults will encourage children to respond actively. Children can be involved in singing refrains or dramatizing song picture books; they can add the narrative or dialogue to wordless books; they can use the illustrations to learn about a place or a group of people.

Illustrators of picture books make choices about the content they will portray, the medium they will use, and the style of art they will employ as they reflect, clarify, or extend the text. Evaluating picture books means looking both at these decisions and the ability of the artist to execute them effectively. Illustrations and text should combine to tell the story, with the illustrations developing the story visually as much as the text does verbally.

When teachers select picture books to share with children, they first want to select books of high quality. Beyond that, however, are considerations of how and why the book might be presented. They may select a book because its content fits the needs of a class or individual or because it will be part of a unit of study. They may select it for its theme or as part of the study of one author or illustrator. They will keep in mind the need to provide multicultural representation in the books they present, and they may select books specifically to explore the lives of various peoples.

Early illustrators, such as George Cruickshank, Walter Crane, Kate Greenaway, and Randolph Caldecott, set the stage for lively art in picture books. As production techniques have become more sophisticated, artists have been able to use more varied media in their illustrations. Children, when guided to look closely at illustrations, respond with increased understanding and appreciation. Picture books can begin their education in the visual arts and contribute to the development of visual literacy, as well as expose children to beautiful language and good stories. Figures 6-12 and 6-13 list many picture books from which teachers can make excellent choices for their students.

Bedard, Michael. *Emily.* Ill. by Barbara Cooney. New York: Doubleday, 1992.

Bowen, Gary. *Stranded at Plimoth Plantation 1626.* New York: HarperCollins, 1994.

Cherry, Lynne. *A River Ran Wild.* San Diego: Harcourt, 1992.

Cowcher, Helen. *Tigress.* New York: Farrar, 1991.

Demi. *Chingis Khan.* New York: Holt, 1992.

Dugan, Barbara. *Loop the Loop.* Ill. by James Stevenson. New York: Greenwillow, 1992.

Gerstein, Mordicai. *The Mountains of Tibet.* New York: Harper, 1987.

Goble, Paul. *Beyond the Ridge.* New York: Bradbury, 1989.

Maruki, Toshi. *Hiroshima No Pika.* New York: Lothrop, 1980.

Rosen, Michael J., ed. *Home. A Collaboration of Thirty Distinguished Authors and Illustrators of Children's Books to Aid the Homeless.* New York: Harper, 1992.

Rylant, Cynthia. *An Angel for Solomon Singer.* Ill. by Peter Catalanotto. New York: Orchard, 1992.

San Souci, Robert D. *Feathertop.* Ill. by Daniel San Souci. New York: Doubleday, 1992.

Sewell, Marcia. *The Pilgrims of Plimoth.* New York: Atheneum,1986.

Shulevitz, Uri. *Toddlecreek Post Office.* New York: Farrar, 1990.

Turner, Ann. *Heron Street.* Ill. by Lisa Desimini. New York: Harper, 1989.

Van Allsburg, Chris. *The Stranger.* Boston: Houghton Mifflin, 1986.

Figure 6-12   Picture books for older children.

Aardema, Verna. *Why Mosquitoes Buzz in People's Ears.* Ill. by Leo and Diane Dillon. New York: Dial, 1975. This retelling of a West African folktale is illustrated with paintings reminiscent of African folk art.

Allard, Harry. *Miss Nelson Is Missing.* Ill. by James Marshall. Boston: Houghton Mifflin, 1977. The children in Miss Nelson's class regret their bad behavior when Miss Viola Swamp arrives to substitute.

Cooney, Barbara. *Island Boy.* New York: Viking, 1988. Matthais was born on the island and died at sea, a grandfather, in this story about the New England land he loved.

Crews, Donald. *Freight Train.* New York: Morrow, 1978. Simple text and illustrations name the cars on a freight train and capture its motion.

de Paola, Tomie. *Strega Nona.* Englewood Cliffs, NJ: Prentice Hall, 1975. In this folktale, Big Anthony hears the words *Strega Nona* used to cause her magic pasta pot to boil but does not notice the three kisses that will cause it to stop.

Ehlert, Lois. *Feathers for Lunch.* New York: Harcourt, 1990. The cat is out, but even though it sees many birds, it gets only feathers for lunch in this rhyming story with brilliantly colored illustrations.

Fox, Mem. *Hattie and the Fox.* Ill. by Patricia Mullins. New York: Bradbury, 1988. Hattie the hen keeps noticing parts of the fox in this cumulative tale but is not frightened until the whole animal appears.

Goble, Paul. *The Girl Who Loved Wild Horses.* New York: Macmillan, 1978. A Plains Indian girl loves horses so much that she chooses to live with them and be transformed into one in this book illustrated with stylized paintings that invoke Native American artistic traditions.

Henkes, Kevin. *Chrysanthemum.* New York: Greenwillow, 1991. Chrysanthemum loves her name until she goes to school where she is teased about it, but acceptance comes with assurance from her parents and the knowledge that her music teacher, Mrs. Delphinium Twinkle, is planning to name her baby Chrysanthemum.

Hutchins, Pat. *Rosie's Walk.* New York: Macmillan, 1968. When Rosie the hen goes for a walk, she is oblivious to the fox that is stalking her and to all the trouble it encounters.

Figure 6-13   Touchstone picture books.

Keats, Ezra Jack. *The Snowy Day.* New York: Viking, 1962. Collage illustrations show Peter's day in the snow, even the snowball he puts in his pocket to save.

Lionni, Leo. *Swimmy.* New York: Pantheon, 1968. Swimmy and the other small fish learn that they can frighten the big fish away when they swim together like one huge fish.

McCloskey, Robert. *Make Way for Ducklings.* New York: Viking, 1941. For over 50 years children have been enjoying Mrs. Mallard's search in Boston for a home for her ducklings.

Marshall, James. *George and Martha.* Boston: Houghton Mifflin, 1972. These two good hippopotamus friends appear in a series of adventures within this book and in the books that follow, as their friendship endures their various foibles.

Say, Allen. *Grandfather's Journey.* Boston: Houghton Mifflin, 1993. A young boy describes his grandfather's life in Japan and in California, and then tells how he himself has come to love two countries.

Sendak, Maurice. *Where the Wild Things Are.* New York: Harper, 1963. Max is sent to bed without his supper, but once in his bedroom he sets sail for the land of the wild things, where he can be king.

Steig, William. *Doctor DeSoto.* New York: Farrar, 1962. Dr. DeSoto is a very good dentist, and a clever one too, since even though he is a mouse, he finds a way to treat the fox and not be eaten.

Williams, Vera. *A Chair for My Mother.* New York: Greenwillow, 1982. After a fire, the family saves their coins to buy one comfortable chair where the mother can rest when she comes home from work.

Van Allsburg, Chris. *The Polar Express.* Boston: Houghton Mifflin, 1985. On a Christmas Eve trip to the North Pole, a little boy is given a silver bell by Santa, a bell that only those who truly believe can hear.

Yolen, Jane. *Owl Moon.* Ill. by John Schoenherr. New York: Philomel, 1987. Soft watercolor illustrations show the night woods as a young child and her father go looking for owls.

Figure 6-13 *continued*

⌒ EXPLORE ON YOUR OWN

1. **Explore Your Personal Response.** Compare the same book in two different formats, such as hardcover and paperback, paper and board book, or original size and reduced size. Which format do you prefer? Why?
2. **Apply Literary Criteria.** Compare a Caldecott winner with the honor books of the same year. Select the book you think has the best illustrations. Write one to two pages defending your choice.

or

Read any four picture books illustrated by the same artist. Describe the style and apparent media; analyze any differences that you notice in the artwork.

3. **Prepare to Share Literature With Children.** Select three picture books. Order them from the easiest to the most difficult and explain your rankings. You might want to try this with wordless books.

⌒ EXPLORE WITH CHILDREN

1. **Explore Children's Responses.** Ask three children in grade 4 or above to tell about a book they liked when they were in kindergarten or grade 1. What do they remember about it? What made it special for them?

or

Share a picture book with a group of primary grade children. After reading it, ask them to close their eyes and picture something from the book and imagine the words they hear. Then have them share the images and phrases. Why do you think these particular images and words came to their minds?

2. **Engage Children With Literature.** Share a picture book with a small group of children.

After reading the story, go back through the book, asking children what they notice in the illustrations (both content and the artist's use of line, space, and color).

or

Select three picture books by two different illustrators. Cover the names of the authors and illustrators. Ask the children to sort the books into two groups and explain why they grouped them as they did. See if the artists' styles were a factor. You might want to try having the children do a second grouping after they have explained the method they used first.

⌒ SUGGESTED PROFESSIONAL REFERENCES

Bader, Barbara. *American Picturebooks from Noah's Ark to The Beast Within.* New York: Macmillan, 1976. § This book, enhanced by numerous illustrations, provides a clear sense of the background of the contemporary picture book.

Benedict, Susan, and Lenore Carlisle, eds. *Beyond Words: Picture Books for Older Readers and Writers.* Portsmouth, NH: Heinemann, 1992. § Contributors to this book explore the value of picture books for older students, and teachers from grade 1 through high school describe how they have used picture books in their classrooms.

Brown, Marcia. *Lotus Seeds: Children's Pictures and Books.* New York: Scribner's, 1986. § Brown writes about her own work, on picture books in general, and about the publishing process in this collection of essays and speeches.

Cianciolo, Patricia. *Picture Books for Children.* 3rd ed. Chicago: American Library Association, 1990. § After discussing the picture book as a literary form, Cianciolo provides an annotated list of books, often suggesting books for comparison.

Cummings, Julie, ed. *Children's Book Illustration and Design.* Glen Cove, NY: PBC International, Inc.,

1992. § The work of over 80 contemporary illustrators of children's books is carefully photographed, showing a broad range of style and media.

Hall, Susan. *Using Picture Storybooks to Teach Literary Devices.* Phoenix: Oryx Press, 1990. § After briefly introducing which terms are defined and explaining the rationale for using picture books with older children, Hall lists books, with annotations, under the literary devices they employ.

Kiefer, Barbara Z. *The Potential of Picturebooks: From Visual Literacy to Aesthetic Understanding.* Englewood Cliffs, NJ: Prentice-Hall, 1995. § How children respond to picture books, how picture books are created, and how they can be used in the classroom are discussed within the context of the picture book as art.

Marcus, Leonard S. *Awakened by the Moon.* Boston: Beacon Press, 1992. § This biography of Margaret Wise Brown explores the role this author and illustrator played in developing the modern picture book through her work in the 1930s and 1940s.

Martin, Douglas. *The Telling Line.* New York: Delacorte, 1989. § The author presents interviews with 15 twentieth-century British illustrators.

Meyer, Susan. *A Treasury of Great Children's Book Illustrators.* New York: Abrams, 1983. § This book describes how social and economic conditions influenced the publication of illustrated children's books and analyzes the work of 13 illustrators of the Victorian period.

Nodelman, Perry. *Words About Pictures: The Narrative Art of Children's Picture Books.* Athens: University of Georgia Press, 1988. § Nodelman analyzes how images and words elicit responses, identifying interpretive skills necessary for understanding how illustrations in picture books provide narrative.

Schwarcz, Joseph, and Chava Schwarcz. *The Picture Book Comes of Age: Looking at Childhood Through the Art of Illustration.* Chicago: American Library Association, 1991. § In a series of essays, the authors look at the messages within illustrations in children's picture books, drawing on illustrators from many countries and looking in depth at three of Maurice Sendak's books.

Sendak, Maurice. *Caldecott & Co.: Notes on Books and Pictures.* New York: Farrar, 1988. § These articles, speeches, interviews, and book reviews, which Sendak produced over a period of 30 years, give a comprehensive picture of his approach to creating children's books.

Shulevitz, Uri. *Writing with Pictures: How to Write and Illustrate Children's Books.* New York: Watson-Guptill, 1985. § Shulevitz clearly describes what picture books are, how they are created both aesthetically and technically, and what he sees as the illustrator's responsibility.

Stewig, John Warren. *Looking at Picture Books.* Fort Atkinson, WI: Highsmith, 1995. § Stewig addresses the visual elements in illustration, the selection of medium, book design, and the influence of various art movements on children's book illustration as he writes of the importance of visual literacy.

⌘ CHILDREN'S BOOKS CITED

Aliki. *Go Tell Aunt Rhody.* New York: Macmillan, 1974.

Alexander, Lloyd. *The Fortune Tellers.* Ill. by Trina Schart Hyman. New York: Dutton, 1992.

Baylor, Byrd. *Hawk, I'm Your Brother.* Ill. by Peter Parnall. New York: Scribner's, 1976.

Bemelmans, Ludwig. *Madeline.* New York: Viking, 1939.

Brett, Jan. *Berlioz the Bear.* New York: Putnam, 1991.

Bridwell, Norman. *Clifford, the Big Red Dog.* New York: Scholastic, 1963.

Briggs, Raymond. *The Snowman.* New York: Random House, 1978.

Browne, Anthony. *The Tunnel.* New York: Knopf, 1989.

Bunting, Eve. *Smoky Night.* Ill. by David Diaz. San Diego: Harcourt, 1994.

Caines, Jeanette. *Just Us Women.* Ill. by Pat Cummings. New York: Harper, 1982.

Carrick, Carol. *The Accident.* Ill. by Donald Carrick. New York: Seabury, 1974.

Carrick, Carol. *The Foundling.* Ill. by Donald Carrick. New York: Seabury, 1977.

Carrick, Carol. *Lost in the Storm.* Ill. by Donald Carrick. New York: Seabury, 1974.

Cherry, Lynne. *A River Ran Wild.* San Diego: Harcourt, 1993.

Clifton, Lucille. *Everett Anderson's Goodbye.* Ill. by Ann Grifalconi. New York: Holt, 1983.

Clifton, Lucille. *Everett Anderson's Nine Month Long.* Ill. by Ann Grifalconi. New York: Holt, 1978.

Clifton, Lucille. *Everett Anderson's 1-2-3.* Ill. by Ann Grifalconi. New York: Holt, 1973.

Clifton, Lucille. *Some of the Days of Everett Anderson.* Ill. by Evaline Ness. New York: Holt, 1970.

Cohen, Miriam. *Jim Meets the Thing*. Ill. by Lillian Hoban. New York: Greenwillow, 1981.

Cooney, Barbara. *Miss Rumphius*. New York: Viking, 1982.

Cowper, William. *The Diverting History of John Gilpin*. Ill. by Randolph Caldecott. London: Warne, 1878.

Crane, Walter. *The Baby's Opera*. London: Warne, 1877.

Cummings, Pat. Comp. *Talking with Artists*. New York: Bradbury, 1992.

De Sutter, Hank. *Who Says a Dog Goes Bow-wow?* Ill. by Suse MacDonald. New York: Doubleday, 1993.

Dragonwagon, Crescent. *Half a Moon and One Whole Star*. Ill. by Jerry Pinkney, New York: Macmillan, 1987.

Flanders, Michael. *The Hippopotamus Song: A Muddy Love Story*. Ill. by Nadine Westcott. Boston: Joy Street, 1991.

Geisert, Arthur. *Oink*. Boston: Houghton Mifflin, 1991.

Goffin, Josse. *OH!* New York: Abrams, 1991.

Goffin, Josse. *Who Is the Boss?* New York: Clarion, 1992.

Goode, Diane. *Diane Goode's Book of Silly Stories and Songs*. New York: Dutton, 1992.

Grifalconi, Ann. *Osa's Pride*. Boston: Little, Brown, 1990.

Hammerstein, Oscar, and Richard Rodgers. *A Read Nice Clambake*. Ill. by Nadine Bernard Westcott. Boston: Little, 1992.

Howe, James. *I Wish I Were a Cricket*. Ill. by Ed Young. San Diego: Harcourt, 1987.

Innocenti, Roberto. *Rose Blanche*. Mankato, MN: Creative Education, 1985.

Janovitz, Marilyn. *Look Out Bird!* New York: North-South Books, 1994.

Johnston, Tony. *Yonder*. Ill. by Lloyd Bloom. New York: Dial, 1988.

Lankford, Mary D. *Hopscotch Around the World*. Ill. by Karen Milone. New York: Morrow, 1992.

Locker, Thomas. *Family Farm*. New York: Dial, 1988.

Macaulay, David. *Black and White*. Boston: Houghton Mifflin, 1990.

Marshall, James (reteller). *Goldilocks and the Three Bears*. New York: Dial, 1988.

Maxner, Joyce. *Nicholas Cricket*. Ill. by William Joyce. New York: Harper, 1989.

McDermott, Gerald. *Zomo the Rabbit*. San Diego: Harcourt, 1992.

McKissack, Patricia. *Flossie & the Fox*. Ill. by Rachel Isadora. New York: Dial, 1986.

Mayer, Mercer, and Marianna Mayer. *One Frog Too Many*. New York: Dial, 1975.

McPhail, David. *Farm Boy's Year*. New York: Atheneum, 1992.

Mennen, Ingrid, and Niki Daly. *Somewhere in Africa*. Ill. by Nicolaas Maritz. New York: Dutton, 1990.

Munsch, Robert. *Thomas' Snowsuit*. Ill. by Michael Martchenko. Toronto: Annick Press, 1985.

Numeroff, Laura Joffe. *If You Give a Mouse a Cookie*. Ill. by Felicia Bond. New York: Harper, 1985.

Provensen, Alice, and Martin Provensen. *Shaker Lane*. New York: Viking, 1987.

Rylant, Cynthia. *Appalachia, the Voices of the Singing Birds*. Ill. by Barry Moser. San Diego: Harcourt, 1991.

Sendak, Maurice. *Where the Wild Things Are*. New York: Harper, 1963.

Sharmat, Marjorie. *Gila Monsters Meet You at the Airport*. 1980. Ill. by Byron Barton. New York: Puffin, 1983.

Spier, Peter. *People*. Garden City, NY: Doubleday, 1980.

Steptoe, John. *Mufaro's Beautiful Daughters*. New York: Morrow, 1987.

Tejima. *Owl Lake*. New York: Philomel, 1987.

Wiesner, David. *Tuesday*. New York: Clarion, 1991.

Williams, Vera. *"More, More, More," Said the Baby*. New York: Greenwillow, 1990.

Wisneiwski, David. *Rain Player*. New York: Clarion, 1991.

Yashima, Taro. *Crow Boy*. New York: Viking, 1955.

Yolen, Jane. *Letting Swift River Go*. Ill. by Barbara Cooney. Boston: Little, Brown, 1992.

Yolen, Jane. *Owl Moon*. Ill. by John Schoemherr. New York: Philomel, 1987.

☙ CHAPTER REFERENCES

Aoki, Elaine. "Turning the Page: Asian Pacific American Children's Literature." Ed. Violet Harris. *Teaching Multicultural Literature in Grades K–8*. Norwood, MA: Christopher-Gordon, 1992, 109–135.

Baird, Shirley B. "The Popularization of Folk Songs Through Children's Picture Books." *Children's Literature Association Quarterly* 11.3 (Fall 1986): 142–144.

Cai, Mingshui. "Images of Chinese and Chinese Americans Mirrored in Picture Books." *Children's Literature in Education* 25.3 (Sept. 1994): 169–188.

Carus, Marianne. "Randolph Caldecott, Father of the Modern Picture Book." *Journal of Youth Services in Libraries* 1.2 (Winter 1988): 143–151.

Diaz, David. "1995 Caldecott Acceptance Speech." *Journal of Youth Services in Libraries* 8.4 (Summer 1995): 343–346.

Elleman, Barbara. "Picture Book Potential." *Book Links* 5.4 (Mar. 1996): 5.

Flatley, Joannis, and Adele Rutland. "Using Wordless Picture Books to Teach Linguistically/Culturally Different Students." *The Reading Teacher* 40.3 (Dec. 1986): 276–281.

Jalongo, Mary Renck, and Karen D'Angelo Bromley. "Developing Linguistic Competence Through Song Picture Books." *The Reading Teacher* 37.9 (May 1984): 840–845.

Kiefer, Barbara. "Picture Books as Contexts for Literary, Aesthetic, and Real World Understandings." *Language Arts* 65.3 (Mar. 1988): 260–271.

Lindauer, Shelley L. "Wordless Books: An Approach to Visual Literacy." *Children's Literature in Education* 19.3 (Fall 1988): 136–142.

Stewig, John Warren. "Book Illustration: Key to Visual and Oral Literacy." Eds. John Stewig and Sam Sebesta. *Using Literature in the Elementary Classroom.* Urbana, IL: National Council of Teachers of English, 1989, 55–74.

Stewig, John Warren. "Reading Pictures, Reading Texts: Some Similarities." *The New Advocate* 5.1 (Winter 1992): 11–22.

Yokota, Junko. "Issues in Selecting Multicultural Literature." *Language Arts* 70.3 (Mar. 1993): 156–167.

Chapter Seven

Poetry: Bringing Poems for Children to Life

Poet Lilian Moore has written about a mouse named Adam, a country mouse who loves his home, its proximity to the garden, the quiet, and the view he has of the sky. Sometimes he thinks aloud. Looking at the old stone wall he loves, he says to his friend Junius:

See how these stones
trust
one another.
Stone resting on
stone
fitting curve and
edge
together.
Nothing but
stone
on
stone
shaping a wall
against
wind and weather. (4)

Junius simply agrees that it's true and carries on with his plan to get Adam to accompany him to the city. The next day on the ride to town in the back of a truck, Adam stares at a river below them and the sky above, and says:

The cloud
in the sky is
the cloud
in the river.

The sky's
blueness
lies there
too.

Tonight
the river will
receive a white
moon.

The sky is the
giver of
light
to the river." (24)[1]

Junius comments, "You do make a fellow look twice, Adam" (25). And this, of course, is what poets do—they make us look twice.

Moore's book, titled *I'll Meet You at the Cucumbers,* has much to say about poetry within the context of the story. When Amanda, Adam's pen friend in the city, takes him to the library and shows him several poems so that he will recognize his own "thoughts" as poetry, he reads "Grass" by Valerie Worth and says that poet really knows grass, and reads "Lumps" by Judith Thurman and says that poet really knows lumps. Moore shows that poets write about things they know and care about and that they often help the reader see objects or experiences in a new light.

Amanda has told Adam that what he writes is poetry and has shown him the work of other poets. But what exactly *is* poetry? Perhaps she has given the best answer by showing examples, for there is no *single* characteristic that differentiates poetry from prose. Poetry may express a depth of emotion, have an imaginative quality, use both the sound of the words and their meaning to communicate, but so does some prose. Much poetry rhymes but not all does. Many poems have a strong or regular rhythm, but not every one does.

Laurence Perrine writes that poetry

> is a kind of multidimensional language. Ordinary language—the kind that we use to communicate information—is one dimensional. It is directed at only part of the listener, his understanding. Its one dimension is intellectual. Poetry, which is language used to communicate experience, has at least four dimensions. If it is to communicate experience, it must be directed at the *whole* man, not just at

Look for more of Adam Mouse's poems in *Don't Be Afraid, Amanda* (New York: Atheneum, 1992) and *Adam Mouse's Book of Poems* (New York: Atheneum, 1992), both by Lilian Moore.

---

[1] *Source:* "See how these stones" poem; "The cloud . . . " poem and "You do make a fellow look twice, Adam" reprinted with the permission of Atheneum Books for Young Readers, an imprint of Simon & Schuster from I'LL MEET YOU AT THE CUCUMBERS by Lilian Moore. Text copyright © 1988 Lilian Moore.

In 1978, Eloise Greenfield published a small book of poetry entitled *Honey I Love and Other Love Poems* with illustrations by Leo and Diane Dillon (New York: Crowell, 1978). The first poem was also titled "Honey I Love," and in it the narrator told about the things she loved. She loved the way her cousin from the South talked; the way her dad would turn the hose on and let the children play in the spray on hot days; playing and laughing with her friend Renee; riding in her uncle's car; sitting quietly beside her mother on the sofa. What she doesn't love is having to go to sleep at night. The poem concludes

> I love a lot of things,
> a whole lot of things
> And honey,
> I love you, too. (n.p.)

In 1995, the initial poem was reissued as a single book, part of the *Let's Read Aloud* series for preschoolers (New York: HarperCollins, 1995). It is illustrated by Jan Spivey Gilchrist. The text is presented in smaller segments and is more fully illustrated. This time the poem concludes

> I love a lot of things,
> a whole lot of things
> And honey,
> I love ME, too. (n.p.)

The change in a single word changes the impact and theme of the poem. In the first edition, the focus is on the child's love of particular activities and the people around her. There is a sense of quiet satisfaction and warmth, of giving love to others. In the second edition, the focus is on self-esteem, the child's love of activities and people, but especially that she sees herself as worthy of love, and that she feels very good about herself. Changing just one word in the poem changes the entire theme; every word counts.

his understanding. It must involve not only his intelligence but also his senses, emotions, and imagination. Poetry, to the intellectual dimension, adds a sensuous dimension, an emotional dimension, and an imaginative dimension. (10)[2]

He adds that poetry achieves these extra dimensions by drawing more fully than ordinary language on such resources as imagery, sound repetition, rhythm, and other elements often associated with poetry, even though they are not unique to poetry. In sum, poetry relies on very concentrated language, with words carefully chosen and arranged, to communicate an idea or feeling. It is a succinct form of expression in which every word counts.

Figure 7-1 shows how changing just one word in a new edition of "Honey I Love" changes the theme of the poem.

---

[2] *Source:* Excerpt from SOUND AND SENSE; AN INTRODUCTION TO POETRY, Fifth Edition by Laurence Perrine, Copyright © 1977 by Harcourt Brace & Company, reprinted by permission of the publisher.

ELEMENTS OF POETRY

Here is a poem by the inventive and popular author, Eve Merriam.

Cheers
The frogs and the serpents each had a football team,
And I heard their cheer leaders in my dream:
"Bilgewater, bilgewater," called the frog,
"Bilgewater, bilgewater,
Sis, boom, bog!
Roll 'em off the log,
Slog 'em in the sog,
Swamp 'em, swamp 'em,
Muck mire quash!

"Sisyphus, Sisyphus," hissed the snake,
"Sibilant, syllabub,
Syllable-loo-ba-lay.
Scylla and Charybdis,
Sumac, asphodel,
How do you spell Success?
With an S-S-S!" (22)[3]

If it were written in prose, "Cheers" might sound something like this: "There were two football teams in a dream, one of frogs and one of snakes. They each had cheers for their team, one based on Greek mythology (for example, referring to Sisyphus, the cruel king of Corinth condemned for eternity to roll a stone up a hill in Hades only to have it roll down again when he neared the top) and the other based on swamps." The poem makes much more sense. Part of the reason for its power is Merriam's use of several strong poetic materials, among them rhyme and sound, rhythm, connotation, and denotation.

Rhyme and Sound

"Cheers" begins with a **couplet,** two successive lines ending in rhyming words; the rhyme scheme then varies throughout the poem. Rhymes help bind the poem together and make it pleasant to read aloud.

There are other powerful sounds. A series of *b*'s breaks up the first few lines of the frog chant, like little croaks. The cheer of the snakes is replete with the hiss of *s*'s. This repetition of a consonant is called **alliteration.** Merriam also repeats a vowel sound, the short *i* in "Sisyphus," in the first four lines of the snake cheer. This vowel repetition is called **assonance.** Some of the words carry extra power because they sound like what they mean. *Slog,* for instance, means

---

[3] *Source:* "Cheers" from IT DOESN'T ALWAYS HAVE TO RHYME by Eve Merriam. Copyright © 1964 Eve Merriam. Copyright Renewed 1992 Eve Merriam. Reprinted by permission of Marian Reiner.

Children enjoy saying rhyming poems and verses aloud.

"to strike with a heavy blow." Use of the word is an example of **onomatopoeia;** words such as *buzz, cuckoo, crack,* and *plink* are also onomatopoetic.

Merriam also uses **repetition,** repeating the *bilgewater* cheer of the frog and the "Sisyphus" of the snake. This repetition gives the poem the feel of a football cheer. In other poems, repetition may be used for emphasis or to give structure to a poem.

Rhythm

After the first slightly irregular couplet, the cheering animals come on with locomotive rhythms driven home by alliteration. In other poems, rhythms can suggest the light steps of dancing, the slow cadence of a funeral march, or the stop-and-start movements of a baseball player caught between bases during an attempted steal. In "Cheers," the rhythm is foot-stomping and heavy, like the steady waves of noise from a crowd of football fans. The beat, or meter, is congruent with the meaning of the poem.

Denotation and Connotation

The words in "Cheers" do double duty, juggling both meanings and feelings. For instance, *bilgewater* **denotes**—identifies, labels—water in the bottom of a boat. But it means much more than that. It **connotes**—suggests or implies—"Nonsense! and also "Phooey!" The several messages in the word make it an extraordinarily good cheer for a frog.

Poets often select words for their connotation as well as their denotation. A single word can thus then bring forth both emotional and intellectual responses in the reader. Carefully chosen, such words give poetry a powerful density of expression.

Imagery

Descriptions of sensory experiences are called **imagery.** Poets use language to help us imagine how things looked, felt, tasted, sounded, or smelled. Poet Barbara Esbensen writes in the introduction to *Cold Stars and Fireflies,* "All my life I have been storing up images of weather and the seasons. Years ago I told a friend that I could probably write forever on the theme: It is snowing. . . . Painters use colors and a brush to put a season on canvas. When I sit down with a clean, white sheet of paper I paint with words" (n.p.). Here is one of her "paintings":

First Snowfall
Out of the grey
pinched air
it falls.

We hear it in the oak trees
hissing
through the brown tongues
of leaves
whispering
and sifting down.

Soon it will erase
the way to school
and our feet will blunder
in blind boots.

Lashes will be fringed
with snowflakes
and our tongues will taste
the cold vanilla
of this early winter day. (1984, 15)[4]

Esbensen has not just painted a visual image, however. She has described snow using sound, taste, and touch as well as sight. The sensuous-

---

[4] *Source:* Abridged poem selection "First Snowfall" from COLD STARS AND FIREFLIES; POEMS OF THE FOUR SEASONS by Barbara Juster Esbensen. Text Copyright © 1984 by Barbara Juster Esbensen. Selection reprinted by permission of HarperCollins Publishers.

ness of her language, the vividness of her words, and the juxtaposition of sensory images combine to deliver a sharp representation of experience. And as is often the case with effective imagery, the emotion connected with the event is implied within the description. Figure 7-2 shows how a group of first graders prepared a color web for imagery.

Figurative Language

Here is how poet Valerie Worth sees a safety pin.

Safety Pin
Closed, it sleeps

Here is how a class of first graders thought about colors as they began webbing their ideas as they prepared to write poems. They were engaging in an activity that would help them use imagery in their writing.

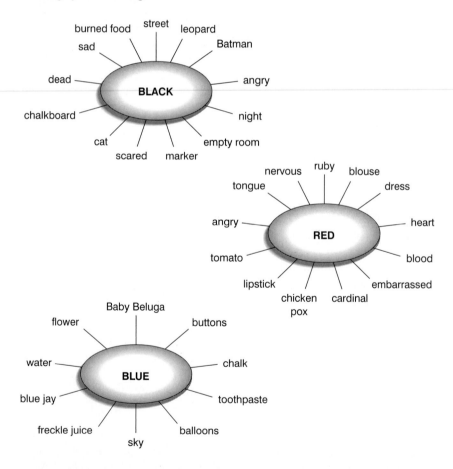

Figure 7-2   A color web for imagery.

On its side
Quietly,
The silver
Image
Of some
Small fish;

Opened, it snaps
Its tail out
Like a thin
Shrimp, and looks
At the sharp
Point with a
Surprised eye. (48)[5]

A safety pin is the silver image of a small fish: That surprising, direct comparison is called a **metaphor.** When the pin is open, it snaps its tail out *"like* a thin shrimp:" That indirect comparison, bridged by the word *like,* is called a **simile.** Both metaphor and simile are figures of speech that compare things that are basically unlike. The safety pin also sleeps on its side and looks at the point with a surprised eye. Giving human characteristics or behavior to objects or animals is called **personification,** also a figure of speech. Generally speaking, figurative language is language that is not to be taken literally. Poets, and often people just in conversation, use figurative language because it helps them express an idea more forcefully or share an insight in a way that will cause others to take notice.

Read the poems in *Out in the Dark and Daylight* by Aileen Fisher (New York: Harper, 1980) to see examples of personification in poetry.

Shape and Spacing

Poets arrange their words on paper with keen consciousness of how the poem looks as well as how it sounds. They may shape the outline of the poem so that it suggests the topic. Lillian Morrison did this in the following poem.

Two Points
Ball,I'mgonnawashyou
in the shower of the
net *Whoosh!* you
gonna come
through
clean
(49)[6]

---

[5] *Source:* "Safety Pin" from MORE SMALL POEMS by Valerie Worth. Copyright © 1976 by Valerie Worth. Reprinted by permission of Farrar, Straus & Giroux, Inc.

[6] *Source:* "Two Points" from THE BREAK DANCE KIDS by Lillian Morrison (Lothrop). Copyright © 1985 Lillian Morrison. Reprinted by permission of Marian Reiner for the author.

The words that run together make the outline work and also enhance the mood of confidence and anticipation. The *Whoosh!* in italic print stands out, centered just as the ball would be as it came through the net. The whooshing sound is emphasized in the repetition of the *sh* and will be heard by the listener, but this is a poem that should be seen as well as heard.

Poets may also use capitalization, punctuation, and spacing as poetic devices. They may indicate a pause through double spacing or emotion through the use of capitals letters. They may place words on the page in ways that control how the poem is read or that enhance the visual impact. When copying poems for children to read, it is important to maintain the original layout.

Poems may take many forms, some strangely shaped, some curt, some disciplined, some relaxed. But the materials available to the poet remain the same no matter what the form. The poet selects those that seem to best fit the idea being presented.

FORMS OF POETRY

Jump rope rhymes are a good example of verse. So too is the "folk poetry from everyone" collected by Alvin Schwartz in *And the Green Grass Grew All Around* (New York: Harper-Collins, 1992).

A young reader's perception may be that all lines of poetry are smooth on the left and bumpy on the right. But many forms of poetry do not follow that form, and some lines that do are not poetry, lines such as the "Roses are red" type of greeting card rhyme. The best of such poemlike writing is sometimes called **verse**, rhymes with steady rhythm but lacking the power of real poetry. The distinction between **verse** and **poetry** can at times be difficult to make, and once made may not be agreed on by all observers.

Narrative

Narrative poetry tells a story, like this poem by Richard Margolis.

Cold Potato
To be a second class scout
you have to pass cooking.
My brother and me,
we make a fire in the backyard
and I shove a potato inside.
When it gets all black
I roll it out with a stick.
"It's hard like a baseball," I say.
"You cooked it, you eat it," he says.

There's a lot you have to swallow
when your brother's the patrol leader. (n.p.)[7]

---

[7] *Source:* Poem "Cold Potato" reprinted with the permission of Simon & Schuster Books for Young Readers from SECRETS OF A SMALL BROTHER by Richard Margolis. Text Copyright © 1984 Richard J. Margolis.

Narrative poetry is popular with children, and many traditional favorites fall into this category. *The Night Before Christmas* (Moore), *Little Orphant Annie* (Riley), *Paul Revere's Ride* (Longfellow), *The Cremation of Sam McGee* (Service), *Hiawatha* (Longfellow), and *The Owl and the Pussycat* (Lear) are all narrative poems that are available in picture book format. In addition, many of the humorous poems of both Shel Silverstein and Jack Prelutsky are narrative.

Ballad

A **ballad** is a long narrative poem that usually relates a single incident, spinning out the story at a leisurely pace, sometimes with dialogue between characters. Repeated refrains or choruses may stretch out the action. Usually the narrative advances in four-line stanzas (blocks of poetry) such as this one, the beginning of the traditional English ballad "Robin Hood and Allan-a-Dale":

> Come listen to me, you gallants so free,
> All you that love mirth for to hear,
> And I will tell of a bold outlaw
> That lived in Nottinghamshire.

In 27 stanzas, Robin Hood rescues Allan-a-Dale's true love, who has been kidnapped by a king. The lovers are married by Little John:

> And thus having ended this merry wedding,
> The bride lookt as fresh as a queen,
> And so they return'd to the merry green-wood,
> Amongst the leaves so green. (44–47)

Ballads originated as folk songs and were for all the people, not just children. The authors of traditional ballads, such as Robin Hood, are unknown.

Lyric

Lyric poetry describes something—an object, scene, personal feeling—in lines with a singing quality; you can imagine them set to music. The word *lyric* comes from the Greek word *lura*, a stringed instrument. The Greeks often strummed a lyre as a poet read, mingling voice with music. Here is a famous children's lyrical poem, titled "The Swing," by Scottish poet Robert Louis Stevenson:

> Oh do you like to go up in a swing,
>   Up in the air so blue?
> Or, I do think it the pleasantest thing
>   Ever a child can do!
>
> Up in the air and over the wall,
>   Till I can see so wide,
> Rivers and trees and cattle and all

Over the countryside.
Till I look down on the garden green,
    Down on the roof so brown—
Up in the air I go flying again,
    Up in the air and down! (17)

Lyric poetry, while not sung, gives the sense that it could be.

Haiku

Haiku, the Japanese name for the poem, comes from ancient Chinese words meaning, literally, "amusement sentence." Haiku are unrhymed lyric poems with 3 lines and a total of 17 syllables: 5 in the first line, 7 in the second, and 5 in the third. Here is a haiku written by an American, Rebecca Caudill.

Forsythia blooms,
and little winds of springtime
Ring the golden bells. (18)

Haiku usually refer to a moment in nature or a sudden insight. Often they connect two things in nature, in this example the grasshopper and the dew:

Grasshopper,
Do not trample to pieces
The pearls of bright dew. (n.p.)

> Children in grades 3 through 6 often enjoy writing within the structure of haiku, focusing on nature rather than philosophic insight for the content.

These lines were written by Issa, well-known haiku poet who was born in central Japan in 1762. The syllable count is off because of the problem of translation.

The photo below shows a child making collage illustrations for haiku he has written. He is working to present an idea in both words and pictures.

Nonsense Verse

Nonsense verse is humorous or whimsical verse that plays with the absurd in ideas or language. Anderson and Apseloff argue that "Nonsense is not the absence of sense but a clever subversion of it that heightens rather than destroys meaning. The very notion of topsy-turvy implies that there is a right side up" (5).[8]

Many nonsense verses appear in a collection illustrated by Wallace Tripp, called *A Great Big Ugly Man Came Up and Tied His Horse to Me.* Here is the title verse, author unknown:

---

[8] *Source:* Excerpt From NONSENSE LITERATURE FOR CHILDREN, AESOP TO SEUSS by Celia Anderson & Marilyn Apseloff. Copyright © 1989 Library of Professional Publications. Reprinted by permission of The Shoestring Press, Inc.

This child is cutting shapes for a collage illustration of a poem he wrote.

As I was standing in the street
As quiet as could be,
A great big ugly man came up
and tied his horse to me.

In Tripp's cover drawing, the "I" is a badger wearing a red coat with gold buttons, looking alarmed but stoical. The horse appears concerned about being tied up to a badger. The situation is carried to a logical conclusion when the horse walks away, with dignity, carrying the badger in a bundle under its chin.

Tripp's spirited animals complement the rhymes. A raccoon in a stocking cap stops a doctor in a snow-covered field and announces:

I do not love thee, Doctor Fell,
The reason why I cannot tell,
But this alone I know full well,
I do not love thee, Doctor Fell.

Perhaps the reason is that the doctor is wearing a coonskin cap.

Nonsense poetry can be complex in its play with language and meaning. In Paul Coltman's *Tog the Ribber or Granny's Tale,* nonsense words abound, giving sense through their sound, their similarity to other words, and the context. Granny has a terrible fright as she passes Tog's tomb on her way home through the woods. She begins her tale:

> I shuddud in the glavering goom
> as homing through the only wood
> I skibbed and teetered past Tog's tomb. (n.p.)[9]

Granny makes it home, but not before a hair-raising chase by Tog's skeleton. The illustrations capture the eerie mood and spooky atmosphere. It is nonsense poetry in the tradition of Lewis Carroll's *Jabberwocky*.

Limerick

The **limerick** is a form of nonsense poetry, five lines of carefully organized silliness. The name comes from a line of old verse that goes "Will you come up to Limerick?" which, oddly, would not fit into the rhythm of a genuine limerick. In classical form, the first, second, and fifth lines of a limerick rhyme; the third and fourth have a rhyme and rhythm of their own. The acknowledged master of the form was Edward Lear, a writer who often embellished his verse with funny drawings. A typical piece of nonsense from Lear looks and sounds like this:

> There was an Old Man with a beard,
> Who said, "It's just as I feared!—
> Two owls and a Hen,
> Four larks and a Wren,
> Have all built their nests in my beard.

Arnold Lobel continued this tradition of humor and form in his book of "pigericks," limericks written, the first one tells us, by a pig.

> There was an old pig with a pen
> Who wrote stories and verse now and then.
> To enhance these creations,
> He drew illustrations
> With brushes, some paints and his pen. (9)[10]

The illustrations show the pig at work at his drawing board, a pig whose moustache and glasses make him strongly resemble Lobel himself. All of the rhymes that make up the book are about pigs.

Free Verse

In contrast to limericks and haiku, **free verse** has no formal governing rules, no required rhythm, no rhyme, no prescribed length of line. The form is not

---

[9] *Source:* Excerpt from TOG THE RIBBER by Paul Coltman. Copyright © 1985 by Paul Coltman. Reprinted by permission of Farrar, Straus & Giroux, Inc.

[10] *Source:* Poem "There Was An Old Pig With A Pen" from THE BOOK OF PIGERICKS; PIG LIMERICKS by Arnold Lobel, Copyright © 1983 by Arnold Lobel. Selection reprinted by permission of HarperCollins Publishers.

THE COMPLETE NONSENSE BOOK

Edward Lear is an acknowledged master of the limerick. (Source: Illustration from THE COMPLETE NONSENSE BOOK written and illustrated by Edward Lear.)

new. "We have heard much in our time about free verse being modern," Carl Sandburg wrote, "as though it is a new-found style for men to use in speaking and writing, rising out of the machine age, skyscrapers, high speed and jazz" (24).[11] But, as Sandburg points out, free verse is older than alphabets. Much of the Bible and many of the poems of Native Americans are free verse. The following poem is from the Chippewa people:

> As my eyes
> Search the Prairie,
> I feel the summer in the spring. (Jones n.p.)

Venerable as it is, free verse can adapt to tell a contemporary story, like this poem by Nikki Giovanni.

parents never understand
well i can't 'cause
yesterday when mommy had
this important visitor she said
run along joey and let mommy talk
and i ran along upstairs to see
bobby and eddie and we were playing
and i forgot and i had to come down

Nikki Giovanni, Richard Margolis, and Arnold Adoff are three poets who have written free verse appropriate for children.

---

[11] *Source:* Excerpt from EARLY MOON by Carl Sandburg, Copyright © 1930 by Harcourt Brace & Company and renewed 1958 by Carl Sandburg, reprinted by permission of the publisher.

stairs and get dry clothes and mommy said how
could an eight year old boy wet his pants
and i looked at the visitor and smiled a really nice
smile and said i guess in america anything
can happen
so mommy said i have to
stay in today (n.p.)[12]

Concrete Poetry

Concrete poetry uses the shapes of words or lines to make a poem, so that the work illustrates itself. Some concrete poetry is built out of conventional forms, like Sylvia Cassedy's *Elevator* (14).

Source: "Elevator" from ROOM-RIMES by Sylvia Cassedy, Text Copyright © 1987 by Sylvia Cassedy, Illustrations Copyright © 1987 by Michele Chessare. Selection reprinted by permission of HarperCollins Publishers.

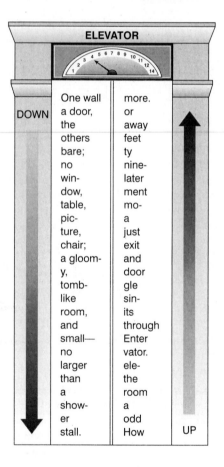

[12] *Source:* "Parents Never Understand" from SPIN A SOFT BLACK SONG by Nikki Giovanni. Copyright © 1971, 1985 by Nikki Giovanni. Reprinted by permission of Farrar, Straus & Giroux, Inc.

Sometimes a concrete poem is made of a few key words, like Froman's "On the Beach." (n.p.)

ON THE BEACH

WAVE
WAVE WAVE
WAVE WAVE WAVE
FOAM FOAM FOAM

SAND SAND SAND... CLAM SHELL... STARFISH... HARD GREY ROCK... PEBBLES...

Source: Poem "On The Beach" by Robert Froman from SEEING THINGS. Copyright © 1974. Reprinted with the permission of the Estate of Robert Froman.

Rap

The word *rap* originated as a Black English word that means to talk, though usually to talk in a way that convinces the listener of the speaker's confidence as well as of the content. It is primarily an oral form of poetry that depends on tone and pitch as well as rhythm and rhyme and is often performed against a rhythmic background (Padgett 155). Eloise Greenfield's *Nathaniel Talking* is a collection of raps in which nine-year-old Nathaniel tells about his world. Here is the opening selection:

Nathaniel's Rap

It's Nathaniel talking
and Nathaniel's me
I'm taking about
My philosophy
About the things I do
And the people I see
All told in the words
Of Nathaniel B. Free
That's me
And I can rap
I can rap
I can rap, rap, rap
Till your earflaps flap
I can talk that talk
Till you go for a walk
I can run it down
Till you get out of town

I can rap
I can rap
Rested, dressed and feeling fine
I've got something on my mind
Friends and kin and neighborhood
Listen now and listen good
Nathaniel's talking
Nathaniel B. Free
Talking about
My philosophy
Been thinking all day
I got a lot to say
Gotta run it down
Nathaniel's way
Okay!
I gotta rap

Gotta rap
Gotta rap, rap, rap
Till your earflaps flap
Gotta talk that talk
Till you go for a walk
Gotta run it down
Till you get out of town
Gotta rap
Gotta rap
Rested, dressed and feeling fine
I've got something on my mind
Friends and kin and neighborhood
Listen now and listen good
I'm gonna rap, hey!
Gonna rap, hey!
Gonna rap, hey!
I'm gonna rap!

Source: Text of "Nathaniel's Rap" from NATHANIEL TALKING Copyright © 1988 by Eloise Greenfield. Reprinted by permission of Scott Treimel New York for the Author.

The rhyme, rhythm, and fast pace of rap make it popular with children. (Source: Text and illustration of "Nathaniel's Rap" from NATHANIEL TALKING Copyright © 1988 by Eloise Greenfield. Reprinted by permission of Scott Treimel New York for the Author.)

Rap for children does not have the violence, sexual aggression, or the profanity that often characterizes adult rap.

Other Forms

Other forms are as disciplined as the steps of formal ballet, with names that sound as fluid and spicy as poetry: villanelle, tercet, quatrain, clerihew, and cinquain. A tercet is 3 rhymed lines; quatrains have 4 lines. A villanelle has 19 lines comprising 5 tercets and a final quatrain governed by rules about what lines are repeated. Clerihews are humorous quatrains, usually about a person identified in the first line. And a cinquain is a 5-line stanza like this one, written to teach what the form is, by David McCord:

This is
The form of the
Cinquain. The five lines have
2,4,6,8,2 syllables
As here.
(1973 n.p.)[13]

EVALUATING POETRY

Neither the form chosen nor the presence of any specific technical devices of poetry determines a poem's quality. The quality is measured by the overall impact and the creative use of ideas and language. Figure 7-3 lists five criteria to apply when assessing a poem.

Here are two poems about water, both from publications intended for primary age children. The author of the first poem was not listed.

Turn Off the Water All the Way
Water is so useful
For drink and bath and play
When your hands are dirty,
Water saves the day.

So when you're taking water,
Even a little taste,
Turn off the faucet all the way
So none will go to waste.[14]

This second poem is by British author and illustrator Shirley Hughes.

Squirting Rainbows
Bare legs,

---

[13] *Source:* Excerpt from PEN, PAPER AND POEM by David McCord, Copyright © 1973 by Holt, Rinehart and Winston, Inc. Reprinted by permission of the publisher.

[14] *Source:* Reprinted from the June, Series 1 issue of *Your Big Backyard* magazine, with the permission of the publisher, the National Wildlife Federation. Copyright 1980 by the National Wildlife Federation.

> 1. A fresh or original view of the subject is presented.
> 2. Insight or emotion is shown or felt.
> 3. Poetic devices are used effectively.
> 4. Language is used effectively.
> 5. The voice or persona within the poem appears to be sincere.

Figure 7-3   Criteria for evaluating a poem.

Bare toes,
Paddling pool,
Garden hose.
Daisies sprinkled
In the grass,
Dandelions
Bold as brass.
Squirting rainbows,
Sunbeam flashes,
Backyard full
Of shrieks and splashes! (n.p.)[15]

Nothing in the first poem is fresh or original, nothing helps the reader see the subject in a new light. One senses the didactic intent—to teach children to conserve water—rather than any real emotion on the part of the poet. In fact, the tone of the poem is almost patronizing. The poetic devices used are rhyme and rhythm, but at the expense of natural language. Saying "Turn off the faucet all the way" keeps the meter regular, but sounds awkward. Saying that "water saves the day" fits the rhyme scheme, but is a trite expression.

The second poem, by contrast, succinctly captures the essence of an experience. It gives fresh images of children playing with water in a backyard. Hughes has also used rhythm and rhyme but in this case has achieved a singing quality. The lines progress from two syllables, to three, to four. Alliteration—*B*are legs, *b*are toes, and *p*addling *p*ools, for example—makes the poem fun to say aloud. The imagery is effective as daisies are described as being "sprinkled" in the grass, and the backyard is full of "shrieks and splashes!" Hughes does use a cliche, "Bold as brass," in describing the dandelions, but it fits with the earlier alliteration and has a double figurative quality in that the dandelions *are* bold as brass in both color and persistence. Hughes' poem also seems to reflect the attitude of the poet that backyard water play is fun.

While many people may sympathize more with the message of the first poem than that of the second as water shortages become increasingly serious, the second is by far the better poem.

---

[15] *Source:* Text from OUT AND ABOUT by Shirley Hughes. Copyright © 1988 by Shirley Hughes. By permission of Lothrop, Lee & Shepard Books, a division of William Morrow and Company.

Squirting Rainbows

Bare legs,
Bare toes,
Paddling pool,
Garden hose.
Daisies sprinkled
In the grass,
Dandelions
Bold as brass.
Squirting rainbows,
Sunbeam flashes,
Backyards full
Of shrieks and splashes!

Shirley Hughes captures the experience of playing with water in succinct and expressive language. (Source: Illustration Copyright © 1988 by Shirley Hughes. Reprinted by permission of Lothrop, Lee & Shepard Books, a division of William Morrow and Company, Inc.)

Reading poetry that professionals consider to be of high quality can help sharpen one's own critical skills. The National Council of Teachers of English gives an Award for Excellence in Poetry for Children to a living American poet for the body of his or her work. Figure 7-4 lists the past winners. Their work is an excellent introduction to outstanding poetry for children.

These poets have each won the Award for Excellence in Poetry for Children given by the National Council of Teachers of English.

1977	David McCord
1978	Aileen Fisher
1979	Karla Kuskin
1980	Myra Cohn Livingston
1981	Eve Merriam
1982	John Ciardi
1985	Lilian Moore
1988	Arnold Adoff
1991	Valerie Worth
1994	Barbara Esbensen

Figure 7-4   Poetry award winners.

POETRY COLLECTIONS

The first criterion for selecting an anthology is that it include good poetry. For most teachers and parents, a general anthology, one that includes poems on a variety of topics by many poets, is essential. *The Random House Book of Poetry for Children* (Prelutsky) has 572 poems grouped into categories such as "Dogs and Cats and Bears and Bats" and "Children, Children Everywhere." A second criterion is that the anthology have a thorough index. In the *Random House* collection, there is an index by title, an index of first lines, an index of authors, and a subject index. Thus, readers can find a specific poem as well as a section on a particular topic.

Sing a Song of Popcorn (de Regniers) is a general anthology with fewer poems, but it has the unique factor of having been illustrated by 11 different Caldecott Medal artists. The section "Mostly Weather" has watercolors by Marcia Brown that give a softness to the seasons; the section "Seeing, Feeling, Thinking" has illustrations by Leo and Diane Dillon that they describe as "images a bit misty to give readers a chance to develop their own pictures" (140).

Make a Joyful Sound: Poems for Children by African-American Poets, edited by Deborah Slier, presents the work of many black poets, with content that speaks to children of all racial and ethnic backgrounds. The emphasis is on hopes, dreams, and plans for the future.

A second type of collection focuses on a particular topic or form, with poems by many different authors. An example of this type of collection is *Cats Are Cats* compiled by Nancy Larrick and illustrated by Ed Young. Forty-

> Children can build an appreciation for poetry by creating their own anthologies, copying poems they especially like, and adding their own illustrations.

Marcia Brown's watercolor illustrations for the poems about weather give a softness to the seasons. (Source: Illustration by Marcia Brown from SING A SONG OF POPCORN by Beatrice Schenk de Regniers et al. Illustrations Copyright © 1988 by Marcia Brown. Reprinted by permission of Scholastic Inc.)

four poems present the stance, the haughtiness, the soft fur, the soft purr, the cleverness of cats. Seven of the NCTE Poetry Award winners are represented in this book. Specialized collections range from general topics such as weather to more narrow topics such as dinosaurs. There are many such collections of holiday poems, humorous poems, and poems about animals.

The forms most often collected in specialized anthologies are haiku, limericks, and concrete poetry. Sometimes these also fit into a third category, poems by a single poet. This is because some poets write or wrote many poems of the same type, such as Edward Lear's limericks, Robert Froman's concrete poetry, and Issa and Basho's haiku. Such a collection provides an opportunity for children to make their own generalizations about the form based on the many examples presented.

Collections of a single poet's work can show patterns in topic or style and sometimes evolution in an author's approach. Children may develop favorite poets just as they come to have favorite authors. Valerie Worth's poems are collected in a volume titled *All the Small Poems,* and David McCord's *One at a Time* contains a large portion of his published work.

Several anthologists have developed strong reputations for their ability to select quality poetry. Among these are Nancy Larrick, Lee Bennett Hopkins, Myra Cohn Livingston, and Jack Prelutsky. Not surprisingly, most are poets themselves.

POEM PICTURE BOOKS

Some poems, often narrative, have been fully illustrated and appear in picture book format. The idea is not new; Kate Greenaway illustrated *The Pied Piper of Hamelin* (Browning) in 1888. Yet poem picture books seem to be becoming increasingly popular. Classic poems such as *Jabberwocky, The Owl and the Pussycat, Hiawatha,* and also many nursery rhymes have been illustrated by several different artists. Other newer poems, such as Siebert's *Heartland,* have been published originally in picture book format.

Those who favor such publications argue that the format increases reader appeal, enticing children to read poetry they might otherwise overlook. The illustrations may help children to understand the poem and present quality art in context.

Those who are concerned about poem picture books argue that illustrations can suppress a child's imagination, providing the images that the words should suggest. The child, they argue, accepts the artist's interpretation rather than developing a personal interpretation. They note also that graphics may overinterpret or overshadow the poem.

One way to avoid these problems is for adults to read poem picture books to children the first time without showing the illustrations. After the child has had time to think about the poem and form his or her own images, the adult could reread the poem and show the illustrations. This is especially important in poems where the artist has given a concrete interpretation to ambiguous lines.

In selecting poem picture books, look for high quality poetry that delights the ear and stimulates the mind. Poor poetry can be masked but not improved by strong art. Look for illustrations that are of a style and medium that capture the tone and significance of the poem and help establish a link between poet and reader.

Graeme Base used a medieval setting for his illustrations of *Jabberwocky*, enhancing the sense of period with embellished first letters on each page. The illustrations burst out of their frames onto the facing page giving flow and drama to the story. Other illustrations are full double-page spreads that allow for both the scaley details of all those creatures gyring and gimbling in the wabe, and the peace of a huge blue sky and view of distant valleys and mountains as our hero "stood awhile in thought." The artist captured the sense of quest as well as the tongue-in-cheek quality of the poem. Base has hidden contemporary artifacts within his villages and forests. One can find clocks and television antennae, a buzzer beside the portcullis, a telephone in the throne room. And one of the final illustrations shows the head of the jabberwocky, mounted and hanging on the trophy wall. Children who have heard the poem, described their own picture of how these creatures looked and sounded, and imagined for themselves a setting could then appreciate this artist's interpretation.

The illustrations for *Heartland* are landscape paintings that show the farms, fields, towns, and people of this lyric tribute to the American Midwest. Both poem and pictures are strong in delivering the feeling of pride in the "patchwork quilt whose seams are etched by miles of wood and wire" (Siebert n.p.). In this book, both the illustrations and poetry convey the message.

Single poems in picture book format can offer a rich source of poetry and art.

Illustrations for poetry collections as well as single editions may influence a reader's reaction. Compare the illustrations of Leonard Weisgard for Mary O'Neill's *Hailstones and Halibut Bones* (New York: Doubleday, 1961) with those of John Wallner for the same text (New York: Doubleday, 1989). Which edition would you be most likely to read? Why?

Look for modern objects in this medieval setting for the poem "Jabberwocky." (*Source:* Illustration from JABBERWOCKY by Lewis Carroll, illustration by Graeme Base. Copyright © 1989. Reprinted by permission of Harry N. Abrams, Inc.)

SELECTING POETRY FOR CHILDREN
Quality

If children are to learn about poetry, respond to its sound and its meaning, and appreciate it, then the poetry selected must be of high quality. Otherwise children are shortchanged. They cannot appreciate the power of language to stimulate the imagination if the poems they hear are neither powerful nor stimulating.

Children's Poetry Preferences

Neither will children appreciate poetry if they dislike the poems presented. Ann Terry studied the poetry preferences of fourth, fifth, and sixth graders. During her survey, teachers played tapes of 113 selected poems read by a radio announcer. The teachers asked children to evaluate each poem, using a five-point scale ranging from "great" to "hated." Snoopy, the dog from Charles Schulz's "Peanuts" comic strip, illustrated the children's response forms: dancing for joy to represent *great* and slumped in dejection for *hated*.

Children listened to 10 to 12 poems a day for two weeks, hearing each poem twice. At the end of each session, they wrote comments on the last poem. Terry also surveyed teachers' preferences and asked about poetry use in the classroom.

Terry tallied the returns to find the 25 most popular poems and the 25 most unpopular. She also analyzed content, poetic elements, poetic form, and age of the poem to try to discover whether there were general characteristics children liked or disliked. The most popular poem was "Mummy Slept Late and Daddy Fixed Breakfast" by John Ciardi.

Mummy Slept Late and Daddy Fixed Breakfast
Daddy fixed the breakfast.
He made us each a waffle.
It looked like gravel pudding.
It tasted something awful.

"Ha, ha," he said, "I'll try again.
This time I'll get it right."
But what I got was in between
Bituminous and anthracite.

"A little too well done? Oh well,
I'll have to start all over."
That time what landed on my plate
Looked like a manhole cover.

I tried to cut it with a fork:
The fork gave off a spark.
I tried a knife and twisted it
Into a question mark.

I tried it with a hack-saw.
I tried it with a torch.
It didn't even make a dent.
It didn't even scorch.

The next time Dad gets breakfast
When Mommy's sleeping late,
I think I'll skip the waffles.
I'd sooner eat the plate. (18)[16]

Least popular was William Carlos Williams' "The Red Wheelbarrow," often cited by critics as a successful adult poem.

so much depends

upon

a red wheel

barrow

glazed with rain

water

beside the white

chickens (277)[17]

Terry found that a poem's content, age, poetic elements, and form all had bearing on children's preferences. The most and least popular poems exemplify many of the patterns in the children's responses.

Terry divided the poetry in the study into nine categories of content, including humor, familiar experience, people, animals, nature, fantasy, historical events, adventure, and social commentary. Students showed a strong preference for humor, familiar experience, and animals. Sometimes young listeners liked or disliked a poem because of their experience with the subject. One boy disliked a poem about daffodils because he was allergic to flowers.

Students favored contemporary poems written within the last 15 or 20 years to older classics. They enjoyed poems with strong rhythm and rhyme, but not those that relied heavily on figurative language and imagery. Williams' use of imagery fell flat with children, and the poem does not rhyme. Terry theorized that the poem was too sophisticated for elementary school children. Another strike against "Wheelbarrow" was probably its form; intermediate grade children tended not to enjoy free verse. Neither did they like haiku. In comments about their ratings, many children stated that they disliked haiku because it was too short and they didn't understand it.

---

[16] *Source:* "Mummy Slept Late" poem from YOU READ TO ME, I'LL READ TO YOU by John Ciardi, Copyright © 1962 by John Ciardi. Selection reprinted by permission of Harper-Collins Publisher.

[17] *Source:* William Carlos Williams from COLLECTED POEMS: 1909–1939, Volume I. Copyright © 1938 by New Directions Publishing Corp. Reprinted by permission of New Directions Publishing Corp.

Carol Fisher and Margaret Natarella replicated the study with primary grade children and poems selected as appropriate for that age level. Their findings were nearly the same at those of Terry. Primary grade children liked humorous poems and poems about children and about animals; they liked rhythm and rhyme; they liked narrative poetry but not haiku or free verse. The age of the poem was not a strong factor in their reaction to it, but the traditional poems in the study all rhymed. The primary children marked the poem with a star, as OK, or with a No. Seventy-six percent of the responses were either a star or an OK, indicating a very strong positive response to poetry. And every poem had at least one star.

Another approach to determining children's poetry preferences was taken by Kutiper and Wilson, who looked at the circulation of poetry books in three metropolitan elementary school libraries rather than having students listen to and rate poems. The three books most frequently checked out in all three schools were *The New Kid on the Block* by Jack Prelutsky and *Where the Sidewalk Ends* and *A Light in the Attic,* both by Shel Silverstein. Kutiper and Wilson noted that this was consistent with the findings of Terry and Fisher and Natarella in that all three of these books contain much poetry that is humorous, narrative, and has strong rhythm and rhyme. They go on to express a serious concern, however. Visual imagery and figurative language require readers to process the reading of poetry at higher cognitive levels. Preference studies (Kutiper, 1993; Terry, 1972) have shown that readers do not like poetry in which figurative language interferes with the instant understanding that most young readers desire. This is not a problem with the poetry of Prelutsky and Silverstein. Their poetry is straightforward, literal in content, and requires little higher level thinking to understand, which undoubtedly contributes to their popularity. These are reasons for both the appeal of their poetry and also for moving beyond Prelutsky and Silverstein to poetry that does ask readers to expand their critical thinking skills (32).

Thus they call for teachers to draw children's attention to other types of poetry.

A discouraging discovery in the earlier Terry data was that these teachers seldom read poetry in their classes. Only one teacher in 42 who responded read poems every day; 34 out of the 42 presented poems approximately once a month or less. This means that the vast majority of these children participated in classroom poetry sessions less than 9 times a year. Thus the preferences Terry discovered grew out of sparse exposure to poetry, at least in the classroom. The studies by Terry and Fisher and Natarella give direction for selecting poetry for children whose background and experience with poetry may be limited.

When Kutiper and Wilson looked at the number of volumes of poetry by the poets who had received the National Council of Teachers of English Award for Excellence in Poetry for Children owned by the libraries of the three schools, they found that some of these award-winning poets were not represented at all in two of the three libraries. If children are to grow in their appreciation for diverse types of poetry, schools must have good collections for children to read, and teachers must help children become aware of the wide range of high quality poetry.

Age and Background of the Children

The age of the children and their background with poetry specifically and life in general will influence their response to poems. Toddlers respond to the sound of Mother Goose rhymes, and much of their own speech may reflect an interest in the sound as well as the meaning of words. Kornei Chukovsky, a leading Russian children's poet and linguistic scholar, wrote that children as young as age three begin to pair words, learning their meanings and discovering rhymes. A mother asks where the broom is and her son answers, "Over there, on the stair," and then begins to chant, "Over there, on the stair; over there, on the stair . . . " (62). The rhyming is fun. "In the beginning of our childhood we are all 'versifiers,'" Chukovsky writes. "It is only later that we begin to learn to speak in prose" (64).[18]

Young children respond to the sound of the words in rhymes such as Bruce Degan's *Jamberry,* which begins

> One berry
> Two berry
> Pick me a blueberry
>
> Hatberry
> Shoeberry
> In my canoeberry (n.p.)[19]

Children need to be somewhat older to follow and appreciate Russell Hoban's description of a sparrow hawk pursuing a mouse.

> **The Sparrow Hawk**
> Wings like pistols flashing at his sides,
> Masked, above the meadow runway rides,
> Galloping, galloping with an easy rein.
> Below, the fieldmouse, where the shadow glides,
> Holds fast the small purse of his life, and hides. (3)[20]

---

[18] *Source:* From Kornei Chukovsky, from *Two to Five,* pp. 62–64, translated edition by Morton Miram. Copyright © 1963 The Regents of the University of California. Reprinted by permission of University of California Press.

[19] *Source:* Abridgement of poem "One Berry . . . Canoeberry" from JAMBERRY by Bruce Degan, Copyright © 1983 by Bruce Degan. Selection reprinted by permission of Harper-Collins Publishers.

[20] *Source:* Poem "Wings . . . " from THE PEDALING MAN AND OTHER POEMS by Russell Hoban. Reprinted by permission of Harold Ober Associates Incorporated. Copyright © 1968 by Russell Hoban.

Young children respond to the sound of the words in Jamberry *by Bruce Degan. Source:* Illustration from JAMBERRY by Bruce Degan. Selection reprinted by permission of HarperCollins Publishers. Copyright © 1983.)

Poems do not come coded for age levels, so teachers must judge where and when a poem fits in. This means knowing the children, their experiences, what makes sense to them, and what touches them. Sharing poems about families might include several selections from Margolis' *Secrets of a Small Brother,* quoted earlier in this chapter. These poems show the emotional reactions of the younger brother within what appears to be a strong nuclear family. Many children will identify with this. Many children will also identify with the following poem by Myra Cohn Livingston:

HOME
Yelling,
shouting,
arguing,
their faces scrunch up tight.

Slamming doors,
clenching fists,
they battle half the night.

Cursing,
hissing,
screaming out
their hates, their rights, their wrongs—

Who am I?
What am I?
Where do I belong? (26)[21]

Cultural Diversity

Poetry offers the opportunity for children to glimpse the reactions and emotions of the poet. Choosing poetry by and about many cultural groups lets children see events from the inside, through different sets of eyes. They look at a painting by Amos Ferguson and see three people, each balancing an object on his or her head. They read Eloise Greenfield's accompanying poem and they gain insight and appreciation of life in the Bahamas:

Tradition

Pineapples! pumpkins! chickens! we
carry them on our heads you see
we can glide along forever
and not drop a thing, no never
never even use our hands
never put a finger to it
you know how we learned to do it?
knowledge came from other lands
Africans of long ago
passed it down to us and so
now we pass it on to you
for what is old is also new
pineapples, pumpkins, chickens, we
carry more than the things you see
we also carry history (1)[22]

The following contemporary Native American poem, recorded by Nancy Wood, lets readers enjoy the humor of this resident of the Taos Pueblo:

My dog barks because he cannot speak.
My horse whinnys because he cannot laugh.
My sheep bleats because he cannot cry.
My rooster crows because he cannot boast.
But my cat just goes to sleep because
He is too old to complain. (40)[23]

---

[21] *Source:* Poem "Home" reprinted with the permission of Margaret K. McElderry Books, an imprint of Simon & Schuster from THERE WAS A PLACE AND OTHER POEMS by Myra Cohn Livingston. Copyright © 1988 Myra Cohn Livingston.

[22] *Source:* "Tradition" from UNDER THE SUNDAY TREE by Eloise Greenfield. Text Copyright © 1988 by Eloise Greenfield. Selection reprinted by permission of HarperCollins Publishers.

[23] *Source:* From MANY WINTERS by Nancy Wood. Copyright © 1974 by Nancy Wood, Illustrations © 1974 by Frank Howell. Used by permission of Bantam Doubleday Dell Books for Young Readers.

Nancy Wood has collected con-
temporary Native American
poems in Many Winters.
(Source: Illustration from
MANY WINTERS by Nancy
Wood. Copyright © 1974 by
Nancy Wood, Illustrations ©
1974 by Frank Howell. Used
by permission of Bantam
Doubleday Dell Books for
Young Readers.)

In the poem picture book, *Father and Son,* poet Denize Lauture describes the many things the father and son do together, from kite flying to attending church. It is the full color oil paintings by illustrator Jonathan Green, however, that fill the scenes with details from Green's Gullah heritage and present cultural information.

Variety in Form and Content

Adults help children grow in their enjoyment and appreciation of poetry by starting with what children know and like and then gradually introducing new forms and varied content. For example, children must hear nonrhyming poetry to learn that not all poetry rhymes, yet free verse was not a form they enjoyed according to the studies by Terry and Fisher and Natarella. Sharing "parents never understand," quoted earlier, would be a good choice because it has humor, is a favorite with children, and is about an experience they can understand. These factors help offset an initial dislike for unrhymed poetry.

The gradual and continuous introduction of new forms broadens children's perspectives about poetry.

Current Experiences

Some childhood experiences are as common in Lost Nation, Iowa, as in New York City. And there are poems to match each experience—sudden loneliness, fright at the first clap of thunder, even dismay at a runny nose. Teachers can have poems ready, perhaps even memorized, for such occurrences.

Poetry can also enrich units of study, such as space exploration, natural phenomena, different parts of the country, and caring for animals. Poetry fits naturally into many ongoing topics of discussion. For example, suppose it is spring and the class is about to begin a study of pond life. The teacher begins looking specifically for poetry about frogs. The search involves looking through several basic anthologies, checking the library for specialized collections, and using the *Index to Poetry for Children and Young People* (Brewton, Meredith, and Blackburn), which lists poems by title, author, subject, and first line. This reference is in several volumes, each for a specific time period. Figure 7-5 shows how that teacher might assess several "frog" poems that she has found.

The teacher is now ready to select the poems based on the age and background of the children and the activities she hopes to encourage.

PRESENTING POETRY

After the selection has been made, it is crucial that the poems be presented well. This means reading them effectively and practicing so that you can add pauses to help express the meaning. It is often helpful to tape-record yourself reading poetry and then listen for strengths and for places needing improvement. The goal is to capture the sound of the language in meaningful units. If children are going to discuss the poem, consider making copies for them or putting the poem on a chart, which makes it easier to think about phrases or thoughts within a poem. And, as is the case with several of the frog poems, note whether children need to see the poem to get the full impact. If so, use an overhead transparency, chart, or individual copies.

Even well-read poetry can be undermined by reading too much poetry at one session. Space the poems so children can concentrate on what they're hearing. You might read a new poem and then have children select two or three favorites that they'd like you to read again. One second-grade teacher presents poetry in her classroom and then has the books available so that children can pick poems for her to reread as they wait for the call to come to their buses at dismissal time. Poetry is like music: As we hear the same melodies or phrases several times, we enjoy

Here is how a teacher might assess several poems about frogs as she looks for poetry to include in a unit on pond life.

Frogs in Spring

Maybe they're glad
for the warmth of spring—
that's why frogs
in the frog pond sing.

Maybe they're glad
to jump and leap
after their long cold
winter sleep.

Maybe they're glad
to see their friends—
that's why they sing
when winter ends.

Maybe they're glad
to *eat* once more.
That's what *I*
would be gladdest for.

       Aileen Fisher (142)

This poem will be understood easily by the children. It uses repetition effectively, has rhythm and rhyme, and is humorous. It is likely to be an instant favorite.

My Frog Is a Frog

My frog is a frog that is hopelessly hoarse,
my frog is a frog with a reason, of course,
my frog is a frog that cannot croak a note,
my frog is a frog with a frog in its throat.

       Jack Prelutsky (1990, 82)

This light verse is also humorous. The idiom of having a "frog in your throat" is common enough that it does not require an explanation. It doesn't refer to any part of "frog life" as the Fisher poem does.

Figure 7-5   Selecting poems to enhance a unit.

Sources: Poem "Frogs in Spring" by Aileen Fisher reprinted by permission of the author who controls all rights. § Text from "My Frog Is A Frog" from SOMETHING BIG HAS BEEN HERE by Jack Prelutsky. Text Copyright © 1990 by Jack Prelutsky. Reprinted by permission of Greenwillow Books, a division of William Morrow and Company, Inc. § "Frog" by Mary Ann Hoberman from A LITTLE BOOK OF LITTLE BEASTS, 1973, published by Simon & Schuster. Reprinted by permission of Gina Maccoby Literary Agency. Copyright © 1973 by Mary Ann Hoberman. § Text of "For Kermit" from GREENS: POEMS by Arnold Adoff. Text Copyright © 1988 by Arnold Adoff. Reprinted by permission of Lothrop, Lee & Shepard Books, a division of William Morrow and Company, Inc. § "Touch It With" poem from WORDS WITH WRINKLED KNEES by Barbara Juster Esbensen, text Copyright © 1986 by Barbara Juster Esbensen. Selection reprinted by permission of HarperCollins Publishers.

Frog

Pollywiggle	Wet skin
Pollywog	Cold blood
Tadpole	Squats in
Bullfrog	Mucky mud
Leaps on	Leaps on
Long legs	Long legs
Jug-o-rum	Jug-o-rum
Jelly eggs	Jelly eggs
Sticky tongue	Laid in
Tricks flies	Wet bog. . .
Spied by	Pollywiggle
Flicker eyes	Pollywog.

Mary Ann Hoberman (18)

The poem is marvelous for word play, and it contains accurate information about frogs as well. It should be put on a chart or overhead transparency so the children can see it as it's being read. This poem lends itself well to choral reading, perhaps having the children discuss and try several different ways of reading it.

This next poem is untitled. It is the first poem, and reads as a dedication, to Adoff's book of poetry titled *Greens*.

For
Ker
Mit
The
    Frog
    With
    This
    Kiss
And
Hug
For
    Being
    Green
And
For
His
    Green Song
    Live Long
        Arnold Adoff (n.p.)

Figure 7-5 *continued*

All the poems in Adoff's book are about things that are green. This poem should also be seen by the children. A teacher might ask them what they notice about the poem and lead them to recognize the pattern of words with the same number of letters being written in groups. This approach requires background knowledge and would probably elicit different levels of understanding and response. Children would know who Kermit is. They might or might not know the Green Song. If they did, some might take the lyrics at face value, the idea that "It's not easy bein' green," and concluding with "It's beautiful and I think it's what I want to be" (Raposa). Others might see the relationship of these lyrics to racial and ethnic identities. If the children knew other works of Adoff, such as *Brown is Black is Tan* or *All the Colors of the Race*, they might further see why Adoff began his book with this poem. While the poem seems to be about a frog, it's import is not really related to pond life.

Here is a final "frog" poem, untitled.

Touch it with your
pencil
Splat!   The word lands   wet
and squat
upon the page   F R O G

Feed it something light
with wings   Here's one!
Tongue flicks   bright
wing   caught!
Small poem
gone (Barbara Esbensen 1986 n.p.)

This is a very sophisticated poem that is taken from a collection in which each poem is about a different animal. Children might need a brief explanation of the premise of the book. They would need to see the poem and examine the poet's use of space and positioning of the words. A teacher might introduce the poem without explanation and ask the children, "What do you think the poet is doing?" Children could discuss how they think the poem should be read and might even illustrate it. A comparison with the Hoberman poem could give added insight.

The teacher is now ready to select the poems she will present.

Figure 7-5 *continued*

them even more. Figure 7-6 gives some suggestions for helping children love poetry.

Have poetry books available for children to read on their own. If there is a listening center, record poems or purchase tapes of poems so children can listen. We must provide these opportunities if we want children to read poetry, develop their own taste, and expand their knowledge and enjoyment of poetry.

As has been implied, children should be involved with the poetry, dramatizing it, illustrating it, comparing poems, and writing poetry of their

Julie keeps a journal of the events that happen in her third-grade class-room and of her responses to the situations. Here is an entry from late March that it shows an approach to teaching that encourages children to participate in and to love poetry.

Poetry is an integral part of my third-grade reading curriculum. My students and I start every day chorally reading our five poems of the month. First we read them together; then the child of the day is allowed to choose two poems he/she would like to read aloud independently. My students will not let me forget to read the poems.

The most thrilling thing happened the other day when about six of my students came up to my desk and said, "Miss Butler, we remember the poem 'Peter the Snowman' from January's poems. Can we say it for you?" This poem had not been up for two months. They recited it beautifully, even giving the author and illustrator. Most of my students can do this with all of the poems we've read since September.

Figure 7-6   Helping children love poetry.

own. They should not be forced to analyze a poem, telling "what the poet really meant" or counting the beats to see if it is iambic pentameter. Poetry is not dressed up or covered up prose, and paraphrasing poems and parsing lines discourage children from further interest. Active, creative responses allow children to interact with poetry in ways that increase their interest.

INVOLVING CHILDREN WITH POETRY

Here are some of the ways children can interact with poetry in a classroom setting.

Choral Speaking and Reading

Children can begin to engage in choral speaking as they listen to Mother Goose rhymes, chiming in on the refrains or saying those lines that they have learned just from listening. Many will have enjoyed finger plays and will have repeated the refrains of predictable books. Children learn the lines because they have heard them often and because the sound of the language is pleasing. This type of unison choral speaking is nonthreatening since children participate when they are comfortable doing so.

Choral speaking is particularly valuable if children themselves decide how a poem should be read. This means that they are attending to the meaning and the mood; they are interpreting the poem themselves. The teacher will introduce different ways of approaching choral reading as he or she introduces particular poems; doing so demonstrates possibilities. Children might then suggest and try other ways, or they may simply have learned about and enjoyed an approach that they may use later.

Decisions about choral reading involve deciding who will say or read which parts and how they will read them. Some poems can be read with two groups in a question-and-answer format; some have refrains, so a group might do the chorus with single voices reciting verses. Other poems have lines that can be given to individuals. Still others may have words that seem to echo or to contain a sound effect that can be made as background accompaniment. Paul Fleischman has written poems for "two voices" that are intended to be read by two people or groups. One group reads the words in the left column and the other the words in the right. The poems capture the noise of the insects described in his book *Joyful Noise*.

Teachers can encourage small groups of children to interpret and read poems and then compare how and why they chose to present it as they did.

Figure 7-7 shows how one kindergarten teacher introduced a poem from *The Tamarindo Puppy* to her class, and how she reflected on the children's responses.

> Writing the "parts" for choral speaking in different colors can help children keep track of the part they are to read.

Drama

Choral reading and speaking seems to lead naturally to dramatization. Young children delight in adding the motions to such verses as this one from *Whiskers & Rhymes*.

> Gaily afloat,
> Three men in a boat,
> In the sun on the waves of the ocean.
> But their faces got burned
> And their stomachs were turned
> By the rollicking, frolicking motion. (n.p.)[24]

Sometimes poems can be pantomimed, with one child reading while others do the acting. Shel Silverstein's "Boa Constrictor" begs to have its action dramatized. One group of children used the space under their tables as the "boa." They began with only their feet in that space, and as the poem continued, they moved more and more of their bodies beneath the tables.

> **BOA CONSTRICTOR**
> Oh, I'm being eaten
> By a boa constrictor,
> A boa constrictor,
> A boa constrictor,
> I'm being eaten by a boa constrictor,
> And I don't like it—one bit.

---

[24] *Source:* Text of "Gaily Afloat" from WHISKERS & RHYMES by Arnold Lobel. Text Copyright © 1985 by Arnold Lobel. Reprinted by permission of Greenwillow Books, a division of William Morrow and Company, Inc.

FIRE HOUSE

Parque de bombas—boom boo.
Parque de vacas—moo moo.
Parque de perros—bow wow.
Parque de gatos—meow meow.

   Parque de fire engines pumping,
   Parque de bombas, bombas, boo.
   Parque de vacas, vacas, vacas,
   Parque de cows and moo, moo, moo.
   Parque de perros, perros, perros,
   Parque de dogs and bow wow wow.
   Parque de gatos, gatos, gatos,
   Parque de cats and meow, meow, meow.

     Parque de bombas—boom boo.
     Parque de vacas—moo moo.
     Parque de perros—bow wow.
     Parque de gatos—meow meow. (Charlotte Pomerantz 9)

THE LESSON, AS PLANNED AND TAUGHT	REFLECTIONS . . .

Rationale

Sondra wanted her kindergarten class to enjoy a poem, to take part in saying the words when they felt comfortable doing so, and to learn to read some of the words. She also wanted her Spanish-speaking children to see and hear their native language in the school context, and her English-speaking students to gain an appreciation of other languages, particularly Spanish. She decided to use "Fire House" in *The Tamarindo Puppy* (New York: Greenwillow, 1993 [1980]) with its combination of English and Spanish within the same poem and its rhythm, rhyme, and repetition.

Both the full book of poetry and the specific poem fit Sondra's purposes well. The rhyme and repetition added to the predictability of the poem, and the two languages are equally important in the sound and the meaning of the poem.

The Lesson

Sondra introduced the poem by telling the children that it had both English and Spanish words. Then she asked the children what the Spanish words *bombas, vacas, perros,* and *gatos* would be in English and wrote both the Spanish and the English on chart paper. She played a game where she would give a definition and the children would find the word in both English and Spanish.

Once the children seemed to know the words, she read the poem and displayed it on chart paper. She read it several times and invited the children to read as much of it with her as they could. Then children came up and cupped their hands around any word they knew. They recognized both English and Spanish words.

Sondra was pleased that the children had learned the words so quickly, and that they seemed to enjoy the poem. Still, she felt that the experience was more of a lesson in reading than a literary activity, and she wasn't sure how the children felt about the languages or speakers of other languages.

As Sondra reread and thought about the poem, she realized that the meaning of many of the words could be inferred from the context. By presenting the words as a vocabulary list, she had not given the children the chance to use their knowledge of how languages work, nor had she focused on the rhythm, rhyme, and fun of the poem.

She decided that the next time she would read the poem several times to the children, ask them to say parts when they knew them, and ask in general what they thought the poem was about.

Then she would show the poem on chart paper, read it several times with her hand moving under the words and have the children chime in on words or phrases they knew. Only then would she have children isolate a word and tell what it meant. She might have the children find both English and Spanish words for the same object. She would encourage the children to find words in the language that was not their native tongue.

Sondra decided to try this approach when she introduced "The Tea Party," another poem from the same collection.

Figure 7-7   On second thought: Let children discover.

Source: Text of "Fire House" from THE TAMARINDO PUPPY by Charlotte Pomerantz. Copyright © 1980 by Charlotte Pomerantz. Reprinted by permission of Greenwillow Books, a division of William Morrow and Company, Inc.

Well, what do you know?
It's nibblin' my toe.
Oh gee,
It's up to my knee.
Oh my,
It's up to my thigh.
Oh fiddle,
It's up to my middle.
Oh heck,
It's up to my neck.
Oh dread,
It's upmmmmmmmmmmmmfffffffffff . . . (45)[25]

And just as in reading, children can decide how they will dramatize a poem and may try it several different ways.

Art

Responding to poetry through art, whatever the medium, again involves interpretation. Children may approach the creation of a painting, or draw-

Responding to poetry through art involves interpretation.

[25] *Source:* "Boa Constrictor" from WHERE THE SIDEWALK ENDS by Shel Silverstein, Copyright © 1974 by Evil Eye Music, Inc. Selection reprinted by permission of Harper-Collins Publishers.

ing, or three-dimensional piece, to accompany a poem just as a professional artist would. That is, they must make a decision about what to paint. They may focus on content, depicting just what the poem says, which means selecting what is central to the poem. Perhaps their art will go beyond the poem, bringing in elements that came to the child as he or she listened to the poem. Perhaps the painting will capture the mood of the poem through colors and images not actually mentioned in the poem. Ask children to listen as you read a poem. Then ask them to close their eyes and describe the image they see—what it was that stuck with them from the poem. This can get them started in trusting and exploring their responses and provides a beginning point for artistic interpretation.

Writing

When poet Georgia Heard works with children, she tells them about how she creates a poem, showing drafts and discussing decisions she made. She writes, "Poems come from something deeply felt; it's essential for student poets to be able to choose their own topics according to what's important to them" (14). Thus she begins by talking with the children about their feelings and what is important to them.

Poetry writing is likely to be more successful if children begin by focusing on what they want to say. Trying to make a poem rhyme or fit a specific scheme often results in strange-sounding sentences that at best are awkward and at worst have no meaning at all. Figure 7-8 describes how one teacher encouraged his students to write poetry.

Strategies that apply for prose writing also work well with poetry writing. A teacher may have a small group of children discuss their ideas, cluster their ideas on a chart, or do a free-write. And the writing of poetry remains a viable choice during writing time.

Children who are involved with poetry build an appreciation for it. Erin, a fourth grader, is in a school and classroom where poetry is valued. She and several of her classmates read *I'll Meet You at the Cucumbers* and decided to write to poet Lilian Moore. Erin's letter appears in Figure 7-9.

Erin has responded to the story and has appreciated the poems within this context. She recognizes that writing poetry is not easy. And she is open and eager for more—more poetry and more stories and poems about Adam and Amanda. (She got her wish. There is a sequel and also a collection of Adam's poems.)

SUMMARY

No single characteristic differentiates poetry from prose, but most poetry relies on very concentrated language, with words carefully chosen and arranged, to communicate an idea. Children learn about these qualities from hearing and reading poetry and from writing poetry of their own. Poets use

Rich's group of second graders had not read much poetry and had not written any when they came into his class. He began reading to them immediately and now was ready to engage them in the writing of a class poem. He began by suggesting they think of something they knew about, perhaps something they liked to do. So the children brainstormed and Rich recorded their ideas on chart paper. Then they began to narrow the topic. Most seemed interested in talking about dancing and singing, and they went on to tell about what music they liked to listen to, particularly which groups.

"Let's write about music," they said. So Rich began a second list, this time of the phrases and feelings that came to mind when they thought about music. This time, though, the phrases were written on strips of paper and put on the chalkboard with masking tape. Rich explained that after they had listed many feelings and thoughts, they would select some of them, organize them into a poem, and make changes that might make their poem sound better.

The writing threatened to get off course when an argument began between the girls, who wanted New Kids on the Block listed, and the boys, who did not want the group even to be considered for the poem. The group was listed on a strip of paper as Rich explained that this was a "phrase-gathering" stage and that they would use only some of the words in their poem.

As they neared the bottom of the third column of phrases, Rich announced that they would stop when that section of the board was filled. Then they all read over the phrases. Rich asked them to select one that would make a good first line for their poem. They wanted to start with naming the kinds of music they liked. Rich began moving the strips of paper onto a fresh area of the board as the children made choices.

With each choice they checked to see that the meaning was clear. They read the whole poem over several times to see how it sounded.

Figure 7-8   Writing their own poetry.

elements such as sound, rhyme, rhythm, figurative language, imagery, shape, and spacing to help in this communication.

Much poetry for children is narrative, telling a story. This is one of the forms most popular with children. Lyric poetry, which describes something in lines with a singing quality, is also very common. Haiku, nonsense poetry, limericks, free verse, concrete poetry, and rap are just some of the forms used in poetry for children.

Good poetry has fresh or original ideas, insight or emotion, effective poetic devices and language, and a sincere voice. Teachers selecting poems for children look first at the quality of the poem. Then they consider the age and background of the children, their poetry preferences, representation of cultural diversity, variety in form and content, and

This is Room #5's poem:

Music to Your Ear

  Rap
    Rock 'n roll
      Pop
Really cool.
They're all rich
  Michael Jackson
    M.C. Hammer
      Vanilla Ice
Kris Kross is gonna make you jump.
      JUMP!

Rich divided the class into four groups by the way their tables were arranged, and they read the poem chorally, with each group reading one line from each stanza, then the entire class reading the last two lines—and jumping as they said "JUMP!"

The children were pleased with their poem. It expressed ideas they had about music. Rich was pleased that the poem said things the children cared about and that they had been attentive to the sound of the language. They added the title last, trying to find words that would relate to the content of the poem. Later in the week, when the children were copying the poem individually and adding illustrations, Rich noticed that most did not copy the spacing and indentation he had used. He noted to himself that he would want to talk about how a poem looked as well as how it sounded as the class continued to read and write poetry.

Figure 7-8   *continued*

the relationship of the poem to children's experiences and to classroom activities.

Children react positively to poetry when they are encouraged to respond through such activities as art, drama, choral reading, writing, and singing. Books of poetry should be readily available in the classroom, with poetry shared regularly. Figure 7-10, a list of recommended poetry books, can be used as a starting point for becoming familiar with quality poetry for children.

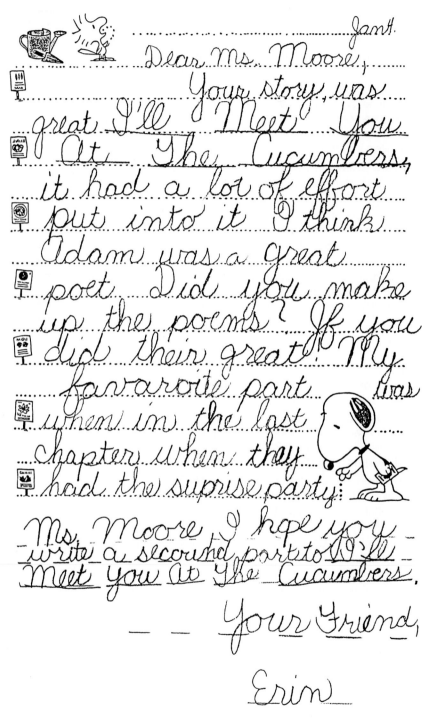

Jan 4.

Dear Ms. Moore,

Your story was great. I'll Meet You At The Cucumbers, it had a lot of effort put into it. I think Adam was a great poet. Did you make up the poems? If you did their great! My favaroite part was when in the last chapter when they had the suprise party.

Ms. Moore I hope you write a secound part to I'll Meet you At The Cucumbers.

— — Your Friend,

Erin

Figure 7-9 Letter to a poet.

Adoff, Arnold. *Sports Pages*. Ill. by Steve Kuzma. New York: Lippincott, 1986. Adoff writes of the pleasures and the pain of participation in sports, evoking rhythm and movement through the placement of the words on the page as well as through their meanings.

Behn, Harry. *Cricket Songs*. Ill. with pictures "from Sesshu and other Japanese masters." New York: Harcourt Brace Jovanovich, 1964. An introduction to haiku by a variety of poets.

Bierhorst, John, ed. *On the Road of Stars: Native American Nights Poems and Sleep Charms.* Ill. by Judy Pedersen. New York: Macmillan, 1994. Poems and sleep charms from various Native peoples are presented with effective illustrations.

Brooks, Gwendolyn. *Bronzville Boys and Girls*. Ill. by Ronni Solbert. New York: Harper, 1956. Set in Chicago, each poem is about a different child's feelings.

Ciardi, John. *Doodle Soup*. Ill. by Merle Nacht. Boston: Houghton Mifflin, 1985. Ciardi's poems are light and humorous, some nonsense, and some tongue-in-cheek cautionary.

Clifton, Lucille. *Everett Anderson's Year*. Ill. by Ann Grifalconi. New York: Holt, 1974. One of several books about Everett Anderson, this offers a poem for each month, recounting special events in 7-year-old Everett's life and his reactions to them.

de Regniers, Beatrice Schenk. *Sing a Song of Popcorn*. Ill. by Marcia Brown, Leo and Diane Dillon, Richard Egielski, Trina Schart Hyman, Arnold Lobel, Maurice Sendak, Marc Simont, and Margot Zemach. New York: Scholastic, 1988. This collection, divided into nine sections, combines the poetry of renowned poets with illustrations by Caldecott Award-winning illustrators.

Dunning, Steven, Edward Lueders, and Hugh Smith, eds. *Reflections on a Gift of Watermelon Pickle . . .* New York: Lothrop, Lee & Shepard, 1967. The modern poems in this collection range from the serious to the lighthearted and present a variety of forms.

Esbensen, Barbara Juster. *Who Shrank My Grandmother's House?* Ill. by Eric Beddows. NY: HarperCollins, 1992. Esbensen stretches the imagination with her poems about discoveries in everyday life. Spaces in the text play an important role in these poems.

Fisher, Aileen. *Out in the Dark and Daylight*. Ill. by Gail Owens. New York: Harper, 1980. Fisher writes about nature, often from a child's point of view.

Fleischman, Paul. *Joyful Noise, Poems for Two Voices*. Ill. by Eric Beddows. New York: Harper, 1988. Each of these poems about insects is designed to be read by two persons, one reading the left column and one reading the right.

Greenfield, Eloise. *Honey, I Love and Other Love Poems.* Ill. by Leo and Diane Dillon. New York: Crowell, 1972. These 16 short poems capture the reactions of a young black child to everyday experiences.

Figure 7-10   Touchstones of poetry for children.

Hall, Donald. *I Am the Dog. I Am the Cat*. Ill. by Barry Moser. New York: Dial, 1994.This contrasting picture of the dog and the cat provides much humor, and lends itself to choral reading.

Hughes, Langston. *Don't You Turn Back*. Poems selected by Lee Bennett Hopkins. Ill. by Ann Grifalconi. New York: Knopf, 1969. Hopkins selected poems by Hughes that evoked strong feelings in children from many different parts of the country.

Hughes, Shirley. *Out and About*. New York: Lothrop, Lee & Shepard, 1988. Hughes presents rich ideas and images in these poems for young children about seasons and the elements of earth, air, fire, and water.

Janeczko, Paul B., sel. *The Place My Words Are Looking For*. New York: Bradbury, 1990. Thirty-nine poets share both one of their poems and their thoughts about poetry and ways of writing.

Kennedy, X. J., and Dorothy Kennedy, eds. *Knock on a Star: A Child's Introduction to Poetry*. Ill. by Karen Ann Weinhaus. Boston: Little, Brown, 1982. This anthology helps children learn about and enjoy poetry.

Koch, Kenneth, and Kate Farrell, sel. *Talking to the Sun*. Ill. with works of art from the Metropolitan Museum of Art. New York: Holt, Rinehart & Winston, 1985. Poems from a wide range of sources and periods are matched with paintings and other art from the Metropolitan Museum of Art.

Kuskin, Karla. *Dogs & Dragons Trees & Dreams*. New York: Harper, 1980. Many of Kuskin's most popular poems are in this collection, from the light to the serious, and in a variety of forms.

Livingston, Myra Cohn. *Celebrations*. Ill. by Leonard Everett Fisher. New York: Holiday House, 1985. Each of the poems about a holiday is embedded in a mood-capturing illustration.

Lobel, Arnold. *Whiskers & Rhymes*. New York: Greenwillow, 1985. These contemporary nursery rhymes are filled with rhythm, rhyme, and humor.

McCord, David. *One At a Time*. Ill. by Henry B. Kane. Boston: Little, Brown, 1977. This collection of McCord's previously published poems includes many of the best known.

Margolis, Richard J. *Secrets of a Small Brother*. Ill. by Donald Carrick. New York: Macmillan, 1984. In unrhymed poetry Margolis expresses the thoughts of the younger brother about life with his older sibling.

Merriam, Eve. *Blackberry Ink*. Ill. by Hans Wilhelm. New York: William Morrow & Co., 1985. In this collection Merriam plays with the sounds and rhythms of language and the use of refrains and repetition.

Moore, Lilian. *Something New Begins*. New York: Atheneum, 1982. Moore's use of figurative language brings new ways of seeing everyday experiences and events in nature.

Morrison, Lillian. *The Break Dance Kids*. New York: Lothrop, Lee & Shepard, 1985. Morrison's poems capture the rhythm and movement in sports and dance.

Figure 7-10 *continued*

Myers, Walter Dean. *Brown Angels.* New York: HarperCollins, 1993. Myers has written poems to accompany snapshots of black children, part of his collection of old photos. Each celebrates the pride of the adults who dressed them for the sitting.

O'Neill, Mary. *Hailstones and Halibut Bones.* 1961. Ill. by John Wallner. New York: Doubleday, 1989. Each poem is about a different color, its look, its feel, its mood.

Prelutsky, Jack. *The Dragons are Singing Tonight.* Ill. by Peter Sis. New York: Greenwillow, 1993. Sis's illustrations capture perfectly the diverse personalities of each of the dragons Prelutsky describes.

Prelutsky, Jack, sel. *The Random House Book of Poetry for Children.* Ill. by Arnold Lobel. New York: Random House, 1983. This useful anthology organizes the poems by themes.

Prelutsky, Jack. *Something BIG Has Been Here.* Ill. by James Stevenson. New York: Greenwillow, 1990. Prelutsky's light and zany verse keeps children laughing.

Read, Herbert, comp. *This Way Delight.* Ill. by Juliet Kepes. New York: Pantheon, 1956. A wide selection of works by adult poets, from Shakespeare to T. S. Eliot, is organized to lead "gradually from the simpler poems to the more difficult."

Silverstein, Shel. *Where the Sidewalk Ends.* New York: Harper, 1974. This is a representative sampling of Silverstein's zany wit in poetry and in illustration.

Slier, Deborah, ed. *Make a Joyful Sound: Poems for Children by African-American Poets.* New York: Checkerboard Press, 1991. These poems by both well-known poets (such as Nikki Giovanni, Gwendolyn Brooks, and Langston Hughes) and "new" poets are upbeat and joyful in tone.

Soto, Gary. *Neighborhood Odes.* San Diego: Harcourt, 1992. Soto's poems explore the lives of children in a Mexican American neighborhood.

Willard, Nancy. *A Visit to William Blake's Inn.* Ill. by Alice and Martin Provensen. New York: Harcourt Brace Jovanovich, 1981. Willard's poems about visitors to an imaginary inn were inspired by Blake's work. This book won the Newbery Medal for the text and was a Caldecott Honor Book for the illustrations.

Worth, Valerie. *All the Small Poems.* Ill. by Natalie Babbitt. New York: Farrar, 1987. This volume contains all four of Worth's earlier books, all presenting poetry focused on nature and strong in imagery and figurative language.

Figure 7-10 *continued*

∞ EXPLORE ON YOUR OWN

1. **Explore Your Personal Response.** Select three theme-oriented books of poetry, such as *Cats* compiled by Nancy Larrick, *Sports Pages* by Arnold Adoff, or *Roomrimes* by Sylvia Cassedy. Note two poems in each that you respond to strongly, either positively or negatively. For each, try to identify factors that may have contributed to your response.

2. **Apply Literary Criteria.** Study the work of one poet, reading at least three of his or her books. What characterizes the work? Assemble the books in the order of their publication. Has the poet's work changed over time? If so, how?

   or

   Evaluate the quality of poetry that appears in several home subscription magazines for children; for example, in *Cricket, Ladybug, Highlights for Children, Your Big Backyard, Ranger Rick, Humpty Dumpty, Jack and Jill, Turtle, Children's Playmate,* or *Sesame Street.*

   or

   Compare two picture book editions of a single poem. Do the interpretations differ? Which seems to better capture the mood of the poem? There are at least two picture book editions of *Jabberwocky, The Owl and the Pussycat, Paul Revere's Ride, The Night Before Christmas, The Highwayman,* and *Casey at the Bat.*

3. **Prepare to Share Literature With Children.** List 10 experiences you would expect elementary school children to have or events that might occur during the year. Using an anthology such as *The Random House Book of Poetry for Children* (Prelutsky) or *Sing a Song of Popcorn* (de Regniers), select an appropriate poem to share during or immediately after each experience.

∞ EXPLORE WITH CHILDREN

1. **Explore Children's Responses.** Interview at least five children. Ask them to tell you what they know about poetry. Record their responses. See if any patterns emerge.

   or

   Read the haiku poem "I Stare at the Rain" by Rebecca Caudill to children of several different ages. Ask them to pretend they are preparing a book of poetry and are to illustrate this poem. When they have finished their drawings, ask them to tell why they illustrated it as they did. What do their responses tell you about their understanding of metaphoric language?

   "I stare at the rain,
   And rain, like our old gray cat,
   Stares coldly at me."

   or

   Find poems for either primary or intermediate grade children that are on the same topic but represent three different forms of poetry. Read them to several children and record their preferences. Analyze their likes and dislikes.

2. **Engage Children With Literature.** Share a poem with children and ask them to respond to it through art, writing, or drama.

   or

   Engage a group of children in a choral reading or speaking experience, one in which they help plan how the poem is to be presented.

∽ SUGGESTED PROFESSIONAL REFERENCES

Chukovsky, Kornei. *From Two to Five*. Trans. and ed. Miriam Morton. Berkeley: University of California Press, 1963. § Chukovsky describes children's enjoyment of and own natural use of poetic language.

Ciardi, John. *How Does a Poem Mean?* 2nd ed. Boston: Houghton Mifflin, 1975. § Ciardi looks at the characteristics and structure of poetry, with a final chapter on how the criteria can be applied to the comprehension of a total poem.

Copeland, Jeffrey S. *Speaking of Poets: Interviews With Poets Who Write for Children and Young Adults*. Urbana, IL: National Council of Teachers of English, 1993. § The 16 poets who talk with Copeland reveal their approaches to writing poetry and share their understanding of and concern for the child reader's response.

Copeland, Jeffrey S. *Speaking of Poets 2: More Interviews With Poets Who Write for Children and Young Adults*. Urbana, IL: National Council of Teachers of English, 1994. § This book continues Copeland's project of interviewing poets about their work, presenting the thoughts of 20 more poets.

Cullinan, Bernice, Marilyn Scala, and Virginia Schroder. *Three Voices: An Invitation to Poetry Across the Curriculum*. York: ME: Stenhouse, 1995. § The authors describe strategies for guiding children's exploration of poetry and give specific examples of poetry integrated into various curricular areas.

Fisher, Carol J., and Margaret A. Natarella. "Young Children's Preferences in Poetry: A National Survey of First, Second and Third Graders." *Research in the Teaching of English* 16 (Dec. 1982): 339–354. § The primary children in this study showed nearly the same poetry preferences as intermediate children in the earlier study by Terry.

Denman, Gregory A. *When You've Made It Your Own . . .* Portsmouth, NH: Heinemann, 1988. § Denman presents techniques for sharing poetry with children and for helping them write poetry themselves.

Dunn, Sonja, with Lou Pamenter. *Butterscotch Dreams*. Markham, Ontario: Pembroke Publishers, 1987. § Dunn presents over 60 original chants with suggestions for involving children in saying, singing, and miming them.

Heard, Georgia. *For the Good of Earth and Sun*. Portsmouth, NH: Heinemann, 1989. § Heard presents a way of teaching poetry that emphasizes its meaning and emotional power.

Hopkins, Lee Bennett. *Pass the Poetry, Please!* rev. ed. New York: Harper, 1987. § Hopkins focuses on ways of integrating poetry into the classroom, with many specific suggestions. Interviews of contemporary poets are included.

Koch, Kenneth. *Wishes, Lies, and Dreams*. New York: Chelsea House, 1970. § Koch describes the techniques he used to teach children in P.S. 61 in New York City to write poetry. Emphasis is on collaboration and on patterned poems.

Larrick, Nancy. *Let's Do a Poem*. New York: Delacorte, 1991. § Larrick shows how to introduce poetry to children through choral reading, listening, singing, movement, and dramatization.

Livingston, Myra Cohn. *Poem-Making: Ways to Begin Writing Poetry*. New York: Harper, 1991. § Livingston describes the elements of poetry and with many examples shows how structure helps to make a poem effective.

Livingston, Myra Cohn. *When You Are Alone/It Keeps You Capone*. New York: Atheneum, 1973. § Livingston describes her own successful work in guiding children in the writing of poetry.

McClure, Amy A., with Peggy Harrison and Sheryl Reed. *Sunrises and Songs*. Portsmouth, NH: Heinemann, 1990. § McClure describes the process used by two elementary school teachers to teach poetry to the children in their multi-age, rural class.

Padgett, Ron. ed. *The Teachers & Writers Handbook of Poetic Forms*. New York: Teachers & Writers Collaborative, 1987. § Seventy-four forms are defined, with history and examples of each form.

Perrine, Laurence. *Sound and Sense: An Introduction to Poetry*. 5th ed. New York: Harcourt Brace Jovanovich, 1977. § Elements of poetry are defined and then illustrated with many examples.

Terry, Ann. *Children's Poetry Preferences: A National Survey of Upper Elementary Grades*. Urbana, IL: National Council of Teachers of English, 1974, reissued 1984. § The preferences found by Terry provide guidelines for selecting poems children will enjoy.

∾ CHILDREN'S BOOKS CITED

Adoff, Arnold. *All the Colors of the Race*. Ill. by John Steptoe. New York: Lothrop, Lee & Shepard, 1982.

Adoff, Arnold. *Brown Is Black Is Tan*. Ill. by Emily McCully. New York: Harper, 1973.

Adoff, Arnold. *Greens*. Ill. by Betsy Levin. New York: Lothrop, Lee & Shepard, 1988.

Adoff, Arnold. *Sports Pages*. Ill. by Steve Kuzma. New York: Lippincott, 1986.

Browning, Robert. *The Pied Piper of Hamelin*. Ill. by Kate Greenaway. London: Warne, 1988.

Carroll, Lewis. *Jabberwocky*. Ill. by Graeme Base. New York: Abrams, 1989. Copyright 1987.

Cassedy, Sylvia. *Roomrimes*. Ill. by Michele Chessare. New York: Crowell, 1987.

Caudill, Rebecca. *Come Along!* Ill. by Ellen Raskin. New York: Holt, Rinehart & Winston, 1969.

Ciardi, John. *You Read to Me, I'll Read to You*. Ill. by Edward Gorey. New York: Lippincott, 1962.

Coltman, Paul. *Tog the Ribber or Granny's Tale*. Ill. by Gillian McClure. New York: Farrar Strauss Giroux, 1985.

Degan, Bruce. *Jamberry*. New York: Harper & Row, 1983.

de Regniers, Beatrice Schenk, sel. *Sing a Song of Popcorn*. New York: Scholastic, Inc., 1988.

Esbensen, Barbara Juster. *Cold Stars and Fireflies*. Ill. by Susan Bonners. New York: Crowell, 1984.

Esbensen, Barbara. *Words with Wrinkled Knees*. Ill. by John Stadler. New York: Crowell, 1986.

Fisher, Aileen. *Out in the Dark and Daylight*. Ill. by Gail Owens. New York: Harper, 1980.

Fleischman, Paul. *Joyful Noise*. Ill. by Eric Beddows. New York: Harper, 1988.

Froman, Robert. *Seeing Things*. New York: Crowell, 1974.

Giovanni, Nikki. *Spin a Soft Black Song*. Ill. by Charles Bible. New York: Hill and Wang, 1971.

Greenfield, Eloise. *Nathaniel Talking*. Ill. by Jan Spivey Gilchrist. New York: Black Butterfly Children's Books, 1988.

Greenfield, Eloise. *Under the Sunday Tree*. Ill. by Amos Ferguson. New York: Harper, 1988.

Hoban, Russell. *The Pedaling Man and Other Poems*. Ill. by Lillian Hoban. New York: Norton, 1968.

Hoberman, Mary Ann. *A Little Book of Little Beasts*. Ill. by Peter Parnall. New York: Simon & Schuster, 1973.

Hughes, Shirley. *Out and About*. New York: Lothrop, Lee & Shepard, 1988.

Issa. "Grasshopper" haiku in Lewis, Richard. Ed. *In a Spring Garden*. Ill. by Ezra Jack Keats. New York: Dial, 1965.

Jones, Hettie. Selector. *The Trees Stand Shining*. 1971. Ill. by Robert Andrew Parker. New York: Dial, 1993.

Larrick, Nancy, comp. *Cats Are Cats*. Ill. by Ed Young. New York: Philomel, 1988.

Lauture, Denize. *Father and Son*. Ill. by Jonathan Green. New York: Philomel, 1993.

Lear, Edward. *The Owl and the Pussycat*. Ill. by Paul Galdone. New York: Clarion, 1987.

Livingston, Myra Cohn. *There Was a Place and Other Poems*. New York: Macmillan, 1988.

Lobel, Arnold. *The Book of Pigericks*. New York: Harper, 1983.

Lobel, Arnold. *Whiskers & Rhymes*. New York: Greenwillow, 1985.

Longfellow, Henry Wadsworth. *Hiawatha*. Ill. by Susan Jeffers. New York: Dial, 1983.

Longfellow, Henry Wadsworth. *Paul Revere's Ride*. Ill. by Nancy Winslow Parker. New York: Greenwillow, 1985.

McCord, David. *One at a Time*. Ill. by Henry B. Kane. Boston: Little, Brown, 1986.

McCord, David. *Pen, Paper and Pencil*. New York: Holt, Rinehart & Winston, 1973.

Margolis, Richard. *Secrets of a Small Brother*. Ill. by Donald Carrick. New York: Macmillan, 1984.

Merriam, Eve. *It Doesn't Always Have to Rhyme*. Ill. by Malcolm Spooner. New York: Atheneum, 1966.

Moore, Clement. *The Night Before Christmas*. Ill. by James Marshall. New York: Scholastic, 1986.

Moore, Lilian. *I'll Meet You at the Cucumbers*. Ill. by Sharon Wooding. New York: Atheneum, 1988.

Morrison, Lillian. *The Break Dance Kids, Poems of Sport, Motion, and Locomotion*. New York: Lothrop, Lee & Shepard, 1985.

Pomerantz, Charlotte. *The Tamarindo Puppy and Other Poems*. Ill. by Bryon Barton. New York: Greenwillow, 1980.

Prelutsky, Jack. *The New Kid on the Block*. Ill. by James Stevenson. New York: Greenwillow, 1984.

Prelutsky, Jack. Selector. *The Random House Book of Poetry for Children*. Ill. by Arnold Lobel. New York: Random House, 1983.

Prelutsky, Jack. *Something BIG Has Been Here*. Ill. by James Stevenson. New York: Greenwillow, 1990.

Riley, James Whitcomb. *Little Orphant Annie*. Ill. by Diane Stanley. New York: Putnam, 1983.

"Robin Hood and Allan-a-Dale," in Manning-Sanders, Ruth. Comp. *A Bundle of Ballads*. London: Oxford University Press, 1959.

Sandburg, Carl. *Early Moon*. 1930. New York: Harcourt, 1958.

Service, Robert. *The Cremation of Sam McGee*. Ill. by Ted Harrison. New York: Greenwillow, 1987.

Siebert, Diane. *Heartland*. Ill. by Wendell Minor. New York: Crowell, 1989.

Silverstein, Shel. "Boa Constrictor" in *Where the Sidewalk Ends*. New York: Harper, 1974, p. 45.

Silverstein, Shel. *A Light in the Attic*. New York: Harper-Collins, 1981.

Silverstein, Shel. *Where the Sidewalk Ends*. New York: Harper, 1974.

Slier, Deborah, ed. *Make a Joyful Sound: Poems for Children by African-American Poets*. New York: Checkerboard Press, 1991.

Stevenson, James. *Sweet Corn*. New York: Greenwillow, 1995.

Stevenson, Robert Louis. *A Child's Garden of Verses*. Ill. by Brian Wildsmith. London: Oxford University Press, 1966.

Tripp, Wallace. *A Great Big Ugly Man Came Up and Tied His Horse to Me*. Boston: Little, Brown, 1973.

"Turn Off the Water All the Way," author unlisted. *Your Big Backyard* (June 1980).

Williams, William Carlos. *Collected Earlier Poems*. New York: New Directions Publishing Corporation, 1938.

Wood, Nancy. *Many Winters*. Garden City, New York: Doubleday, 1974.

Worth, Valerie. *All the Small Poems*. Ill. by Natalie Babbitt. New York: Sunburst (Farrar), 1987.

∾ CHAPTER REFERENCES

Anderson, Celia, and Apseloff, Marilyn. *Nonsense Literature for Children, Aesop to Seuss*. Hamden, CT: Library Professional Publications, 1989.

Brewton, John, G. Meredith, and Lorraine Blackburn, comps. *Index to Poetry for Children and Young People 1976–1981*. New York: Wilson, 1984.

Chukovsky, Kornei. *From Two to Five*. Trans. and ed. by Miriam Morton. Berkeley: University of California Press, 1963.

Fisher, Carol, and Margaret A. Natarella. "Young Children's Preferences in Poetry: A National Survey of First, Second and Third Graders." *Research in the Teaching of English* 16 (Dec. 1982): 339–353.

Heard, Georgia. *For the Good of the Earth and Sun*. Portsmouth, NH: Heinemann, 1989.

Kutiper, Karen, and Wilson, Patricia. "Updating Poetry Preferences: A Look at the Poetry Children Really Like." *The Reading Teacher* 47.1 (Sept. 1993): 28–35.

Padgett, Ron, ed. *The Teachers & Writers Handbook of Poetic Forms*. New York: Teachers & Writers Collaborative, 1987.

Perrine, Laurence. *Sound and Sense*. 5th ed. New York: Harcourt Brace Jovanovich, 1977.

Raposa, Joe. *Green (Bein' Green)*. Copyright 1970 and 1977, Jonico Music.

Terry, Ann. *Children's Poetry Preferences: A National Survey of Upper Elementary Grades*. Urbana, IL: National Council of Teachers of English, 1972.

Chapter Eight

Traditional Literature: Familiar Tales, Different Voices

Six fourth graders decided that they would respond to the class literature unit on folktales by writing a newspaper about the happenings in the stories and about related events that may have been "unreported" previously. They titled their paper *The Daily Fairy Tale* and created the features, worked on layout, and finally published copies for all their classmates. Each student contributed several features. Billy reported on an interview with the shoemaker, who was quoted as saying, "At first I liked the elves. They were funny and interesting, and they helped me get way ahead in my work. But then they started stealing my leather, and I had to report them to the police."

A real estate ad showed that there was a "Gingerbread House" on the market. "It has been sitting in the woods for years now. It is a great house to live in with a small family. It has three bedrooms and a kitchen with an oven big enough for cooking anything." In the divorce column was the news, that, sadly, Cinderella and her prince were not living happily ever after and had signed divorce papers on March 14. On the sports page was the story of an exciting climbing race. It was close, but Rapunzel's prince made it up the beanstalk even faster than Jack. And among the comics was a strip about the Three Little Pigs. In the first segment there is a pig, with an arrow pointing to it and the words, "Artificial coloring." In the next block, another pig and the words, "Artificial flavor." In the third, the wolf, looking dejected, declares in a dialogue balloon, "Everything is artificial." Ah, but in the last block, the third pig, safely ensconced in his house, announces, "Bricks are for real!"

These young newspaper writers could be fairly certain that not only their class, but a much wider audience, would understand their articles and cartoons. All were based on tales that are part of western folk literature and that many adults and older children recall from their own childhood.

LITERATURE WITH MANY VOICES

In one classic German story, a girl named Ashputtel cannot go to a ball because her stepmother orders her to pick lentils out of cinders. Magically, she gets a pair of slippers and silver robe, goes to several balls, loses a slipper, and gains a prince. In a Chinese tale, first written down during the T'ang dynasty (618–907 A.D.), a young orphan girl living in her stepmother's home is given golden slippers and a beautiful gown so she can sneak off to the village festival. The slipper she loses is sold to a merchant and eventually to the king, who sets out in search of its owner. When he finds the girl, Yeh-Shen, he is struck by her beauty and her tiny feet, and not long after marries her (Louie).

In an Algonquin tale (*The Rough-Faced Girl* by Martin), a girl whose face and arms are scarred by sparks from the fire she is forced to attend, sees, when her older sisters do not, the face of the Invisible Being. It is she who can describe him and who marries him, but both he and his sister saw her beauty even before her scars were washed away by a bath in the lake. These are just three of the estimated 600 or more versions of the Cinderella story.

Figure 8-1 shows how one class and their teacher approached a study of folktale variants.

Three variants of the Little Red Riding Hood story are *Red Riding Hood* retold by James Marshall (New York: Dial, 1987), *Lon Po Po* translated and illustrated by Ed Young (New York: Philomel, 1989), and *Red Riding Hood* retold by Beatrice Schenk de Regniers and illustrated by Edward Gorey (New York: Macmillan, 1990).

Definition of Traditional Literature

Cinderella is a character of **traditional literature.** In some ways her story is typical of all the stories in this chapter. No one knows for sure where the story began. It was carried from country to country in the voices of thousands of tellers who changed it as they spoke it. Listeners, mainly adults, heard the tale for centuries before anyone wrote it down.

"Cinderella" is a fairy tale, a fast-moving story of magic, part of a large body of short stories called **folktales.** Several other categories of traditional literature were also centuries old before the printing press was invented in the middle of the fifteenth century. **Fables** are stories, usually about animals, that teach a lesson, often summarized in a one-line moral at the end of the tale. **Myths** are longer stories that explain how the universe and its contents came into being; myths focus on gods, ancient heroes, ancestors, and natural phenomena. **Epics** are narratives of mortal heroes whose lives are closely watched and often directed by the heavens.

Some of this traditional literature is closely related to poetry. Classic epics were long poems following strict rules of style. Folktales often use repetitive phrases (for instance, "Little pig, little pig, let me come in./ Not by the hair of my chinny-chin chin") that sound similar to the choruses of ballads. And like poetry, much of traditional literature is meant to be spoken.

Art decided to introduce a unit on folktales by reading *The Rough-Faced Girl,* an Algonquin version of the Cinderella story, told by Rafe Martin and illustrated by David Shannon (New York: Putnam's, 1992). When he had completed the story, he asked the students what the story reminded them of and why. They immediately identified Cinderella and began to state similarities between the *Cinderella* they knew and the story they had just heard. Art suggested they make a list and began writing their comments in chart form. Here is the beginning of their chart.

Cinderella	*The Rough-Faced Girl*
Sat by the fire and had to do all the work.	Sat by the fire and had to keep it burning.
Had two cruel older sisters.	Had two cruel older sisters.
Had to show that the shoe fit to marry the prince.	Had to be able to see the Invisible Being to marry him.
Lots of women, including the sisters, wanted to marry the prince.	Lots of women, including the sisters, wanted to marry the Invisible Being.
The sisters dressed up and went to the ball.	The sisters dressed up and went to the wigwam of the Invisible Being.
The sisters tried to squeeze their feet into the slipper.	The sisters tried to describe the Invisible Being's bow and the runners on his sled.
Went from ugly to beautiful with clothes from the fairy godmother.	Went from ugly to beautiful when she bathed in the lake and got clothes from the Invisible Being.

At this point, the students began talking about differences, noting particularly that Cinderella was beautiful the first time the prince saw her, whereas the Rough-Faced Girl still had her scars and burns. The prince saw a beautiful maiden; the Invisible Being and his sister saw a good heart and inner beauty.

Art led the students in naming categories for each statement on their chart. Their categories were

What the Cinderella character was like

Family members and what they were like

What the test was

How others tried to pass the test

How the Cinderella character passed the test

Important ideas in the story

Figure 8-1   Comparing variants of a folktale.

Background of Traditional Literature

No one knows exactly when the **oral tradition,** passing on stories by telling them out loud, originated, but all cultures have engaged in story-telling. Modern scholars have tried to explore how the stories began and how they migrated. Why, investigators have wondered, does Cinderella appear in different clothing in different countries? One explanation, called

These categories were added to the left side of the chart, and extra space was left at the bottom in case the children wanted to add new categories. In the days that followed, Art read four other versions of the Cinderella tale and the students filled in each category. The other books read were *The Egyptian Cinderella,* retold by Shirley Climo and illustrated by Ruth Heller (New York: Crowell, 1989); *The Korean Cinderella,* retold by Shirley Climo and illustrated by Ruth Heller (New York: HarperCollins, 1993); *Yeh-Shen, A Cinderella Story from China,* retold by Ai-Ling Louie and illustrated by Ed Young (New York: Philomel, 1982); and *Cinderella,* retold by Barbara Karlin and illustrated by James Marshall (Boston: Little, Brown, 1989). The children added four categories to the chart:

Where the story takes place

What the magic was

What the "prince" character was like

How the story made you feel

Although the children had not identified the story elements of characterization, plot, theme, setting, and style, their categories reflected all of these. The filled-in chart also let the students look at both story structure and motifs.

Art suggested that they write their own version of the Cinderella tale as a group, and that to do this, they identify the essential elements of the story by looking at their chart. They decided that the story needed a beautiful young girl mistreated by her family, a handsome young man of position and wealth, a test to find the "right" wife for the young man, some sort of magic to aid the young girl, and a marriage between the young woman and young man.

Using these guidelines, the students composed this story.

Singerella

In the time when music was heard on all the good channels, there lived a beautiful young girl named Singerella who could sing like the birds. Her two older sisters made her do the dishes and clean the house and buy the groceries.

One day a handsome rock star was walking past the grocery story and heard Singerella humming. "What beautiful music," he thought. "I'd like to marry that person and have her sing on my next video." But when he went into the store, he couldn't find her anywhere. She was so shy that she had run outside when he came in. For days he walked past the grocery, but he never heard the singing again. Finally he announced an audition in the parking lot.

Lots and lots of people sang, even Singerella's two sisters, but all the voices were awful. Singerella knew she was the one he had heard, but she was afraid to sing before a crowd. She was just about to go home when three birds began to chirp the song she had been humming in the grocery. She began to laugh and to hum along with them. The rock star heard the humming, and ran into the audience and found her. He said that he wanted to marry her and sing with her. They got married and sang happily ever after, one on TV and the other around the house.

Figure 8-1 *continued*

monogenesis, is that originally just one society (in this case, a Middle Eastern society) knew the story; its tellers passed it on to other societies while traveling. The listeners then changed the story to suit their own tastes and their audience as they told it. Another explanation of why so many tales are alike is called **polygenesis:** Similar stories grew spontaneously in separate countries because societies, though different, shared the same needs and emotions.

Whatever their origin, folk literature did travel in different voices and dialects. Storytellers slung musical instruments on their backs, crossing cultural lines and mixing and blending heritages from many lands as they collected and spread stories all over the world. Joseph Jacobs, a pioneer in publishing folktales for children, once said that he had discovered "an English version of an Italian adaptation of a Spanish translation of a Latin version of a Hebrew translation of an Arabic translation of an Indian original" (Colwell 178).

You will add a dimension to your study of stories from the oral tradition if you read them aloud and imagine the way they sounded when audiences first encountered them centuries ago. You may also want to help your students understand how storytellers changed and adapted tales. Figure 8-2 shows one way of doing this.

One source of folklore for all of us is stories that have been told and retold within our families. See if you can think of a story within *your* family that others might find entertaining.

As she listened to the students in her class, Tricia realized that while they knew and enjoyed folktales, they really had no concept of the oral tradition underlying the stories that were so familiar to them. She decided to incorporate a lesson about the history of folk literature into an ongoing unit on folktales.

She began by dividing the students into three groups. Each student in group 1 was to write *The Three Little Pigs* from memory. Those in group 2 were to write *Jack and the Beanstalk* and in group 3 *Little Red Riding Hood.* The students in each group read and compared their versions, then presented the results to the total group, telling what similarities and what differences they found.

The students were told that no one version was "right" and began to discuss why there were differences in their memories of the stories. Tricia than talked with them about how these tales were originally told orally and were retold by many different storytellers. The reasons they gave for their different versions—how they heard it, what they remembered, what they liked—may well have influenced those ancient storytellers as well.

Then Tricia introduced the idea that storytellers sometimes changed a story or its presentation to fit their audience. Each group was to prepare and tell their story as though it were for a different audience. *The Three Little Pigs* was to be told to a group of preschool children; *Jack and the Beanstalk* to elementary children who were still in the process of learning English; and *Little Red Riding Hood* to a group of campers sitting around a campfire at night. Each group presented its story and then told how and why they had adapted their retelling to their specific audience.

An unexpected bonus of the lessons was the children's awareness of cultural information in variants of a folktale from different countries and from different regions within the United States. They saw how both what the storyteller and the intended audience knew influenced details of a story, even when the structure and the motifs remained constant.

Figure 8-2   Teaching about the oral tradition.

FOLKTALES

Folktales provide a rich source of literature for children even though they were originally told for adults. Authors and illustrators have researched and retold, bringing to children good stories and often introducing them to new countries and peoples.

Collectors of Folktales

Some tales have come to be associated with the person or persons who first wrote them down. Thus we talk about "Grimm's Fairy Tales" because it was Jakob and Wilhelm Grimm who began to collect and then write folktales told in their native Germany. They published three editions of their folktale collection, the first in 1812, and the others in 1816 and 1856. Kamenetsky notes that as they revised, "They weeded out needless repetitions, simplified the plot structure, substituted for indirect speech some lively conversations, added some action where the description became too involved, and even modified the titles of the tales" (318). Although they were primarily interested in recording the grammar and language used in the tales as part of a linguistic study of the Germanic language and in attempting to learn more about the migration of early Europeans, their careful writing brought to the world such tales as "The Frog Prince," "Snow White," "Hansel and Gretel," and "Rumpelstiltskin."

Jakob and Wilhelm Grimm began collecting folktales such as Rumpelstiltskin *to study the German language. (Source:* Illustration from RUMPEL-STILTSKIN by Paul O. Zelinsky. Copyright © 1986 by Paul O. Zelinsky. Used by permission of Dutton Children's Books, a division of Penguin Books USA Inc.)

Charles Perrault published *Contes de ma Mere l'Oye* in 1697, which comprised eight folktales including "Puss in Boots" and "Sleeping Beauty." In Norway, Peter Christian Asbjornsen and Jorgen E. Moe began collecting tales. In 1859 Sir George Dascent translated them into English, and Norwegian tales such as "The Three Billy Goats Gruff" reached a wider audience. Joseph Jacobs, quoted earlier, was one of the first to collect folktales with a child audience in mind. He made certain adaptations of the British tales, noted in the back of his books, and is responsible for introducing stories such as "The Three Bears," "The Three Little Pigs," and "Henny Penny."

Outstanding contemporary collections of folktales are listed in Figure 8-11 at the end of this chapter. Generally these authors built their collections from written sources.

An Example

As you read the Norwegian tale in Figure 8-3, listen to the sound effects, the alliteration, and the rhythm, particularly near the climatic confrontation between the troll and the biggest Gruff.

The Folktale Formula

The Three Billy Goats Gruff exemplifies many of the characteristics of folktales. The story begins quickly. Characters are uncomplicated. Plots move swiftly along well-trod paths, and all questions are answered before the story ends. Still, there is room for flexibility, from beginning to happy ending.

Patterned Openings and Closings

"Once upon a time . . . " tells the reader or listener that the story happened in the past, but not exactly when, and the words do not give away any of the plot. The phrase is like theme music, rhythmically signaling to listeners that if they are not quiet, they will miss something.

There are many versions. "Many years ago when the earth was nearer the sky than it is today" begins the Hmong tale, *Nine-in-One Grr! Grr!* (Xiong), *The Frog Prince* begins, "In olden times, when wishing was still of some use . . . " (Ehrlich 94).[1] Once the patterned opening ends, the plot begins immediately. The stage has been set.

When the story is over, another phrase signals the listener that it is safe to stretch or sigh. It may be the ubiquitous " . . . and they lived happily ever after" or it may be the storytellers' phrase, the "Snip, snap, snout, This tale's told out," as was used in *The Three Billy Goats Gruff.* Folktales were meant to be spoken. Storytellers, as performers, had no

Try having children read and compare the first line in several folktales. Have them decide which opening lines they think are the most effective.

---

[1] *Source:* From THE RANDOM HOUSE BOOK OF FAIRY TALES by Amy Ehrlich, Illustrations by Diane Goode. Copyright © 1985, Random House, Inc.

Once upon a time there were three billy-goats who were to go up to the hillside to make themselves fat, and the name of all three was "Gruff."

On the way up was a bridge over a burn they had to cross; and under the bridge lived a great ugly Troll, with eyes as big as saucers and a nose as long as a poker.

So first of all came the youngest billy-goat Gruff to cross the bridge.

"Trip, trap; trip, trap!" went the bridge.

"WHO'S THAT tripping over my bridge?" roared the Troll.

"Oh, it is only I, the tiniest billy-goat Gruff; and I'm going up to the hillside to make myself fat," said the billy-goat, with such a small voice.

"Now I'm coming to gobble you up," said the Troll.

"Oh no, pray don't take me. I'm too little, that I am," said the billy-goat; "wait a bit till the second billy-goat comes; he's much bigger."

"Well, be off with you," said the Troll.

A little while after came the second billy-goat Gruff to cross the bridge.

"Trip, Trap! Trip, Trap! Trip, Trap!" went the bridge.

"Who's that tripping over my bridge?" roared the Troll.

"Oh, it's the second billy-goat Gruff, and I'm going up to the hillside to make myself fat," said the billy-goat, who hadn't such a small voice.

"Now I'm coming to gobble you up," said the Troll.

"Oh no, don't take me; wait a little till the big billy-goat Gruff comes; he's much bigger."

"Very well, be off with you," said the Troll.

"TRIP, TRAP! TRIP, TRAP! TRIP, TRAP!" went the bridge, for the billy-goat was so heavy that the bridge creaked and groaned under him.

"WHO'S THAT trampling over my bridge?" roared the Troll.

"IT'S I! THE BIG BILLY-GOAT GRUFF," said the billy-goat, who had an ugly voice of his own.

"Now I'm coming to gobble you up," roared the Troll.

"Well, come along! I've got two spears
And I'll poke your eyeballs out at your ears:
I've got besides two curling-stones,
and I'll crush you to bits, body and bones."

That was what the big billy-goat said; and so he flew at the Troll and poked his eyes out with his horns, and crushed him to bits, body and bones, and tossed him out into the burn, and after that he went up to the hillside. There the billy-goats got so fat they were scarce able to walk home again; and if the fat hasn't fallen off them, why, they're still fat; and so—

Snip, snap, snout,
This tale's told out.

Figure 8-3 The *Three Billy Goats Gruff.*

The first line of this Hmong tale, "Many years ago when the earth was nearer the sky than it is today," signals that this is a folktale. (Source: Excerpt and illustration from NINE-IN-ONE GRR! GRR! by Blia Ziong, adapted by Cathy Spagnoli, illustrations by Nancy Hom, Copyright © 1989. Reprinted with permission from Children's Book Press, San Francisco, CA.)

curtains or blackouts to cut them off from their audiences at the end of a tale. Instead they used familiar devices—short verses, sayings, asides to the reader, or phrases built on "happily ever after"—to let listeners know they were done.

Quick Presentation of the Problem

As soon as the words signaling the beginning of a folktale have been heard, the plot begins. Within the first few sentences, the audience knows the characters, often by name, and what their problem is. The confrontation is set up in the first two sentences: goat versus a great ugly troll. Another story, *Princess Furball,* opens with: "Once upon a time there was a beautiful young Princess whose hair was the color of pure gold. She was frequently lonely and unhappy, for her mother had died when she was a baby, and her father paid little attention to her" (Huck).[2] The Ashanti tale entitled "Talk" begins:

---

[2] *Source:* Text excerpt from PRINCESS FURBALL by Charlotte Huck. Illustrated by Anita Lobel. Illustrations Copyright © 1989 by Anita Lobel. Reprinted by permission of Greenwillow Books, a division of William Morrow and Company, Inc.

Once, not far from the city of Accra on the Gulf of Guinea, a country man went out to his garden to dig up some yams to take to market. While he was digging, one of the yams said to him:

"Well, at last you're here. You never weeded me, but now you come around with your digging stick. Go away and leave me along." (Goode 31)[3]

In each story there is a problem or challenge faced by a single or a small number of characters. And in each story, the problem is quickly identified.

Uncomplicated Characters

A four-year-old listening to the story of the three goats Gruff interrupted with a question after the first sentence. Gruff was a frightening name, she said. "Are the goats good or bad?"

She had learned that characters in folktales are uncomplicated. They tend to be either good or bad and are generally not believable by ordinary standards. Meet the characters in *The Talking Eggs,* retold by San Souci.

Rose, the older sister, was cross and mean and didn't know beans from birds' eggs. Blanche was sweet and kind and sharp as forty crickets. But their mother liked Rose the best, because they were alike as two peas in a pod—bad-tempered, sharp-tongued, and always putting on airs. (n.p.)[4]

The characters in folktales tend to be either completely good like Blanche, described as "sweet and kind," or very bad like her sister Rose, described as "cross and mean." (Source: Illustration from THE TALKING EGGS by Robert D. San Souci, pictures by Jerry Pinkney. Text Copyright © 1989 by Robert D. San Souci. Pictures Copyright © 1989 by Jerry Pinkney. Used by permission of Dial Books for Young Readers, a division of Penguin Books USA Inc.)

---

[3] *Source:* "Talk," from DIANE GOODE'S BOOK OF SILLY STORIES AND SONGS by Diane Goode. Copyright © 1992 by Dutton Children's Books, collection. Illustrations copyright © 1992 by Diane Goode. Used by permission of Dutton Children's Books, a division of Penguin Books USA Inc.

[4] *Source:* Excerpt from THE TALKING EGGS by Robert D. San Souci. Copyright © 1989 by Robert D. San Souci. Used by permission of Dial Books for Young Readers, a division of Penguin Books USA Inc.

Many other characters are not merely good; they tower over normal mortals, like the girl in *The Frog Prince* who "was so beautiful that the sun itself was amazed each time it shone upon her face" (Ehrlich 94).[5]

Descriptions give the reader a clear and immediate picture of a character. "Zomo. Zomo the rabbit. He is not big. He is not strong. But he is very clever." McDermott, in his retelling, gets right to the point about this trickster from West Africa.

There is seldom any growth or change in folktale personalities. Unlike characters in a novel or some modern fantasy, evil daughters never repent and bad witches refuse to recant cruel spells. Fools never grow in wisdom. When a poor boy becomes a king, or the tattered girl by the fire wins the heart of a prince, it is only because their true natures have emerged. They have not changed.

Quick Pace of the Plot

A life-and-death confrontation between the poker-nosed troll and the first goat develops within the first 200 words of the billy goats Gruff story. Within 500 words, three goats have risked their lives and the troll has been horribly dispatched. If you read the story silently, episodes flip by quickly like jerky scenes from an old silent movie. Even read out loud the story develops quickly, arouses suspense, and builds to a climax: " . . . crushed him to bits, body and bones." The plots are tightly structured and move along quickly. They also lend themselves to dramatization because the focus is on the action. Figure 8-4 shows how a teacher worked with seven kindergarten children as the enacted *The Three Billy Goats Gruff*.

The Inevitable Fate of Villains

The troll is crushed. The wicked queen in *Snow White*, the story goes, "had to put on the red-hot slippers and dance till she dropped down dead." The teller does not linger over the punishment, nor does the story give so much detail about the fate of the villain that the punishment becomes the focus of the story. The characters are symbols for good and evil, and evil gets punished. Critic Lillian Smith writes, "Both the child's attitude and the characteristic narrative method of the folktale have an impersonal quality important to remember. In the telling, it is a matter of emphasis and intention; in the listener, the child, it is a recognition that the events all belong to the realm of story, of imagination" (Smith 59). This understanding between storyteller and listener makes the violence meaningful in abstract terms—justice prevails—rather than brutal in realistic terms.

Recognizable Motifs

Some characters and certain elements in folktales appear regularly in story after story. The youngest and smallest of siblings is successful after others in

---

[5] *Source:* From THE RANDOM HOUSE BOOK OF FAIRY TALES by Amy Ehrlich, Illustrations by Diane Goode. Copyright © 1985, Random House, Inc.

Janet sat with the seven kindergartners seated around her. They knew she was going to share a story. She opened by holding up the copy of *The Three Billy Goats Gruff* and asking the children to look at the cover illustration. As they did, she asked, "What do you think the story might be?" and "Does anyone recognize these characters?" One child said she knew them from the zoo and another noted that "Dogs can't stand up like that." Janet responded, "Let's take a closer look at the cover." "Oh, goats," they said. And again, "I see that one at the zoo."

Janet then read the title and the name of the illustrator and explained why this story was listed on the title page as being "retold." She also said, "How the characters talk is very important. We'll see, later on, if some of you would like to be some of the goats or other characters in the story." As she read, Janet stopped to let the children describe the facial expressions of the characters and how they thought the characters were feeling. They also made some suggestions of how the Billy Goats Gruff might solve their problem of having a troll block their way on the bridge.

After the story was finished, Janet suggested that they pretend to be the characters and had children volunteer for which part they would like. They moved furniture to represent the bridge. Then Janet narrated the story line, and the children acted out the parts. She used her narration to provide hints for children who were hesitant. She paused for each character to say his or her lines. The children changed characters and enacted the story three times. Here is the dialogue from the first two times.

First Dramatization

Billy Goat Gruff #1 starts across the bridge.

Troll:	Who's that walking on my bridge?
Goat #1:	I'm the littlest Billy Goat Gruff.
Troll:	I'll eat you up.
Goat #1:	No. I'm too small for you to eat me.
Troll:	Go!

Billy Goat Gruff #2 starts across the bridge.

Troll:	Who's walking on my bridge? (pause) I'm going to eat you up!
Goat #2:	Don't eat me. Eat my brother. Here he comes!

Figure 8-4   Dramatizing *The Three Billy Goats Gruff.*

the family fail. Wishes are granted. A trickster ends up being the one who is tricked. Magic objects such as rings, beans, or tablecloths serve as props that are critical to the plot. These elements are called **motifs.** They recur so frequently that a well-known folklorist, Stith Thompson, was able to index them. He found, for instance, that fools appeared in more than a thousand stories. He counted and categorized the variety of fools and "other unwise persons" in his *Motif-Index of Folk Literature.*

Billy Goat Gruff #3 starts across the bridge.

Troll: Who's walking on my bridge?
Goat #3: It's the Big Billy Goat Gruff.
Troll: I'm going to eat you up!
Goat #3: Try it. I'm ready for you.

Billy Goat Gruff #3 pretends to butt the Troll into the river. All the children clap for themselves.

Second Dramatization
Billy Goat Gruff #1 starts across the bridge.

Troll: Who's that walking on my bridge?
Goat #1: Me. I'm the little one.
Troll: I'm going to eat you up!
Goat #1: No. I'm the little one. Here comes the medium one.

Billy Goat Gruff #2 starts across the bridge.

Troll: Who's walking over my bridge?
Goat #2: It's me. It's the middle (pause) medium one.
Troll: I'm going to eat you up.
Goat #2: Not yet. Here comes the big one.

Billy Goat Gruff #3 starts across the bridge.

Troll: Who's that walking on my bridge?
Goat #3: I'm the big goat.
Troll: I'm going to eat you up.
Goat #3: Come on up.

Once again the goat manages to knock the troll off the bridge, and again the children clap.

Janet was pleased that the children took the roles seriously, walking lightly or heavily and making their voices small or loud. They were able to give dialogue that kept the story moving. She noticed that some of the "goats" used size when describing the next goat to come, and others used the relationship. For the third dramatization, every child wanted to be involved, so they had "twin" trolls and more goats. This short folktale with its clear action was a good introduction to story dramatization.

Figure 8-4   *continued*

Fools (and other unwise persons)
Fools (general)

Absurd misunderstandings

Absurd disregard of facts . . .

Gullible fools

Talkative fools

Inquisitive fools

Foolish imitation

Literal fools

Foolish extremes

Thankful fools

Cowardly fools

Bungling fools . . . (Thompson 8)

The longer and more involved the tale, the more motifs. In *The Three Billy Goats Gruff*, there are four motifs. Animals talk. There is a monster (the troll). The goats use trickery. And the number three is significant.

Why three? No one is sure, but no one questions its appeal. Repeatedly, folktale heroes from many cultures face three tasks. Families have three children. Spirits grant three wishes or give three gifts. Even phrases come in waves of three—the three goats have similar lines for the troll and the bridge makes the same noise three times. From a literary standpoint, this repetition gives continuity to the story. From the standpoint of the child listener, the repetition of refrains delights the ear and the repetition of incidents builds suspense and anticipation. However, three is not the magic number in all folktales. In Native American folktales, for example, four is the magic number.

Seven is also a popular number in folktales. Examples are *The Seven Ravens, Snow White and the Seven Dwarfs,* and *The Seven Chinese Brothers.*

Reflection of a Culture

Many cultural beliefs and attributes appear in folktales. In *The Frog Prince*, the king tells his daughter, "What you have promised you must perform" and "You must not despise any one who has helped you in your need." The

The witch Strega Nona has a magic pasta pot that will fill at her command. (Source: Illustration by Tomie dePaola reprinted by permission of G. P. Putnam's Sons from STREGA NONA MEETS HER MATCH, Copyright © 1993 by Tomie dePaola.)

Algonquin maiden in *The Rough-Faced Girl* (Martin) sees the face of the Invisible Being in the beauty of the sky and of the earth, of all nature that surrounds her. African Americans expressed their longing for freedom in tales such as "The People Could Fly." (Hamilton 166–172)

Even the animals, objects, and events of folktales often grew out of the experiences and knowledge of the peoples who told the tales. Thus the witch *Strega Nona* (dePaola) in an Italian tale has a magic pasta pot that will fill at her command, whereas Xiao Sheng, the young Chinese boy in *The Dragon's Pearl* (Lawson) has a magic pearl that increases the quantity of whatever surrounds it.

TYPES OF FOLKTALES

There are as many variations as there are voices, but some types of folk-tales—groups of stories distinguished by a motif—are particularly popular with children. Figure 8-12 at the end of this chapter lists single folktales in picture book format, giving the tale's country of origin.

Tales of Talking Animals

The Three Billy Goats Gruff is a talking animal tale, often called a **beast tale.** Animals talk and have human feelings, although not as profound as talking animals in modern fantasy. Frequently folktale animals are caught in competition and depend on cleverness to see them through.

These three picture books editions of Anansi tales vary in tone and in style of art. *Anansi Goes Fishing* by Eric Kimmel, illustrated by Janet Stevens (New York: Holiday, 1992); *Anansi the Spider* by Gerald McDermott (New York: Holt, 1972); and *Anansi Finds a Fool: An Ashanti Tale* by Verna Aardema (New York: Dial, 1992).

Anansi, for example, is a wily and mischievous spider in West African folk-tales who enjoys playing tricks on other animals. (Storytellers pronounce his name "ah-NAN-cy," although sometimes it appears in print as "Ananse.") When Turtle comes to visit him just at dinner, Anansi is forced by custom to invite him to stay. Reluctantly, the spider sets out a steaming platter of fish. But as Turtle reaches for a piece, Anansi reminds him to wash his paws because "in my country it is ill-mannered to come to the table without first washing." Turtle complies, but gets his paws dusty as he returns from the stream. Again Anansi send him to wash, and by the time Turtle has come back to dinner, the spider has eaten all the fish. Turtle thanks him sarcastically for his "wonderful hospitality," tells Anansi he must come and visit, and leaves in a huff.

Anansi tries to visit Turtle at the bottom of a river, but has trouble sinking. He fills his jacket pocket with pebbles. The extra weight drags him down to the dinner table. Before he can eat any of the oysters or clams, Turtle announces that "in my country it is ill-mannered to come to the table wearing a jacket. Please take it off." Anansi does, and floats slowly away from the feast (Kaula 26–31).

Tales That Tell Why

Pourquoi tales (*pourquoi,* pronounced "poor-QUAH, is the French word for *why*) give imaginative explanations to childlike questions about why things are the way they are. Why do moles burrow tunnels underground and come out only at night? A Peruvian tale, *Moon Rope: A Peruvian Folktale/Un lazo a la*

A good story keeps children enthralled.

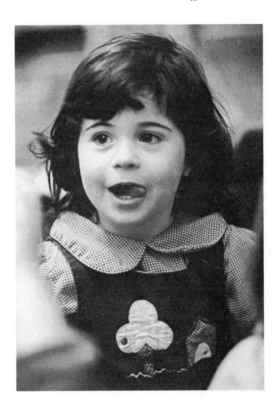

luna: Una leyenda peruana (Ehlert), provides an answer. Mole was taking a break from digging worms when Fox came up and asked what he'd like if he could have anything in the world. "Worms, worms, more worms," Mole answers. But Fox wants to go to the moon, and he convinces Mole to go along by telling him that there are huge worms up there. After getting the birds to loop his grass rope over the crescent moon, Fox begins climbing with mole following after. Mole isn't such a good climber and he falls. He had hoped no one would notice, but they do, and they tease him. Mole is upset, so he burrows underground and comes out only at night so he can avoid the other animals.

Ehlert's illustrations were inspired by ancient Peruvian artwork on textiles, on jewelry, and in architectural detail. She use a silvery color for the Fox, the grass rope, and the moon because a pre-Columbian legend proclaimed that gold was the sweat of the sun and silver the tears of the moon. The initial moon is a flat silvery color. The final illustration, after the text that says the birds say they can see the fox in the full moon, shows the same large silvery circle, but this time a face appears when the light catches the sheen at a particular angle. The text is in both English and Spanish.

Tales of Wonder

In every version of *Cinderella*, the poor kitchen maid obtains a beautiful gown by magic, even if it isn't always given by a magical person. In *Snow*

White, a girl falls asleep and wakes up under terms of a magic spell. A boy named Jack climbs to the sky on a stalk grown from magic beans and discovers a giant in *Jack and the Beanstalk.* Each of these stories is commonly called a **fairy tale,** but more accurately each is a tale of magic, wonder, or the supernatural. Wonder tales frequently have the hero or heroine go on a long journey or quest, and they always return home successful.

Cumulative Tales

"Old MacDonald Had a Farm" and "The Little Old Lady Who Swallowed a Fly" are songs with cumulative structures.

Like songs or poems with refrains, cumulative tales encourage listeners to join in the telling when the words become familiar. Plots are particularly simple. In *All in the Morning Early,* as told by Sorche Nic Leodhas, a boy named Sandy starts walking to the grinding mill with his sack of corn. He meets people and animals along the way, and as each decides to join him, a new line is added to the refrain, which always ends:

> . . . down the road that leads to the mill,
> Where the old mill wheel is never still—
> Clicketty-clicketty-clicketty-clack!
> All in the morning early. (Leodhas)[6]

The group with Sandy grows after each refrain until 55 people and animals have joined his march to the mill. This odd collection of travelers includes three Gypsies, six hares, eight ladybugs, and nine larks, among others.

Tales of Foolishness

Fools in folktales never change, but they survive, single-minded and simple-minded, against all laws of evolution. Sometimes they prosper.

In a story called "The Snows in Chelm," told by Isaac Bashevis Singer, village elders demonstrate their right to rule as "oldest and greatest fools." Snow falls one Hanukkah evening, and the flakes look like silver, pearls, and diamonds in the moonlight. The elders decide it is a treasure and that all the people must be warned not to walk on it until it can be collected. A problem: The messenger himself may trample the treasure.

The elders have a subtle plan. The messenger will stand on a table, carried by four men. But in the morning, they find that the feet of the four who carried the table have trampled the treasure. Ah, but already they have thought of a solution in case it should snow next Hanukkah: They will employ four others to carry the four who bore the table that carted the messenger.

We laugh as the fools of folktales fail to see the obvious, but we warm to their good intentions and naive trust.

---

[6] *Source:* Excerpt from ALL IN THE MORNING EARLY by Sorche Nic Leodhas. Copyright © 1963 by Leclaire G. Alger. Reprinted by permission of Henry Holt and Co., Inc.

In this Japanese folktale, Taro learns that his mother is not going to let him continue in his lazy ways. (Source: Illustration from THE BOY OF THE THREE-YEAR NAP by Dianne Snyder. Illustrations copyright © 1988 by Allen Say. Reprinted by permission of Houghton Mifflin Company. All rights reserved.)

Tales That Could Happen

A few folktales are **realistic,** with events that could happen and characters who could be real. *Dick Whittington and His Cat* is one of the best known of such tales and is based on a real Richard Whittington, who was indeed a mayor of London. Another is *The Boy of the Three-Year Nap*, retold by Dianne Snyder and illustrated by Allen Say. In this Japanese tale, a widow works hard to earn a living while her lazy son, Taro, sleeps the day away, always saying he will work after his nap. Taro tricks a wealthy merchant into thinking that his daughter is destined to marry him. While Taro dreams of the easy life to come, his mother talks with the merchant, consenting to the marriage of her son only after the merchant agrees to give Taro a job managing his storehouse. When Taro says that working was not part of his plan, his mother responds by asking him if he thinks he is the only one who makes plans.

The story uses elements of the culture, such as the patron god of the town, *ujigami,* whom Taro impersonates in order to trick the merchant, but there is no magic—only the threat of magic.

After children have read or listened to many folktales, they may enjoy reading stories in which authors have played with literary elements within the tale, changing the point of view, for example, or combining two tales. Figure 8-5 gives examples. Martinez and Nash note that such language play can stimulate creativity in children (62). These examples might well provide the stimulus for children to try such approaches in their own storytelling or writing.

Folktale spin-offs, as well as being great fun, encourage children to see what happens when one or more elements of a story are changed. They often provide the stimulus for children to write their own spin-offs.

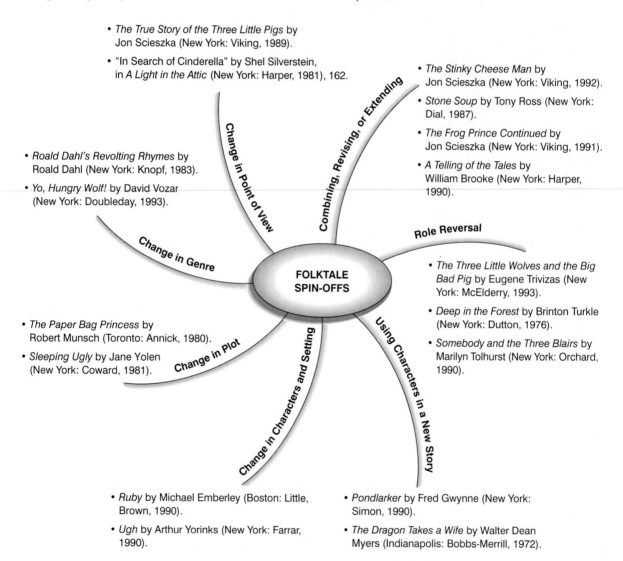

Change in Point of View
- *The True Story of the Three Little Pigs* by Jon Scieszka (New York: Viking, 1989).
- "In Search of Cinderella" by Shel Silverstein, in *A Light in the Attic* (New York: Harper, 1981), 162.

Combining, Revising, or Extending
- *The Stinky Cheese Man* by Jon Scieszka (New York: Viking, 1992).
- *Stone Soup* by Tony Ross (New York: Dial, 1987).
- *The Frog Prince Continued* by Jon Scieszka (New York: Viking, 1991).
- *A Telling of the Tales* by William Brooke (New York: Harper, 1990).

Change in Genre
- *Roald Dahl's Revolting Rhymes* by Roald Dahl (New York: Knopf, 1983).
- *Yo, Hungry Wolf!* by David Vozar (New York: Doubleday, 1993).

Role Reversal
- *The Three Little Wolves and the Big Bad Pig* by Eugene Trivizas (New York: McElderry, 1993).
- *Deep in the Forest* by Brinton Turkle (New York: Dutton, 1976).
- *Somebody and the Three Blairs* by Marilyn Tolhurst (New York: Orchard, 1990).

Change in Plot
- *The Paper Bag Princess* by Robert Munsch (Toronto: Annick, 1980).
- *Sleeping Ugly* by Jane Yolen (New York: Coward, 1981).

FOLKTALE SPIN-OFFS

Change in Characters and Setting
- *Ruby* by Michael Emberley (Boston: Little, Brown, 1990).
- *Ugh* by Arthur Yorinks (New York: Farrar, 1990).

Using Characters in a New Story
- *Pondlarker* by Fred Gwynne (New York: Simon, 1990).
- *The Dragon Takes a Wife* by Walter Dean Myers (Indianapolis: Bobbs-Merrill, 1972).

Figure 8-5   Folktale spin-offs.

FOLKTALES OF DIFFERENT CULTURES

Diane Wolkstein is a storyteller, a teacher, and an author of many books of folktales. She describes her work in learning to tell stories from Africa, from Haiti, and from India, when she began to work with musicians from different cultures, creating programs of stories and music.

> Every story is rooted in a culture, and the world of culture is limitless—music, dance, religion, art. I was beginning to understand that to truly tell a story in all its depth requires a lifetime of preparation. Storytelling is a challenge, an art, a possibility, a doorway into other cultures, a momentary opening into the universal. (Wolkstein 704)

Those who retell folktales have the challenge of preserving the cultural attributes of the stories. Verna Aardema, in retelling *Bimwili & the Zimwi,* a tale from Zanzibar, preserves the use of **ideophones,** words used to represent sounds, that is a common literary device in many African tales. The swamp is noisy with the "wurrr wurrr wurrr" of frogs, and Bimwili sniffles, "hih, hih, hih." The use of this device helps to maintain authenticity in form, and the result is pleasing aesthetically as well as honest in representation. Children hearing several tales from the same country or culture can begin to look for similarities. If they listened to *Why Mosquitoes Buzz in People's Ears* (Aardema) and *A Story A Story* (Haley) in addition to *Bimwili,* they would have many examples of ideophones and could begin to make generalizations about this element of storytelling. They might even decide to use it themselves in their own writing. At the same time, they are growing in their appreciation for aspects of another culture. Figure 8-6 outlines an approach in which children learn about a culture through its folktales.

Conscientious authors and illustrators can introduce young readers and listeners to a variety of cultures through the content of their stories and the artistic representation. Paul Goble has studied the Plains Indians of North America and illustrates his retellings of the oral literature of various tribes with pictures that capture both the settings and the style of art. In *The Love Flute,* Goble begins by talking about courtship rituals and then gives his source as a Santee Dakota myth. The illustrations show variations in the design of the flutes as the story describes how a shy young man was given the flute by the Elk Men and how he was able to express his love with it. In *Iktomi and the Ducks,* Goble encourages audience participation, as was common with Iktomi stories, by having parts of the text in gray italic, a signal for listeners to express their opinions. In an author's note, he also explains that "in former time, Iktomi lived in people's minds"; he is brought into everyday conversation in relation to characteristics he at times exemplified—greed, insincerity, or ambition.

A caution is in order, however. Cultures grow and change. Because folktales have been handed down from generation to generation, they may reflect what once was rather than what is. This is one argument given by people who are concerned that many western fairy tales are sexist, presenting women as

Very young children can listen to folktales and simply accept that many people enjoy stories and tell good stories. It is the beginning of appreciation for diversity as the teacher introduces the tale with the title, reteller, and country or culture of origin.

Older children, however, may use folktales within their studies of various cultures. In this case, it can be helpful for a teacher to guide their study by suggesting an approach for gathering and interpreting data. The teacher should also guide the children to be specific about the country or culture; that is, recording which country in Africa or which group of Native Americans rather than using the larger and more inclusive classifications.

Here is a chart that students may use as they read various folktales.

Title:

Reteller:

Country or Culture Represented:

What I noticed in the text	What I noticed in the illustrations	What this seems to tell about the country or culture

After individual children or groups of children have completed the chart for a book, they can compare their observations and interpretations with the notations of other groups. They would then want to use other references to corroborate their findings.

Figure 8-6   Learning about a culture through folktales.

valuable only if they are beautiful and successful only if they marry. When children compare folktales and look for cultural information, they need to verify their deductions with data from other sources and to be aware that what they are seeing and hearing may not reflect contemporary customs and beliefs.

WHY CHILDREN LIKE FOLKTALES

The basic appeal of folktales is that they are good stories. The action is quick and suspenseful; the characters are easily identified; conclusions are dramatic and just.

Beyond that, they appeal to the imagination. Tolkien says that folktales appeal to the "subcreator function," the ability to create a new and secondary world. Carl Jung argued that the appeal is in their ability to liberate the archetypes that exist in the collective unconscious. Bruno Bettleheim vali-

Paul Goble's illustrations capture both the settings and the style of art of the Plains Indians of North America. (Source: Illustration adapted with the permission of Simon & Schuster Books for Young Readers from LOVE FLUTE by Paul Goble. Copyright © 1992 by Paul Goble.)

dated folktales for the help they give children in dealing with anger and frustration and for their symbolic representation of fear of separation, or "separation anxiety." The "happily ever after" ending implies that the characters will never be deserted. Thus the tales are entertaining, but also imbued with a deeper meaning, one that has psychological significance. Trousdale, in talking with children about "Snow White" and "The Sleeping Beauty," found that "They selected and emphasized elements in the tales which seemed to have personal significance for them and ignored or deleted elements which apparently had little significance for them, or were painful to them" (38).

THE VALUE OF FOLKTALES

A child's enjoyment is one good reason to keep folktales alive in the classroom and home. Other reasons are described in the following sections.

Many teachers tell as well as read folktales to their classes. Figure 8-7 describes the steps one teacher uses as she prepares to tell a story. Each year she adds one or two stories to her repertoire.

Fostering the Imagination

One value of sharing traditional literature with children is that it provides an opportunity to strengthen their imaginations. The ability to conjure up what one has never seen is necessary to all new invention.

A well-known Russian poet and translator, Kornei Chukovsky, wrote that fantasy is essential to science:

> Without imaginative fantasy there would be complete stagnation in both physics and chemistry, because the formulation of new hypotheses, the

Figure 8-7   Learning to tell a story.

Selecting a Story

1. Evaluate the tale and select only retellings of high literary quality.
2. Look for stories that have a compact plot and much action.
3. Look for stories that have a strong beginning and a satisfying ending.
4. Look for stories that have only a few characters.
5. As you read, see if you think the text can be paraphrased without damaging the story.
6. Decide if the story is appropriate for the intended audience.
7. Select a story you like.

Preparing to Present the Story

1. Read through the story several times.
2. Think about blocks of action within the story and their sequence. (Some storytellers make notecards with the blocks of action.)
3. Visualize the story as you think about the sequence.
4. Memorize the beginning sentence, the concluding sentence, and any phrases or refrains that you plan to use.
5. Practice telling the story aloud several times.

Telling the Story

1. Make certain that your audience is settled and that everyone can see before you begin.
2. Make eye contact with your audience immediately.
3. Let your voice express the emotion of the characters and the mood of the story.
4. Tell your audience why you selected the story either at the beginning or the end of your retelling.
5. Let your own enjoyment of the story show.

invention of new implements, the discovery of new methods of experimental research, the conjecturing of new chemical fusions—all of these are products of imagination and fantasy. (124)

Almost every folktale begins with a problem and ends with a solution. Exposure to many tales may encourage children to act to solve their own problems in imaginative ways and keep up hope for a happy outcome.

Simplifying Moral Questions

Folktales also encourage respect for human greatness and an identification with characters who represent the good and the just. The charge of a single goat can crush the troll, and even the smallest child can cast a stone at an evil giant. Unlike many modern stories, folktales put clear labels on right and wrong and enable children to simplify moral questions. The abstract battles in folktales, writes Elizabeth Cook, remind us of modern struggles against evil; dragons, for instance, symbolize injustice, corruption, and hatred when they occur in tales. (Cook was talking about western tales. In eastern tales, this does not hold true. In China, for example, the dragon may be either good or bad and is often thought of as a god of the sea, the rivers, and the lakes (Cai 79).) That is why, she writes, "it is a great mistake to feel sorry for the dragon, as some adult readers do if they have not been brought up on fairy tales" (Cook 4).

Promoting Multicultural and Global Awareness

Folktales promote an awareness of other cultures and countries, particularly if a teacher or other adult calls attention to the source of the story. For preschoolers, this may simply be including in the introduction a statement such as, "This is a folktale from the country of Laos. The Hmong people who live there told this story for many years, and the person who told it, Blia Xiong, first heard it when she was a small child living in Laos." This is the beginning of the concept that people in many countries tell and enjoy stories.

Later children can compare folktales and perhaps locate countries on a map or globe. Where is Norway, home of the three Billy Goats Gruff? Does the land there really have mountains and streams?

Opportunities to show that the retellers appreciate cultures other than their own and to give examples of international cooperation may appear if you look at the information about the reteller and the illustrator. Such an opportunity might take the form of learning that Molly Bang, reteller and illustrator of the Japanese tale *The Paper Crane,* was born in the United States but has lived in Europe, Japan, and India. It might take the form of pointing out that one retelling of the Russian tale *Vasilissa the Beautiful* was adapted by Elizabeth Winthrop, an American, and illustrated by Alexander Koshkin, a Russian. But whatever the approach, the tales themselves speak to human problems and needs and show children both universal themes and cultural uniqueness.

Many approaches are valid in studying folktales. Figure 8-8 describes several and suggests appropriate folk literature for each.

APPROACH	PURPOSE	EXAMPLE
Group titles from the same country or culture (for example, tales from Russia).	To learn customs, values, and information about a culture To build appreciation for diversity	**Russian tales:** Ginsburg, Mirra. *The King Who Tried to Fry an Egg on His Head.* Ill. by Will Hildebrand. New York: Macmillan, 1994. Hastings, Selina. *The Firebird.* Ill. by Reg Cartwright. Cambridge, MA: Candlewick, 1993. Kimmell, Eric. *Baba Yaga.* Ill. by Megan Lloyd. New York: Holiday, 1991. Langton, Jane. *Salt: A Russian Folktale.* Ill. by Ilse Plume. New York: Hyperion, 1992. Winthrop, Elizabeth. *Vasilissa the Beautiful.* Ill. by Alexander Koshkin. New York: HarperCollins, 1991.
Select several versions of the same tale as told in different countries.	To show how different peoples can enjoy and find meaning in the same story To listen or read critically for similarities and differences	**Tales about a magic pot:** dePaola, Tomie. *Strega Nona.* Englewood Cliffs, NJ: Prentice Hall, 1975. Galdone, Paul. *The Magic Porridge Pot.* New York: Seabury, 1976. Hong, Lily Toy. *Two of Everything.* Niles, IL: Whitman, 1993. Mosel, Arlene. *The Funny Little Woman.* Ill. by Barry Moser. New York: Dutton, 1972.
Group tales by type (for example, pourquoi tales).	To help students recognize story structure To provide a stimulus for writing	**Pourqoui tales:** Aardema, Verna. *Why Mosquitoes Buzz in People's Ears.* Ill. by Leo and Diane Dillon. New York: Dial, 1975. Bryan, Ashley. *The Cat's Purr.* New York: Atheneum, 1985. Gerson, Mary-Joan. *Why the Sky Is Far Away: A Nigerian Folktale.* Ill. by Carla Golembe. Boston: Joy Street, 1992. Goble, Paul. *Crow Chief: A Plains Indian Story.* New York: Orchard, 1992. Rosen, Michael. *How Giraffe Got Such a Long Neck . . . and Why Rhino Is So Grumpy.* Ill. by John Clementson. New York: Dial, 1993.

Figure 8-8 Approaches to folktale study.

APPROACH	PURPOSE	EXAMPLE
Group tales by motif (for example, trickery).	To help students recognize patterns within a story and story structure To provide a stimulus for writing	**Tales with trickery:** Aardema, Verna. *Borreguita and the Coyote: A Tale from Ayutila, Mexico*. Ill. by Petra Mathers. New York: Knopf, 1991. Goble, Paul. *Iktomi and the Ducks: A Plains Indian Story*. New York: Orchard, 1992. Greene, Jacqueline Dembar. *What His Father Did*. Ill. by John O'Brien. Boston: Houghton, 1992. Knutson, Barbara. *Sungura and Leopard: A Swahili Trickster Tale*. Boston: Little, Brown, 1993. Shute, Linda. *Clever Tom and the Leprechaun*. New York: Lothrop, 1988.
Present the same folktale interpreted by different retellers and illustrators.	To show how the storyteller influences the story To demonstrate the role of illustrations in the understanding of character and setting and in the development of mood	**Versions of Beauty and the Beast:** Brett, Jan. *Beauty and the Beast*. Boston: Houghton, 1989. Gerstein, Mordicai. *Beauty and the Beast*. New York: Dutton, 1989. Hague, Michael. *Beauty and the Beast*. New York: Holt, 1988. Hutton, Warwick. *Beauty and the Beast*. New York: Atheneum, 1985. Willard, Nancy. *Beauty and the Beast*. Ill. by Barry Moser. New York: Harcourt, 1992.
Present several works by a single reteller or illustrator.	To show how an author or artist incorporates the origin of the tale into the retelling or the illustrations	**Folktales retold and illustrated by Gerald McDermott:** *Arrow to the Sun: A Pueblo Indian Tale*. New York: Viking, 1974. *Daniel O'Rourke: An Irish Tale*. New York: Viking, 1986. *The Stonecutter: A Japanese Folktale*. New York: Penguin, 1975. *Raven: A Trickster Tale from the Pacific Northwest*. San Diego: Harcourt, 1993. *Zomo the Rabbit: A Trickster Tale from West Africa*. San Diego: Harcourt, 1992.
Share chapter books or novels of contemporary realism or fantasy that have a basis in folktales.	To show how a basic tale can be expanded or embellished To help students recognize the structure within a chapter book or novel	**Novels based on folktales:** Hamilton, Virginia. *The Magical Adventures of Pretty Pearl*. New York: Harper, 1983. (African American folk hero John de Conquer) McKinley, Robin. *Beauty: A Retelling of the Story of Beauty and the Beast*. New York: Harper, 1978.

Figure 8-8 *continued*

FABLES

If we were to play a game of word association and the word given was *fable,* the chances are that many of us would respond immediately with "Aesop." Certainly many of the best-known fables are attributed to him. Scholars are not certain if there really was an Aesop, and if there was, if he was the author of the fables or simply the collector. However, they do tend to agree on the characteristics he was supposed to have had. If he existed, he was a hunchbacked Greek slave born around 620 B.C.; he was quick-witted and engaged in political satire; and he was eventually sentenced to death, executed by being hurled off a cliff. His fables survived, first in Greek, then in Latin, and were finally translated into English, French, German, and many other languages.

Less well known to Americans is the French poet Jean de la Fontaine (1621–1695), who used Latin versions of Aesop to create his own fables in verse. La Fontaine also drew on venerable—and long—stories from ancient India. The earliest of these collections is called *The Panchatantra* ("the book of five headings"), a guide in poetry to proper living originally intended for sons of royalty, a combination of stories and philosophic stanzas. Another set of Indian stories, called the *Jatakas,* relates events in the lives of Buddha, the title of the philosopher Gautama Siddhartha who was supposedly born in India at roughly the same time Aesop died in Greece. Buddhist religious belief holds that Gautama Buddha died and was reborn many times in different animal forms. In the *Jatakas,* animals act out lessons of ancient folk wisdom, often so that errant humans will learn.

In fact, this "lesson" is the marker of the fable. Most **fables** are beast tales, but they differ from folktales in leading the reader toward a lesson, often summarized at the end by a one-line moral. Fables have few characters (more than three is unusual) and few twists of plot. And—as with folktales—there are many different versions of each fable.

Here is the fable of *The Fox and the Grapes* as told by Joseph Jacobs and first published in 1894.

> One hot summer's day a Fox was strolling through an orchard till he came to a bunch of Grapes just ripening on a vine which had been trained over a lofty branch. "Just the thing to quench my thirst," quoth he. Drawing back a few paces, he took a run and a jump, and just missed the bunch. Turning round again with a One, Two, Three, he jumped up, but with no greater success. Again and again he tried after the tempting morsel, but at last had to give it up, and walked away with his nose in the air, saying, "I am sure they are sour."
>
> It is easy to despise what you cannot get. (76–77)[7]

This fable is the source of the expression "sour grapes." Other fables from Aesop generated the expressions "don't count your chickens before

Two Jataka tales retold in picture book format are *Once a Mouse* by Marcia Brown (New York: Scribner's, 1961) and *Foolish Rabbit's Big Mistake* by Rafe Martin (New York: Putnams, 1985).

---

[7] *Source:* Excerpt from THE FABLES OF AESOP by Joseph Jacobs, Schocken, Copyright © 1966. Random House, Inc., New York.

The expression "sour grapes" comes from a fable by Aesop in which a fox who cannot reach some grapes says that they were probably sour anyway. (Source: Illustration and text excerpt from ANIMAL FABLES FROM AESOP by Barbara McClintock, reprinted by permission of DAVID R. GODINE, PUBLISHER, INC. Copyright © 1991 by Barbara McClintock.)

they're hatched" (from "The Milkmaid and Her Pail") and "cry wolf" (from "The Boy Who Cried Wolf").

Fables are generally most appropriate for children aged eight or nine and older. Although the stories are short, the meaning may be complex and the moral difficult for preschoolers to understand, particularly when stated in abstract terms. Look at the language, the content, and the use of illustrations as you determine age-level appropriateness.

Barbara McClintock has adapted and illustrated fables from Aesop, using descriptive language and illustrations that capture the action and show the emotions of the characters. Her retelling of "The Fox and the Grapes" begins:

> One hot summer's day a gentleman Fox was strolling along, when suddenly he spied a beautiful bunch of grapes hanging high on a vine overhead.[8]

The moral is given when one observer to the fox's attempts and "sour grapes" statement calls out, "It's easy to hate what you can't have." The contemporary language helps to make the story clear.

---

[8] *Source:* Excerpt from ANIMAL FABLES FROM AESOP by Barbara McClintock reprinted by permission of David R. Godine, Publishers, Inc. Copyright © 1991 by Barbara McClintock.

Tony Ross, in *Foxy Fables*, lengthens several fables, gives them a modern setting, and imbues them with his own sense of humor. *The Hare and the Tortoise* begins,

> One night the Hare was having a quiet drink with the Tortoise, and as usual the conversation turned to sports. Also as usual the Hare was bragging about how good he was at shuffleboard, croquet, darts . . . everything. As he spoke he kept poking the Tortoise on the shell. At last the Tortoise snapped, "You may be okay at all the *easy* sports, but I'm a better *athlete* than you."[9]

The challenge is on, and—no surprise—the Tortoise wins the race.

Single editions of fables can expand a story and make it accessible to primary age children. Ed Young, in *Seven Blind Mice,* tells the Indian fable about the blind men and the elephant, where each touches a different part of the animal and each has a different interpretation of what it might be like, by making the characters mice. Each mouse is a different color, and each goes exploring on a succeeding day of the week. Brilliant collage illustrations on a black background emphasize the color, and on the seventh day, when the last mouse investigates the whole animal, all the mental pictures are put together. The animal is "as sturdy as a pillar, supple as a snake, wide as a cliff, sharp as a spear, breezy as a fan, stringy as a rope."[10]

Collections of fables let children become familiar with many different tales and set the stage for comparisons. Children who had heard McClintock's tellings of several of Aesop's fables could compare those with the collection of Chinese fables retold and illustrated by Demi. Titled *A Chinese Zoo: Fables and Proverbs,* the book has 13 fables, each with a stated moral. *Feathers and Tails, Animal Fables From Around the World* (Kherdian) introduces children to a wide range of sources, from LaFontaine to Yurok Indian to West African. One group of fourth graders, whose teacher read fables regularly in those "two minutes free" moments of the day, thought of it as a game when they could relate one fable to another. Hearing "Anansi Rides Tiger" from *Feathers and Tails,* the children immediately tied Anansi's trickery— his covering his boast that he could ride the tiger by pleading illness so that the tiger would carry him to the king to confess his lie—with the fable in *A Chinese Zoo* in which a fox announces that he is king of the forest so the tiger will not eat him and then proves it by having the tiger walk after him and see how all the animals flee.

Fables lend themselves to quick retellings and to dramatization. With only a few characters and a single-incident plot, they are simple enough for small groups of children just learning to work together cooperatively to plan and enact without teacher intervention.

Fables from Aesop that lend themselves to dramatization are "The Lion and the Mouse" and "The Fox and the Crow," each with two characters, and "The North Wind and the Sun" and "The Grasshopper and the Ants," each with three characters.

---

[9] *Source:* Excerpt from FOXY FABLES by Tony Ross. Copyright © 1986 by Tony Ross. Used by permission of Dial Books for Young Readers, a division of Penguin Books USA Inc.

[10] *Source:* Excerpt from SEVEN BLIND MICE, Copyright © 1992 by Ed Young. Reprinted by permission of Philomel Books.

MYTHS

Fables are short, moralistic forms of the beast tale; **myths** are similar to pourqoui tales. They answer fundamental "why?" questions about the origins of the earth and natural phenomena. Usually the characters are gods and goddesses, though some humans may appear, and usually the setting is the home of the gods. Often elements in nature are personified.

Myths From Many Cultures

Virginia Hamilton, in her introduction to her collection of creation myths entitled *In the Beginning: Creation Stories from Around the World,* notes that creation myths are considered to be actual accounts by the people who believe in them. They take place before anything else has happened, explaining how the universe came to be.

Often early peoples were isolated. In their desire to discover and understand, they created stories that explained who they were and how they came to be. Usually humans fit between the animals and the gods, being higher than animals but lower than gods. Myths helped to give a purpose to existence.

Sharing such ideas with children would help them accept the seriousness of myth and understand that its truth is not in how close it comes to provable facts. Joseph Campbell quotes a small boy who described a myth as "something that's a lie on the outside and is truth on the inside" (Larsen and Larsen 552). Campbell felt that the boy's insight deserved "a prize from the Smithsonian," and he used the quotation often.

Another collection of myths is *Moon Was Tired of Walking on Air* by Natalia Belting, retellings of South American Indian myths. In "How Averiri Made the Night and the Seasons," a Campas Indian myth, in "the time before this time," there were earth and sky and water, people and villages, but no night and no seasons. After Averiri had eaten at his sister's house, he took out his pipes and played and sang. With his music he created night and the wet and the dry seasons.

> He took the sounds of thunder crashing, of rain rattling and pounding, of the rising river throwing itself against its rocky banks; he took the soft sounds of feet sinking in wet sand and the plop of mud bubbling up, put words to the sounds, sang them. He played his pipes and sang. And with his music Averiri made the wet season. (36)[11]

Like folktales, storytellers passed on myths for centuries before anyone wrote them down. When they were collected and ordered logically, the resulting **mythology** presented an entire universe. Unlike the factual universe, there is no vacuum in the elaborate universe of mythology. The story-

[11] *Source:* Excerpt and text from MOON WAS TIRED OF WALKING ON AIR by Natalia M. Belting. Text copyright © 1992 by Natalia M. Belting. Illustration copyright © 1982 by Will Hillenbrand. Reprinted by permission of Houghton Mifflin Company. All rights reserved.

Averiri plays his pipes and sings to create the night and the seasons in a Campas Indian myth. (Source: Excerpt and text from MOON WAS TIRED OF WALKING ON AIR by Natalia M. Belting. Text copyright © 1992 by Natalia M. Belting. Illustration copyright © 1982 by Will Hillenbrand. Reprinted by permission of Houghton Mifflin Company. All rights reserved.)

tellers filled the heaven and earth with restless populations of gods and humans, monsters and spirits.

Two of the most famous mythologies, one southern, one northern, do reflect the air and earth of the countries where they developed. Both mythologies are a mother lode of stories, and both have been mined by contemporary writers for fresh retellings.

Greek Mythology: Stories From a Golden Land

The Greeks called their universe a *cosmos,* a system that, in the beginning of creation, brought order out of primordial chaos. The home of the gods, called Olympus, is sometimes described as a mountain top and sometimes as a mysterious, unearthly place.

The god Zeus presided over Olympus with awful power. Zeus was lord of the sky, armed with thunder and lightning and respected by all other gods. He did have weaknesses; one was beautiful women. He constantly angered his wife, Hera, with his infidelity, and to avenge herself she pursued his lovers without mercy. This endeared her to wives in ancient Greece, and her daughter Ilithyia was said to help women in childbirth.

Zeus had two brothers. One, Poseidon, ruled the sea, carrying his three-pronged spear called a trident and battering waves into submission by riding over the waters in a golden chariot. The second brother, Hades, ruled the dead in a dark underworld kingdom.

The Greek poet Hesiod collected the myths about these and other gods about 800 B.C. Later, around the time of Christ, the Roman poet Ovid translated the Greek stories into Latin. He changed the names of the characters as he wrote his mythology, called the *Metamorphoses*. In Ovid's version, Zeus became Jupiter; Poseidon, Neptune; Hera, Juno; and Hades, sometimes called Pluto, was named Dis, a Latin work for rich, because he presided over all the gold in the earth. A good reference source for students is Leonard Everett Fisher's *The Olympians* because it describes each of the deities and gives both the Greek and Roman names.

Several Greek myths have been retold and illustrated by Warwick Hutton and are appropriate for both primary grade and older children. *Persephone,* the myth that explains the seasons, is simply yet effectively told.

Northern Myths: Stories From a Land of Frost

Where the gods of Olympus had sunshine and warmth, the gods in the Scandinavian countries had cold air and a long winter season. The earth seemed made of frost, and life, even for gods, was vulnerable.

In northern creation myths, the world we know was made from parts of the great frost giant Ymir. Three brothers, the gods Odin, Vili, and Ve, dismembered Ymir and created the seas from his blood, mountains from his bones, and clouds heavy with hail from his brain. After this violent beginning, the gods fought with the other giants in a continual war; eventually the gods died in a final all-out battle.

In contrast to Olympus, the home of the northern gods rings with the disharmonious sounds of armed fighting. The land of the gods is called Asgard. In Valhalla, the great hall of Odin in Asgard, warriors who died bravely in battles on earth continue to fight with each other.

Norse myths, as far as we know, came together in a mythology more than a millennium after the Greeks had collected their ancient stories. The *Poetic Edda* is a book of old Norse verse recorded in the tenth and eleventh centuries A.D. Sometimes this collection of narrative poetry is called the Elder Edda, because a second collection, the younger or *Prose Edda,* was written down by Snorri Sturluson in the early part of the thirteenth century.

These two works are the sources for modern retellings. The stories of Loki, god of the kindled fire, who had been taken into the family by Odin, is frequently told for children. Loki, armed with magic and crafty intelligence, often made trouble among the gods, playing on their weaknesses. His adventures and trickery make stories about him appealing to young readers.

LEGENDS AND TALL TALES

Legends are stories based on the lives of real, or supposedly real, people. They range from the full cycle of Arthurian legends, based on medieval lore about King Arthur of Britain and his knights, to the stories of such characters as Paul Bunyan and John Henry, filled with exaggeration and referred to as **tall tales.**

Arthurian Legends

In the fifteenth century, Sir Thomas Malory wrote *Morte d'Arthur,* a work that became the source for most later retellings of the Arthurian legend. Tales and poems that involved a mighty warrior, a conquering king, and the ideals of chivalric romance had merged over several centuries into a coherent group of stories with all the characters related in some way to King Arthur.

There are also picture book editions of single tales. *Sir Gawain and the Loathly Lady,* retold by Selina Hastings, relates with humor and suspense how Arthur was challenged by the Black Knight to find out what it is that most women desire. It was the Loathly Lady who gave him the answer—that what most women want is to have their own way—but in return he promised that one of his knights would become her husband. Sir Gawain, volunteering to serve his king, is the one who agrees to wed this ugly creature. After the wedding, Sir Gawain learns that his bride can be beautiful either by day or by night, but not both. She asks him to choose. First he suggests night, then day, and finally says she must decide which she prefers. This, of course, is the correct answer for it lets the woman have her own way, and she becomes beautiful all the time.

Picture book editions often give further information about medieval times because the illustrations reflect life at that period and are often carefully researched. Jamichael Henterly, the illustrator of the picture book *Young Guinevere* (San Souci) used the style of the decorations in the *Book of Kells* because it was created by monks in the British Isles in the same period as the story is thought to have originated. Young readers can see elements of medieval life as they learn about Camelot and the Knights of the Round Table.

Tall Tales

In **tall tales,** the dimensions of legendary heroes are exaggerated, often with humorous intent. Many of the tall tales originated in the United States. Paul Bunyan, for example, was not an ordinary lumberjack. When he must move the cut trees from Minnesota to the sawmill in New Orleans, he decides the

Paul Bunyan takes just a few days to dig the St. Lawrence River and the Great Lakes in this tall tale. (Source: Illustration from PAUL BUNYAN by Steven Kellogg, Copyright © 1984 by Steven Kellogg. Reprinted by permission of Morrow Junior Books, a division of William Morrow and Company, Inc.)

best route would be a river. But there is no river. So after a lunch of 19 pounds of sausage, 7 hams, 8 loaves of bread, and 231 flapjacks, each slathered with a pound of butter and a quart of maple syrup, he digs a river and names it the Mississippi.

He dug the St. Lawrence River and the Great Lakes so that barges could get maple syrup to the camp, and he created the Grand Canyon when his ax fell from his shoulder and he dragged it along the ground while crossing Arizona.

Again, the retelling helps the tale. Parts of Bunyan's story may be hard to swallow. It may be hard to believe that frontiersman Davy Crockett rode a bear or that legendary cowboy, Pecos Bill, rode a cyclone from Texas to the West Coast or that John Henry could dig a tunnel faster than a steam drill. What saves exaggeration in many surviving tall tales is clever expression or an unexpected twist. When Paul Bunyan was a lad, "he could blow out a candle and leap into bed before the room became dark" (Kellogg n.p.). And Mike Fink, King of the Keelboatmen, was "such a crackerjack marksman that he could shoot the shell off an egg" (Kellogg n.p.). Figure 8-13 at the end of this chapter lists strong retellings of fables, myths, legends, and epics.

Teachers help children learn about tall tales and other folk literature by sharing many examples. Figure 8-9 shows one teacher's planning and her later reflection as she guided students in making generalizations.

THE LESSON, AS PLANNED AND TAUGHT	REFLECTIONS . . .
Rationale: Gayle wanted her students to compare two versions of *John Henry,* learn about exaggeration as a technique in storytelling, and identify the characteristics of a tall tale. She saw her main goal as one of having them enjoy listening to stories, however.	Two versions of a tall tale or other folk literature are a good choice for making comparisons, and talking about the voice of the teller in literature.

The Lesson:
Gayle read one version on Monday and then continued the lesson on Tuesday with the second book. She made a list of similarities and differences on chart paper as the children discussed the topic.
 	
On Wednesday, Gayle brought both versions of *John Henry* and a version of *Paul Bunyan* that she had read to the class the previous week. She informed them that both stories were called tall tales. Then she asked them to identify what the stories had in common, planning for them to learn the characteristics of a tall tale inductively.
 	
The children offered such commonalities as these:
 	
    "They were both about men."
    "People worked hard at something in them."
    "Good deeds were done by good people."
    "They died at the end."
 	
Gayle realized that her students were finding commonalities, but that the idea of exaggeration was not being addressed, nor were the characteristics of a tall tale being identified. They did enjoy the stories, though and did ask her to read them again.
	Gayle's use of time eliminated the concern that children would be asked to listen too long and lose interest. The children enjoyed the stories and were eager to participate in the discussion. Their responses showed that they had listened and understood both stories.
	
	The difficulty with this lesson was that the children were not given enough examples to generalize. Gayle decided to read more tall tales to the class, selecting tales that had women, that did not have the character die, and that may not have had all actions be good deeds. The children then would have more data to draw upon, and the focus of exaggeration would be more pronounced.

Figure 8-9   On second thought: Helping children make generalizations.

EPICS

In 1872, the last of the 12 tablets telling the epic story of a young king named Gilgamesh was found in Iraq. The story was first recorded more than 3,000 years before Christ and was most certainly told orally before that. The tablets preserved in hard clay some of the familiar foundations of all later epics, including the stories of the legendary Greek poet Homer and epic Indian poems. After his best friend is killed by an angry goddess, Gilgamesh sets out on a long and perilous journey to search for an old man, Utnapishtim, who was said to hold the secret of life and death. When he finally finds the old man, he is told about a worldwide flood, a time in which Utnapishtim had built a ship and taken aboard the "seed of every living thing" (Bryson 79) and was given eternal life as his reward. Gilgamesh does not find the secret of life and death, nor can he bring his friend back from the dead. At the end, Gilgamesh wills his own death so that he may join his friend.

Two characteristics of this story define **epics.** First, the hero is human, though the gods watch over him and sometimes intervene. He is similar to characters in tall tales in that his dimensions are bigger than life. Second, despite his high standing as a king and favored son of the heavens, Gilgamesh is vulnerable.

Time and again in great epics, the hero risks his life in tests or battles while the story's audience watches over the shoulders of the gods. Battles have great moments partly because heroes are powerful and partly because the enemy appears even stronger.

An epic hero of northern mythology, Sigurd, is directly descended from the god Odin and slays the scaly dragon Fafnir with his sword. Beowulf, hero of the oldest-known English epic, written down some time in the eighth century after Christ, faces a similar contest with a supernatural, spell-casting monster named Grendel. Beowulf almost loses. Even Robin Hood, the spirited outlaw of the Middle Ages who robs the rich for the sake of the poor, must face death. In Howard Pyle's version, *The Merry Adventures of Robin Hood,* the apparently indomitable Robin is betrayed by a nun and killed.

The *Iliad* and the *Odyssey,* two Greek epics, were recorded thousands of years after Gilgamesh. They weave dozens of subplots, intrigues between gods, quests, and battles into a labyrinthine narrative. Legend has it that Homer, a blind Greek poet, composed the two works and sang them as he traveled from city to city some time within the last 1000 year before Christ. No one is sure exactly when, or whether, Homer was the only author. However, around 1200 B.C., there *was* a battle between Greeks and the residents of Troy that lasted 10 years and generated the epic stories.

According to the *Iliad,* the conflict begins with an abduction. Paris, son of the king of Troy, steals the beautiful Helen, wife of the Greek king Menelaus. The Greeks come by sea to rescue Helen; they lay siege to Troy and years later enter the city through trickery. They build a wooden horse, hide soldiers inside it, and present it as a gift to the Trojans who admit the horse through their gates. Troy falls. The *Odyssey* picks up the story after the Greek victory as one of the warriors, Odysseus, travels home. It takes a decade of grueling tests and temptations before he arrives back in Greece.

The works are a challenge to modern writers for children because it is difficult to simplify the story without killing its spirit. Warwich Hutton has approached the problem by focusing on specific incidents. For example, his picture book *The Trojan Horse* quickly explains the war and then describes just one incident. This approach allows him to present it clearly and simply and to use the watercolor illustrations to emphasize the enormity of the wooden horse, to provide information, and to further the story.

All the best retellings of epics for children do preserve the story line, the power of the hero, and the possibility of the hero's death.

EVALUATING TRADITIONAL LITERATURE

Figure 8-10 list guidelines for evaluating traditional literature. When these are applied to the Navaho folktale *Ma'ii and Cousin Horned Toad,* which is retold and illustrated by Shonto Begay, the high quality of the book becomes apparent. In the story, Ma'ii, the coyote trickster, is hungry and so decides to visit his cousin on the other side of the mountain. In the meantime, Horned Toad is continuing his hard work in his cornfield, knowing he will have food for himself and his friends. When Ma'ii arrives, Horned Toad, "being the nice fellow he was," gets a sack of corn for him. But Ma'ii is still hungry, and after finally eating his fill, thinks of a trick to get the farm for himself. Complaining that he has a piece of corn stuck in his teeth, he gets Horned Toad to climb in his mouth, and he promptly swallows him. Ah, but he is later awakened by a voice that sounds like that of Horned Toad—and it is, from inside his stomach. Horned Toad likes it there and refuses to leave, even though Ma'ii tries to drown him by drinking lots of water and even contemplates jumping over the edge of the canyon to crush him. When Horned Toad begins tugging on Ma'ii's heart, Ma'ii faints. Horned Toad crawls out, pulling Ma'ii's tongue on his way out. Ma'ii runs off screaming. "And even to this day, Ma'ii leaves his cousin Horned Toad alone."

The story has action and humor, giving it great appeal for children. It preserves the cultural integrity of the traditional tale. Begay, a Navaho, has drawn on his own intimate knowledge of the Navaho culture and weaves into his retelling Navaho words and several songs that include Navaho

Figure 8-10 Guidelines for evaluating traditional literature.

1. The story should be appealing to children. Some tales are excellent in themselves but may have a theme that is too advanced for children and thus does not interest them, or are too long and involved for children to enjoy.

2. The story should preserve the cultural integrity of the original.

3. The story should preserve the stylistic integrity of the original. Criteria 2 and 3 do not mean that no adaptations can be made. They do mean that the reteller tries to keep the flavor of the dialect and to use the literary devices indigenous to the area.

4. The language used to tell the story should flow smoothly and tell the story clearly.

5. The retelling should be an authentic retelling of the original. Storytellers adapt and embellish stories to fit their audiences, but the "facts" of the story should not be altered so drastically that the meaning of the story is changed.

6. In an illustrated edition, the pictures should be of superior quality and should help the child interpret the story's setting, plot, and perhaps characters.

phrases. "Shil na aash. Shil na aash . . . " hears Ma'ii. And he says to himself, "Sounds like someone is saying, 'My cousin. My cousin' " (n.p.).

The language is effective, with rhythm and repetition in the song/chants and in phrasing. First Horned Toad's phrase "being the nice fellow he was" is repeated as he shares his corn with Ma'ii. Then it is repeated when Ma'ii hears the voice calling to him. Active verbs—Ma'ii "bolted"—build the action.

The illustrations combine stylized symbols in the background of the pictures with the depiction of the characters in the foreground. The result is that the story retains its urgency while still seeming to be a part of the ancient past. Particularly impressive is the illustration in which the Horned Toad faces the reader, the paw of the coyote coming after him and the shadow of the coyote covering him.

A reteller and illustrator can capture or change the mood of a story. When Gerald McDermott interpreted the Greek myth of Daedalus and Icarus, he showed the climax, when Icarus, having ignored his father's warnings, flies too close to the sun, with Icarus outlined against a golden sphere and Daedalus pleading and calling in fear. The colors are predominately reds, oranges, and yellows, and the art is stylized and symbolic. It is a powerful rendition.

When Marcia Williams retold the same myth, she used a cartoon style, with the text under the picture unchanged but with dialogue added. Icarus's complaint of the "wobble wing" and the birds' flying around him asking, "You know what pride comes before?" make this a humorous story. McDermott preserves the power of the myth; Williams makes it amusing. If you were going to introduce this myth to a group of fourth graders, which would you use?

The cartoon style of this retelling of Daedalus and Icarus changes the mood of the original and makes it a humorous story. (Source: Extract from GREEK MYTHS by Marcia Williams reproduced with permission of Walker Books, Ltd. Copyright © 1992 Marcia Williams. Published in the US by Candlewick Press, Cambridge, MA.)

Aardema, Verna, reteller. *Misoso: Once Upon a Time Tales from Africa.* New York: Knopf, 1994. These 12 tales, each with its country of origin noted, abound with onomatopoetic languge and cultural detail.

Chase, Richard. *The Jack Tales.* 1943. Boston: Houghton Mifflin, 1971. Chase collected these tales about Jack and his brothers from people living in the mountains of North Carolina and captured much of the dialect in his recording of them.

Courlander, Harold. *The King's Drum and Other African Stories.* New York: Harcourt, 1962. Courlander has captured the humor in African folktales in his retelling of these 29 brief stories.

Ehrlich, Amy, adapter. *The Random House Book of Fairy Tales.* Ill. by Diane Goode. New York: Random House, 1985. Ehrlich retells tales from the Brothers Grimm and from Perault, as well as several literary folktales written by Hans Christian Andersen.

Goode, Diane. *Diane Goode's Book of Silly Stories and Songs.* New York: Dutton, 1992. Goode presents 11 humorous folktales from a variety of countries.

Haley, Gail E. *Mountain Jack Tales.* New York: Dutton, 1992. The 9 tales about Jack show his trickster ways with humor and verve.

Hamilton, Virginia. *The People Could Fly: American Black Folktales.* Ill. by Leo and Diane Dillon. New York: Knopf, 1985. Tales from American blacks represent many sources and dialects, from animal tales to slave tales of freedom.

Leodhas, Sorch Nic. *Thistle and Thyme: Tales and Legends from Scotland.* Ill. by Evaline Ness. New York: Holt,1962. Leodhas has captured the rhythm of the original Gaelic in these tales of magic and humor set in Scotland.

Figure 8-11   Touchstone folktale collections.

SUMMARY

Traditional literature such as folktales, fables, myths, legends, and epics had its beginnings in oral tellings passed down from generation to generation and from storyteller to storyteller. Folktales are frequently identified and described by motifs, such as beast tales or pourquoi tales. Fables are like beast tales in that they are usually about animals, but they have a moral at the end. Myths explain the origin of the universe and natural phenomena and are much like pourqoui tales. Legends focus on people rather than gods, though the people are extraordinary, and epics too are narratives of mortals, though often the gods watch over and sometimes direct them.

With their emphasis on plot and their repetitive structure, folktales provide excellent vehicles for both dramatization and storytelling. Their

Minard, Rosemary, ed. *Womenfolk and Fairy Tales*. Ill. by Suzanna Klein. Boston: Houghton Mifflin, 1975. These 18 tales focus on women who are active and decisive—characters such as Molly Whuppie.

Pushkin, Aleksandr. *The Golden Cockerel and Other Fairy Tales*. 1925. Ill. by Boris Zvorykin. New York: Doubleday, 1989. These four tales were recorded by Pushkin, considered by some to have been Russia's greatest poet.

Sadler, Catherine Edwards, reteller. *Heaven's Reward: Fairy Tales from China*. Ill. by Cheng Mung Yun. New York: Atheneum, 1985. These six tales span over 2,000 years of Chinese history, with the first reflecting Confucian philosophy and the last having been changed to reflect Communist ideals.

Singer, Isaac Bashevis. *Zlateh the Goat and Other Stories*. Ill. by Maurice Sendak. New York: Harper, 1966. The seven tales in this book are based on middle-European Jewish folklore.

Voake, Charlotte. *The Three Little Pigs and Other Favorite Nursery Stories*. Cambridge, MA: Candlewick, 1992. The 10 folktales in this collection are appropriate for preschool children, with appealing rhythm and repetition.

Watkins, Yoko Kawashima. *Tales from the Bamboo Grove*. Ill. by Jean Tseng and Mou-sien Tseng. New York: Bradbury, 1992. Watkins retells folktales she heard in North Korea and gives background that makes the stories particularly interesting.

Yellow Robe, Rosebud. *Tonweya and the Eagles and Other Lakota Tales*. 1979. Ill. by Jerry Pinkney. New York: Dial, 1992. The 10 tales tell of the education of Chano in the ways and beliefs of the Lakota Sioux.

Figure 8-11   *continued*

quick action and dramatic conclusions are popular with children even though they were originally told to adult audiences. Fables, with morals sometimes stated in abstract terms, and many myths are more appropriate for children of at least eight or nine years of age than for very young children.

Central to evaluating traditional literature is the degree to which the retelling maintains the original version's cultural content and style. When authenticity is maintained, children learn about the beliefs and values of peoples of many cultures and can begin to develop an appreciation for diversity.

Figure 8-11, 8-12, and 8-13 provide lists of many excellent folktales, fables, myths, legends, and epics.

Aardema, Verna. *Why Mosquitoes Buss in People's Ears.* Ill. by Leo and Diane Dillon. New York: Dial, 1975. (West African). Mosquito starts a chain of events among the animals that makes everyone angry in this pourquoi tale.

Begay, Shonto. *Maii and Cousin Horned Toad.* New York: Scholastic, 1992. (Native American—Navaho). Maii, the trickster coyote, swallows Horned Toad in order to take over his farm, but is himself outsmarted.

Brett, Jan. *The Mitten.* New York: Putnam's, 1989. (Ukranian). One by one the animals squeeze into Nicki's lost mitten—until at last the bear sneezes, the mitten flies off, and the animals are once again in the snow.

Bruchac, Joseph, reteller. *Gluskabe and the Four Wishes.* Ill. by Christine Shrader. New York: Cobblehill, 1995. (Native American—Abenaki). Four men travel to Gouskabe who has said he will grant each one wish, but only the man who makes an unselfish wish gets to enjoy it.

Bryan, Ashley. *Turtle Knows Your Name.* New York: Atheneum, 1989. (Antilles). Upsilimana Tumpalerado has trouble remembering his name, but his granny says it just takes time, and Turtle will listen and help.

dePaola, Tomie. *Strega Nona.* Englewood Cliffs, NJ: Prentice Hall, 1975. (Italy). Big Anthony watches how Strega Nona gets the magic pasta pot to begin its production of pasta, but he neglects to learn how she stops it.

Hooks, William H. *The Ballad of Belle Dorcas.* Ill. by Brian Pinkney. New York: Knopf, 1990. (African American). Belle Dorcas agrees to do what the "conjure" woman tells her in order to keep her husband Joshua from being sold and learns what the old woman meant when she said that Belle would have to give him up to keep him.

Hyman, Trina Schart. *The Sleeping Beauty.* Boston: Little, Brown, 1977. (Germany). In this classic fairy tale, the king's daughter lies sleeping in the castle, to be awakened eventually by a kiss from a handsome prince.

Figure 8-12   Touchstone folktales—Single editions.

Kwon, Holly H. *The Moles and the Mireuk: A Korean Folktale.* Ill. by Woodleigh Hubbard. Boston: Houghton, 1993. (Korea). Papa Mole seeks the most powerful being in the whole universe to help him find the best husband for his "perfect" daughter.

McDermott, Gerald. *Raven: A Trickster Tale from the Pacific Northwest.* San Diego: Harcourt, 1993. (Native American). Raven changes his shape in a very clever fashion to steal the sun from the Sky chief and bring light to the world.

Paterson, Katherine. *The Tale of the Mandarin Ducks.* Ill. by Leo and Diane Dillon. New York: Lodestar, 1990. (Japan). The kitchen mail and servant are rewarded for their compassion in releasing a captured mandarin duck.

San Souci, Robert D. *The Talking Eggs.* Ill. by Jerry Pinkney. New York: Dial, 1989. (Southern U.S.—Creole). Blanche, kind and sweet, gains riches from an old woman she helps and whose directions she follows, while her scheming mother and older sister are punished for their greed.

Willard, Nancy. *Beauty and the Beast.* Ill. by Barry Moser. San Diego: Harcourt, 1992. (French). Beauty's capacity to love changes the beast into a handsome young man.

Yolen, Jane. *Tam Lin.* Ill. by Charles Mikolaycak. San Diego: Harcourt, 1990. (Scotland). Through her courage and spirit, Jennet wins back her home and saves the life of the handsome Tam Lin.

Zelinsky, Paul O. *Rumpelstiltskin.* New York: Dutton, 1986. (Germany). In this familiar Grimm tale, the queen can save her first-born child only by guessing the name of the little man who spun straw into gold for her.

Zemach, Margot. *It Could Always Be Worse.* New York: Farrar, 1977. (Jewish). When the farmer worries because his house is too crowded, the rabbi advises him to bring his animals, one at a time, into the house.

Figure 8-12   *continued*

Anno, Mistumasa. *Anno's Aesop.* New Orchard, 1989. (Fable).The top two thirds of the book give the fable and its illustration, and in the bottom third, Mr. Fox gives his interpretation of the illustrations.

Belting, Natalie. *Moon Was Tired of Walking on Air.* Ill. by Will Hillenbrand. Boston: Houghton Mifflin, 1992. (Myth). Belting retells 14 origin myths, each from a different group of South American Indians.

Bierhorst, John. *Doctor Coyote: A Native American Aesop's Fables.* Ill. by Wendy Watson. New York: Macmillan, 1987. (Fable). These fables about the trickster Coyote are based on Aztec sources.

Bierhorst, John, reteller. *The Woman Who Fell From the Sky. The Iroquois Story of Creation.* Ill. by Robert Andrew Parker. New York: Morrow, 1993. (Myth). This creation myth tells how the sky woman fell to earth, created the earth, the sun, and the stars, and and with her sons Sapling and Flint created seasons, rivers, birds, and animals.

DeGerez, Toni. *Louhi, Witch of North Farm.* Ill. by Barbara Cooney. New York: Viking, 1986. (Epic). Louhi has stolen the sun and the moon and darkness covers the land in this tale from the Finnish epic, the *Kalevala.*

Hodges, Margaret. *St. George and the Dragon.* Ill. by Trina Schart Hyman. Boston: Little, Brown, 1984. (Legend). This retelling of the story of George the Red Cross Knight and his quest to slay the dragon is a winner of the Caldecott Award.

Kellogg, Steven. *Mike Fink.* New York: Morrow, 1992. (Tall Tale). Kellogg matches the daring and exaggerated deeds of Mike Fink, King of the Keelboatmen, with equally humorous illustrations.

Kherdian, David. *Feathers and Tails, Animal Fables from Around the World.* Ill. by Nonny Hogrogian. New York: Philomel, 1992. (Fable). These 19 fables represent stories from a wide variety of cultures.

Figure 8-13   Touchstone fables, myths, legends, and epics.

Lester, Julius. *John Henry.* Ill. by Jerry Pinkney. New York: Dial, 1994. (Tall Tale). Details of both text and illustration make this a strong and exciting retelling of John Henry and his sledgehammer digging a tunnel faster than the steam drill.

McClintock, Barbara. *Animal Fables From Aesop.* Boston: Godine, 1991. (Fable). These 9 fables are retold in clear and expressive language and enhanced by detailed and action-filled illustrations.

Martin, Rafe. *Foolish Rabbit's Big Mistake.* Ill. by Ed Young. New York: Putnam's, 1985. (Fable). This Jataka tale is perhaps the oldest version of "Henny-Penny," as rabbit begins to wonder what would happen if the earth broke up.

San Souci, Robert D. *Cut From the Same Cloth. American Women of Myth, Legend, and Tall Tale.* Ill. by Brian Pinkney. New York: Philomel, 1993. These stories, organized by regions in North America, show strong and clever women from various ethnic backgrounds.

San Souci, Robert D. *The Samurai's Daughter.* Ill. by Stephen T. Johnson. New York: Dial, 1992. (Legend). Tokoyo follows her father, a samurai nobleman, to the island where he has been exiled and uses her diving skill and bravery to free the ruler of Japan from a curse and her father from exile.

Young, Ed, reteller. *Seven Blind Mice.* New York: Philomel, 1992. (Fable). The seven blind mice find that wisdom comes from knowing the whole rather than individual parts as they try to describe an elephant when each has only experienced a part of the animal.

Figure 8-13 *continued*

∽ EXPLORE ON YOUR OWN

1. **Explore Your Personal Response.** Read two folktales from your own cultural background. Identify at least three values and or beliefs that seem to be expressed. The examples on pages 329 and 331 to 335 will give an idea of beliefs demonstrated in several folktales. What could others learn about your culture from these tales? (Look in the subject index of issues of *The Horn Book Guide* to locate tales from specific countries or cultural groups.)

2. **Apply Literary Criteria.** Select a Greek myth and read its retelling in two different collections. Using the criteria for evaluating traditional literature listed in Figure 8-10, which is the better retelling and why?

3. **Prepare to Share Literature With Children.** Select two creation myths and decide how you would introduce them to children. What would you say if a child asked you which of the two myths was true? You may want to reread pages 339 to 341 of the text as you plan your response.

∽ EXPLORE WITH CHILDREN

1. **Explore Children's Responses.** Read a fairy tale to a child of six to eight years of age. Ask the child to retell the story. What parts does the child emphasize? What parts were left out? When the child has finished, ask if what happened to the characters was "fair." Describe the child's response.

2. **Engage Children With Literature.** Try having children retell a folktale or other piece of traditional literature changing one element, such as the setting or the point of view. You might want to read to them one of the stories listed in Figure 8-5 on Folk Tale Spin-Offs to demonstrate what you mean.

∽ SUGGESTED PROFESSIONAL REFERENCES

Bettelheim, Bruno. *The Uses of Enchantment*. New York: Knopf, 1976. § Bettelheim used his background as a child psychologist to explore the content of fairy tales and the importance they have in the emotional development of children.

Blatt, Gloria, ed. *Once Upon a Folktale: Capturing the Folklore Process With Children*. New York: Teachers College Press, 1993. § Contributing authors describe bringing children and folklore together, understanding folklore, and connecting folklore to other literary genre.

Bosma, Berry. *Fairy Tales, Fables, Legends, and Myths: Using Folk Literature in Your Classroom*. 2nd ed. New York: Teachers College Press, 1992. § Bosma suggests ways to use folk literature in the classroom and includes a bibliography and a special section on multicultural folktales.

Butler, Francelia, and Margaret Higonnet, eds. *Children's Literature, Volume 13: Annual of the Modern Language Association Division on Children's Literature and The*

Children's Literature Association. New Haven: Yale University Press, 1985. § This issue is devoted to essays on aspects of the fairy tale.

Butler, Francelia. *Skipping Around the World: The Ritual Nature of Folk Rhymes*. New York: Ballentine, 1989. § These skip-rope rhymes collected from children in various parts of the world are an example of the oral tradition as it functions for children.

Campbell, Joseph. *The Hero With a Thousand Faces*. Princeton, NJ: Princeton University Press, 1949, 1968. § Campbell presents a single hero, the archetype of all myth, by comparing protagonists of myth and religion.

Campbell, Joseph, and Bill Moyers. *The Power of Myth*. New York: Doubleday, 1988. § Campbell and Moyers discuss myths across cultures and the role of myth in contemporary society.

Cook, Elizabeth. *The Ordinary & the Fabulous*. 2nd ed. Cambridge, England: Cambridge University Press,

1976. § Cook describes and analyzes myths, legends, and fairy tales to show how they can be presented to children.

Favat, F. Andre. *Child and Tale: The Origins of Interest.* Urbana, IL: National Council of Teachers of English, 1977. § Favat examines the characteristics of children ages six to eight and of fairy tales, showing how and why children's interest in this genre peaks at this period in their lives.

Hearne, Betsy. *Beauty and the Beast: Visions and Revisions of an Old Tale.* Chicago: University of Chicago Press, 1989. § Hearne selects versions of the tale appearing from 1740 to 1985, presents them in chronological order for close examination of their structure and form, compares masculine with feminine versions of nineteenth-century retellings, and even looks at mass media productions.

Pellowski, Anne. *The Story Vine: A Source Book of Unusual and Easy-to-Tell Stories from Around the World.* New York: Macmillan, 1984. § Many of these simple yet interesting stories have directions for easy drawings the storyteller can do as part of the presentation. Background for the stories is provided.

Smith, Ron. *Mythologies of the World.* Urbana, IL: National Council of Teachers of English, 1981. § This resource book organizes the study of mythology by geographic regions, with extensive listings of sources for exploring mythology in depth.

Yolen, Jane. *Tough Magic: Fantasy, Faerie and Folklore in the Literature of Childhood.* New York: Philomel, 1981. § The author, through a series of essays, explores both the history of folklore and its relation to the social and intellectual growth of children.

∾ CHILDREN'S BOOKS CITED

Aardema, Verna. *Anansi Finds a Fool: An Ashanti Tale.* Ill. by Bryna Waldman. New York: Dial, 1992.

Aardema, Verna. *Bimwili & the Zimwi.* Ill. by Susan Meddaugh. New York: Dial, 1985.

Begay, Shonto. *Ma'ii and Cousin Horned Toad.* New York: Scholastic, 1992.

Bang, Molly. *The Paper Crane.* New York: Greenwillow, 1985.

Belting, Natalia. *Moon Was Tired of Walking on Air.* Ill. by Will Hillenbrand. Boston: Houghton Mifflin, 1992.

Bryson, Bernarda. *Gilgamesh.* New York: Holt, 1967.

Demi. *A Chinese Zoo.* San Diego: Harcourt, 1987.

dePaola, Tomie. *Strega Nona.* Englewood Cliffs, NJ: Prentice Hall, 1975.

Ehlert, Lois. *Moon Rope: A Peruvian Folktale/ Un lazo a la luna: Una leyenda peruana.* New York: Harcourt, 1993.

Ehrlich, Amy. *The Random House Book of Fairy Tales.* Ill. by Diane Goode. New York: Random House, 1985.

Fisher, Leonard Everett. *The Olympians.* New York: Holiday, 1984.

Goble, Paul. *Iktomi and the Ducks.* New York: Orchard, 1990.

Goble, Paul. *The Love Flute.* New York: Bradbury, 1992.

Goode, Diane. *Diane Goode's Book of Silly Stories and Songs.* New York: Dutton, 1992.

Hamilton, Virginia. *In the Beginning: Creation Stories from Around the World.* Ill. by Barry Moser. San Diego: Harcourt, 1988.

Hamilton, Virginia. *The People Could Fly: American Black Folktales.* New York: Knopf, 1985.

Hastings, Selina. *Sir Gawain and the Loathly Lady.* Ill. by Juan Wijngaard. New York: Lothrop, 1985.

Haley, Gail. *A Story, A Story.* New York: Atheneum, 1970.

Huck, Charlotte. *Princess Furball.* Ill. by Anita Lobel. New York: Greenwillow, 1989.

Hutton, Warwick. *Persephone.* New York: McElderry, 1994.

Hutton, Warwick. *The Trojan Horse.* New York: McElderry, 1992.

Jacobs, Joseph. *The Fables of Aesop.* 1894. New York: Schocken, 1966.

Kaula, Edna Mason. *African Village Folktales.* Cleveland: World, 1968.

Kellogg, Steven. *Mike Fink.* New York: Morrow, 1992.

Kellogg, Steven. *Paul Bunyan.* New York: Morrow, 1984.

Kherdian, David. *Feathers and Tails, Animal Fables from Around the World.* Ill. by Nonny Hogrogian. New York: Philomel, 1992.

Lawson, Julie. *The Dragon's Pearl.* Ill. by Paul Morin. New York: Clarion, 1993.

Leodhas, Sorche Nic. *All in the Morning Early.* Ill. by Evaline Ness. New York: Holt, 1963.

Louie, Ai-Ling. *Yeh-Shen, A Cinderella Story from China.* Ill. by Ed Young. New York: Philomel, 1982.

McClintock, Barbara. *Animal Fables From Aesop.* Boston: Godine, 1991.

McDermott, Gerald. *Sun Flight.* New York: Four Winds Press, 1980.

McDermott, Gerald. *Zomo the Rabbit.* San Diego: Harcourt, 1992.

Martin, Rafe. *Foolish Rabbit's Big Mistake.* Ill. by Ed Young. New York: Putnam's, 1985.

Martin, Rafe. *The Rough-Faced Girl.* Ill. by David Shannon. New York: Putnam's, 1992.

Pyle, Howard. *The Merry Adventures of Robin Hood.* New York: Scribner's, 1946.

Ross, Tony. *Foxy Fables.* New York: Dial, 1986.

San Souci, Robert. *Young Guinevere.* Ill. by Jamichael Henterly. New York: Doubleday, 1993.

San Souci, Robert D. *The Talking Eggs.* Ill. by Jerry Pinkney. New York: Dial, 1989.

Singer, Isaac Bashevis. *Slateh the Goat and Other Stories.* Ill. by Maurice Sendak. New York: Harper, 1966.

Snyder, Dianne. *The Boy of the Three-Year Nap.* Ill. by Allen Say. Boston: Houghton Mifflin, 1988.

Winthrop, Elizabeth. *Vasilissa the Beautiful.* Ill. by Alexander Koshkin. New York: HarperCollins, 1991.

Xiong, Blia. Adapted by Cathy Spagnoli. *Nine-in-One Grr! Grr!* Ill. by Nancy Hom. San Francisco: Children's Book Press, 1989.

Young, Ed, reteller. *Seven Blind Mice.* New York: Philomel, 1992.

CHAPTER REFERENCES

Bettelheim, Bruno. *The Uses of Enchantment.* New York: Knopf, 1976.

Cai, Mingshui. "Folks, Friends and Foes: Relationships Between Humans and Animals in Some Eastern and Western Folktales." *Children's Literature in Education* 24.2 (June 1993): 73–83.

Chukovsky, Kornei. *From Two to Five.* 1925. Trans. and ed. Miriam Morton. Berkeley: University of California Press, 1971.

Colwell, Eileen. "Folk Literature: An Oral Tradition and an Oral Art." *Top of the News* 24 (Jan. 1968): 175–180.

Cook, Elizabeth. *The Ordinary and the Fabulous.* Cambridge, England: Cambridge University Press, 1969.

Favat, F. Andre. *Child and Tale: The Origins of Interest.* Urbana, IL: National Council of Teachers of English, 1977.

Jung, C. G. *The Essential Jung.* (Selected by Anthony Storr). Princeton, NJ: Princeton University Press, 1983.

Kamenetsky, Christa. "The Brothers Grimm: Folktale Style and Romantic Theories." *Jump Over the Moon.*

Pamela Petrick Barron and Jennifer Burley. New York: Holt, 1984. 316–322.

Larsen, Stephen, and Robin Larsen. *A Fire in the Mind: The Life of Joseph Campbell.* New York: Doubleday, 1991.

Martinez, Miriam, and Marcia Nash. "Spinoffs and Extensions of Folk Literature: Language Play at Its Best." *Language Arts* 69.1 (Jan. 1992): 62–68.

Smith, Lillian. *The Unreluctant Years.* Chicago: American Library Association, 1991.

Thompson, Stith. *Motif-Index of Folk Literature.* Bloomington, IN: Indiana University Press, 1955.

Tolkien, J. R. R. *Tree and Leaf.* Boston: Houghton, 1965.

Trousdale, Ann. M. "Let the Children Tell Us: The Meanings of Fairy Tales for Children." *The New Advocate* 2.1 (Winter 1989): 37–48.

Wolkstein, Diane. "Twenty-Five Years of Storytelling: The Spirit of the Art." *The Horn Book Magazine* Vol. LXVIII, No. 6 (Nov./Dec. 1992): 702–708.

Yashinsky, Dan. "Libraries and Storytellers: Keeping Folk Tales Alive." *Wilson Library Bulletin* 65.5 (Jan. 1991): 53–55.

Chapter Nine

Modern Fantasy: A Small Step From Reality

Elizabeth was reading *The Cricket in Times Square* (Selden) to her group of second and third graders, whom she describes as "above average achievers." Her original intent had been to read the book simply for their enjoyment, but activities "sort of cropped up spontaneously" when Amanda, one of the third graders, came in from recess with a live cricket.

They put the cricket in a jar and named it Chester, after the cricket in the book. The Chester in the book spends one summer in New York City, learns about urban living from a cat named Harry and a mouse named Tucker, and saves a family from bankruptcy by giving concerts. All the children got a good look at their own Chester, and Elizabeth explained that rather than confine the cricket, she would tip the jar on its side and hope that the cricket would come and go freely, just like the book Chester.

The next morning the jar was empty, but while the students were arriving, the kindergarten teacher stopped by. She had a cricket in a bug-viewing jar and wondered if it was theirs. While the children were admiring that cricket, the custodian arrived with his fist loosely clenched. "I found your cricket in the hallway. Where do you want me to put him?" he asked. Chester #2 was put in a jar.

A few minutes later, a child just entering the room glanced down at the floor and exclaimed, "Chester came back! There he is!" As the startled cricket was captured, Chester #1 began chirping in his jar. Elizabeth saw the interest of the children and gave as a prompt for journal writing the question, "Which of the three Chesters is really ours, and how can you tell?"

The children observed all three crickets carefully. "Not surprisingly," said Elizabeth, "all the children wanted to talk about that morning was crickets." So after recess, she guided the children in creating a comparison chart. On the left side they put what Chester could do, on the right what real crickets could do, and in the middle what both the fantasy cricket and a real cricket could do. Their chart is shown in Figure 9-1.

As they reviewed their chart, Elizabeth and the children talked about distinguishing real from make-believe and how authors may use real animals or objects in their stories, but create fantasy by letting those animals or

Here is the chart Elizabeth and her second and third graders created as they compared Chester from *The Cricket in Times Square* with the real crickets they found and observed. The children referred to the chart as they discussed fantasy literature and as they wrote their own stories.

Chester	Both	Real Crickets
talks	jump	sleep in stumps and grass
travels to a new town	hop	live in the real world
drinks from a glass	chirp	hop away from people
feels emotions	run fast	
thinks	cross streets	
is friends with a cat and a mouse	have six legs, wings	

Not included on the chart was the descriptor, "Brings good luck," because the children differed in their assessments. All said that Chester had definitely brought good luck in the story, but some argued that real crickets also brought good luck and others said that nothing really "brought good luck." They decided that this item needed further investigation.

Figure 9-1 A comparison chart on crickets.

objects do things they can't or don't really do. In the next few days, the children added to the chart and listened to more of *A Cricket in Times Square*. When the book was completed, the children wrote their own fantasy stories about a cricket in their school. They looked at the chart for characteristics of real crickets and then brainstormed fantasy ideas.

Elizabeth had taken advantage of her choice of good literature and a teachable moment to engage the children in enjoying a story, observing an insect carefully, comparing real and make-believe crickets, extending their understanding of fantasy as a genre, and writing their own stories.

Fantasy is made up of elements that do not exist outside of the imagination. One elf, one child who can fly, one animal that talks, and the book is fantasy. Realistic fiction, by contrast, is based on what happened or could have happened. If someone in the Park Snoot Hotel complains about seeing a mouse, as happens in *Do You See a Mouse?* (Waber), well, that could happen. It's possible that everyone who works at the hotel, from Mary Alice at the front desk, to Gaston the chef, to Yolanda in the gift shop, might have missed seeing it, even though sharp-eyed readers will find a mouse in every illustration. A hotel owner might even hire a pair of detectives to look into the matter. What makes this humorous story a fantasy is that the mouse assumes human characteristics in its poses and as it stands in line with all the hotel employees, answering with them that there is no mouse. As the detectives leave the hotel after having certified that there is no mouse—the mouse waves good-bye from the window.

Chester's adventures continue in several sequels, the first of which is *Tucker's Countryside* (New York: Farrar, 1969). How Harry and Tucker met is told in the prequel *Harry Kitten and Tucker Mouse* (New York: Farrar, 1986).

This story is fantasy, not because there is a mouse in the hotel, but because the mouse assumes human characteristics. (Source: Illustration from DO YOU SEE A MOUSE? Copyright © 1995 by Bernard Waber. Reprinted by permission of Houghton Mifflin Co. All rights reserved.*)*

Much of fantasy literature, however, *appears* plausible. Characters, even when they are rats or rabbits or crickets, behave something like people. Maybe they are able to disappear under certain circumstances, or fly, or change from one form to another, but they cannot escape normal human sadness, longing for love, or other real human emotions.

HOW FANTASY BEGINS

Some writers lead readers to accept the fantasy by beginning the story in reality and then having the fantasy occur, sometimes in a sudden leap, other times in small doses. Often writers start the story in fantasy, simply presenting it as the way the world is.

An activity to follow the reading of *Jumanji* would be for children to work in pairs and create a board game of their own, incorporating ideas from the story into it.

Van Allsburg begins *Jumanji* with Peter and Judy, realistic children whose parents who tell them they are to keep the house neat. Becoming bored as they play with their toys, they decide to go to the park. Once there they find a board game titled *Jumanji, a Jungle Adventure Game*. They take it home and begin playing, not impressed with the notice in the directions that once a game has begun, it cannot end until one of the players has reached the golden city. This bit of information takes on significance once they find that when they land on a space, whatever it says will happen—REALLY happens. When Peter lands on a square that says he will have to move back two spaces because of a lion attack, readers see in the illustration what his sister facing him, sees, a lion on the piano behind him. Monkeys steal food, the monsoon season arrives, and rhinos stampede.

In the game of Jumanji, *whatever happens on the board happens in real life. (Source:* Illustration from JUMANJI. Copyright © 1981 by Chris Van Allsburg. Reprinted by permission of Houghton Mifflin Co. All rights reserved.)

The fantasy is accepted by the reader because the action is just as horrifying to the children *in* the story as it is to the children *reading* the story. And the trap is set. Peter and Judy must continue this frightening game, because, as the instructions say, it will not end until someone wins.

Kevin Henkes, on the other hand, introduces his story about *Chrysanthemum* by explaining that the day she was born was the happiest in her parents' lives. They thought she was perfect. The opening illustration shows her in her bassinet, and this is how the reader knows that she is a mouse. That the mice parents are talking immediately defines this book as fantasy. It continues with the entire cast of characters being personified mice. Chrysanthemum loves her "flower" name—the way it sounds and the way it looks when written. But when she starts school, her classmates immediately begin to make fun of her name. Even though her parents assure her each night that her name is beautiful, each day she becomes more unhappy. She is vindicated, however, when the beloved music teacher, Mrs. Twinkle, reveals that *her* first name is Delphinium.

Chrysanthemum celebrates her perfect name. (Source: Illustration and text excerpt from CHRYSANTHEMUM by Kevin Henkes, Copyright © 1991 by Kevin Henkes. Reprinted by permission of Greenwillow Books, a division of William Morrow and Company, Inc.)

The fantasy is accepted because it is presented in a matter-of-fact way. Children identify with the emotions of the characters and suffer with Chrysanthemum as she endures the ridicule, reveling with her as the others select new names, all flowers. Many fantasy picture books for young children feature animals or toys that take on human characteristics.

Children can look for what makes a book fantasy and for how the fantastic elements are introduced. With animal fantasy, they might also look for times when a personified animal maintains some of its animal characteristics. In *Chrysanthemum,* Henkes plays with the mouse idea in humorous ways, such as having *cheese* and *rodent* among the words the class knows and showing a picture hanging in the kitchen, a Picasso-style painting of two mice.

In another Henkes book, *Julius, the Baby of the World,* the characters are also mice, but big sister Lilly is not at all happy with the arrival of her new sibling, Julius, much as human children do not always welcome competition from a tiny newcomer. The feelings are human, but the descriptions reflect their animal characteristics.

Children can chime in on the refrain about Julius' nose, eyes, and fur—it appears five times.

But her parents loved him.
They kissed his wet pink nose.
They admired his small black eyes.
And they stroked his sweet white fur.
"Julius is the baby of the world," chimed Lilly's parents.
"Disgusting," said Lilly. (Henkes, n. pag.)[1]

---

[1] *Source:* Text excerpt from JULIUS: BABY OF THE WORLD by Kevin Henkes, Text Copyright © 1990 by Kevin Henkes. Reprinted by permission of Greenwillow Books, a division of William Morrow and Company, Inc.

CATEGORIZING FANTASY

This chapter focuses mainly on modern fantasy and science fiction, although writers today sometimes draw on traditional fantasy—myths, legends, fables, and folktales—for form or content. Fantasy clearly cannot be pigeon-holed into neat categories.

One way to try to organize such books, however, is to identify the primary element of fantasy. Is it a toy that is alive, an animal that talks, a two-inch tall person? Or is the primary departure from the real world a series of curious occurrences—do people fly, travel through time, or perform inhuman tasks? Here is a sampling of books to illustrate these elements.

Talking Toys

Winnie-the-Pooh (Milne) is a stuffed bear and a companion of a little boy named Christopher Robin. Pooh ordinarily lives by himself in a forest near a pessimistic donkey friend named Eeyore and a homey collection of other stuffed animals including Piglet, Rabbit, Owl, Kanga, and Little Roo. The none-too-bright bear is always affable and only mildly surprised at the indignities he continually suffers, often of his own doing. His songs, poems, and antics provide enjoyment for many children. Each chapter is a separate story. In one, Pooh leaves home with a birthday gift, a jar of honey, for Eeyore. But he eats the honey on the way, so Eeyore gets instead a Useful Pot to Keep Things in.

Inanimate toys also come alive in *The Tub Grandfather*, a continuation of the adventures of the tub people created by Pam Conrad. In this adventure the family of wooden dolls are parading around the rug, which the grandmother remembers from times past as a "sunny field." When their ball rolls under the radiator, they discover the long-missing grandfather, lying on his side and covered with dust and spider webs. Their attempts to revive him are unsuccessful, including the trip to the bathtub in an attempt to jog his memory, until the radiator begins to whistle. This, combined with the grandmother's soft humming, awakens him. The story closes as the grandmother and grandfather dance in that sunny field remembered from long ago.

Personified Animals

Stories about talking animals, like those of talking toys, often explore the human condition. In fact, some personified animals become almost like family members or friends to the children who read about them and understand their feelings.

Preschool and primary age children can identify with a young badger named Frances in a series by Russell Hoban. In *A Birthday for Frances,* which was first published in 1968 and reissued with new color in the illustrations in 1995, Frances suffers jealousy over birthday celebrations for her sister Gloria. She decides to give Gloria a Chompo bar and four pieces of bubble gum, and she buys the presents with her father at a store. On the way home,

A family of wooden dolls finds their long missing grandfather and attempts to revive him. (Source: Illustration from THE TUB GRANDFA-THER, text Copyright © 1993 by Pam Conrad. Illustration Copyright © 1993 by Richard Egielski. Cover Copyright © 1993 by Richard Egielski. Cover Copyright © 1993 by HarperCollins Publishers. Reprinted by permission of HarperCollins Publishers.)

the wily Frances begins to question whether a whole Chompo bar might not be too much for Gloria, and when her father worries that she might eat the candy, Frances comments that the candy is not yet Gloria's.

The party begins. The group sings "Happy Birthday" to Gloria, all except Frances, who sings her own words to the tune. Gloria's wish as she blows out the candles is that Frances will be nice to her. And Frances tries, singing "Happy Birthday" again, with the right words, when she gives Gloria the present.

Just as Frances becomes known to children through many books about her, so too do the friends George and Martha, and Frog and Toad. *George and Martha* (Marshall) is the first book about two hippopotamus friends, and it, like all the ones that follow, is divided into five short stories.

Story number three in this book has only five lines. The first explains that George likes to peek in windows, and the second that once he peeked in on Martha. The illustration for this text shows that Martha is in the bathtub when George peeks in. Lines three, four, and five indicate that he doesn't do it again because an angry Martha lets him know that even though they are friends, he is not to intrude on her privacy. The illustration shows Martha glaring from the bathroom window at George, who is outside with the tub having been thrown on his head.

Story number one has much more text. It tells how Martha loves making split pea soup and serves it often to George—who hates it but doesn't

Frances doesn't even notice that she has begun to eat the presents she has bought for her sister Gloria. (Source: Illustration from A BIRTHDAY FOR FRANCES by Russell Hoban, Illustrations by Lillian Hoban. Copyright © 1968, Harper-Collins Publishers. Reprinted with permission.)

want to hurt Martha's feelings. One day, after 10 bowls of the soup, George has had enough. He pours the remaining soup into his loafers. When Martha confronts him, he confesses, only to have Martha tell him that friends tell each other the truth and that from now on, no more pea soup. How about chocolate chip cookies?

Frog and Toad also have a friendship that continues through several books. In *Frog and Toad Are Friends* (Lobel), Frog bursts into Toad's cozy house with the announcement that it is spring. Toad, still hibernating, is uninterested. It is only by changing Toad's calendar that Frog convinces him to get up.

Despite their realistically grimacing expressions and the moist, root-level scenery, it is easy to forget that these are animals. In a later story about a swimming expedition, Toad makes Frog hide his eyes until Toad gets in the water because he says he looks funny in a bathing suit. Toad's embarrassment arouses the curiosity of several animals who gather to look and laugh at Toad. And when he emerges from the water, he does look funny in a bathing suit.

Both George and Martha and Frog and Toad explore the dimensions of friendship with sympathetic understanding and clever language. The books present an opportunity for teachers and children to discuss, role-play, and write about friendship. One second-grade teacher used these books to plan a writing lesson with her students. First the children talked about these pairs of friends, then made a list of other pairs of friends, some real and some imaginary. Following this, they talked about their favorite chapters, each a complete story, and *where* the action took place. They talked about what had happened and why it made a good story. Again the teacher recorded their comments on a list. The children had addressed characterization, setting, and plot in their responses. During their writing for that

When engaging children in role playing, before they begin, ask them to think about how the character feels and why the character behaves as he or she does.

Frog and Toad are friends who have many adventures together. (Source: Illustration from FROG & TOAD TOGETHER by Arnold Lobel. Copyright © 1971, HarperCollins Publishers. Reprinted with permission.)

week, the teacher encouraged them to look at the lists they had made and to create a "friendship" story of their own.

Personified animals can be as fully developed as their human counterparts. The English writer and illustrator Beatrix Potter created entire farms of animals with human traits, including the mischievous Peter Rabbit. One of her small books, *The Tale of Jemima Puddle-Duck,* is about a naive duck who trusts a fox intent on roast duck for dinner. The leering fox offers a shed to Jemima as a nesting place and even talks her into bringing him herbs to flavor the roast. A friendly collie and two foxhound puppies save Jemima, but the ending is melancholy. The exuberant puppies cannot be stopped from eating the duck eggs. When Jemima tries again to sit on a new batch of eggs, only four hatch. "Jemima Puddle-Duck said that it was because of her nerves, but she had always been a bad sitter," the book concludes. Readers can recognize rationalization, even if they cannot name it. And they can feel affection for Jemima, trying hard to be a mother in her shawl and bonnet, even when she fails.

More sophisticated is one of the most popular children's books in history, E. B. White's *Charlotte's Web.* Wilbur, the runt pig, first meets the gray spider, Charlotte A. Cavatica, when she offers to be his friend. She proves the value of her friendship when Wilbur is slated for slaughter. She weaves the words "some pig" into her web, and Wilbur is saved: Who could butcher a special pig under an advertisement like that? One character's comment that the spider seems more special than the pig is ignored, and Wilbur wins a prize at a local fair. He is assured of a long life. Charlotte, however, lives only long enough to make her egg sac, which she entrusts to Wilbur. She dies alone.

White, a long-time writer with the *New Yorker* magazine, has been famous for his clear, deceptively simple style and his love for the New England farm where he lived. *Charlotte's Web* captures the scents and sounds of barnyard living at the same time it explores themes of life and death, friendship and selfishness. Charlotte's lonely death is all the more poignant to children because of their earlier laughter at the terse and silky messages in her web. Though Wilbur makes friends with some of her children the following spring, he will never forget Charlotte, a true friend.

Figure 9-2 shows how one class of children compared the book of *Charlotte's Web* to a movie version.

Chris had read *Charlotte's Web* to her third graders, who enjoyed it thoroughly. Several children mentioned having seen a movie of the book and enjoying that too. Chris decided to borrow the video from the library and show it to the class, but also to involve them in making a comparison of the book and the movie version.

She contemplated approaches to the comparison. She knew some students would have difficulty sitting quietly for the full movie, but she also knew that seeing it in its entirety would make a better and more coherent comparison. She could have students look for specific points of comparison, such as how each character was portrayed, or she could leave it open to what the students noticed. She could have students work individually or in groups.

Chris decided to have students work individually but be free to talk with others and to leave the comparison openended. Her procedure was to place large sheets of white paper on the side and back walls of the classroom, with magic markers by each sheet. While the video was being shown, children could get up and make a note of a difference between movie and book on the white paper. The notation did not need to be in a complete sentence. Children were also permitted to have quiet discussions with classmates during the movie. Chris said afterwards, "This freedom to discuss before or as they wrote was important because it helped them clarify ideas they wrote."

After the movie, the children read what they had recorded and categorized their comments. Then they made generalizations. For example, they decided that while most of the characters retained their book personalities in the movie, some were different. "The sheep was a snob in the book but not in the movie." "Wilbur did not seem as sad in the movie because he did not fall asleep crying in it." "Avery is funnier in the book." Their final generalization was that a movie doesn't have to follow a book exactly to be good, but that some changes can be annoying.

Figure 9-2 *Charlotte's Web*— Comparing the book with the video.

Imaginary Animals

Dragons are perhaps the most popular of the imaginary animals that appear in books for children—and in mythology for that matter. A close second would be the unicorn, also with roots in ancient myth and storytelling. Often these age-old characters bring with them their symbolic meanings and distinctive descriptions.

In contemporary fantasy, however, the imaginary animal is often one of the protagonists, so it is developed fully rather than simply fulfilling the role of villain. In Tomie dePaola's *The Knight and the Dragon,* for example, parallel stories are told about the title characters. The knight prepares to fight the dragon by getting a book at the castle library on dragon fighting, while the dragon prepares by reading his own book, *How to Fight Knights.* Both attempt to hone their skills, but the actual battle shows them to be equally clumsy. The solution to their ineptness in battle is provided by the castle librarian, whose books on outdoor cooking inspire them to open their own barbecue restaurant. After all, lances make excellent skewers, and a fire-breathing dragon can grill to perfection.

Margaret Shannon goes even further in developing a dragon that does not fit the stereotype or fit with family members for that matter. *Elvira* likes making daisy chains and dresses. The other dragons tease her and burn her daisy chains, making her so angry that she packs her suitcase and goes to live with the princesses, soul mates even though they are frightened of her initially. Once they are assured that she does not plan to eat them, the princesses think she is a marvelous pet. They even paint her claws. When Elvira encounters her family in the forest, they take her home, where she stuns the other dragons with the beautiful dress she has made. At their request, she makes dresses for the other dragons, and everyone is happy. Well, not exactly everyone. The princesses are not delighted since the dragons have not changed completely—they still chase the princesses; they just look prettier while they do it.

Stories of imaginary animals often provide the stimulus for art projects. Children can create their own imaginary animals or build on how illustrators have captured the personalities of the animals they portray. Figure 9-3 shows how an art teacher and a classroom teacher collaborated to guide first graders in a comparison of dragon stories and dragon characters.

Tiny People

Other characters in modern fantasy spring from the imagination in miniature human form. Some are small enough to hide under flowers but yet impinge on the world of full-grown people, often without being detected.

These characters have a long tradition in English literature for adults. Elves, small magical people, appear in Shakespeare's *A Midsummer-Night's Dream,* and Lilliputians, hand-sized people, overwhelm a sleeping man in *Gulliver's Travels* by the English satirist Jonathan Swift.

Martha, the school's art teacher, often coordinated her projects with the reading being done in the children's classrooms. When she talked with the first-grade teacher, she learned that the class was reading about fantastic animals and would be looking at several books about dragons. Among them were *Demi's Dragons* by Demi (New York: Holt, 1993); *The Knight and the Dragon* by dePaola (New York: Putnam's, 1980); *Saint George and the Dragon* by Hodges (Boston: Little, 1984); a newly illustrated edition of *The Tale of Custard the Dragon* by Nash (Boston: Little, 1995); and the poems in *The Dragons Are Singing Tonight* by Prelutsky (New York: Greenwillow, 1993).

For art, she engaged the children in creating mixed media collages that included a dragon. The children first compared the dragons in the books, noting the shapes of the dragons' bodies, describing how they looked when walking and when flying, paying particular attention to how scales were shown. Then they drew their own dragons, using crayons to create line and pattern. After this they used payons (water color crayons) to add more color to their dragons. Finally, the children created color backgrounds on construction paper, cut out their dragons, and placed them on their collages.

After the children had walked around the room looking at the many dragons, they talked about how artists can create their own vision of a subject. As she had planned with the classroom teacher, Martha had the children take their pictures back to their class. Once there, they told stories about their dragons and talked about how writers can create stories about make-believe animals.

Figure 9-3   The art teacher and the classroom teacher collaborate on dragon pictures and stories.

In this tradition is the chapter book *The Borrowers* by British writer Mary Norton. The borrowers are tiny people living under a grandfather clock. They squirrel away items they "borrow" from residents of an old but elegant house. They cook soup in a thimble. A chest of drawers is made of matchboxes. Queen Victoria's portrait, hung on a wall, is a postage stamp. Pod and Homily Clock and their daughter Homily live comfortably in their quarters under the timepiece, but Arriety longs to see more of the world. This worries her parents, since the worst thing that can happen to a borrower is to be seen by a human. Humans do not like the little people and are liable to call in a cat to get rid of them. Arriety ignores her parents' fears and goes exploring anyway, becoming friends with a boy. The friendship pays off. When the grumpy cook in the house discovers the borrowers and calls in a rat-catcher, the boy helps the Clock family escape. The characters are small but not sentimentalized, and the careful description of details adds to the believability.

Making a diorama of actual objects that Borrowers might find and use can be a creative and challenging extension of this book.

Curious Occurrences

A fantastic character is likely to undergo extraordinary experiences. Pod, the borrower, can climb curtains using a hatpin as a kind of piton, and Toad (in *Frog and Toad Are Friends)* can put on a bathing suit and be embarrassed about how he looks. But neither adventure seems particularly fantastic once the reader's natural inclination to doubt has been overcome. Once you accept a talking toad, it is a fairly small step to allow it to wear a bathing suit.

In another major class of fantasy, the characters are comparatively normal. The fantastic element is what happens to them, the curious occurrence in which they are turned temporarily into someone else, are carted through time, or experience strange happenings. Characters in such books almost always pass through periods of questioning, surprise, and doubt.

Monsieur Bibot, the dentist in Van Allsburg's *The Sweetest Fig,* has no difficulty extracting a tooth from an old woman who has no appointment when he thinks of the extra francs he may earn, and he has no regret at withholding pain pills when she has no money to pay. Nor does he pay attention to her words that the two figs she gives him are magic and can make his dreams come true. Only when he finds himself in his underwear as he walks his dog, Marcel, does he remember eating one of the figs and dreaming of standing in front of the cafe in just such clothing. He is astounded, yet understands as he notices that other elements of his dream have come true.

Bibot initiates a plan to make himself dream of being the richest man on earth, looking into a mirror to hypnotize himself before falling asleep. Alas, on the very night Bibot is to eat the fig, Marcel gulps it down. In the morning, Bibot awakens underneath his bed, and as a man with his own face reaches toward him, all he can do is bark. Readers share his surprise, and then infer what Marcel must have dreamed after having snatched the fig from his master's plate.

A group of third graders discussed what Bibot's life as a dog might be like. Some thought the magic was temporary and that he might become a nicer person when transformed back to human form. Others said that the magic was permanent, and that since Bibot was still Bibot, even in Marcel's body, he might become renowned as the "Amazing Dog Dentist."

In a nearly wordless book, David Wiesner shows what happens on a *Tuesday.* Three panels before the title page show frogs first sleeping peacefully on their lily pads and then looking startled as the pads rise into the air. Once the text has announced that it is a Tuesday, readers see frogs first floating above the water on their pads and then flying wildly through the sky. Animals that see this action are stunned; a man having a late night snack glances furtively at the frogs flying by his window; a woman asleep in front of her television misses the group that has joined her. That is not a problem for the frogs, however, because one is holding the remote control and changing the channel with its tongue.

When morning comes, the frogs are back in the swamp, and the once levitating lily pads lie limp on the street. Police and bystanders look at them

Some very strange events occur in the wordless book Tuesday. *(Source:* Illustration from TUESDAY. Text and illustrations Copyright © 1991 by David Wiesner. Reprinted by permission of Houghton Mifflin Co./Clarion Books. All rights reserved.)

in puzzlement. The book closes on the next Tuesday, again at nearly eight o'clock. A shadow on the barn shows that a pig is flying by, and in the final illustration, airborne pigs somersault in the night sky.

One class decided to make their own books with each student continuing the story. They used Wiesner's technique of panels to continue Tuesday adventures with pigs. When the book was completed, they wrote their dedication: "This book is dedicated to all the moms who say we can do things . . . when pigs fly."

Curious occurrences in fantasy may be flying frogs or magic figs. Characters may travel through time to another period or see money grow on trees. In *The Mountains of Tibet* (Gerstein), time travel is a chance to choose a second life. Figure 9-4 shows how one class responded to this fantasy.

Often books include more that one element of fantasy. In *Zeke Pippin* (Steig), for example, one element of fantasy is Zeke himself—a personified pig who talks, runs away from what he thinks is his unappreciative family, and escapes from three dogs who attack him and call him "porky." A second element is the magic harmonica he finds, an instrument that causes audiences to fall asleep when they hear it being played. Zeke, clever pig that he is, recognizes the supernatural qualities of his harmonica. Eventually he is reunited with his family, attains another harmonica, and plays his sleep-inducing instrument only for hospital patients and restless children at bedtime.

Randall was intrigued with the illustrations in *The Mountains of Tibet* by Mordicai Gerstein (New York: Harper, 1987) and the opportunity for discussion that the text provides. The story opens with a little boy born in Tibet, tells about his life as a woodcutter, and explains how he never left his valley. After his death, a voice tells him that he may become a part of the endless universe or live another life. He chooses another life; then he must make a series of other choices—which galaxy, which star, which planet, which creature, which race, which country, which parents, and which sex? All his choices match his previous life except for his last choice. This time he will be born a girl.

The illustrations depicting his life as a woodcutter are enclosed in squares centered within the white space of each page, like pictures hung on a wall. When he is making his choices, he is shown within a small blue circle on the left page, and his choices are in circles on a blue background on the right page, mandala-like.

After looking at the illustrations and noticing the patterns in size, shape, and color, the children talked about what choices they might make and their reasons for each choice. Then one child said that she wondered what it was really like to die. Other children began volunteering questions they had and things they wondered about.

Randall was at the close of his planned reading and discussion of the book, and it was near the end of the day. Still, he didn't want this new topic of discussion to be lost. He suggested that for their journal writing for the next few days, children record what they "wondered" about. They could choose whether to share their writing just with him or with their classmates.

Later that week, as he read their journals and as they shared their ideas, he was struck by the diversity and depth of their "wonderings." Here is a sampling:

I wonder: why people kill animals.
   how many people are in the world.
   if the earth will blow up sometime.
   what I'll be when I grow up.
   how people make ink.
   if my mom will be home when I get home.
   when I'll die.
   who made me.
   why my parents make me work.
   how my uncle is doing in heaven.
   what Santa looks like in Korea.
   if I will ever get a horse.
   if I will be very smart one day.
   what the earth will look like in 1,000,000 years.
   why people kill each other.
   if I will get a job when I grow up.
   if Nicole will ever be my friend again.

Figure 9-4   Children write, "I wonder. . . . "

SCIENCE FICTION

If fantasy is hard to classify, science fiction is next to impossible. "It is the literature of pure escapism," writes Sheila Egoff, "and it may also be the vehicle of biting criticism of contemporary society . . . If you will, it is often children's literature for adults and it may equally well be the child's easiest entry into speculations that trouble the adult mind" (384).

The field includes stories of monsters stalked by cliches. (Are you saying, doctor, that—that **thing** is alive?) It also includes stories that make serious comment on where we are really going in society and what we are likely to be when we get there. Both approaches rely on scientific possibility, on what **might** happen in the future based on our current scientific knowledge.

A large number of books, often incorporating the fantasy elements of curious occurrences and odd characters, are woven around space travel. They range from pleasantly silly stories to serious social comment. In general, books for children in preschool to grades 2 or 3 are of the lighter variety.

In *The Long Blue Blazer* (Willis), a child describes a boy named Wilson who was in her class for one day. He wore his long blue blazer, refusing to remove it for painting, for gym, or for anything else. When it was time to go home and Wilson's mother had not come for him, he just stood outside gazing at the sky. The child and her mother take Wilson home with them, where he has dinner, in his blazer, and finally goes to bed on the top bunk. The child awakens to see Wilson looking out the window at a space ship, and the last time she ever sees him is when he jumps from the window and she can see his long blue tail extending out from under his long blue blazer as he swoops through the sky. A final illustration shows Wilson outside the saucer-shaped space ship handing his mother the picture of her he had painted in school. After readers have responded to the surprise ending, they can go back and identify clues, foreshadowing, within the story that hint at Wilson's ancestry.

A different mood pervades *UFO Diary* (Kitamura), another science fiction story with a visitor from space. This time the visitor tells the tale. He made a wrong turn in the Milky Way and found himself approaching a blue planet. The illustrations show his bell-shaped craft as it comes closer and closer to Earth, finally landing in a field of grass. As he looks down he sees a creature looking up. The creature, a small boy, smiles, and he knows they will be friends, even though he cannot understand the boy's language. They play all afternoon, and before leaving for good, he takes the boy for a ride in his spacecraft, letting him circle the earth. The traveler is pleased when the boy gives him a present that is yellow and that grew in the field where they met. He promises he will plant it. The text shifts the point of view to that of the visitor, and the illustrations show Earth in space, a tiny dot in a vast blue universe.

Children in fourth grade (and older) can be introduced to serious science fiction with a book such as *The Green Book* (Walsh). This chapter

Most serious, or high, fantasy as it is often called, that explores issues of good versus evil or that critiques societal norms and mores is appropriate for children in grades 5 and up rather than for primary grade children.

This is a good point to stop and have children make predictions about the story. Try it with the cover of the book hidden so that children do not have clues about the setting.

book opens with Father telling the family that they will be able to take very little with them, only a few tools, one or two personal belongings, and one book. They make their selections, and Father shows some old slides since he will not be able to take the projector. They are aboard the space craft only a short time when the disaster anticipated for Earth occurs. They are alone in space on a rather old ship since they are from one of the poorer countries, searching for a new planet that will support life. After four years, they land on a red and shiny planet that Pattie, the youngest child, names Shine. There they must try to grow crops with the seeds they have brought, construct shelter, and make rules to govern themselves. If they fail, they have "last resort" pills to end their lives. They will find whether this handpicked group of people, a group designed to have the minimum number of people necessary to survive and grow, will indeed prosper. The book closes as the settlers discover that Pattie, whom they had teased about her choice of bringing a green bound notebook for writing rather than a book to read, has kept a history of their group. Her notebook begins with the first sentence of *The Green Book,* and readers realize that what they have been reading is Pattie's journal.

The book can stimulate consideration of issues such as the importance of books in a society. If children could take only one book for the rest of time, what book would each choose? They can talk about how individuals serve a society. If they were selecting people by occupations that would be needed for a society to function, which occupations would they want represented and why?

Here are rules for governing that one fourth-grade class agreed on. They made their rules at the point in the story where the ship was landing and the characters had not yet devised their governance system.

Government: Leader to be person who knows the most, determined by taking a test. Also a person who is "cool headed."

Laws: Citizens will not be permitted to murder or steal. They will be required to work and to share materials.

Punishments: People who break the laws will have extra work, no lunch, no breaks during work. The punishment for murder will be banishment from the settlement.

Rations: Food and other rations to be divided equally per person. Certain people are to find food and resources on certain days. Leftover rations will be kept for emergencies.

Jobs: Jobs include farmer, resource finder/developer, carpenter, newscarrier, technician, explorer.

Work Period: Generally five to six days per week, four to five hours per day. Ten days off every month; five weeks off every year.

Emergencies: Have a protection force for things like fires, vicious animals.

Language Play in Science Fiction

The genre of science fiction may lend itself to cliches, but it also includes some very creative use of language. Jane Yolen has written a series of space adventures about Commander Toad, using clever puns and taking gentle gibes at the genre. Commander Toad's ship is the *Star Warts,* with a crew that includes Mr. Hop, Lieutenant Lily, Doc Peeper, and Jake Skyjumper. In one book, they search for an intergalactic spy—Agent 007½, a master of disguise known as Tip Toad. In another, their ship is invaded by Commander Salamander and his pirates who force the crew to play Hop the Plank. The humor in the text is matched by that in the illustrations. Bruce Degen's pictures show that the crew reads such books as *Long John Slither* and *The Lizard of Oz,* as well as *Slime* magazine, which features on its cover the frog of the year.

Jeanne Willis has an alien—a five-eyed, two-tentacled hairy green professor—teach his class about Earth creatures before they make a visit to the planet. In *Earthlets as Explained by Professor Xargle,* for example, he tells his class about the tiny creatures that inhabit the Earth. They come in several colors, have only two eyes, and leak. They don't even have enough fur on their heads to keep them warm, but that is not really a problem since they can be wrapped in the fuzz from sheep. "Earthlings called Grandmas unravel the fuzz. Then with two pointed sticks, they make it into Earthlet wrappers" (n. pag.)[2]. The illustration shows one of these Grandmas watching television, surrounded by yarn, her knitting needles whipping back and forth in a flurry of activity.

> Giving children time to look at the illustrations themselves lets them discover details often missed at the distance and speed of a class reading.

MODERN MYTHMAKERS

Science fiction often looks toward the future. Another major category of fantasy uses stories drawn from past forms.

Unlike classic tales, myths, or epics (described in Chapter 8), narratives from modern mythmakers appear in print before they are widely told. The stories may borrow mermaids or other motifs from traditional literature, but they grow out of a known author's own experiences and feelings.

Some of the stories by Hans Christian Andersen, for example, seem to be about him, even though they have the form of the fairy tale. Andersen, who was born into a poor shoemaker's family, became a straggly young man with an oversized nose and ill-fitting clothes. As a teenager in Copenhagen, he sought out well-known artists and entertainers and bored them with his songs and poetry. He was said to have loved several women, among them a famous Swedish singer names Jenny Lind. He never married.

---

[2] *Source:* Text excerpt from EARTHLETS AS EXPLAINED BY DR. XARGLE by Jeanne Willis, illustrated by Rony Ross. Copyright © 1988 by Jeanne Willis. Used by permission of Dutton Children's books, a division of Penguin Books USA Inc. First published by Andersen Press Ltd. London.

The Hans Christian Andersen Award is give biennially by the International Board on Books for Young People to one author and one illustrator worldwide in recognition of his or her entire body of work.

Finally he began to publish plays and poems with some success, but his first fairy tales did not appear in print until he was in his thirties. Then, at last, his reputation began to grow. In his late thirties, he began to invent his own plots.

Andersen seems to have put his own life into one of his most famous stories, *The Ugly Duckling.* Duck society mocks the awkward little bird, just as Danish society had spurned Andersen. In the story, the ugly duckling leaves the nest and meets wild ducks in the marsh. They tell him that he is a "scarecrow," but it doesn't matter as long as he doesn't marry into their family. This is probably a commentary on Copenhagen society, just as there is in *The Emperor's New Clothes,* another Andersen tale about a proud emperor who parades before his people in the buff until a small boy has the courage to tell him he is naked.

Other Andersen stories are closer to traditional fairy tales. *The Snow Queen* is made of hearty traditional stock: lost children, a quest, a witch, talking beasts, and magic. The story involves two close friends, Kay and Gerda, who are divided when Kay gets a glass splinter in his eye. The splinter also stabs Kay's heart, turning it cold as ice and making him angry and critical of his friend. He goes to live in the Snow Queen's cold palace where Gerda, after an adventurous quest, finds him and melts the cold and crippling splinter with her tears. Love and courage conquer, just as they do in classic folktales.

Literary folktales are reissued with new illustrators just as those from the oral tradition are. James Thurber's *The Great Quillow,* in which a small toymaker, Quillow, outwits the giant who has been demanding food and clothing from village after village, is available in older editions with Thurber's original illustrations and in a newer edition with illustrations by Steven Kellogg. Students might compare the illustrations in *Quillow,* just as they might look at several editions of Andersen's tales.

Some families have a tradition of storytelling, often in folktale format, and these tales may be reworked and written down, another source of modern mythmaking. Patricia McKissack's *Flossie and the Fox* is a delightful trickster tale. Flossie Finley, the spunky heroine, starts off through the woods to deliver a basket of fresh eggs to Miz Viola at the McCutchin Place. Before long she is accosted by a fox. Flossie, with her soft Black dialect of the rural south, manages to keep the fox, with his elegant and educated language, at bay by pretending that she doesn't believe he actually *is* a fox. Only when the McCutchin Place is in sight, and the hounds are after the fox, does she admit—with a grin—that she knows what he is.

In an interview with Rudine Bishop, McKissack described how a story her grandfather told came to be a published book for children.

> It came from my grandfather. He used to tell wonderful stories. That man could mesmerize us. But if I told it the way he had told it, it would not be publishable because it was so long and rambling. Her name was not Flossie; it was Pat. He always named his characters after me, or my sister, or my brother, which was wonderful, too, because we became a part of this magical world that he had created. In his story, Flossie encountered a bear, a wolf, a snake—all the evil creatures that children might encounter—and then a fox. But she did basically the same thing each time, and it would ramble on and on and on. So I developed Flossie from that. (73)

McKissack based her story about Flossie tricking a fox on a tale her grandfather told. (Source: Illustration from FLOSSIE AND THE FOX by Patricia C. McKissack, pictures by Rachel Isadora. Copyright © 1986 Rachel Isadora for pictures. Used by permission of Dial Books for Young Readers, a division of Penguin Books USA Inc.)

McKissack goes on to tell about hearing the language her grandfather used in his storytelling and adopting it for her own rendition of the tale.

Modern mythmakers may draw heavily on the culture of a group as well as on traditional folk tale form. Matthew Gollub's original tale, *The Moon Was a Fiesta,* incorporates the love of festivals and the historic study of the cosmos by the people of Oaxaca, Mexico. For hundreds of years, the story tells us, the sun and moon were separate, with the sun watching over people's work and the moon over their dreams. Then the moon overhears some stars wishing that they could come out with the sun because that's when all the games and feasts take place. The moon tries to see just what the sun does but keeps falling asleep. Finally she is awakened by a "great commotion" and sees a fiesta in progress. The moon decides to have her own fiesta, even though the sun warns of dire consequences. The moon names *padrinos* who get animals to bring food and who decorate the village in preparation for the festival. The people come to the fiesta, wearing their wooden masks, and happily celebrate all night. But as the moon eats and drinks, she gives off less light, causing the people to lose track of time. Even the moon herself forgets to go "behind the sky," and thus the moon and sun are in the sky at the same time. No work at all gets done, and the moon is sorry—but does remember the fun of the fiesta. And the moon still likes to celebrate. That is why, the story concludes, that when people in Oaxaca see the sun and moon together in the sky, they say that the moon was a fiesta.

The street experiences of a modern black child in Harlem play against traditional African folktales in Virginia Hamilton's *The Time-Ago Tales of Jahdu.* Where young Lee Edward lives, the air is filled with stories about a mythical character named Jahdu. Lee Edward points to a plot floating in the air, and Mama Luka, who takes care of him after school, grabs the story and tells it. In

The Moon Was a Fiesta *draws heavily on the culture of the people of Oaxaca, Mexico. (Source: Quote and one illustration from THE MOON WAS A FIESTA by Matthew Gollub. Illustrated by Leovigildo Martinez. Text Copyright © 1994 by Matthew Gollub. Illustration Copyright © 1994 by Leovigildo Martinez. Reprinted by permission of Tambourine Books, a division of William Morrow and Company, Inc.)*

the last story, Jahdu takes the form of a small black child who stays in the Harlem neighborhood awhile and, like Lee Edward, enjoys living there.

Fables appear in modern form too. Arnold Lobel has written 20 contemporary fables *(Fables),* complete with morals at the end. In "The Bad Kangaroo," a small kangaroo behaves so badly at school, putting tacks on the teacher's chair and throwing spitballs in the classroom, that the principal makes an appointment to visit the parents. When he sits down in their living room, he is startled to find himself sitting on a thumbtack. Mr. Kangaroo is not surprised, though. He put it there. After observing the parents' behavior and attitude, the principal makes a quick exit. The moral is that children's conduct reflects that of their parents.

Some of these contemporary stories, of course, will be adopted as personal property by the people who hear them. The original authors may become anonymous. Many of Andersen's tales are no longer associated with him. They are told in the company of Grimm's collected stories as if the oral tradition had generated them.

Jane Yolen, who coined the phrase "modern mythmakers," and who has written many such tales herself, reported that one of her stories, *Greyling,* had been read over British Broadcasting Company radio for several years as "a folk tale from the Shetland Islands," although she made it up" (492).

THE VALUE OF FANTASY

The shelf of fantasy and science fiction we have explored includes an odd collection of talking toys and toads, tiny people, and a trove of narratives about impossible occurrences. All of this can be valuable in helping children to understand real life. Some even argue that fantasy is more illuminating than realistic fiction. How is that possible? C. S. Lewis answers:

> I think what profess to be realistic stories for children are far more likely to deceive them. I never expected the real world to be like the fairy tales. I think I did expect school to be like the school stories. The fantasies did not deceive me; the school stories did. (464)

Good fantasy does not deceive; more than that, it tells truths that children could not understand unless coded in imaginary stories. Nine-year-olds may never have talked about human death, but many can understand death as treated in Natalie Babbitt's fantasy *Tuck Everlasting,* the story of a family that will never die. Tuck, his wife Mae, and two sons, Miles and Jesse, have all looked the same for four score and seven years, since they drank the waters of a mysterious spring. The spring, hidden away in a forest near the house of a 10-year-old girl named Winnie Foster, gives immortality to all who sip it. It remains a Tuck family secret until Winnie, running away from home, encounters the spring and learns the secret. The Tucks carry her away before she has time to tell anyone else. After a hard journey, the family and a frightened Winnie arrive at the Tuck homestead, a dusty little house on the edge of a pond. Tuck takes Winnie for a rowboat ride and explains the family's situation and death almost entirely in images. He tells Winnie that everything is a wheel, continually turning, with new creatures coming in and old ones going out. The Tucks, he says, have dropped off the wheel. But Winnie hasn't. She'll go from child to woman, then move on to make room for new children.

The image is too powerful for Winnie and she feels sudden rage and helplessness. She does not want to die. But Tuck presses on, telling her that death is a part of the wheel.

At 10, Winnie comes to understand that she must die—unless she decides to drink some of the spring water Jesse has given her. In an understated but triumphant ending, the indestructible Tucks return to Winnie's village decades later and find a tall monument in a cemetery over Winnie's grave. She had lived 78 years and had been a loving wife and mother. Tuck says "good girl" aloud.

Winnie learned through images. Readers can, too. They can begin to understand their own feelings and to recognize that they are not alone in their experiences. Figure 9-5 describes how a teacher might have strengthened children's encounter with fantasy as a genre by attending more to their comments about a specific book. They were grappling with the theme, the deeper meanings of the book.

Fantasy helps explain the way things really are, and it can help readers explore how things should be. Lynne Cherry presents her concern for the environment, specifically the Amazon rain forest, in *The Great Kapok Tree.* A man has been sent into the forest to cut down the kapok tree. He begins his task, but tires, so he sits at the base of the tree to rest. He falls asleep, and one by one the forest animals come to tell him why he should not cut down the tree. The boa constrictor tells him that the tree is its home; the monkey

THE LESSON, AS PLANNED AND TAUGHT	REFLECTIONS . . .

Janie knew her second graders enjoyed experimenting with different art materials. She decided that their experiences with both art and literature might be enhanced by having them look at books in which the illustrator had used techniques the children were using.

The Lesson

The children had created pictures using crayon resist and had looked at Brian Pinkney's scratchboard illustrations in *The Ballad of Belle Dorcas*. They had also tried their hands at making Styrofoam prints, seeing how their work compared with the woodblock illustrations in *Whaling Days*. Now they were using collage techniques. Janie read *Frederick* by Leo Lionni. She and the children looked at the mice in the story, noting how they were constructed. They also noted how Frederick, the protagonist who works at saving the memory of sunshine and colors and warmth rather than storing food for the winter as they other mice do, could be distinguished from other mice in the illustrations. The children noticed that Frederick was often placed away from the other mice, but that all the mice were the same size and color. Then Robert said, "But Frederick wasn't the same. He was a poet and he knew that stories can make you feel good."

"I wouldn't let him have my food when he didn't work, even if he did tell good stories," offered Melissa.

"But stories and poems are important, and they helped the mice keep warm," countered Robert.

Janie decided she needed to keep their comments focused on the art, so she said, "Some of the edges of objects are sharp and were probably cut. Look again at the pictures. What other kinds of edges do you see? How do you think Lionni made them?" The children noticed the bodies of the mice and decided that Lionni had torn the paper, giving the mice a rougher, hairier look.

Janie planned to move to collage using more varied materials for the next lesson.

Combining the art and the literature seemed to enhance both—the children looked more closely at their own work and at the illustrations in picture books. They seemed to appreciate how artists used media for particular effects.

Janie's choice of examples worked well because the media were clear and because the books were interesting to the children. Also, having the children experiment with the media first and then look at the books both kept them from imitating and made them more readily appreciative of the artist's work.

Janie was so intent on studying the artistic techniques that she missed a perfect opportunity to let the children explore the themes of the book. Robert had identified one, and Melissa, among others, was ready to discuss it. Theme can be a rather abstract concept for young children, so when they identified this level of meaning, Janie might have asked them what they thought the important ideas in the story were. She could have gone back to the art by looking for more ways in which Lionni showed that Frederick was different from the other mice, yet was appreciated by them and essential to their survival.

Figure 9-5   On second thought: An opportunity to discuss theme.

Lynne Cherry's fantasy The Great Kapok Tree *stimulates readers to think about environmental choices. (Source:* Illustration from THE GREAT KAPOK TREE; A TALE OF THE AMAZON RAIN FOREST, Copyright © 1990 by Lynne Cherry, reproduced by permission of Harcourt Brace & Company.)

mentions that the roots hold the earth in place; the anteater wants him to think of the future; and the sloth questions how much beauty is worth. The man is awakened by a child from the Yanomamo tribe who asks him to look upon all of them with fresh eyes. As he sits up, all the creatures who have spoken to him are now staring at him. He picks up his ax, hesitates, then drops it and leaves the forest. The man has made what Cherry believes to be the right choice. It can stimulate children to think themselves about endangered environments and choices they may someday have to make.

Anne Jordan writes:

> Fantasy, because it requires its readers to go beyond the normal into imaginative worlds where anything is possible, fuels imaginative development and progress in the real world. There would be no space program, for instance, had not someone, somewhere imagined waking on the moon and flying to distant planets. (19)

Figures 9-6 and 9-7, at the end of this chapter, give examples of fantasy picture books and chapter books.

EVALUATING FANTASY

The freedom to take readers into forests where animals talk or introduce them to odd characters does not give writers of fantasy license to write wildly. There are, to begin with, the disciplines of all good writing. Good fantasy tells an original story well. Yet fantasy must meet other tests, too. These are the basic criteria.

The fantastic element must be believable. In *Tuck Everlasting,* the story takes its first jog away from reality while Mae Tuck is getting dressed, a simple everyday ritual filled with lulling detail. She puts on three petticoats, a skirt, a cotton jacket, a shawl, and leather boots and winds her hair into a bun, without looking into the mirror.

She does not need a mirror for a simple, yet fantastic, reason. She and her husband and her sons have looked exactly the same for the last 87 years. The details in the scene help put readers' disbelief to rest.

In addition to the details in this credible introduction, the Tuck's varied reactions to their lives everlasting—Jesse is pleased, his father feels useless—lend authenticity throughout the book.

The elements of fantasy must be central to the story. A collection of unrelated happenings, no matter how interesting, is not fantasy. The entire plot in *Tuck* and its theme of life and death revolve around the element of immortality.

Details must be consistent with the fantastic element. The one touch of fantasy explains details small and large throughout the whole story: why the Tuck's house on the pond is so dusty, why they are afraid to tie themselves emotionally to mortals, and why they fear someone else will find the spring and pass the water around. Jesse hesitates when Winnie asks him how old he is before she knows the Tuck's secret. He cannot answer directly. Mr. Tuck stops in midsentence to ask if she knows before saying anything revealing.

No matter how fantastic the story, main characters must be plausible and familiar. The best characters in fantasy remain humanlike, even when cloaked in animal identities, flung into weird lands, or placed under magical spells. They are fearful when readers would likely be afraid. They are unpredictable up to a point, just like real people. By refusing to drink the water, Winnie remains vulnerable and mortal, choosing fragile life over the certainty of everlasting existence. We last see her pouring Jesse's gift of spring water on the back of a toad.

Characters in realistic fiction make choices, too, of course. They are fearful, sometimes unpredictable, kind, and cruel; and their adventures challenge them. They are believable. But only in fantasy—magic made by just a small step from reality—can a little girl choose to confer immortality on a toad.

SUMMARY

Fantasy is made up of elements that do not exist outside the imagination. One talking animal or one child who can fly and the story is classified as fantasy. Writers make fantasy believable in several ways, but two common ones are (a) to begin the story in realism and then introduce the fantastic element, with the reader identifying with the book characters' reactions; or (b) to have the fantasy presented as the way the world is from page one.

Often fantasy is classified by the primary elements of fantasy. For young children these fall into the categories of talking toys, personified animals, imaginary animals, tiny people, and curious or strange occurrences.

Science fiction is fantasy in that it contains elements impossible in the world today. Usually it is keyed to scientific and technological knowledge but extends what might happen with that knowledge. Much science fiction revolves around space travel, with Earth both sending and receiving travelers.

Another form of fantasy is the literary folktale, fable, or myth. These stories draw on traditional literature for form or content, but they have known authors. Yolen has termed writers of such stories—Hans Christian Andersen is one—"modern mythmakers."

Children can explore difficult truths through fantasy. Its images enhance understanding and encourage consideration of new ideas. Fantasy can be judged using four basic criteria in addition to the disciplines of all good writing.

1. The fantastic element is made believable.
2. The elements of fantasy are central to the story.
3. Details are consistent with the fantastic element.
4. No matter how fantastic the story, main characters are plausible and familiar.

Asch, Frank. *Here Comes the Cat!* Ill. by Vladimir Vagin. New York: Scholastic, 1989. The mice are frightened by the message that the cat is coming in this book with text in English and Russian and a surprise ending.

Brown, Marc. *Arthur's Chicken Pox.* Boston: Little, Brown, 1994. One of many books about Arthur, this one has him sick a week before a planned trip to the circus and his sister D. W. jealous of the attention he is getting.

Burningham, John. *Mr. Gumpy's Outing.* New York: Holt, 1971. Mr. Gumpy invites the animals, one by one, to ride on his boat, but they don't behave and the boat tips.

Burton, Virginia. *The Little House.* Boston: Houghton Mifflin, 1942. Built in a rural area, the little house finds herself surrounded by city as times change and the urban area expands.

Carle, Eric. *A House for a Hermit Crab.* Saxonville, MA: Picture Book Studio, 1987. Each month hermit crab decorates the shell he has moved into more elaborately, but each month he also grows, so that in December he has to move on to a larger house.

Conrad, Pamela. *Call Me Ahnighito.* Ill. by Richard Egielski. New York: HarperCollins, 1995. A giant meteorite tells about its discovery in Greenland and its eventual trip to the American Museum of Natural History in New York City.

de Brunhoff, Jean. *The Story of Babar.* New York: Random House, 1960. The first of many stories about Babar, this one sees the elephant after running away, return to the jungle, resplendent in his new clothing.

Figure 9-6   Touchstone fantasy picture books.

Dorros, Arthur. *Abuela.* Ill. by Elisa Kleven. New York: Dutton, 1991. Rosalba imagines what it would be like if she and her grandma, her abuela, could fly over the city, looking down at the places they know.

Fox, Mem. *Hattie and the Fox.* Ill. by Patricia Mullins. New York: Bradbury, 1988. Hattie the hen sees the fox emerging bit by bit, but doesn't recognize it until the last minute.

Freeman, Don. *Corduroy.* New York: Viking, 1968. A small toy bear, Corduroy searches all night in the department store for a replacement button for his overalls.

Geisel, Theodor. (Dr. Seuss) *And to Think That I Saw It on Mulberry Street.* New York: Vanguard, 1937. A little boy lets his imagination run wild as he tells what he has seen on the way home from school.

Hutchins, Pat. *Rosie's Walk.* New York: Macmillan, 1968. When Rosie the hen goes for a walk, she escapes disaster after disaster, completely unaware of the dangers.

McCloskey, Robert. *Make Way for Ducklings.* New York: Viking, 1941. Mrs. Mallard gets her ducklings safely from the Charles River to the Boston Public Garden, where they decide to make their home.

Rey, H. A. *Curious George.* Boston: Houghton Mifflin, 1941. A very inquisitive monkey, George is frequently in trouble, even though his intentions are only to satisfy his curiosity.

Ringgold, Faith. *Tar Beach.* New York: Crown, 1991. One night Cassie's dream of being free to go whereever she wants comes true as the stars lift her from the rooftop of her Harlem apartment and she learns to fly.

Figure 9-6   *continued*

Avi. *Poppy.* Ill. by Brian Floca. New York: Orchard, 1995. Poppy, a tiny deer mouse, has the courage to explore New Farm as a possible home for her family and to confront the Mr. Ocax, the owl.

Babbitt, Natalie. *Knee-knock Rise.* New York: Farrar, 1970. Young Egan climbs to the top of the mountain in search of the Megrimum, but the villagers don't want to hear what he discovers.

Bond, Michael. *A Bear Called Paddington.* Ill. by Peggy Fortnum. Boston: Houghton, 1960. Paddington is found in a railway station in London and taken home by the Brown family where his efforts to be helpful usually end up with less than satisfactory results.

Brittain, Bill. *Shape-Changer.* New York: HarperCollins, 1994. Frank meets a talking fire hydrant named Zymel who says he is a detective from a distant planet seeking an escaped criminal who could destroy Earth.

Cameron, Eleanor. *The Wonderful Flight to the Mushroom Planet.* Ill. by Robert Henneberger. Boston: Little, Brown, 1954. This is the first in a series of easy reading science fiction stories about Mr. Bass, resident of the planet Basidium.

Cleary, Beverly. *Ralph S. Mouse.* Ill. by Paul Zelinsky. New York: Morrow, 1982. Ralph, a mouse who enjoys riding his motorcycle, but not fending off his noisy cousins, has an adventurous trip to school.

Dahl, Roald. *James and the Giant Peach.* Ill. by Nancy Burkert. New York: Knopf, 1961. James' adventures begin when he drops the bag holding the magic green things under the peach tree, causing a peach and its insect inhabitants to grow to giant size.

Graham, Kenneth. *The Wind in the Willows.* 1908. Ill. by E. H. Shepard. New York: Scribner's, 1940. Four animal friends, Badger, Ratty, Mole, and Toad, have a series of adventures in this classic animal fantasy.

Figure 9-7   Touchstone fantasy chapter books.

Howe, James and Deborah. *Bunnicula*. Ill. by Leslie Morrill. New York: Atheneum, 1983. The Monroe family, after seeing a movie of Dracula, begin to notice events that make them think the bunny they found in the theatre may be a vampire rabbit.

Jansson, Tove. *Moominpappa at Sea*. 1967. Translated by Kingsley Hart. New York: Farrar, 1993. This is one of several stories about the tiny Moomin family, this time setting up housekeeping on an island.

King-Smith, Dick. *Babe: the Gallant Pig*. Ill. by Mary Rayner. New York: Crown, 1985. Babe is a motherless pig when the old sheepdog takes over; what she teaches him later helps him effectively herd the sheep, who admire his ability to talk with them.

Le Guin, Ursula K. *Catwings*. Ill. by S. D. Schindler. New York: Orchard, 1988. The four kittens who are born with wings fly from the city to the country, where they learn that some humans can be very kind.

Lewis, C. S. *The Lion, the Witch, and the Wardrobe*. Ill. by Pauline Baynes. New York: Macmillan, 1961. In this religious allegory, which can be read on many levels, four children find their way to Narnia and attempt to break the spell of the wicked Snow Queen.

Lindgren, Astrid. *Pippi Longstocking*. Ill. by Louis Glanzman. New York: Viking, 1950. Pippi is an adventuresome orphan who lives with her monkey and her horse and does whatever she wants in this first of a series of books about her.

Slote, Alfred. *My Robot Buddy*. New York: Lippincott, 1975. Jack's perfect birthday gift of a robot that looks just like him makes a great playmate and leads to adventure.

Figure 9-7 *continued*

☙ EXPLORE ON YOUR OWN

1. **Explore Your Personal Response.** Read three books of animal fantasy and three books in which animals are portrayed realistically. Which type of animal story do you prefer and why?
2. **Apply Literary Criteria.** Read five books of fantasy. For each, identify the techniques the author uses to make the fantasy believable and decide how successfully the techniques worked.
3. **Prepare to Share Literature With Children.** Select a book of fantasy. Then write a paragraph that would have children picture in their minds situations or events that fit the role of fantasy and that relate to the book. For example, a guided imagery exercise preceding a book about visitors from space might include such suggestions as, "Imagine you are looking out the window of your bedroom. You see a space vehicle land. It opens. Picture in your mind the creatures that come out. See what they look like. Picture what they are doing. If you were writing a story about them, what would you have happen?"

☙ EXPLORE WITH CHILDREN

1. **Explore Children's Responses.** Ask a group of children to name books of fantasy they have read or heard. Write the titles they name on strips of paper. Then ask the children to group the books by moving the strips of paper so that like books are together. Have them identify the criteria they are using in their categorization.
2. **Engage Children With Literature.** Read a book of fantasy to a group of children without showing the illustrations. Ask the children to make an illustration for the book of any scene they like, but their pictures must in some way show that the book is a fantasy. When they are finished, encourage the children to show and explain their pictures.

☙ SUGGESTED PROFESSIONAL REFERENCES

Anderson, Celia Catlett, and Marilyn Fair Apseloff. *Nonsense Literature for Children: Aesop to Seuss.* Hamden, CT: Library Professional Publications, 1989. § This scholarly text explores how authors and illustrators have played with language and pictures to create nonsense, using both historical and contemporary examples.

Edinger, Monica. *Fantasy Literature in the Elementary Classroom: Strategies for Reading, Writing, and Responding.* Jefferson City, MO: Scholastic, 1995. § The author presents strategies for guiding children's responses to fantasy and describes thematic units focusing on fantasy texts.

Goldthwaite, John. *The Natural History of Make-Believe.* New York: Oxford University Press, 1996. § Goldthwaite surveys three centuries of fantasy literature for children, showing how early folktales and nursery rhymes evolved into modern fantasy and fairy tales in Britain, Europe, and America.

Neumeyer, Peter F. *The Annotated Charlotte's Web.* New York: HarperCollins, 1994. § Neumeyer analyzes *Charlotte's Web,* commenting on the text itself, noting the literary traditions in which the book was written, and referring to original drafts of the manuscript and other writings by White.

CHILDREN'S BOOKS CITED

Andersen, Hans Christian. *The Emperor's New Clothes.* Retold and ill. by Anne Rockwell. New York: Harper-Collins, 1982.

Andersen, Hans Christian. *The Snow Queen.* Retold by Caroline Peachey. Ill. by P. J. Lynch. New York: Gulliver, 1994.

Andersen, Hans Christian. *The Ugly Duckling.* Trans. by Anthea Bell. Ill. by Alan Marks. Saxonville, MA: Picture Book Studio, 1989.

Babbitt, Natalie. *Tuck Everlasting.* New York: Farrar, 1975.

Cherry, Lynne. *The Great Kapok Tree.* New York: Harcourt, 1990.

Conrad, Pam. *The Tub Grandfather.* Ill. by Richard Egielski. New York: HarperCollins, 1993.

dePaola, Tomie. *The Knight and the Dragon.* New York: Putnam, 1980.

Gerstein, Mordicai. *The Mountains of Tibet.* New York: Harper & Row, 1987.

Gollub, Matthew. *The Moon Was a Fiesta.* Ill. by Leovigildo Martinez. New York: Tambourine, 1994.

Hamilton, Virginia. *The Time-Ago Tales of Jahdu.* Ill. by Nonny Hogrogian. New York: Macmillan, 1969.

Henkes, Kevin. *Chrysanthemum.* New York: Greenwillow, 1991.

Henkes, Kevin. *Julius, the Baby of the World.* New York: Greenwillow, 1990.

Hoban, Russell. *A Birthday for Frances.* 1968. Ill. by Lillian Hoban. New York: HarperCollins, 1995.

Kitamura, Satoshi. *UFO Diary.* New York: Farrar, 1989.

Lobel, Arnold. *Fables.* New York: Harper, 1980.

Lobel, Arnold. *Frog and Toad Together.* New York: Harper, 1971.

McKissack, Patricia. *Flossie & the Fox.* Ill. by Rachel Isadora. New York: Dial, 1986.

Marshall, James. *George and Martha.* Boston: Houghton, 1972.

Milne, A.A. *Winnie-the-Pooh.* 1926. New York: Dutton, 1954.

Norton, Mary. *The Borrowers.* New York: Harcourt, 1953.

Potter, Beatrix. *The Tale of Jemima Puddle-Duck.* London: Warne.

Selden, George. *The Cricket in Times Square.* Ill. by Garth Williams. New York: Farrar, 1960.

Shannon, Margaret. *Elvira.* New York: Ticknor, 1993.

Steig, William. *Zeke Pippin.* New York: HarperCollins, 1994.

Thurber, James. *The Great Quillow.* Ill. by Steven Kellogg. New York: Harcourt, 1995.

Van Allsburg, Chris. *Jumanji.* Boston: Houghton, 1981.

Van Allsburg, Chris. *The Sweetest Fig.* Boston: Houghton Mifflin, 1993.

Waber, Bernard. *Do You See a Mouse?* Boston: Houghton, 1995.

Walsh, Jill Paton. *The Green Book.* New York: Farrar, 1982.

White, E. B. *Charlotte's Web.* Ill. by Garth Williams. New York: Harper, 1952.

Wiesner, David. *Tuesday.* New York: Clarion, 1991.

Willis, Jeanne. *Earthlets as Explained by Professor Xargle.* Ill. by Tony Ross. New York: Dutton, 1988.

Willis, Jeanne. *The Long Blue Blazer.* Ill. by Susan Varley. New York: Dutton, 1987.

Yolen, Jane. *Commander Toad and the Intergalactic Spy.* Ill. by Bruce Degen. New York: Coward, 1986.

Yolen, Jane. *Commander Toad and the Space Pirates.* Ill. by Bruce Degen. New York: Coward, 1987.

CHAPTER REFERENCES

Bishop, Rudine Sims. "A Conversation with Patricia McKissack." *Language Arts* 69.1 (Jan. 1992): 69–74.

Egoff, Sheila, G. T. Stubbs, and L. F. Ashley, eds. *Only Connect.* Toronto: Oxford University Press, 1969.

Jordan, Anne Devereaux. "Tell Me Where Fancy is Bred: Fantasy." *Teaching and Learning Literature* 4.4 (Mar./Apr. 1995): 16–20.

Lewis, C. S. "On Three Ways of Writing for Children." *The Horn Book* 39.5 (Oct. 1963): 459–469.

Yolen, Jane. "The Modern Mythmakers." *Language Arts* 53.5 (May 1976): 491–495.

 **Chapter Ten**

Realism: Fiction Out of Fact

Julie held up the book and read the title to the children surrounding her—
Aunt Flossie's Hats (and Crab Cakes Later) by Elizabeth Fitzgerald
Howard. "Look at the picture on the cover and tell me what you notice."

"Everyone's wearing a hat."

"The girls look like they're dancing."

"The woman looks tired but happy."

"You can see brushmarks in the picture."

After they had discussed what they had noticed, talked about the illustrations, and made predictions about the story's content, they listened as
Julie read the book. The story tells about Sarah and Susan on their regular
Sunday afternoon visit to their Great-great-aunt Flossie. The girls have tea
and cookies and then persuade Aunt Flossie to tell the story that accompa-
nies each of the hats they select from her many hatboxes. One she was
wearing as she ran outside to see the great fire in Baltimore. Another she
wore in the parade marking the end of The Great War. And there is their
favorite—the hat that blew off on a Sunday afternoon walk with Sarah and
Susan and their parents and which was retrieved by a dog that had been
taught to fetch. The day ends with another favorite activity, eating crab
cakes in a restaurant.

Julie asks the children what they think Aunt Flossie meant when she
said that her hats were her memories. They respond that she remembered
where she was and what she did when she wore each hat. Some say that perhaps she was just making up the stories because she had to stop and think

before she started a story. Others argue that she "was old and old people need time to think so they get things straight. She was telling what really happened." The children are enthralled when Julie puts on her mother's old straw beach hat and tells about it.

The children then each create a collage hat, writing the "memory" that goes with it, some real and some imagined. Jeannette writes about a bonnet, "I wore this hat when I was a baby. It was for a party for Christmas." Carl says, "I wore this hat to Dr. Martin Luther King, Jr.'s famous speech 'I Have a Dream'." Caroline's felt hat is covered with buttons and ribbons and small objects. "When I was little, every time I did a good deed I added something to my hat. I love this hat."

Later in the week, Julie puts the hats and stories together in a class book, one that proves to be very popular. Children read it themselves in pairs and ask her to read it to the class many times.

REALISM BEGINS WITH REFLECTION

Realistic fiction tells a story that could happen or could have happened in the past. In **contemporary realism,** the setting is the present. Realistic stories with settings in the past are called historical realism or, more commonly, **historical fiction.** *Aunt Flossie's Hats* is contemporary realism because it has a modern setting. Sarah and Susan are children in the 1990s, with both text and illustrations establishing time and place. If the author had chosen to tell about Aunt Flossie and the great fire in Baltimore or Aunt Flossie celebrating the end of World War II, then the story would have been historical fiction.

Writers begin with reality and then apply imagination and artistic skill to write fiction. They choose and enliven facts. The Aunt Flossie of the book was a real person, a teacher in the Baltimore public schools. At a family outing to the Inner Harbor in Baltimore, the real Aunt Flossie's hat blew away. Flossie lived in the same house for most of her life and was always willing to tell stories about the past. With this as her base, Elizabeth Howard shaped her story.

Realism for children involves reflection, both as a mirror showing real life and as a mode of thought in which the meaning of that life is contemplated. Some portrayals are light, built on familiar sights, sounds, and smells. Shirley Hughes explores the world of a toddler and her baby brother in *Giving,* showing that one can give a present or a kiss, but also an angry look!

Writer Miriam Cohen explores the world of primary grade children in her stories about Jim and his classmates. The titles express many of the themes and topics—*When Will I Read?, No Good in Art,* and *Lost in the Museum.* Yet all is not perfect in this world and there are realities to be faced. In *Jim's Dog Muffins,* Jim must cope with the death of his beloved dog. In

A book of contemporary realism may become historical fiction as time passes, particularly if the setting includes specific details or is keyed to a public event.

Carol Carrick, Lucille Clifton, and Charlotte Zolotow have many books of realism focusing on common childhood experiences and emotions.

Shirley Hughes portrays young children engaged in familiar activities in many of her books. (*Source:* Illustration and text from GIVING by Shirley Hughes reproduced with permission of Walker Books Ltd. Copyright © 1993 Shirley Hughes. Published in the US by Candlewick Press, Cambridge, MA.)

It's George, Jim and his classmates come to appreciate George, who can't write, but who makes the evening news when he knows to call 911 to get help for an elderly friend who has fallen from his rocker.

Audrey Wood played with language in *Quick as a Cricket*. Figure 10-1 shows how one class of first graders built on this clever language and everyday observations.

Figure 10-1   As creative as a simile.

> The children in Marie's first-grade class loved listening to Audrey Wood's book *Quick as a Cricket* (New York: Child's Play, 1982) and looking at the illustrations by Don Wood. Marie encouraged them to play with creating similes of their own, at first using animals as the book does. Then she asked the children to dictate adjectives, in her terms "words that describe," for a list she wrote on chart paper.
>
> The children then began working in pairs to write three similes, using either adjectives they thought of or ones from the list. This time their comparison could use anything but animals. Marie wanted to encourage original thinking and to structure the lesson so that cliches would be avoided. By working together, children stimulated each other and had an instant evaluation of ideas presented.
>
> Here are some of the children's similes:
>
> *   fast as a space ship
> *   shiny as a whistle
> *   loose as a rubber band
> *   hard working as a steam shovel
> *   colorful as a rainbow

ISSUES IN REALISTIC FICTION

Writers of realistic fiction must do more than reflect reality or introduce facts lightly cloaked in fiction. They must organize and shape their stories. They must make choices about what they will emphasize. As they engage in these activities, recurring issues arise.

Reflecting Reality

Stories that merely reflect reality are not literature any more than car repair manuals or biology textbooks are literature. But adults sometimes become entranced by a play or a book just because it models life exactly to scale. Realistic fiction may win favor solely because it introduces readers to real difficulties, such as physical handicaps or racial prejudice. For readers like this, books function as museums or zoos; the readers get to watch realistic people trying to cope with their problems.

On the other hand, adults reading children's books sometimes ignore literary qualities such as theme or character development and see only the slice of life, the realistic street talk or the setting in an urban ghetto. The realism may be objectionable to some tastes.

Authors of good realistic fiction present information that is accurate but do so in a creative and artistic format. Barbara Dugan, for example, writes about Anne and her friendship with an elderly woman, Mrs. Simpson, in *Loop the Loop*. Anne is playing outside with her doll Eleanor when she first meets Mrs. Simpson, who is being pushed in her wheelchair by her nurse Bonnie. Mrs. Simpson is enthusiastic and witty, but as their friendship develops, readers see that Mrs. Simpson is forgetful and that there are notes in her kitchen to remind her to take her pills and to turn off the stove. When Mrs. Simpson breaks her hip and is hospitalized, Anne goes to visit, but Mrs. Simpson doesn't remember who Anne is. The situation is real. Mrs. Simpson does not have a miraculous recovery, but she maintains her sense of humor, noting, for example, that Anne probably isn't her doctor because she's too short. Dugan carefully crafts the dialogue to show Mrs. Simpson's mental state and lets readers see Anne's understanding and compassion when she gives her doll to Mrs. Simpson so she won't be lonely. The pathos of the situation is felt as Mrs. Simpson responds to Anne's comment that she is going home by stating that home is a great place. Readers know that Mrs. Simpson is unlikely to see that great place again.

History Remembered, History Researched

Some historical fiction is written from memory. Perhaps the best known of such memory-based books are those in the *Little House* series by Laura Ingalls Wilder. These stories are based on her life, starting when she was six in Wisconsin (in *Little House in the Big Woods*). Later books take the family through difficult moves, and the last in the series, *The First Four Years,* describes what happened after her marriage in 1885.

Most historical fiction, however, grows out of research. Archaic church records, diaries, tombstones, crumbling newspapers, accounts by eyewitnesses long passed away—all provide facts for realistic fiction set in the past. It is the writer's responsibility to weave enough detail into a story to let readers picture the scene and understand life in that period, at least the life of the book characters. Of course, even the most careful library research may not answer all the questions an author has. The author may never know exactly what a person said or what the weather was on a particular day, but careful research should keep an author from contradicting known events.

Invention plays an even greater role when an author writes of a period or place about which very little is known—or at least recorded. Claude Clement's *Musician from the Darkness* is a story of a group of prehistoric people. It tells of the men's pursuit of game with primitive weapons and of one man's listening to the calls of the birds. He makes a flute from a reed to try to copy their sound. When he blows it, some of the birds fly toward the song but are killed by the other hunters. When the man refuses to use his flute again to attract birds, he is chased from the tribe. Alone during the night, he plays his flute and discovers the many sounds he can make. He and a young boy who had been watching from a hiding place have learned the power of music to dispel fear, and together they start off on their own. This writer has used "what might have been" to full advantage.

Stereotyping, Sexism, Racism

One way history can be misrepresented is to base a story and characters on stereotypes rather than on fact. In children's books of an earlier era, Native Americans were usually the villains in books. Members of Indian tribes appeared as either blood-loving warriors, simpering sidekicks to white masters, or noble but naive savages. When the one-dimensional Indian in these stories had to choose between living with the tribe or joining white civilization, the "right" choice was to go with the whites.

The viewpoint of Plains Cree artist George Littlefield about the history of his people and about his own experiences growing up is explicated in the text and symbolized in the pictures in *This Land is My Land* (Emeryville, CA: Children's Book Press, 1993).

While fewer books with blatant stereotyping are being published for children today, it is still necessary to be a careful reader and to encourage children to question and read critically. When *Brother Eagle, Sister Sky*, subtitled *A Message from Chief Seattle* (illustrated by Jeffers), was first released, it was hailed as a moving environmental message for children, relying as it did on the words of a Native American chief about the sacredness of the earth and its creatures. The poetic words were moving, and the illustrations showed first the beauty of the land and then the devastation that could befall it. On closer examination, however, some phrases did not make sense. In particular, Chief Seattle talked about having seen buffalo rotting on the prairie, but he had lived in the Pacific Northwest and would never have seen a buffalo. Further investigation showed that the words had been written by a screenwriter for a film about ecology (Jones and Sawhill) and attributed to Chief Seattle. Critics still disagree on the value of the book, but that any Native American other than Plains Indians would know about buffalo shows that stereotyping still occurs.

Another problem facing writers of historical fiction is how, and if, to portray the racist or sexist attitudes of characters. If this was a character's belief, how does the writer show it truthfully while still letting readers know that the attitude is unacceptable? Mildred Taylor, in *The Well*, has a white character call the black protagonist a "nigger," a reality for the time and place of the book. However, David, the young black, is resentful, and while his family knows that they cannot confront and change the words, that they are unfair and hurtful is clear.

A useful strategy for teachers is to pair books so that if characters are portrayed with racist or sexist beliefs in one book, a challenge to those beliefs is presented in another.

COMMON THEMES IN REALISTIC FICTION

If we look at the lives of contemporary children we would likely see patterns in their thoughts and feelings and the challenges facing them. Literature for children reflects these patterns, with some topics and themes occurring often. The following sections address some of the most common themes in realistic fiction for young children.

Common Experiences

Many books for young children capture the everyday events of life. Keats' book *The Snowy Day* opens as Peter wakes up and sees the snow that has fallen during the night. Once outside, he looks at his tracks in the snow, slides down a hill, makes snow angels, and then brings a snowball inside with him to save for the next day. Although he is sad when he finds the pocket where he had put the snowball is empty, the next day brings more snow and new adventures.

The Snowy Day was published in 1962, but the universality of the experience makes it an enduring favorite. One kindergarten teacher describes reading it every year on the first snowfall. This year she added *Snowballs* by Ehlert. The children collect objects to use in making snowmen and snowwomen of their own, just as Ehlert shows the bottle caps, buttons, bells, yarn, seeds, ribbon, and other materials that can be used to give snowpeople added personality.

Books about common experiences encourage children to make connections between books and their own lives and to tell and write about experiences important to them.

Personal Growth

Other books focus on the challenges that are a part of maturing—some physical, others emotional. Pat Hutchins' many books about *Titch* show what it is like to be the youngest, to get hand-me-down clothes and always be the shortest, but assure the reader that growth will come. After all, even

Peter gazes at fresh snow in The Snowy Day, *an enduring favorite for over thirty years.* (*Source:* Illustration from THE SNOWY DAY by Ezra Jack Keats. Copyright © 1962 by Ezra Jack Keats, renewed © 1990 by Martin Pope. Used by permission of Viking Penguin, a division of Penguin Books USA Inc.)

though Pete has the spade and Mary has the flowerpot, it is Titch who has the tiny seed, a seed that grows into a plant taller than all three children.

Canadian writer Jan Andrews shows how Eva Padlyat overcomes her fear when she is under the ice collecting mussels and the tide begins to come in. Even though her candle has blown out, she does not panic. She finds her way out, and this is the *Very Last First Time* that she will walk under the ice alone.

Esperanza works to learn the skill of weaving from her grandmother, her abuela, and then must face her fear that people in the marketplace where the two plan to sell their goods will prefer machine-made articles or may be frightened by the birthmark on Abuela's face. Like Eva, she faces her fears and takes a step toward maturity in doing so.

Relationships

For children, the world of relationships is the world of family and friends. Grandparents appear in many books for children, perhaps because these are adults who often have very special relationships with children, and sibling rivalry abounds. Love shows itself in many ways. It may be in the serious

Esperanza and her grandmother take their weaving to the marketplace to sell. (Source: Illustration from ABUELA'S WEAVE by Omar S. Castaneda, illustrations by Enrique O. Sanchez. Copyright © 1993 Lee & Low Books, Inc. New York. Reprinted by permission.)

and respectful interaction between Esperanza and her grandmother in *Abuela's Weave.* It may also be in Tomie dePaola's depiction of his grandfather in *Tom.* This is a grandfather who had a twinkle in his eye and a trick up his sleeve. Tom shows young Tommy in his butcher shop how to pull the tendon on a chicken's foot so that the claws will close. Tommy decides to put a chicken foot protruding from each sleeve at school and to pull the tendons to move the claws—to the horror of his classmate and his teacher.

Children in third and fourth grade will enjoy chapter books about family life. Getting along with siblings is a common theme, as is getting along with friends in school.

In *Lator Gator* (Yep), the older brother feels that it is up to him to provide his younger brother with experiences that will build character, and the first is to get him a baby alligator, rather than the turtle their mother recommends, for his birthday. In *Partners* (Waggoner), the younger brother must convince his older brother that the mice are to be pets. They are not to be raised and sold as food for snakes.

Getting along with friends, both children and adults, has many interpretations in literature for children. In *Mrs. Katz and Tush* (Polacco), young Larnel comes first to understand Mrs. Katz, his Jewish neighbor, and then to love her as she shares her memories with him. Children can even view and discuss friendships among adults. They can see the posturing and the attempts to repair a friendship as well as a piece of clothing, in *Clancy's Coat* (Bunting). Figure 10-2 suggests some books that describe problems in relationships and lend themselves to discussion and to role play.

Tommy has a special relation-
ship with his grandfather.
(Source: Illustration by Tomie
dePaola reprinted by permission of G. P. Putnam's Sons
from TOM, Copyright ©
1993 by Tomie dePaola.)

Problems

The problems in books for young children need to be presented in terms a child can understand, even if the problems themselves are anything but childlike. In *Losing Uncle Tim* (Jordan), a young boy named Daniel tells in first person about the things he enjoyed doing with his Uncle Tim. Then he describes how his uncle became very ill, and that he saw changes as the AIDS affected his uncle's strength. His mother explains that most AIDS patients do die, but that it is safe for him to visit, even to hug, his uncle. Watching someone die is difficult, and that fact is not glossed over. At the funeral, Tim wishes his uncle could come back, but knows it will not happen. His memories will stay alive, though, through the special toys his uncle left him and the love they shared.

Books that present problems let children see how others react and show ways of approaching difficulties. Figure 10-3 reports the responses of a group of second graders to *A Chair for My Mother* (Williams). The teacher encouraged the children to think about their own questions as they heard how a family tries to cope following a fire that has destroyed the home and personal belongings of a family.

Even when the problems are far removed from the daily life of the children, books let them think about how they might react. In *Sami and the Time of the Troubles* (Heide), they see a character living in war-ravaged Beirut in his uncle's basement, coming outside only a few days each month when the shooting subsides. The children did not create the problem, but they must live with it.

Many realistic books present problems in relationships and in understanding others that are challenging to the characters and can be
challenging to young readers. In the following suggested books with
role-play situations, the teacher reads until the problem is explained but
not solved. Then children take the roles of the characters and act out
what the next action might be, what the characters could say or do to
resolve the situation. The books present the problems clearly and have
only two or three characters, so children can be put in pairs or triads to
role-play the situation simultaneously. After they finish, the children talk
about what was tried and how well it seemed to work. The purpose is to
explore alternative courses of action, so the discussion focuses on actions
and their consequences rather than attempts to guess how the author has
the characters resolve their problems.

Books With Role Play Possibilities:

Blos, Joan. *Old Henry.* (New York: Morrow, 1987)
Bunting, Eve. *Clancy's Coat.* (New York: Warne, 1984)
Fleischman, Sid. *The Scarebird.* (New York: Greenwillow, 1987)
Grifalconi, Ann. *Osa's Pride.* (Boston: Little, 1990)
Guback, Georgia. *Luka's Quilt.* (New York: Greenwillow, 1994)
Kellogg, Steven. *Can I Keep Him?* (New York: Dial, 1971)
Steptoe, John. *Stevie.* (New York: Harper, 1969)
Stevenson, James. *What's Under My Bed?* (New York: Greenwillow, 1983)
Viorst, Judith. *Alexander, Who's Not (Do You Hear Me? I Mean it!) Going
    to Move.* (New York: Atheneum, 1995)
Zolotow, Charlotte. *William's Doll.* (New York: Harper, 1972)

Figure 10-2   Role play: What would you do?

Life in a Pluralistic Society

Realism shows children the lives of people who are both like them and different from them. A balanced literature program includes books with characters from a variety of backgrounds. Children who hear *The Lotus Seed*
(Garland), for example, can appreciate elements of Vietnamese culture as the
child tells how her grandmother had plucked a seed from a lotus pod in the
Imperial Garden and kept it wrapped in silk because it made her think of the
brave emperor. She marries, loses her husband in the war, and emigrates to
the United States. She is heartbroken when a grandson plants the seed, but
the seed germinates. Eventually she gives a seed to each grandchild, a
reminder of the day she saw the emperor.

Life styles can be compared, using the stories as resources. In *Working Cotton*, Sherley Williams describes, in a black dialect, her family as
they go to the fields near Fresno to pick cotton. Another story of a
migrant family's life over several weeks, is *Radio Man* by Arthur Dorros,
a story about a migrant family picking fruits and vegetables, and told in

Kerri and her second graders were reading about families. They had explored the question of what makes a family, looking at different family structures. They had talked about how family members care about and help each other. They had each written a postcard to a family member.

Now they were going to hear *A Chair for My Mother* by Vera Williams. In this book, a fire has destroyed the the home and personal belongings of the family, and a little girl, her mother, and grandmother have saved for more than a year to buy a special chair so that the mother can sit and relax when she returns home from her job as a waitress.

Kerri chose the book because it included several ideas they had already discussed. She wanted the children to relate their own lives to what they were hearing and reading, and she wanted to set the stage for children to work in small discussion groups. Before beginning the book, Kerri asked the children to close their eyes and think of a special chair in their houses. They were to picture just how it looked, and to see themselves sitting in it.

James: I have a special chair at the dinner table. I use it at dinner.
Marissa: My favorite chair is a white couch. It is great for reading. I sit in it when I read.
Meredith: I have a special chair. It is a mauve colored beanbag chair. I sit in my family room and watch TV.
Jeffrey: My special chair is the recliner. It is very comfortable. I like to sit in it all the time.

After hearing the story, the children compared their special chairs to that of the little girl and her mother and grandmother. They talked about times they had saved money themselves, and compared *Something Special for Me,* also by Vera Williams, with *A Chair for My Mother,* seeing the similarity of characters and plot, but noting that the characters were saving for different purposes.

Then Kerri asked the children to each think of one question they had about the book, a question that the group could discuss. They were given time to write their questions, then asked them with the group responding.

Tara: Where is the Dad in this story?
Justin: How did the house burn down?
James: Why did the grandmother say she felt like Goldilocks trying out all of the chairs?
Jeffrey: Why did it take so long to save up enough money for a chair?
Marissa: Why couldn't they each buy a chair or a couch big enough for all of them to sit in?

The questions lead the children to talk again about the concept of family, to see how one story relates to another, and to build on comments made by one another.

Figure 10-3   Children ask the questions.

both English and Spanish. Descriptions of the fields, attitudes, and language can all be compared.

The pluralistic society is not just the United States but the world. Figure 10-4 shows the responses of a group of children to their teacher's reading of books from other countries and how it stimulated children to bring books in to share.

Both illustrations and text can help children understand other places and perhaps other customs. In *Boundless Grace* (Hoffman), Grace barely remembers her father and is frightened to travel to Africa to visit when her father

THE LESSON, AS PLANNED AND TAUGHT	REFLECTIONS . . .
Rationale Jim's second grade class had been reading realistic stories set in other countries and locating each country on a classroom map. They had enjoyed *Saturday Market* by Patricia Grossman (Ill. by Enrique Sanchez. Lothrop, 1994) set in Mexico, *The Day Adam Got Mad* by Astrid Lindgren (Ill. by Marit Tornqvist. R & S Books, 1993) set in Sweden and originally published there, and *Where Are You Going Manyoni?* by Catherine Stock (Morrow, 1993) set in Zimbabwe.	Reading stories from or set in other countries is one way to help children learn to appreciate other cultures, both for the information in the realistic stories and for the idea that children of many countries tell and enjoy stories. As Jim helped the children find the countries on the map, he was also introducing the children to map usage in a natural and purposeful manner.
On Monday morning, Dana brought in a book from England and asked Jim to read it to the class. It had been a gift to Dana from his grandfather.	Dana's bringing in the book showed that he understood that the books Jim had been reading were from other countries and that he wanted to contribute to the class.
The Lesson Jim was delighted at Dana's interest and agreed to read the book to the class. That afternoon, Jim skipped the book he'd planned to read, let Dana tell about his book, and then read it aloud.	
Midway through the book Jim realized that he had probably made a mistake. The book was poorly written and the children were becoming restless. He decided to read only key sentences from each of the remaining pages in order to finish the book quickly. The strategy worked and he returned the book to Dana and thanked him for bringing it in.	Jim's choices once the problem arose were to stop reading, to skim and read only parts of the book, or to plunge ahead reading the rest of the book. His choice to skim gave a sense of completion, speeded up the process, and supported Dana's desire to share the book.
However, on Tuesday, three other students came to Jim with books they wanted him to read to the class. He was pleased with their interest, but concerned about the quality of the literature and how he would work these books into the day's schedule.	Jim needs a way to allow the children to share their books, yet not have the rest of the class bored if the books are not interesting. He might have each child tell about the book and select one page for him to read aloud; he might help the children set up a display of the books, labeling where each takes place, and marking a favorite illustration. He may want to have the children locate the setting of each of these stories. The strategy should highlight the book, reward the child who brought it in, and be interesting to the class.

Figure 10-4   On second thought: Children sharing books from home.

Grace travels to Africa to visit her father and meet his new wife. (Source: Illustration from BOUNDLESS GRACE by Mary Hoffman, illustrated by Caroline Binch. Copyright © 1995 by Mary Hoffman, text; Copyright © 1995 by Caroline Binch, illustrations. Used by permission of Dial Books for Young Readers, a division of Penguin Books USA Inc. and Frances Lincoln Limited.)

Look for picture books by Omar Castanda for settings in Guatemala, by Mairi Hedderwick for settings in Scotland, by Ann Blades and Jan Andrews for settings in Canada, by Mem Fox for settings in Australia, by Niki Day for settings in South Africa, and Taro Yashima for settings in Japan.

sends tickets. But her Nana goes with her, and once there she begins to appreciate the beauty of the designs in the clothing fabrics and the food her father's new wife prepares. In fact, those are easier to accept than the fact that her father has a new family, including a young son and daughter. Acceptance is not immediate, but it does come.

FICTION ABOUT DIFFERENT TIMES AND PLACES

Realism set in the past builds on human emotion and relationships just as contemporary realism does. The story, not the setting, is compelling to children, although historical fiction provides the opportunity for children to learn about life in different times. Ann Turner, author of many historical books for children, explains her approach.

Turner writes both picture books and chapter books, with a range of complexity in language and content.

> Whenever I write a piece of historical fiction, I try and imagine myself, as a child, alive in that time and place. I wonder: What would I do then? How would I feel and react? Through my imaginative identification with the past, I want to create a personal moment in history, something children can live through, too. (11)

As children live through historical events or periods in the books they read, they learn what life was like and how people felt and often must consider the problems and issues of the day. In Patricia Polacco's *Pink and Say,*

Pinkus Aylee rescues the wounded Shelton Curtis in Pink and Say. *(Source:* Illustration by Patricia Polacco reprinted by permission of Philomel Books from PINK AND SAY, Copyright © 1994 by Patricia Polacco.)

readers meet Sheldon Curtis, called Say by his family in Ohio, as he lays wounded in Georgia. He is just a boy, though he is fighting with the Union army. He is found by another soldier, also just a boy, who is also wearing a Union uniform. Pinkus Aylee, called Pink, has gotten lost from his company, the Forty-Eighth Colored. He rescues Say, taking him home to his mother, Moe Moe Bay, who nurses him back to health.

Reading a map, Say figures that they can rejoin his company and responds to his mother's distress at their leaving by saying that the war has to be won to get rid of the "sickness," his term for slavery. Before they can leave, however, marauders attack, killing Moe Moe Bay while the boys hide in the root cellar. The boys bury her and set out but are soon accosted by Confederate soldiers and taken prisoner. At Andersonville prison camp they are separated. At this point the narration, which had been in first person by Say, ends. The final two pages explain that Say was released several months later, but that Pink was hung within hours of his arrival. The story had been handed down in Say's family.

In the context of this story of friendship, trust, and sacrifice, young readers imagine how it would feel to be wounded and frightened; to see the life of a woman living on the deserted planation where she had recently been a slave; to sense the importance of Abraham Lincoln in the lives of both boys; and to learn about the fighting in the Civil War. The pain and loss are not glossed over or minimized. The issues of slavery, war, treatment of enemy soldiers, and action against civilians are all presented through the viewpoint of child whose life is affected by them. A teacher sharing this book with children has a rich source for discussion and response.

Combining Books

Often children gain a deeper understanding of different times and places if books are grouped. Different combinations of time and place can give new insights to young readers.

Sewell's book *People of the Breaking Day* (Atheneum, 1990) describes the life of the Wampanoags at the time the Pilgrims landed. This is an interesting companion book to *The Pilgrims of Plimoth.*

Same Time/Same Place.   When more than one book with the same setting in both time and place are presented, children can begin to generalize about that setting. Fourth graders who have read *Stranded at Plimoth Plantation 1626* by Gary Bowen and *The Pilgrims of Plimoth* by Marcia Sewell can compare information on the same topic, such as how corn was planted, how the houses were constructed, or the role Squanto played. They will get a fuller picture from the two books, the first in diary format and the second told through narration as though by one of the Pilgrims, than they would from either book alone.

Books with the same or similar setting may also show children that there is variety in how people lived in the past, just as there is in the present. *In Coal Country* by Judith Hendershot is set in Ohio and *No Star Nights* by Anna Smucker in West Virginia. Both take place in the 1930s, and they are companion books in that they show families in two related industries, each dependent on the other, within the same geographic area. There are many similarities between Hendershot's coal mining family missing the father when he works nights, fighting coal dust, and watching and hearing the trains with their heavy black loads, and Smucker's steel mill family, also missing the father when he works nights, seeing school windows closed to keep out the graphite and smoke, and watching trains filled with slag.

Same Time/Different Place.   Sharing stories with a similar time frame but with different geographic settings helps to give children a sense of the period and an appreciation for differences dependent on place and circumstance. *Death of the Iron Horse* by Paul Goble is based on an actual incident in 1867, when a Union Pacific freight train was derailed by Cheyennes. The story is told from the Cheyenne point of view as scouts arrive in camp having seen an Iron Horse. The white men are making a road for it, and it is breathing smoke. A group of warriors, intent on protecting their people, derail and burn the train. The illustrations show the landscape, the dress of the Cheyenne, previous attacks on tipi villages by white soldiers, as well as the successful stopping of this train, if not the many that would follow.

When reading *Emily,* you might want to share some of Dickinson's poems that are appealing to children, such as "I'm Nobody! Who Are You?," "A Word," or "A Bird."

This picture of life on the plains can be contrasted with *Emily* by Michael Bedard, with its setting in Amherst, Massachusetts. The "Emily" of the title is Emily Dickinson, and the story is told by a young girl who lives across the street from the reclusive Dickinson and whose mother plays the piano for Emily to hear. The elegant colonial houses, the flowers, the poetry, and the music are a contrast to life on the American plains of the same period. It is not necessary that children know exact dates, and for young children the dates will not have much meaning anyway. What they might do is recognize that these stories took place at the same time. Worldviews can also be added. For a slightly earlier time period, that of the first half of the nineteenth century, a teacher might read *The Giraffe That Walked to Paris* by Nancy Milton. In 1826, the pasha of Egypt gave a giraffe to the king of France as a gift. The giraffe's journey, first by boat across the Mediterranean Sea and then by foot from Marseilles to Paris, created a sensation. Life in France could be compared with that in New England in *Celia's Island Journal* (Thaxter), an adaptation of a journal kept by Celia Thaxter during the seven years she lived on White Island where her father was the lighthouse keeper. Fitting in this same time frame would be *Sweet Clara and the Freedom Quilt* by Deborah Hopkinson. When the book opens, Clara is 12 and has just been sent to a different planation because they needed another field hand. She is cared for by Rachel, who teaches her to sew so that she can work in the Big House rather than the fields. As Clara does her work as a seamstress, she hears the slaves talking about escaping and about their need for a map. Clara begins a quilt, using patches to represent the pond and fields she can see, and adding to it the information she can glean from those who have been beyond the plantation. Eventually Clara escapes, leaving the quilt with Rachel for others to look at, and for Rachel, too old to travel, to sleep under and dream of freedom.

Certainly life in Paris, life on an island as the lighthouse keeper's daughter, and life as a slave on a southern plantation show children a wide variety of experiences.

Clara's freedom quilt is a map that helps slaves learn an escape route. (Source: Illustration from SWEET CLARA AND THE FREEDOM QUILT by Deborah Hopkinson, illustrated by James Ransome. Illustrations copyright © 1993 by Alfred A. Knopf, Inc. Reprinted by permission of Alfred A. Knopf, Inc.)

Different Time/Same Place. Keeping the place constant but having different time periods represented lets children see changes that have occurred. Natalie Kinsey-Warnock and Helen Kinsey retell a family story in *The Bear That Heard Crying*. The time is 1783 and the place is New Hampshire. Three-year-old Sarah Whitcher gets lost in the woods and spends the night and the next three days alone . . . well, not totally alone. She snuggles up to a bear for warmth and is not harmed. Neighbors searching for her have found her tracks and those of a bear, and they have little hope for her. Then a stranger arrives and says he can find Sarah. He has had a dream that she is lying by Berry Brook with a bear guarding her. They find her there, surrounded by bear tracks. Sarah tells how a big, black dog took care of her.

Sarah and her family live in a log cabin and go barefoot inside the house. Cooking is done over an open hearth.

In *Ox-Cart Man* by Donald Hall, the setting is still New Hampshire, but the time is now the early 1800s. A farmer packs his cart in October for the trip to Portsmouth market, where he will see the products the family has grown and made: the wool, the yarn, the candles, the linen, the shingles and birch brooms, potatoes and apples, and maple sugar. He will even sell the cart and the ox that pulls it. He buys the supplies his family needs and walks home, where his family awaits. They will begin the yearly farm cycle again.

Barbara Cooney's illustrations show changes in the landscape since the time of *The Bear That Heard Crying* as villages have grown up and forested

Three-year-old Sarah tells her family that while she was lost a big black "dog" kept her warm. (Source: Illustration from THE BEAR THAT HEARD CRYING by Natalie Kinsey-Warnock, illustrated by Ted Rand. Copyright © 1993 by Ted Rand on illustrations. Used by permission of Cobblehill Books, an affiliate of Dutton Children's Books, a division of Penguin USA Inc.)

land has been converted to fields. Not everything has changed, however. Paths have become roads, but cooking is still done on the open hearth.

In a second book by Donald Hall, *The Farm Summer 1942,* Peter has come to spend the summer with his grandparents on their New Hampshire farm. Cooking is done on a wood burning stove in the kitchen. His grandparents talk about the changes in the farmhouse since Peter's father was a boy—they now have indoor plumbing—and Peter also sees differences between his grandparents' home and his more modern home in San Francisco.

Children reading these three books could list similarities and differences, perhaps looking at specific categories for comparison such as clothing, animals raised, or expectations for family members.

In *Seminole Diary* by Dolores Johnson, a contemporary child finds her mother in the attic reading a diary she has found. The diary is of a slave named Libbie and begins in March of 1834, when she has been whipped and her father announces they are going to escape. Libbie, her sister Clarissa, and her father leave, later to join a group of Seminoles. Life is good there, but it is not to last. They, and their Seminole benefactors, must make a choice—either to go deeper into the Florida swamps to hide or to allow themselves to be relocated to Oklahoma. Father and Libbie head for Oklahoma. *Dancing With the Indians* by Angela Medearis has a young girl in the 1930s going with her family to an Indian pow-wow. They still celebrate together because the girl's grandfather was rescued from slavery by the Seminoles and accepted by them.

Combined, the two books show the events happening, African Americans joining with Seminoles to escape slavery and certain results of that union, in this case a continued celebration of freedom.

Patterns Throughout Time. Historical fiction is filled with stories that show patterns throughout time and that can be grouped by theme, content, or style rather than by setting. Members of one race helping people of another are shown in *Pink and Say, Seminole Diary,* and *Dancing With the Indians.*

Historical fiction can also be grouped with contemporary realism. *Leah's Pony* by Elizabeth Friedrich is based on the practice of "penny" auctions, in which neighbors would help friends keep their possessions by buying the items very cheaply at foreclosure sales and then returning them to the original owners. In this story set in the 1930s in the Dust Bowl, Leah helps her family keep their possessions by selling her pony and then bidding her one dollar for their tractor. No one will bid against her, and soon neighbors are bidding tiny amounts for livestock, which they will then give back to Leah's family.

Friedrich's book would fit well with a discussion of problem solving, of difficulty in making a living on a farm, and of family solidarity when paired with a book such as *Family Farm* by Thomas Locker. This book of contemporary realism shows a farm family worried about the low price of milk and corn, their crops. To keep from losing their home, their mother had at first worked in a restaurant in town and then planted flowers and pumpkins to

Leah helps her family keep their possessions during the Depression by selling her pony and using the money to bid on the family's tractor at a foreclosure sale. (Source: Illustration and Text from LEAH'S PONY. Text by Elizabeth Friedrich, Illustrations by Michael Garland. Copyright © 1996 by Boyds Mills Press. Reprinted by permission of Boys Mills Press, Honesdale, PA.)

sell. Dad takes a job in a factory. Neighbors help out. Finally, they decide that they will have to grow what they can sell, flowers and pumpkins.

Figure 10-5 suggests books that could be used for an exploration of immigration to the United States, crossing time periods and countries of origin. Books such as these give both a broad view of the people and their various reasons for coming to the United States and help readers appreciate the feelings involved in such a move.

When selecting a book of historical fiction, see what connections you can help children make. Suppose you were reading *Farmboy's Year* by David McPhail, which is set in New England in the 1800s and shows farm life through the eyes of a young boy. It could be grouped with other books in several ways: with other books about farm life; with other books in its time period; with other books with New England settings; or with other books that have a similar style of writing. It is in diary format. Here is one entry.

> October 19
>   Picked apples today. It was warm for October. Mother made a half dozen pies (can't wait for supper).
>   Father took a cart full of the apples to the barn to press them into cider. I helped. He says I drink it almost as fast as he makes it.
>   It tastes good now, and it will taste good next summer when we're haying.[1]

---

[1] *Source:* Excerpt from FARM BOY'S YEAR by David McPhail reprinted with the permission of Atheneum Books for Young Readers, an imprint of Simon & Schuster. Text copyright © 1992 David McPhail.

Coming to the United States in the Past
Bartone, Elisa. *Peppe the Lamplighter.* Ill. by Ted Lewin. New York: Lothrop, 1993.
Cohen, Barbara. *Molly's Pilgrim.* Ill. by Michael Deraney. New York: Lothrop, 1983.
Johnson, Dolores. *Now Let Me Fly: The Story of a Slave Family.* New York: Macmillan, 1993.
Kroll, Steven. *Mary McLean & the St. Patrick's Day Parade.* Ill. by Michael Dooling. New York: Scholastic, 1991.
Say, Allen. *Grandfather's Journey.* Boston: Houghton, 1993.

Coming to the United States in the Present
Anzaldua, Gloria. *Friends from the Other Side/Amigoes del otro lado.* Ill. by Consuelo Mendez. San Francisco: Children's Book Press, 1993.
Bunting, Eve. *How Many Days to America? A Thanksgiving Story.* Ill. by Beth Peck. New York: Clarion, 1988.
Turner, Ann. *Through Moon and Stars and Night Skies.* Ill. by James Graham Hale. New York: Harper, 1990.

Adapting to Life in a New Land
Bunting, Eve. *A Day's Work.* Ill. by Ronald Himler. New York: Clarion, 1994.
Levine, Ellen. *I Hate English!* Ill. by Steve Bjorkman. New York: Scholastic, 1989.
Stanek, Muriel. *I Speak English for My Mother.* Ill. by Judith Friedman. Morton Grove, IL: Whitman, 1989.
Surat, Michele Maria. *Angel Child, Dragon Child.* Ill. by Vo-Dinh Mai. Milwaukee: Raintree, 1983.

Keeping Memories and Culture Alive
Bonners, Susan. *The Wooden Doll.* New York: Lothrop, 1991.
Garland, Sherry. *The Lotus Seed.* Ill. by Tatsuro Kiuchi. San Diego: Harcourt, 1993.
Joose, Barbara. *The Morning Chair.* Ill. by Marcia Sewall. New York: Clarion, 1995.
Oberman, Sheldon. *The Always Prayer Shawl.* Ill. by Ted Lewin. Honesdale, PA: Boyds Mills, 1994.

Figure 10-5　　Coming to America: Past and present.

Celia's Island Journal and *Seminole Diary* are also in diary format. Children could look at the language used, how it differs and why it differs. They might compare some of their own journal entries with those in these three books. Figure 10-6 shows how a group of children created a role story based on the diary entries in *Pedro's Journey* by Pam Conrad. Diary format can stimulate a variety of forms of response.

Bethany's class had been reading several books, some fiction and some nonfiction, in which characters kept journals of their travels. The latest was *Pedro's Journal* by Pam Conrad (New York: Scholastic, 1991). In this fictional account, young Pedro de Sadcedo is a ship's boy who sails with Christopher Columbus. The diary entries record what happened on selected days, and particularly what was sighted.

The children talked about ways of showing and telling what was seen. They considered various types of projects they had done in the past— art galleries, class books, travel brochures. They decided that they would create a roll story, each drawing and labeling one of the day's events, then mounting the illustrations on a long roll of paper. They could then unroll the paper so that the pictures appeared as a filmstrip.

First they made a list of days on the trip that would be good to illustrate. Each date was written on a separate piece of paper and put into a shoebox. Children drew a date, reread that date's journal entry in the book, then created a picture. Here is the illustration for October 11, 1492, the day before land was sighted. The text describes the crew finding a stick that seemed to them to be man-made floating near by.

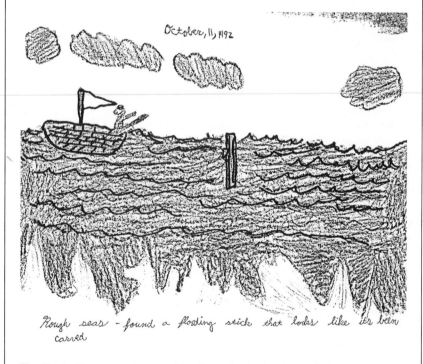

The illustrations were mounted in chronological order, and the roll story placed in the classroom library, with projects related to the other books in journal format that they had read. The children planned to keep their own journals for the week of school vacation.

Figure 10-6 Significant sightings from Pedro's journal.

SPECIAL CATEGORIES OF REALISM

A few topics in realism are so popular that they sometimes earn their own displays or special shelves in libraries. Many of the books in the special categories of sports, animals, mystery and humor are good literature; like other works of realism, they deal with significant themes such as the child's drive for independence. Others books on these special shelves are escapist fare; flat characters beat all odds or outwit bumbling adults in the course of precut plots.

Sports Stories

Many sports stories suffer from formula writing. The main character frequently faces impossible odds in the last seconds of the big game. The clock is running . . . the crowd is on its feet . . . the ball/hockey puck is in the air . . . touchdown!/goal!/basket! The game ends with a bang or a buzz, and readers seldom get to see the losers' locker room.

Yet such books are often popular with children, in part because of the subject and in part because they are predictable. Matt Christopher is a prolific writer of sports stories, usually in chapter book format with easy to read text. There are few surprises. In *Zero's Slider,* for example, young baseball player Zero Ford, potentially out of Friday's game after slamming a car door on his finger, practices his pitching, and while he cannot depend on his slider, the pitch that curves sharply in front of the batter, he does improve. And his finger has healed enough for him to pitch. On Friday, Zero heads for the mound filled with confidence. He also gains the courage to ask his Uncle Pete, an out-of-work sports announcer, to act as substitute coach for the two weeks the regular coach is on vacation. This allows the team to play the three games scheduled during that time.

It is fortunate, and some might argue a bit contrived, that Uncle Pete has the needed background, is living with Zero and his mother temporarily, and gets a job that will begin in two weeks—just after the period when a coach is needed.

Beman Lord and Marion Renick are two other writers of sports stories who keep action levels high and give explanations of games and their rules so those who have never played or watched before know what is happening. The action is interesting to intermediate grade readers, and the books provide an introduction to chapter books for some and an easy read for older students with reading problems. Good third- and fourth-grade readers may enjoy the stories of Alfred Slote, whose sports stories are enriched by depth of characterization and development of theme.

Christopher has several books about the Peach Street Mudders baseball team, all part of the "Springboard Books" series.

Animal Stories

Most children in sports stories win their major battles, showing up disbelievers and taking further steps toward adulthood. Children in realistic stories about animals often show similar control over the world around them.

In books for children from prekindergarten to grade 2, animal stories often depict a child who wants a pet, convinces parents, and becomes master or mistress. Mary Jo, for instance, wants a puppy and promises to take care of it. In *What Mary Jo Wanted,* by Janice Udry, the puppy turns out to be demanding, but the little girl takes the responsibility, even sleeping in the kitchen so the dog will stop crying at night.

In an opposite plot line, the protagonist in *Wilderness Cat* (Kinsey-Warnock) has a pet but must give it up. Serena loves her cat Moses and does not want to leave him behind when the family moves from Vermont to Canada in the late 1700s. Father explains that Moses will not like to ride in the cart and that 50 miles is too far for him to walk. They can get a new cat in Canada. When Serena says she doesn't want another cat, father says that there are to be no more outbursts. The cat is left with a neighbor.

The family treks to Canada and settles into the cabin father has built. Winter brings deep snow and difficulty getting enough food. But winter also bring Moses to their door, thin and with a piece of one ear missing, but bearing a snowshoe hare he has caught. Now when Serena asks if they will ever move again, father says they might, but that if they do, Moses will come with them.

In a more complex story, *Willa and Old Miss Annie,* three animal stories are woven into a single book. In the first section, Willa, a very shy little girl who has moved and has no friends in her new home, meets Miss Annie, a very old neighbor, who tells her she has a ghost in her garden. The ghost turns out to be Joshua, Miss Annie's goat. In the second section, a peddlar known as Sly Old Silas tries to trick Silly Molly Pickleby into buying a rocking chair. She, in turn, tricks him by offering to trade her horse for the chair. When Silas discovers that the horse is really a Shetland pony, he ties it to a tree and leaves. Weeks later, when the horse is nearly starved, a young boy finds it, and Annie, Annie's father, the boy, and Old Miss Annie rescue it. Annie gets to keep the pony, a friend for her and a friend for Joshua. In the last section, Willa and another young girl, Ruth, each conquer their jealousy of the attention Miss Annie pays to the other and become best friends, watching as Ruth's pet fox uses the run constructed by Miss Annie.

All of the sections show the value of animals as friends, the importance of kindness and appropriate care for animals, and how animals can enrich people's lives.

Fourth-grade readers will encounter ethical issues in stories such as *Shiloh* by Phyllis Reynolds Naylor. Eleven-year-old Marty knows that the dog he calls Shiloh belongs to his neighbor Judd Travers; he remembers that he has promised Judd to return the dog if it runs away. But there it is in his yard, and if he returns it, he knows Judd will once again beat and mistreat it. How can he reconcile conflicting feelings about what is right?

Young children also enjoy reading series books about characters and their animals. Rylant's stories about Henry and his dog Mudge are easy-to-read books that feature Henry and his family and everyday adventures. In *Henry and Mudge and the Long Weekend,* the problem is that it is cold and rainy outside, and Henry is bored. The solution is for Henry, his dad, and Mudge, who is covered with paint, to make an old refrigerator box into a castle. It is a family project, a family story, and the dog is an essential member of the family.

Animal stories may also address the issue of the death of a pet. In *I'll Always Love You* (Wilhelm), the young narrator describes his dog Elfie. We see Elfie grow older and fatter and the narrator develop from a toddler to a child of six or seven. The narrator tells about how he always told Elfie that he loved her, even as she grew rounder and slower and could no longer climb the stairs. Finally one morning the family finds that Elfie has died during the night. They bury her, and when a neighbor boy offers the narrator a new puppy, he refuses. The book closes with the boy saying that someday he will have another pet, and that he will always tell it he loves it, just as he always told Elfie.

Mysteries

Like sports stories, mysteries often combine action with suspense about how things are going to come out. Who outsmarts whom? Again, the child character has a major effect on the outcome, sometimes confounding adults with deft deduction. Again, children reading the stories can find young heroes or heroines who master the world of their neighborhoods.

The dearly loved Nancy Drew, who appears in book after best-selling book, has become a caricature of mystery-book characters. The stories are always roughly the same. Nancy, a one-dimensional character, unravels a mystery that baffles adults, never doubting she can do it. Of course, one of the mysteries about the Nancy Drew books centers on the writing itself. Who did it? You never know. "Carolyn Keene," the author credited on the title pages, is a pseudonym for many different writers hired to fill out outlines supplied to them.

Children in the primary grades enjoy three mystery series that use a predictable format and are easy to read. The *Nate the Great* series by Marjorie Sharmat features young Nate, who speaks detective-eze as he goes about solving his cases. In *Nate the Great and the Fishy Prize,* the case is one of a missing prize for the smartest pet, an empty tuna can with the word *Smartest* painted in gold letters by Nate's friend Rosamond. Nate finds the prize in time for the contest by putting clues together, such as the ruckus when everyone came to Rosamond's to sign up for the contest; the memory of Fang, her dog, wagging his tail by the open window where the can had been set to dry; knowing he had ridden past the window on his bike; and seeing his dog Sludge sniff the grocery bag he had carried home on his bike. It has been knocked from the window sill and fallen into his grocery bag. Nate's humor and bravado keep children laughing and also guessing about the outcome of the case.

The Cam Jansen mysteries by David Adler feature young Jennifer Jansen, called Cam for "Camera" because she has a photographic memory, a trait that allows her to solve the mysteries. She simply closes her eyes and says "click," visualizing scenes at various times and, by comparing changes, deduces what has happened.

Series books such as these most often appear in paperback editions.

Patricia Reilly Giff has a mystery series called *The Polka Dot Private Eye.* In these books, Dawn Bosco is the child detective who helps her friends and classmates from the Polk Street School solve problems and often finds something that has been lost, such as a cat in *The Powder Puff Puzzle.* Dawn, like Nate, must use logic as she goes about her work. Children just beginning to read chapter books find these books an easy read.

Author Donald Sobol writes for slightly older children. His protagonist, Encyclopedia Brown, a 10-year-old whose real name is Leroy Brown, is the son of the Idaville chief of police. Young Brown has his own detective agency, charging 25 cents a day plus expenses for his work. Each case takes about six pages, and the reader is let in on all the facts needed to solve the case. Encyclopedia puzzles out solutions, and the reader is asked "How did he know?" There are answers at the back of the book.

Humorous Stories

A pleasant collection of credible nonsense offers an alternative to the serious themes underlying much realism. Children and adults alike appreciate Miss Nelson, the lovable and gentle teacher of *Miss Nelson Is Missing* and its sequels. The children in her class are rude to her, even during story hour, and Miss Nelson knows that something has to be done. The next day she is absent, and in her place is Miss Viola Swamp, a substitute who makes the children behave, loading them down with homework and eliminating story

Kind Miss Nelson is replaced by Viola Swamp, a substitute teacher who means business. (Source: Illustration from MISS NELSON IS MISSING! by Harry Allard and James Marshall. Illustration Copyright © 1977 by James Marshall. Reprinted by permission of Houghton Mifflin Co. All rights reserved.)

hour. Ah, how the children long for Miss Nelson. But she is not to be found, even by Detective McSmogg. Finally, when all hope seems lost, Miss Nelson returns. Not surprisingly, the children now behave beautifully. And though Miss Nelson does not tell her class where she has been, readers see an ugly black dress, just like the one worn by Viola Swamp, hanging in her closet.

How to Eat Fried Worms by Thomas Rockwell can make slightly older readers giggle and groan. A boy named Billy makes a bet that he can eat 15 worms, one a day for 15 days. The payoff will be $50 from his friend Alan, or a about $3.33 per worm. Billy begins with workaday seasonings such as mustard, ketchup, salt, pepper, and lemon, and then samples more advanced cuisine, such as his mother's own "Whizbang Worm Delight," made by stuffing ice cream cake with a single worm. Author Rockwell assures readers that he checked with a doctor and eating worms is not dangerous, so go ahead, have a bite.

Much of humor for children depends on exaggeration. Pippi Longstocking, a creation of author Astrid Lindgren, carries independence to an extreme. She lives with her horse and pet monkey and does what she wants with no adult interference. Her self-sufficiency was assured when her father, a sea captain turned king of cannibals, left her a supply of gold pieces. In *Pippi Goes on Board,* Pippi goes shopping with a style most children envy. She buys candy in 36-pound lots.

And certainly Shirley, in *Fat Chance, Claude* (Nixon), is a character to be reckoned with. Set in the days of the Gold Rush, the stories show Shirley from the time she joins a wagon train and heads west, able to save Claude from a rattlesnake by dumping hot stew on it, able to fix a rip in the canvas with a string from the corset she wasn't going to wear anyway, to her finding gold on her claim and agreeing to marry Claude. The humor is enhanced by the Western drawl and figurative expressions, and by the repetition of the phrase "fat chance" at the appropriate times. Shirley and Claude's adventures continue in several other books, each with a special phrase used in the title and throughout the book.

Sometimes it is the situation that brings the humor. Jenny, in *Nibble, Nibble Jenny Archer* (Ellen Conford), manages to annoy her family and friends as she practices for a TV commercial. She had been chosen because she was willing to sample a snack at the mall, and now she is to tell how good it is. Only when her commercial airs does she discover that the snack was intended for gerbils.

In humorous books for younger readers, illustrations are often a major source of humor. The text of Reeve Lindbergh's *If I'd Known Then What I Know Now* has its own humor as the narrator tells about his dad's yearly projects, from building a house to getting farm animals to giving a party. It is the illustrations, however, that show just how bad things were. The plumbing is a maze of pipes angling and intertwining, with the tub literally above it all. When the tub drains and the soap bubbles go down the lane, the neighbors watch in astonishment. Although Dad insists that things would have been different if he'd known then what he knows now, the child agrees that that may be so, but that they wouldn't want any other dad, even if they'd known then what they know now.

EVALUATING REALISM

Writer Don Freeman wrote *Mop Top* in 1955 when short hair was the fashion. It is about a little boy who does not want a haircut. When his head gets shaggy, other children call him Moppy, and when he gets a haircut, the text tells how trim, neat, and tidy he looks. Children in the late 1970s thought Moppy was much better looking with his hair hanging halfway down his ears, and children in the 1990s think he looks first "funny" and then "nerdy." It could be argued that the book, contemporary realism when it was written, is now historical fiction.

Hair styles, clothing, and speech patterns change over time. Books of contemporary realism that rely solely on what is current for their popularity will go out of fashion when the fashion changes for they have nothing else to recommend them.

So the first criterion for evaluating both contemporary and historical realism is literary quality. Good realism must meet the basic standards for plot, characterization, setting, theme, and style. Other considerations also pertain particularly to this genre.

1. *The style must match the story.* The author's choice of language must fit with the characters and the setting. Good writing need not always follow the conventions of standard English. For example, incomplete sentences, used with care, can establish mood or character artistically. And especially in presenting dialogue, an author may choose to show a character's background, personality, or emotional state through how the character speaks. Authors of historical fiction sometimes face the problem of deciding whether characters should speak in accurate language, using the vocabulary of their day or more easily understood contemporary English. Most opt for giving the flavor of the language rather than a fully accurate rendition of it. Brinton Turkle, for example, uses *thee* and *thy* in the speech of Obadiah Starbuck and his Quaker family.

2. *Content should be free of cliché.* Clichés can weaken individual sentences and entire stories. They show an absence of original thought and language. If you feel you've heard that comment many times before or read that plot in exactly the same way, look for another book.

3. *Books should avoid didacticism.* The temptation to teach something beckons many writers of children's literature. For writers of realism, the temptation often seems to be irresistible. However, the ideas or morals presented should emanate naturally from the plot and characterization and should be inherent in the theme. A book becomes didactic when the teaching function overpowers the telling of a good story. In historical fiction, with its reliance on setting, this may show up when an author attempts to include all the facts, as though attempting to have a hidden history lesson sneak up on the reader.

4. *The setting must be accurate.* The writer of both contemporary and historical realism must present the "facts" of the time period as they are known. That is, the houses, clothes, and food of the main characters must be accurate. If the setting is a specific place, a writer may even use a map to

plan the movements of characters in the story. The writer is free to create characters and plot, but not free to change historical events or places.

The illustrator has the same responsibility for accuracy in pictures as the author has in text. Props in pictures must be accurate, but the whole illustration must support the spirit the author is trying to convey. Peter Spier's illustrations for songs add historical data to the words. In *The Erie Canal,* Spier shows the cargo of barrels, bottles, and produce on the boat. He tells about society, too: A woman does washing atop the deckhouse of one boat while another boat carrying wealthy gentry passes by.

Figure 10-7 lists Touchstone realistic picture books, and Figure 10-8 lists touchstone realistic chapter books. Look at some of the books on these lists to find strong examples of good realistic fiction.

THE VALUE OF REALISM

The key values in sharing realism with children may sound like opposites. That is, realism illustrates differences, and realism illustrates similarities.

Through realism, readers gain the experience of living somewhere else, living with strangers, smelling exotic foods cooking, or seeing flashes of color in dress and personality. They see that societies are not all alike and

Realism has been attacked and censored more often than other genres. Why do you think this is so?

Through realism young readers experience lives both similar to and different from their own.

Baylor, Byrd. *One Small Blue Bead.* Ill. by Ronald Himler. New York: Scribner, 1992. (Original with illustrations by Symeon Shimin. New York: Macmillan, 1965) A young cave dweller in the prehistoric Southwest wonders if there are other people like him and sets out with an old man of the tribe to find out.

Blos, Joan. *Old Henry.* Ill. by Stephen Gammell. New York: Morrow, 1987. Henry and his neighbors disagree about how his house and yard should be kept, and only when he moves away do both sides decide to reach a middle ground for agreement.

Bunting, Eve. *The Wall.* Ill. by Ronald Himler. New York: Clarion, 1990. A little boy and his father search for, find, and make a rubbing of the boy's grandfather's name on the Vietnam Veterans Memorial in Washington.

Cohen, Miriam. *Jim Meets the Thing.* Ill. by Lillian Hoban. New York: Greenwillow, 1981. In one of many stories about Jim and his classmates, Jim learns that nearly everyone is afraid of something, just not always the same something.

Crews, Donald. *Sail Away.* New York: Greenwillow, 1995. A family goes out for a day's sail, beginning in clear and sunny weather but having to cope with a sudden storm.

dePaola, Tomie. *The Art Lesson.* New York: Putnam's, 1989. Tommy has his own ideas about art, and they don't always match those of Mrs. Bowers, the first-grade art teacher.

Flournoy, Valerie. *The Patchwork Quilt.* Ill. by Jerry Pinkney. New York: Dial, 1985. When Tanya's grandmother becomes ill, Tanya, her mother, and the whole family help complete the quilt she was making.

Hall, Donald. *Lucy's Summer.* Ill. by Michael McCurdy. New York: Harcourt, 1995. Lucy visits a New Hampshire farm in the early 1900s.

Figure 10-7   Touchstone realistic picture books.

that there are values in each. They can explore different family structures, different systems of child rearing, and variations in customs, and by extension learn more about what forces affect people.

But realism also shows similarities. Problems recur. They may be as simple as how to cope with the teasing of brothers and sisters or as complex and difficult as realizing that sometimes one must be brave enough to be different from one's peers.

They can show that people of many times and places have aspirations, some very similar to their own. In *The Day of Ahmed's Secret* (Heide and Gilliland), they see a young boy in Cairo whose special secret, which he shares with pride, is that he has learned to write his name. In *At the Beach* (Lee), they learn with Xiao Ming to write Chinese characters in the sand. And in *More Than Anything Else* (Bradby) they see a young Booker T. Washington asking a man reading a newspaper to teach him to read and learning to write "Booker." Young children

Hughes, Shirley. *Hiding.* Cambridge, MA: Candlewick, 1994. The meaning of the title is shown in many ways as young children engage in everyday games and activities.

Kellogg, Steven. *Pinkerton, Behave!* New York: Dial, 1979. In this, the first of several books about Pinkerton, the huge dog catches a burglar once the family has learned the right commands.

McCloskey, Robert. *Time of Wonder.* New York: Viking, 1957. A summer on an island in Maine is poetically described, complete with a hurricane and its aftermath.

Mora, Pat. *Pablo's Tree.* Ill. by Cecily Lang. New York: Macmillan, 1994. Pablo's *abuelito* decorates a special tree each year and retells his grandson the story of the tree as a celebration of his adoption.

Polacco, Patricia. *Just Plain Fancy.* New York: Bantam, 1990. Naomi and Ruth get their wish for something fancy when the egg they find hatches into a peacock, but they worry about how the Amish elders may react.

Ringgold, Faith. *Tar Beach.* New York: Crown, 1991. Opening with a realistic setting in 1939, this story quilt shows Cassie's dream adventures as she flies above Harlem.

Viorst, Judith. *Alexander and the Terrible, Horrible, No Good, Very Bad Day.* Ill. by Ray Cruz. New York: Atheneum, 1972. Alexander recounts all the things that happened to make his day terrible, with the recurring threat that he may move to Australia.

Yee, Paul. *Roses Sing on New Snow: A Delicious Tale.* Ill. by Harvey Chan. New York: Macmillan, 1992. This book is strong in its portrayal of a Chinatown in the late 19th century, where Maylin finally gets the recognition she deserves as primary cook in her father's restaurant.

Zolotow, Charlotte. *William's Doll.* Ill. by William Pene du Bois. New York: Harper, 1972. When his father tries to dissuade William from his wish to have a doll, his grandmother buys one for him, so he can learn to be a father.

Figure 10-7　*continued*

can relate their own achievements in literacy with the accomplishments of these characters, realizing that people of different nationalities, ethnic groups, or periods of history may have as many commonalities as differences.

SUMMARY

Realistic fiction tells a story that could happen or could have happened in the past. In contemporary realism, the setting is the present. Realistic stories with settings in the past are called historical realism or, more commonly, historical fiction.

Writers begin with reality and then apply imagination and skill to write fiction. They choose and enliven facts, building on human emotion and interrelationships. Good realistic fiction is accurate in its setting, avoids

Blume, Judy. *Tales of a Fourth Grade Nothing*. Ill. by Roy Doty. New York: Dutton, 1972. Peter's life with his two-year-old brother Fudge is difficult for him but humorous for the reader.

Byars, Betsy. *The 18th Emergency*. Ill. by Robert Grossman. New York: Viking, 1973. Mouse likes to draw cartoons, but when the school bully is not amused, Mouse has a real emergency on his hands.

Cleary, Beverly. *Ramona Quimby, Age 8*. Ill. by Alan Tiegreen. New York: Morrow, 1981. In a series of episodes, Ramona shows her individuality and her spunk.

Dalgliesh, Alice. *The Courage of Sarah Noble*. Ill. by Leonard Weisgard. New York: Scribner's, 1954. This is based on a true story of an eight-year-old girl who goes with her father to the wilderness of Connecticut to cook for him as he builds the family cabin.

Hamilton, Virginia. *Zeely*. Ill. by Symeon Shimin. New York: Macmillan, 1967. Geeder is convinced that Zeely Tabor is really a Watusi queen until Zeely talks with her about the source of real beauty.

Henry, Marguerite. *Misty of Chincoteague*. Ill. by Wesley Dennis. New York: Macmillan, 1947. Paul and Maureen buy a colt in the annual sale of wild horses from Assateague Island.

Lowry, Lois. *Attaboy, Sam!* Ill. by Diane de Groat. Boston: Houghton Mifflin, 1992. Sam decides to create a perfume of his mother's favorite smells as a gift for her birthday in this book, one of the many stories about Anastasia Krupnik and her family.

Figure 10-8   Touchstone realistic chapter books.

cliché in both language and content, has a style that is consistent with the setting and the characterization, and is not didactic.

Contemporary realism for young children often explores common situations and experiences. Problems in growing up, relationships with family and friends, making decisions, and learning about people who differ from oneself are frequent themes. Books of historical fiction, sometimes researched and sometimes based on the experiences and memory of the author, can be grouped so that children examine different places within the same time period, changes in a single place over time, or varied views of a particular time and place.

MacLachlan, Patricia. *Sarah, Plain and Tall.* New York: Harper, 1985. Anna and Caleb hope feverishly that Sarah from Maine will decide to marry their father and stay with them in their prairie home.

Paterson, Katherine. *The Great Gilly Hopkins.* New York: Crowell, 1978. Gilly realizes too late the love she felt for Maime Trotter, her foster parent, but has the capacity to heal.

Reeder, Carolyn. *Shades of Gray.* New York; Macmillan, 1989. The issue of conscientous objectors is raised in Will Page's dislike of his uncle who refused to fight in the War Between the States.

Smith, Doris Buchanan. *A Taste of Blackberries.* Ill. by Charles Robinson. New York: Crowell, 1973. The narrator of the story must cope with the death of his friend Jamie.

Speare, Elizabeth. *The Sign of the Beaver.* Boston: Houghton Mifflin, 1983. Matt learns survival skills from the grandson of the chief of the Beaver Clan when he stays in the Maine territory to take care of his family's cabin.

Taylor, Mildred. *The Well.* New York: Dial, 1995. The Logan's share their well water with all who need it, black and white alike, but this is no protection from Charlie Simms' anger and ability to taunt the Logan sons.

Wilder, Laura Ingalls. *Little House on the Prairie.* Ill. by Garth Williams. New York: Harper, 1953 (1935). This is one of nine books in which Wilder tells about her life in the 1870s and 1880s as part of a loving pioneer family.

Yep, Laurence. *Later, Gator.* New York: Hyperion, 1995. Teddy decides to get his younger brother a baby alligator for his birthday and is disappointed to find that his brother likes the pet.

Figure 10-8   *continued*

A few topics in realism are so popular that they are often given special shelves in libraries. Among these are sports stories, animal stories, mysteries, and humorous stories. Like other works of realism, some of these have serious themes, while others are light, with predictable endings.

Realism helps children see both similarities and differences among peoples. They may see life styles and beliefs very different from their own, broadening their outlook and building a respect for others. They may also see that they are very much like other people in their wishes and aspirations, their dreams and worries.

∽ EXPLORE ON YOUR OWN

1. **Explore Your Personal Response.** Read a book of contemporary realism that has characters of the same cultural background as you in terms of your ethnicity, race, gender, or socioeconomic or religious background. Are you pleased with the portrayal? What seems to account for your reaction?
2. **Apply Literary Criteria.** In historical fiction, the setting often affects plot and characterization. Read two books of historical fiction and describe the role of the setting in each. How might the characters' actions be different if the story had a contemporary setting?
3. **Prepare to Share Literature With Children.** In a chapter book of either contemporary or historical fiction, select one scene that would provide the basis for a role play. Mark where you would stop reading and write what you would say to children to introduce the role play.

∽ EXPLORE WITH CHILDREN

1. **Explore Children's Responses.** Read to a small group of children books set in two different historical periods. Ask the children to say which period they would live in if they were sent back in time. List the reasons they give to support each period. You might want to try this with a different group of children using different books set in the same two historical periods and compare the children's responses.
2. **Engage Children With Literature.** Share with a group of children three books of realism in which the main character has the same or similar problems, such as being afraid, moving to a new home, or coping with changes in family structure. Create a web in which you record the children's descriptions of the various ways characters responded to the problem. Conclude by having the children list other possible responses to the problem.

∽ SUGGESTED PROFESSIONAL REFERENCES

Fisher, Margery. *The Bright Face of Danger: An Exploration of the Adventure Story*. Boston: The Horn Book, 1986. § Fisher examines the special characteristics of the adventure story and compares stories written in that genre for adults with those written for children.

Paterson, Katherine. *Gates of Excellence: On Reading and Writing Books for Children*. New York: Elsevier, 1981. § Paterson describes many of her experiences which she eventually used in her books in this collection of her speeches and essays.

Paterson, Katherine. *The Spying Heart: More Thoughts on Reading and Writing for Children*. New York: Lodestar, 1989. § Paterson writes with wit and insight about serious themes in literature for children in this second collection of essays.

∽ CHILDREN'S BOOKS CITED

Allard, Harry. *Miss Nelson Is Missing*. Ill. by James Marshall. Boston: Houghton Mifflin, 1977.

Andrews, Jan. *Very Last First Time*. Ill. by Ian Wallace. New York: Atheneum, 1986.

Bedard, Michael. *Emily*. Ill. by Barbara Cooney. New York: Doubleday, 1992.

Bowen, Gary. *Stranded at Plimoth Plantation 1626*. New York: HarperCollins, 1994.

Bradby, Marie. *More Than Anything Else*. Ill. by Chris Soentpiet. New York: Orchard, 1995.

Bunting, Eve. *Clancy's Coat*. Ill. by Lorinda Cauley. New York: Warne, 1984.

Castaneda, Omar. *Abuela's Weave*. Ill. by Enrique Snaches. New York: Lee & Low, 1993.

Christopher, Matt. *Zero's Slider*. Ill. by Molly Delaney. Boston: Little, Brown, 1994.

Clement, Claude. *Musician From the Darkness*. Ill. by John Howe. Boston: Little, 1990.

Cohen, Miriam. *It's George!* Ill. by Lillian Hoban. New York: Greenwillow, 1988.

Cohen, Miriam. *Jim's Dog Muffins*. Ill. by Lillian Hoban. New York: Greenwillow, 1984.

Cohen, Miriam. *Lost in the Museum*. Ill. by Lillian Hoban. New York: Greenwillow, 1979.

Cohen, Miriam. *No Good in Art*. Ill. by Lillian Hoban. New York: Greenwillow, 1980.

Cohen, Miriam. *When Will I Read?* Ill. by Lillian Hoban. New York: Greenwillow, 1977.

Conford, Ellen. *Nibble, Nibble, Jenny Archer.* Ill. by Diane Palmisciano. Boston: Little, Brown, 1993.

dePaola, Tomie. *Tom*. New York: Putnam, 1993.

Doherty, Berlie. *Willa and Old Miss Annie*. Ill. by Kim Lewis. Cambridge, MA: Candlewick, 1994.

Dorros, Arthur. *Radio Man*. New York: HarperCollins, 1993.

Dugan, Barbara. *Loop the Loop*. Ill. by James Stevenson. New York: Greenwillow, 1992.

Ehlert, Lois. *Snowballs*. New York: Harcourt, 1995.

Freeman, Don. *Mop Top*. New York: Viking, 1955.

Friedrich, Elizabeth. *Leah's Pony*. Ill. by Michael Garland. Honesdale, PA: Boyds Mills, 1996.

Garland, Sherry. *The Lotus Seed*. Ill. by Tatsuro Kiuchi. New York: Harcourt, 1993.

Giff, Patricia Reilly. *The Powder Puff Puzzle*. Ill. by Blanche Sims. New York: Dell, 1987.

Goble, Paul. *Death of the Iron Horse*. New York: Bradbury, 1987.

Hall, Donald. *The Farm Summer 1942*. Ill. by Barry Moser. New York: Dial, 1994.

Hall, Donald. *Ox-Cart Man*. Ill. by Barbara Cooney. New York: Viking, 1979.

Heide, Florence, and Judith Gilliland. *The Day of Ahmed's Secret*. Ill. by Ted Lewin. New York: Lothrop, 1990.

Heide, Florence, and Judith Gilliland. *Sami and the Time of the Troubles*. Ill. by Ted Lewin. New York: Clarion, 1992.

Hendershot, Judith. *In Coal Country*. Ill. by Thomas B. Allen. New York: Knopf, 1987.

Hoffman, Mary. *Boundless Grace*. Ill. by Caroline Binch. New York: Dial, 1995.

Hopkinson, Deborah. *Sweet Clara and the Freedom Quilt*. Ill. by James Ransome. New York: Knopf, 1993.

Howard, Elizabeth Fitzgerald. *Aunt Florrie's Hats (and Crab Cakes Later)*. Ill. by James Ransome. New York: Clarion, 1991.

Hughes, Shirley. *Giving*. Cambridge, MA: Candlewick, 1993.

Hutchins, Pat. *Titch*. New York: Macmillan, 1971.

Johnson, Dolores. *Seminole Diary, Remembrances of a Slave*. New York: Macmillan, 1994.

Jordan, MaryKate. *Losing Uncle Tim*. Ill. by Judith Friedman. Niles, IL: Whitman, 1989.

Keats, Ezra Jack. *The Snowy Day*. New York: Viking, 1962.

Kinsey-Warnock, Natalie, and Helen Kinsey. *The Bear That Heard Crying*. Ill. by Ted Rand. New York: Dutton, 1993.

Kinsey-Warnock, Natalie. *Wilderness Cat*. Ill. by Mark Graham. New York: Dutton, 1992.

Lee, Huy Voun. *At the Beach*. New York: Holt, 1994.

Lindbergh, Reeve. *If I'd Known Then What I Know Now*. Ill. by Kimberly Root. New York: Viking, 1994.

Lindgren, Astrid. *Pippi Goes on Board*. Trans. by Florence Lamborn. Ill. by Louse Glanzman. New York: Viking, 1957.

Locker, Thomas. *Family Farm*. New York: Dial, 1988.

McPhail, David. *Farmboy's Year*. New York: Atheneum, 1992.

Medearis, Angela Shelf. *Dancing With the Indians*. Ill. by Samuel Byrd. New York: Holiday, 1991.

Milton, Nancy. *The Giraffe That Walked to Paris*. Ill. by Roger Roth. New York: Crown, 1992.

Naylor, Phyllis Reynolds. *Shiloh*. New York: Atheneum, 1991.

Nixon, Joan Lowrey. *Fat Chance, Claude*. Ill. by Tracey Campbell Pearson. New York: Viking, 1987.

Polacco, Patricia. *Mrs. Katz and Tush*. New York: Bantam, 1992.

Polacco, Patricia. *Pink and Say*. New York: Philomel, 1994.

Rockwell, Thomas. *How to Eat Fried Worms*. Ill. by Emily McCully. New York: Watts, 1973.

Rylant, Cynthia. *Henry and Mudge and the Long Weekend*. Ill. by Sucie Stevenson. New York: Macmillan, 1992.

Seattle, Chief. *Brother Eagle, Sister Sky*. Ill. by Susan Jeffers. New York: Dial, 1991.

Sewell, Marcia. *The Pilgrims of Plimoth*. New York: Atheneum, 1986.

Thaxter, Celia. *Celia's Island Journal*. Adapted and Ill. by Loretta Krupinski. Boston: Little, Brown, 1992.

Sharmat, Marjorie. *Nate the Great and the Fishy Prize*. Ill. by Marc Simont. New York: Putnam, 1985.

Smucker, Anna Egan. *No Star Nights*. Ill. by Steve Johnson. New York: Knopf, 1989.

Spier, Peter. *The Eric Canal*. New York: Doubleday, 1970.

Taylor, Mildred. *The Well*. New York: Dial, 1995.

Turkle, Brinton. *Obadiah the Bold*. New York: Viking, 1965.

Udry, Janice. *What Mary Jo Wanted*. Ill. by Eleanor Mill. New York: Whitman, 1968.

Waggoner, Karen. *Partners*. Ill. by Cat Bowman Smith. New York: Simon, 1995.

Wilhelm, Hans. *I'll Always Love You.* New York: Crown, 1985.

Williams, Sherley Anne. *Working Cotton.* Ill. by Carole Byard. New York: Harcourt, 1992.

Williams, Vera. *A Chair for My Mother.* New York: Greenwillow, 1982.

Wood, Audrey. *Quick as a Cricket.* Ill. by Don Wood. New York: Child's Play, 1982.

Yep, Laurence. *Later, Gator.* New York: Hyperion, 1995.

◌ CHAPTER REFERENCES

Jones, Malcolm, and Ray Sawhill. "Just Too Good to Be True." *Newsweek* 4 May 1992: 68.

Turner, Ann. "On Writing *Katie's Trunk.*" *Book Links* 2.5 (May 1993): 11.

 ***Chapter Eleven***

Biography and Informational Books: Factual Portraits and Explorations

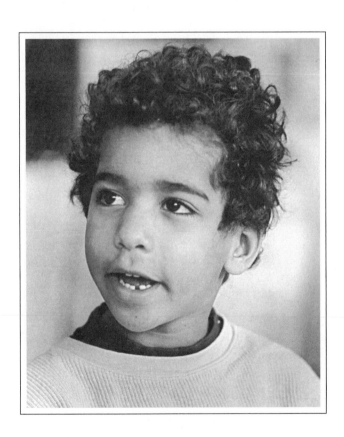

Cheryl's third-grade class had been studying ocean life. She invited Mr. Delmont, an instructor in scuba diving, to talk with the class about his experiences "underwater" and to show the class scuba diving equipment. Here is how the discussion and demonstration began.

Mr. D.:   Does anybody have any questions before we start?

St: Have you ever gone skin diving? (Mr. D. nods yes.)

St: Have you ever seen a shark?

Mr. D: That's one thing I wanted to talk to you about. How many of you have seen *Jaws?* (Several hands go up.) That story is all wrong. It's not true. That movie was not very fair to sharks, and when it came out it scared a lot of grown-ups. So adults went out and killed sharks. But sharks are not dangerous; they do not eat people. Do you know what sharks do eat?

St: They eat fish?

Mr. D: What do you think?

St: Well, in the book I read, they eat tiny, tiny fish.

Mr. D: Some do. Sharks basically eat dead or dying animals, like a seal or walrus that is sick, or fish. What do you suppose would happen to all those dead or dying fish if there weren't any sharks?

St: They would probably make a big smell in the ocean.

St: They wash up onto the water's edge, to the shore.

St: I know. I know. They're beached.

Mr. D: Bingo! So sharks are very important. They follow around beaches and keep the beaches and the ocean clean. What else do you know about sharks?

St: If you swim around, they will come after you.

Mr.D: But the big secret is, they are cowards. They're scaredy cats. If they're aggressive, all you have to do is go like this. (Demonstrates swimming toward them.) If you swim toward them, they will go away. Why do you suppose sharks sometimes attack? You'll notice that often people who have been attacked by the great white sharks are surfers. Why do you suppose that is?

St: Because fish sometimes surface.

Mr. D: Close, you're real close.

St: Like if you're a shark underwater . . . up, uh, oh forget it.

Mr. D:	A surfer is laying on a board. When a shark looks up, it looks like a dead seal. That's why surfers sometimes get attacked. If you just swim around, sharks won't notice. But if you get scared and start swimming around real fast, you'll look like something's wrong. You won't be going smooth and steady. It tells the shark something's wrong, like you're wounded.
St:	Are sharks cowards like the lion in the *Wizard of Oz?*
Mr. D:	Well, kind of. They try to look brave, but they're really not. Yes?
St:	In my book there's a shark, called a carpet shark. And it stays in the mud and blends in with the dirt, and when the fish come by, it snaps at them. And it's really bad because they don't know if it's grass or what.
Mr. D:	There are many kinds of sharks. Anyone know what a basking shark is?
St:	It's black.
Mr. D:	Mostly black and gray.
St:	I think it's a big fish and it's almost the biggest fish, shark.
St:	Almost the biggest shark.
Mr. D:	It is the biggest shark.
St:	I thought the great white shark was.
Mr. D:	The basking shark is the size of a whale, of a school bus, and it doesn't eat meat. It goes along with its mouth open. Thousands and thousands of gallons of water pass through, and it filters out the plankton.
St:	When I saw this underwater show, there was this fish called a rock fish. And it was ugly. The fish goes under the rock, and it looked like a rock.
St:	That's why they're called rock fish.
St:	I was wondering. We have a book on the back shelf, and it has all kinds of fish. Can I go get it please?

These children are gathering information from a variety of sources. They are learning from a guest speaker who has expertise in the area, from television, and from informational books. Notice that several students refer to what they've read, weaving that knowledge naturally into the discussion.

INFORMATIONAL BOOKS: DIVERSE EXPLORATIONS

Good nonfiction both supplements and stimulates direct experience. The third graders had been reading about undersea life and about diving equipment. They were prepared to talk with Mr. Delmont and to see for themselves what his diving suit looked like and how it functioned. After his visit, the class read more about sharks and began reading about compasses, fascinated with his talk of finding directions on the ocean floor. Cheryl borrowed compasses from the science room and set up an orienteering experience in

This was a natural time for the teacher and librarian to help the children learn to use library reference tools.

which teams of students were on the ocean floor—the multipurpose room—and had to follow written compass directions to find their way to a sunken treasure. The question "What makes a compass work?" emerged from several of the groups, and the class began another search for information in nonfiction books.

Definition

Informational books present facts, concepts, and generalizations about a particular topic rather than tell a story, although they may do both. Chapter 5 introduced a small collection of concept books with pictures; all of them are informational books. Informational, or **nonfiction,** books may deal with rudimentary knowledge, such as the shape of numerals, or may cover subjects foreign to many adults, such as atomic research or prehistoric art.

There are more nonfiction books than any other kind of writing for children. Of the over 40,000 books listed in *Subject Guide to Children's Books in Print,* the clear majority are nonfiction. Their quality is determined by how these books present facts and principles and how they draw readers in and stimulate thought. Looking carefully at nonfiction books to assess both their quality and their potential uses in your classroom can help you present these books effectively. Figure 11-1 shows how one teacher could have strengthened a lesson by previewing more assiduously the book he planned to share.

Evaluating Informational Books: The Quality of the Exploration

Good informational books launch readers on a kind of exploration. They offer a clear idea, with their own kind of markers, of where the journey is going before the reader sets off. They carry children along, accurately charting what is known and unknown. They rouse interest in further exploration. Illustrations, comparable to colorful vistas opening up to travelers, add to the excitement of the trip. Sometimes they are the reason for going.

The standards for evaluating informational books are closely related to those for fiction—an overall plan, truthfulness, a stimulating style, and illustrations that extend the text.

Where Is the Book Going?
Good informational books are generous with information about themselves. Unless a nonfiction book is short, a beginning concept book or one with a very narrow focus, for example, it should contain a table of contents and give detailed data on what it offers in an index. From the title and table of contents alone, readers should know whether the book surveys a broad field. Scanning the index gives a more detailed idea of the scope.

Skimming is a reading strategy that needs to be modeled and taught directly.

Most informational books center on one clearly defined territory. Books for younger readers seldom offer a **table of contents,** but most of these books are so short that the plan and scale of the book are apparent after brief skimming.

THE LESSON, AS PLANNED AND TAUGHT	REFLECTIONS . . .
Rationale Stan's fourth-grade class had been enthralled by a visit from a local string quartet. He decided that this was the perfect time to show how non-fiction books could supplement other knowledge. He would bring in books that extended what the players had told the children about their instruments and their music.	The idea was a good one, especially since the children's interest was high. Stan might have brought books about the music the children had heard as well as the instruments, even though he was not planning any sort of lengthy unit study on the topic.
The Lesson Stan made a quick trip to the library, collecting 10 books on violins, violas, and cellos. He decided to read *Music in the Wood* by Cornelia Cornelissen (New York: Delacorte, 1995) to the entire class because in skimming it he recognized that the many photographs and the concise text clearly demonstrated the steps in the construction of a baroque cello and the high degree of craftsmanship involved.	
He was correct about the photographs, but he made two discoveries while reading the book to his class. First, there were many technical terms. Most meanings could be determined by the children by using the photographs and clues within the text, but the reading took twice as long as he had expected. And second, as he was closing the book, he found that it included a CD of music being played on the cello shown in the book. Stan told the class that they'd listen to the CD on their next scheduled visit to the media center, where the school's computers with CD ROM were housed.	A more careful reading of the book would have helped Stan be prepared to work with the vocabulary. In addition, had he seen the glossary, he could have had children check their guesses and learn how to use a glossary within a meaningful situation. Also, had he seen the CD, he could have planned the reading to coincide with a trip to the media center, thus heightening the children's awareness of the relationship of the text in the book, the sound of the cello, and the music and discussion of the visiting string quartet.

Figure 11-1   On second thought: Plan ahead for a better lesson.

The classroom of the third graders studying ocean life had many books on ocean life. The Eyewitness book *Shark* (MacQuitty) shows in its table of contents that it will begin with a definition of sharks, look at the body of a shark, at how sharks reproduce, at their danger, at specific types of sharks, and finally at how sharks are studied and can be kept from extinction. Several children who wanted to know about sharks' teeth knew from the table of contents that there were two pages about that topic. When they looked in the **index,** they found 10 different references to teeth.

Another book in the classroom, *Tracks in the Sand* by Loreen Leedy, has a much narrower focus and has neither table of contents nor index. It

These children are learning to use a table of contents.

describes the life cycle of the loggerhead sea turtle, opening with the turtles swimming in the ocean and mating and then showing the female coming ashore to lay her eggs. The eggs hatch and the tiny turtles head into the ocean, where they will grow for several seasons before they too mate, thus continuing the cycle. A series of pictures on one double-page spread show how the cells divide within each egg as the turtles grow and develop.

Both books have a place in the classroom. *Shark* gives a broad view of the topic of sharks; *Tracks in the Sand* gives a narrow view of a specific turtle, but that view is representative of the life of many types of sea turtles. Assessing the scope of a book can help a teacher match it to readers' current interests.

Most books provide other indications, easily checked, of how good the exploration will be. The **copyright date,** for instance, can reveal quickly whether the material is likely to be dated. Sometimes the date is irrelevant: books of history, for example, have a better chance of long-range survival than books about space exploration. Dates on the books about sharks and turtles may not matter if the reader is interested in how species differ or how they reproduce. Data on the amount and type of ocean pollution, however, are perishable. Theories and information about the effect of oil spills on the environment grow and change yearly. The date of the book may be a warning sign to doubt some of the information. Children themselves should learn to look at the book's age and try to decide how time may have affected accuracy.

The **author's qualifications,** the way the author gained his or her information, and the people who have checked the information can all be clues to the quality of the exploration. Can you trust the information in *Shark?* Yes, you probably can. In the Acknowledgments, the publisher lists and thanks scientists and curators at six museums and three professional organizations. Can you

Show children that when two or more copyright dates appear, such as "© 1969, 1996," this means that the book was published first in 1969 and again in 1996, when the copyright was renewed. They should see if the book has been revised or updated.

trust the information is *Tracks in the Sand?* Yes, you probably can. The author lists four professors of biology and the director of Sea World in Orlando and notes that her illustrations are based on photographs she took of nesting turtles.

Notes, copyright date, table of contents, index, and even the title all indicate the direction the book will take, partially answering whether the exploration will be worthwhile. Further evaluation depends on reading the text and studying illustrations.

Is the Exploration Accurate?

A collection of verifiable facts does not necessarily give an accurate view of a subject any more than a jet flight over the Grand Canyon gives insight into the life of former cave dwellers there. Of course, the basic facts must be correct. But while facts can be grouped and analyzed so that the reader can see principles, generalizations, and patterns, they can also be simplified, abridged, or selected until they are meaningless or misguiding.

Blumberg groups facts and tells far more than the story of an item of women's clothing in her book *Bloomers!* She writes about how in 1851 Libby Miller wore these ballooning trousers, which she had purchased in Switzerland to wear hiking, to visit her friend Elizabeth Stanton. She describes how Elizabeth then had some made for herself and told her friend Amelia Bloomer about them. In showing the relationship and concerns of these women, she shows the significance of bloomers as a symbol for women's demand for equal rights, especially the right to vote. The story, told with humor, takes on added meaning when the facts are organized and put into context.

Bloomers! *shows the significance of this style of clothing as a symbol for women's demands for equal rights. (Source:* Illustration reprinted with the permission of Atheneum Books for Young Readers, an imprint of Simon & Schuster from BLOOMERS! by Rhoda Blumberg, illustrated by Mary Morgan. Illustrations Copyright © 1993 Mary Morgan.)

Peter and Connie Roop have published several books based on journals or diaries, among them *I Columbus: My Journal* (New York: Walker, 1990).

Authors must select which facts to include. In *Off the Map,* Peter and Connie Roop tell the story of the journey of Meriwether Lewis and William Clark on their expedition to explore the Louisiana Territory by selecting entries from their journals. A prologue and an epilogue set the context, but entries themselves tell the story. The journals of Lewis and Clark were first published in eight volumes. Thus the Roops had to be extremely selective in what they kept, so that the central facts of the trip were preserved, so that the excerpts formed a coherent whole, and so that the facts did not misrepresent what had happened because significant details had been omitted. Here is one of the entries:

> *August 29, 1804.* We had a violent storm of wind and rain last evening. Sergeant Pryor and his party arrived, attended by five chiefs and 70 men and boys. As a mark of great respect, they were presented with a fat dog, already cooked, of which they partook heartily and found it well flavored. The lodges of the Sioux are of a conical form, covered with buffalo robes painted with various figures and colors, with a hole in the top for the smoke to pass through. The lodges contain from 10 to 15 persons. The interior arrangement is compact and handsome. (Roop 13)[1]

Teachers discussing this book with children have the opportunity not just to talk about the journey of 8,000 miles, but also to discuss how Lewis and Clark viewed the new land and new people they were seeing and how customs may have differed. In this excerpt, for example, there is the matter-of-fact description of the lodges, the judgment that the lodges were handsome, and the statement that dog is flavorful. One fourth-grade teacher found that the excerpts elicited much discussion and provided a natural time to explore how different peoples can appreciate one another. Figure 11-2 shows how another teacher engaged children in an activity to help them learn about and appreciate different styles of art.

Authors of good nonfiction not only select their facts carefully and embed them in an understandable context, but they also identify when facts are unknown or where theories are still being developed. Philip Isaacson, in *A Short Walk Around the Pyramids & Through the World of Art,* describes works of art in relation to their creators as well as to their aesthetic appeal. Here is his description of a funerary figure made by the Kota, a group of tribes from the West African country of Gabon:

> We are not certain what the figure meant to the Kota. Perhaps it was magical, a figure that possessed power and could help in some way when help was needed. Or perhaps it was something quite different. We may never know the answer, for the Kota, like many of the tribes of Africa, have changed their old ways, and the meaning of many of their traditions has been lost. (Isaacson 18)[2]

---

[1] *Source:* Text excerpt from OFF THE MAP: The Journals of Lewis and Clark edited by Peter and Connie Roop, Illustrations by Tim Tanner, Copyright © 1993 by Walker and Company. Reprinted with permission.

[2] *Source:* Text from A SHORT WALK AROUND THE PYRAMIDS by Philip M. Isaacson, Copyright © 1993 by Philip M. Isaacson. Reprinted by permission of Alfred A. Knopf, Inc.

Mary Beth had read Konigsburg's *From the Mixed-Up Files of Mrs. Basil E. Frankweiler* (New York: Atheneum, 1967) to her fourth-grade class. During the reading of the book, in which two children hide in an art museum, she had placed books about artists on a special table and encouraged the children to browse through them. Several of the books were from the series about artists by Ernest Raboff (New York: Harper, 1987 and 1988).

Once she had finished the oral reading, she began a study of the artists, using the nonfiction books on the table. Children in groups of four or five looked at books about, and pictures by, a single artist. From the works shown, they discussed the artist's use of color, style, and subject. They reached these conclusions:

Van Gogh used many bright colors, painted more things than people, and his works became darker as he got older.

Picasso used the color blue a lot in many of his works, shapes were important to him, and his work was cartoon-like.

Rembrandt used mostly dark colors, the subjects seemed to blend into the background, people were his main focus, his strokes were soft and round, and his works were photograph-like.

Renoir used many colors, his works were more action-oriented than that of the other artists, and his works often seemed blurred.

Then the next day, as a total group, the children viewed some of the works of **Michelangelo** (Richmond, Robin. *Introducing Michelangelo.* Boston: Little, 1992). They compared his style to that of the other artists. Mary Beth told them that his most famous work was on the ceiling of the Sistine Chapel and asked the children to think of ways he could have painted a picture on the ceiling of a building. One child said that he could have painted it on paper then pasted it on the ceiling; another suggested that he simply used a ladder to reach the ceiling; a third used the term *scaffolding.* Mary Beth then showed a drawing depicting Michelangelo at work, and the class described times they had seen workmen using scaffolding.

Each child was then given a piece of manilla paper to sketch a picture, a picture that they would paint the next day. They would experience lying on their backs and painting, just as Michelangelo had. They were to wear old clothes even though they would also be wearing their painting smocks.

On the third day, the children taped their pictures to the undersides of their desks. They made palettes of cardboard, added blobs of thickly mixed powdered tempera paint, and with their brushes stretched out under their desks to paint their own ceiling masterpieces. When they had finished painting, the children discussed the difficulties they had encountered, reviewed the pictures from the Sistine Chapel, and hypothesized about the difficulties Michelangelo must have experienced.

Figure 11-2 Learning about styles in art.

Acknowledging the fact that some things are unknown adds credibility to statements of what is known. Isaacson even anticipates where readers might form unwarranted conclusions. He notes that many African tribes could copy the human figure perfectly, so this abstract figure is not the result of an inability to make a realistic sculpture. He also states that while art made by people who live in groups called tribes was once called primitive art, it is not primitive in the feelings it expresses or how it is made. These warnings help prevent readers from forming erroneous or stereotypical assumptions.

Sometimes writers stray from accuracy by trying to dress up facts in a misguided attempt to make them more appealing to children. Two common errors in informational books are called **anthropomorphism** and **teleology. Anthropomorphism** means giving human characteristics to things that are not human. Animals act certain ways in order to be happy, for instance, or a teapot feels better after it blows its whistle and "lets off steam." In fiction, this approach is called personification, and it is an effective literary technique. In nonfiction, it is misleading and confusing.

The word *teleology* refers to the belief that there is an overall design or plan in nature. Teleological explanations assume that all of nature, or Mother Nature, knows the plan and works toward certain goals or ends. Vultures eat carrion because it is part of Mother Nature's plan to help clean up the landscape, for example. The difficulty with teleology is that it confuses cause with effect.

Does the Book Propel the Reader to Turn the Page?

Travel agents help people get where they want to go, but they also entice people to visit places they may have never considered on their own. Informational books may answer readers' questions; they may also capture readers and take them on an unexpected journey. They do both through interesting subjects and effective writing styles. Jim Brandenburg begins *An American Safari: Adventures on the North American Prairie* on a very personal note. He tells about growing up in southern Minnesota, always aware of the land and the grasses and the wildflowers. He tells about his first camera, a $3 Argus from the local drugstore. His first picture was of a red fox, and when it—and the seven others he took of the same fox from the same vantage point—was developed, he discovered the magic of preserving a moment in time, of being able to relive that moment when viewing the photograph. The reader feels Brandenburg's enthusiasm, and sets out with him to explore the prairie through vivid descriptions and artistic photos.

Dick King-Smith shows in the title, and in his opening sentences, just where he stands regarding his subject. *All Pigs Are Beautiful* begins

An effective writing experience for children is for them to take photographs or make sketches and then write the narrative to accompany their visual representation.

> I love pigs. I don't care if they're little pigs or big pigs, with long snouts or short snouts, with ears that stick up or ears that flop down. I don't mind if they're black or white or ginger or spotted. I just love pigs. (King-Smith n. pag.)[3]

[3] *Source:* Text from ALL PIGS ARE BEAUTIFUL by Dick King-Smith, Illustrated by Anita Jeram reproduced with permission of Walker Books Ltd. Illustrations © 1993 Anita Jeram. Text © 1993 Foxbuster Ltd. Published in the US by Candlewick Press, Cambridge, MA.

Wouldn't we all like that kind of unconditional love! The statement says to readers that this will be an adventure of warmth and caring and gentle humor.

Inside and Outside Snakes (Markle) uses questions within the text. After noting that snakes can move without arms or legs, the question of how they can do that is raised. Readers wonder. And they can swallow food larger than their heads. How can they do that? Readers wonder. The books answers these questions and poses others. Even the pictures are captioned with questions and answers.

The wide variety of styles in contemporary nonfiction lets readers choose formats they enjoy and experience many different writing styles. Teachers often use these books as models for how to organize and write a report. The writer may describe personal observations as a beginning point. The writer may want to use a question-and-answer format, cause and effect, or chronology. Children can see how topic and purpose may affect organizational structure by looking at different books on related nonfiction topics. For example, *How a Book Is Made* (Aliki) is organized chronologically, an effective approach since the book is describing a process. *Write It Down* (Cobb) separates each topic into its own chapter—paper, ballpoint pens, pencils, and the crayon, since each really has a story of its own. Children might even predict how a book is organized before they look at the table of contents or skim the text.

Organization within one or two paragraphs also provides a model for children's writing. Berger, for example, uses very clear organization with the topic sentence first in many of the paragraphs in *Germs Make Me Sick!* In one paragraph he begins by defining germs and then describes them. In the next, he writes that there are many kinds of germs but that bacteria and viruses are the two that usually make people sick. Paragraph three tells about bacteria and paragraph four about viruses. Just analyzing these four paragraphs will help children understand that a logical organization to writing aids the reader's comprehension.

The Crinkleroot books by Jim Arnosky provide a useful format for class books. In them an old man named Crinkleroot explores his environment, and every few pages a full-page spread gives information about something he has seen. In *Crinkleroot's Guide to Walking in Wild Places,* he explores the forest. The interspersed pages describe ticks, ferns, objects found, stinging insects, and poisonous plants. A class can dictate their own story of exploration, with teams of students researching and creating the informational pages.

Clearly organized writing can also be used to teach note-taking techniques. Have a child read the paragraph while you write notes from that paragraph on the board or on chart paper. Then explain why you wrote what you did in the way that you did.

Do the Illustrations Improve the View?

Good illustrations are more than rest stops in informational books. They add information. Like a new view opening up as a hiker rounds a bend, good illustrations give readers a sense of where they are in ways that words cannot.

Perhaps the new information is scale. Readers immediately understand just how tiny a five-day-old mouse is when they see it nestled in a teaspoon in Jerome Wexler's photograph in *Pet Mice.*

The teaspoon is this photograph provides scale for the size of a five-day-old mouse. (Source: Illustration from PET MICE by Jerome Wexler reprinted by permission of the author.)

Perhaps the new information is detail, for instance, exactly what poison ivy leaves look like, or how the scales on a snake may be either ridged or smooth. Although photographs may appear to be the most objective medium for nonfiction illustration, all illustration involves choice on the part of the illustrator. The photographer decides what to record on film, and children can learn to look for point of view expressed in photography as in other media (Barrett and Marantz).

Illustrations can clarify information by presenting it in diagram form. In *Who Eats What?,* Patricia Lauber describes the food chain, giving several specific examples, then shows how disruptions in the chain have far-reaching

A flow chart shows four links in a food chain in this illustration. (Source: Illustrations and text from WHO EATS WHAT? FOOD CHAINS AND FOOD WEBS by Patricia Lauber. Text copyright © 1995 by Patricia Lauber, Illustrations Copyright © 1995 by Holly Keller. Reprinted by permission of HarperCollins Publishers.)

Here a cutaway drawing shows the same four links in the food chain shown in the previous illustration. (Source: Illustrations and text from WHO EATS WHAT? FOOD CHAINS AND FOOD WEBS by Patricia Lauber. Text copyright © 1995 by Patricia Lauber, Illustrations Copyright © 1995 by Holly Keller. Reprinted by permission of HarperCollins Publishers.)

effects. Holly Keller's illustrations show who is eating what in two different ways. One is like a flow chart, with arrows showing that the leaf is eaten by the caterpillar, which is eaten by the wren, which is eaten by the hawk. These are four links in one food chain. This same information is shown in a cutaway drawing in which each link is inside the creature that ate it; leaf inside caterpillar inside wren inside hawk.

As you share books with children, you may want to talk with them about their interpretations of diagrams rather than simply assuming they understand. Figure 11-3 shows a kindergarten teacher working with her children in interpreting a very basic cutaway illustration. By having the children actually remove soil to expose the bulb and roots of a plant, she built on concrete experience to help them comprehend the more abstract representation.

Drawings, paintings, or photographs in informational books should stand on their own as good art. It is important to recognize, however, that photographs are not necessarily more "factual" than other modes of illustra-

The kindergartners in Kanha's class were excited about the tulips they were growing. If all went well, the flowers would be in bloom by Mother's Day and would become beautiful gifts. Each child had labeled his or her pot, decorated it, and was in charge of watering it every Monday and Friday. Five extra pots with bulbs were designated as replacements if any were needed, or as flowers for the classroom.

Kanha had read *Giving* by Shirley Hughes (Cambridge, MA: Candlewick, 1993) and the class had discussed many ways that people can give to one another, especially the hugs, smiles, and help that children can give. They had also talked about what plants need to grow and were monitoring water and sunlight.

Kanha found several informational books about plants. As she perused them, she recognized an opportunity to help children learn to read diagrams. In the books were several cutaway drawings, even one that showed a tulip in bloom and the bulb and root system beneath the ground. Holding up the page with that illustration, she asked the children what it showed. They readily responded that it was a tulip and that the artist had drawn what showed and what was "underneath the dirt." "How did he know what was underneath the dirt?" she asked.

They answered that he must have dug up a tulip. "If we dig up one of ours, do you think it would look this way?" Most said yes. They then took one of the five extra plants and checked their predictions.

The following week, Kanha brought in three books by Gallimard Jeunesse: *The Tree* (New York: Scholastic, 1992), *Fruit* (New York: Scholastic, 1992), and *Vegetables in the Garden* (New York: Scholastic, 1994), all in the First Discovery series. The books feature transparent pages interspersed between the regular pages so that color on those pages will cover part of an illustration. Thus a tree can be seen with grass under it, but when the transparent page with the grass is turned, the soil under the tree and the tree's root system are revealed. Children delighted in making predictions about what they would see and then turning the page to see what remained when layers had been removed.

Figure 11-3   Reading diagrams.

tion. Barrett and Marantz caution that photographs may vary in how much they stress the factuality of the medium.

> Photographs can be said to fit on a continuum with two poles: at one end are those that are straight-forward, direct, and realistic renderings of actual objects, people, or places; at the other end are those that are overtly and obviously directed, manipulated, and fictional, using props and models and actors. (227)

Illustrations should also blend with the text, capturing the same joy of discovery that propels text readers from page to page. That means, to begin with, that illustrations should be near passages they illustrate or extend. They should be accurate, like the text, and the media and style of the artwork should match the nature of the material. Some books profit from photographic realism, others from diagrams or elaborate paintings. The illustrator's basic responsibility is not much different from the obligation of the writer. Art and text in informational books encourage readers to travel down a foreign road, observing and learning throughout the trip.

The Value of Informational Books

For many children, nonfiction is the genre of choice. That is, they would select it rather than fiction for pleasure reading. Making nonfiction readily available in the classroom is a recognition of these children's preferences. Many teachers select nonfiction books as read-alouds, often combining them with fiction books on the same or a similar topic (Moss 124).

Reading nonfiction lets children explore topics in a context that strives to make it meaningful. As teachers present information in integrated units, they need books that address the various facets of a topic (Doiron) and that allow children to select what most interests them. These same books provide models for report writing (Freeman). Robb (241) stresses the usefulness of giving children time to browse through books, perhaps talking with partners about what they are discovering, as a first step in researching a topic. In fact,

---

A. **Accuracy**
   The facts presented are accurate.
   The facts are shown in context and are used to support
     generalizations.
   Important facts are not omitted.
   Opinions and theories are differentiated from facts.
   Sources of information are documented.

B. **Organization**
   The material is organized logically.
   The organization is easily discernable.
   Specific information can be found, often through an index or
     table of contents.

C. **Writing Style**
   The writing is interesting and understandable.
   The tone of the writing shows the author's attitude toward the
     subject.
   The author avoids anthropomorphism and teleology.

D. **Illustrations**
   The illustrations are accurate.
   The illustrations enhance and extend the text.
   The illustrations have artistic merit.

Figure 11-4   Guidelines for evaluating nonfiction.

she had the second-grade students with whom she was working spend several days browsing before they began collecting information.

Informational books even lend themselves to author studies, where children see how particular nonfiction writers approach their subjects, how they organize their information, and how they use illustrations to extend the text (Duthie).

Figure 11-6 at the end of this chapter lists a sampling of outstanding informational books for children. Look also in the Appendix A for the list of winners of the Orbis Pictus Award for Outstanding Nonfiction for Children, given annually by the National Council of Teachers of English for the most outstanding nonfiction book of the previous year.

BIOGRAPHY: FACTUAL PORTRAITS

Stanley has written biographies of Shaka, the Zulu King, of William Shakespeare, of Queen Elizabeth I of England, and of Cleopatra.

Biography is a story centering on a person who actually existed or exists. As such, there is almost a built-in narrative structure. But writers of a biography must do more than list the chronology of important events in a person's life. Diane Stanley, who has written several biographies in picture book form, selected Peter the Great as the subject for her first biography. She had studied Russian history in college, read Russian novels, and had visited Moscow and Leningrad. It seemed a perfect choice, given her knowledge.

Soon the difficulties became apparent. How to write this man's story in a 32-page picture book was the first. It meant being very selective, telling what it was that made Peter "great," and telling it in a way children could understand. Then there were some aspects of his life that seemed rather boring, and others that seemed inappropriate for young children. Diane Stanley writes:

> I did not discuss Peter's family life, since I would have had to explain that he put his first wife away in a nunnery in order to make room for his mistress, Catherine, whom he only married after they had lived together openly for years. I would also have been forced to explain that his son died in prison under suspicious circumstances, probably as a result of torture inflicted on Peter's orders—perhaps even by his own hand. This material seemed a bit shocking for the target age group (though they probably hear worse on the evening news), and I personally believe in protecting our children from some of life's harsher realities, at least for a while.
>
> Because the absence of Peter's family from the narrative has been mentioned in reviews, I have wondered since whether the better approach would have been to mention some, but not all, of that story. Yet I am uncomfortable with that option since it would leave a false impression. (213)

Stanley goes on to note the change in biographies for young children, from writing only about "spotless heroes after whom the young readers would want to model their lives" (213) to writing about complex personalities with both strengths and weaknesses. While it is likely that biographers will continue to portray important people—men and women whose lives can stir ambitions, perk interest in the period in which they lived, and raise ideals—they may also portray interesting and influential people who were not paragons.

Biography in Many Forms

There are many ways to write biography, and not all of them depend on presenting a "whole" person. Biographers are not required to tell every known fact about a subject from birth to death. They may focus on a few years in their subject's life and may fictionalize part of the account of those years. They may even write in the first person to create a narrative as if told by the subject. Some biographies deal with one person; others present the lives of several people grouped around a single theme. So biography may be sorted out in several ways.

Use of Factual Data

Nonfiction Biography.   Jean Fritz's *You Want Women to Vote, Lizzie Stanton?* has reliable sources for all its information. The book presents her early years, her travels around the country supporting women's rights and women's suffrage, her marriage to Henry Stanton, and her friendship and political alliance with Susan B. Anthony. The relationship between the two women is documented through letters and actual quotes, with the sources noted at the back of the book. This is a scholarly work, with all the care and notation of a research paper, but with a lively writing style that pulls readers in. Children who had read *Bloomers!* would find this book an extension of the characters' lives and a more thorough analysis. The two books also present the opportunity to explore how two different authors selected part of the same "story" to tell and how they approached their tellings. This type of activity works well with children comparing several biographies of the same person, too. Another approach to biography in picture book form, shown in Figure 11-5, is for children to read a biography and then describe what they have learned from the illustrations that was not in the text.

Fictionalized Biography.   The most common type of biography for young readers, fictionalized biography, is similar to historical fiction: The author is bound by what is known from historical research and may not change these facts. But the writer does create some scenes, dialogue, or thoughts to mesh reasonably with what is known. Author Kathryn Laskey, for example, had no personal documents, no diaries, no letters, no records of conversations to use in her biography of Eratosthenes, the mathematician and librarian who figured out a way to measure the circumference of the earth in the third century B.C. His measurements were within 200 miles of the figure determined with modern technology. So in *The Librarian Who Measured the Earth,* she creates the kind of inquisitive child he must have been and fills in the personal aspects of his life around what is known of his accomplishments. In her author's note, she explains to readers that there is much that is not known about Eratosthenes himself, but that much *is* known about the time and place he lived. This helps a biographer imagine what might have been.

The story of Eratosthenes' life is easily understood by children in the primary grades, but the mathematics he used in measuring the earth is too abstract for most young children. Thus primary grade teachers usually focus on the story and the importance of what he did, not on how he did it.

The second graders in Varda's class were reading and sharing biographies. They had listened as the school media specialist read *A Boy Called Slow: The True Story of Sitting Bull* (Joseph Bruchac. Ill. by Rocco Baviera. New York: Philomel, 1995) to them, and now wanted to read about "real" people. They had learned where the section on biographies was located and had each selected at least one biography. As Varda listened to the children talking about their books, she realized that illustrations had played a key role in their selections. She decided to use this opportunity to extend their observation and appreciation of illustrations in biography and nonfiction.

Varda called the class together and asked the children to tell her what they had learned about Sitting Bull from *A Boy Called Slow.* After they had responded, she held up the book and asked them to look as she slowly showed each illustration and to identify new information presented in the pictures. The children described details and made generalizations based on what they'd observed.

She then asked the children to prepare for their next small-group discussion by looking again at the biography each had chosen and listing in their response journals at least three things they'd learned from the illustrations that were not in the text. The next day, the children shared their journal entries and showed the illustrations. A child who had read *A Letter from Phoenix Farm,* an autobiography of Jane Yolen (Ill. by Jason Stemple. Katonah, New York: Owen, 1992), said:

1. She has lots of books in her house.
2. She likes to walk in the country.
3. She listens to what her husband says about her books, but it's not always easy.
4. Sometimes she wears her glasses and sometimes she doesn't.
5. She must have a lot of money because she lives in a big house.

As she moved around from group to group, Varda encouraged the children to point out the details they had observed (learning at a literal level) and to tell how they had reached other conclusions (often at the inferential level). For example, the child who had been reading about Jane Yolen could point to some pictures in which she was wearing glasses and others in which she wasn't, a literal-level observation. In explaining that it wasn't always easy for her to listen to her husband's comments, the child pointed to the third in a series of photographs in which Jane is listening to her husband as he is pointing to specific places in a manuscript. "See how she has her hand over her eyes. That's what you feel like doing when someone keeps telling you what's wrong. It's not easy."

Varda felt that the children were becoming more aware of the information conveyed through illustrations and that they were using high-level thinking skills as they made and explained generalizations and inferences.

Figure 11-5   Learning from the illustrations in biographies.

A fictional character, Danny O'Riley, helps John Thompson, a man who lived in California in the 1850s, make skis in this fictionalized biography. (Source: Illustration FROM SHOW-SHOE THOMPSON by Nancy Smiler Levinson. Illustration Copyright © 1992 by Joan Sandlin. Reprinted by permission of HarperCollins Publishers.)

Some fictionalized biographies are more fiction than fact and are sometimes termed **biographical fiction.** In the I-Can-Read book *Snowshoe Thompson* (Levinson), the author creates a young boy named Danny O'Riley, who wants to send a letter from his home in California to his father, who is digging gold in Nevada. Set in the 1850s, the story is based on the true story of John Thompson, who moved to Placerville, California, from Norway during the gold rush days. He could carry bags of mail weighing as much as 100 pounds.

Thompson tells Danny he can make it across the Sierra Nevada Mountains, even though the snow is deep. He makes a pair of skis, and Danny helps to sand them. Thompson travels across the mountains and back in five days, delivering Danny's letter and bringing a response to Danny from his father. This book is almost totally fiction, although the story centers on a famous person.

Stage of Life

Childhood   It was once widely held that children do not like to read about adults, that young readers cannot understand what is happening in books about grown-ups. For that reason, biographies usually told stories about great people as children. Some of what resulted was lopsided and trivial.

Lincoln was depicted as not more than honest, hard-working, and, occasionally, funny. Some of what resulted was myth. George Washington, in fact, never chopped down the cherry tree.

Now that view has changed, and children can choose understandable stories about the adult life of interesting people. Some good books, however, still focus on the subject as a child. It makes sense in *Kate Shelley: Bound for Legend* (San Souci) because the action for which Shelley is known occurred when she was 15-years-old. Kate lived on an Iowa farm, and knew about the railroad because her father had been a section foreman on the Chicago & North Western Railway. Even after her father's death, Kate was fascinated by trains. One night in 1881, in the midst of a fierce rain storm, Kate and her mother heard a steam engine crash on the bridge close to their home. Kate realized that the men would be in trouble and that the midnight train with hundreds of passengers was due soon. Kate crawled across the bridge, from railroad tie to railroad tie, to reach the station in an attempt to stop the passenger train and get help for the men floundering in the creek. Her heroism made her a local legend, even though the train had been stopped before she arrived at the station. In this biography, only two pages describe her later life, for the action that made Kate known was done when she was young.

Adulthood.   The biography *Cleopatra* by Diane Stanley, on the other hand, opens when Cleopatra is 18 years old and has become Queen of Egypt. This is when the events for which she became famous began. In the preface, Stanley explains that although many people think of Cleopatra as Egyptian, she was in fact Greek and lived after the time of the Pharaohs. Cleopatra's story is complex, for her desire to see Egypt returned to its former power and glory was opposed by Julius Caesar and his successors, who envisioned the world under Roman rule. Stanley notes that if Cleopatra had been successful, she and her descendants, rather than the emperors of Rome, would have ruled the Western world.

A preface, an epilogue, and a page of author's notes give readers background about this highly political story. In addition, within the text itself, Stanley identifies areas where it is difficult to know what really happened or why characters acted as they did. At the battle of Actium, both Cleopatra and Marc Antony deserted their fleets. Perhaps Cleopatra was, as the Romans believed, fleeing for her life. Yet her ships were equipped with sails, so they could function in the open seas, and baggage and treasure were stored on board. Perhaps Cleopatra had planned to return to Egypt as part of an agreement by which Antony's officers would be appeased and she could save her ships. And what about Antony, whose fleet surrendered to the Roman Octavian after he left to follow Cleopatra? Was he acting on a plan he and Cleopatra had made, or was he a coward as Octavian later said?

Adult lives make more complex narratives than do childhood ones, both for the writer, who must select and explain, and the reader, who must make a greater experiential leap in order to understand.

Complete or Nearly Total Lifespan.   Complete biographies trace the most significant events in a subject's life from birth to death. They enable readers to see such things as the effects of a harsh childhood and to understand the complex forces that shape personality as a person matures.

Andrea Pinkney, in her biography of *Alvin Ailey,* selects highlights in his life. When the book opens, he is a child in Texas, where he responds to the gospel music at the True Vine Baptist Church. Then he and his mother move to Los Angeles, where he sees Katherine Dunham and her dancers, and is enthralled by the fact that this group of black performers are showcasing the dances of black people. Ailey begins to study dance and to develop his own style. Finally, the book shows his move to New York to continue studying, his formation of the Alvin Ailey American Dance Theater, and the many awards and honors he and his company won.

Readers see how this gifted dancer and choreographer developed over a lifetime. The illustrations by Brian Pinkney capture his grace and strength. In fact, both the Pinkneys took dance lessons from Ella Thompson Moore, who had been a dancer in Ailey's company, as preparation for creating this biography (Bishop 46).

In a picture book biography of Betsy Ross, author Alexandra Wallner shows how what was basically one moment of glory—sewing the American flag—fit into a full lifetime. Betsy was born into a Quaker family, the eighth of 17 children. At home all the children had chores and Betsy's was sewing. At the Quaker school she attended, she enjoyed making quilts with complicated designs and won prizes for her needlework. Eventually she married John Ross, and they set up their own shop.

George Washington learned about her from Colonel George Ross, John's uncle, and they brought a design for the flag to Betsy. She redesigned the flag before sewing it, and it was her design that was accepted on June 14, 1777, as the official flag. She continued with her sewing, and after John died, remarried and ran an upholstery shop with the help of her daughter, granddaughter, and nieces.

Partial Biography.   Partial biography offers only a portion of the subject's life or relates a few incidents grouped around one theme, giving readers a taste and stimulating their appetite for more. Jean Fritz's *Why Don't You Get a Horse, Sam Adams?* is based on Adams' refusal to ride horseback, even when he has to escape from the British at Lexington. John Adams argues that great statesmen of great nations have always ridden horses, and since Sam is a great statesman of a great nation, he ought to get a horse, too. Sam Adams does, and rides it, and along the comparatively short and humorous trail the reader travels through some of the events leading to the American Revolution.

Single or Collective Biographies.   Some biographical books comprise stories of several subjects—great black scientists, for example, or war heroes. Pat Cummings, in *Talking With Artists,* interviewed 14 illustrators of children's books, asking them the same set of questions. They tell about their work, where they get their ideas, and how they got to do their first book. Each section includes examples of the illustrators' work and pictures of them as children and as adults.

Collected biographies can provide a strong introduction to biography because children can read about different people who have something in common and then describe and answer questions about "their person."

Betsy Ross's redesigning and sewing of the American flag fit into a lifetime of sewing and upholstery work. (Source: Illustration from BETSY ROSS Copyright © 1994 by Alexandria Wallner. All rights reserved. Reprinted from BETSY ROSS by permission of Holiday House, Inc.)

Children can compare the process of writing autobiography with that of writing biography by writing first about themselves and then about a classmate.

Point-of-View

First Person.   The biographical sketches in *Talking With Artists* are in first person, as each artist talks about his or her life. And, obviously, **autobiographies,** life stories written by the person they are about, are in first person. The "Meet the Author" series, published by Richard C. Owen, features different authors of children's books in separate autobiographies, illustrated with color photographs that reflect the writers' homes and lives.

Third Person.   The narrator of an autobiography is free to tell a tale without qualification or credential. "I was there" usually replaces research. The narrator of a nonfictional third person story has to reflect the historical record and let the reader know when the record has blank pages, as Stanley does in *Cleopatra.*

Evaluating Biography

Accuracy and Honesty.   By letting readers know that she did not have all the answers about Cleopatra, Stanley was supporting the authenticity of her book. For the same reason, most authors of good biography list sources and often tell which parts of the story, if any, are fiction. This allows readers to judge the accuracy of a book themselves.

There is more to accuracy than supporting detail, however. Individual dress may look right, and there may be several witnesses to what was said, but the overall picture may be flawed, sometimes by what is left out.

The central character in *Kit Carson* (Gleiter and Thompson), one in a series of "First Biographies," the "life stories of legendary American heroes," learned to respect Native Americans while still a child. He traveled to New Mexico where he learned Spanish and several Native American languages, was a trapper for 12 years, married an Arapaho woman, explored with and was a guide for Charles Fremont, and finally became a messenger between the government and the Utes. The last illustration in the book shows a large portrait of Carson in soft colors, with a smaller image of a Native American couple superimposed on it.

Jeanette Winter illustrated her biography of Diego Rivera with pictures that mirror the style and content of his paintings. (Source: Illustration and text from DIEGO by Jeanette Winter and Jonah Winter, Copyright © 1991 by Alfred A. Knopf, Inc. Reprinted by permission of Alfred A. Knopf, Inc.)

Demi uses gold tones and large white spaces to depict events in the life of Ghengis Khan. (Source: Illustration from CHINGIS KHAN by Demi. Copyright © 1991 by Demi. Reprinted by permission of Henry Holt and Co., Inc.)

Kit Carson fails to mention that in June 1863, Carson invaded the Navaho country of northern Arizona, under orders from the United States government. He destroyed crops and livestock and killed Indians who fought back.

Real people have faults. And for the sake of honesty, biographers have a responsibility to present these faults. Good biography does not eulogize. Figure 11-7 at the end of this chapter lists Touchstone biographies for children.

Accuracy and Honesty in Illustration.   Illustrators share the responsibility for accuracy. Details must be correct and must support the spirit of the writing. Trina Schart Hyman, for instance, drew a funny picture of Sam Adams thumbing his nose at a portrait of King George standing outside "Ye George" tavern in *Why Don't You Get a Horse, Sam Adams?* Buildings, wharves, and the dress of Boston residents appear as quiet background, just as historical detail flavors the humorous text by Jean Fritz.

Jeanette Winter illustrated *Diego,* about Mexican artist Diego Rivera, with illustrations that mirror the style and content of his paintings.

Demi uses gold tones and large white spaces to show the life of Ghengis Khan *(Chingis Khan)* in her biography, based on both fact and legend, of the Mongol chieftain who conquered Persia and China. In the illustration shown, five-year-old Temujin is herding camels to protect them from wolves. The illustrations match the epic quality of this fictionalized biography.

Quality of Writing.   Accuracy does not count for much if the writing is second-rate. A good story is much more important to a young reader than the weight of the research, the number of footnotes, or even the name of the subject. A child who has never considered modern dance or knows little of jazz may be caught up in the story of *Alvin Ailey,* with its clear and flowing language and strong narration. That same child, who may well have seen movies about Kit Carson, may not want to read further than page one of *Kit Carson* by Gleiter and Thompson. There are 11 sentences on that first page, all following the same "subject—verb—object" pattern and all but three having only five to seven words. The style is stilted and boring.

Context.   Milton Meltzer, author of many biographies and nonfiction books, writes about biography as one form of history.

> If biography is well done, it is also social history. As a biographer, I don't believe my only subject is the man or woman I am writing about. If my book is any good, it must tell the story of my subject's time and of the people who live through that time. If all I were to manage is a closeup of one figure against a blank wall, I would not be doing my job. (1–2)

Good biography provides the social context for its subject. Fisher gives two contexts for the life and work of Johann Gutenberg *(Gutenberg),* that of 15th-

Leonard Fisher provides a social context for the life and work of Johann Gutenberg, the subject of this biography. (Source: Illustration reprinted with the permission of Atheneum Books for Young Readers, an imprint of Simon & Schuster from GUTENBERG by Leonard Everett Fisher. Copyright © 1993 Leonard Everett Fisher.)

century Europe in which he lived and that of the history of modern printing, into which his work fit. Readers are presented with his insight into business dealings of the day, from Gutenberg's secret work on developing movable type, with hopes of becoming the only master printer in Europe, to his eventual loss of all his materials and his print shop to his partner, who completed the printing of Gutenberg's Bible and kept all the profits from the sale of copies. They also learn of the importance of this printing press in making books available to ordinary people in Europe and thus encouraging them to learn to read.

The Value of Biography

In her book *Learning About Biographies,* Myra Zarnowski opens with a clear position statement:

> Biography is appropriate material for children because it bridges what they already know and understand with what they need—and even *want*—to learn. This is so for several reasons. First, biography resembles other narratives children enjoy, making it an easy transition from fiction to history. Second, biography teaches children information about the world in an accessible, engaging way. Third, reading and writing biography teaches children about the role of interpretation in nonfiction writing. Children begin to realize that more than "facts" are involved. (6)

Biography is enjoyable reading and a way for children to learn about the world as well as about the process used by historians and biographers to select and present their material. Close contact with strangers from another time or place and with public figures they may see on television or hear their parents discuss can dramatize to children the possibilities for human choice and show the constraints of human society. It can show how human emotions are constant through changing times and customs.

Jean Fritz talks about biographies as if they are charts revealing hidden countries we may never actually see. "In actual experience," she writes, "we are able to see so few lives in the round and to follow them closely from beginning to end. I for one need to possess a certain number of relatively whole lives in the long span of history" (193). Biography lets children see lives in context, with an immediacy and intimacy that makes whole periods and whole places come alive.

SUMMARY

Informational, or nonfiction, books are designed to present concepts and generalizations about a particular topic rather than tell a story, although they may do both. Good nonfiction both supplements and stimulates direct experience. It broadens children's knowledge as they research topics of interest, and it presents new topics that capture their attention.

Nonfiction can be judged by four basic criteria. First, its pattern of organization and accuracy is shown through such markers as a table of contents, index, and author's qualifications. Second, the facts it presents are grouped and analyzed so readers can see principles, generalizations, and patterns, and the facts are not misleading because of simplification or selection. Third, the writing is compelling. And fourth, the illustrations are accurate and add information.

Biography is a story centering on the life of a person who exists or existed. It comes in many forms. Biography may be authentic, with only documented information and dialogue or fictionalized, with scenes and dialogue created. Biography may encompass only the subject's childhood, only his or her adult life, the total lifespan, or specific times or incidents. Biographies may be single, about one person, or collective, usually several people grouped by a common quality or accomplishment. And biographies may be told in first person or third person.

Biographies can be evaluated by the accuracy and honesty of both text and illustrations, with attention to what is omitted as well as what is included, the quality of the writing, and the degree to which the subject of the biography is portrayed in context. Like other informational books, biography can both initiate and extend a child's interest in a particular person or topic.

Ancona, George. *Powwow*. San Diego: Harcourt, 1993. These photographs of many different Native American dances being performed at a powwow on the Crow Reservation in Montana are accompanied by clear and descriptive text.

Arnosky, Jim. *All About Owls*. New York: Scholastic, 1995. The life-size illustration of a great-horned owl takes up the first three pages of the book and sets the tone for this informative book about owls.

Brandenberg, Aliki. *I'm Growing*. New York: HarperCollins, 1992. This simple picture book shows how people grow and explains differences in size and appearance.

Bryan, Ashley. *All Night, All Day: A Child's First Book of African American Spirituals*. New York: Atheneum, 1991. The vivid illustrations capture the mood of the 20 spirituals, with piano and guitar accompaniments included.

Burleigh, Robert. *Flight: The Journey of Charles Lindbergh*. Ill. by Mike Wimmer. New York: Philomel, 1991. Lindbergh's transatlantic flight, with all its suspense and loneliness, is presented in an accurate narrative.

Cole, Joanna. *The Magic School Bus on the Ocean Floor*. Ill. by Bruce Degen. New York: Scholastic, 1992. Mrs. Frizzle, the science teacher, once again takes her class on a memorable field trip that combines the fantasy of the trip with nonfiction in charts and reports that her students create.

French, Vivian. *Caterpillar Caterpillar*. Ill. by Charlotte Voake. Cambridge, MA: Candlewick, 1993. A young girl learns about caterpillars from her grandfather in this book that combines text with carefully labeled illustrations.

Figure 11-6 Touchstone informational books.

Fritz, Jean. *Shh! We're Writing the Constitution.* Ill. by Tomie dePaola. New York: Putnam's, 1987. The writing of this important document is described in the context of both its political importance and the details of real people working under difficult conditions.

Heller, Ruth. *Chickens Aren't the Only Ones.* New York: Scholastic, 1981. This very simple rhyming text explains that chickens aren't the only animals that lay eggs; it also presents animal classifications.

Johnson, Sylvia A. *Raptor Rescue!* Ill. by Ron Winch. New York: Dutton, 1995. The veterinarians in this book have birds of prey as patients, treating as many as 600 raptors each year.

Lankford, Mary D. *Hopscotch Around the World.* Ill. by Karen Milone. New York: Morrow, 1992. Nineteen different versions of hopscotch are described, with rules for playing and a little about the country where each is played.

Markle, Sandra. *Measuring Up!: Experiments, Puzzles, and Games Exploring Measurement.* New York: Atheneum, 1995. Readers are encouraged to try various experiments and to solve puzzles that involve measurement for their solutions.

Simon, Seymour. *Snakes.* New York: HarperCollins, 1992. This smoothly flowing narrative gives much information about snakes and is accompanied by full-page color photographs.

Wexler, Jerome. *Sundew Stranglers: Plants That Eat Insects.* New York: Dutton, 1995. Wexler's close-up color photographs enhance a topic already fascinating to children.

Wolf, Bernard. *Homeless.* New York: Orchard, 1995. One family's life as they search for affordable housing in New York is portrayed realistically and sympathetically.

Figure 11-6 *continued*

Adler, David. *A Picture Book of Helen Keller.* Ill. by John and Alexandra Wallner. New York: Holiday, 1990. Helen Keller's life and accomplishments are clearly and simply presented.

Aliki. *The King's Day: Louis XIV of France.* New York: Crowell, 1989. The focus is one day in the life of the king, showing him and his courtiers engaged in their regular rituals.

Bruchac, Joseph. *A Boy Called Slow: The True Story of Sitting Bull.* Ill. by Rocco Baviera. New York: Philomel, 1995. This coming-of-age story shows how Slow earned the name of Sitting Bull.

Fritz, Jean. *What's the Big Idea, Ben Franklin?* Ill. by Margot Tomes. New York: Putnam, 1976. In this well-researched narrative, Fritz shows the course of Franklin's career from apprentice to renowned inventor and statesman.

Giblin, James Cross. *George Washington: A Picture Book Biography.* Ill. by Michael Dooling. New York: Scholastic, 1992. The author simplifies without distorting major events in Washington's life.

Hoyt-Goldsmith, Diane. *Hoang Anh: A Vietnamese-American Boy.* Ill. by Lawrence Migdale. New York: Holiday, 1992. Chau tells about his life in Vietnam and in America, with rich details of family life and cultural traditions.

Krull, Kathleen. *Lives of the Musicians.* Ill. by Kathryn Hewitt. San Diego: Harcourt, 1993. In this collective biography, Krull describes the daily lives and the music of 19 musicians, from Bach to Woody Guthrie.

Mahy, Margaret. *My Mysterious World.* Katonah, NY: Owen, 1995. One of the "Meet-the-Author" series, this book lets Mahy share her personality and zany actions with children as she tells about her writing.

Figure 11-7 Touchstone biographies.

McKissack, Patricia, and Fredrick McKissack. *Mary McLeod Bethune: A Great Teacher.* Ill. by Ned O. Hillside, NJ: Enslow, 1991. This is one in a series of short biographies of African American achievers.

Miller, William. *Frederick Douglass: The Last Days of Slavery.* Ill. by Cedric Lucas. New York: Lee, 1995. Text and illustrations portray the harsh realities of slavery that prompted Douglass to rebel and led to his career in the antislavery movement.

Provensen, Alice, and Martin Provensen. *The Glorious Flight: Across the Channel with Louis Bleriot, July 25, 1909.* New York: Viking, 1983. Louis Bleriot's struggles to construct an airplane are rewarded when he makes his successful flight across the English Channel.

Raimondo, Lois. *The Little Lama of Tibet.* New York: Scholastic, 1994. Ling Rinpoche, six-years-old and believed to be the reincarnation of a great teacher, is shown living in a monastery in Northern India.

Say, Allen. *El Chino.* Boston: Houghton, 1990. Billy Wong, a Chinese American, succeeds in becoming a matador in spite of the many obstacles in his way.

Stanley, Diane, and Peter Vennema. *Good Queen Bess: The Story of Elizabeth I of England.* Ill. by Diane Stanley. New York: Four Winds, 1990. The personality of Queen Elizabeth I shows as the authors present her intelligence, judgment, and love of the arts.

Whiteley, Opal. *Only Opal: The Diary of a Young Girl.* Selected by Jane Boulton. Ill. by Barbara Cooney. New York: Philomel, 1994. This biography is an adaptation of the diary of Opal Whiteley, who was taken in by a family in Oregon after she was orphaned at age five.

Figure 11-7 *continued*

∽ EXPLORE ON YOUR OWN

1. **Explore Your Personal Response.** Select a historical or public figure you admire and list three of their qualities or actions that you admire. Read a children's biography about the person you selected and see if the characteristics you noted appear in the book.
2. **Apply Literary Criteria.** Select a nonfiction children's book on a topic you know very little about. Evaluate how clearly the information is

presented. Assess how the book's organization either helped or hindered your understanding of the material.
3. **Prepare to Share Literature With Children.** Select an informational book to share with children. Write how you would introduce the book to draw the children's background knowledge of the subject into the discussion.

∽ EXPLORE WITH CHILDREN

1. **Explore Children's Responses.** Ask several children to list topics they find interesting. Then ask them if they have ever read a book about any of these topics. If so, how did they locate the book and what did they think of it? If not, what would they hope to find in a book about this topic?
2. **Engage Children With Literature.** Select two short informational books on the same topic or two biographies of the same person. Ask chil-

dren to suggest four things they would like to know about that topic or person. Show the two books and ask students to predict which of the two is the more likely to have the answers to their questions. Have them give the rationale for their predictions. With them check their predictions by using the index and table of contents and reading portions of the book.

∽ SUGGESTED PROFESSIONAL REFERENCES

Carr, Jo, Compiler. *Beyond Fact: Nonfiction for Children and Young People.* Chicago: American Library Association, 1982. § Well-known authors and critics write about nonfiction and biography for children, emphasizing criteria for selection and controversies stimulated by the genre.

Freeman, Evelyn B., and Diane Goetz Person, eds. *Using Nonfiction Trade Books in the Elementary Classroom: From Ants to Zeppelins.* Urbana, IL: National Council of Teachers of English, 1992. § In three sections the writers in this book address the genre of nonfiction, the use of nonfiction in specific subject areas, and nonfiction at the primary and the middle school level.

Graves, Donald. *Investigate Nonfiction.* Portsmouth, NH: Heinemann, 1989. § Graves shows how teachers and children alike both write and read nonfiction, with clear suggestions for actions that can be taken to develop nonfiction writing.

Saul, E. Wendy, ed. *Nonfiction for the Classroom: Milton Meltzer on Writing, History, and Social Responsibility.*

New York: Teachers College Press, 1994. § Saul has compiled and edited a series of articles, interviews, and speeches by Meltzer in an organized collection that shows Meltzer's approach to writing nonfiction and his concern for the study of history.

Tunnell, Michael O., and Richard Ammon, eds. *The Story of Ourselves: Teaching History Through Children's Literature.* Portsmouth, NH: Heinemann, 1993. § Children's writers and educators at the elementary/secondary and college levels describe both the difficulties in writing good historical fiction and the promise it provides for stimulating studies in history.

Zarnowski, Myra. *Learning About Biographies: A Reading-and-Writing Approach for Children.* Urbana, IL: National Council of Teachers of English, 1990. § Many practical suggestions for engaging children in both reading and writing biographies are woven into a clear theoretical framework.

CHILDREN'S BOOKS CITED

Aliki. *How a Book Is Made.* New York: Crowell, 1986.

Arnosky, Jim. *Crinkleroot's Guide to Walking in Wild Places.* New York: Bradbury, 1990.

Arnosky, Jim. *I See Animals Hiding.* New York: Scholastic, 1995.

Berger, Melvin. *Germs Make Me Sick!* Ill. by Marylin Hafner. New York: Crowell, 1985.

Blumberg, Rhoda. *Bloomers!* Ill. by Mary Morgan. New York: Bradbury, 1993.

Brandenburg, Jim. *An American Safari: Adventures on the North American Prairie.* New York: Walker, 1995.

Cobb, Vicki. *Writing It Down.* Ill. by Marylin Hafner. New York: Lippincott, 1989.

Cummings, Pat, compiler and ed. *Talking With Artists.* New York: Bradbury, 1992.

Demi. *Chingis Khan.* New York: Holt, 1991.

Fisher, Leonard Everett. *Gutenberg.* New York: Macmillan, 1993.

Fritz, Jean. *Why Don't You Get a Horse, Sam Adams?* Ill. by Trina Schart Hyman. New York: Coward, 1974.

Fritz, Jean. *You Want Women to Vote, Lizzie Stanton?* Ill. by DyAnne DiSalvo-Ryan. New York: Putnam's, 1995.

Gibbons, Gail. *Sharks.* New York: Holiday House, 1992.

Gleiter, Jan, and Kathleen Thompson. *Kit Carson.* Ill. by Rick Whipple. Austin, TX: Raintree, 1995.

Isaacson, Philip. *A Short Walk Around the Pyramids & Through the World of Art.* New York: Knopf, 1993.

King-Smith, Dick. *All Pigs Are Beautiful.* Ill. by Anita Jeram. Cambridge, MA: Candlewick, 1995.

Lasky, Kathryn. *The Librarian Who Measured the Earth.* Ill. by Kevin Hawkes. Boston: Little, Brown, 1994.

Lauber, Patricia. *Who Eats What?* Ill. by Holly Keller. New York: HarperCollins, 1995.

Leedy, Loreen. *Tracks in the Sand.* New York: Doubleday, 1993.

Levinson, Nancy Smiler. *Snowshoe Thompson.* Ill. by Joan Sandin. New York: HarperCollins, 1992.

MacQuitty, Miranda. *Shark.* Eyewitness Books. New York: Knopf, 1992.

Markle, Sandra. *Outside and Inside Snakes.* New York: Macmillan, 1995.

Pinkney, Andrea. *Alvin Ailey.* Ill. by Brian Pinkney. New York: Hyperion, 1993.

Roop, Peter, and Connie Roop. *Off the Map: The Journals of Lewis and Clark.* Ill. by Tim Tanner. New York: Walker, 1993.

San Souci, Robert. *Kate Shelley: Bound for Legend.* Ill. by Max Ginsburg. New York: Dial, 1995.

Stanley, Diane. *Cleopatra.* Ill. by Peter Vennema. New York: Morrow, 1994.

Wallner, Alexandra. *Betsy Ross.* New York: Holiday, 1994.

Wexler, Jerome. *Pet Mice.* Niles, IL: Whitman, 1989.

Winter, Jonah. *Diego.* Ill. by Jeanette Winter. New York: Knopf, 1991.

CHAPTER REFERENCES

Barrett, Terry, and Kenneth Marantz. "Photographs as Illustrations." *The New Advocate* 2.4 (Fall 1989): 227–238.

Bishop, Rudine Sims. "The Pinkney Family: In the Tradition." *The Horn Book Magazine* 72.1 (Jan./Feb. 1996): 42–49.

Doiron, Ray. "Using Nonfiction in a Read-Aloud Program: Letting the Facts Speak for Themselves." *The Reading Teacher* 47 (May 1994): 616–624.

Duthie, Christine. "Nonfiction: A Genre Study for the Primary Classroom." *Language Arts* 71.8 (Dec. 1994): 588–595.

Freeman, Evelyn. "Informational Books: Models for Student Report Writing." *Language Arts* 68.6 (Oct. 1991): 470–473.

Fritz, Jean. "George Washington, My Father, and Walt Disney." *The Horn Book* (Apr. 1976): 191–198.

Meltzer, Milton. "Selective Forgetfulness: Christopher Columbus Reconsidered." *The New Advocate* 5.1 (Winter 1992): 1–9.

Moss, Barbara. "Using Children's Nonfiction Tradebooks as Read-Alouds." *Language Arts* 72.2 (Feb. 1995): 122–126.

Robb, Laura. "Second Graders Read Nonfiction: Investigating Natural Phenomena and Disasters." *The New Advocate* 7.4 (Fall 1994): 239–252.

Stanley, Diane. "Picture Book History." *The New Advocate* 1.4 (Fall 1988): 209–220.

Zarnowski, Myra. *Learning About Biographies: A Reading-and-Writing Approach for Children.* Urbana, IL: National Council of Teachers of English, 1990.

 **Chapter Twelve**

Changes Over Time: Society's View of the Child

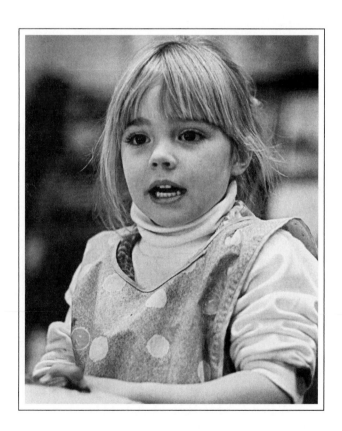

The trustees of the Seekonk, Massachusetts, Public Library scheduled a meeting for the nearly 50 residents of the town who had signed a petition expressing concern about a children's book recently purchased by the library and the equally large number of residents who circulated their own petition countering what they saw as an attempt at censorship. At the end of the meeting, the trustees voted to keep the book in the library and in the children's section. The chairwoman of the board stated that it was a picture book for children, and it belonged in the children's room of the library. "Parents have the right to choose, but that means they can choose to read it to their children or not," she stated (Borg A1).

The book in question was *Daddy's Roommate* by Michael Willhoite. It tells about a young boy's visit with his father, who is gay. The boy lives with his divorced mother and visits Daddy and Daddy's roommate Frank on weekends. The boy, Daddy, and Frank go to ballgames and watch movies together. His mother explains that Daddy and Frank are gay and that being gay is "just one more kind of love."

Some of the residents wanted the book banned totally, believing that homosexuality is evil and not an appropriate topic for children. "Ten years from now, you'll be debating whether to put books on pedophilia in the library. Even a good humanist would take a stand on this. Homosexuality is aberrant behavior. God calls it an abomination and a loathing," said one resident.

Another countered that children need to know about homosexuality. "Eight to ten million children have gay and lesbian parents. Children need to know that there are different kinds of families. We need to create an atmosphere of tolerance. It doesn't matter what we think; children need to be protected from racism, sexism, and homophobia."

Still another talked about his fear that if this book were banned, others might follow. "Reading is fundamental. It is not fundamentalist. It's very frightening when any library starts censoring books."

WHAT SHOULD A CHILD READ?

Issues of censorship are not new in the world of literature for children. Adults have strong and often differing beliefs about what is appropriate for children, and many of these beliefs are based on deeply held values. The parents at the Seekonk Library differed in their beliefs about homosexuality and therefore about whether *Daddy's Roommate* was an appropriate book for children. A parent in Brookville, Pennsylvania, complained about an illustration of a mug of beer in a book that played on words that sound alike but have different meanings. The child is saying how her father says that there is a head on his beer. The illustration shows the child's visualization of this statement. The parent was concerned about alcohol appearing in a book for children.

Some individuals are willing to have *their* values serve as guidelines for choosing reading material for all children. Others see the overriding issue as free access to materials and the need for each person—child or adult—to make selections. Keeping certain books out of a collection limits this access, so is not an acceptable solution to concerns about specific books.

Censors have been trying to ban books as long as there have been books, and you will read several examples in this chapter. The frank and explicit nature of some realism today means that the problem of censorship is likely to arise again and again. Both contemporary and historical realism will continue to offend people, and some books—sexist or racist stories, for instance—will offend many people. But every time a group bans a book, other books are threatened. Where censorship takes hold, opposing groups can claim with equal authority the right to decimate school or library shelves.

In its annual *Attacks on the Freedom to Learn* report, the People for the American Way reported 395 incidents of censorship in 44 states during the 1992–1993 school year. Censorship pressures on schools have been rising steadily during the 1980s and 1990s.

Librarians and teachers can take precautions against such actions by establishing a clear policy for dealing with complaints before they arise. The National Council of Teachers of English suggests printing a form for complainants to fill out, with space to specify objections. The form (shown in Figure 12-1) asks for recommendations about what should be done. It asks whether the complainant has read the whole book. The form clarifies objections, weeds out frivolous gripes, and helps ensure that the book's accuser will be aware of the context around offensive passages. It also ensures that the complaint will be seriously considered. Completed forms can be referred to a committee of concerned parents and school personnel. Many schools take the position that parents may prohibit their own children from reading certain books, but that they have no authority over what other people's children can read.

SOCIETY'S VIEW OF THE CHILD

In the 15th century, almost as soon as there were printed books, there was tension between teaching and entertaining as the purpose of literature. There has been no resolution of the tension, although throughout the intervening centuries a number of critics have urged that children's books should do both—instruct *and* delight. It is worth following the old debate over how books should be used because the arguments recur century after century. School boards and teachers, librarians and parents, continue to take sides today.

How adults have defined children has helped determine how they used literature in their times. Changing patterns of use, in other words, can be traced by exploring how adults in each age, from the invention of the printing press on, viewed their children.

The National Council of Teachers of English, in its publication *The Students' Right to Read* (revised, 1982), recommends that persons whose complaint about a book cannot be satisfied with a conversation with the teacher be asked to complete the following form. The form is then given to a review committee that evaluates the book and the complaint. Such a procedure assures the objector that the complaint is being taken seriously and allows the school to resist unreasonable pressures.

Citizen's Request for Reconsideration of a Work

Paperback _____

Author_____Hardcover _____

Title _____

Publisher (if known) _____

Request initiated by _____

Telephone _____Address _____

City _____Zip Code _____

Complainant represents

_____   Himself/Herself

_____   (Name organization)_____

_____   (Identify other group)_____

1.   Have you been able to discuss this work with the teacher or librarian who ordered it or who used it?
     _____ Yes _____ No

2.   What do you understand to be the general purpose for using this work?
     a.   Provide support for a unit in the curriculum?   _____ Yes _____ No
     b.   Provide a learning experience for the reader in one kind of literature?   _____ Yes _____ No
     c.   Other _____
          _____

3.   Did the general purpose for the use of this work, as described by the teacher or librarian, seem a suitable
     one to you?   _____ Yes _____ No
     If not, please explain. _____
     _____

Figure 12-1   Citizen's request for reconsideration of a book.
Source: The National Council of Teachers of English. *The Student's Right to Read.* Urbana, IL: Author. rev. 1982.

It is possible to chart at least four different philosophies over the past few centuries about who the child is. Young readers have been seen in many lights, some dark, some bright. Puritans viewed their offspring as sinners headed for hell. In later ages, unspoiled goodness and humor came to dominate the portraits of young people. Many observers today have adopted what is in some ways an earlier view: The child is again like an adult in facing heavy social problems.

Ideas about children, of course, do not suddenly change at midnight on a specific day. The dates used here to mark philosophies are somewhat arbi-

4. What do you think is the general purpose of the author in this book? _____

5. In what ways do you think a work of this nature is not suitable for the use the teacher or librarian wishes to carry out?

_____

_____

6. Have you been able to learn what is the students' response to this work?   _____ Yes _____ No

7. What response did the students make? _____

_____

8. Have you been able to learn from your school library what book reviewers or other students of literature have written about this work? _____ Yes _____ No

9. Would you like the teacher or librarian to give you a written summary of what book reviewers and other students have written about this book or film? _____ Yes _____ No

10. Do you have negative reviews of the book? _____ Yes _____ No

11. Where were they published? _____

12. Would you be willing to provide summaries of the reviews you have collected? _____ Yes _____ No

13. What would you like your library/school to do about this work?
    _____ Do not assign/lend it to my child.
    _____ Return it to the staff selection committee/department for reevaluation.
    _____ Other—Please explain. _____

14. In its place, what work would you recommend that would convey as valuable a picture and perspective of the subject treated? _____

_____

Signature _____

Date _____

Figure 12-1 *continued*

trary and indicate merely that a group of people in that time viewed their daughters and sons in a certain way. And their views strongly affected what young people got to read, just as your concept of your students will determine what books you offer them.

Inevitably your own philosophy will be shaped by the thinking of people in other eras. As you explore the thinking of the last few centuries, see if you can recognize fragments of earlier philosophies in your own feelings about children today. Imagine the child you will teach. Ask: Who are you?

Here are some answers.

The Child in Need of Salvation: 1671

At the time the printing press was invented in the mid-15th century, children were seen as little adults. They were dressed like adults, sat in on adult parties in the great halls of kings in the late Middle Ages, and listened to the old, sometimes bawdy stories told by wandering minstrels.

But then in the early 17th century, strong religious forces in England and in the American colonies put a dark cloak on the child. The Puritans in England believed that children were born sinners. Their beliefs traveled to America with early New England settlers.

In the harsh new land, children frequently died young. The pressing danger, however, was not death, but eternal damnation. So out of love and concern for their children's souls, Puritan parents decided that they should be saved as soon as possible. Books favored by the Puritans warned constantly of brimstone and extolled the joy of death after a sinless life on earth.

The warnings in *A Token for Children,* published by an English minister names James Janeway about 1671 (and in many later editions), were typical. As in most books of the age, the actual title covered almost half a page and previewed the contents: *An Exact Account of the Conversion, Holy and Exemplary Lives, and Joyful Deaths of Several Young Children.* Janeway's book contains about a dozen stories of children, each a diminutive preacher and moralist and each dwelling on death and the release it will provide. Printers in Boston adapted the book in the 18th century, adding passages Puritans thought important for New England children.

Instructional Tools

To frighten children away from sin with such material, the Puritans had to teach reading skills. So one result of conservative Puritan discipline was progressive legislation designed to ensure literacy. In 1647, 17 years after the founding of Boston, legislators passed a law about reading in Massachusetts. The law mandated that where schools were lacking, parents were required to teach "their children and apprentices perfectly to read the English tongue." And any town of 100 families had to set up a grammar school.

New England Primer.   The foremost book of instruction in reading was the *New England Primer.* Primers were originally books of private prayer, but the *New England Primer,* first published some time before 1690, included a section on the alphabet with rhymes for each letter (except, for unknown reasons, *I* and *V,* which were omitted) and a catechism—a summary of religious belief in question-and-answer form. The catechism was taken from an earlier tome by John Cotton called *Spiritual Milk for Boston Babes in Either England Drawn from the Breasts of Both Testaments for Their Souls' Nourishment.* Children had to memorize the answers. Even the alphabet section of the *Primer* taught the faith:

6

N.
Nightingales sing
In time of Spring.

O.
The Owl at night
Hoots out of sight.

P.
Peter denied
His Lord, and cry'd.

Q.
Queens & kings must
Lie in the dust.

R.
The Rose in bloom
Sheds sweet perfume.

S.
Samuel anoints
Whom God appoints.

7

T.
Time cuts down all,
Both great and small.

U.
Urns hold, we see,
Coffee and tea.

W.
Whales in the sea
God's voice obey.

X.
Xerxes the great
Shar'd common fate.

Y.
Youth should delight
In doing right.

Z.
Zaccheus, he
Did climb the tree
His Lord to see.

The New England Primer *was the foremost book of instruction in reading for Puritan children. (Source:* Illustration from BEAUTIES OF THE NEW-ENGLAND PRIMER, New York: Published by Samuel Wood & Sons, 1818, in YANKEE DOODLES LITERARY SAMPLER OF PROSE, POETRY, & PICTURES by Virginia Haviland and Margaret Couglin, eds., Crowell, 1974.)

A
In Adam's fall
We sinned all.

Another version was:

A
Adam and Eve
Their God did grieve.

Forms of the primers, like Janeway's *Token,* lasted decades. For a while in the 18th century, a picture of King George III appeared on the frontispiece, but after the revolution, he was deposed in American primers and replaced by George Washington. The lessons inside remained unflaggingly religious despite minor changes in wording.

Hornbooks. Puritan schoolchildren used another device to learn to read, called a **hornbook,** though it was neither a book nor a horn. It was a single

The lesson sheet was nearly the same on all horn books, but the "book" itself was sometimes made of ivory, metal, or leather rather than wood and might be elaborately carved, tooled, or embossed.

sheet of paper glued to a piece of wood cut in the shape of a small paddle, about 3 inches wide by 5 inches long. A transparent shaving of animal horn covered and protected the paper. Thin brass strips held the horn in place. Again, the contents blended religion with basic skills needed for reading: The paper displayed the alphabet and the Lord's Prayer.

Adventure Stories

Ballads and fairy tales were banned by unwritten law in Boston and all over the new colonies. But the religious fare of the 17th century occasionally offered some adult-approved adventure and excitement to young readers. The most popular author of the century among children was probably John Bunyan (1628–1688), a Puritan preacher in England who grew up tormented by nightmares about hellfire. Bunyan was jailed because of his nonconformist sermons, and began to write his famous *Pilgrim's Progress* (1678) in a cell. The story grew out of his own dramatic dreams, forged into a story by his prison experience.

The book was about Christian, a pilgrim on an epic journey through life. Like all epics, there were snares and battles along the way, including lions, a monster named Apollyon, a jail cell in Doubtful Castle, and a happily-ever-after destination, and the glimmering gate of the King's Palace.

The view of the child as sinner in need of emergency instruction lasted well into later centuries. Lessons to save souls, however, got lively competition, at least from England, from several sources.

Chapbooks

One competitor was the small-time salesman call the chapman, who carried his goods with him as he wandered, peddling necklaces, trinkets, beads—and inexpensive books. These **chapbooks** (*chap* comes from an Old English word meaning "trade," *chapbook* means "trade book") were published to appeal to large audiences. They were printed like modern newspapers, with no binding, and—like newspapers—they put into print what people were talking about: some of the tales that had come down through the Middle Ages in the voices of storytellers. The earliest printed version of *Tom Thumb* was a chapbook. In contrast to most of the Puritans' tracts, these chapbooks brought adventure, fantasy, and humor to children who had never seen books before. Avi, a children's author, notes the irony of chapbooks being considered a part of childhood literature, but their contemporary counterparts, comic books, often being ignored by literature specialists (43). Yet chapbooks and comic books share the qualities of having been designed for wide audiences, being relatively inexpensive, and providing an underground literature for children. The lesson described in Figure 12-2 shows how one teacher built on the knowledge her students had about the conventions of print used in comic books and in newspaper cartoons.

Nonfiction

In the middle of the 17th century, a Moravian educator named John Amos Comenius came up with another idea extraordinary for the times. Comenius's *Orbis Pictus* (meaning "illustrated world"), first published in 1657,

Jenna listened as her second graders talked about how *Emma* by James Stevenson (New York: Greenwillow, 1985) was "sort of like the comics." They pointed to the dialogue balloons and the way pages had several "squares" with action in each.

Jenna decided to see just what her students knew by making a chart with them showing conventions used to help tell a story in a comic. After a child had drawn the symbol, the class discussed what it meant, and Jenna wrote their words on the chart. On the first day, the chart had five symbols.

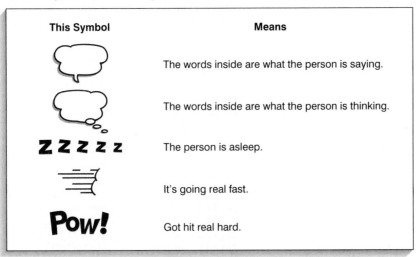

As the children remembered or found other symbols, they added them to the chart. Here are some they added.

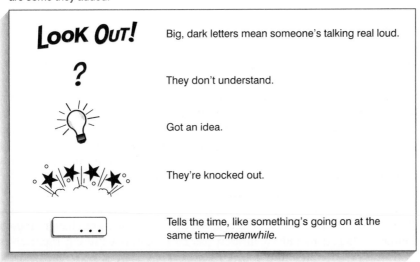

During Writing Workshop several children wrote their stories in comic book format. Jenna also began bringing in books that used that style. She shared books by James Stevenson, Marc Brown, and Raymond Briggs and put them and the stories the children had written on the bookshelf below the chart. She planned to refer back to the dialogue balloons when she talked with the children about quotation marks.

Figure 12-2   A lesson on conventions in comics.

(104)

LI.

Piscatio.

Fiſhing.

| The Fiſher-man 1. catcheth fiſh, either on the ſhoar, with an Hook, 2. which hangeth by a line from the angling-rod, and on which the bait ſticketh; or with a Cleek-Net, 3. which hanging on a Pole, 4. is put into the water; or in a Boat, 5. with a Trammel-Net 6. or with a Weel, 7. which is laid in the water by Night. | *Piſcator* 1. captat piſces, ſive, in littore, *Hamo*, 2. qui ab *arundine* filo pendet, & cui inhæret *Eſca*; ſive *Fundâ*, 3. quæ pendens *Perticâ*, 4. aquæ immittitur; ſive, in *Cymba*, 5. *Reti*, 6. ſive *Naſſa*, 7. quæ per Noctem demergitur. |

John Amos Comenius published Orbis Pictus, *a book of facts for children, in 1657.*
(Source: Illustration COMENIUS, John Amos. ORBIS PICTUS, Syracuse, NY:
C. W. Bardeen, 1887. Reissued by Singing Tree Press, Detroit, MI, 1968.
Reprinted by permission of Oxford University Press, Oxford, England.)

was a book of facts for children. As far as we know, no one before Comenius had devoted a book to teachings about the world. Almost half of each page was a woodcut, marked with numbers. The text above told what was happening, more or less accurately, in English and Latin (for example, see the photo above). The pictures made this pleasurable reading in an age when adults put little stock in pleasure.

Reading for Pleasure

But toward the end of the 17th century, there were signs of change. Puritan influence began to fade. Children passed chapbooks among themselves; some of the little unbound books were sneaked aboard ships to the colonies. In 1693, a widely respected English philosopher named John Locke seemed to put his blessing on reading for fun. In *Some Thoughts Concerning Education,* Locke said that children should begin to learn to read as soon as they begin talking. "Great care is to be taken that it be never made as a business," he wrote. Locke also suggested: "There may be dice and playthings, with the letters on them to teach the children the alphabet by playing; and twenty other ways may be found, suitable to their particular tempers, to make this kind of learning a sport to them" (332–333).

By the end of the century, American children still toted their hard horn-books and memorized their religious catechism. But then other books and new ideas, Locke's among them, began drifting into the colonies. Over the next century, children's literature changed. Many adults on both sides of the Atlantic during the 1700s came to agree with Locke. That, of course, meant a change in the adult view of the child. Children might be sinners, but adults no longer had to drum salvation into them. Children had some inherent ability to learn, even when acting like children and having fun.

The Child as Sensible Student: 1765

The Business and Pleasure of John Newbery

In 1765, *The History of Little Goody Two-Shoes* came off the press of a London printer, writer, businessman, patron of writers, and promoter of cure-all medicines. His name was John Newbery.

His shop, called The Bible and Sun, began issuing books written expressly for children. The first of these, *A Little Pretty Pocket-Book,* laid down principles Newbery was to follow in all his path-breaking books. *Pocket-Book,* the title page announced, was "intended for the Instruction and Amusement of Little Master Tommy and Pretty Miss Poll, with an agreeable Letter to read from Jack the Giant Killer . . . " Like 17th-century publications, the book was meant to teach. But breaking with Puritan philosophy, Newbery intended his books to amuse and be agreeable at the same time, just as Locke has suggested.

Newbery was one of the first to recognize the possibilities for profit in children's books, and he was a master of selling techniques. The *Pocket-Book* was a package deal. The book cost sixpence; for just twopence more, you could get a cushion to tote up children's good and bad deeds by sticking pins in one side or the other. In one of his ads in 1755, Newbery as huckster offered a *free* book for boys called *Nurse Truelove's New Year Gift.* All boys had to do was buy the *binding,* twopence a book.

Newbery probably wrote many books himself. He enjoyed making up tripping titles and funny names, such as Peregrine Puzzlebrains and Giles Gingerbread. He also employed a stable of writers to turn out bound books and chapbooks. Among them was Oliver Goldsmith (1728–1774), the English poet, dramatist, and novelist. Goldsmith often gets credit for Newbery's most famous publication, *The History of Little Goody Two-Shoes.*

Modern children find *Goody Two-Shoes* melodramatic and overly moralistic. But in its time, the story seemed believable, and its morals were disguised a bit by a fast-paced plot.

Newbery's books began infiltrating the American colonies around the time of the American Revolution. His importer was a Massachusetts printer, Isiah Thomas of Worcester. Thomas piously passed on Newbery's moral lessons ["Know this (which is enough to know)/ Virtue is Happiness below"] while picking the Englishman's *Pocket-Book.* Years later, Newbery officially won the credit Thomas had failed to give him in America when, in

Being called a "Goody Two-Shoes" comes from this book because the protagonist, Margery Meanwell, was unfailingly kind and forgiving.

1922, an annual award for the best children's book written by an American author was set up in his name.

Newbery was not the only publisher to produce books for amusement as well as instruction; nor was he the first. But he was the best known of his time and probably did more than any other person to establish children's books as a separate, flowering field. No longer, in Newbery's view, was the child a miniature adult corrupted by sin and headed toward damnation. Now children had time to be children, even though they still had much to learn.

The Legacy of Jean Jacques Rousseau: Moral Tales.   About the time *Goody Two-Shoes* appeared, French philosopher Jean Jacques Rousseau (1712–1778) added his voice in support of the view that children were different from parents and had their own needs. In *Emile,* published in 1762, Rousseau argued that children learn for themselves through experience and activity. *Emile* is the story of a boy who lives mostly without books; he reads only *Robinson Crusoe* and learns with enthusiasm by following natural inclinations, his thinking shaped by a lone teacher.

Rousseau might not have been pleased to see what came of his thinking toward the end of the century. His philosophy helped to spawn a whole series of somber books written to teach moral customs. These "moral tales" often had an all-knowing adult, older sibling, or a pair of children—one good, one bad—and focused on the child discovering truths about good and evil through his or her own common sense and experience.

Sanford and Merton, by Britisher Thomas Day (1748–1789), and *Fabulous Histories, or, The Story of the Robins* by Sarah Trimmer were typical moral tales.

During this period, textbooks on arithmetic, geography, and spelling appeared for the first time in American schools. In England, Mrs. Trimmer and a contemporary, Mrs. Letitia Barbault, condemned fairy tales and Mother Goose rhymes. And there were still sermonizing authors who propounded the Gospel. Hannah More, another Englishwoman, produced conservative religious lessons for children, which she termed "Cheap Repository Tracts," aimed at Sunday School readers.

The Legacy of England: American Literature Almost Comes of Age
Early in the 1800s, for the first time, American literature began to set off on its own, breaking with English domination. However, the writings of the two countries had been so closely allied for centuries that the first steps toward independence were taken with many backward glances.

Samuel Goodrich Teaches.   In 1822, a young American named Samuel Goodrich was having a bad year. His wife died; his business ventures were failing; he fell off a horse and was lamed. So he decided to go to Europe to try to relax and also to search for books he might import to the United States.

He made a pleasant tour of Europe and then traveled to Bristol, England, where he met 79-year-old Hannah More. Goodrich told More that he had grown up admiring her writing. The two talked of how authors could use fiction to convey truth and good moral conduct. They agreed there was little value in imaginative stories of giants, fairies, and monsters.

In 1827, inspired by More's philosophy, he wrote the first of what would become a series of books. By the end of his career, he boasted of having written 116 Peter Parley books (Hearn 34). The first was titled *The Tales of Peter Parley About America,* and it began:

> Here I am. My name is Peter Parley. I am an old man. I am very grey and lame. But I have seen a great many things, and had a great many adventures, and I love to talk about them . . . .

Parley went on about how New England was settled and about the war with Britain. He also told Indian stories, at times with direct honesty. The white man, Goodrich wrote,

> " . . . killed the children of the red men, they shot their wives, they burned their wigwams, and they took away their lands . . . The red men were beaten. They ran away into the woods. They were broken-hearted, and they died. They are all dead or gone far over the mountains, except a few. . . . " (56)

The Parley books were so popular that they were pirated—Newbery's revenge—by English printers. In the United States, there were many imitators and even some who dressed like Parley and gave lectures.

Peter Parley was meant to teach lessons, and Goodrich's English counterparts continued to turn out their didactic tales as the 19th century began. Another American writer, New Englander Jacob Abbott, carried on the tradition in a series about an American boy named Rollo. In early books, published from 1834 on, Rollo learned to talk and read; he then set off on travels, picking up a heavy load of moral instruction wherever he went.

Young readers were shown how Peter Parley supposedly looked, and many of them took the description quite literally. (Source: Illustration of Peter Parley from THE TALES OF PETER PARLEY, ABOUT AMER-ICA [by Samuel Goodrich (1793–1860)]. Boston: S. G. Goodrich, 1827.)

Another angelic American character, young Elsie Dinsmore, was created by Martha Farquharson (a pseudonym for Finley) in 1867. Elsie is so pious in *Elsie Dinsmore* that she refuses her father's order to play the piano on the Sabbath. In a battle of wills, she sits silently at the piano for hours. Finally, she faints, hitting her head on the piano on the way down. She might have died, the reader learns. Her father relents. He carries her to bed, but she refuses to lie down until she has said her prayers.

America may have won the revolution, but for the first half of the 19th century, at least, much of children's literature was still tied to the mother country.

Not everyone in the 18th and 19th centuries was pleased with the view of the child as sensible student. Newbery had added some whimsy to his lessons, but as the 19th century ended, he had been gone for more than 30 years. Children's literature seemed to have awakened from Newbery's comparatively amusing dreams into an age of sugar-coated reason.

Charles Lamb Entertains.   Where were Giles Gingerbread and Peregrine Puzzlebrains? Charles Lamb, an English essayist at the turn of the century, grumbled about what had happened. On October 23, 1802, he wrote a complaint about the times to the English poet Samuel Taylor Coleridge.

> *Goody Two-Shoes* is almost out of print. Mrs. Barbauld's stuff has banished all the old classics of the nursery; and the shopman at Newbery's hardly deigned to reach them off an old exploded corner of the shelf . . . Mrs. B's and Mrs. Trimmer's nonsense lay in piles about . . . Science has succeeded in Poetry no less in the little walks of children than with men. Is there no possibility of averting this sore evil? Think what you would have been now, if instead of being fed with Tales and old wives' fables in childhood, you had been crammed with geography and natural history?
>
> Damn them!—I mean the cursed Barbauld Crew . . . (326)

Lamb himself decided to do something. Four years after his letter to Coleridge, he and his wife Mary published *Tales from Shakespeare,* retelling the stories of many of the plays with such imagination that the book became an immediate success. Two years later, in 1808, Lamb brought out his version of Homer's *Odyssey* in *The Adventures of Ulysses.* The old tales and the imaginative dreams behind them were beginning to make a comeback. Astonishingly for the times, it was hard to find the lessons in them.

The Child Out of School: 1865

Lewis Carroll Entertains

The signs of change during the 19th century are easy to read in Lewis Carroll's *Alice's Adventures in Wonderland,* first published in 1865. There was no moral instruction in this story; neither was there a tutor or wise guardian to help the little girl through Wonderland. Her guides were a harried rabbit and a sometimes-invisible cat. Carroll's book even made fun of authors he thought had loaded their writing with lessons.

This is one of the original illus-trations created by John Tenniel for the two books about Alice.

In 1715, an English poet and author of hymns named Isaac Watts had written a poem about industry in a book called *Divine and Moral Songs for Children.* In one scene of *Alice,* she tries to remember the old Watts song, written 150 years before, but it comes out garbled. Figure 12-3 shows the way Watts wrote it and how Alice recalled it.

The view of the child had softened. The moralistic writings of Watts had turned into odd images that seem like remnants of a dream. But children were still regarded as students; there were plenty of books around to instruct them in morals, manners, and science. But now there were respectable alter-natives. Authors like Carroll seemed to want to give children books to enter-tain them when school was out. The new child of the 19th century, many adults thought, was free to dream a little.

There were at least two kinds of dreams in the 19th century. Some dreams were fantastic; folktales had come alive again in print, and several new stories of fantasy appeared, including *Alice.*

Other new dreams were based on what was happening in the world. Factories began encroaching on farmland on both sides of the Atlantic. Americans were moving, encountering adventures and freedom from many of the Puritan restrictions. The first railroad in the United States was built in 1827. By 1840, there were nearly 3,000 miles of track. The first wagon train arrived in California in 1841, and seven years later, 100 dragoons and the United States Navy claimed California.

In 1800, just 3 percent of the American population lived in urban areas. By 1860, the percentage had more than tripled. In the course of

Figure 12-3   Carroll
rewrites Watts.

> **Watts (1715)**
>
> How does the busy little bee
> Improve each shining hour,
> And gather honey all the day
> From every opening flower.
>
> How skillfully she builds her cell!
> How neat she spreads her wax!
> And labours hard to store it well
> With the sweet food she makes . . .
>
> **Carroll (1865)**
>
> How doth the little crocodile
> Improve his shining tail,
> And pour the waters of the Nile
> On every golden scale!
>
> How cheerfully he seems to grin
> How nearly spreads his claws,
> And welcomes little fishes in,
> With gently smiling jaws.
>
> Carroll 17

migrations, children began to gain freedom to dream up adventures for themselves. Struggles at the frontier, battles to survive in the burgeoning cities—real life generated romantic stories to rival fairy tales in action and suspense.

Folktales and Fairy Tales

Charles Lamb helped to start the movement back to old, imaginative tales partly to combat the "sore evil" he saw in 17th-century children's literature. Ironically, others who explored traditional literature were probably encouraged by the same cold scientific spirit that irked Lamb.

The Grimm Brothers

Jakob and Wilhelm Grimm in Germany were historical linguists. They studied language scientifically hoping to find clues about the migrations of Europeans. The brothers collected and published folktales for adults. They worked like archeologists to dig up fragments of folk art and preserve them for future study.

But the Grimms also recognized that many of the stories had been told to children, and so they called their collections *Kinder und Haus Marchen (Children and Household Tales)*.

Whatever the Grimms' intention, children claimed the tales for themselves. Right after they were published, a translator named Edgar Taylor presented them to young readers with the title *Household Tales,* and soon they fit into English and American households as naturally as a kitchen table.

The Grimms opened the door and other European writers and translators followed, In the 1850s, several versions of Greek legends were published in England. In 1859, Sir George Dasent brought English readers the wintery Scandinavian folklore in *Popular Tales from the Norse.*

Folklore in America

In America, later in the century, Joel Chandler Harris collected and published folktales from southern plantations, many of which had roots in traditional folklore from other parts of the world. The stories of how a clever rabbit repeatedly tricks his enemies are similar to stories about clever animals found in African and Native American folklore.

The narrator of Harris's *Uncle Remus, His Songs and His Sayings* was an old slave, Uncle Remus, who speaks in what is supposed to be a southern slave dialect, but which many modern readers consider insulting (as well as the portrayal of Uncle Remus himself). Virginia Hamilton, in her introduction to *The People Could Fly: Black American Folktales,* writes: "Harris and his contemporaries used phonetic dialect as a literary device. They felt that an exaggerated colloquial language best symbolized what they regarded as the quaint appeal of lowly, rural people" (xi). Harris's Uncle Remus stories are still the largest collection of African American folklore ever published (Church 244).

Another contemporary retelling of these stories is *The Tales of Uncle Remus* by Julius Lester, illustrated by Jerry Pinkney (New York: Dial, 1987).

In one of the stories, "The Tar Baby," Uncle Remus explains to a little boy that a tar baby is a rabbit-sized figure made of tar and turpentine. Brer Fox sets the Tar Baby in the road and then hides in the bushes to wait for Brer Rabbit to come along. Here is a sample of the dialect:

> . . . Bimemby here come Brer Rabbit pacin/ down de road— lippity-clippity, clippity-lippity—dez ez sassy ez a jay-bird. Brer Fox, he lay low . . . (Haviland 274–275 showing Harris 23–24)

Here is a sample from Hamilton's retelling:

> And he spied Tar Baby just sittin, gazin out on the water.
>   "What you doin here, baby rabbit?" Rabbit asked Tar Baby.
>   Tar Baby wouldn't say. Too stuck up. "You better speak to me," Doc Rabbit said, "or I'll have to hurt you."
>   But the Tar Baby wasn't gone speak to a stranger. (15)

Brer Rabbit turns angry when the figure does not respond. His anger comes to blows, but his fists and finally his head get stuck in the tar. The fox saunters out of hiding, comments that the rabbit looks "stuck up," (Harris 25), and rolls on the ground laughing.

Where is the moral? There is none. There is not even a definite ending to the original. Did the fox eat the rabbit? the little boy asks. "Dat's all the fur de tale goes," Uncle Remus replies (25).

Fantasy and Adventure

Other 19th century writers took off from traditional literature to write wholly new imaginative stories. In Denmark, the young Hans Christian

Virginia Hamilton uses moderate colloquialisms in her retelling of Tar Baby story. (Source: Illustration from THE PEOPLE COULD FLY by Virginia Hamilton, illustrated by Leo & Diane Dillon. Illustrations copyright © 1985 by Leo & Diane Dillon. Reprinted by permission of Alfred A. Knopf, Inc.)

Andersen gathered material for his later writing: He grew up listening to tales told by old women in a poorhouse where his grandmother gardened. Then he wrote and told his own stories, including *The Ugly Duckling* and *The Little Mermaid.* Mary Howitt translated them in England in 1846; they have appeared in new translations every few years since then.

The first *Alice* book came out less than a decade after Howitt's translation, and *Through the Looking Glass,* another of Lewis Carroll's fantastic trips, was published in 1871. The same year Alice jumped into her first journey down the rabbit hole, 1865, the French writer Jules Verne took readers on a submarine ride, *Twenty Thousand Leagues Under the Sea,* generally considered the first book of science fiction.

And that is just a sampling. By the 1870s and the 1880s, on both sides of the Atlantic, there were some new rules of writing for children. Two women, one American and one English, presented some of the rewritten standards in separate critical essays.

"Stop preaching" was the call that began to sound in America a decade after the Civil War. In 1873, *Scribner's Magazine* put forth the new approach in an unsigned piece written by Mary Mapes Dodge, an author and editor. Children's magazines of the day, she wrote, were sometimes a "milk and water" version of adult journals.

But, in fact, the child's magazine needs to be stronger, truer, bolder, more uncompromising than [adult magazines]. Its cheer must be the cheer of the bird song, not of condescending editorial babble . . . No sermonizing either, no wearisome spinning out of facts, nor rattling of the dry bones of history . . . The ideal child's magazine is a pleasure ground. (Lanes 18)

Shortly after her article appeared, she began editing a new children's magazine, *St. Nicholas*. It lasted until 1940 and drew contributions from generations of well-known imaginative writers. Children wrote for *St. Nicholas* also, and contributors included Robert Benchley, who grew up to be a famous humorist, and E. B. White, who would later spin *Charlotte's Web*. How a contemporary teacher used an issue of *St. Nicolas* magazine to stimulate her students to explore several curricular areas is described in Figure 12-4.

"Beguile, amuse," was what Charlotte Yonge, an Englishwoman, asked of children's books when she compiled *What Books to Give and What to Lend* in 1887. An outspoken Christian in the tradition of Mrs. Trimmer, Yonge boldly parted company with the critics of the early years of the century. Young readers must be exposed to fairy tales, she argued, and that includes modern stories by Andersen and Carroll. Adventure is good for boys, and romance refines girls— even without an overt Christian message. With recommendations like these— doughty Mrs. Trimmer would have been apoplectic over them—it is no wonder Yonge found that "Many stories have become obsolete." For instance, "the stories of the good children who are household supports and little nurses, picking up chance crumbs of instruction, have lost all present reality" (Avery 17).

Didactic literature had not died by any means. There were still plenty of lessons, sometimes lurking in newly mined fantasy. In 1887, the same year Charlotte Yonge compiled her booklist, the American Tract Society published *Mother Goose for Temperance Nurseries,* which included this verse:

Ding, dong, bell!
Paddy's in the well!
What threw him in?
Half a glass of gin. (Coughlin 38)

But by the early part of the 20th century, many adults thought that the real Mother Goose, Alice, and legendary Greek and Norse heroes had become respectable companions for children.

Realism

Twain and Alcott.   Some adults were not quite so sure Mark Twain's *Tom Sawyer* and *Huckleberry Finn* were respectable. These stories about believable Missouri boys, both of them rebels against repressive or disreputable adults, were initially banned in some libraries as trashy and dangerous. After the Brooklyn Public Library removed Huck Finn, Twain (a pseudonym for Samuel Clemens) responded with pretended indignation that anyone should have considered *Huck* a children's book. In a letter sent in 1905 to Asa Dickinson at the Brooklyn library, he contended:

I wrote Tom Sawyer and Huck Finn for adults exclusively, and it always distresses me when I find that boys and girls have been allowed access to them. The mind that becomes soiled in youth can never again be washed

Eula's fourth-grade class had a subscription to *Cricket* magazine, and the children read it and several other magazines regularly. She had begun the subscription several years earlier to provide short stories for children who were not yet settling down with books during the period for Sustained Silent Reading.

One Saturday Eula found a copy of *St. Nicholas* magazine for children at a yard sale. It was the December 1902 issue. She thought she would share it with the children just for fun. When she got home and began reading it, however, she realized that it had the potential to stimulate serious discussion and study. There were works by Howard Pyle and Louisa May Alcott in it. It had ads for products still available—Ivory soap, Gorham silver polish, Postum. Books for children published by Harpers, Scribner's, Lee and Shepard, Doubleday, and Little, Brown were annotated in advertisements. And it showed the social consciousness of the time—a heavy emphasis on "the good old-fashioned Christmas," a story that used the term *nigger* and included caricatures of an African American child and phonetic colloquial dialect, and several stories, both fiction and nonfiction, with international settings.

Eula took the magazine to school and gave the students a week to look through it. Each student was to note how it was like and different from *Cricket*. Eula explained that both magazines published stories for children, although *St. Nicholas* was for ages "six to sixteen" whereas *Cricket* was generally thought of as for children in elementary and middle school, not into high school. Each student was also to note a part of the magazine he or she would like to read in full or have Eula read to the class.

Then the class came together and created a chart comparing the two magazines.

Ways *Cricket* and *St. Nicholas* Are Alike

Some stories are complete.
Some stories are chapters from books.
Pictures go with the stories.
Not much color in any of the pictures.
Poems.
Letters from kids.
Puzzles and contests.
Stories and poems written by children and contests for children's writing and drawing.
Stories or authors we've heard of.

Ways *Cricket* and *St. Nicholas* Are Different

St. Nicholas has stories that are longer and harder.
St. Nicholas has ads for adult stuff; *Cricket* has ads only on the back cover for books or magazines
    it publishes.
St. Nicholas is bigger.
St. Nicholas looks old fashioned.
St. Nicholas used the word *nigger* and made fun of the girl in the pictures.
St. Nicholas had a write-in column for questions and answers about science and nature.
Cricket tells what happened earlier when they continue a story. *St. Nicholas* just began with the chapter.

Figure 12-4   A Comparison of *St. Nicholas* and *Cricket* Magazines

Eula then had the students tell the story or part of *St. Nicholas* they'd like to read and announced that they'd be working in pairs. She made one photocopy of the specific section for each pair. She moved around the room as the pairs worked, helping students with the reading when necessary. When they had completed reading their section, each pair was to discuss it and to write two things that they wondered about in relation to their section. Among the "wonderings" were these:

1. How come the story about ski jumping in Norway spells ski "skee?"
2. Why do they only have Christmas stories and poems—no Hanukkah or Kwanzaa?
3. Why would Louisa May Alcott describe a girl as pretty by saying she had "beady black eyes?"
4. How come they can call a girl a *nigger* and make fun of her in a story and no one says it's wrong?
5. Is it really possible to make a sled with just one runner and use it like it shows in "The Jumper?"
6. How come we know some stories, like *King Arthur,* and not others in *St. Nicholas*?
7. Were the books they were advertising really any good?

The children explored their "wonderings" for nearly three weeks, with Eula guiding both discussion and research. In the course of the study, the students explored how language and usage change over time, how social and political factors may affect what is written, how recognition of and sensitivity to parallel cultures within the United States has changed and is continuing to change, and why certain works of literature are read by generations of readers. Several children went to the library and reported that, of all the books advertised in *St. Nicholas* in that 1902 edition, only 3 were still available in their local library. The 3 were *The Jungle Book* (Kipling), *The Just So Stories* (Kipling), and *Little Women* (Alcott). However, of the 10 books on the winning list in a contest for children to list the "best" books for children, 7 were available. Of these 7, at least one child in the class had heard of *Hans Brinker* (Dodge), *Alice in Wonderland* (Carroll), *A Child's Garden of Verses* (Stevenson), and *The Prince and the Pauper* (Twain).

Figure 12-4 *continued*

clean; I know this by my own experience, and to this day I cherish an unappeasable bitterness against the unfaithful guardians of my young life, who not only permitted but compelled me to read an unexpurgated Bible through before I was 15 years old . . . I wish I could say a softening word or two in defence [sic] of Huck's character, since you wish it, but really in my opinion it is no better than those of Solomon, David, Satan, and the rest of the sacred brotherhood . . . (Clemens 335–336)

In spite of would-be censors, Twain's warm, funny, suspenseful portrayals of growing up in the American midwest triumphed well into the present.

Some adults grumbled against other realistic books, such as Louisa May Alcott's *Little Women.* The story of the March family as told by Jo, one of four affectionate but sometimes willful daughters, was based roughly on the plot of *Pilgrim's Progress,* but not enough to suit critics who thought the adventures of Jo were not religious enough.

Dime Novels. Some critics could not restrain the 19th-century authors who wrote realistic stories of frontier adventures, modern war epics, and rags-to-riches sagas. A century before, chapbooks had brought fantasy to young readers. Now the new **dime novel,** written for adults but read by children, brought "true-life" stories that in some ways were just as dreamy. But chapmen of the 1860s were more sophisticated. Instead of hawking their wares on the street, they put ads in the newspapers.

One appeared June 7, 1860, in the New York *Tribune.* "BOOKS FOR THE MILLION!" the ad's headline said. The idea for the ad was not new. Within the previous decade or so, roughly the same headline had been used to sell clothing, dry goods, and coffee, all "for the million!"

Malaeska, the first of the dime novels, came out in an orange wrapper that became characteristic of the vastly successful Beadle books.

One man who had been a boy in the 1860s told in an *Atlantic Monthly* article in 1907 what it had been like when the books hit the streets, one book every two weeks. Charles M. Harvey rhapsodized:

> How the boys swarmed into and through stores and newsstands to buy copies as they came hot from the press! And the fortunate ones who were there before the supply gave out—how triumphantly they carried them off to the rendezvous, where eager groups awaited their arrival! What silver-tongued orator of any age or land ever had such sympathetic and enthusiastic audiences as did the happy youths at those trysting places, who were detailed to read those wild deeds of forest, prairie and mountain! (Avi 155–156)

Perhaps none of the Beadles ever actually sold a million copies, but the most popular sold in the hundreds of thousands (Johannsen 33). At a dime a book, that was more than enough to make a booming profit for publisher Beadle. More expensive ($1 each), but also mass-produced were the rags-to-riches books of Horatio Alger, Jr. set in the *other* frontier of the 19th century, the city.

Horatio Alger.   Alger (1834–1899), son of a Unitarian minister, graduated from Harvard and proceeded under family pressure to divinity school. But after a year's work in Brewster, Massachusetts, he quit the ministry, went to New York, and stored up impressions for a series of books whose theme he trotted out than one hundred times.

Ragged Dick is a 14-year-old bootblack. After a Sunday school teacher has encouraged him toward greater self-discipline and reading, he heroically saves the son of a rich man who has fallen off the Staten Island Ferry and is himself rewarded.

The realists of the late 19th century presented an exciting world and created adventurous children to explore it. But much of the mass-produced realism such as Alger's work was built of clichés and shallow thinking. Ragged Dick's extraordinary luck was as implausible as a visit from a fairy godmother. It was not until the 20th century that the honest realism pioneered by Twain and a few others matured. At the same time, new lines were added to the portrait of the child.

The Child as Customer and Critic: 1919, 1995

By the turn of the century, childhood had become golden. Many adults looked with longing at the carefree years of their youth. Compared with the stiff model child of Mrs. Trimmer's day, children in the early 20th century seemed younger. The new ideal in 1900 was an innocent child who might do naughty things, but was a "scamp" rather than a sinner.

Yet in the course of the 20th century, views of the child became much more complicated. For one thing, children and their literature now got much more attention. In 1880, fewer than 300 books were written for children. By 1930, the number of children's books produced each year had tripled, to about 1,000 (Johnson 68), and by the 1990s it hovered at the 5,000 mark. As the one-room schoolhouse yielded to schools with many rooms, books and magazines began to specialize. There were books for two- to four-year-olds, easy-to-read books for primary school children just learning to read, and books with nearly adult sophistication for older children.

Children themselves had become specialties. Sigmund Freud (1856–1939), the founder of modern psychoanalysis, spawned generations of experts on children with his theories that childhood deeply affected adulthood, often unconsciously. Child psychologists took posts next to teachers, teachers themselves specialized in children of particular ages, and libraries set apart children's rooms. And as children's rooms became more prominent and were included in the design of new libraries, a philosophy of service to children developed (Thomas 83). Also, for the first time, publishing houses hired editors whose only job was to reach the rapidly growing children's market.

The Child as Valued Customer: 1919

Louise Seaman Bechtel was working in the advertising office at the Macmillan Company at the end of World War I when she was offered a department of her own. The company astutely recognized that postwar prosperity would stimulate interest in children's books. So in 1919, Bechtel was assigned a secretary and a budget and told to run the country's first children's department.

From then on, she recalled in 1969, the 50th anniversary of her promotion,

> My secretary—Gertrude Blumenthal—and I were the entire department. Alone we accomplished everything: editing, manuscript reading, bookmaking, interviewing artists, laying out books, advertising, preparing catalogues. From the beginning we usually received fifty to one hundred unsolicited manuscripts a week . . .
>
> One discovered books in many places. Of course, one such place was the children's room of a public library. At the New York Public Library children's room on 42nd Street, I found ten little boys absorbed in a book in Italian, "the big Pinocchio." So we sent to Italy to have it printed for us in English; and it was a great success. (Silberberg and Donovan 704)

Early editors set high standards for writing for children. Louise Bechtel recalls meeting many of the best authors of the day as they came and went from the Macmillan offices, writers such as John Mansfield, poet laureate in England, and William Butler Yeats, Irish poet and playwright. Encounters with them encouraged her to seek the best from authors and artists for children.

Quality Becomes Important.   Over the next decade, a comradeship devoted to quality began to grow among editors. Alice Dalgliesh, who became children's editor at Charles Scribner's Sons in 1935, recalls that even during the Depression of the 1930s, when editors thought twice before taking new books, they kept faith "that if it was a *good* book it would sell" (Silberberg 706). By the 1950s, children's editors no longer felt like stepchildren in the publishing house.

There were other people behind the improved quality of children's books in the early 20th century. Anne Carroll Moore became head of the children's room at the New York Public Library in 1906. Amid stacks of papers and books in room 105, editors, authors, and illustrators came to talk about children's books and how they might be better. Anne Moore also set stringent literary standards in a regular column in the *New York Herald Tribune.*

Many states and organizations give annual awards to authors and illustrators of children's books. You might want to see what awards are given in your area of the country.

Newbery and Caldecott Awards.   Meanwhile, Franklin K. Mathiews, librarian of the Boy Scouts of America, convinced publisher Frederic G. Melcher to institute a national Children's Book Week in 1919 to encourage adults to recognize good books for children. A few years later, in 1922, in an era when several publishers were beginning to agree with John Newbery that children's literature could stand on its own, Melcher led the Children's Book Council to establish the Newbery Award. It was the first of many prizes established in this century to encourage quality. The Caldecott Award, named after the witty 19th-century artist Randolph Caldecott, was begun in 1938 for the best illustrations by an American artist. Both awards are now given by the Association of Library Services to Children of the American Library Association. Specialization crept into the world of prizes; in 1977, the National Council of Teachers of English (NCTE) gave their first annual children's poetry award to David McCord.

Committed editors, publishers, and librarians, as well as the incentive of the marketplace, helped to boost interest in children's books in the first few decades of the century. Fortunately, at the same time, a growing group of talented writers and artists chose to work in the children's field. Of course many popular books in the 1920s and 1930s had been written decades before. Alcott's *Little Women* remained a favorite; so did Twain's books. But after World War I, new authors on both sides of the Atlantic began producing works that would be classics.

New Authors, New Horizons.   The English author A. A. Milne created the simple-minded teddy bear, *Winnie-the-Pooh,* for his son in 1926. Two years later, Wanda Gag told the still-popular story of the man who went out

Gag's Millions of Cats, *first published in 1928, is still popular today. (Source:* Illustration by Wanda Gag reprinted by permission of Coward-McCann, Inc. from MILLIONS OF CATS by Wanda Gag, copyright 1928 by Coward-McCann, Inc. © 1956 by Robert Janssen.)

to get his wife a cat, could not settle on which was best, and came home with *Millions of Cats.* In the early 1930s, the American writer Laura Ingalls Wilder wrote the first in a series of books about log cabin life in Wisconsin, *Little House in the Big Woods.*

American children benefited after World War I from an influx of authors and artists from Europe who crossed the ocean seeking artistic freedom; many turned to children's books. Padraic Colum from Ireland, who was to provide elegant retellings of Greek and Norse myths, was one. Kurt Wiese from Germany, who was to illustrate the story of the runaway duck in Marjorie Flack's *The Story About Ping,* was another.

The New Dime Novel.   Other publishers and writers after the turn of the century were less interested in quality for young customers than cash. A successor to the chapman was a writer and business genius named Edward Stratemeyer (1862–1930). Educated on dime novels (he grew up on Alger's stories and never went to college), he wrote his first story on brown wrapping paper while working at a tobacco store and sold it for $75. In a short time, equipped with pen name Arthur M. (for "Million") Winfield, he began selling stories to children's magazines as fast as he could write them. He then turned to dime novels signed with other pseudonyms, such as Jim Bowie, Nat Woods, and Jim Daly.

Stratemeyer's biggest break came when Admiral George Dewey routed the Spanish fleet in Manila Bay in May, 1898. At the time, Stratemeyer's latest book, about boys on a battleship, was in a safe at Lothrop, Lee and Shepard, a Boston publishing house where Stratemeyer had submitted it. After Dewey's victory, an editor remembered the manuscript and asked the author to rewrite it with Dewey at the helm. The request was no real challenge for plot-wise Stratemeyer; in a few days he produced *Under Dewey at Manila,* which sold out edition after edition.

In a few more years, Stratemeyer had set up his own syndicate to turn out books. He sat in a small New York office, dictated plot outlines, hired writers to turn them into books, and sold the manuscripts to publishers. The Rover Boys, Tom Swift, the Bobbsey Twins, the Hardy Boys, and Nancy Drew all sprang from Stratemeyer's dime-novel mind. All sold, and still sell today, at prices children can afford without asking parents for the money or the approval to read them. The Stratemeyer Syndicate produced over 1,600 series books using nearly 100 pseudonyms (Keeline 41).

For a thorough analysis of the Nancy Drew books, read Vol. 18.1 (July 1994) of the journal *The Lion and the Unicorn.* All of the articles focus on these books.

At his death in 1930, Stratemeyer had conceived or written more than 800 books, and he left an estate of $1 million (Egoff, Stubbs, and Ashley 41–61). His characters outlived him. Nancy Drew books have been translated into 15 languages, are sold worldwide, and are a firm participant in the popular culture. Was his work good literature? No, Stratemeyer did not add to high-quality literature of the 20th century. Profit was his passion, and the mass market was the way to profit. His work foreshadowed such series as the contemporary *Babysitters-Club* and *Sweet Valley Twins.*

The Child as Critic: 1995

The field of children's books exploded in the 20th century. By 1995, the number of children's books in print was 94,330 according to *Children's Books in Print.* Who was the child in these books? There were many. Psychologists and teachers alike had spread the word in the course of the century that each child was different and that childhood itself divided into many phases. Some, like children in the *Little House* books, grew up in a family nest. Others, like Mark Twain's Tom Sawyer and Huck Finn, rebelled against family and struck out on their own. And still others, particularly in the 1960s and the 1990s, appeared on the page as young adults, often independent of their parents, facing real social problems with no magic sword or Sunday School lesson to save them.

The "New" Realism.   The benchmark for such books is *Harriet the Spy,* published in 1964, Louise Fitzhugh's story of a New York City girl. Harriet's parents are so busy they entrust their daughter to a nurse. By the time she turns 11, Harriet has settled on a career plan: She wants to be a writer. She begins by keeping observations about people she knows in a notebook. She writes honestly and alienates classmates when they find her notebook and read about themselves.

Harriet was too real for some adults. At one point, Harriet says, "I'll be *damned* if I'll go to dancing school" (83). In some libraries, the book was kept off the shelf. Other libraries required a note from home before children could read the book. The furor settled down, at least for the time being, and books on sex, drugs, divorce, racial discrimination, and death followed Harriet into the thicket of what came to be called **"new realism."**

There was nothing new about the controversy over new realism. Twain's books had faced similar attempts at censorship about 60 years before. A century before that, Mrs. Trimmer had given uncompromising directions about what children should not read. School boards today often debate about what books are fit for children's eyes, arguing from cultural or religious criteria just the way the Puritans did. Reread the statements about *Daddy's Roommate* that open this chapter to see a more contemporary discussion that hinges on cultural and religious beliefs.

Parents and educators today also pull out well-worn threads of argument from John Newbery's time about whether books should enlighten or entertain. Masha Rudman, in writing about the number of books on the Holocaust published for children in the 1980s, looked at the enlightened side of the argument.

> It is no accident that a great number of books dealing with the Holocaust have been published in the past several years. Most survivors of those tragic times are now 70 years old or older. Actual witnesses to the events are feeling an urgency to make their stories known, because they recognize that even though memories are painful, the truth must be conveyed to current generations. If our children learn about the Holocaust early, then perhaps they can think critically about these historical events, recognize the symptoms of despotism, and fight against them. (163)

Multicultural Content.   Literature could serve an instructional function, and the focus was on what *should* be available rather than what should not. By the 1970s and 1980s, social and political concerns of the country and of the adults who were concerned with books for children focused on multicultural content.

Rudine Sims states succinctly:

> Educators and parents alike maintain a strong belief in the power of literature to affect the minds and hearts of its readers, particularly when those readers are children and youth. Multicultural literature is one of the most powerful components of a multicultural education curriculum, the underlying purpose of which is to help make the society a more equitable one. (40)

New Approaches/New Ideals.   The selection of books was highlighted as schools moved to teach reading with children's books rather than basal readers. In 1986, California published its literature framework, *Literature: Recommended Readings in Kindergarten Through Grade Eight*. The list had "core" readings and "extended" readings, identified the cultural or ethnic groups represented, and set the publishing world jumping. Now there was a market—in a large state whose buying power had made its

Multicultural literature is a powerful component of multi-cultural education. (Source: Illustration from HUE BOY by Rita Phillips Mitchell, illustrated by Caroline Binch. Copyright © 1993 by Rita Phillips Mitchell on text; Pictures copyright © 1993 by Caroline Binch. Used by permission of Dial Books for Young Readers, a division of Penguin Books USA Inc.)

textbook adoptions pivotal in textbook development—for children's books. Older books were reissued in paperback. Textbook publishers began including copies of the books with textbook packages of basal readers, workbooks, and testing materials. The market for children's books was financially strong.

As children read more literature—more of what educators came to call "real" books (to differentiate them from abridged or rewritten stories in reading textbooks and anthologies)—the methods for teaching children to read in school changed. Now children began selecting books, talking about them with classmates, and offering their own opinions. The child became the critic, experiencing and assessing self-chosen literature. Children were viewed as readers of books, and their response groups had the tone of a group of friends exchanging ideas and asking questions. The focus was on the ability to read critically, to relate literature to other readings and to one's own life.

The Child as Global Citizen: 2000+

How is society's view of the child changing? And are children themselves changing? Certainly the advent of the computer and the capability it gives

In contemporary classrooms, children read books together and exchange ideas about their reading.

for communication and information gathering have had and probably will continue to have a major impact on both children and adults.

Enhanced Communication. As children use the Internet to write to other people, their world expands. Exchanging views with a child in England becomes no more difficult than doing so with a child in the next classroom. This personal contact is likely to heighten interest in wider and more diverse populations. Book discussions now cross national boundaries, and recommendations for reading will include titles from many countries.

The reference tools available through the World Wide Web will let children research topics in great detail and are likely to be used in conjunction with nonfiction and bibliography.

In addition, more children will be experiencing literature through CD-ROM. The interactive nature of such programs may change the way children think about story, at least in this format. For example, many of the stories for young children on CD are set up so that the viewer may click on almost any object in the illustration, and that object will move or make a sound or interact with another object. Viewers intent on all the action they can elicit may find the story line and character motivation less compelling

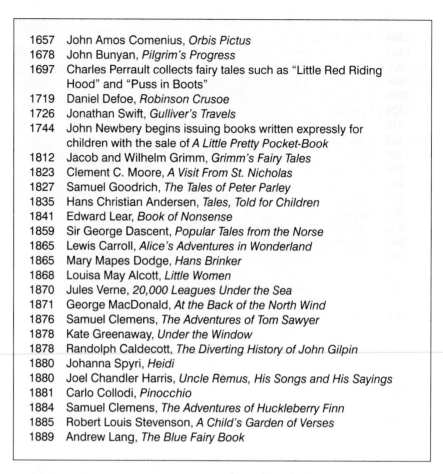

1657	John Amos Comenius, *Orbis Pictus*
1678	John Bunyan, *Pilgrim's Progress*
1697	Charles Perrault collects fairy tales such as "Little Red Riding Hood" and "Puss in Boots"
1719	Daniel Defoe, *Robinson Crusoe*
1726	Jonathan Swift, *Gulliver's Travels*
1744	John Newbery begins issuing books written expressly for children with the sale of *A Little Pretty Pocket-Book*
1812	Jacob and Wilhelm Grimm, *Grimm's Fairy Tales*
1823	Clement C. Moore, *A Visit From St. Nicholas*
1827	Samuel Goodrich, *The Tales of Peter Parley*
1835	Hans Christian Andersen, *Tales, Told for Children*
1841	Edward Lear, *Book of Nonsense*
1859	Sir George Dascent, *Popular Tales from the Norse*
1865	Lewis Carroll, *Alice's Adventures in Wonderland*
1865	Mary Mapes Dodge, *Hans Brinker*
1868	Louisa May Alcott, *Little Women*
1870	Jules Verne, *20,000 Leagues Under the Sea*
1871	George MacDonald, *At the Back of the North Wind*
1876	Samuel Clemens, *The Adventures of Tom Sawyer*
1878	Kate Greenaway, *Under the Window*
1878	Randolph Caldecott, *The Diverting History of John Gilpin*
1880	Johanna Spyri, *Heidi*
1880	Joel Chandler Harris, *Uncle Remus, His Songs and His Sayings*
1881	Carlo Collodi, *Pinocchio*
1884	Samuel Clemens, *The Adventures of Huckleberry Finn*
1885	Robert Louis Stevenson, *A Child's Garden of Verses*
1889	Andrew Lang, *The Blue Fairy Book*

Figure 12-5 Touchstones in the development of literature for children.

than they are in book format. However, because the computer allows for nonlinear presentation and exploration of ideas, it may encourage storytelling in which parallel plots and subplots are included.

Visual Literacy. The emphasis on visual presentation of information that is a hallmark of computer-accessed material and of video will continue to be central in book publishing for children. Picture books received increased attention in the 1990s with an expanded audience and ever more elaborate colors and designs. This is likely to continue, both because children will be more visually oriented and because picture books sell well to adults who are buying for children. In her analysis of trends in children's book publishing, Barbara Elleman notes that nonfiction also is marked by "high visual content," particularly the use of photographs (Elleman 157).

1894	Rudyard Kipling, *The Jungle Book*	
1900	L. Frank Baum, *The Wonderful Wizard of Oz*	
1901	Beatrix Potter, *The Tale of Peter Rabbit*	
1904	James Barrie, *Peter Pan*	
1908	Kenneth Graham, *The Wind in the Willows*	
1909	Lucy Montgomery, *Anne of Green Gables*	
1910	Frances Hodgson Burnett, *The Secret Garden*	
1922	Carl Sandburg, *Rootabaga Stories*	
1926	A. A. Milne, *Winnie-the-Pooh*	
1928	Wanda Gag, *Millions of Cats*	
1932	Laura Ingalls Wilder, *Little House in the Big Woods*	
1937	J. R. R. Tolkien, *The Hobbit*	
1939	Ludwig Bemelmans, *Madeline*	
1943	Esther Forbes, *Johnny Tremain*	
1943	Virginia Lee Burton, *The Little House*	
1950	C. S. Lewis, *The Lion, The Witch, and the Wardrobe*	
1952	E. B. White, *Charlotte's Web*	
1957	Dr. Seuss, *The Cat in the Hat*	
1963	Maurice Sendak, *Where the Wild Things Are*	
1964	Louise Fitzhugh, *Harriet the Spy*	
1969	Langston Hughes, *Don't You Turn Back*	
1969	John Steptoe, *Stevie*	
1970	Judy Blume, *Are You There God? It's Me, Margaret*	
1976	Verna Aardema, *Why Mosquitoes Buzz in People's Ears*	
1985	Chris Van Allsburg, *The Polar Express*	
1986	Patricia MacLachlan, *Sarah, Plain and Tall*	
1990	Gary Soto, *Baseball in April*	
1990	David Macaulay, *Black and White*	

Figure 12-5 *continued*

Cultural Heritage. As American society comes to view itself as a mosaic and not a melting pot, and as groups celebrate their background and customs, children are likely to identify with their cultural heritage with pride. Books by authors of diverse backgrounds and with characters of many nationalities and ethnic groups will show the lifestyles and feelings, values and beliefs, of many peoples, allowing children both to identify with a group and to understand other groups.

The increase in books about Latinos, and with both English and Spanish text, will continue. The Census Bureau predicts that by the year 2050, over one-fifth of the United States population will be of Hispanic origin. Further exploration will be done with bilingual books, both those originally written in two languages and those with a new translation added.

Books can help children proudly identify with their cultural heritage. (Source: Illustration from THE WHISPERING CLOTH written by Pegi Deitz Shea and illustrated by Anita Riggio, Copyright © 1995 Boyds Mill Press. Reprinted by permission.)

THE CONSTANTS IN A CHANGING WORLD

Teachers and librarians today share certain beliefs and concerns with the teachers and critics of periods past. Running through all the arguments and discussions is the belief that literature matters and that what children read influences what and how they think. This means that adults who select books for children will do so with an end in mind, whether to develop a child who is pious and repentant or skilled in the effective use of language; a child who can focus on important realistic topics or can use his or her imagination; or a child who will know about the places Peter Parley visited or know about alternative lifestyles.

Society's view of the child, and society's values, will influence what books seem appropriate for children. Fairy tales have come in and out of favor as the perceived importance of fanciful literature waxes and wanes. Adults have differed with one another within a single time period, and attempts have been made to censor literature for children. Children continue to have an underground literature, those stories that they read even if the adults in their lives do not approve, whether these were chapbooks in the 1600s or horror stories in the 1900s.

Publishing remains a business, with its bottom line of profit. John Newbery packaged *The History of Little Goody Two-Shoes* with the cushion and pins for tallying good and bad deeds, and contemporary publishers tie their books to movies, TV, videos, and action figures. When times are good, more books are published. When finances are strained, as in the depression of the 1930s, the number of trade books published declines (Karl 261). And publishers must make decisions based on who buys and what sells. Thus attractive picture books fill the shelves of bookstores; paperback books appear in book club advertisements; favorite titles are reissued, often with new illustrations.

The basic tension between the role of literature as entertainment and its role in instruction continues. Some teachers feel guilty when they select books "just for fun." Others look at how they might use books in their teaching of science and social studies topics, but worry about the possibility of destroying the aesthetic value of the literature. Teachers are plagued by questions such as

"Should I use a mediocre book if it teaches something important?"

"Should I eliminate a well-written book if I do not approve of the message?"

The decisions are not easy, but it helps to see them in historical perspective and to see our own reasoning as it relates to the reasoning of others.

SUMMARY

Adults are influenced by the society in which they live and how that society at that time views its children. Changes in what has been deemed appropriate for children have occurred from time to time and place to place. In the early 17th century, in both Britain and the United States, literature for children was designed to help children be saved so that should they die an early death—not uncommon at that time—they would not die sinners. Literature for children in the 1990s in the United States still is still instructive, but now it is more about how people live and why they make the decisions they do.

The question of whether the purpose of literature is to instruct or to delight has permeated each generation's view of what literature is best for children. Adults selecting books for children can gain insight into their own beliefs by seeing how people in the past have addressed the issue. They will also see that issues of censorship are not new, but must still be dealt with seriously.

∞ EXPLORE ON YOUR OWN

1. **Explore Your Personal Response.** Read two books that were first published in the years when you were eight- or nine-years-old. You can find the titles by looking at reviews of new books in *The Horn Book Magazine* for those years. What is the view of childhood that seems to be represented? How do you feel about the values expressed in each of the books?

2. **Apply Literary Criteria.** Read two books from a series such as Nancy Drew, The Hardy Boys, or The Babysitters-Club. Evaluate them using the literary criteria described in Chapter 2.

3. **Prepare to Share Literature With Children.** Write down how you might introduce a book that has significance in the history of literature for children to an audience of children. How much information would you give them? Why?

∞ EXPLORE WITH CHILDREN

1. **Explore Children's Responses.** Find a book published before 1960 and share it with a child or group of children. Analyze their responses in light of the book's content and presentation and what you know of the child or children. Did the age of the book make a difference?

or

Ask several fourth graders to tell you the titles of three of their favorite books. What percent of the titles are series books? Is there any pattern—by gender or perhaps specific books mentioned?

2. **Engage Children With Literature.** Read to a group of children a book or an excerpt from a book published before 1900. See Figure 12-5 for possible titles. Tell them the publication date. Have them design a cover for the book that they think is consistent with the content *and* that would make the book appealing to today's readers.

∞ SUGGESTED PROFESSIONAL REFERENCES

Avery, Gillian. *Behold the Child: American Children and Their Books 1621–1922*. Baltimore: Johns Hopkins, 1995. § American children's books are frequently compared to British books for children in this heavily illustrated volume.

Bader, Barbara. *American Picture Books from Noah's Ark to the Beast Within*. New York: Macmillan, 1976. § This history of American picture books includes the influence of popular culture and social views on books for children.

Bingham, Jane, and Grayce Scholt. *Fifteen Centuries of Children's Literature*. Westport, CT: Greenwood Press, 1980. § Dividing the history of American and British books for children into six time periods, the authors show the development of the books and the attitudes of the people for each segment.

Carpenter, Humphrey. *Secret Gardens. The Golden Age of Children's Literature*. Boston: Houghton Mifflin, 1985. § Both biographical and critical, this book explores the lives and writing of children's authors from 1865 to 1926, from *Alice's Adventures in Wonderland* to *Winnie-the-Pooh*.

Demers, Patricia, and Gordon Moyles, eds. *From Instruction to Delight*. Toronto: Oxford University Press, 1982. § This anthology includes illustrations and text from books read to children from medieval times through the mid-19th century, with notes about each of the authors and works.

Goldthwaite, John. *The Natural History of Make-Believe: Tracing the Literature of Imagination for Children*. New York: Oxford University Press, 1995. § The author describes and critiques fantasy and nonsense books for children, ranging from folktales to *The Chronicles of Narnia*.

Hunt, Peter, ed. *Children's Literature: An Illustrated History*. New York: Oxford University Press, 1995. § With contributors from several nations, this book shows the development of literature for children in English-speaking countries, from Aesop to Sendak.

Lehr, Susan, ed. *Battling Dragons: Issues and Controversy in Children's Literature*. Portsmouth, NH: Heinemann, 1995. § Writers, editors, publishers, sellers, and teachers of literature for children examine areas of controversy within the field in a series of essays.

Lurie, Alison. *Don't Tell the Grown-ups: Subversive Children's Literature*. Boston: Little, Brown, 1990. § The essays in this collection show that works of literature for children that have remained popular often went against the values of the times in which they were published.

Marcus, Leonard S. *75 Years of Children's Book Week Posters*. New York: Knopf, 1994. § Marcus' commentary as he traces the posters designed for Book Week celebrations show social changes as they are reflected in the works depicted.

Meigs, Cornelia, et al. *A Critical History of Children's Literature,* rev. ed. New York: Macmillan, 1969. § Social trends that affected British and American children's literature are described for each of four chronological periods.

Moffett, James. *Storm in the Mountains: A Case Study of Censorship, Conflict, and Consciousness*. Carbondale, IL: Southern Illinois University Press, 1988. § Although describing the conflicts over textbook, not trade book, selection in Kanawha County, West Virginia, the author's analysis of the cultural conflicts involved in censorship issues in the United States has application to book selection in general.

Reichman, Henry. *Censorship and Selection: Issues and Answers for School*. Chicago: American Library Association, 1988. § An excellent reference, this book provides guidelines for establishing selection policies and for dealing with censorship issues.

Silvey, Anita, ed. *Children's Books and Their Creators*. Boston: Houghton, 1995. § Focusing on books published within the last 50 years, this volume includes biographical sketches of authors and illustrators, descriptions of literary genre and history, and essays by children's book authors.

Simmons, John S., ed. *Censorship: A Threat to Reading, Learning, Thinking*. Newark, DE: International Reading Association, 1994. § Specific censorship cases are presented with an analysis of their effects and a plan for dealing with complaints and challenges.

∽ CHILDREN'S BOOKS CITED

Alcott, Louisa May. *Little Women*. Boston: Little, Brown, 1868.

*Alger, Horatio. *Ragged Dick*. Boston: Loring, 1868.

Carroll, Lewis. *Alice in Wonderland*. New York: Norton, 1971. (*Alice's Adventures in Wonderland* was first published in 1865; *Through the Looking Glass* in 1871.)

Comenius, John Amos. *Orbis Pictus*. Syracuse, NY: C. W. Bardeen, 1887. (Reissued by Singing Tree Press, Detroit, MI, 1968.)

*Farquharson, Martha (pseudonym for Martha Farquharson Finley). *Elsie Dinsmore*. New York: M. W. Dodd, 1867.

Fitzhugh, Louise. *Harriet the Spy*. New York: Harper, 1964.

Flack, Marjorie. *The Story About Ping*. Ill. by Kurt Wiese. New York: Viking, 1933.

Gag, Wanda. *Millions of Cats*. New York: Coward-McCann, 1928.

*Goodrich, Samuel Griswold. *The Tales of Peter Parley About America*. Boston: S. G. Goodrich, 1827.

Hamilton, Virginia. *The People Could Fly*. Ill. by Leo and Diane Dillon. New York: Knopf, 1985.

*Harris, Joel Chandler. *Uncle Remus, His Songs and His Sayings*. Ill. by Frederick S. Church and James H. Moser. New York: D. Appleton and Co., 1881.

Haviland, Virginia, and Margaret N. Coughlin, eds. *Yankee Doodle's Literary Sampler of Prose, Poetry, and Pictures*. New York: Crowell, 1974.

The History of Little Goody Two-Shoes. New York: H. W. Hewit, Co. 1855.

*Janeway, James. *A Token for Children*. Boston: Z. Fowle, 1771.

**A Little Pretty Pocket-Book*. Worcester, MA: Isaiah Thomas, 1787.

Milne, A.A. *Winnie-the-Pooh*. Ill. by Ernest Shepard. New York: Dutton, 1926.

Twain, Mark (pseudonym for Samuel Clemens) *The Adventures of Huckleberry Finn*. New York: Harper, 1884.

————. *The Adventures of Tom Sawyer*. New York: Harper, 1876.

Wilder, Laura Ingalls. *Little House in the Big Woods*. Ill. by Garth Williams. New York: Harper, 1953 (1932).

Willhoite, Michael. *Daddy's Roommate*. Boston: Alyson, 1990.

---

* Excerpts of the books preceded by an asterisk appear in Haviland and Coughlin's *Yankee Doodle's Literary Sampler of Prose, Poetry, and Pictures*. New York: Crowell, 1974.

∽ CHAPTER REFERENCES

Avery, Gillian. "Fashions in Children's Fiction." *Children's Literature in Education* 12 (1973): 10–19.

Avi. "The Child in Children's Literature." *The Horn Book* 69.1 (Jan./Feb. 1993): 40–50.

Borg, Linda. "Book on Gay Life Won't Be Restricted." *The Providence Journal* 22 Apr. 1993: A1, A10.

California State Department of Education. *Recommended Readings in Literature, Kindergarten Through Grade Eight*. Sacramento: California State Department of Education, 1986.

Children's Books in Print. New York: R. R. Bowker, 1995.

Church, Phyllis. "Sassy as a Jaybird: Brer Rabbit in Children's Literature." *Journal of Youth Services to Children* 4.3 (Spring 1991): 243–247.

Clemens, Samuel L. *Autobiography*. Vol. 2. New York: Harper, 1924.

Coughlin, Margaret. "Guardians of the Young." *Top of the News* 43.2 (Winter 1977): 137–148.

Egoff, Sheila, G. T. Stubbs, and L. F. Ashley, eds. *Only Connect: Readings on Children's Literature*. New York: Oxford University Press, 1969.

Elleman, Barbara. "Toward the 21st Century—Where Are Children's Books Going?" *The New Advocate* 8.3 (Summer 1995): 151–163.

Hamilton, Virginia. *The People Could Fly*. Ill. by Leo and Diane Dillon. New York: Knopf, 1985.

Haviland, Virginia, and Margaret N. Coughlin (eds.) *Yankee Doodle's Literary Sampler of Prose, Poetry and Pictures*. New York: Harper, 1974.

Hearn, Michael Patrick. "What Ever Happened to 'Peter Parley?'" *Teaching and Learning Literature with Children and Young Adults* 4.5 (May/June 1995): 34–40.

Johannsen, Albert. *The House of Beadle and Adams and Its Dime and Nickel Novels*. Vol. 1. Norman, OK: University of Oklahoma Press, 1950.

Karl, Jean. "A History of Children's Book Publishing." *Youth Services in Libraries* 8.3 (Spring 1995): 259–265.

Keeline, James D. "The Stratemeyer Syndicate and its Role in Creating Series Books that Children Actually Read." *Teaching and Learning Literature* 5.3 (Jan./Feb. 1996): 39–50.

Lamb, Charles, in E. V. Lucas, ed. *Letters of Charles Lamb*. New Haven: Yale University Press, 1935.

Lanes, Selma. *Down the Rabbit Hole*. New York: Atheneum, 1971.

Locke, John. *On Politics and Education*. Roslyn, NY: Walter J. Black, 1947. *(Some Thoughts Concerning Education* was first published in 1693).

Miller, Janet, and June H. Schlessinger. "Trends in the Portrayal of Minorities in the Nancy Drew Series." *Journal of Youth Services in Libraries* 1.3 (Spring 1988): 329–333.

Rudman, Masha, and Susan Rosenberg. "Confronting History: Holocaust Books for Children." *The New Advocate* 4.3 (Summer 1991): 163–177.

Silberberg, Sophie C., and John Donovan. "Fifty Years of Children's Book Week: Fifty years of Independent American Children's Book Publishing," *The Horn Book* (Dec. 1969): 702–711.

Simora, Filomena, ed. *The Bowker Annual of Library and Book Trade Information*. New York: R. R. Bowker, 1988.

Sims, Rudine Bishop. "Multicultural Literature for Children, Making Informed Choices." *Teaching Multicultural Literature in Grades K–8*. Ed. Violet J. Harris. Norwood, MA: Christopher-Gordon, 1992.

Thomas, Fannette H. "Early Appearances of Children's Reading Rooms in Public Libraries." *Journal of Youth Services in Libraries* 4.1 (Fall 1990): 81–85.

 **Appendix A**

Children's Book Awards

THE RANDOLPH CALDECOTT MEDAL

The Randolph Caldecott Medal, named in honor of a nineteenth-century British illustrator of books for children, is given annually to the illustrator of the most distinguished picture book for children published in the United States in the year preceding the award. It is presented by a committee of the Association of Library Service to Children of the American Library Association. Eligibility for the award is limited to U.S. citizens and permanent residents. The following list includes both award winners and honor books for each year. If the illustrator is not cited then the book was written and illustrated by the same person.

1938

Animals of the Bible, a Picture Book. Text selected from the King James *Bible* by Helen Dean Fish. Illustrated by Dorothy P. Lathrop. Lippincott.

Honor Books:
Seven Simeons: A Russian Tale by Boris Artzybasheff. Viking.

Four and Twenty Blackbirds compiled by Helen Dean Fish. Illustrated by Robert Lawson. Stokes/Lippincott.

1939

Mei Li by Thomas Handforth. Doubleday.

Honor Books:
The Forest Pool by Laura Adams Armer. McKay/Longmans.

Wee Gillis by Munro Leaf. Illustrated by Robert Lawson. Viking.

Snow White and the Seven Dwarfs. Translated and illustrated by Wanda Gág. Coward-McCann.

Barkis by Clare Turlay Newberry. Harper.

Andy and the Lion by James Daugherty. Viking.

1940

Abraham Lincoln by Ingri d'Aulaire and Edgar Parin d'Aulaire. Doubleday.

Honor Books:
Cock-a-Doodle-Doo by Berta and Elmer Hader. Macmillan.

Madeline by Ludwig Bemelmans. Viking.

The Ageless Story by Lauren Ford. Dodd.

1941

They Were Strong and Good by Robert Lawson. Viking.

Honor Book:
April's Kittens by Clare Turlay Newberry. Harper.

1942

Make Way for Ducklings by Robert McCloskey. Viking.

Honor Books:
An American ABC by Maud and Miska Petersham. Macmillan.

In My Mother's House by Ann Nolan Clark. Illustrated by Velino Herrera. Viking.

Paddle-to-the-Sea by Holling Clancy Holling. Houghton Mifflin.

Nothing at All by Wanda Gág. Coward-McCann.

1943

The Little House by Virginia Lee Burton. Houghton Mifflin.

Honor Books:
Dash and Dart by Mary and Conrad Buff. Viking.

Marshmallow by Clare Turlay Newberry. Harper.

1944

Many Moons by James Thurber. Illustrated by Louis Slobodkin. Harcourt.

Honor Books:
Small Rain: Verses from the Bible. Text arranged from the Bible by Jessie Orton Jones. Illustrated by Elizabeth Orton Jones. Viking.

Pierre Pigeon by Lee Kingman. Illustrated by Arnold Edwin Bare. Houghton Mifflin.

The Mighty Hunter by Berta and Elmer Hader. Macmillan.

A Child's Good Night Book by Margaret Wise Brown. Illustrated by Jean Charlot. Scott.

Good Luck Horse by Chih-Yi Chan. Illustrated by Plato Chan. Whittlesey.

1945

Prayer for a Child by Rachel Field. Illustrated by Elizabeth Orton Jones. Macmillan.

Honor Books:
Mother Goose: Seventy-Seven Verses With Pictures. Illustrated by Tasha Tudor. Walck.

In the Forest by Marie Hall Ets. Viking.

Yonie Wondernose by Marguerite de Angeli. Doubleday.

The Christmas Anna Angel by Ruth Sawyer. Illustrated by Kate Seredy. Viking.

1946

The Rooster Crows selected and illustrated by Maud and Miska Petersham. Macmillan.

Honor Books:
Little Lost Lamb by Golden MacDonald. Illustrated by Leonard Weisgard. Doubleday.

Sing Mother Goose by Opal Wheeler. Illustrated by Marjorie Torrey. Dutton.

My Mother Is the Most Beautiful Woman in the World retold by Becky Reyher. Illustrated by Ruth Gannett. Lothrop.

You Can Write Chinese by Kurt Wiese. Viking.

1947

The Little Island by Golden MacDonald. Illustrated by Leonard Weisgard. Doubleday.

Honor Books:
Rain Drop Splash by Alvin Tresselt. Illustrated by Leonard Weisgard. Lothrop.

Boats on the River by Marjorie Flack. Illustrated by Jay Hyde Barnum. Viking.

Timothy Turtle by Al Graham. Illustrated by Tony Palazzo. Viking.

Pedro, the Angel of Olvera Street by Leo Politi. Scribner's.

Sing in Praise: A Collection of the Best Loved Hymns by Opal Wheeler. Illustrated by Marjorie Torrey. Dutton.

1948

White Snow, Bright Snow by Alvin Tresselt. Illustrated by Roger Duvoisin. Lothrop.

Honor Books:
Stone Soup: An Old Tale by Marcia Brown. Scribner's.

McElligot's Pool by Dr. Seuss (pseud. for Theodor Geisel). Random.

Bambino the Clown by George Schreiber. Viking.

Roger and the Fox by Lavinia Davis. Illustrated by Hildegard Woodward. Doubleday.

Song of Robin Hood edited by Anne Malcolmson. Illustrated by Virginia Lee Burton. Houghton Mifflin.

1949

The Big Snow by Berta and Elmer Hader. Macmillan.

Honor Books:
Blueberries for Sal by Robert McCloskey. Viking.

All Around Town by Phyllis McGinley. Illustrated by Helen Stone. Lippincott.

Juanita by Leo Politi. Scribner's.

Fish in the Air by Kurt Wiese. Viking.

1950

Song of the Swallows by Leo Politi. Scribner's.

Honor Books:
America's Ethan Allen by Stewart Holbrook. Illustrated by Lynd Ward. Houghton Mifflin.

The Wild Birthday Cake by Lavinia R. Davis. Illustrated by Hildegard Woodward. Doubleday.

The Happy Day by Ruth Krauss. Illustrated by Marc Simont. Harper.

Henry-Fisherman by Marcia Brown. Scribner's.

Bartholomew and the Oobleck by Dr. Seuss (pseud. for Theodor Geisel). Random.

1951

The Egg Tree by Katherine Milhous. Scribner's.

Honor Books:
Dick Whittington and His Cat. Translated and illustrated by Marcia Brown. Scribner's.

The Two Reds by Will (pseud. for William Lipkind). Illustrated by Nicolas (pseud. for Nicolas Mordvinoff). Harcourt.

If I Ran the Zoo by Dr. Seuss (pseud. for Theodor Geisel). Random.

T-Bone, the Baby-Sitter by Clare Turlay Newberry. Harper.

The Most Wonderful Doll in the World by Phyllis McGinley. Illustrated by Helen Stone. Lippincott.

1952

Finders Keepers by Will (pseud. for William Lipkind). Illustrated by Nicolas (pseud. for Nicolas Mordvinoff). Harcourt.

Honor Books:
Mr. T. W. Anthony Woo by Marie Hall Ets. Viking.

Skipper John's Cook by Marcia Brown. Scribner's.

All Falling Down by Gene Zion. Illustrated by Margaret Bloy Graham. Harper.

Bear Party by William Pène du Bois. Viking.

Feather Mountain by Elizabeth Olds. Houghton Mifflin.

1953

The Biggest Bear by Lynd Ward. Houghton Mifflin.

Honor Books:
Puss in Boots. Translated and illustrated by Marcia Brown. Scribner's.

One Morning in Maine by Robert McCloskey. Viking.

Ape in a Cape: An Alphabet of Odd Animals by Fritz Eichenberg. Harcourt.

The Storm Book by Charlotte Zolotow. Illustrated by Margaret Bloy Graham. Harper.

Five Little Monkeys by Juliet Kepes. Houghton Mifflin.

1954

Madeline's Rescue by Ludwig Bemelmans. Viking.

Honor Books:
Journey Cake, Ho! by Ruth Sawyer. Illustrated by Robert McCloskey. Viking.

When Will the World Be Mine? by Miriam Schlein. Illustrated by Jean Charlot. Scott.

The Steadfast Tin Soldier by Hans Christian Andersen. Translated by M. R. James. Illustrated by Marcia Brown. Scribner's.

A Very Special House by Ruth Krauss. Illustrated by Maurice Sendak. Harper.

Green Eyes by Abe Birnbaum. Capitol.

1955

Cinderella, or the Little Glass Slipper by Charles Perrault. Translated and illustrated by Marcia Brown. Scribner's.

Honor Books:
Book of Nursery and Mother Goose Rhymes compiled and illustrated by Marguerite de Angeli. Doubleday.

Wheel on the Chimney by Margaret Wise Brown. Illustrated by Tibor Gergely. Lippincott.

The Thanksgiving Story by Alice Dalgliesh. Illustrated by Helen Sewell. Scribner's.

1956

Frog Went A-Courtin' retold by John Langstaff. Illustrated by Feodor Rojankovsky. Harcourt.

Honor Books:
Play With Me by Marie Hall Ets. Viking.

Crow Boy by Taro Yashima. Viking.

1957

A Tree Is Nice by Janice May Udry. Illustrated by Marc Simont. Harper.

Honor Books:
Mr. Penny's Race Horse by Marie Hall Ets. Viking.

1 Is One by Tasha Tudor. Walck.

Anatole by Eve Titus. Illustrated by Paul Galdone. McGraw.

Gillespie and the Guards by Benjamin Elkin. Illustrated by James Daugherty. Viking.

Lion by William Pène du Bois. Viking.

1958

Time of Wonder by Robert McCloskey. Viking.

Honor Books:

Fly High, Fly Low by Don Freeman. Viking.

Anatole and the Cat by Eve Titus. Illustrated by Paul Galdone. McGraw.

1959

Chanticleer and the Fox by Chaucer. Adapted and illustrated by Barbara Cooney. Crowell.

Honor Books:

The House That Jack Built ("La Maison Que Jacques a Bâtie"): A Picture Book in Two Languages by Antonio Frasconi. Harcourt.

What Do You Say, Dear? A Book of Manners for All Occasions by Sesyle Joslin. Illustrated by Maurice Sendak. Scott.

Umbrella by Taro Yashima. Viking.

1960

Nine Days to Christmas by Marie Hall Ets and Aurora Labastida. Illustrated by Marie Hall Ets. Viking.

Honor Books:

Houses from the Sea by Alice E. Goudey. Illustrated by Adrienne Adams. Scribner's.

The Moon Jumpers by Janice May Udry. Illustrated by Maurice Sendak. Harper.

1961

Baboushka and the Three Kings by Ruth Robbins. Illustrated by Nicolas Sidjakov. Parnassus.

Honor Book:

Inch by Inch by Leo Lionni. Obolensky.

1962

Once a Mouse retold by Marcia Brown. Scribner's.

Honor Books:

The Fox Went Out on a Chilly Night: An Old Song by Peter Spier. Doubleday.

Little Bear's Visit by Else Minarik. Illustrated by Maurice Sendak. Harper.

The Day We Saw the Sun Come Up by Alice Goudey. Illustrated by Adrienne Adams. Scribner's.

1963

The Snowy Day by Ezra Jack Keats. Viking.

Honor Books:

The Sun Is a Golden Earring by Natalia Belting. Illustrated by Bernarda Bryson. Holt.

Mr. Rabbit and the Lovely Present by Charlotte Zolotow. Illustrated by Maurice Sendak. Harper.

1964

Where the Wild Things Are by Maurice Sendak. Harper.

Honor Books:

Swimmy by Leo Lionni. Pantheon.

All in the Morning Early by Sorche Nic Leodhas (pseud. for Leclaire Alger). Illustrated by Evaline Ness. Holt.

Mother Goose and Nursery Rhymes by Philip Reed. Atheneum.

1965

May I Bring a Friend? by Beatrice Schenk de Regniers. Illustrated by Beni Montresor. Atheneum.

Honor Books:

Rain Makes Applesauce by Julian Scheer. Illustrated by Marvin Bileck. Holiday House.

The Wave by Margaret Hodges. Illustrated by Blair Lent. Houghton Mifflin.

A Pocketful of Cricket by Rebecca Caudill. Illustrated by Evaline Ness. Holt.

1966

Always Room for One More by Sorche Nic Leodhas (pseud. for Leclaire Alger). Illustrated by Nonny Hogrogian. Holt.

Honor Books:

Hide and Seek Fog by Alvin Tresselt. Illustrated by Roger Duvoisin. Lothrop.

Just Me by Marie Hall Ets. Viking.

Tom Tit Tot adapted by Joseph Jacobs. Illustrated by Evaline Ness. Scribner's.

1967

Sam, Bangs and Moonshine by Evaline Ness. Holt.

Honor Book:

One Wide River to Cross adapted by Barbara Emberley. Illustrated by Ed Emberley. Prentice Hall.

1968

Drummer Hoff adapted by Barbara Emberley. Illustrated by Ed Emberley. Prentice Hall.

Honor Books:

Frederick by Leo Lionni. Pantheon.

Seashore Story by Taro Yashima. Viking.

The Emperor and the Kite by Jane Yolen. Illustrated by Ed Young. World.

1969

The Fool of the World and the Flying Ship: A Russian Tale by Arthur Ransome. Illustrated by Uri Shulevitz. Farrar.

Honor Book:

Why the Sun and the Moon Live in the Sky: An African Folktale by Elphinstone Dayrell. Illustrated by Blair Lent. Houghton Mifflin.

1970

Sylvester and the Magic Pebble by William Steig. Windmill.

Honor Books:

Goggles! by Ezra Jack Keats. Macmillan.

Alexander and the Wind-Up Mouse by Leo Lionni. Pantheon.

Pop Corn and Ma Goodness by Edna Mitchell Preston. Illustrated by Robert Andrew Parker. Viking.

Thy Friend, Obadiah by Brinton Turkle. Viking.

The Judge: An Untrue Tale by Harve Zemach. Illustrated by Margot Zemach. Farrar.

1971

A Story, a Story: An African Tale by Gail E. Haley. Atheneum.

Honor Books:

The Angry Moon retold by William Sleator. Illustrated by Blair Lent. Atlantic/Little, Brown.

Frog and Toad Are Friends by Arnold Lobel. Harper.

In the Night Kitchen by Maurice Sendak. Harper.

1972

One Fine Day by Nonny Hogrogian. Macmillan.

Honor Books:

If All the Seas Were One Sea by Janina Domanska. Macmillan.

Moja Means One: Swahili Counting Book by Muriel Feelings. Illustrated by Tom Feelings. Dial.

Hildilid's Night by Cheli Duran Ryan. Illustrated by Arnold Lobel. Macmillan.

1973

The Funny Little Woman retold by Arlene Mosel. Illustrated by Blair Lent. Dutton.

Honor Books:

Hosie's Alphabet by Hosea Baskin, Tobias Baskin, and Lisa Baskin. Illustrated by Leonard Baskin. Viking.

When Clay Sings by Byrd Baylor. Illustrated by Tom Bahti. Scribner's.

Snow-White and the Seven Dwarfs by the Brothers Grimm. Translated by Randall Jarrell. Illustrated by Nancy Ekholm Burkert. Farrar.

Anansi the Spider: A Tale from the Ashanti adapted and illustrated by Gerald McDermott. Holt.

1974

Duffy and the Devil retold by Harve Zemach. Illustrated by Margot Zemach. Farrar.

Honor Books:

Three Jovial Huntsmen adapted and illustrated by Susan Jeffers. Bradbury.

Cathedral: The Story of Its Construction by David Macaulay. Houghton Mifflin.

1975

Arrow to the Sun adapted and illustrated by Gerald McDermott. Viking.

Honor Book:

Jambo Means Hello: Swahili Alphabet Book by Muriel Feelings. Illustrated by Tom Feelings. Dial.

1976

Why Mosquitoes Buzz in People's Ears retold by Verna Aardema. Illustrated by Leo and Diane Dillon. Dial.

Honor Books:

The Desert Is Theirs by Byrd Baylor. Illustrated by Peter Parnall. Scribner's.

Strega Nona retold and illustrated by Tomie dePaola. Prentice Hall.

1977

Ashanti to Zulu: African Traditions by Margaret Musgrove. Illustrated by Leo and Diane Dillon. Dial.

Honor Books:

The Amazing Bone by William Steig. Farrar.

The Contest by Nonny Hogrogian. Greenwillow.

Fish for Supper by M. B. Goffstein. Dial.

The Golem: A Jewish Legend retold and illustrated by Beverly Brodsky McDermott. Lippincott.

Hawk, I'm Your Brother by Byrd Baylor. Illustrated by Peter Parnall. Scribner's.

1978

Noah's Ark by Peter Spier. Doubleday.

Honor Books:
Castle by David Macaulay. Houghton Mifflin.

It Could Always Be Worse retold and illustrated by Margot Zemach. Farrar.

1979

The Girl Who Loved Wild Horses by Paul Goble. Bradbury.

Honor Books:
Freight Train by Donald Crews. Greenwillow.

The Way to Start a Day by Byrd Baylor. Illustrated by Peter Parnall. Scribner's.

1980

Ox-Cart Man by Donald Hall. Illustrated by Barbara Cooney. Viking.

Honor Books:
Ben's Trumpet by Rachel Isadora. Greenwillow.

The Treasure by Uri Schulevitz. Farrar.

The Garden of Abdul Gasazi by Chris Van Allsburg. Houghton Mifflin.

1981

Fables by Arnold Lobel. Harper.

Honor Books:
The Bremen-Town Musicians retold and illustrated by Ilse Plume. Doubleday.

The Grey Lady and the Strawberry Snatcher by Molly Bang. Four Winds.

Mice Twice by Joseph Low. Atheneum.

Truck by Donald Crews. Greenwillow.

1982

Jumanji by Chris Van Allsburg. Houghton Mifflin.

Honor Books:
A Visit to William Blake's Inn: Poems for Innocent and Experienced Travelers by Nancy Willard. Illustrated by Alice and Martin Provensen. Harcourt.

Where the Buffaloes Begin by Olaf Baker. Illustrated by Stephen Gammell. Warne.

On Market Street by Arnold Lobel. Illustrated by Anita Lobel. Greenwillow.

Outside Over There by Maurice Sendak. Harper.

1983

Shadow by Blaise Cendrars. Translated and illustrated by Marcia Brown. Scribner's.

Honor Books:
When I Was Young in the Mountains by Cynthia Rylant. Illustrated by Diane Goode. Dutton.

A Chair for My Mother by Vera B. Williams. Greenwillow.

1984

The Glorious Flight: Across the Channel with Louis Blériot, by Alice and Martin Provensen. Viking.

Honor Books:
Ten, Nine, Eight by Molly Bang. Greenwillow.

Little Red Riding Hood by the Brothers Grimm. Retold and illustrated by Trina Schart Hyman. Holiday House.

1985

Saint George and the Dragon adapted by Margaret Hodges. Illustrated by Trina Schart Hyman. Little, Brown.

Honor Books:
Hansel and Gretel adapted by Rika Lesser. Illustrated by Paul O. Zelinksy. Dodd.

The Story of Jumping Mouse retold and illustrated by John Steptoe. Lothrop.

Have You Seen My Duckling? by Nancy Tafuri. Greenwillow.

1986

The Polar Express by Chris Van Allsburg. Houghton Mifflin.

Honor Books:
The Relatives Came by Cynthia Rylant. Illustrated by Stephen Gammell. Bradbury.

King Bidgood's in the Bathtub by Audrey Wood. Illustrated by Don Wood. Harcourt.

1987

Hey, Al by Arthur Yorinks. Illustrated by Richard Egielski. Farrar.

Honor Books:
The Village of Round and Square Houses by Ann Grifalconi. Little, Brown.

Alphabatics by Suse MacDonald. Bradbury.

Rumpelstiltskin by the Brothers Grimm. Retold and illustrated by Paul O. Zelinsky. Dutton.

1988

Owl Moon by Jane Yolen. Illustrated by John Schoenherr. Philomel.

Honor Book:
Mufaro's Beautiful Daughters retold by John Steptoe. Lothrop.

1989

Song and Dance Man by Karen Ackerman. Illustrated by Stephen Gammell. Knopf.

Honor Books:
Free Fall by David Wiesner. Lothrop.

Goldilocks and the Three Bears retold and illustrated by James Marshall. Dial.

Mirandy and Brother Wind by Patricia McKissack. Illustrated by Jerry Pinkney. Knopf.

The Boy of the Three-Year Nap by Diane Snyder. Illustrated by Allen Say. Houghton Mifflin.

1990

Lon Po Po: A Red-Riding Hood Story from China translated and illustrated by Ed Young. Philomel.

Honor Books:
Hershel and the Hanukkah Goblins by Eric Kimmel. Illustrated by Trina Schart Hyman. Holiday House.

The Talking Eggs adapted by Robert D. San Souci. Illustrated by Jerry Pinkney. Dial.

Bill Peet: An Autobiography by Bill Peet. Houghton Mifflin.

Color Zoo by Lois Ehlert. Lippincott.

1991

Black and White by David Macaulay. Houghton Mifflin.

Honor Books:
Puss 'n Boots by Charles Perrault. Illustrated by Fred Marcellino. Farrar.

"More, More, More," Said the Baby: 3 Love Stories by Vera B. Williams. Greenwillow.

1992

Tuesday by David Wiesner. Clarion.

Honor Book:
Tar Beach by Faith Ringgold. Crown.

1993

Mirette on the High Wire by Emily Arnold McCully. Putnam.

Honor Books:
Seven Blind Mice by Ed Young. Philomel.

The Stinky Cheese Man & Other Fairly Stupid Tales by Jon Scieszka. Illustrated by Lane Smith. Viking.

Working Cotton by Sherley Anne Williams. Illustrated by Carole Byard. Harcourt.

1994

Grandfather's Journey by Allen Say. Houghton Mifflin.

Honor Books:
Peppe the Lamplighter by Elisa Bartone. Illustrated by Ted Lewin. Lothrop.

In the Small, Small Pond by Denise Fleming. Holt.

Owen by Kevin Henkes. Greenwillow.

Raven: A Trickster Tale from the Pacific Northwest by Gerald McDermott. Harcourt.

Yo! Yes? by Chris Raschka. Orchard.

1995

Smoky Night by Eve Bunting. Illustrated by David Diaz. Harcourt.

Honor Books:
Swamp Angel by Anne Isaacs. Illustrated by Paul O. Zelinsky. Dutton.

John Henry by Julius Lester. Illustrated by Jerry Pinkney. Dial.

Time Flies by Eric Rohmann. Crown.

1996

Office Buckle and Gloria by Peggy Rathman. Putnam.

Honor Books:
Alphabet City by Stephen Johnson. Viking.

Zin! Zin! Zin! a Violin by Lloyd Moss. Illustrated by Marjorie Priceman. Simon.

The Faithful Friend by Robert San Souci. Illustrated by Brian Pinkney. Simon.

Tops and Bottoms by Janet Stevens. Harcourt.

THE JOHN NEWBERY MEDAL

The John Newbery Medal, named in honor of an eighteenth- century British publisher and bookseller, is given annually to the author of the most distinguished contribution to literature for children publishéd in the United States in the year preceding the award. It is presented by a committee of the Association of Library Service to Children of the American Library Association. Eligibility for the award is limited to U.S. citizens and permanent residents. The following list includes both award winners and honor books for each year.

1922

The Story of Mankind by Hendrik Willem Van Loon. Liveright.

Honor Books:
The Great Quest by Charles Boardman Hawes. Little, Brown.

Cedric the Forester by Bernard G. Marshall. Appleton.

The Old Tobacco Shop by William Bowen. Macmillan.

The Golden Fleece and the Heroes Who Lived Before Achilles by Padraic Colum. Macmillan.

Windy Hill by Cornelia Meigs. Macmillan.

1923

The Voyages of Doctor Dolittle by Hugh Lofting. Lippincott. (No record of the honor books.)

1924

The Dark Frigate by Charles Boardman Hawes. Little, Brown. (No record of the honor books.)

1925

Tales from Silver Lands by Charles J. Finger. Illustrated by Paul Honoré. Doubleday.

Honor Books:
Nicholas by Anne Carroll Moore. Putnam.

Dream Coach by Anne and Dillwyn Parrish. Macmillan.

1926

Shen of the Sea by Arthur Bowie Chrisman. Illustrated by Else Hasselriis. Dutton.

Honor Book:
The Voyagers by Padraic Colum. Macmillan.

1927

Smoky, the Cowhorse by Will James. Scribner's. (No record of the runners-up.)

1928

Gay-Neck, The Story of a Pigeon by Dhan Gopal Mukerji. Illustrated by Boris Artzybasheff. Dutton.

Honor Books:
The Wonder Smith and His Son by Ella Young. McKay/Longmans.

Downright Dencey by Caroline Dale Snedeker. Doubleday.

1929

The Trumpeter of Krakow by Eric P. Kelly. Illustrated by Angela Pruszynska. Macmillan.

Honor Books:
The Pigtail of Ah Lee Ben Loo by John Bennett. McKay/Longmans.

Millions of Cats by Wanda Gág. Coward-McCann.

The Boy Who Was by Grace T. Hallock. Dutton.

Clearing Weather by Cornelia Meigs. Little, Brown.

The Runaway Papoose by Grace P. Moon. Doubleday.

Tod of the Fens by Eleanor Whitney. Macmillan.

1930

Hitty: Her First Hundred Years by Rachel Field. Illustrated by Dorothy P. Lathrop. Macmillan.

Honor Books:
The Tangle-Coated Horse and Other Tales: Episodes from the Fionn Saga by Ella Young. Illustrated by Vera Brock. Longmans.

Vaino: A Boy of New Finland by Julia Davis Adams. Illustrated by Lempi Ostman. Dutton.

Pran of Albania by Elizabeth C. Miller. Doubleday.

The Jumping-Off Place by Marian Hurd McNeely. McKay/Longmans.

A Daughter of the Seine by Jeanette Eaton. Harper.

Little Blacknose by Hildegarde Hoyt Swift. Illustrated by Lynd Ward. Harcourt.

1931

The Cat Who Went to Heaven by Elizabeth Coatsworth. Illustrated by Lynd Ward. Macmillan.

Honor Books:
Floating Island by Anne Parrish. Harper.

The Dark Star of Itza by Alida Malkus. Harcourt.

Queer Person by Ralph Hubbard. Doubleday.

Mountains Are Free by Julia Davis Adams. Dutton.

Spice and the Devil's Cave by Agnes D. Hewes. Knopf.

Meggy McIntosh by Elizabeth Janet Gray. Doubleday.

Garram the Hunter: A Boy of the Hill Tribes by Herbert Best. Illustrated by Allena Best (Erick Berry). Doubleday.

Ood-Le-Uk, The Wanderer by Alice Lide and Margaret Johansen. Illustrated by Raymond Lufkin. Little, Brown.

1932

Waterless Mountain by Laura Adams Armer. Illustrated by Sidney Armer and Laura Adams Armer. McKay/Longmans.

Honor Books:
The Fairy Circus by Dorothy Lathrop. Macmillan.

Calico Bush by Rachel Field. Macmillan.

Boy of the South Seas by Eunice Tietjens. Coward-McCann.

Out of the Flame by Eloise Lownsbery. McKay/Longmans.

Jane's Island by Marjorie Hill Alee. Houghton Mifflin.

The Truce of the Wolf and Other Tales of Old Italy by Mary Gould Davis. Harcourt.

1933

Young Fu of the Upper Yangtze by Elizabeth Foreman Lewis. Illustrated by Kurt Wiese. Holt.

Honor Books:
Swift Rivers by Cornelia Meigs. Little, Brown.

The Railroad to Freedom by Hildegarde Swift. Harcourt.

Children of the Soil by Nora Burglon. Doubleday.

1934

Invincible Louisa: The Story of the Author of "Little Women" by Cornelia Meigs. Little, Brown.

Honor Books:
The Forgotten Daughter by Caroline Dale Snedeker. Doubleday.

Swords of Steel by Elsie Singmaster. Houghton Mifflin.

ABC Bunny by Wanda Gág. Coward-McCann.

Winged Girl of Knossos by Erick Berry. Appleton.

New Land by Sarah L. Schmidt. McBride.

The Apprentice of Florence by Anne Kyle. Houghton Mifflin.

The Big Tree of Bunlahy: Stories of My Own Countryside by Padraic Colum. Illustrated by Jack Yeats. Macmillan.

Glory of the Seas by Agnes D. Hewes. Illustrated by N.C. Wyeth. Knopf.

1935

Dobry by Monica Shannon. Illustrated by Atanas Katchamakoff. Viking.

Honor Books:
The Pageant of Chinese History by Elizabeth Seeger. McKay/Longmans.

Davy Crockett by Constance Rourke. Harcourt.

A Day on Skates: The Story of a Dutch Picnic by Hilda Van Stockum. Harper.

1936

Caddie Woodlawn by Carol Ryrie Brink. Illustrated by Kate Seredy. Macmillan.

Honor Books:
Honk: The Moose by Phil Strong. Illustrated by Kurt Wiese. Dodd.

The Good Master by Kate Seredy. Viking.

Young Walter Scott by Elizabeth Janet Gray. Viking.

All Sail Set by Armstrong Sperry. Winston.

1937

Roller Skates by Ruth Sawyer. Illustrated by Valenti Angelo. Viking.

Honor Books:
Phoebe Fairchild: Her Book by Lois Lenski. Lippincott.

Whistler's Van by Idwal Jones. Viking.

The Golden Basket by Ludwig Bemelmans. Viking.

Winterbound by Margery Bianco. Viking.

Audubon by Constance Rourke. Harcourt.

The Codfish Musket by Agnes D. Hewes. Doubleday.

1938

The White Stag by Kate Seredy. Viking.

Honor Books:
Bright Island by Mabel L. Robinson. Random.

Pecos Bill by James Cloyd Bowman. Little, Brown.

On the Banks of Plum Creek by Laura Ingalls Wilder. Harper.

1939

Thimble Summer by Elizabeth Enright. Holt.

Honor Books:
Leader by Destiny: George Washington, Man and Patriot by Jeanette Eaton. Harcourt.

Penn by Elizabeth Janet Gray. Viking.

Nino by Valenti Angelo. Viking.

"Hello, the Boat!" by Phyllis Crawford. Holt.

Mr. Popper's Penguins by Richard and Florence Atwater. Little, Brown.

1940

Daniel Boone by James H. Daugherty. Viking.

Honor Books:
The Singing Tree by Kate Seredy. Viking.

Runner of the Mountain Tops by Mabel L. Robinson. Random.

By the Shores of Silver Lake by Laura Ingalls Wilder. Harper.

Boy with a Pack by Stephen W. Meader. Harcourt.

1941

Call It Courage by Armstrong Sperry. Macmillan.

Honor Books:
Blue Willow by Doris Gates. Viking.

Young Mac of Fort Vancouver by Mary Jane Carr. Crowell.

The Long Winter by Laura Ingalls Wilder. Harper.

Nansen by Anna Gertrude Hall. Viking.

1942

The Matchlock Gun by Walter D. Edmonds. Illustrated by Paul Lantz. Dodd.

Honor Books:
Little Town on the Prairie by Laura Ingalls Wilder. Harper.

George Washington's World by Genevieve Foster. Scribner's.

Indian Captive: The Story of Mary Jemison by Lois Lenski. Lippincott.

Down Ryton Water by Eva Roe Gaggin. Illustrated by Elmer Hader. Viking.

1943

Adam of the Road by Elizabeth Janet Gray. Illustrated by Robert Lawson. Viking.

Honor Books:
The Middle Moffat by Eleanor Estes. Harcourt.

"Have You Seen Tom Thumb?" by Mabel Leigh Hunt. Lippincott.

1944

Johnny Tremain by Esther Forbes. Illustrated by Lynd Ward. Houghton Mifflin.

Honor Books:
These Happy Golden Years by Laura Ingalls Wilder. Harper.

Fog Magic by Julia L. Sauer. Viking.

Rufus M. by Eleanor Estes. Harcourt.

Mountain Born by Elizabeth Yates. Coward-McCann.

1945

Rabbit Hill by Robert Lawson. Viking.

Honor Books:
The Hundred Dresses by Eleanor Estes. Harcourt.

The Silver Pencil by Alice Dalgliesh. Scribner's.

Abraham Lincoln's World by Genevieve Foster. Scribner's.

Lone Journey: The Life of Roger Williams by Jeanette Eaton. Illustrated by Woodi Ishmael. Harcourt.

1946

Strawberry Girl by Lois Lenski. Lippincott.

Honor Books:
Justin Morgan Had a Horse by Marguerite Henry. Follett.

The Moved-Outers by Florence Crannell Means. Houghton Mifflin.

Bhimsa, the Dancing Bear by Christine Weston. Scribner's.

New Found World by Katherine B. Shippen. Viking.

1947

Miss Hickory by Carolyn Sherwin Bailey. Illustrated by Ruth Gannett. Viking.

Honor Books:
The Wonderful Year by Nancy Barnes. Messner.

The Big Tree by Mary and Conrad Buff. Viking.

The Heavenly Tenants by William Maxwell. Harper.

The Avion My Uncle Flew by Cyrus Fisher. Appleton.

The Hidden Treasure of Glaston by Eleanore M. Jewett. Viking.

1948

The Twenty-One Balloons by William Pène du Bois. Lothrop.

Honor Books:
Pancakes-Paris by Claire Huchet Bishop. Viking.

Li Lun, Lad of Courage by Carolyn Treffinger. Abingdon.

The Quaint and Curious Quest of Johnny Longfoot, The Shoe-King's Son by Catherine Besterman. Bobbs-Merrill.

The Cow-Tail Switch, And Other West African Stories by Harold Courlander and George Herzog. Holt.

Misty of Chincoteague by Marguerite Henry. Illustrated by Wesley Dennis. Rand.

1949

King of the Wind by Marguerite Henry. Illustrated by Wesley Dennis. Rand.

Honor Books:
Seabird by Holling Clancy Holling. Houghton Mifflin.

Daughter of the Mountains by Louise Rankin. Viking.

My Father's Dragon by Ruth S. Gannett. Random.

Story of the Negro by Arna Bontemps. Knopf.

1950

The Door in the Wall by Marguerite de Angeli. Doubleday.

Honor Books:
Tree of Freedom by Rebecca Caudill. Viking.

The Blue Cat of Castle Town by Catherine Coblentz. McKay/Longmans.

Kildee House by Rutherford Montgomery. Doubleday.

George Washington by Genevieve Foster. Scribner's.

Song of the Pines by Walter and Marion Havighurst. Holt.

1951

Amos Fortune, Free Man by Elizabeth Yates. Illustrated by Nora Unwin. Dutton.

Honor Books:
Better Known as Johnny Appleseed by Mabel Leigh Hunt. Lippincott.

Gandhi, Fighter Without a Sword by Jeanette Eaton. Morrow.

Abraham Lincoln, Friend of the People by Clara I. Judson. Follett.

The Story of Appleby Capple by Anne Parrish. Harper.

1952

Ginger Pye by Eleanor Estes. Harcourt.

Honor Books:
Americans Before Columbus by Elizabeth Chesley Baity. Viking.

Minn of the Mississippi by Holling Clancy Holling. Houghton Mifflin.

The Defender by Nicholas Kalashnikoff. Scribner's.

The Light at Tern Rock by Julia L. Sauer. Viking.

The Apple and the Arrow by Mary and Conrad Buff. Houghton Mifflin.

1953

Secret of the Andes by Ann Nolan Clark. Illustrated by Jean Charlot. Viking.

Honor Books:
Charlotte's Web by E. B. White. Harper.

Moccasin Trail by Eloise J. McGraw. Coward-McCann.

Red Sails to Capri by Ann Weil. Viking.

The Bears on Hemlock Mountain by Alice Dalgliesh. Scribner's.

Birthdays of Freedom, Vol. 1 by Genevieve Foster. Scribner's.

1954

And Now Miguel by Joseph Krumgold. Illustrated by Jean Charlot. Crowell.

Honor Books:
All Alone by Claire Huchet Bishop. Viking.

Shadrach by Meindert DeJong. Harper.

Hurry Home, Candy by Meindert DeJong. Harper.

Theodore Roosevelt, Fighting Patriot by Clara I. Judson. Follett.

Magic Maize by Mary and Conrad Buff. Houghton Mifflin.

1955

The Wheel on the School by Meindert DeJong. Illustrated by Maurice Sendak. Harper.

Honor Books:
The Courage of Sarah Noble by Alice Dalgliesh. Scribner's.

Banner in the Sky by James Ramsey Ullman. Lippincott.

1956

Carry on, Mr. Bowditch by Jean Lee Latham. Houghton Mifflin.

Honor Books:
The Golden Name Day by Jennie D. Lindquist. Harper.

The Secret River by Marjorie Kinnan Rawlings. Scribner's.

Men, Microscopes and Living Things by Katherine B. Shippen. Viking.

1957

Miracles on Maple Hill by Virginia Sorensen. Illustrated by Beth and Joe Krush. Harcourt.

Honor Books:
Old Yeller by Fred Gipson. Harper.

The House of Sixty Fathers by Meindert DeJong. Harper.

Mr. Justice Holmes by Clara I. Judson. Follett.

The Corn Grows Ripe by Dorothy Rhoads. Viking.

The Black Fox of Lorne by Marguerite de Angeli. Doubleday.

1958

Rifles for Watie by Harold Keith. Illustrated by Peter Burchard. Crowell.

Honor Books:
The Horsecatcher by Mari Sandoz. Westminster.

Gone-Away Lake by Elizabeth Enright. Harcourt.

The Great Wheel by Robert Lawson. Viking.

Tom Paine, Freedom's Apostle by Leo Gurko. Crowell.

1959

The Witch of Blackbird Pond by Elizabeth George Speare. Houghton Mifflin.

Honor Books:
The Family Under the Bridge by Natalie S. Carlson. Harper.

Along Came a Dog by Meindert DeJong. Harper.

Chucaro: Wild Pony of the Pampa by Francis Kalnay. Harcourt.

The Perilous Road by William O. Steele. Harcourt.

1960

Onion John by Joseph Krumgold. Illustrated by Symeon Shimin. Crowell.

Honor Books:
My Side of the Mountain by Jean George. Dutton.

America Is Born by Gerald Johnson. Morrow.

The Gammage Cup by Carol Kendall. Harcourt.

1961

Island of the Blue Dolphins by Scott O'Dell. Houghton Mifflin.

Honor Books:
America Moves Forward by Gerald Johnson. Morrow.

Old Ramon by Jack Schaefer. Houghton Mifflin.

The Cricket in Times Square by George Selden. Farrar.

1962

The Bronze Bow by Elizabeth George Speare. Houghton Mifflin.

Honor Books:
Frontier Living by Edwin Tunis. World.

The Golden Goblet by Eloise J. McGraw. Coward.

Belling the Tiger by Mary Stolz. Harper.

1963

A Wrinkle in Time by Madeleine L'Engle. Farrar.

Honor Books:
Thistle and Thyme by Sorche Nic Leodhas (pseud. for Leclaire Alger). Holt.

Men of Athens by Olivia Coolidge. Houghton Mifflin.

1964

It's Like This, Cat by Emily Cheney Neville. Harper.

Honor Books:
Rascal by Sterling North. Dutton.

The Loner by Esther Wier. McKay/Longmans.

1965

Shadow of a Bull by Maia Wojciechowska. Atheneum.

Honor Book:
Across Five Aprils by Irene Hunt. Follett.

1966

I, Juan de Pareja by Elizabeth Borten de Treviño. Farrar.

Honor Books:
The Black Cauldron by Lloyd Alexander. Holt.

The Animal Family by Randall Jarrell. Pantheon.

The Noonday Friends by Mary Stolz. Harper.

1967

Up a Road Slowly by Irene Hunt. Follett.

Honor Books:
The King's Fifth by Scott O'Dell. Houghton Mifflin.

Zlateh the Goat and Other Stories by Isaac Bashevis Singer. Harper.

The Jazz Man by Mary H. Weik. Atheneum.

1968

From the Mixed-Up Files of Mrs. Basil E. Frankweiler by E. L. Konigsburg. Atheneum.

Honor Books:
Jennifer, Hecate, Macbeth, William McKinley, and Me, Elizabeth by E. L. Konigsburg. Atheneum.

The Black Pearl by Scott O'Dell. Houghton Mifflin.

The Fearsome Inn by Isaac Bashevis Singer. Scribner's.

The Egypt Game by Zilpha Keatley Snyder. Atheneum.

1969

The High King by Lloyd Alexander. Holt.

Honor Books:
To Be a Slave by Julius Lester. Dial.

When Shlemiel Went to Warsaw and Other Stories by Isaac Bashevis Singer. Farrar.

1970

Sounder by William H. Armstrong. Harper.

Honor Books:
Our Eddie by Sulamith Ish-Kishor. Pantheon.

The Many Ways of Seeing: An Introduction to the Pleasure of Art by Janet Gaylord Moore. World.

Journey Outside by Mary Q. Steele. Viking.

1971

Summer of the Swans by Betsy Byars. Viking.

Honor Books:
Kneeknock Rise by Natalie Babbitt. Farrar.

Enchantress from the Stars by Sylvia Louise Engdahl. Atheneum.

Sing Down the Moon by Scott O'Dell. Houghton Mifflin.

1972

Mrs. Frisby and the Rats of NIMH by Robert C. O'Brien. Atheneum.

Honor Books:
Incident at Hawk's Hill by Allan W. Eckert. Little, Brown.

The Planet of Junior Brown by Virginia Hamilton. Macmillan.

The Tombs of Atuan by Ursula K. LeGuin. Atheneum.

Annie and the Old One by Miska Miles. Little, Brown.

The Headless Cupid by Zilpha Keatley Snyder. Atheneum.

1973

Julie of the Wolves by Jean Craighead George. Harper.

Honor Books:
Frog and Toad Together by Arnold Lobel. Harper.

The Upstairs Room by Johanna Reiss. Crowell.

The Witches of Worm by Zilpha Keatley Snyder. Atheneum.

1974

The Slave Dancer by Paula Fox. Bradbury.

Honor Book:
The Dark Is Rising by Susan Cooper. Atheneum/McElderry.

1975

M. C. Higgins, the Great by Virginia Hamilton. Macmillan.

Honor Books:
Figgs & Phantoms by Ellen Raskin. Dutton.

My Brother Sam Is Dead by James Lincoln Collier and Christopher Collier. Four Winds.

The Perilous Gard by Elizabeth Marie Pope. Houghton Mifflin.

Philip Hall Likes Me, I Reckon Maybe by Bette Greene. Dial.

1976

The Grey King by Susan Cooper. Atheneum/McElderry.

Honor Books:
The Hundred Penny Box by Sharon Bell Mathis. Viking.

Dragonwings by Lawrence Yep. Harper.

1977

Roll of Thunder, Hear My Cry by Mildred D. Taylor. Dial.

Honor Books:
Abel's Island by William Steig. Farrar.

A String in the Harp by Nancy Bond. Atheneum/McElderry.

1978

Bridge to Terabithia by Katherine Paterson. Crowell.

Honor Books:
Anpao: An American Indian Odyssey by Jamake Highwater. Lippincott.

Ramona and Her Father by Beverly Cleary. Morrow.

1979

The Westing Game by Ellen Raskin. Dutton.

Honor Book:
The Great Gilly Hopkins by Katherine Paterson. Crowell.

1980

A Gathering of Days: A New England Girl's Journal, 1830–32 by Joan Blos. Scribner's.

Honor Book:
The Road from Home: The Story of an Armenian Girl by David Kherdian. Greenwillow.

1981

Jacob Have I Loved by Katherine Paterson. Crowell.

Honor Books:
The Fledgling by Jane Langton. Harper.

A Ring of Endless Light by Madeleine L'Engle. Farrar.

1982

A Visit to William Blake's Inn: Poems for Innocent and Experienced Travelers by Nancy Willard. Illustrated by Alice and Martin Provensen. Harcourt.

Honor Books:
Ramona Quimby, Age 8 by Beverly Cleary. Morrow.

Upon the Head of the Goat: A Childhood in Hungary, 1939–1944 by Aranka Siegal. Farrar.

1983

Dicey's Song by Cynthia Voigt. Atheneum.

Honor Books:
The Blue Sword by Robin McKinley. Greenwillow.

Dr. DeSoto by William Steig. Farrar.

Graven Images by Paul Fleischman. Harper.

Homesick: My Own Story by Jean Fritz. Putnam.

Sweet Whispers, Brother Rush by Virginia Hamilton. Philomel.

1984

Dear Mr. Henshaw by Beverly Cleary. Morrow.

Honor Books:
The Sign of the Beaver by Elizabeth George Speare. Houghton Mifflin.

A Solitary Blue by Cynthia Voigt. Atheneum.

Sugaring Time by Kathryn Lasky. Photographs by Christopher Knight. Macmillan.

The Wish Giver by Bill Brittain. Harper.

1985

The Hero and the Crown by Robin McKinley. Greenwillow.

Honor Books:
Like Jake and Me by Mavis Jukes. Illustrated by Lloyd Bloom. Knopf.

The Moves Make the Man by Bruce Brooks. Harper.

One-Eyed Cat by Paula Fox. Bradbury.

1986

Sarah, Plain and Tall by Patricia MacLachlan. Harper.

Honor Books:
Commodore Perry in the Land of the Shogun by Rhoda Blumberg. Lothrop.

Dogsong by Gary Paulsen. Bradbury.

1987

The Whipping Boy by Sid Fleischman. Greenwillow.

Honor Books:
On My Honor by Marion Dane Bauer. Clarion.

Volcano: The Eruption and Healing of Mount St. Helens by Patricia Lauber. Bradbury.

A Fine White Dust by Cynthia Rylant. Bradbury.

1988

Lincoln: A Photobiography by Russell Freedman. Clarion.

Honor Books:
After the Rain by Norma Fox Mazer. Morrow.

Hatchet by Gary Paulsen. Bradbury.

1989

Joyful Noise: Poems for Two Voices by Paul Fleischman. Harper.

Honor Books:
In the Beginning: Creation Stories from Around the World by Virginia Hamilton. Harcourt.

Scorpions by Walter Dean Myers. Harper.

1990

Number the Stars by Lois Lowry. Houghton Mifflin.

Honor Books:
Afternoon of the Elves by Janet Taylor Lisle. Orchard.

Shabanu, Daughter of the Wind by Suzanne Fisher Staples. Knopf.

The Winter Room by Gary Paulsen. Orchard.

1991

Maniac Magee by Jerry Spinelli. Little, Brown.

> **Honor Book:**
> *The True Confessions of Charlotte Doyle* by Avi. Orchard.

1992

Shiloh by Phyllis Reynolds Naylor. Atheneum.

> **Honor Books:**
> *Nothing But the Truth* by Avi. Orchard.
>
> *The Wright Brothers: How They Invented the Airplane* by Russell Freedman. Holiday House.

1993

Missing May by Cynthia Rylant. Orchard.

> **Honor Books:**
> *The Dark-Thirty: Southern Tales of the Supernatural* by Patricia McKissack. Illustrated by Brian Pinkney. Knopf.
>
> *Somewhere in Darkness* by Walter Dean Myers. Scholastic.
>
> *What Hearts* by Bruce Brooks. Laura Geringer Books (Harper).

1994

The Giver by Lois Lowry. Houghton Mifflin.

> **Honor Books:**
> *Crazy Lady* by Jane Leslie Conly. Harper.
>
> *Dragon's Gate* by Laurence Yep. Harper.
>
> *Eleanor Roosevelt: A Life of Discovery* by Russell Freedman. Clarion.

1995

Walk Two Moons by Sharon Creech. Harper.

> **Honor Books:**
> *Catherine, Called Birdy* by Karen Cushman. Clarion.
>
> *The Ear, the Eye and the Arm* by Nancy Farmer. Orchard.

1996

The Midwife's Apprentice by Karen Cushman. Clarion.

> **Honor Books:**
> *What Jamie Saw* by Carolyn Coman. Front Street.
>
> *The Watsons Go to Birmingham - 1963* by Christopher Paul Curtis. Delacorte.
>
> *Yolanda's Genius* by Carol Fenner. McElderry.

The Great Fire by Jim Murphy. Scholastic.

OTHER U.S. AWARDS

Boston Globe/Horn Book Award   Presented annually by the *Boston Globe* and *The Horn Book Magazine* for outstanding fiction or poetry, outstanding nonfiction, and outstanding illustration.

Coretta Scott King Awards   Presented annually by the Social Responsibilities Round Table and the Association of Library Service to Children of the American Library Association to an outstanding African-American author and illustrator.

International Reading Association Children's Book Award   Presented annually to an author of a book for older readers and an author of a books for younger readers published in the preceding year for writing that shows unusual promise.

Laura Ingalls Wilder Award   Presented every three years by the Association of Library Service to Children of the American Library Association to an author or illustrator whose books, published in the United States, have made a substantial and lasting contribution to literature for children.

Mildred L. Batchelder Award   Presented annually by the Association of Library Service to Children of the American Library Association to the publisher of the most outstanding book of the year, first published in another country, and published in translation in the United States.

NCTE Excellence in Poetry for Children Award   Presented every three years by the National Council of Teachers of English to a living American poet in recognition of an aggregate body of work for children.

Orbis Pictus Award for Outstanding Nonfiction for Children   Presented annually by the National Council of Teachers of English to an author for the most outstanding nonfiction book published the previous year.

Phoenix Award   Presented annually by the Children's Literature Association to the author of a book published twenty years before that has not received a major children's book award.

AWARDS IN OTHER COUNTRIES

Carnegie Medal (Great Britain)   Presented to the author of a children's book of outstanding merit, written in English and first published in the United Kingdom during the preceding year.

Kate Greenaway Medal (Great Britain)   Presented to the illustrator of the most distinguished picture book first published in the United Kingdom during the preceding year.

Amelia Frances Howard-Gibbon Medal (Canada) Presented to the illustrator of the most outstanding artwork in a children's book published in Canada during the preceding year.

Canadian Librarian Association Book of the Year for Children Award (Canada)   Presented to the authors of the most outstanding English-language and French-language children's books published during the preceding year.

Children's Books of the Year Awards (Australia)   Presented to authors and illustrators who are Australian citizens or residents for books of outstanding merit. There are three awards: The Picture Book of the Year Award, The Children's Book for Younger Readers Award, and The Children's Book of the Year for Older Readers.

Russell Clark Award (New Zealand)   Presented for the most distinguished illustrations in a children's book, usually given for a book published the previous year.

Esther Glen Award (New Zealand)   Presented to the author of the most distinguished contribution to New Zealand literature for children published in the previous year.

The Hans Christian Andersen Prize   This international award is presented to one author and one illustrator biennially for his or her entire body of work. It is sponsored and administered by the International Board on Books for Young People. Americans who have won the Anderson Medal are Meindert DeJong (1962), Maurice Sendak (1970), Scott O'Dell (1972), Paula Fox (1978), and Virginia Hamilton (1992).

Publishers' Addresses

Publishers' addresses may change as a result of mergers and acquisitions. For the most up-to-date information, check the current edition of *Literary Market Place* or *Children's Books in Print*.

Abrams
100 Fifth Ave.
New York, NY 10010

Addison-Wesley Publishing Co., Inc.
One Jacob Way
Reading, MA 01867

Aladdin Books
1230 Avenue of the Americas
New York, NY 10020

Atheneum Publishers
1230 Avenue of the Americas
New York, NY 10020

Avon Books
1350 Avenue of the Americas
New York, NY 10019

Bantam Books, Inc.
666 Fifth Ave.
New York, NY 10103

Peter Bedrick Books, Inc.
2112 Broadway, Suite 318
New York, NY 10023

Beechtree Books
1350 Avenue of the Americas
New York, NY 10019

Berkley Publishing Group
200 Madison Ave.
New York, NY 10010

Boyds Mills Press
815 Church St.
Honesdale, PA 18431

Bradbury Press
1230 Avenue of the Americas
New York, NY 10020

Camelot
1350 Avenue of the Americas
New York, NY 10019

Candlewick Press
2067 Massachusetts Ave.
Cambridge, MA 02140

Carolrhoda Books, Inc.
241 First Ave. N.
Minneapolis, MN 55401

Chelsea House Publishers
95 Madison Ave.
New York, NY 10016

Children's Book Press
6400 Hollis St.
Emeryville, CA 94608

Children's Press
5440 N. Cumberland Ave.
Chicago, IL 60656

Chronicle Books
275 Fifth St.
San Francisco, CA 94103

Clarion Books
215 Park Ave. S.
New York, NY 10003

Cobblehill Books
375 Hudson St.
New York, NY 10014

Creative Education, Inc.
Box 227
123 S. Broad St.
Mankato, MN 56001

Crestwood House
1230 Avenue of the Americas
New York, NY 10020

Crowell
10 East 53rd St.
New York, NY 10022

Crown Publishers
201 E. 50th St.
New York, NY 10022

Dell Publishing Co., Inc.
666 Fifth Ave.
New York, NY 10103

Dial Books for Young Readers
Imprint of Penguin USA
375 Hudson St.
New York, NY 10014

Dillon Press
1230 Avenue of the Americas
New York, NY 10020

Doubleday
666 Fifth Ave.
New York, NY 10103

Dutton
375 Hudson St.
New York, NY 10014

Farrar, Straus & Giroux, Inc.
19 Union Square W.
New York, NY 10003

Four Winds Press
1230 Avenue of the Americas
New York, NY 10020

David R. Godine, Publisher, Inc.
Horticulture Hall

300 Massachusetts Ave.
Boston, MA 02115

Green Tiger Press
1230 Avenue of the Americas
New York, NY 10020

Greenwillow Books
1350 Avenue of the Americas
New York, NY 10019

Grosset & Dunlap
200 Madison Ave.
New York, NY 10016

Gulliver Books
1250 Sixth Ave.
San Diego, CA 92101

Harcourt Brace and Co.
1250 Sixth Ave.
San Diego, CA 92101

HarperCollins Children's Books
10 E. 53rd St.
New York, NY 10022

Harper Trophy
10 East 53rd St.
New York, NY 10022

Holiday House, Inc.
425 Madison Ave.
New York, NY 10017

Henry Holt & Co.
115 W. 18th St.
New York, NY 10011

Houghton Mifflin Co.
2 Park St.
Boston, MA 02108

Hyperion Books for Children
114 Fifth Ave.
New York, NY 10011

Ideals Publishing Corp.
Egmont, Inc., U.S.A.
565 Marriot Dr.
Nashville, TN 37210

Jewish Publication Society
1930 Chestnut St.
Philadelphia, PA 19103

Joy Street Books
34 Beacon St.
Boston, MA 02108

Kane/Miller Book Publishers
Box 529
Brooklyn, NY 11231

Alfred A. Knopf, Inc.
201 E. 50th St.
New York, NY 10022

Lerner Publications Co.
241 First Ave. N.
Minneapolis, MN 55401

Lippincott
10 East 53rd St.
New York, NY 10022

Little, Brown & Co., Inc.
34 Beacon St.
Boston, MA 02108

Lodestar Publishing
375 Hudson St.
New York, NY 10014

Lothrop, Lee & Shepard Books
1350 Avenue of the Americas
New York, NY 10014

Macmillan Publishing Co.
1230 Avenue of the Americas
New York, NY 10020

Margaret K. McElderry Books
1230 Avenue of the Americas
New York, NY 10020

McGraw-Hill Book Co.
1221 Avenue of the Americas
New York, NY 10020

William Morrow & Co., Inc.
1350 Avenue of the Americas
New York, NY 10019

Morrow Junior Books
1350 Avenue of the Americas
New York, NY 10019

John Muir Publications
P. O. Box 613
Santa Fe, NM 87504

Mulberry Books
1350 Avenue of the Americas
New York, NY 10019

North-South Books
1133 Broadway, Suite 1016
New York, NY 10019

Orchard Books
387 Park Ave.
New York, NY 10016

Oxford University Press, Inc.
200 Madison Ave.
New York, NY 10016

Pantheon Books, Inc.
201 E. 50th St. 27th Floor
New York, NY 10022

Penguin USA
375 Hudson St.
New York, NY 10014

Philomel Books
200 Madison Ave.
New York, NY 10016

Picture Book Studio
Box 9139
10 Central St.
Saxonville, MA 01701

Price Stern Sloan, Inc.
11150 Olympic Blvd.
Suite 650
Los Angeles, CA 90064

Puffin Books
375 Hudson St.
New York, NY 10014

G. P. Putnam Sons
200 Madison Ave.
New York, NY 10016

Random House, Inc.
201 E. 50th St.
New York, NY 10022

Scholastic, Inc.
555 Broadway
New York, NY 10012

Charles Scribner's Sons
1230 Avenue of the Americas
New York, NY 10020

Simon & Schuster Books for Young Readers
1230 Avenue of the Americas
New York, NY 10020

Tambourine Books
1350 Avenue of the Americas
New York, NY 10019

Troll Associates
100 Corporate Dr.
Mahwah, NJ 07430

Tundra Books
Box 1030
Plattsburgh, NY 12901

Viking Penguin
375 Hudson St.
New York, NY 10014

Walker & Co.
720 Fifth Ave.
New York, NY 10019

Frederick Warne & Co., Inc.
375 Hudson St.
New York, NY 10014

Franklin Watts, Inc.
95 Madison Ave.
New York, NY 10016

Western Publishing Co., Inc.
1220 Mound Ave.
Racine, WI 53404

Albert Whitman & Co.
6340 Oakton St.
Morton Grove, IL 60053

 # Name Index

This index includes names of authors, illustrators, and titles.

 # Subject Index

 *About the Author*

Joan Glazer is a Professor in the Department of Elementary Education at Rhode Island College where she teaches courses in children's literature, language arts, and teacher research. She has taught in grades one through four, worked with Head Start, and taught in both English and Education Departments at the college level. In 1994–1995 she served as President of the Special Interest Group on Reading and Children's Literature of the International Reading Association, and in 1997 as President of the United States Board on Books for Young People. She is the author of *Literature for Young Children* (Merrill, 1991) and articles published in *The Reading Teacher, Language Arts, The Children's Literature Association Quarterly,* and *The Dragon Lode,* and is a regular presenter at regional and national conferences.

Montgomery

Rm 309